American History told by Contemporaries

BY THE SAME EDITOR

A Source-Book of American History

The *Source-Book* is independent of the four volumes of *Contemporaries*, and contains no articles which appear in the larger series.

THE MACMILLAN COMPANY

60 FIFTH AVENUE, NEW YORK

American History told by
Contemporaries

VOLUME IV

WELDING OF THE NATION

1845–1900

THE MACMILLAN COMPANY
NEW YORK · BOSTON · CHICAGO · DALLAS
ATLANTA · SAN FRANCISCO

MACMILLAN AND CO., Limited
LONDON · BOMBAY · CALCUTTA · MADRAS
MELBOURNE

THE MACMILLAN COMPANY
OF CANADA, Limited
TORONTO

American History told by Contemporaries

VOLUME IV

WELDING OF THE NATION

1845–1900

EDITED BY

ALBERT BUSHNELL HART

PROFESSOR OF HISTORY IN HARVARD UNIVERSITY
MEMBER OF THE MASSACHUSETTS HISTORICAL SOCIETY
AUTHOR OF "FORMATION OF THE UNION," "EPOCH MAPS,"
"SALMON P. CHASE," ETC.

NEW YORK

THE MACMILLAN COMPANY

LONDON: MACMILLAN & CO., LTD.

42-25-2

24859

Preface

IN taking leave of a work which has called for much time and consideration during the past five years, I feel first of all a sense of gratitude to the good worthies who had sufficient interest in the affairs of their times, and sufficient sense of their own importance in the eyes of posterity, to provide such rich material for our use. Theirs is the delineator's task throughout the *American History told by Contemporaries:* if the pupils in schools, the readers in libraries and at home, teachers and searchers, find the books useful, it is because our forefathers did interesting things and left entertaining records. In my own mind I find the story of the nation's development clearer for the suggestions made by the writers of these four volumes. They are prejudiced; they see but a part of what is going on; they leave many gaps; but, after all, they tell the story.

The selection has been difficult because of the mass of excellent materials, and much that is valuable had to be left aside for lack of space. I have tried to let advocates of both sides speak on all great contested questions; to call upon the best informed and best disposed witnesses; to give examples of the writings of the nation's leaders; to let no significant episode pass unpresented. In the latter part of this volume it has not been possible to appeal to many diaries and collections of letters, for they have not yet come into print, or even into collections of manuscripts; but there are plenty of other forms of available writings. Official documents have, as in the previous volumes, been left for the most part to other collections.

At this stage of the work it is not necessary to apologize for the system of literal transcripts from the originals; changes of spelling and grammar would in any case be few in the writings of the last half century, and the simplest rule is to stick to the copy. Beyond reasons of convenience is the lesson of accurate use of materials, of looking exactly to what a man said, and not to what an editor makes him say.

The ground covered by this volume includes many stirring events. It begins with the Mexican War and the consequent renewal of the slavery contest, and it leads through the exciting "Fifties." Then comes the Civil War, which is treated in detail; on the causes, conditions, and progress of that titanic struggle, the participants, both civil and military, speak with directness and cogency. The troubled and confused Reconstruction period is illustrated by extracts which bring out the main events and scenes; there is no attempt to restate the wearisome debates, or to bring out the details of party and personal controversy. For the period since 1875 I have found the usual difficulty of the searcher into recent history: it is hard to get a right perspective, and impossible to include all the thronging activities of a nation; but the main currents of public thought are illustrated.

In this volume, as in all the others of the series, my expert aids have been Mr. David M. Matteson and Miss Addie F. Rowe; and the Harvard College Library, Boston Athenaeum, and Boston Public Library have been hospitable.

Acknowledgments have been made throughout to the volumes from which extracts have been taken. Especial mention is due of the courtesy of Houghton, Mifflin & Co., authorized publishers of the works of Dr. Holmes, Longfellow, and Whittier, and of the *Atlantic Monthly*. I have drawn much from their rich stores of contemporary material.

'Tis only a mosaic at the best — fragments which in themselves feebly shine with the glow of their original stones; but the effectiveness of a mosaic is not to be judged altogether by the tesseræ, nor by single figures; it depends on the color sense, the grouping, the broad scheme. The workman knows better than anybody else the defects of his materials; and he cannot judge how far they fit together into an illuminating whole.

ALBERT BUSHNELL HART.

CAMBRIDGE, December 13, 1900.

Contents

PART I

PRACTICAL INTRODUCTION
FOR TEACHERS, LIBRARIES, AND STUDENTS

CHAPTER I—SOURCES AND THEIR USES

PART II

EXPANSION AND SLAVERY

CHAPTER II—THE MEXICAN WAR

CHAPTER III—WILMOT PROVISO AND COMPROMISE

CHAPTER IV—CONDITIONS OF SLAVERY

CHAPTER V—FUGITIVE SLAVES

PART III

CONTEST RENEWED

CHAPTER VI — "BLEEDING KANSAS"

CHAPTER VII — THE CRISIS ARRIVES

PART IV

CAUSES OF CIVIL WAR

CHAPTER VIII — ELECTION OF 1860

PART VI

PROGRESS OF THE WAR

CHAPTER XVIII—YEAR OF PREPARATION

CHAPTER XIX—YEAR OF DISCOURAGEMENT

CHAPTER XX—YEAR OF ADVANCE

PART IX

AMERICAN PROBLEMS

CHAPTER XXX — THE SPANISH WAR

CHAPTER XXXI — QUESTIONS OF COLONIZATION

American History told by Contemporaries

PART I

PRACTICAL INTRODUCTION
FOR TEACHERS, LIBRARIES, AND STUDENTS

CHAPTER I — SOURCES AND THEIR USES

1. Educative Value of Sources

THE question of the availability and use of sources for those who are not expert investigators has been discussed recently in many other places, and needs no special treatment here. The Committee of Seven of the American Historical Association has considered it in its *Study of History in Schools;* the New England History Teachers' Association is shortly to publish a *Report on the Use of Sources,* which will be a guide both to the methods of using sources and also to the materials available in English. In Hart's *Source-Book of American History* are practical introductions, by various hands, on the use of sources in schools and colleges. James Ingersoll Wyer, *Bibliography of the Study and Teaching of History* (in the *Report* of the American Historical Association for 1899), prints an elaborate list of books and articles on historical methods. The editor of the *Contemporaries* has developed his views on the subject in the Introductions to the previous volumes of this series, and they need not here be repeated.

For the imaginative side of history, Volume IV includes some of the most notable and spirited narratives ever written on American affairs. The period from the beginning of the Mexican War to the outbreak of the

Civil War abounds in deeds of daring and of equally heroic suffering. The controversies over the Wilmot Proviso, the Compromise of 1850, the Kansas-Nebraska Act, and " Bleeding Kansas " are the precursors of the great storm. On the causes, elements, and events of the Civil War there is a wealth of materials. Most of the great military commanders on both sides prepared reports at the time, and wrote memoirs afterward ; there is a literature of soldiers' letters and reminiscences ; and the civil side of the war is hardly less varied and active. For the last part of the volume, there is less of the romantic, yet much that arouses the mind.

------◆------

2. How to Find Sources

FOR the period covered by this volume there is no comprehensive bibliography, least of all on post-bellum events. The most convenient brief bibliography is, William E. Foster, *References to the History of Presidential Administrations ;* Channing and Hart, *Guide to the Study of American History*, comes down only to the end of the Civil War. The foot-notes to the four volumes now published of James Ford Rhodes, *History of the United States from the Compromise of 1850*, are a valuable means of reaching sources from about 1845 to 1864; on the Reconstruction period may be used the foot-notes to W. A. Dunning, *Essays on the Civil War and Reconstruction.* J. M. Larned's forthcoming *Annotated Bibliography of American History*, prepared by the coöperative method, promises to be very helpful. Bowker and Iles, *Reader's Guide*, has many references on current economic and social questions ; and W. E. Foster's *Bulletins of the Providence Public Library* include many serviceable special bibliographies. *Poole's Index* is of course the best approach to the abundant periodical material of the last quarter century, much of it first-hand writings. The collections available for school use are named and described in the *Report on the Use of Sources*, mentioned above.

------◆------

3. Intelligent Use of Sources

THE use of sources as school material has been discussed above : that sources vivify the study of history and tend to fix in the memory the principles best worth remembering, seems established by the experience of schools that have tried it.

Teachers will naturally wish to have and to use the full text of some of the authorities which are represented in this volume in brief extract; but from the pieces here printed they can probably enrich their stock of illustrations and cogent facts.

The ordinary literature of the Civil War is in many ways less available to school children than that of earlier periods; perhaps this volume may therefore be especially helpful for that critical epoch in the topical work which now forms so large a part of the training in history in many schools; the *Contemporaries* is also meant to form a body of suitable parallel reading in connection with text-books.

Little space has been given in the head-notes to a criticism of the writers from whom extracts have been taken. It is assumed that those who use the book are aware of the necessity of considering how far it is the interest and intention of the source-writers to speak the truth. Unless there is a distinct caution to the contrary, it will be understood that the editor selected the extracts because worthy of credit. It must not, however, be inferred that pieces are chosen simply because they express laudable sentiments: it is quite as important to know what were the arguments against a policy as to know those in favor of it. On contested questions both sides have a hearing throughout this series.

---

4. Classification of Extracts in this Volume

AS in previous volumes, it may be convenient in this place to classify materials by their origins, so that the reader or the teacher may easily find pieces illustrating special types or sources or source-writers.

Large use has been made in this volume of extremely valuable material in official records of various kinds: first, the Debates of Congress, from which have been taken speeches by Corwin (No. 11); Wilmot (No. 16); Calhoun (No. 19); Webster (No. 20); Seward (No. 22); Wade (Nos. 46, 65); Toombs (No. 54); Wigfall (No. 55); Vallandigham (No. 129); Stevens (No. 152); Wilson (No. 155); various members (No. 168); Hoar (No. 191). Large use has also been made of the House Reports (Nos. 40, 149, 156); Senate Reports (No. 47); Senate Journals (Nos. 64, 164, 166, 190); House Executive Documents (Nos. 13, 111, 134, 167, 175, 176, 177, 179, 182); Senate Executive Documents (Nos. 99, 143, 144, 178, 185, 187, 195). The magnificent official records of the Union and Confederate armies have furnished extracts

from Jefferson Davis (No. 62) ; Walker, Beauregard, Foster, and Anderson (Nos. 71, 72) ; Prentiss (No. 110) ; "Stonewall" Jackson (No. 113) ;
Burnside (No. 115) ; Lee (No. 117) ; Thomas (No. 123) ; Butler (No.
124) ; Semmes (No. 133) ; Hood (No. 138). Extracts from presidential messages and other official communications are represented by
Polk (No. 10) ; Buchanan (No. 64) ; Lincoln (No. 145) ; Cleveland
(No. 164) ; Harrison (No. 166) ; McKinley (No. 190). Diplomatic
correspondence will be found as follows : Seward (No. 99) ; Slidell (No.
100) ; C. B. Elliott (No. 173) ; Sumner (No. 174) ; Geneva arbitration (No. 175); Fish (No. 176); Blaine (No. 177) ; Bering Sea
(No. 178) ; Olney (No. 179) ; Hay (No. 193).

Next in significance are the official and semi-official utterances of
public men, chiefly in collected correspondence and similar material,
some of them in the official records : as Polk (No. 14) ; Calhoun (No.
19) ; Webster (No. 20) ; Seward (Nos. 22, 45, 97) ; Douglas (No. 34) ;
Benton (No. 43) ; Lincoln (Nos. 44, 66, 97, 101, 127) ; A. H. Stephens
(No. 53) ; Jefferson Davis (Nos. 62, 106) ; Chase (No. 128) Sumner
(Nos. 146, 174) ; Tilden (No. 150) ; Thaddeus Stevens (No. 152) ;
J. G. Blaine (No. 160) ; Olney (No. 192). Of statesmen less famous,
extracts have been made as follows : Edward Everett (No. 79) ; Critten-
den (No. 69) ; John A. Dix (No. 67) ; Wendell Phillips (No. 102) ;
Garrison (No. 126) ; Greeley (No. 127) ; Corwin (No. 11) ; R. J.
Walker (No. 40) ; Wilmot (No. 16); Vallandigham (No. 129) ; Butler
(No. 154) ; Wilson (No. 155) ; H. A. Herbert (No. 158) ; Bryan (No.
171) ; B. F. Wade (Nos. 46, 65) ; Thurlow Weed (No. 63) ; Chittenden
(No. 68) ; Slidell (No. 100) ; Robert Toombs (No. 54) ; John Brown
(No. 48) ; Andrew Johnson (No. 148) ; L. J. Gage (No. 172) ; J. T.
Morgan (No. 178) ; W. R. Day (No. 185) ; Leonard Wood (No. 189) ;
G. F. Hoar (No. 191) ; Theodore Roosevelt (No. 198) ; B. S. Coler
(No. 202) ; Evarts (No. 154) ; John Sherman (No. 169). Less sig-
nificant as public men, but extremely valuable for their testimony, are
Waddy Thompson (No. 8) ; I. P. Walker (No. 17) ; Stringfellow (No.
26) ; Julian (No. 35) ; Wigfall (No. 55) ; E. Hannaford (No. 161) ;
A. F. Walker (No. 165) ; Lacey (No. 167) ; Eckels (No. 167).
Speeches and reports by various members and commissioners will be
found in Nos. 70, 149, 168, 195.

Characteristic extracts are taken from the following renowned generals : Scott (No. 13) ; Grant (Nos. 12, 107, 139, 144) ; Lee (Nos.
47, 117) ; Beauregard (No. 71) ; McClellan (No. 112) ; "Stonewall"

Jackson (No. 113) ; Burnside (No. 115) ; Longstreet (No. 120) ; Hood (No. 138) ; Hancock (No. 159) ; Thomas (No. 123) ; Sheridan (No. 135) ; Sherman (No. 137) ; Farragut (No. 134) ; Dewey (No. 182) ; Porter (No. 118).

The only journals which have seemed available are those of Polk (No. 14) ; Dana (No. 31) ; Jones (No. 83) ; "Bull Run" Russell (No. 96) ; Chase (No. 128) ; Mrs. Lowry (No. 194). In reminiscences and historical work, carefully written later by participants, this field is rich, as will be seen by the following list : Pollard (No. 27) ; Levi Coffin (No. 29) ; Parker (No. 30) ; Cutts (No. 34) ; Julian (No. 35) ; Mrs. Robinson (No. 36) ; John Scott (No. 38) ; Reuben Davis (Nos. 58, 80); Mrs. Livermore (No. 73); Mrs. Clayton (No. 81) ; George Cary Eggleston (No. 82) ; Mosby (No. 95) ; Stevenson (No. 92) ; Billings (No. 84) ; Hosmer (No. 87) ; C. C. Coffin (No. 131) ; Charles A. Dana (No. 132) ; Porter (No. 118) ; Longstreet (No. 120) ; Mrs. Botume (No. 141) ; Sheridan (No. 135) ; General Sherman (No. 137) ; John Sherman (No. 169) ; Grant (No. 139) ; Mrs. Hancock (No. 159). Travellers have been very abundant, but have not been quoted so freely as in other volumes. The only foreign travellers are T. H. Gladstone (No. 39) ; Fremantle (No. 94) ; W. H. Russell (Nos. 96, 103) ; Captain Wilkinson (No. 116) ; Campbell (No. 203). The American travellers are R. H. Dana (No. 7) ; Delano (No. 18). Special observers on the South and slavery are Emily P. Burke (No. 23) ; Nehemiah Adams (No. 25); Pollard (No. 27) ; Godkin (No. 142) ; Schurz (No. 143) ; Pike (No. 157) ; Grady (No. 205) ; Booker T. Washington (No. 208). Observers, correspondents, and critics on the Civil War period are Murat Halstead (Nos. 49, 50); A. H. Stephens (No. 53); Joel Parker (No. 56) ; S. W. Crawford (No. 59) ; Smalley (No. 114) ; Shanks (No. 122). Critics on the academic, social, and political conditions since the war are Poor (No. 163) ; Taussig (No. 170); C. B. Elliott (No. 173); Mahan (No. 183) ; A. L. Lowell (No. 186) ; A. B. Hart (Nos. 196, 209) ; Roosevelt (No. 198) ; Schurz (No. 199) ; Clark (No. 201) ; J. B. Harrison (No. 204) ; Riis (No. 206) ; C. W. Eliot (No. 207) : on our new possessions, Atkins (No. 184) ; Carroll (No. 188).

Satirists are represented by several authors : James Russell Lowell (Nos. 9, 15) ; Brownell (No. 57) ; Richard Grant White (Nos. 74, 140) ; Artemus Ward (No. 75) ; McElroy (No. 197) ; "Mr. Dooley" (No. 200). Closely allied with this group are two novelists, Harriet Beecher Stowe (No. 24) ; Anna Dickinson (No. 121).

Pieces in verse are rather numerous : Whittier (Nos. 21, 125) ; Lucy Larcom (No. 37) ; Brownell (No. 57) ; O. W. Holmes (No. 60) ; Bryant (No. 76) ; Phœbe Cary (No. 78) ; Northern War Songs (No. 85) ; Southern War Songs (No. 91) ; Palmer (No. 93) ; Mrs. Warfield (No. 104) ; Longfellow (No. 108) ; Boker (No. 130) ; T. Buchanan Read (No. 136).

The contributions of women to this volume are as follows : Emily P. Burke (No. 23) ; Harriet Beecher Stowe (No. 24) ; Mary D. Armstead (No. 32) ; Mrs. Robinson (No. 36) ; Lucy Larcom (No. 37) ; Mrs. Livermore (No. 73) ; Mrs. Clayton (No. 81) ; Mrs. Warfield (No. 104) ; Anna Dickinson (No. 121) ; Mrs. Botume (No. 141) ; Mrs. Lowry (No. 194).

Foreign critics and statesmen have contributed some interesting pieces : John Bright (No. 98) ; Comte de Paris (No. 105) ; Peto (No. 162) ; Courcel (No. 178) ; Hannen (No. 178) ; Sawyer (No. 187).

---

5. Reprints and Collections

THE principal collections of sources on the period 1845–1900 are as follows : —

American Annual Cyclopædia (annual volumes, 1861, etc.). New York, 1862–1900. — From Vol. V (1875) on, the title is *Appleton's Annual Cyclopædia*. Contains very valuable materials, especially extracts from public documents.

H. W. Caldwell, *Source Extracts*. 1. *A Survey of American History*. 2. *Great American Legislators*. 3. *American Territorial Development : Expansion*. Chicago, 1900. — 1 and 3 published together, under the title *American History : Unification, Expansion*. Chicago, 1900.

Albert Bushnell Hart, *Source-Book of American History, with Practical Introductions*. New York, 1899. — Nos. 102–145 cover the same chronological field as Vol. IV of the *Contemporaries*, but the two works contain no duplicates.

Albert Bushnell Hart and Edward Channing, editors, *American History Leaflets*. 30 numbers (to be had separately). New York, 1892–1896. — Includes Lincoln's state papers.

Mabel Hill, *Liberty Documents*. New York, 1901. — Contains documents and comments thereon relating chiefly to personal liberty, and showing the derivation of American principles of free government from English traditions.

Alexander Johnston, *American Orations: Studies in American Political History*. (Edited by James Albert Woodburn.) 4 vols. New York, etc., 1896–1897. — Vols. III and IV are parallel with this volume.

William MacDonald, *Select Statutes and other Documents illustrative of the History of the United States*, 1861–1898. — This third volume of Professor MacDonald's series, covering the period from 1861 down, is in preparation.

Edward McPherson, *The Political History of the United States during the Great Rebellion*. Washington, etc., 1864.

Edward McPherson, *The Political History of the United States during the Period of Reconstruction*. Washington, 1871.

Edward McPherson, *A Hand-Book of Politics* (biennial volumes, omitting 1870). Washington, 1868–1894. — The above three series are made up of excellent selections or abstracts from the political documents of the time, — statutes, proclamations, speeches, letters, orders, decisions of the courts, political platforms, debates, etc.

Edmund Clarence Stedman and Ellen Mackay Hutchinson, editors, *A Library of American Literature, from the Earliest Settlement to the Present Time*. 11 vols. New York, 1888–1890. — Vols. VI–XI on the period 1845–1890. These volumes are to a large degree literary rather than historical, but they include some excellent contemporary narratives on the slavery conflict and the Civil War.

United States, *A Compilation of the Messages and Papers of the Presidents*. 10 vols. Washington, 1896–1899. — A valuable official publication, poorly edited by James D. Richardson, containing all the presidents' messages and proclamations except nominations for office. Sold by the government at cost.

United States, *Congressional Globe: containing Sketches of the Debates and Proceedings*. 109 vols. Washington, 1835–1873. — Contains the debates from 1833 to 1873.

United States, *Congressional Record*. 34 vols. Washington, 1873–1901. — Contains the debates and proceedings in full from 1873.

---

6. A Good Library of Sources

FOR an intelligent study of the political history of the United States, the first necessity is access to the most important government records. Exact titles of these publications are found in Channing and Hart's *Guide*, § 30. Odd volumes and partial sets are common and may be very useful.

OFFICIAL RECORDS OF THE UNITED STATES

1790–1854. B. R. Curtis, *Reports of Decisions in the Supreme Court of the United States; with Notes and a Digest.* 22 vols. Boston, 1881. — Condensed reports.

1855–1862. Samuel F. Miller, *Reports of Decisions in the Supreme Court of the United States.* 4 vols. Washington, 1874–1875. — Condensed reports, in continuation of Curtis.

1863–1874. John William Wallace, *Cases Argued and Adjudged.* 23 vols. Washington, 1870–1876.

1875–1882. William T. Otto, *Cases Argued and Adjudged.* 17 vols. Boston, 1876–1883. — Also bears the title, *United States Reports, Supreme Court,* Vols. 91–107.

1882–1899. J. C. Bancroft Davis, *United States Reports.* Vols. 108–178. 71 vols. New York, etc., 1884–1900.

1791–1897. *Official Opinions of the Attorneys-General of the United States.* 21 vols. Washington, 1852–1898.

1833–1873. United States, *Congressional Globe: containing Sketches of the Debates and Proceedings.* 109 vols. Washington, 1835–1873. — Contains the debates from 1833 on.

1789–1900. United States, *Statutes at Large.* 31 vols. Boston, etc., 1850–1900. — The official text of statutes from 1789 to 1900.

1789–1897. United States, *A Compilation of the Messages and Papers of the Presidents.* 10 vols. Washington, 1896–1899. — A valuable official publication, poorly edited by James D. Richardson, containing all the presidents' messages and proclamations except nominations for office. Sold by the government at cost.

1873–1900. United States, *Congressional Record.* 34 vols. Washington, 1873–1901. — Official reports of debates.

DIARIES AND AUTOBIOGRAPHIES

In comparison with earlier times, the period after 1845 is very deficient in materials of this kind, except during the Civil War.

[Thomas Hart Benton], *Thirty Years' View; or, A History of the Working of the American Government for Thirty Years, from 1820 to 1850.* 2 vols. New York, etc., 1854–1856.

James G. Blaine, *Twenty Years of Congress* [1861–1881]. 2 vols. Norwich, Conn., 1884–1886.

[James Buchanan], *Mr. Buchanan's Administration on the Eve of the Rebellion*. New York, 1866.

F[rancis] B[icknell] Carpenter, *Six Months at the White House with Abraham Lincoln*   New York, 1866.

L[ucius] E[ugene] Chittenden, *Personal Reminiscences, 1840–1890, including some not hitherto published of Lincoln and the War*.   New York, 1893.

James Freeman Clarke, *Anti-Slavery Days*.   New York, 1884.

Reuben Davis, *Recollections of Mississippi and Mississippians*.   Boston, etc., 1891.

U[lysses] S. Grant, *Personal Memoirs*.   2 vols.   New York, 1885–1886.

Horace Greeley, *Recollections of a Busy Life*.   New York, etc., 1868.

Joseph E. Johnston, *Narrative of Military Operations during the Late War between the States*.   New York, 1874.

George W. Julian, *Political Recollections, 1840 to 1872*.   Chicago, 1884.

James Longstreet, *From Manassas to Appomattox; Memoirs of the Civil War in America*.   Philadelphia, 1896.

A. K. McClure, *Abraham Lincoln and Men of War Times*.   Philadelphia, 1892.

Hugh McCulloch, *Men and Measures of Half a Century ; Sketches and Comments*.   New York, 1888.

Samuel J[oseph] May, *Some Recollections of our Antislavery Conflict*.   Boston, 1869.

Frederick Law Olmsted, *The Cotton Kingdom*.   2 vols.   New York, etc., 1861.

William Howard Russell, *My Diary North and South* [1861].   2 vols.   London, 1863.

William H. Seward, *Autobiography, from 1801 to 1834, with a Memoir of his Life*.   (Edited by F. W. Seward.)   New York, 1877.

P[hilip] H. Sheridan, *Personal Memoirs*.   2 vols.   New York, 1888.

John Sherman, *Recollections of Forty Years in the House, Senate, and Cabinet*.   2 vols.   Chicago, etc., 1895.

William T[ecumseh] Sherman, *Memoirs. By himself*.   2 vols.   New York, 1875.

John Sherman and William Tecumseh Sherman, *Letters*.   (Edited by Rachel Sherman Thorndike.)   New York, 1894.

Alexander H. Stephens, *A Constitutional View of the Late War between the States*.   2 vols.   Philadelphia, etc. [1868–1870].

Thurlow Weed, *Autobiography*.   (Edited by Harriet A. Weed.)   Boston etc., 1884.

TRAVELS

Books of foreign travels are not so numerous or important as earlier in our history. A long list will be found in Channing and Hart's *Guide*, § 24. The following are of special importance : —

Isabella Bird, *The Englishwoman in America*. London, 1856.

Paul Bourget, *Outre-Mer ; Impressions of America* [1893-1894]. New York, 1895.

Fredrika Bremer, *The Homes of the New World; Impressions of America* [1849-1851]. (Translated by Mary Howitt.) 2 vols. New York, 1853.

William Chambers, *Things as they are in America* [1853]. London, etc., 1854.

Emily Faithfull, *Three Visits to America* [1872, 1882, 1884]. Edinburgh, 1884.

George A. McCall, *Letters from the Frontier. Written during a Period of Thirty Years' Service in the United States Army*. Philadelphia, 1868.

Anthony Trollope, *North America* [1861-1862]. New York, 1862.

Charles Dudley Warner, *Studies in the South and West, with Comments on Canada*. New York, 1889.

WORKS OF STATESMEN

George S. Boutwell, *Speeches and Papers relating to the Rebellion and the Overthrow of Slavery*. Boston, 1867.

Rufus Choate, *Works*. (Edited by S. G. Brown.) 2 vols. Boston, 1862.

George William Curtis, *Orations and Addresses*. (Edited by C. E. Norton.) 3 vols. New York, 1894.

John A. Dix, *Speeches and Occasional Addresses*. 2 vols. New York, 1864.

Joshua R. Giddings, *Speeches in Congress*. Boston, etc., 1853.

Abraham Lincoln, *Complete Works*. (Edited by John G. Nicolay and John Hay.) 2 vols. New York, 1894.

William H. Seward, *Works*. (Edited by G. E. Baker.) 5 vols. New York, etc., 1853-1884.

Charles Sumner, *Works*. 15 vols. Boston, 1875-1883.

Samuel J. Tilden, *Writings and Speeches*. (Edited by John Bigelow.) 2 vols. New York, 1885.

PART II

EXPANSION AND SLAVERY

CHAPTER II — THE MEXICAN WAR

7. On the Coast of California (1835)

BY RICHARD HENRY DANA (1840)

Dana, who afterward became prominent as a lawyer and as a writer on international law, sought to restore his health during his college days by taking a sea voyage as a common sailor. Most of the two years thus spent was employed in sailing up and down the coast of California. The book in which he describes the routine and incidents of this experience acquired great popularity as a vivid and truthful narrative of the life of the common sailor, and is one of the few accounts of Mexican California. — For Dana, see C. F. Adams, *Richard Henry Dana*. — Bibliography: H. H. Bancroft, *History of the Pacific States*, XV, chs. xi-xiv *passim*.

THE bay of Monterey is very wide at the entrance, being about twenty-four miles between the two points, Año Nuevo at the north, and Pinos at the south, but narrows gradually as you approach the town. . . . We came to anchor within two cable lengths of the shore, and the town lay directly before us, making a very pretty appearance ; its houses being plastered, which gives a much better effect than those of Santa Barbara, which are of a mud-color. The red tiles, too, on the roofs, contrasted well with the white plastered sides, and with the extreme greenness of the lawn upon which the houses — about an hundred in number — were dotted about, here and there, irregularly. . . .

. . . The next day we were " turned-to " early, and began taking off the hatches, overhauling the cargo, and getting everything ready for inspection. At eight, the officers of the customs, five in number, came on board, and began overhauling the cargo, manifest, &c. The Mexican revenue laws are very strict, and require the whole cargo to be landed, examined, and taken on board again ; but our agent, Mr. R——, had succeeded in compounding with them for the two last vessels, and saving the trouble of taking the cargo ashore. The officers were dressed in the costume which we found prevailed through the country. A broad-brimmed hat, usually of a black or dark-brown color, with a gilt or figured band round the crown, and lined inside with silk; a short jacket of silk or figured calico, (the European skirted body-coat is never worn;) the shirt open in the neck; rich waistcoat, if any; pantaloons wide, straight, and long, usually of velvet, velveteen, or broadcloth; or else short breeches and white stockings. They wear the deer-skin shoe, which is of a dark-brown color, and, (being made by Indians,) usually a good deal ornamented. They have no suspenders, but always wear a sash round the waist, which is generally red, and varying in quality with the means of the wearer. Add to this the never-failing cloak, and you have the dress of the Californian. This last garment, the cloak, is always a mark of the rank and wealth of the owner. The "*gente de razón*," or aristocracy, wear cloaks of black or dark blue broadcloth, with as much velvet and trimmings as may be; and from this they go down to the blanket of the Indian; the middle classes wearing something like a large table-cloth, with a hole in the middle for the head to go through. This is often as coarse as a blanket, but being beautifully woven with various colors, is quite showy at a distance. Among the Spaniards there is no working class; (the Indians being slaves and doing all the hard work;) and every rich man looks like a grandee, and every poor scamp like a broken-down gentleman. I have often seen a man with a fine figure, and courteous manners, dressed in broadcloth and velvet, with a noble horse completely covered with trappings; without a *real* in his pockets, and absolutely suffering for something to eat. . . .

The Californians are an idle, thriftless people, and can make nothing for themselves. The country abounds in grapes, yet they buy bad wine made in Boston and brought round by us, at an immense price, and retail it among themselves at a *real* (12½ cents) by the small wine-glass. Their hides too, which they value at two dollars in money, they give for something which costs seventy-five cents in Boston; and buy shoes (as like as not, made of their own hides, which have been carried twice round Cape Horn) at three and four dollars, and "chicken-skin" boots at fifteen dollars apiece. Things sell, on an average, at an advance of nearly three hundred per cent upon the Boston prices. This is partly owing to the heavy duties which the government, in their wisdom, with the intent, no doubt, of keeping the silver in the country, has laid upon imports. These duties, and the enormous expenses of so long a voyage, keep all merchants, but those of heavy capital, from engaging in the trade. . . .

. . . Generally speaking, each person's caste is decided by the quality of the blood, which shows itself, too plainly to be concealed, at first sight. Yet the least drop of Spanish blood, if it be only of quatroon or octoon, is sufficient to raise them from the rank of slaves, and entitle them to a suit of clothes — boots, hat, cloak, spurs, long knife, and all complete, though coarse and dirty as may be, — and to call themselves Españolos, and to hold property, if they can get any. . . .

Another thing that surprised me was the quantity of silver that was in circulation. I certainly never saw so much silver at one time in my life, as during the week that we were at Monterey. The truth is, they have no credit system, no banks, and no way of investing money but in cattle. They have no circulating medium but silver and hides — which the sailors call "California bank notes." Everything that they buy they must pay for in one or the other of these things. . . .

Monterey, as far as my observation goes, is decidedly the pleasantest and most civilized-looking place in California. In the centre of it is an open square, surrounded by four lines of one-story plastered buildings, with half a dozen cannon in the centre ; some mounted, and others not. This is the " Presidio," or fort. Every town has a presidio in its centre ; or rather, every presidio has a town built around it; for the forts were first built by the Mexican government, and then the people built near them for protection. The presidio here was entirely open and unfortified. There were several officers with long titles, and about eighty soldiers, but they were poorly paid, fed, clothed and disciplined. The governor-general, or, as he is commonly called, the " general," lives here ; which makes it the seat of government. He is appointed by the central government at Mexico, and is the chief civil and military officer. In addition to him, each town has a commandant, who is the chief military officer, and has charge of the fort, and of all transactions with foreigners and foreign vessels ; and two or three alcaldis and corregidores, elected by the inhabitants, who are the civil officers. Courts and jurisprudence they have no knowledge of. . . . No Protestant has any civil rights, nor can he hold any property, or, indeed, remain more than a few weeks on shore, unless he belong to some vessel. Consequently, the Americans and English who intend to reside here become Catholics, to a man ; the current phrase among them being, — " A man must leave his conscience at Cape Horn." . . .

In Monterey there are a number of English and Americans (English or " Ingles " all are called who speak the English language) who have married Californians, become united to the Catholic church, and acquired considerable property. Having more industry, frugality, and enterprise than the natives, they soon get nearly all the trade into their hands. . . . The people are naturally suspicious of foreigners, and they would not be allowed to remain, were it not that they become good Catholics, and by marrying natives, and bringing up their children as Catholics and Spaniards, and not teaching them the English language, they quiet suspicion, and even become popular and leading men. The chief alcaldis in Monterey and Santa Barbara were both Yankees by birth. . . .

California was first discovered in 1536, by Cortes, and was subsequently visited by numerous other adventurers. . . . No sooner was the importance of the country known, than the Jesuits obtained leave to establish themselves in it, to christianize and enlighten the Indians. They established missions in various parts of the country toward the close of the seventeenth century, and collected the natives about them, baptizing them into the church, and teaching them the arts of civilized life. To protect the Jesuits in their missions, and at the same time to support the power of the crown over the civilized Indians, two forts were erected and garrisoned, one at San Diego, and the other at Monterey. These were called Presidios, and divided the command of the whole country between them. Presidios have since been established at Santa Barbara and San Francisco ; thus dividing the country into four large districts, each with its presidio, and governed by the commandant. The soldiers, for the most part, married civilized Indians ; and thus, in the vicinity of each presidio, sprung up, gradually, small towns. . . . On the expulsion of the Jesuits from the Spanish dominions, the missions passed into the hands of the Franciscans, though without any essential change in their management. Ever since the independence of Mexico, the missions have been going down ; until, at last, a law was passed, stripping them of all their possessions, and confining the priests to their spiritual duties ; and at the same time declaring all the Indians free and independent *Rancheros*. The change in the condition of the Indians was, as may be supposed, only nominal : they are virtually slaves, as much as they ever were. But in the missions, the change was complete. The priests have now no power, except in their religious character, and the great possessions of the missions are given over to be preyed upon by the harpies of the civil power, who are sent there in the capacity of *administradores*, to settle up the concerns ; and who usually end, in a few years, by making themselves fortunes, and leaving their stewardships worse than they found them. . . . The change had been made but a few years before our arrival upon the coast, yet, in that short time, the trade was much diminished, credit impaired, and the venerable missions going rapidly to decay.

The government of the country is an arbitrary democracy ; having no common law, and no judiciary. Their only laws are made and unmade at the caprice of the legislature, and are as variable as the legislature itself. They pass through the form of sending representatives to the congress at Mexico, but as it takes several months to go and return, and there is very little communication between the capital and this distant province, a member usually stays there, as permanent member, knowing very well that there will be revolutions at home before he can write and receive an answer ; and if another member should be sent, he has only to challenge him, and decide the contested election in that way.

Revolutions are matters of constant occurrence in California. They are got up by men who are at the foot of the ladder and in desperate circumstances, just as a new political party is started by such men in our own country. The only object, of course, is the loaves and fishes ; and instead of caucusing, paragraphing, libelling, feasting, promising, and lying, as with us, they take muskets and bayonets, and seizing upon the presidio and custom-house, divide the spoils, and declare a new dynasty. As for justice, they know no law but will and fear. . . .

[Richard Henry Dana], *Two Years before the Mast* (New York, 1840), 87–212 *passim*.

---

8. Condition of Mexico (1842)

BY LATE MINISTER WADDY THOMPSON (1846)

Thompson was a southerner who became minister to Mexico in 1842. His sober estimate of that nation shows the conditions under which she entered upon a war with the United States.— Bibliography: H. H. Bancroft, *History of the Pacific States*, VIII, 249–251; War Department Library, *Index of Publications relating to Mexico*, 28.

WHENEVER the foreigners in California make the movement of separation, it must succeed. The department of Sonora, not half the distance from Mexico, has been in a state of revolt for the last four years, and the government has been unable to suppress it. . . .

A leading member of the Mexican cabinet once said to me that he believed that the tendency of things was towards the annexation of Texas to the United States, and that he greatly preferred that result either to the separate independence of Texas or any connection or dependence of Texas upon England ; that if Texas was an independent power, other departments of Mexico would unite with it either voluntarily or by conquest, and if there was any connection between Texas and England, that English manufactures and merchandise would be smuggled into Mexico through Texas to the utter ruin of the Mexican manufactures and revenue.

In one of my last interviews with Santa Anna I mentioned this conversation. He said with great vehemence, that he " would war for ever for the reconquest of Texas, and that if he died in his senses his last words should be an exhortation to his countrymen never to abandon the effort to reconquer the country ;" and added, " You, Sir, know very well that to sign a treaty for the alienation of Texas would be the same thing as signing the death-warrant of Mexico," and went on to say that " by the same process we would take one after the other of the Mexican provinces until we had them all." I could not, in sincerity, say that I thought otherwise ; but I do not know that the annexation of Texas will hasten that event. That our language and laws are destined to pervade this continent, I regard as more certain than any other event which is in the future. Our race has never yet put its foot upon a soil which it has not only not kept but has advanced. I mean not our English ancestors only, but that great Teuton race from which we have both descended.

There seems to be a wonderful adaptation of the English people to the purpose of colonization. The English colony of convicts at New South Wales is a more prosperous community than any colony of any other country. That the Indian race of Mexico must recede before us, is quite as certain as that that is the destiny of our own Indians, who in a military point of view, if in no other, are superior to them. I do not know what feelings towards us in Mexico may have been produced by recent events, but whatever they may be, they will not last long ; and I believe that the time is not at all distant, when all the northern departments of Mexico, within a hundred miles of the city, will gladly take refuge under our more stable institutions from the constant succession of civil wars to which that country seems to be destined. The feeling is becoming a pretty general one amongst the enlightened and patriotic, that they are not prepared for free institutions, and are incapable themselves of maintaining them. There is very great danger that the drama may close there, as it has so often done in other countries, with anarchy ending in despotism, — such is the natural swing of the pendulum. The feeling of all Mexicans towards us until the revolution in Texas, was one of unmixed admiration; and it is our high position amongst the nations, and makes our mission all the more responsible, that every people, struggling to be free, regard us with the same feelings — we are indeed the "looking-glass in which they dress themselves." As a philanthropist, I have deeply deplored the effects of the annexation of Texas upon the feelings of the people of all classes in Mexico, towards this country, as diminishing their devotion to republican institutions; this should not be so, but it will be. Ours is regarded as the great exemplar Republic in Mexico, as everywhere else, and the act which they regard as such an outrage, must have the prejudicial effect which I have indicated — still more will that effect be to be deprecated, if it should throw Mexico into the arms of any great European power.

The northern departments of Mexico contain all the mines, and more of the wealth of the country than any others; and they all hang very loosely to the confederacy; — they receive no benefit from the central government, which in truth they only know in its exactions. All the money collected from them is expended in the city and elsewhere, and they have not even the satisfaction of knowing that it is beneficially or even honestly used. The security which would be given to property, as well as its great enhancement in value, would be powerful inducements with all the owners of large estates which are now comparatively value- less. The only obstacle that I know to such a consummation, infinitely desirable in my judgment, to the people of those departments, less so to us, would be in the influence of the priesthood. They are well aware that such a measure might very soon be fatal, not only to their own supremacy, but to that of the Catholic religion also, — but they would have on the other hand a powerful motive in the security which it would give them to their large church property — no motive but interest would have any influence with the people of Mexico, for they cer- tainly do not like us. Their feelings towards us may be summed up in two words, jealousy and admiration, — they are not going to declare war against us, I have never doubted for a moment about that. Public opinion in Mexico, to all practical purposes, means the opinion of the army, and the very last thing in the world which the army desires, is such a war, — nor do I believe that one Mexican in a thousand does, however they may vaunt and bluster — as a frightened school-boy whistles as he passes a graveyard in the night.   I have just as little idea that they will negotiate now, or until matters are adjusted between England and this country. . . . nothing would be more convenient to Mexico than that we should have no minister there to trouble the government with complaints.

Waddy Thompson, *Recollections of Mexico* (New York, etc., 1846), 235–241 *passim.*

———◆———

9. "The Present Crisis" (1844)

BY JAMES RUSSELL LOWELL

For Lowell, see No. 15 below. — Bibliography as in No. 11 below.

WHEN a deed is done for Freedom, through the broad earth's aching breast
Runs a thrill of joy prophetic, trembling on from east to west,
And the slave, where'er he cowers, feels the soul within him climb
To the awful verge of manhood, as the energy sublime
Of a century bursts full-blossomed on the thorny stem of Time.

Through the walls of hut and palace shoots the instantaneous throe,
When the travail of the Ages wrings earth's systems to and fro ;
At the birth of each new Era, with a recognizing start,
Nation wildly looks at nation, standing with mute lips apart,
And glad Truth's yet mightier man-child leaps beneath the Future's heart.

.   .   .   .

For mankind are one in spirit, and an instinct bears along,
Round the earth's electric circle, the swift flash of right or wrong ;
Whether conscious or unconscious, yet Humanity's vast frame
Through its ocean-sundered fibres feels the gush of joy or shame ; —
In the gain or loss of one race all the rest have equal claim.

Once to every man and nation comes the moment to decide,
In the strife of Truth with Falsehood, for the good or evil side ;
Some great cause, God's new Messiah, offering each the bloom or blight,
Parts the goats upon the left hand, and the sheep upon the right,
And the choice goes by for ever 'twixt that darkness and that light.

Hast thou chosen, O my people, on whose party thou shalt stand,
Ere the Doom from its worn sandals shakes the dust against our land?
Though the cause of Evil prosper, yet 't is Truth alone is strong,
And, albeit she wander outcast now, I see around her throng
Troops of beautiful, tall angels, to enshield her from all wrong.

. . . .

We see dimly in the Present what is small and what is great,
Slow of faith how weak an arm may turn the iron helm of fate,
But the soul is still oracular ; amid the market's din,
List the ominous stern whisper from the Delphic cave within, —
" They enslave their children's children who make compromise with sin."

Slavery, the earthborn Cyclops, fellest of the giant brood,
Sons of brutish Force and Darkness, who have drenched the earth with
    blood,
Famished in his self-made desert, blinded by our purer day,
Gropes in yet unblasted regions for his miserable prey ; —
Shall we guide his gory fingers where our helpless children play?

. . . .

'Tis as easy to be heroes as to sit the idle slaves
Of a legendary virtue carved upon our fathers' graves ;
Worshippers of light ancestral make the present light a crime ; —
Was the Mayflower launched by cowards, steered by men behind their
    time?
Turn those tracks toward Past or Future, that make Plymouth rock
    sublime?

They were men of present valor, stalwart old iconoclasts,
Unconvinced by axe or gibbet that all virtue was the Past's ;
But we make their truth our falsehood, thinking that hath made us free,
Hoarding it in mouldy parchments, while our tender spirits flee
The rude grasp of that great Impulse which drove them across the sea.

. . . .

New occasions teach new duties ; Time makes ancient good uncouth ;
They must upward still, and onward, who would keep abreast of Truth ;
Lo, before us gleam her camp-fires ! we ourselves must Pilgrims be,
Launch our Mayflower, and steer boldly through the desperate winter sea,
Nor attempt the Future's portal with the Past's blood-rusted key.

[James Russell Lowell], *Poems*, Second Series (Cambridge, etc., 1848), 53-62
passim.

10. Reasons for War (1846)

BY PRESIDENT JAMES KNOX POLK

Polk as president confirmed the annexation of Texas; the war with Mexico which followed might have been averted but for the intention to conquer and annex New Mexico and California. The reasons for war given in this message to Congress do not cover the real grounds. — Bibliography: H. H. Bancroft, *History of the Pacific States*, VIII, 344–345 ; Channing and Hart, *Guide*, § 194.

THE existing state of the relations between the United States and Mexico renders it proper that I should bring the subject to the consideration of Congress. In my message at the commencement of your present session the state of these relations, the causes which led to the suspension of diplomatic intercourse between the two countries in March, 1845, and the long-continued and unredressed wrongs and injuries committed by the Mexican Government on citizens of the United States in their persons and property were briefly set forth. . . .

Mr. Slidell arrived at Vera Cruz on the 30th of November [1845], and was courteously received by the authorities of that city. But the Government of General Herrera was then tottering to its fall. The revolutionary party had seized upon the Texas question to effect or hasten its overthrow. Its determination to restore friendly relations with the United States, and to receive our minister to negotiate for the settlement of this question, was violently assailed, and was made the great theme of denunciation against it. The Government of General Herrera, there is good reason to believe, was sincerely desirous to receive our minister ; but it yielded to the storm raised by its enemies, and on the 21st of December refused to accredit Mr. Slidell upon the most frivolous pretexts. These are so fully and ably exposed in the note of Mr. Slidell of the 24th of December last to the Mexican minister of foreign relations, herewith transmitted, that I deem it unnecessary to enter into further detail on this portion of the subject.

Five days after the date of Mr. Slidell's note General Herrera yielded the Government to General Paredes without a struggle, and on the 30th of December resigned the Presidency. This revolution was accomplished solely by the army, the people having taken little part in the contest ; and thus the supreme power in Mexico passed into the hands of a military leader. . . .

Under these circumstances, Mr. Slidell, in obedience to my direction, addressed a note to the Mexican minister of foreign relations, under date of the 1st of March last, asking to be received by that Government in the diplomatic character to which he had been appointed. This minister in his reply, under date of the 12th of March, reiterated the arguments of his predecessor, and in terms that may be considered as giving just grounds of offense to the Government and people of the United States denied the application of Mr. Slidell. Nothing therefore remained for our envoy but to demand his passports and return to his own country.

Thus the Government of Mexico, though solemnly pledged by official acts in October last to receive and accredit an American envoy, violated their plighted faith and refused the offer of a peaceful adjustment of our difficulties. Not only was the offer rejected, but the indignity of its rejection was enhanced by the manifest breach of faith in refusing to admit the envoy who came because they had bound themselves to receive him. Nor can it be said that the offer was fruitless from the want of opportunity of discussing it ; our envoy was present on their own soil. Nor can it be ascribed to a want of sufficient powers ; our envoy had full powers to adjust every question of difference. Nor was there room for complaint that our propositions for settlement were unreasonable ; permission was not even given our envoy to make any proposition whatever. Nor can it be objected that we, on our part, would not listen to any reasonable terms of their suggestion ; the Mexican Government refused all negotiation, and have made no proposition of any kind.

In my message at the commencement of the present session I informed you that upon the earnest appeal both of the Congress and convention of Texas I had ordered an efficient military force to take a position " between the Nueces and the Del Norte." This had become necessary to meet a threatened invasion of Texas by the Mexican forces, for which extensive military preparations had been made. The invasion was threatened solely because Texas had determined, in accordance with a solemn resolution of the Congress of the United States, to annex herself to our Union, and under these circumstances it was plainly our duty to extend our protection over her citizens and soil.

This force was concentrated at Corpus Christi, and remained there until after I had received such information from Mexico as rendered it probable, if not certain, that the Mexican Government would refuse to receive our envoy.

Meantime Texas, by the final action of our Congress, had become an integral part of our Union. The Congress of Texas, by its act of December 19, 1836, had declared the Rio del Norte to be the boundary of that Republic. Its jurisdiction had been extended and exercised beyond the Nueces. The country between that river and the Del Norte had been represented in the Congress and in the convention of Texas, had thus taken part in the act of annexation itself, and is now included within one of our Congressional districts. Our own Congress had, moreover, with great unanimity, by the act approved December 31, 1845, recognized the country beyond the Nueces as a part of our territory by including it within our own revenue system, and a revenue officer to reside within that district has been appointed by and with the advice and consent of the Senate. It became, therefore, of urgent necessity to provide for the defense of that portion of our country. Accordingly, on the 13th of January last instructions were issued to the general in command of these troops to occupy the left bank of the Del Norte. This river, which is the southwestern boundary of the State of Texas, is an exposed frontier. . . .

The movement of the troops to the Del Norte was made by the commanding general under positive instructions to abstain from all aggressive acts toward Mexico or Mexican citizens and to regard the relations between that Republic and the United States as peaceful unless she should declare war or commit acts of hostility indicative of a state of war. He was specially directed to protect private property and respect personal rights.

The Army moved from Corpus Christi on the 11th of March, and on the 28th of that month arrived on the left bank of the Del Norte opposite to Matamoras, where it encamped on a commanding position, which has since been strengthened by the erection of fieldworks. A depot has also been established at Point Isabel, near the Brazos Santiago, 30 miles in rear of the encampment. The selection of his position was necessarily confided to the judgment of the general in command.

The Mexican forces at Matamoras assumed a belligerent attitude, and on the 12th of April General Ampudia, then in command, notified General Taylor to break up his camp within twenty-four hours and to retire beyond the Nueces River, and in the event of his failure to comply with these demands announced that arms, and arms alone, must decide the question. But no open act of hostility was committed until the 24th of April. On that day General Arista, who had succeeded to the command of the Mexican forces, communicated to General Taylor that " he considered hostilities commenced and should prosecute them." A party of dragoons of 63 men and officers were on the same day dispatched from the American camp up the Rio del Norte, on its left bank, to ascertain whether the Mexican troops had crossed or were preparing to cross the river, "became engaged with a large body of these troops, and after a short affair, in which some 16 were killed and wounded, appear to have been surrounded and compelled to surrender."

The grievous wrongs perpetrated by Mexico upon our citizens throughout a long period of years remain unredressed, and solemn treaties pledging her public faith for this redress have been disregarded. A government either unable or unwilling to enforce the execution of such treaties fails to perform one of its plainest duties.

Our commerce with Mexico has been almost annihilated. It was formerly highly beneficial to both nations, but our merchants have been deterred from prosecuting it by the system of outrage and extortion which the Mexican authorities have pursued against them, whilst their appeals through their own Government for indemnity have been made in vain. Our forbearance has gone to such an extreme as to be mistaken in its character. Had we acted with vigor in repelling the insults and redressing the injuries inflicted by Mexico at the commencement, we should doubtless have escaped all the difficulties in which we are now involved.

Instead of this, however, we have been exerting our best efforts to propitiate her good will. Upon the pretext that Texas, a nation as independent as herself, thought proper to unite its destinies with our own, she has affected to believe that we have severed her rightful territory, and in official proclamations and manifestoes has repeatedly threatened to make war upon us for the purpose of reconquering Texas. In the meantime we have tried every effort at reconciliation. The cup of forbearance had been exhausted even before the recent information from the frontier of the Del Norte. But now, after reiterated menaces, Mexico has passed the boundary of the United States, has invaded our territory and shed American blood upon the American soil. She has proclaimed that hostilities have commenced, and that the two nations are now at war.

As war exists, and, notwithstanding all our efforts to avoid it, exists by the act of Mexico herself, we are called upon by every consideration of duty and patriotism to vindicate with decision the honor, the rights, and the interests of our country.

James D. Richardson, *A Compilation of the Messages and Papers of the Presidents* (Washington, 1897), IV, 437–442 *passim*.

11. An Opponent of the War (1847)

BY SENATOR THOMAS CORWIN

Corwin, elected to the United States Senate in 1844 as a Whig, was persistent in his opposition to the war with Mexico. He was a born orator, and by this courageous but indiscreet speech in the Senate against granting an appropriation with which to buy peace and territory from Mexico, he gained renown, but injured his political advancement. — For Corwin, see A. P. Russell, *Thomas Corwin.* — Bibliography : Channing and Hart, *Guide*, § 194.

MR. PRESIDENT, I . . . beg the indulgence of the Senate to some reflections on the particular bill now under consideration. I voted for a bill somewhat like the present at the last session — our army was then in the neighborhood of our line. I then hoped that the President did sincerely desire a peace. Our army had not then penetrated far into Mexico, and I did hope, that with the two millions then proposed, we might get peace, and avoid the slaughter, the shame, the crime, of an aggressive, unprovoked war. But now you have overrun half of Mexico — you have exasperated and irritated her people — you claim indemnity for all expenses incurred in doing this mischief, and boldly ask her to give up New Mexico and California ; and, as a bribe to her patriotism, seizing on her property, you offer three millions to pay the soldiers she has called out to repel your invasion, on condition that she will give up to you at least one-third of her whole territory. . . .

But, sir, let us see what, as the chairman of the Committee on Foreign Relations explains it, we are to get by the combined processes of conquest and treaty.

What is the territory, Mr. President, which you propose to wrest from Mexico ? It is consecrated to the heart of the Mexican by many a well-fought battle with his old Castilian master. His Bunker Hills, and Saratogas, and Yorktowns, are there ! The Mexican can say, "There I bled for liberty ! and shall I surrender that consecrated home of my affections to the Anglo-Saxon invaders ? What do they want with it ? They have Texas already. They have possessed themselves of the territory between the Nueces and the Rio Grande. What else do they want ? To what shall I point my children as memorials of that independence which I bequeath to them when those battle-fields shall have passed from my possession ?"

Sir, had one come and demanded Bunker Hill of the people of Massachusetts, had England's Lion ever showed himself there, is there a man over thirteen and under ninety who would not have been ready to mee* him? Is there a river on this continent that would not have run red with blood? Is there a field but would have been piled high with the unburied bones of slaughtered Americans before these consecrated battle-fields of liberty should have been wrested from us? But this same American goes into a sister republic and says to poor, weak Mexico, "Give up your territory, you are unworthy to possess it; I have got one-half already, and all I ask of you is to give up the other!" England might as well, in the circumstances I have described, have come and demanded of us, "Give up the Atlantic slope—give up this trifling territory from the Alleghany Mountains to the sea; it is only from Maine to St. Mary's — only about one-third of your republic, and the least interesting portion of it." What would be the response? They would say, we must give this up to John Bull. Why? "He wants room." The Senator from Michigan says he must have this. Why, my worthy Christian brother, on what principle of justice? "I want room!"

Sir, look at this pretence of want of room. With twenty millions of people, you have about one thousand millions of acres of land, inviting settlement by every conceivable argument, bringing them down to a quarter of a dollar an acre, and allowing every man to squat where he pleases. But the Senator from Michigan says we will be two hundred millions in a few years, and we want room. If I were a Mexican I would tell you, "Have you not room in your own country to bury your dead men? If you come into mine, we will greet you with bloody hands, and welcome you to hospitable graves."

Why, says the chairman of this Committee on Foreign Relations, it is the most reasonable thing in the world! We ought to have the Bay of San Francisco. Why? Because it is the best harbor on the Pacific! It has been my fortune, Mr. President, to have practised a good deal in criminal courts in the course of my life, but I never yet heard a thief, arraigned for stealing a horse, plead that it was the best horse that he could find in the country! We want California. What for? Why, says the Senator from Michigan, we will have it; and the Senator from South Carolina, with a very mistaken view, I think, of policy, says you can't keep our people from going there. I don't desire to prevent them. Let them go and seek their happiness in whatever country or clime it pleases them.

All I ask of them is, not to require this Government to protect them with that banner consecrated to war waged for principles — eternal, enduring truth. Sir, it is not meet that our old flag should throw its protecting folds over expeditions for lucre or for land.   But you still say you want room for your people.   This has been the plea of every robber chief from Nimrod to the present hour. . . .

Appendix to the Congressional Globe, 29 Cong., 2 sess. (Blair and Rives, Washington, 1847), 216–217 *passim*, February 11, 1847.

———◆———

12. A Young Officer in the War (1847)

BY SECOND LIEUTENANT ULYSSES SIMPSON GRANT

Young Grant was fresh from West Point; he served throughout the war, first under Taylor and later under Scott.   For his gallantry in the event here described he was brevetted captain and mentioned in several reports, among others in that of Major Robert E. Lee. — For Grant, see Channing and Hart, *Guide*, § 25. — Bibliography: H. H. Bancroft, *History of the Pacific States*, VIII, 550–556; Channing and Hart, *Guide*, § 194.

I WAS with the earliest of the troops to enter the Mills.   In passing through to the north side, looking towards Chapultepec, I happened to notice that there were armed Mexicans still on top of the building, only a few feet from many of our men.   Not seeing any stairway or ladder reaching to the top of the building, I took a few soldiers, and had a cart that happened to be standing near brought up, and, placing the shafts against the wall and chocking the wheels so that the cart could not back, used the shafts as a sort of ladder extending to within three or four feet of the top.   By this I climbed to the roof of the building, followed by a few men, but found a private soldier had preceded me by some other way.   There were still quite a number of Mexicans on the roof, among them a major and five or six officers of lower grades, who had not succeeded in getting away before our troops occupied the building.   They still had their arms, while the soldier before mentioned was walking as sentry, guarding the prisoners he had *surrounded*, all by himself.   I halted the sentinel, received the swords from the commissioned officers, and proceeded, with the assistance of the soldiers now with me, to disable the muskets by striking them against the edge of the wall, and throw them to the ground below. . . .

During the night of the 11th [September] batteries were established which could play upon the fortifications of Chapultepec.   The bombardment commenced early on the morning of the 12th, but there was no further engagement during this day than that of the artillery.   General Scott assigned the capture of Chapultepec to General Pillow, but did not leave the details to his judgment. Two assaulting columns, two hundred and fifty men each, composed of volunteers for the occasion, were formed. They were commanded by Captains McKinzie and Casey respectively. The assault was successful, but bloody. . . .

Worth's command gradually advanced to the front. . . . Later in the day in reconnoitring I found a church off to the south of the road, which looked to me as if the belfry would command the ground back of the garita San Cosme. I got an officer of the voltigeurs, with a mountain howitzer and men to work it, to go with me. The road being in possession of the enemy, we had to take the field to the south to reach the church. This took us over several ditches breast deep in water and grown up with water plants. These ditches, however, were not over eight or ten feet in width. The howitzer was taken to pieces and carried by the men to its destination. When I knocked for admission a priest came to the door, who, while extremely polite, declined to admit us. With the little Spanish then at my command, I explained to him that he might save property by opening the door, and he certainly would save himself from becoming a prisoner, for a time at least ; and besides, I intended to go in whether he consented or not. He began to see his duty in the same light that I did, and opened the door, though he did not look as if it gave him special pleasure to do so. The gun was carried to the belfry and put together. We were not more than two or three hundred yards from San Cosme. The shots from our little gun dropped in upon the enemy and created great confusion. Why they did not send out a small party and capture us, I do not know. We had no infantry or other defences besides our one gun.

The effect of this gun upon the troops about the gate of the city was so marked that General Worth saw it from his position. He was so pleased that he sent a staff officer, Lieutenant Pemberton . . . to bring me to him. He expressed his gratification at the services the howitzer in the church steeple was doing, saying that every shot was effective, and ordered a captain of voltigeurs to report to me with another howitzer to be placed along with the one already rendering so much service. I could not tell the General that there was not room enough in the steeple for another gun, because he probably would have looked upon such a statement as a contradiction from a second lieutenant. I took the captain with me, but did not use his gun.

U. S. Grant, *Personal Memoirs* (New York, 1885), I, 152–159 *passim.*

13. Capture of Mexico (1847)

BY GENERAL WINFIELD SCOTT

Scott served with honor in the War of 1812, and in 1841 became commander-in-chief of the army. Like Taylor, he was a Whig. The Democratic administration with reluctance consented that he should command in person the expedition against Mexico, which he brought to the brilliant close described in the report given below. Scott was punctilious and brave and loyal, and in the Mexican War he showed himself a leader among soldiers. — For Scott, see M. J. Wright, *General Scott, passim,* especially Preface. — Bibliography as in No. 12 above.

HEAD-QUARTERS OF THE ARMY,

National Palace of Mexico, Sept. 18, 1847.

. . . AT the end of another series of arduous and brilliant operations, of more than forty-eight hours continuance, this glorious army hoisted, on the morning of the 14th, the colors of the United States on the walls of this palace. . . .

This city stands upon a slight swell of ground, near the centre of an irregular basin, and is girdled with a ditch in its greater extent — a navigable canal of great breadth and depth — very difficult to bridge in the presence of an enemy, and serving at once for drainage, custom-house purposes, and military defence ; leaving eight entrances or gates over arches, each of which we found defended by a system of strong works, that seemed to require nothing but some men and guns to be impregnable.

Outside, and within the cross-fires of those gates, we found to the south other obstacles but little less formidable.   All the approaches near the city, are over elevated causeways, cut in many places (to oppose us) and flanked on both sides by ditches, also, of unusual dimensions. The numerous cross-roads are flanked in like manner, having bridges at the intersections, recently broken.   The meadows thus chequered, are, moreover, in many spots, under water, or marshy ; for, it will be remembered, we were in the midst of the wet season, though with less rain than usual, and we could not wait for the fall of the neighboring lakes and the consequent drainage of the wet grounds at the edge of the city — the lowest in the whole basin.

After a close personal survey of the southern gates, covered by Pillow's division and Riley's brigade of Twiggs's, with four times our numbers concentrated in our immediate front, I determined, on the

11th, to avoid that net-work of obstacles, and to seek, by a sudden inversion to the southwest and west, less unfavorable approaches. . . .

The first step in the new movement was to carry Chapultepec, a natural and isolated mound, of great elevation, strongly fortified at its base, on its acclivities and heights. Besides a numerous garrison, here was the military college of the republic, with a large number of sub-lieutenants and other students. Those works were within direct gun-shot of the village of Tacubaya, and, until carried, we could not approach the city on the west without making a circuit too wide and too hazardous. . . .

The signal I had appointed for the attack was the momentary cessa-tion of fire on the part of our heavy batteries. About eight o'clock in the morning of the 13th, judging that the time had arrived, by the effect of the missiles we had thrown, I sent an aid-de-camp to Pillow, and another to Quitman, with notice that the concerted signal was about to be given. Both columns now advanced with an alacrity that gave assurance of prompt success. The batteries, seizing opportunities, threw shots and shells upon the enemy over the heads of our men, with good effect, particularly at every attempt to reinforce the works from without to meet our assault.

Major General Pillow's approach, on the west side, lay through an open grove, filled with sharp shooters, who were speedily dislodged; when, being up with the front of the attack, and emerging into open space, at the foot of a rocky acclivity, that gallant leader was struck down by an agonizing wound. The immediate command devolved on Brigadier General Cadwalader, in the absence of the senior brigadier (Pierce) of the same division — an invalid since the events of August 19. On a previous call of Pillow, Worth had just sent him a reinforcement — Colonel Clark's brigade.

The broken acclivity was still to be ascended, and a strong redoubt, midway, to be carried, before reaching the castle on the heights. The advance of our brave men, led by brave officers, though necessarily slow, was unwavering, over rocks, chasms, and mines, and under the hottest fire of cannon and musketry. The redoubt now yielded to resistless valor, and the shouts that followed announced to the castle the fate that impended. The enemy were steadily driven from shelter to shelter. The retreat allowed not time to fire a single mine, without the certainty of blowing up friend and foe. Those who at a distance attempted to apply matches to the long trains were shot down by our men. There was death below, as well as above ground. At length the ditch and wall of the main work were reached ; the scaling-ladders were brought up and planted by the storming parties ; some of the daring spirits first in the assault were cast down — killed or wounded ; but a lodgment was soon made ; streams of heroes followed ; all opposition was overcome, and several of the regimental colors flung out from the upper walls, amidst long-continued shouts and cheers, which sent dismay into the capital. No scene could have been more animating or glorious.

Major General Quitman, nobly supported by Brigadier Generals Shields and Smith (P. F.,) his other officers and men, was up with the part assigned him. . . . The New York and South Carolina volunteers (Shields' brigade) and the 2d Pennsylvania volunteers, all on the left of Quitman's line, together with portions of the storming parties, crossed the meadows in front, under a heavy fire, and entered the outer enclosure of Chapultepec just in time to join in the final assault from the west. . . .

At this junction of roads, we first passed one of those formidable systems of city defences, spoken of above, and it had not a gun ! — a strong proof — 1. That the enemy had expected us to fall in the attack upon Chapultepec, even if we meant anything more than a feint ; 2. That, in either case, we designed, in his belief, to return and double our forces against the southern gates, a delusion kept up by the active demonstrations of Twiggs and the forces posted on that side ; and 3. That advancing rapidly from the reduction of Chapultepec, the enemy had not time to shift guns — our previous captures had left him, comparatively, but few — from the southern gates.

Within those disgarnished works, I found our troops engaged in a street fight against the enemy posted in gardens, at windows and on house-tops — all flat, with parapets. Worth ordered forward the mountain howitzers of Cadwalader's brigade, preceded by skirmishers and pioneers, with pickaxes and crowbars, to force windows and doors, or to burrow through walls. The assailants were soon in an equality of position fatal to the enemy. By 8 o'clock in the evening, Worth had carried two batteries in this suburb. According to my instructions, he here posted guards and sentinels, and placed his troops under shelter for the night. There was but one more obstacle — the San Cosme gate (custom-house) between him and the great square in front of the cathedral and palace — the heart of the city ; and that barrier, it was known, could not, by daylight, resist our siege guns thirty minutes. . . .

I had intended that Quitman should only manœuvre and threaten the Belén or southwestern gate, in order to favor the main attack . . .

Those views I repeatedly, in the course of the day, communicated to Major General Quitman ; but being in hot pursuit — gallant himself, and ably supported by Brigadier Generals Shields and Smith — Shields badly wounded before Chapultepec and refusing to retire — as well as by all the officers and men of the column — Quitman continued to press forward, under flank and direct fires ; — carried an intermediate battery of two guns, and then the gate, before two o'clock in the afternoon, but not without proportionate loss, increased by his steady maintenance of that position. . . .

Quitman, within the city — adding several new defences to the position he had won, and sheltering his corps as well as practicable — now awaited the return of daylight under the guns of the formidable citadel, yet to be subdued.

At about 4 o'clock next morning, (September 14,) a deputation of the *ayuntamiento* (city council) waited upon me to report that the federal government and the army of Mexico had fled from the capital some three hours before, and to demand terms of capitulation in favor of the church, the citizens, and the municipal authorities. I promptly replied, that I would sign no capitulation ; that the city had been virtually in our possession from the time of the lodgments effected by Worth and Quitman the day before ; that I regretted the silent escape of the Mexican army ; that I should levy upon the city a moderate contribution, for special purposes ; and that the American army should come under no terms, not *self*-imposed — such only as its own honor, the dignity of the United States, and the spirit of the age should, in my opinion, imperiously demand and impose. . . .

At the termination of the interview with the city deputation, I communicated, about daylight, orders to Worth and Quitman to advance slowly and cautiously (to guard against treachery) towards the heart of the city, and to occupy its stronger and more commanding points. Quitman proceeded to the great *plaza* or square, planted guards, and hoisted the colors of the United States on the national palace — containing the halls of Congress and executive apartments of federal Mexico. . . .

House Executive Documents, 30 Cong., 1 sess. (Washington, 1848), II, No. 8, pp. 375–383 *passim*.

14. Why the Whole of Mexico was not Annexed (1847–1848)

BY PRESIDENT JAMES KNOX POLK

Polk's public papers on the Mexican War need to be supplemented by his unpublished diary, of which a transcript is available. In all American history we have few such revelations of the inside workings of war and diplomacy. But for Polk's resistance Mexico would probably have disappeared from the list of nations. — Bibliography: E. G. Bourne, *The United States and Mexico*, 1847–1848, in *American Historical Review*, April, 1900; also in American Historical Association, *Report for 1899*.

September 4 [1847]. — I SAID that I would be unwilling to pay the sum which Mr Trist had been authorized to pay, in the settlement of a boundary by which it was contemplated that the United States would acquire New Mexico and the Californias; and that if Mexico continued obstinately to refuse to treat, I was decidedly in favor of insisting on more territory than the provinces named. I expressed the opinion further that as our expenses had been greatly enlarged by the obstinacy of Mexico, in refusing to negotiate, since Mr. Trist's instructions were prepared in April last, if a treaty had not been made when we next heard from Mexico, that his instructions should be modified. . . .

September 7. — The distinct question submitted was whether the amount which Mr. Trist had been authorized to pay for the cession of New Mexico and the Californias, and right of passage through the Isthmus of Tehuantepec should not be reduced, and whether we should not now demand more territory than we now did. All seemed to agree that the maximum sum to be paid for the cessions above described should be reduced. Mr. Buchanan suggested that this sum should be reduced from 30 to 15 millions, and that the cession of the right of passage through the Isthmus of lower, as well as upper California and New Mexico should be made a *sine qua non*. He suggested also that the line should run on the parallel of 31° or 31.° 30' of North Latitude from the Rio Grande to the Gulf of California, instead of on the parallel of 32° which Mr. Trist had been authorized to accept. Upon the question of acquiring more territory than this, there was some difference of opinion. The Secretary of the Treasury and the Attorney General were in favor of acquiring in addition the Department or state of Tamaulipas which includes the port of Tampico. The Postmaster General and the Secretary of the

Navy concurred with him.   I expressed myself as being entirely agreed to reduce the sum to be paid from 30 to 15 millions and to modify the line as suggested by Mr. Buchanan.   I declared myself as being in favor of acquiring the cession of the Department of Tamaulipas, if it should be found practicable. . . .

November 9. — Mr. Buchanan spoke to-day in an unsettled tone, and said I must take one of two courses in my next message : viz. to designate the part of Mexican territory which we intended to hold as an indemnity, or to occupy all Mexico by a largely increased force and subdue the country and promise protection to the inhabitants.   He said he would express no opinion between these two plans ; but after the despatches which were expected from the army were received he would do so.   I remarked that I thought our policy had been settled upon sometime since, but as the subject was now brought up as one that was still open, I would read what I had written on the subject, and I did so.   My views as thus reduced to writing were in substance that we would continue the prosecution of the war with an increased force, hold all the country we had conquered, or might conquer, and levy contributions upon the enemy to support the war, until a just peace was obtained, that we must have indemnity in territory, and that as a part indemnity, the Californias and New Mexico should under no circumstances be restored to Mexico, but that they should henceforward be considered a part of the United States and permanent territorial governments be established over them ; and that if Mexico protracted the war additional territory must be acquired as further indemnity.

His change of opinion will not alter my views ; I am fixed in my course, and I think all the Cabinet except Mr. Buchanan still concur with me, and he may yet do so. . . .

November 18. — I requested Mr. Buchanan to prepare a paragraph for the message to the effect that failing to obtain a peace, we should continue to occupy Mexico with our troops, and encourage and protect the friends of peace in Mexico to establish and maintain a republican government, able and willing to make peace.

In Mr. Buchanan's draft, he stated in that event that "we must fulfill that destiny which Providence may have in store for both countries."

I thought this would be too indefinite and that it would be avoiding my constitutional responsibility.   I preferred to state in substance that we should, in that event, take the measure of our indemnity into our own hands and dictate our own terms to Mexico. . . .

D

November 23. — Mr. Buchanan still preferred his own draft, and so did Mr. Walker, the latter avowing as a reason that he was for taking the whole of Mexico, if necessary, and he thought the construction placed upon Mr. Buchanan's draft by a large majority of the people would be that it looked to that object.

I replied that I was not prepared to go to that extent, and furthermore, that I did not desire that anything I said in the message should be so obscure as to give rise to doubt or discussion as to what my true meaning was; that I had in my last message declared that I did not contemplate the conquest of Mexico, and that in another part of this paper I had said the same thing. . . .

February 21 [1848]. — I announced to the Cabinet that under all the circumstances of the case I would submit it to the Senate for ratification, with a recommendation to strike out the tenth article. I assigned my reasons for this decision. They were, briefly, that the treaty conformed on the main question of limits and boundary to the instructions given Mr. Trist in April last, and that though if the treaty was now to be made I should demand more territory, perhaps, to make the Sierra Madre the line, yet it was doubtful whether this could be ever obtained by the consent of Mexico. I looked to the consequences of its rejection. A majority of one branch of Congress is opposed to my Administration; they have falsely charged that the war was brought on and is continued by me with a view to the conquest of Mexico, and if I were now to reject a treaty made upon my own terms, as authorized in April last, with the unanimous approbation of the Cabinet, the probability is that Congress would not grant either men or money to prosecute the war. Should this be the result, the army now in Mexico would be constantly wasting and diminishing in numbers, and I might at last be compelled to withdraw them, and then lose the two provinces of New Mexico and Upper California, which were ceded to the U. S. by this treaty. Should the opponents of my Administration succeed in carrying the next Presidential election, the great probability is that the country would lose all the advantages secured by this treaty. I adverted to the immense value of Upper California, and concluded by saying that if I were now to reject my own terms as offered in April last I did not see how it was possible for my Administration to be sustained. . . .

Transcript of Polk's Diary, prepared for George Bancroft, in the Lenox Library, New York.

CHAPTER III — WILMOT PROVISO AND COMPROMISE

15. The Doughface's Creed (1848)

BY JAMES RUSSELL LOWELL

The Mexican War opened the eyes of the North to southern intentions, and the opposition to the war found perhaps its most influential expression in Lowell's stinging satire under the name of "The Biglow Papers." Famous as poet, critic, and diplomatist, Lowell did his greatest service for his country when he wrote these verses in the Yankee dialect. — For Lowell, see E. E. Hale, Jr., *James Russell Lowell*, 124–128. — Bibliography as in No. 11 above.

I DU believe in Freedom's cause,
    Ez fur away ez Paris is;
I love to see her stick her claws
    In them infarnal Pharisees;
It's wal enough agin a king
    To dror resolves an' triggers, —
But libbaty's a kind o' thing
    Thet don't agree with niggers.

I du believe the people want
    A tax on teas an' coffees,
Thet nothin' aint extravygunt, —
    Purvidin' I'm in office;
Fer I hev loved my country sence
    My eye-teeth filled their sockets,
An' Uncle Sam I reverence,
    Partic'larly his pockets.

I du believe in *any* plan
    O' levyin' the taxes,
Ez long ez, like a lumberman,
    I git jest wut I axes:

I go free-trade thru thick an' thin,
    Because it kind o' rouses
The folks to vote, — an' keeps us in
    Our quiet custom-houses.

I du believe it 's wise an' good
    To sen' out furrin missions,
Thet is, on sartin understood
    An' orthydox conditions ; —
I mean nine thousan' dolls. per ann.,
    Nine thousan' more fer outfit,
An' me to recommend a man
    The place 'ould jest about fit.

I du believe in special ways
    O' prayin' an' convartin' ;
The bread comes back in many days,
    An' buttered, tu, fer sartin ; —
I mean in preyin' till one busts
    On wut the party chooses,
An' in convartin' public trusts
    To very privit uses.

I du believe hard coin the stuff
    Fer 'lectioneers to spout on ;
The people 's ollers soft enough
    To make hard money out on ;
Dear Uncle Sam pervides fer his,
    An' gives a good-sized junk to all, —
I don't care *how* hard money is,
    Ez long ez mine 's paid punctooal.

I du believe with all my soul
    In the gret Press's freedom,
To pint the people to the goal
    An' in the traces lead 'em ;
Palsied the arm thet forges yokes
    At my fat contracts squintin',
An' withered be the nose thet pokes
    Inter the gov'ment printin' !

I du believe thet I should give
    Wut's his'n unto Cæsar,
Fer it's by him I move an' live,
    Frum him my bread an' cheese air;
I du believe thet all o' me
    Doth bear his souperscription, —
Will, conscience, honor, honesty,
    An' things o' thet description.

I du believe in prayer an' praise
    To him thet hez the grantin'
O' jobs, — in every thin' thet pays,
    But most of all in CANTIN';
This doth my cup with marcies fill,
    This lays all thought o' sin to rest, —
I *don't* believe in princerple,
    But, O, I *du* in interest.

I du believe in bein' this
    Or thet, ez it may happen
One way or t' other hendiest is
    To ketch the people nappin';
It aint by princerples nor men
    My preudunt course is steadied, —
I scent wich pays the best, an' then
    Go into it baldheaded.

I du believe thet holdin' slaves
    Comes nat'ral tu a Presidunt,
Let 'lone the rowdedow it saves
    To hev a wal-broke precedunt;
Fer any office, small or gret,
    I could n't ax with no face,
Without I 'd ben, thru dry an' wet,
    Th' unrizzest kind o' doughface.

I du believe wutever trash
    'll keep the people in blindness, —
Thet we the Mexicuns can thrash
    Right inter brotherly kindness,

Thet bombshells, grape, an' powder 'n' ball
  Air good-will's strongest magnets,
Thet peace, to make it stick at all,
  Must be druv in with bagnets.

In short, I firmly du believe
  In Humbug generally,
Fer it's a thing thet I perceive
  To hev a solid vally;
This heth my faithful shepherd ben,
  In pasturs sweet heth led me,
An' this 'll keep the people green
  To feed ez they hev fed me.

[James Russell Lowell], *The Biglow Papers*, [First Series] (Cambridge, 1848), No. vi., 75–80.

---

16. Defence of the Proviso (1847)

BY REPRESENTATIVE DAVID WILMOT

Wilmot was a Northern Democrat, content to allow the South some of her demands, but unwilling to have any responsibility for more slave territory. His famous proviso, first introduced in 1846, was the bugle-call which aroused the North to the intention of the South to increase the slave states beyond Texas, and thus to extend slavery. Lincoln once boasted that he had voted for the principle of the Wilmot Proviso forty-two times in the two years of his service in the House. — Bibliography : Channing and Hart, *Guide*, § 196.

SIR, it will be recollected by all present, that, at the last session of Congress, an amendment was moved by me to a bill of the same character as this, in the form of a proviso, by which slavery should be excluded from any territory that might subsequently be acquired by the United States from the republic of Mexico.

Sir, on that occasion, that proviso was sustained by a very decided majority of this House. Nay, sir, more, it was sustained, if I mistake not, by a majority of the Republican party on this floor. I am prepared, I think, to show that the entire South were then willing to acquiesce in what appeared to be, and, in so far as the action of this House was concerned, what was the legislative will and declaration of the Union on this subject. It passed this House. Sir, there were no threats of disunion sounded in our ears. It passed here and went to the Senate and it was the judgment of the public, and of men well informed, that, had it not been defeated there for want of time, it would have passed that body and become the established law of the land. . . .

. . . There was then no cry that the Union was to be severed in consequence. The South, like brave men defeated, bowed to the voice and judgment of the nation. No, sir, no cry of disunion then. Why now? The hesitation and the wavering of northern men on this question has encouraged the South to assume a bolder attitude. This cry of disunion proceeds from no resolve of the South. It comes, sir, from the cowardice of the North. . . .

But, sir, the issue now presented is not whether slavery shall exist unmolested where it now is, but whether it shall be carried to new and distant regions, now free, where the footprint of a slave cannot be found. This, sir, is the issue. Upon it I take my stand, and from it I cannot be frightened or driven by idle charges of abolitionism. I ask not that slavery be abolished. I demand that this Government preserve the integrity of *free territory* against the aggressions of slavery — against its wrongful usurpations. Sir, I was in favor of the annexation of Texas. . . . The Democracy of the North, almost to a man, went for annexation. Yes, sir, here was an empire larger than France given up to slavery. Shall further concessions be made by the North? Shall we give up free territory, the inheritance of free labor? Must we yield this also? Never, sir, never, until we ourselves are fit to be slaves. The North may be betrayed by her Representatives, but upon this great question she will be true to herself — true to posterity. Defeat! Sir, there can be no defeat. Defeat to-day will but arouse the teeming millions of the North, and lead to a more decisive and triumphant victory to-morrow.

But, sir, we are told, that the joint blood and treasure of the whole country being expended in this acquisition, therefore it should be divided, and slavery allowed to take its share. Sir, the South has her share already; the instalment for slavery was paid in advance. We are fighting this war for Texas and for the South. I affirm it — every intelligent man knows it — Texas is the primary cause of this war. For this, sir, northern treasure is being exhausted, and northern blood poured out upon the plains of Mexico. We are fighting this war cheerfully, not reluctantly — cheerfully fighting this war for Texas; and yet we seek not to change the character of her institutions. Slavery is there : there let it remain. . . .

Now, sir, we are told that California is ours; that New Mexico is ours — won by the valor of our arms. They are free. Shall they remain free? Shall these fair provinces be the inheritance and homes of the white labor of freemen or the black labor of slaves? This, sir, is the issue — this the question. The North has the right, and her representatives here have the power. . . . But the South contend, that in their emigration to this free territory, they have the right to take and hold slaves, the same as other property. Unless the amendment I have offered be adopted, or other early legislation is had upon this subject, they will do so. Indeed, they unitedly, as one man, have declared their right and purpose so to do, and the work has already begun. Slavery follows in the rear of our armies. Shall the war power of our Government be exerted to produce such a result? Shall this Government depart from its neutrality on this question, and lend its power and influence to plant slavery in these territories? There is no question of abolition here, sir. Shall the South be permitted, by aggression, by invasion of the right, by subduing free territory, and planting slavery upon it, to wrest these provinces from northern freemen, and turn them to the accomplishment of their own sectional purposes and schemes? This is the question. Men of the North answer. Shall it be so? Shall we of the North submit to it? If we do, we are coward slaves, and deserve to have the manacles fastened upon our own limbs.

Appendix to the Congressional Globe, 29 Cong., 2 sess. (Blair and Rives, Washington, 1847), 315 *passim*, February 8, 1847.

---

17. Extension of the Constitution (1849)

BY SENATOR ISAAC P. WALKER

Walker was elected to the Senate as an anti-slavery Democrat; but his love for the Union made him timid; his so-called "peace-offering" amendment was thought to be too favorable to the South. Southern statesmen were not unwilling to accept a tangible enactment which was in harmony with their constitutional theories. The amendment passed in the Senate but was rejected in the House. — Bibliography as in No. 16 above.

USUALLY, sir, these general laws of the United States have been extended over Territories gradually. . . .

But what is the state of the case before us? Let me call the attention of the Senate to this state of the case. Here we see a picture presented

which was never presented before ; we see a country occupying a position which none ever occupied before it.   We are witnessing developments which are new and unprecedented.   Here we see interests of the
most momentous kind growing suddenly into existence, and interests,
too, which in their tendency, since man first existed, have had the effect
more to excite the avarice and the baser passions of the human mind
than any other. . . .

. . . Sir, we find here a more heterogeneous class of population than
perhaps we ever found, or shall ever find, congregated, during the same
space of time, in any region of the world. . . .   Then, sir, this is a state
of things which renders it very necessary indeed that steps extraordinary
and commensurate with the emergency should be taken by us, for the
purpose of accomplishing the end so desirable. . . .

. . . Now, sir, what I propose shall be done, is set forth in the amendment which I have had the honor to offer to the Senate. . . .

"SEC. — *And be it further enacted,* That the Constitution of the United States, and
all and singular the several acts of Congress . . . of a public and general character,
and the provisions whereof are suitable and proper to be applied to the territory west
of the Rio del Norte, acquired from Mexico by the treaty of the second day of February, eighteen hundred and forty-eight, be, and the same are hereby, extended over
and given, and made in full force and efficacy in all said territory."

That is the first provision.   Now, I have remarked that this general
extension of the laws of the United States over the territories has generally taken place gradually, as the interests and necessities of the country
to which they were to be extended grew up.   But, sir, under the peculiar
state of things here, it is proposed now, and in this manner, to extend
them at once.   Suppose, sir, that we were to propose to carry this matter
through a series of years, should we not have the power to do all that is
proposed to be done now? . . .

Here, sir, I beg leave to call the attention of the Senate for a moment
to the remarks of the honorable Senator from New Jersey (Mr. DAYTON)
upon this subject.   He objects to the extension of these laws. . . .

. . . his argument is, that the South claims that the Constitution gives
them the right to take their slaves there and make it a slave country. . . .
Sir, my feelings upon the subject of slavery are, perhaps, as well known here
as those of any other Senator upon this floor.   But, sir, I say before this
Senate, and before high Heaven, that I feel myself incapable of entertaining any such feelings as those entertained by the Senator from New Jersey.
If the Constitution will extend slavery to the land, then let it go.   If by
that Constitution slavery is extended, I am willing to stand by that Con·

stitution. I am unwilling to withhold from our southern brethren any of the rights given to them by that sacred instrument. If by the operation of the Constitution they have any advantage, they may possess it. . . . I am not one to violate a constitution I have sworn to support, merely to cripple an institution which I condemn. No; take it. But let the people of that distant country have the benefit of its protection extended to them. . . .

. . . This is a peace-offering. It is not proposed to organize a government where the Wilmot proviso will be either applicable or inapplicable. That question comes up when we propose to organize a territorial government. This is an intermediate step between anarchy and territorial government. This is to do what little we can for that country to protect the rights of southern men as well as men of the North; to protect the property of the South as well as of the North. . . .

Mr. DAYTON. Would the gentleman say that the Constitution of the United States can be extended by an act of legislation? . . .

Mr. WALKER. I was going to remark that, whether the Constitution *proprio vigore*, extend there or not, or whether it can be extended over it or not by legislation, there would be no doubt as to the extension of the principles of the Constitution as a legislative act of Congress. There is nothing in the Constitution which is unconstitutional; and, therefore, it would not be unconstitutional. And, therefore, to provide that any of its provisions applicable should be extended, would not be in violation of the Constitution. If, then, we approve of the provisions of this measure, it is clearly constitutional, as far as legislation is concerned.

Mr. DAYTON. May I interrupt the Senator for a moment? I supposed it was a clear point that the Constitution of the United States, being a contract and agreement between sovereign States, could be extended no further than it, by its inherent power, extended itself. No act of legislation could make that compact between sovereign States reach further than to these States. . . .

Mr. WALKER. . . . But when we extend the provisions of the Constitution to these territories, we do not extend its vigor and its provisions to these localities as a whole, as a compact, but as a piece of legislation on the part of the supreme power of the nation. . . .

I have before remarked, that so far as the protection of life, liberty, personal security, and the rights of property are concerned, the citizen, as such, had the shield of the Constitution there already thrown before

him ; and that when he went there, he went with these rights, and entitled to this shield of protection.   Now, sir, we propose to enforce these
rights, and protect him in the enjoyment of them.

Appendix to the Congressional Globe, 30 Cong., 2 sess. (Blair and Rives, Washington, 1849), 266–268 *passim*, February 24, 1849.

------◆------

18. A Forty-Niner (1849–1850)

BY ALONZO DELANO (1852)

Delano's work is a truthful and valuable personal account of the hardships endured
in crossing the plains in 1849, and of the trials, failures, and successes of the argo-
nauts, especially in the smaller mining towns. — Bibliography: H. H. Bancroft, *History of the Pacific States*, XVIII, chs. viii–ix *passim*, especially 161–163.

. . . OUR general rendezvous was to be at St. Joseph, on the Missouri, from which we intended to take our departure.   I had
engaged men, purchased cattle and a wagon, and subsequently laid in my
supplies for the trip, at St. Louis.   My wagon I shipped by water to St.
Joseph, and sent my cattle across the country about the middle of March,
[1849] to meet me at the place of rendezvous, in April. . . .

[May 21.]   Our desire to be upon the road induced us to be stirring
early, and we were moving as soon as our cattle had eaten their fill,
when a drive of a mile placed us upon the great thoroughfare of the gold
seekers.

For miles, to the extent of vision, an animated mass of beings broke
upon our view.   Long trains of wagons with their white covers were
moving slowly along, a multitude of horsemen were prancing on the
road, companies of men were traveling on foot, and although the scene
was not a gorgeous one, yet the display of banners from many wagons,
and the multitude of armed men, looked as if a mighty army was on its
march ; and in a few moments we took our station in the line, a compo-
nent part of the motley throng of gold seekers, who were leaving home
and friends far behind, to encounter the peril of mountain and plain. . . .

[June 29.]   On leaving the Missouri, nearly every train was an organized company, with general regulations for mutual safety, and with a
captain chosen by themselves, as a nominal head.   On reaching the
South Pass, we found that the great majority had either divided, or

broken up entirely, making independent and helter-skelter marches towards California. . . .

[August 10.] Reports began to reach us of hard roads ahead; that there was no grass at the Sink, or place where the river disappears in the sands of the desert, and that from that place a desert of sand, with water but once in forty-five miles, had to be crossed. In our worn-out condition this looked discouraging, and it was with a kind of dread that we looked to the passage of that sandy plain. At the same time an indefinite tale was circulated among the emigrants, that a new road had been discovered, by which the Sacramento might be reached in a shorter distance, avoiding altogether the dreaded desert; and that there was plenty of grass and water on the route. . . .

[August 11.] . . . There were a great many men daily passing, who, having worn down their cattle and mules, had abandoned their wagons, and were trying to get through as they might; but their woe-begone countenances and meagre accoutrements for such a journey, with want, and excessive labor staring them in the face, excited our pity, wretched as we felt ourselves. Our own cattle had been prudently driven, and were still in good condition to perform the journey. Although our stock of provisions was getting low, we felt that under any circumstances we could get through, and notwithstanding we felt anxious, we were not discouraged. . . .

[August 15.] . . . It was decided, finally, that we would go the northern route, although some of our company had misgivings. The younger portion being fond of adventure, were loud in favor of the road. . . .

[August 16.] . . . Beyond us, far as we could see, was a barren waste, without a blade of grass or a drop of water for thirty miles at least. Instead of avoiding the desert, instead of the promised water, grass, and a better road, we were in fact upon a more dreary and wider waste, without either grass or water, and with a harder road before us. . . .

[August 17.] As I walked on slowly and with effort, I encountered a great many animals, perishing for want of food and water, on the desert plain. Some would be just gasping for breath, others unable to stand, would issue low moans as I came up, in a most distressing manner, showing intense agony; and still others, unable to walk, seemed to brace themselves up on their legs to prevent falling, while here and there a poor ox, or horse, just able to drag himself along, would stagger towards me with a low sound, as if begging for a drop of water. My sympathies were excited at their sufferings, yet, instead of affording them aid, I was a subject for relief myself.

High above the plain, in the direction of our road, a black, bare mountain reared its head, at the distance of fifteen miles ; and ten miles this side the plains was flat, composed of baked earth, without a sign of vegetation, and in many places covered with incrustations of salt. Pits had been sunk in moist places, but the water was salt as brine, and utterly useless. . . .

The train had passed me in the night, and our cattle traveled steadily without faltering, reaching the spring about nine o'clock in the morning, after traveling nearly forty hours without food or water. If ever a cup of coffee and slice of bacon was relished by man, it was by me that morning, on arriving at the encampment a little after ten.

We found this to be an oasis in the desert. A large hot spring, nearly three rods in diameter, and very deep, irrigated about twenty acres of ground — the water cooling as it ran off. . . .

[August 20.] . . . Through the day there was a constant arrival of wagons, and by night there were several hundred men together ; yet we learned by a mule train that at least one hundred and fifty wagons had turned back to the first spring west of the Humboldt, on learning the dangers of crossing the desert, taking wisely the old road again. This change of route, however, did not continue long, and the rear trains, comprising a large portion of the emigration, took our route, and suffered even worse than we did. It was resolved that several trains should always travel within supporting distance of each other, so that in case of an attack from the Indians, a sufficient body of men should be together to protect themselves. . . . Reports again reached us corroborating the great loss of cattle on the desert beyond the Sink. The road was filled with dead animals, and the offensive effluvia had produced much sickness ; but shortly afterward, our own portion of the desert presented the same catastrophe, and the road was lined with the dead bodies of wornout and starved animals, and their debilitated masters, in many cases, were left to struggle on foot, combatting hunger, thirst and fatigue, in a desperate exertion to get through. . . .

[September 17.] . . . Ascending to the top of an inclined plain, the long-sought, the long-wished-for and welcome valley of the Sacramento, lay before me, five or six miles distant. . . .

In May, 1850, a report reached the settlements that a wonderful lake had been discovered, an hundred miles back among the mountains, towards the head of the Middle Fork of Feather River, the shores of which abounded with gold, and to such an extent that it lay like pebbles on the beach. An extraordinary ferment among the people ensued, and a grand rush was made from the towns, in search of this splendid El Dorado. Stores were left to take care of themselves, business of all kinds was dropped, mules were suddenly bought up at exorbitant prices, and crowds started off to search for the golden lake.

Days passed away, when at length adventurers began to return, with disappointed looks, and their worn out and dilapidated garments showed that they had "seen some service," and it proved that, though several lakes had been discovered, the Gold Lake *par excellence* was not found. The mountains swarmed with men, exhausted and worn out with toil and hunger; mules were starved, or killed by falling from precipices. Still the search was continued over snow forty or fifty feet deep, till the highest ridge of the Siérra was passed, when the disappointed crowds began to return, without getting a glimpse of the grand *desideratum*, having had their labor for their pains. Yet this sally was not without some practical and beneficial results. The country was more perfectly explored, some rich diggings were found, and, as usual, a few among the many were benefitted. A new field for enterprize was opened, and within a month, roads were made and traversed by wagons, trading posts were established, and a new mining country was opened, which really proved in the main to be rich, and had it not been for the gold-lake fever, it might have remained many months undiscovered and unoccupied. . . .

From the mouth of Nelson's Creek to its source, men were at work in digging. Sometimes the stream was turned from its bed, and the channel worked; in other places, wing dams were thrown out, and the bed partially worked; while in some, the banks only were dug. Some of these, as is the case everywhere in the mines, paid well, some, fair wages, while many were failures. One evening, while waiting for my second supply of goods, I strolled by a deserted camp. I was attracted to the ruins of a shanty, by observing the effigy of a man standing upright in an old, torn shirt, a pair of ragged pantaloons, and boots which looked as if they had been clambering over rocks since they were made — in short, the image represented a lean, meagre, worn-out and woe-begone miner, such as might daily be seen at almost every point in the upper mines. On the shirt was inscribed, in a good business hand, "My claim failed — will you pay the taxes?" (an allusion to the tax on foreigners.) Appended to the figure was a paper, bearing the following words:

" Californians — Oh, Californians, look at me ! once fat and saucy as a privateersman, but now — look ye — a miserable skeleton. In a word, I am a used up man. . . . "

Ludicrous as it may appear, it was a truthful commentary on the efforts of hundreds of poor fellows in the " golden land." This company had penetrated the mountain snows with infinite labor, in the early part of the season, enduring hardships of no ordinary character — had patiently toiled for weeks, living on the coarsest fare ; had spent time and money in building a dam and digging a race through rocks to drain off the water ; endured wet and cold, in the chilling atmosphere of the country, and when the last stone was turned, at the very close of all this labor, they did not find a single cent to reward them for their toil and privations, and what was still more aggravating, a small, wing dam, on the very claim below them, yielded several thousand dollars. Having paid out their money, and lost their labor, they were compelled to abandon the claim, and search for other diggings, where the result might be precisely the same. . . .

The population of Independence represented almost every State in the Union, while France, England, Ireland, Germany, and even Bohemia, had their delegates. As soon as breakfast was dispatched, all hands were engaged in digging and washing gold in the banks, or in the bed of the stream. When evening came, large fires were built, around which the miners congregated, some engrossed with thoughts of home and friends, some to talk of new discoveries, and richer diggings somewhere else ; or, sometimes a subject of debate was started, and the evening was whiled away in pleasant, and often instructive, discussion, while many, for whom this kind of recreation had not excitement enough, resorted to dealing monte, on a small scale, thus either exciting or keeping up a passion for play. Some weeks were passed in this way under the clear blue sky of the mountains, and many had made respectable piles. I highly enjoyed the wild scenery, and, quite as well, the wild life we were leading, for there were many accomplished and intelligent men ; and a subject for amusement or debate was rarely wanting. As for ceremony or dress, it gave us no trouble : we were all alike. . . . At length a monte dealer arrived, with a respectable bank.

A change had been gradually coming over many of our people, and for three or four days several industrious men had commenced drinking, and after the monte bank was set up, it seemed as if the long smothered fire burst forth into a flame. Labor, with few exceptions, seemed sus-

pended, and a great many miners spent their time in riot and debauchery.
. . . The monte dealer, who, in his way was a gentleman, and honorable
according to the notions of that class of men, won in two nights three
thousand dollars ! When he had collected his taxes on our bar, he went
to Onion Valley, six miles distant, and lost in one night four thousand,
exemplifying the fact, that a gambler may be rich to-day, and a beggar
to-morrow. . . .

A[lonzo] Delano, *Life on the Plains and among the Diggings* (Auburn, etc.,
1854), 14–351 *passim.*

------◆------

19. Danger of Disunion (1850)

BY SENATOR JOHN CALDWELL CALHOUN

The speech from which this extract is taken was Calhoun's last statement of the
principle for which he had labored constantly during the second half of his political
life, viz., the principle that slavery, as the chief interest of the South, must advance. —
For Calhoun, see Winsor, *Narrative and Critical History*, VII, 324; American Historical Association, *Report for 1899*, Vol. II; *Contemporaries*, III, No. 131. — Bibliography : Channing and Hart, *Guide*, § 197.

. . . I HAVE, Senators, believed from the first that the agitation of
the subject of slavery would, if not prevented by some timely
and effective measure, end in disunion. Entertaining this opinion, I
have, on all proper occasions, endeavored to call the attention of each
of the two great parties which divide the country to adopt some measure
to prevent so great a disaster, but without success. The agitation has
been permitted to proceed, with almost no attempt to resist it, until it
has reached a period when it can no longer be disguised or denied that
the Union is in danger. You have thus had forced upon you the greatest
and the gravest question that can ever come under your consideration :
How can the Union be preserved ?
. . . The first question, then, presented for consideration, in the
investigation I propose to make, in order to obtain such knowledge, is :
What is it that has endangered the Union ? . . .
One of the causes is, undoubtedly, to be traced to the long-continued
agitation of the slave question on the part of the North, and the many
aggressions which they have made on the rights of the South during the
time. . . .
There is another, lying back of it, with which this is intimately con-

nected, that may be regarded as the great and primary cause. That is
to be found in the fact that the equilibrium between the two sections in
the Government, as it stood when the constitution was ratified and the
Government put in action, has been destroyed. . . .

. . . To sum up the whole, the United States, since they declared
their independence, have acquired 2,373,046 square miles of territory,
from which the North will have excluded the South, if she should succeed in monopolizing the newly acquired territories, from about three-
fourths of the whole, leaving to the South but about one-fourth.

Such is the first and great cause that has destroyed the equilibrium
between the two sections in the Government.

The next is the system of revenue and disbursements which has been
adopted by the Government. . . .

But while these measures were destroying the equilibrium between the
two sections, the action of the Government was leading to a radical
change in its character, by concentrating all the power of the system in
itself. . . .

That the Government claims, and practically maintains, the right to
decide in the last resort as to the extent of its powers, will scarcely
be denied by any one conversant with the political history of the
country. . . . It . . . follows that the character of the Government
has been changed, in consequence, from a Federal Republic, as it originally came from the hands of its framers, and that it has been changed
into a great national consolidated Democracy. It has indeed, at present, all the characteristics of the latter, and not one of the former,
although it still retains its outward form.

The result of the whole of these causes combined is, that the North
has acquired a decided ascendency over every department of this Government, and through it a control over all the powers of the system. . . .

As, then, the North has the absolute control over the Government, it
is manifest that on all questions between it and the South, where there is
a diversity of interests, the interests of the latter will be sacrificed to
the former, however oppressive the effects may be, as the South possesses
no means by which it can resist through the action of the Government.
But if there was no question of vital importance to the South, in reference to which there was a diversity of views between the two sections,
this state of things might be endured without the hazard of destruction
to the South. But such is not the fact. There is a question of vital
importance to the southern section, in reference to which the views and

E

feelings of the two sections are as opposite and hostile as they can possibly be.

I refer to the relation between the two races in the southern section, which constitutes a vital portion of her social organization. Every portion of the North entertains views and feelings more or less hostile to it. . . . On the contrary, the southern section regards the relation as one which cannot be destroyed without subjecting the two races to the greatest calamity, and the section to poverty, desolation, and wretchedness ; and accordingly they feel bound by every consideration of interest and safety, to defend it.

This hostile feeling on the part of the North towards the social organization of the South long lay dormant, but it only required some cause to act on those who felt most intensely that they were responsible for its continuance, to call it into action. The increasing power of this Government, and of the control of the northern section over all its departments, furnished the cause. It was this which made an impression on the minds of many that there was little or no restraint to prevent the Government from doing whatever it might choose to do. This was sufficient of itself to put the most fanatical portion of the North in action for the purpose of destroying the existing relation between the two races in the South. . . .

Such is a brief history of the agitation, as far as it has yet advanced. Now, I ask Senators, what is there to prevent its further progress, until it fulfills the ultimate end proposed, unless some decisive measure should be adopted to prevent it ? Has any one of the causes, which has added to its increase from its original small and contemptible beginning until it has attained its present magnitude, diminished in force ? Is the original cause of the movement, that slavery is a sin, and ought to be suppressed, weaker now than at the commencement ? Or is the Abolition party less numerous or influential, or have they less influence over, or control over the two great parties of the North in elections ? Or has the South greater means of influencing or controlling the movements of this Government now than it had when the agitation commenced ? To all these questions but one answer can be given : no, no, no ! The very reverse is true. Instead of being weaker, all the elements in favor of agitation are stronger now than they were in 1835, when it first commenced, while all the elements of influence on the part of the South are weaker. Unless something decisive is done, I again ask what is to stop this agitation, before the great and final object at which it aims — the abolition of slavery in the States — is consummated? Is it, then, not certain that if something decisive is not now done to arrest it, the South will be forced to choose between abolition and secession? . . .

. . . I return to the question with which I commenced, How can the Union be saved ? There is but one way by which it can with any certainty ; and that is, by a full and final settlement, on the principle of justice, of all the questions at issue between the two sections. The South asks for justice, simple justice, and less she ought not to take. She has no compromise to offer but the Constitution, and no concession or surrender to make. She has already surrendered so much that she has little left to surrender. Such a settlement would go to the root of the evil, and remove all cause of discontent, by satisfying the South she could remain honorably and safely in the Union, and thereby restore the harmony and fraternal feelings between the sections which existed anterior to the Missouri agitation. Nothing else can, with any certainty, finally and forever settle the questions at issue, terminate agitation, and save the Union.

But can this be done ? Yes, easily ; not by the weaker party, for it can of itself do nothing — not even protect itself — but by the stronger. The North has only to will it to accomplish it — to do justice by conceding to the South an equal right in the acquired territory, and to do her duty by causing the stipulations relative to fugitive slaves to be faithfully fulfilled — to cease the agitation of the slave question, and to provide for the insertion of a provision in the Constitution, by an amendment, which will restore to the South in substance the power she possessed of protecting herself, before the equilibrium between the sections was destroyed by the action of this Government. There will be no difficulty in devising such a provision — one that will protect the South, and which at the same time will improve and strengthen the Government, instead of impairing and weakening it.

But will the North agree to do this ? It is for her to answer this question. . . .

. . . If you remain silent, you will compel us to infer by your acts what you intend. In that case, California will become the test question. If you admit her, under all the difficulties that oppose her admission, you compel us to infer that you intend to exclude us from the whole of the acquired territories.

Congressional Globe, 31 Cong., 1 sess. (John C. Rives, Washington, 1850), 451-455 *passim*, March 4, 1850.

20. The Middle Way (1850)

BY SENATOR DANIEL WEBSTER

Webster's "seventh-of-March speech" on the Compromise, though it brought upon him an avalanche of criticism from the anti-slavery people, is, on the whole, harmonious with his earlier utterances; for the burden of his argument was always "liberty *and* union," and he considered a compromise necessary to preserve the Union.— For Webster, see Henry Matson, *References for Literary Workers*, 124–125; *Contemporaries*, III, No. 159.— Bibliography as in No. 19 above.

. . . I NOW say, sir, as the proposition upon which I stand this day, and upon the truth and firmness of which I intend to act until it is overthrown, that there is not, at this moment, within the United States, or any territory of the United States, a single foot of land, the character of which, in regard to its being free-soil territory or slave territory, is not fixed by some law, and some irrepealable law, beyond the power of the action of this Government. Now, is it not so with respect to Texas? Why, it is most manifestly so. . . .

But now that, under certain conditions, Texas is in, with all her territories, as a slave State, with a solemn pledge that if she is divided into many States, those States may come in as slave States south of 36° 30', how are we to deal with this subject? I know no way of honorable legislation, when the proper time comes for the enactment, but to carry into effect all that we have stipulated to do. . . .

Now, as to California and New Mexico, I hold slavery to be excluded from those territories by a law even superior to that which admits and sanctions it in Texas — I mean the law of nature — of physical geography — the law of the formation of the earth. That law settles forever, with a strength beyond all terms of human enactment, that slavery cannot exist in California or New Mexico. . . . I look upon it, therefore, as a fixed fact, to use an expression current at this day, that both California and New Mexico are destined to be free, so far as they are settled at all, which I believe, especially in regard to New Mexico, will be very little for a great length of time — free by the arrangement of things by the Power above us. I have therefore to say, in this respect also, that this country is fixed for freedom, to as many persons as shall ever live there, by as irrepealable and a more irrepealable law, than the law that attaches to the right of holding slaves in Texas; and I will say further, that if a resolution, or a law, were now before us, to provide a territorial government for New Mexico, I would not vote to put any prohibition into it whatever. The use of such a prohibition would be idle, as it respects any effect it would have upon the territory; and I would not take pains to reaffirm an ordinance of nature, nor to reënact the will of God. And I would put in no Wilmot proviso, for the purpose of a taunt or a reproach. I would put into it no evidence of the votes of superior power, to wound the pride, even whether a just pride, a rational pride, or an irrational pride — to wound the pride of the gentlemen who belong to the southern States. . . .

Mr. President, in the excited times in which we live, there is found to exist a state of crimination and recrimination between the North and the South. . . . I will state these complaints, especially one complaint of the South, which has in my opinion just foundation; and that is, that there has been found at the North, among individuals and among the Legislatures of the North, a disinclination to perform, fully, their constitutional duties, in regard to the return of persons bound to service, who have escaped into the free States. In that respect, it is my judgment that the South is right, and the North is wrong. Every member of every northern Legislature is bound, by oath, like every other officer in the country, to support the Constitution of the United States; and this article of the Constitution, which says to these States, they shall deliver up fugitives from service, is as binding in honor and conscience as any other article. . . . I put it to all the sober and sound minds at the North, as a question of morals and a question of conscience, What right have they, in all their legislative capacity, or any other, to endeavor to get round this Constitution, to embarrass the free exercise of the rights secured by the Constitution, to the persons whose slaves escape from them? None at all — none at all. Neither in the forum of conscience, nor before the face of the Constitution, are they justified, in my opinion. Of course, it is a matter for their consideration. They probably, in the turmoil of the times, have not stopped to consider of this; they have followed what seemed to be the current of thought and of motives as the occasion arose, and neglected to investigate fully the real question, and to consider their constitutional obligations, as I am sure, if they did consider, they would fulfill them with alacrity. . . .

Then, sir, there are those abolition societies, of which I am unwilling to speak, but in regard to which I have very clear notions and opinions. I do not think them useful. I think their operations for the last twenty years have produced nothing good or valuable. At the same time, I know thousands of them are honest and good men; perfectly well

meaning men. They have excited feelings ; they think they must do
something for the cause of liberty ; and in their sphere of action, they
do not see what else they can do, than to contribute to an abolition
press, or an abolition society, or to pay an abolition lecturer. I do not
mean to impute gross motives even to the leaders of these societies, but
I am not blind to the consequences. I cannot but see what mischiefs
their interference with the South has produced. . . . The bonds of the
slaves were bound more firmly than before ; their rivets were more
strongly fastened. Public opinion, which in Virginia had begun to be
exhibited against slavery, and was opening out for the discussion of the
question, drew back and shut itself up in its castle. . . . We all know
the fact, and we all know the cause, and everything that this agitating
people have done, has been, not to enlarge, but to restrain, not to set
free, but to bind faster, the slave population of the South. . . .

Now, sir, so far as any of these grievances have their foundation in
matters of law, they can be redressed, and ought to be redressed ; and
so far as they have foundation in matters of opinion, in sentiment, in
mutual crimination and recrimination, all that we can do is, to endeavor
to allay the agitation, and cultivate a better feeling and more fraternal
sentiments between the South and the North.

Mr. President, I should much prefer to have heard, from every member on this floor, declarations of opinion that this Union should never
be dissolved, than the declaration of opinion that in any case, under
the pressure of any circumstances, such a dissolution was possible. I
hear with pain, and anguish, and distress, the word secession, especially when it falls from the lips of those who are eminently patriotic,
and known to the country, and known all over the world, for their
political services. Secession ! Peaceable secession ! Sir, your eyes
and mine are never destined to see that miracle. The dismemberment
of this vast country without convulsion ! The breaking up of the fountains of the great deep without ruffling the surface ! Who is so foolish
— I beg everybody's pardon — as to expect to see any such thing?
Sir, he who sees these States, now revolving in harmony around a common centre, and expects to see them quit their places and fly off without
convulsion, may look the next hour to see the heavenly bodies rush from
their spheres, and jostle against each other in the realms of space, without producing the crush of the universe. There can be no such thing
as a peaceable secession. Peaceable secession is an utter impossibility.
Is the great Constitution under which we live here — covering this whole

country — is it to be thawed and melted away by secession, as the snows on the mountain melt under the influence of a vernal sun — disappear almost unobserved, and die off ? No, sir ! no, sir ! I will not state what might produce the disruption of the States ; but, sir, I see it as plainly as I see the sun in heaven — I see that disruption must produce such a war as I will not describe, in its twofold characters.

Appendix to the Congressional Globe, 31 Cong., 1 sess. (John C. Rives, Washington, 1850), 272–276 *passim*, March 7, 1850.

---

21. "Thy Glory is Departed" (1850)

BY JOHN GREENLEAF WHITTIER

Whittier early became identified with the anti-slavery crusade. The pathetic earnestness of these verses on Webster's supposed apostasy in his seventh-of-March speech is typical of the feeling with which the speech was received among the anti-slavery radicals, who had previously considered Webster a stanch advocate and defender of all constitutional measures against slavery. — For Whittier, see W. S. Kennedy, *John G. Whittier, the Poet of Freedom; Contemporaries*, III, No. 178. — Bibliography as in No. 19 above.

SO fallen ! so lost ! the light withdrawn
    Which once he wore !
The glory from his gray hairs gone
    Forevermore !

Revile him not — the Tempter hath
    A snare for all ;
And pitying tears, not scorn and wrath,
    Befit his fall !

Oh ! dumb be passion's stormy rage,
    When he who might
Have lighted up and led his age,
    Falls back in night.

Scorn ! would the angels laugh, to mark
    A bright soul driven,
Fiend-goaded, down the endless dark,
    From hope and heaven !

Let not the land, once proud of him,
    Insult him now,

Nor brand with deeper shame his dim,
    Dishonored brow.

But let its humbled sons, instead,
    From sea to lake,
A long lament, as for the dead,
    In sadness make.

Of all we loved and honored, nought
    Save power remains —
A fallen angel's pride of thought,
    Still strong in chains.

All else is gone ; from those great eyes
    The soul has fled :
When faith is lost, when honor dies,
    The man is dead !

Then, pay the reverence of old days
    To his dead fame ;
Walk backward, with averted gaze,
    And hide the shame !

John G. Whittier, *Ichabod*, in his *Songs of Labor, and other Poems* (Boston, 1850), 93–94.

------◆------

22. An Appeal to the Higher Law (1850)

BY SENATOR WILLIAM HENRY SEWARD

The compromise measures of 1850 caused the only great debate in which the statesmen of both the second and third generations after the Revolution took part. Seward, destined to play so important a part for the next fifteen years as senator and secretary of state, in this discussion made his first appearance as a national legislator. His speech is typical of the moderate northern view ; it attracted great attention for the argument given in this extract, an appeal which voiced a stronger moral feeling than Seward intended. — For Seward, see Channing and Hart, *Guide*, § 25. — Bibliography : Frederic Bancroft, *Life of Seward*, I, 243–263.

. . . IT is insisted that the admission of California shall be attended by a COMPROMISE of questions which have arisen out of SLAVERY.
I AM OPPOSED TO ANY SUCH COMPROMISE, IN ANY AND ALL THE FORMS IN WHICH IT HAS BEEN PROPOSED, because, while admitting the purity and the patriotism of all from whom it is my misfortune to differ, I think all legislative compromises radically wrong and essentially vicious. . . .
Nor would success attend any of the details of the compromise. And,

first, I advert to the proposed alteration of the law concerning fugitives from service or labor. . . .

We deem the principle of the law for the recapture of fugitives . . . unjust, unconstitutional, and immoral; and thus, while patriotism with-holds its approbation, the consciences of our people condemn it.

You will say that these convictions of ours are disloyal. Grant it for the sake of argument. They are, nevertheless, honest; and the law is to be executed among us, not among you; not by us, but by the Fed-eral authority. Has any Government ever succeeded in changing the moral convictions of its subjects by force? But these convictions imply no disloyalty. We reverence the Constitution, although we perceive this defect, just as we acknowledge the splendor and the power of the sun, although its surface is tarnished with here and there an opaque spot.

Your Constitution and laws convert hospitality to the refugee, from the most degrading oppression on earth, into a crime, but all mankind except you esteem that hospitality a virtue. The right of extradition of a fugitive from justice, is not admitted by the law of nature and of nations, but rests in voluntary compacts. . . .

. . . The law of nations disavows such compacts; the law of nature, written on the hearts and consciences of freemen, repudiates them. Armed power could not enforce them, because there is no public con-science to sustain them. I know that there are laws of various sorts which regulate the conduct of men. There are constitutions and statutes, codes mercantile and codes civil; but when we are legislating for States, especially when we are founding States, all these laws must be brought to the standard of the laws of God, and must be tried by that standard, and must stand or fall by it. . . .

To conclude on this point: We are not slaveholders. We cannot, in our judgment, be either true Christians or real freemen, if we impose on another a chain that we defy all human power to fasten on ourselves. You believe and think otherwise, and doubtlessly with equal sincerity. We judge you not, and He alone who ordained the conscience of man and its laws of action, can judge us. Do we, then, in this conflict, demand of you an unreasonable thing in asking that, since you will have property that can and will exercise human powers to effect its escape, you shall be your own police, and in acting among us as such, you shall conform to principles indispensable to the security of admitted rights of freemen? If you will have this law executed, you must alleviate, not increase, its rigors. . . .

But there is yet another aspect in which this principle must be examined. It regards the domain only as a possession, to be enjoyed, either in common or by partition, by the citizens of the old States. It is true, indeed, that the national domain is ours ; it is true, it was acquired by the valor and with the wealth of the whole nation ; but we hold, nevertheless, no arbitrary power over it. We hold no arbitrary authority over anything, whether acquired lawfully, or seized by usurpation. The Constitution regulates our stewardship ; the Constitution devotes the domain to union, to justice, to defence, to welfare, and to liberty.

But there is a higher law than the Constitution, which regulates our authority over the domain, and devotes it to the same noble purposes. The territory is a part — no inconsiderable part — of the common heritage of mankind, bestowed upon them by the Creator of the universe. We are his stewards, and must so discharge our trust as to secure, in the highest attainable degree, their happiness. . . .

This is a State, and we are deliberating for it, just as our fathers deliberated in establishing the institutions we enjoy. Whatever superiority there is in our condition and hopes, over those of any other " kingdom " or " estate," is due to the fortunate circumstance that our ancestors did not leave things to " take their chance," but that they " added amplitude and greatness " to our commonwealth, " by introducing such ordinances, constitutions, and customs, as were wise." We, in our turn, have succeeded to the same responsibilities ; and we cannot approach the duty before us, wisely or justly, except we raise ourselves to the great consideration of how we can most certainly " sow greatness to our posterity and successors."

And now the simple, bold, and even awful question which presents itself to us, is this : Shall we, who are founding institutions, social and political, for countless millions — shall we, who know by experience the wise and the just, and are free to choose them, and to reject the erroneous and unjust — shall we establish human bondage, or permit it, by our sufferance, to be established ? Sir, our forefathers would not have hesitated an hour. They found slavery existing here, and they left it only because they could not remove it. There is not only no free State which would now establish it, but there is no slave State, which, if it had had the free alternative, as we now have, would have founded slavery. . . .

Appendix to the Congressional Globe, 31 Cong., 1 sess. (John C. Rives, Washington, 1850), 262–265 *passim*, March 11, 1850.

CHAPTER IV — CONDITIONS OF SLAVERY

23. The Poor Whites (1850)

BY EMILY P. BURKE

The writer of the reminiscences from which this extract is taken was a New Hampshire teacher, who taught school in various parts of Georgia between 1840 and 1850. Though she looked at things through New England eyes, her descriptions are eminently fair. — Bibliography: Channing and Hart, *Guide*, §§ 186, 204.

ALTHOUGH praise-worthy attempts have been made in various parts of Georgia, to diffuse the means of education more extensively than was formerly thought necessary, still there is a class of people in that State, as also in the Carolinas, who have never been benefitted by any of these privileges ; and these individuals, though degraded and ignorant as the slaves, are, by their little fairer complexions entitled to all the privileges of legal suffrage. These people are known at the South by such names as crackers, clay-eaters, and sand-hillers. I have previously mentioned the circumstance from which they derived the appellation of crackers. They are called clay-eaters, because all this class of people, from the oldest to little children, are as much addicted to the eating of clay as some communities are to the use of tobacco and snuff. This senseless habit is indulged in to such an extent, that when a person has once seen a clay-eater, he can, ever after, instantly recognize any one of their number by their sickly, sallow, and most unnatural complexions, let them be seen in never so large a crowd. Children, by the time they are ten or twelve years of age, begin to look old, their countenances are stupid and heavy and they often become dropsical and loathsome to the sight. Those who survive this practice thirty or forty years, look very wrinkled and withered, their flesh shrunken to their bones like that of very aged people. They are also called sand-hillers from the grounds they usually occupy, which are the barren and sandy districts of Georgia and South Carolina, to which these poor wretched beings have been driven by the powerful and rich planters, who have wealth and avarice sufficient to secure to themselves all the best soil.

This part of the population of Georgia and some of the contiguous States, are the lineal descendents of those paupers from England, whom Gen. Oglethorpe brought to this country and by whom Georgia was first settled. The same crushed spirit that will ever suffer one to accept of a home in an alms house, seems to have been transmitted down to the present posterity of these emigrants, and their situation has always been such, they never have had the power to acquire education or wealth sufficient to raise them above their original degradation or enable them to shake off that odium they have inherited from their pauper ancestry. They have no ambition to do any thing more than just what is necessary to procure food enough of the coarsest kind to supply the wants of the appetite, and a scanty wardrobe of a fabric they manufacture themselves. If they should ever cherish a desire for any other life than such as the brutes might lead, it would be all in vain, for the present institutions and state of society at the South are calculated to paralyze every energy of both body and mind. They are not treated with half the respect by the rich people that the slaves are, and even the slaves themselves look upon them as their inferiors. I have seen the servants when one of these poor women came into a planter's house, dressed in her homespun frock, bonnet and shawl, collect together in an adjoining room or on the piazza and indulge in a fit of laughter and ridicule about her "cracker gown and bonnet," as they would call them.

Slavery renders labor so disreputable, and wages of slave labor so low, that if places could be found where they might hire out to service, there would be but little inducement to do so. Sometimes a young man who has a little more ambition than usually falls to the lot of his people, will succeed in obtaining a situation as overseer on a plantation. As such an office is to them quite honorable, they will almost give their services for it. I knew one young man about the age of nineteen who took the entire charge of a large plantation, and even labored with his own hands in the time of preparing the cotton for market, for the paltry sum of fifty dollars per year besides his board.

The sand-hillers usually cultivate a few acres of that barren land they are allowed to live upon, in the labor of which the females are obliged to take a part as well as the man. In this way they raise their corn, vegetables, and cotton, sufficient for domestic manufacture and sometimes a small quantity for market. When they do this, they can provide themselves with such luxuries as coffee, tea, sugar, etc., though besides coffee they seldom use any thing that is not the product of their own industry.

While I was residing in the interior of Georgia, one of these women sent her little daughter for me on horseback to go and make her a visit. I returned with the child on the beast with her ; in the evening she carried me home in the same way. I found this woman living in a small log house, very neat, but there was nothing belonging to it, to which the term comfortable could be applied. She had a bed, a table, two or three benches that were used instead of chairs and a very little crockery. The kitchen was a separate little building, of course scantily supplied with cooking utensils. The entertainment she prepared for me, while I sat with her in her little kitchen on a stool, consisted of coffee without sugar, fried bacon and corn bread mixed with water only. She had neither vegetables, or butter, or any other condiment we consider essential to any repast. In the course of the afternoon she showed me a roll of cloth she had just taken from the loom, which she told me, was all the product of her own hard labor, commencing with the cotton seed. On inquiring if she could not purchase cloth much cheaper than she could manufacture it, she replied, " she could if her time was worth any thing, but there was no labor she could perform that would bring her any money."

At that age when the youth of the North are confined at hard lessons for six hours a day from one season to another, these children are wasting the spring time of their lives, in the fields and woods, climbing trees, robbing bird's nests, or breaking up the haunts of squirrels, and engaged in every such kind of mischief, enough of which is always to be found for idle hands to do. These are the children and youth that the advantages of education which some enjoy at the South, have never yet reached, and probably never will, till some special effort is made in their behalf by missionary labor. As long as the present feeling between the rich and poor exists, they can never be brought together into the same schools and if this could be effected it would not be expedient. I have seen the results of such an experiment in my own school. While I was teaching in the north part of Georgia, I gave two little girls belonging to one of these poor families, their tuition for the purpose of encouraging them to come to school, but the neglect and scornful treatment they received from those who considered themselves their superiors, because they had wealthy parents and servants and could dress fashionably while they were obliged to wear their coarse homespun dresses, contributed to make them so miserable they could derive but little advantage from their instruction, and such will always be the case if attempts are made to bring them into the schools of the wealthy.

Efforts have been made to persuade these parents to put their sons to useful trades, but if they do this they are obliged to labor in the shops with the slaves, and this being placed on a level with the colored people, they feel is a degradation they can not submit to, therefore they choose to bring up their sons to hunting and fishing.

Emily P. Burke, *Reminiscences of Georgia* (n. p., 1850), 205–211.

---

24. Death of Uncle Tom (1852)

BY HARRIET BEECHER STOWE

Mrs. Stowe lived in Cincinnati for many years, frequently visited the slave states, and acquired an accurate knowledge of slave life. She was greatly impressed with the effect of the fugitive-slave law passed in 1850, and wrote *Uncle Tom's Cabin* with the hope of bringing to the public mind a realizing sense of the actual condition of slavery. The popularity and influence of the book speedily made it a factor in the advancement of the anti-slavery cause. Its influence over women and the rising generation was especially cogent. — For Mrs. Stowe, see Mrs. Annie Fields, *Life and Letters of Harriet Beecher Stowe.* — Bibliography : George Bullen, *Bibliographical Account of Uncle Tom's Cabin*, in Harriet Beecher Stowe, *Uncle Tom's Cabin* (Houghton, Mifflin, & Co., Boston, 1884).

THE hunt was long, animated, and thorough, but unsuccessful ; and, with grave, ironic exultation, Cassy looked down on Legree, as, weary and dispirited, he alighted from his horse.

"Now, Quimbo," said Legree, as he stretched himself down in the sitting-room, "you jest go and walk that Tom up here, right away ! The old cuss is at the bottom of this yer whole matter ; and I'll have it out of his old black hide, or I'll know the reason why ! " . . .

Tom heard the message with a forewarning heart ; for he knew all the plan of the fugitives' escape, and the place of their present concealment ; — he knew the deadly character of the man he had to deal with, and his despotic power. But he felt strong in God to meet death, rather than betray the helpless.

He sat his basket down by the row, and, looking up, said, "Into thy hands I commend my spirit ! Thou hast redeemed me, oh Lord God of truth ! " and then quietly yielded himself to the rough, brutal grasp with which Quimbo seized him.

"Ay, ay ! " said the giant, as he dragged him along ; " ye'll cotch it, now ! I'll boun' Mas'r's back's up *high !* No sneaking out, now !

Tell ye, ye'll get it, and no mistake ! See how ye'll look, now, helpin Mas'r's niggers to run away ! See what ye'll get ! "

The savage words none of them reached that ear ! — a higher voice there was saying, " Fear not them that kill the body, and, after that, have no more that they can do." Nerve and bone of that poor man's body vibrated to those words, as if touched by the finger of God ; and he felt the strength of a thousand souls in one. As he passed along, the trees and bushes, the huts of his servitude, the whole scene of his degradation, seemed to whirl by him as the landscape by the rushing car. His soul throbbed, — his home was in sight, — and the hour of release seemed at hand.

" Well, Tom ! " said Legree, walking up, and seizing him grimly by the collar of his coat, and speaking through his teeth, in a paroxysm of determined rage, " do you know I've made up my mind to KILL you ? "

" It's very likely, Mas'r," said Tom, calmly.

" I *have*," said Legree, with grim, terrible calmness, " *done — just — that — thing*, Tom, unless you'll tell me what you know about these yer gals ! "

Tom stood silent.

" D'ye hear ? " said Legree, stamping, with a roar like that of an incensed lion. " Speak ! "

" *I han't got nothing to tell, Mas'r*," said Tom, with a slow, firm, deliberate utterance.

" Do you dare to tell me, ye old black Christian, ye don't *know ?* " said Legree.

Tom was silent.

" Speak ! " thundered Legree, striking him furiously. " Do you know anything ? "

" I know, Mas'r ; but I can't tell anything. *I can die !* "

Legree drew in a long breath ; and, suppressing his rage, took Tom by the arm, and, approaching his face almost to his, said, in a terrible voice, " Hark 'e, Tom ! — ye think, 'cause I've let you off before, I don't mean what I say ; but, this time, I've *made up my mind*, and counted the cost. You've always stood it out agin' me : now, I'll *conquer ye, or kill ye !* — one or t'other. I'll count every drop of blood there is in you, and take 'em, one by one, till ye give up ! "

Tom looked up to his master, and answered, " Mas'r, if you was sick, or in trouble, or dying, and I could save ye, I'd *give* ye my heart's blood ; and, if taking every drop of blood in this poor old body would save your precious soul, I'd give 'em freely, as the Lord gave his for me. O, Mas'r! don't bring this great sin on your soul! It will hurt you more than 'twill me! Do the worst you can, my troubles'll be over soon; but, if ye don't repent, yours won't *never* end!"

Like a strange snatch of heavenly music, heard in the lull of a tempest, this burst of feeling made a moment's blank pause. Legree stood aghast, and looked at Tom; and there was such a silence, that the tick of the old clock could be heard, measuring, with silent touch, the last moments of mercy and probation to that hardened heart.

It was but a moment. There was one hesitating pause, — one irresolute, relenting thrill, — and the spirit of evil came back, with seven-fold vehemence; and Legree, foaming with rage, smote his victim to the ground.

*   *   *   *   *   *   *   *

Scenes of blood and cruelty are shocking to our ear and heart. What man has nerve to do, man has not nerve to hear. What brother-man and brother-Christian must suffer, cannot be told us, even in our secret chamber, it so harrows up the soul! And yet, oh my country! these things are done under the shadow of thy laws! O, Christ! thy church sees them, almost in silence!

But, of old, there was One whose suffering changed an instrument of torture, degradation and shame, into a symbol of glory, honor, and immortal life; and, where His spirit is, neither degrading stripes, nor blood, nor insults, can make the Christian's last struggle less than glorious.

Was he alone, that long night, whose brave, loving spirit was bearing up, in that old shed, against buffeting and brutal stripes?

Nay! There stood by him ONE, — seen by him alone, — "like unto the Son of God."

The tempter stood by him, too, — blinded by furious, despotic will, — every moment pressing him to shun that agony by the betrayal of the innocent. But the brave, true heart was firm on the Eternal Rock. Like his Master, he knew that, if he saved others, himself he could not save; nor could utmost extremity wring from him words, save of prayer and holy trust.

"He's most gone, Mas'r," said Sambo, touched, in spite of himself, by the patience of his victim.

"Pay away, till he gives up! Give it to him! — give it to him!" shouted Legree. "I'll take every drop of blood he has, unless he confesses!"

Tom opened his eyes, and looked upon his master. "Ye poor miserable critter!" he said, "there an't no more ye can do! I forgive ye, with all my soul!" and he fainted entirely away.

"I b'lieve, my soul, he's done for, finally," said Legree, stepping forward, to look at him. "Yes, he is! Well, his mouth's shut up, at last, —that's one comfort!"

Yes, Legree; but who shall shut up that voice in thy soul? that soul, past repentance, past prayer, past hope, in whom the fire that never shall be quenched is already burning!

Harriet Beecher Stowe, *Uncle Tom's Cabin* (Boston, etc., 1852), II, 271–275 *passim.*

---◆---

25. A Northern Apologist (1854)

BY REVEREND NEHEMIAH ADAMS

Adams was a prominent clergyman of Boston, whose favorable comments on slavery, based on personal inspection, were strongly condemned by his anti-slavery neighbors, and gave him the nickname of "South-Side Adams." — Bibliography as in No. 23 above.

TAKING all the favorable features and all the evils of southern slavery together simply as to their bearing upon the slave, it appears that, leaving out of view the liabilities to separation, to be a slave at the south is an evil or not according to the character or habits of the master. The master or mistress can make the relation of a slave the very best on earth for one who must be dependent. One can not be long at the south, and not see for himself that the perfection of human happiness in a serving class is found among certain slaves. There is nothing that approaches to it except the relation of certain servants and dependants of noble families in Great Britain; but at the south the relation and the happiness do not depend upon family and wealth; every householder may be a master or mistress to whom it will be a privilege to belong. Instances come to mind of servants in whose condition nothing is wanting to promote happiness in this world and preparation for the next; and the only source of disquietude in such cases you will hear thus expressed: "Master may die, and then I shall have to be free. I have laid up money, and am mentioned in the will, and my free papers are made out." Such servants sometimes select new masters, and pre-

F

vail on them to buy them, preferring the feeling of protection, the gratification of loving and serving a white person, to abstract liberty.

Then there is another side to this picture. It is in the power of a
master or mistress to make the condition of the slave a perpetual sorrow.
It would be well if some men, and women too, could be debarred by law
from having authority over a human being. One looks with pity even
upon the animal that belongs to them. Imperative, fierce, threatening
in their tones, petulant and cruel in their dispositions, capricious and
contradictory in their orders, and full of scolding, the word and blow
coming together, they wear out the patience of their servants. No wonder that the slaves of such men and women run away, that white boys
in similar circumstances betake themselves to the sea, and girls elope or
go to service, as a refuge from such dispositions and tongues. A certain
distinguished slave owner seriously entertains the desire, for which his
friends banter him, that every one proposing to be a slaveholder shall
bring certificates of good temper, and be examined. To one who was
a most thorough lover of the system of slavery I put the question, in a
favorable moment, " What, in your view, is the greatest objection that
can be made to slavery?" "O," said he, " this irresponsible power.
You can not prevent its abuse while human nature is what it is. Good
and kind men and women can make a slave happier than he could be
any where; but certain masters and mistresses of slaves are the worst
of tyrants."

There are some men to whom a negro is merely an ox or an ass.
They buy, sell, work, treat, talk about, their "niggers" as about cattle
— hard, sharp, vulgar men. . . .

It will generally be expected that punishment by whipping should be
mentioned among the revolting features of slavery. In a well-regulated
southern household, as in a well-ordered family of children, or a good
school, the rod is out of sight. It is seldom alluded to; threatenings
are rare; but the knowledge on the part of each servant, child, and
pupil, that there is a punishment in reserve for the last resort, will have
a salutary effect. Southern ladies, when they meet insolence or disobedience in their slaves, have not our easy means of relief in dismissing
them at once, and repairing to the intelligence offices for others. They
must have them punished, or they must continue to bear with them,
as they often do, with long and exemplary patience, shrinking as we
should from subjecting them to punishment; or they must sell them,
as incorrigible, to the slave trader, which is far worse than chastise-

ment, however severe.   In good hands this power is exercised without abuse.

This power is also in the hands of the cruel and unprincipled, and is fearfully abused.   Slaves, however, are not the only subjects of these cruelties, nor masters of slaves the only transgressors. . . .

Passing by a plantation, I saw a white man standing in a field near the road, with his arms folded, and a large whip in his hand.   A little farther on, I came to a row of fifteen or twenty negroes, hoeing industriously, without lifting their heads to look at those who were going by. Had I told this overseer how I felt on seeing him, he would probably have replied, that my feelings were northern prejudices; that he never strikes the negroes, and is on good terms with them; that his whip is partly in self-defence in case of need, and partly to enforce, by its bare presence, his orders, in refractory cases, should they occur.   But he was a revolting sight.

Many planters do not employ white overseers, but use some of the hands in their stead, paying them for this responsibility.   Touching instances of faithfulness are related of these colored head men.   The white overseers have it in their power, of course, to perpetrate many tyrannical and cruel acts; but we must not suppose that southern masters are indifferent to wrongs and outrages committed against their slaves. There is a public sentiment to which they are amenable; a cruel, neglectful master is marked and despised; and if cruel or neglectful by proxy, he does not escape reprobation.   It was not unusual to hear one say of another, " I have been told that he does not use his people well." This is a brand upon a man which he and his family are made to feel deeply.   But this is true only of certain states of society.

Slaveholding, like every relation, is a net which gathers of every kind. There are elements in it, at the south, fitted to promote the highest happiness and welfare, temporal and spiritual, of the negro; and it can make him perfectly miserable.   Many things charged against slavery are chargeable to ' construction account ' in human nature.

The most common expression at the south, with regard to slavery, is, " It is a great curse."   An intelligent gentleman, a slaveholder, said, in answer to a question, that unquestionably four-fifths of the people of his State, one of the oldest slave States, would be entirely free from it were it possible. . . .

A southern correspondent of the New York Observer thus expresses himself: " Though born and raised among the Green Mountains, I have been more than thirty years at the south, and I hold slaves ; yet I think I can do justice to the feelings of north and south. I believe slavery is a curse to the south, and many others believe it, who will not own it, on account of the fanatic efforts of the abolitionists. When I speak of it as a curse, I mean in all its relations of master and servant — the bad influence it has upon our passions, upon our children, destroying that sense of moral responsibility which ought to bear upon us."

Nehemiah Adams, *A South-Side View of Slavery* (Boston, 1854), 91–99 *passim.*

---

26. Slavery a Positive Good (1854)

BY GENERAL BENJAMIN F. STRINGFELLOW

Stringfellow, a Missourian, a militia officer, and prominent as a radical advocate of slavery, distinguished himself as a leader of the "border ruffians." These assertions as to the mutual benefits of slavery, although somewhat tinged by the author's characteristic bombast, contain the usual arguments on the benefits of that institution. — Bibliography : Channing and Hart, *Guide*, § 187.

WE assert that negro-slavery, as it exists in the United States, is neither a moral nor a political evil, but on the contrary, is a blessing to the white race and to the negro. . . .

Slavery is no evil to the negro. If we look at the condition of the negro in Africa, the land of his nativity, we find the most pitiable victim of a cruel master, the most wretched slave in America, when contrasted with a prince of his tribe in the deserts of Africa, is as a man contrasted with a beast ! The mightiest of the negro race, in his native land, not only sacrifices his human victims to his Gods of stone, but is so loathsome in his filth and nakedness, that Giddings, or Gerrit Smith, would fly from his presence. Mrs. Stowe could not in fancy picture him a kinsman of poor Topsy ; Fred Douglass would disown him as a countryman. It is not for us to question God's purposes, but it is certain that from our first knowledge of the negro race, those only have been rescued from the lowest stage of heathen barbarity, who have been made slaves to the white man — those only have learned to know the God of the Christian, who have been instructed by their masters. Ages have rolled on, and still the labour of the pious missionary has been in vain ; the African in his native land is still an idolator ! Even now the only hope of his elevation in the scale of humanity, is by means of the liberated slave. . . .

But we go further and say that, wherever the negro has been the slave of the white man, his condition has been better, not only than that of his race in the deserts of Africa, but better than when freed from the control of the white man, in whatever land the comparison be made. . . .

Negro slavery is no evil to the white race. . . .

. . . there are effects procured by negro slavery, which are not exhibited in the census, can not be set down in figures, of far more importance than the acquisition of wealth, as [or] mere increase of population. These are, its tendency to elevate the character of the white race, to give to that race a more exalted tone of moral sentiment ; and in a republic of vital importance is its influence in giving to the white race a higher, holier, more stern and unyielding love of liberty ; in making the white race emphatically a race of Sovereigns, fit members of a free government. . . .

. . . Not only does the institution of slavery elevate the character of the master, and where the master is free render his devotion to liberty a high and holy feeling, fortify it and render it invincible, but, where, as in our country, the slave is of a different race, marked and set apart by his colour, it elevates the character not only of the master, the actual owner of slaves, but of all who wear the colour of the freeman. With us, colour, not money marks the class : black is the badge of slavery ; white the colour of the freeman : and the white man, however poor, whatever be his occupation, feels himself a sovereign. Though his estate be but an empty title, he will not disgrace his station by stooping for moneys' sake to become the slave of another : he will treat with others as his equals, exchange his labour for their money, not honoured by their service, but reciprocating the favour of equal to equal. His class respects him, with the jealousy of rank will stand by him, and for the sake of their order will sustain him.

Not only does negro slavery thus elevate the character of the white man, it ennobles woman. Relieved by the slave from the abject toil, the servile condition to which the white woman is so often subjected by necessity where negro slavery does not exist, and which strip her of womans' greatest charm, modesty ; which make of her the rude drudging, despised servant of a harsh master ; the white woman becomes, as she is fitted to be, not the slave, but the queen of her household, fit mate for a sovereign.

Virtuous, modest, sensitive, retiring, her only ambition to merit the love of her husband, her only pride to point to her children and say, " these are my jewels ; " worshipped in her sphere, her gentle sway undisputed, the white woman in the slave-holding States needs no conventions to give her, her rights. Whether she be the mistress of a mansion, or the humble tenant of a cabin, to her the seat of honour is ever accorded — at home or abroad, every son of the south deems himself her champion. . . .

. . . Where negro slavery exists, money is not necessary to make the freeman ; the white man takes rank by his colour ; it is his patent of nobility, and until forfeited for dishonour, entitles him and commands for him all the privileges of his class.

Not so can it be, where " all the exterior of servitude " attaches to the nominal freeman : there of necessity money must distinguish the classes — mark the master, separate him from the servant. There colour gives no privilege, but the white man and the white woman driven to "service," are excluded from the presence of their masters, dare not claim to be their equals. Where money gives honour, poverty is looked upon as disgrace. To those who envy the negro his position, we urge no argument ; but to those who would see their race respected, fit to be free, we confidently appeal to reflect upon the difference which is thus effected in the condition of the white race. With all the pride and haughtiness attributed by the abolitionist to the slave-holder, we challenge a comparison of the rank in society held by the poor white man in the slave-holding, and non-slave-holding States. The northern mechanic, who has once put foot within the limits of a slave-holding State, has felt this vast difference, and can bear witness to it. The humble seamstress, the despised chambermaid, whose fortune has led her to the home of the slave-holder, has had cause to remember his courtesy to woman. Slave holders are proud of their colour, they can not but respect it.

But the influence of negro-slavery on the future destiny of our Republic, is even more potent than its effects upon the character of those who compose the government. We have said that the preservation of our Republic in its purity, depends on the institution of slavery. . . .

Politically the pauper, and the man of wealth are equal : labour has thus the power of numbers ; while on the other hand wealth has the power of money, the command of talent. The contest has ever proved unequal ; the brute force of numbers may prevail for a time, it effects a mere convulsion : Agrarian laws may be called for, a distribution of property demanded ; in the end talent and wealth will conquer ; and then, to protect itself, to guard against a like convulsion, strong laws will be enacted, a government of force be established. The scenes of the French revolution but illustrate the issue of this contest : Anarchy under the cry of " Liberty, Equality, Fraternity," rules for a day, to be followed on the morrow by an Empire ! . . .

Let the influx of foreign labourers continue, daily reducing the rate of wages ; let, as is threatened, the prisons and poorhouses of Europe be emptied on us ; let thus labour be consumed by its own strength, capital be thus still further monopolised by the few, until the thousand famished victims of excessive population cry out for bread, rise in the power of numbers and demand their " equal rights," their " equal share ; " what then shall save the Republic from wreck ? . . .

Upon the South, as upon the strong arm of a brother, so long as negro slavery exists, the North can rely ; it will furnish materials to its workshops, a market for its manufactures ; wealth to its capitalist, wages to the labourer. In the South no struggle between labour and capital can arise. Where slavery exists, capital and labour are one, for labour is capital. There the capitalist, instead of exhausting his labourer, must strengthen, protect and preserve him, for he is his money. The interest of the labourer and the capitalist, the slave and his master, are identical ; they cannot conflict. The prosperity of the master is the happiness of the slave, for his condition is improved as his master prospers ; the master prospers, as his slave is healthy, vigorous and happy.

To negro slavery is the South indebted for its unrivalled prosperity, its exemption from the fearful struggle of wealth and poverty ; the happy equality in the condition of its people ; its practical enjoyment of the full blessings of republican government.

Let abolitionists succeed, let slavery be abolished, the negroes turned loose : the whites, driven from their homes, will seek a refuge among the crowded population of the North ; or else the whites victorous in the conflict which would follow, the miserable negroes would fly to their professed friends ; the northern labourer would find a ruinous competitor ; the northern capitalist a fearful addition to the strength of his enemy. In either event the struggle would be hastened to an issue. The fall of the South would bring ruin on the North ; the Republic would give place to Anarchy, to be followed by the rich man's rule, a despotism.

B. F Stringfellow, *Negro-Slavery, no Evil* (St. Louis, 1854), 9–35 *passim*.

27. A Good-Natured Slaveholder's View of Slavery (1858)

BY EDWARD ALBERT POLLARD

Pollard is best known as a sprightly, prejudiced, and unscientific writer on the Civil War from the southern point of view. He was a journalist by profession and an extreme pro-slavery advocate. This extract is from letters originally addressed to David M. Clarkson, of New York. — Bibliography as in No. 23 above.

AND here, dear C., let me meet an objection which has been eloquently urged against the proposition to import into this country slaves from Africa. It is said that our slave population has attained a wonderful stage of civilization; that they have greatly progressed in refinement and knowledge, and that it would be a great pity to introduce among them, from the wilds of Africa, a barbarous element which would have the effect of throwing back our Southern negroes into a more uncivilized and abject condition.

What is pleaded here as an objection I adopt as an argument on my side of the question — that is, in favor of the African commerce. What we want especially in the South, is that the negro shall be brought down from those false steps which he has been allowed to take in civilization, and reduced to his proper condition as a slave. I have mentioned to you, dear C., what an outrage upon the feelings of poor white men, and what a nuisance generally, the *slave gentry* of the South is. It is time that all these gentlemen of color should be reduced to the uniform level of the slave; and doubtless they would soon disappear in the contact and admixture of the rude African stock.

Most seriously do I say, dear C., that numbers of the negro slaves of the South display a refinement and an ease which do not suit their condition, and which contrast most repulsively with the hard necessities of many of the whites. I have often wished that the abolitionists, instead of hunting out among the swamps and in the raggedest parts of the South, some poor, exceptional victim to the brutality of a master, and parading such a case as an example of slavery, would occasionally show, as a picture of the institution, some of the slave gentry, who are to be found anywhere in the cities, towns, and on the large farms of the South, leading careless, lazy, and impudent lives, treating white freemen with superciliousness if they happen to be poor, and disporting themselves with airs of superiority or indifference before everybody who does not happen to be their particular master. Pictures drawn as equally from this large class of our slave population, as from the more abject, would, I am sure, soon convert some of your Northern notions of the institution of slavery.

. . . My blood boils when I recall how often I have seen some poor "cracker," dressed in striped cotton, and going through the streets of some of our Southern towns, gazing at the shop windows with scared curiosity, made sport of by the sleek, dandified negroes who lounge on the streets, never unmindful, however, to touch their hats to the "gem'men" who are "stiff in their heels," (*i. e.* have money) ; or to the counter-hoppers and fast young gents with red vests and illimitable jewelry, for whom they pimp. And consider that this poor, uncouth fellow, thus laughed at, scorned and degraded in the estimate of the slave, is a freeman, beneath whose humble garb is a heart richer than gold — the heart of a mute hero, of one who wears the proud, though pauper, title of the patriot defender of the South.

I love the simple and unadulterated slave, with his geniality, his mirth, his swagger, and his nonsense ; I love to look upon his countenance, shining with content and grease ; I love to study his affectionate heart ; I love to mark that peculiarity in him, which beneath all his buffoonery exhibits him as a creature of the tenderest sensibilities, mingling his joys and his sorrows with those of his master's home. . . . But the "genteel" slave, who is inoculated with white notions, affects superiority, and exchanges his simple and humble ignorance for insolent airs, is altogether another creature, and my especial abomination.

I have no horror, dear C., of imported savage slaves from Africa. I have no doubt that they would prove tractable, and that we would find in them, or would soon develop, the same traits of courage, humor, and tenderness, which distinguish the character of the pure negro everywhere.

When I was last through the country here, I made the acquaintance of a very old "Guinea negro," Pompey by name, who had been imported at an early age from the African coast ; and a livelier, better-dispositioned and happier old boy I have never met with. . . .

Pompey had married a "genteel" slavewoman, a maid to an old lady of one of the first families of Carolina, and lived very unhappily with his fine mate, because she could not understand "black folks' ways." It appears that Pompey frequently had recourse to the black art to inspire his wife with more affection for him ; and having in his hearing dropped the remark, jokingly, one day, that a good whipping made a mistress love her lord the more, I was surprised to hear Pompey speak up suddenly, and with solemn emphasis, " Mass'r Ed'rd, I bleve dar *is* sumthin' in dat.   When de 'ooman get *ambitious* " — he means high-notioned and passionate — " de debble is sot up against you, and no use to honey dat chile ; you jest got to beat him out, and he bound to come out 'fore the breath come out, anyhow."   I am inclined to recommend Pompey's treatment for all " ambitious " negroes, male or female. . . .

. . . I agree with Pompey, as to what constitutes a useful and respect-able negro, and tell him that we shall soon have some such from the country from which he came, at which prospect he is greatly pleased. " Ah, Mass'r," says he, " dat is de nigger dat can do your work ; he de chile dat can follow arter the beast, like dis here," tugging away and gee-hawing while he speaks, at the hard mouth of a stupid mule, with which he is plowing in the garden.   " But I tells you what, Mass'r Ed'rd," continues Pompey, impressively, " no matter how de dam proud black folks hold der head up, and don't love de mule, and don't love de work, and don't love nothing but de ownselves, I tells you what, I ain't but nigger nohow ; and I tells you, and I tells 'em all, *de nigger and de mule am de axle-tree of de world.*"

The truth is, my dear friend, we want more such slaves in the South as Pompey, who while they can speak such honest and brilliant senti-ments, will also be as humble in their hearts and as faithful to their work as he, and who will sustain the car of progress over all obstacles in the path of Southern destiny. . . .

After a round of visits to others of " the kin," I at last find myself the guest of that most excellent and beloved old lady, Miss R. . . .

I find the old, familiar, black faces about the house.   Uncle Jeames, the dining-room servant, is an old, decayed family negro, wearing a roundabout, and remarkable for an unctuous bald head, unadorned by hat or cap.   Miss R., who has known him since he was a boy, still ad-dresses him by the name of " Jimboo."   Uncle Jimboo has a good deal of slave-pride, and is anxious to appear to visitors as one of great dignity and consequence in household affairs.   He is especially proud of his position as general conservator of the order and security of the household, and any interruption of his stilted dignity is very painful to nim.   Devoted to his mistress, he assumes the office of her protector. Having in one of his winter patrols, according to his account, been chased by some forgotten number of " black bars," and having valiantly whipped "the king bar," and put the others to flight, it remains that he is afraid of nothing in the world "but a gun."

Peace to Uncle Jimboo! May his days never be shortened by the accidents of his valiant service! I can never expect to see the old man again; he is passing away; but, thanks to God, he, the slave, has not to go down to the grave in a gloomy old age, poverty-stricken and forgotten; he has a beloved mistress near by to provide for him in the evening of his life — a rare mistress, who, distinguished in her neighborhood for hospitality and munificence, has delighted also to adorn herself with simple and unblazoned charities to the humblest of all humanity — the poor, dependent, oft-forgotten slave.

Edward A. Pollard, *Black Diamonds Gathered in the Darkey Homes of the South* (New York, 1859), 55–74 *passim.*

---

28. A Slave Auction (1859)

FROM THE NEW YORK TRIBUNE

The *New York Tribune*, with Horace Greeley at its head, was at this time the most influential newspaper in the United States, through its weekly and semi-weekly editions moulding the opinions of the farmers and village people. It was sternly anti-slavery, and by publishing facts connected with the existence of slavery it made that institution speak against itself. — For Greeley and his newspaper, see Whitelaw Reid, *Memorial of Horace Greeley.* — Bibliography: Channing and Hart, *Guide*, § 186.

THE largest sale of human chattels that has been made in Star-Spangled America for several years took place on Wednesday and Thursday of last week, at the Race Course near the City of Savannah, Georgia. The lot consisted of four hundred and thirty-six men, women, children and infants, being that half of the negro stock remaining on the old Major Butler plantations which fell to one of the two heirs to that estate. . . .

The sale had been advertised largely for many weeks, and as the negroes were known to be a choice lot and very desirable property, the attendance of buyers was large. The breaking up of an old family estate is so uncommon an occurrence that the affair was regarded with unusual interest throughout the South. For several days before the sale every hotel in Savannah was crowded with negro speculators from North and South Carolina, Virginia, Georgia, Alabama and Louisiana,

who had been attracted hither by the prospects of making good bar-
gains. Nothing was heard for days, in the bar-rooms and public rooms
but talk of the great sale, criticisms of the business affairs of Mr. Butler,
and speculations as to the probable prices the stock would bring. The
office of Joseph Bryan the negro broker who had the management of
the sale, was thronged every day by eager inquirers in search of
information, and by some who were anxious to buy, but were uncertain as to whether their securities would prove acceptable. Little
parties were made up from the various hotels every day to visit the
Race-Course, distant some three miles from the city, to look over the
chattels, discuss their points, and make memoranda for guidance on
the day of sale. The buyers were generally of a rough breed, slangy,
profane and bearish, being for the most part, from the back river and
swamp plantations, where the elegancies of polite life are not perhaps
developed to their fullest extent. . . .

The negroes came from two plantations, the one a rice plantation
near Darien . . . and the other a cotton plantation. . . .

None of the Butler slaves have ever been sold before, but have been
on these two plantations since they were born. . . .

It is true they were sold " in families ; " but let us see : a man and
his wife were called a "family," their parents and kindred were not
taken into account. . . . And no account could be taken of loves
that were as yet unconsummated by marriage, and how many aching
hearts have been divorced by this summary proceeding, no man can
ever know. . . .

The slaves remained at the race-course, some of them for more than
a week and all of them for four days before the sale. They were brought
in thus early that buyers who desired to inspect them might enjoy that
privilege, although none of them were sold at private sale. For these
preliminary days their shed was constantly visited by speculators. The
negroes were examined with as little consideration as if they had been
brutes indeed ; the buyers pulling their mouths open to see their teeth,
pinching their limbs to find how muscular they were, walking them up
and down to detect any signs of lameness, making them stoop and bend
in different ways that they might be certain there was no concealed
rupture or wound; and in addition to all this treatment, asking them
scores of questions relative to their qualifications and accomplishments.
All these humiliations were submitted to without a murmur, and in
some instances with good-natured cheerfulness — where the slave liked

the appearance of the proposed buyer, and fancied that he might prove a kind " mas'r."

The following curiously sad scene is the type of a score of others that were there enacted :

" Elisha," chattel No. 5 in the catalogue, had taken a fancy to a benevolent looking middle-aged gentleman, who was inspecting the stock, and thus used his powers of persuasion to induce the benevolent man to purchase him, with his wife, boy and girl, Molly, Israel and Sevanda, chattels Nos. 6, 7 and 8. The earnestness with which the poor fellow pressed his suit, knowing, as he did, that perhaps the happiness of his whole life depended on his success, was interesting, and the arguments he used were most pathetic. He made no appeal to the feelings of the buyer ; he rested no hope on his charity and kindness, but only strove to show how well worth his dollars were the bone and blood he was entreating him to buy.

" Look at me, Mas'r ; am prime rice planter ; sho' you won't find a better man den me ; no better on de whole plantation ; not a bit old yet ; do mo' work den ever ; do carpenter work, too, little ; better buy me, Mas'r ; I'se be good sarvant, Mas'r. Molly, too, my wife, Sa, fus rate rice hand ; mos as good as me. Stan' out yer, Molly, and let the gen'lm'n see."

Molly advances, with her hands crossed on her bosom, and makes a quick short curtsy, and stands mute, looking appealingly in the benevolent man's face. But Elisha talks all the faster.

" Show mas'r yer arm Molly — good arm dat mas'r — she do a heap of work mo' with dat arm yet. Let good mas'r see yer teeth Molly — see dat mas'r, teeth all reg'lar, all good — she'm young gal yet. Come out yer Israel, walk aroun' an' let the gen'lm'n see how spry you be " —

Then, pointing to the three-year-old girl who stood with her chubby hand to her mouth, holding on to her mother's dress, and uncertain what to make of the strange scene.

" Little Vardy's on'y a chile yet ; make prime gal by-and-by. Better buy us mas'r, we'm fus' rate bargain " — and so on. But the benevolent gentleman found where he could drive a closer bargain, and so bought somebody else. . . .

Mr. Walsh mounted the stand and announced the terms of the sale, " one-third cash, the remainder payable in two equal annual installments, bearing interest from the day of sale, to be secured by approved mortgage and personal security, or approved acceptances on Savannah, Ga., or Charleston, S. C. Purchasers to pay for papers." The buyers, who were present to the number of about two hundred, clustered around the platform; while the negroes, who were not likely to be immediately wanted, gathered into sad groups in the background to watch the progress of the selling in which they were so sorrowfully interested. The wind howled outside, and through the open side of the building the driving rain came pouring in; the bar down stairs ceased for a short time its brisk trade; the buyers lit fresh cigars, got ready their catalogues and pencils, and the first lot of human chattels are led upon the stand, not by a white man, but by a sleek mulatto, himself a slave, and who seems to regard the selling of his brethren, in which he so glibly assists, as a capital joke. It had been announced that the negroes would be sold in "families," that is to say, a man would not be parted from his wife, or a mother from a very young child. There is perhaps as much policy as humanity in this arrangement, for thereby many aged and unserviceable people are disposed of, who otherwise would not find a ready sale. . . .

. . . The expression on the faces of all who stepped on the block was always the same, and told of more anguish than it is in the power of words to express. Blighted homes, crushed hopes and broken hearts was the sad story to be read in all the anxious faces. Some of them regarded the sale with perfect indifference, never making a motion save to turn from one side to the other at the word of the dapper Mr. Bryan, that all the crowd might have a fair view of their proportions, and then, when the sale was accomplished, stepping down from the block without caring to cast even a look at the buyer, who now held all their happiness in his hands. Others, again, strained their eyes with eager glances from one buyer to another as the bidding went on, trying with earnest attention to follow the rapid voice of the auctioneer. Sometimes, two persons only would be bidding for the same chattel, all the others having resigned the contest, and then the poor creature on the block, conceiving an instantaneous preference for one of the buyers over the other, would regard the rivalry with the intensest interest, the expression of his face changing with every bid, settling into a half smile of joy if the favorite buyer persevered unto the end and secured the property, and settling down into a look of hopeless despair if the other won the victory. . . .

The auctioneer brought up Joshua's Molly and family. He announced that Molly insisted that she was lame in her left foot, and perversely would walk lame, although, for his part, he did not believe a word of it. He had caused her to be examined by an eminent physician in Savannah, which medical light had declared that Joshua's Molly was not lame, but was only shamming. However, the gentlemen must judge for themselves and bid accordingly. So Molly was put through her paces, and compelled to trot up and down along the stage, to go up and down the steps, and to exercise her feet in various ways, but always with the same result, the left foot *would* be lame. She was finally sold for $695.

Whether she really was lame or not, no one knows but herself, but it must be remembered that to a slave a lameness, or anything that decreases his market value, is a thing to be rejoiced over. A man in the prime of life, worth $1,600 or thereabouts, can have little hope of ever being able, by any little savings of his own, to purchase his liberty. But, let him have a rupture, or lose a limb, or sustain any other injury that renders him of much less service to his owner, and reduces his value to $300 or $400, and he may hope to accumulate that sum, and eventually to purchase his liberty. Freedom without health is infinitely sweeter than health without freedom.

And so the Great Sale went on for two long days, during which time there were sold 429 men, women and children. There were 436 announced to be sold, but a few were detained on the plantations by sickness. . . .

The total amount of the sale foots up $303,850 — the proceeds of the first day being $161,480, and of the second day $142,370. . . .

Leaving the Race buildings, where the scenes we have described took place, a crowd of negroes were seen gathered eagerly about a man in their midst. That man was Mr. Pierce M. Butler of the free city of Philadelphia, who was solacing the wounded hearts of the people he had sold from their firesides and their homes, by doling out to them small change at the rate of a dollar a head. To every negro he had sold, who presented his claim for the paltry pittance, he gave the munificent stipend of one whole dollar, in specie ; he being provided with two canvas bags of 25 cent pieces, fresh from the mint, to give an additional glitter to his munificent generosity.

New-York Daily Tribune, March 9, 1859.

CHAPTER V — FUGITIVE SLAVES

29.   On the Underground Railroad (*circa* 1850)

BY LEVI COFFIN (1876)

Although the amount of organization which the Underground Railroad possessed may never be made clear, Coffin enjoyed the reputation of being president of the line. He was a Quaker, and lived in Cincinnati during most of the time that the "Road" was in active operation. This extract shows the methods that the management was sometimes forced to adopt in order to secure connections northward. — Bibliography: W. H. Siebert, *Underground Railroad*, Appendix D; Marion G. McDougall, *Fugitive Slaves*, Appendix E; Channing and Hart, *Guide*, § 198. — For similar materials, see Hart, *Source-Book*, Nos. 97–100.

THE fugitives generally arrived in the night, and were secreted among the friendly colored people or hidden in the upper room of our house. They came alone or in companies, and in a few instances had a white guide to direct them.

One company of twenty-eight that crossed the Ohio River at Lawrenceburg, Indiana — twenty miles below Cincinnati — had for conductor a white man whom they had employed to assist them. The character of this man was full of contradictions. He was a Virginian by birth and spent much of his time in the South, yet he hated slavery. He was devoid of moral principle, but was a true friend to the poor slave. . . .

. . . The company of twenty-eight slaves referred to, all lived in the same neighborhood in Kentucky, and had been planning for some time how they could make their escape from slavery. This white man — John Fairfield — had been in the neighborhood for some weeks buying poultry, etc., for market, and though among the whites he assumed to be very pro-slavery, the negroes soon found that he was their friend.

He was engaged by the slaves to help them across the Ohio River and conduct them to Cincinnati. They paid him some money which they had managed to accumulate. The amount was small, considering the risk the conductor assumed, but it was all they had. Several of the men had their wives with them, and one woman a little child with her, a few months old. John Fairfield conducted the party to the Ohio River opposite the mouth of the Big Miami, where he knew there were several skiffs tied to the bank, near a wood-yard.   When I asked him afterward if he did not feel compunctions of conscience for breaking these skiffs loose and using them, he replied : " No ; slaves are stolen property, and it is no harm to steal boats or anything else that will help them gain their liberty."   The entire party crowded into three large skiffs or yawls, and made their way slowly across the river.   The boats were overloaded and sank so deep that the passage was made in much peril.   The boat John Fairfield was in was leaky, and began to sink when a few rods from the Ohio bank, and he sprang out on the sand-bar, where the water was two or three feet deep, and tried to drag the boat to the shore.   He sank to his waist in mud and quicksands, and had to be pulled out by some of the negroes.   The entire party waded out through mud and water and reached the shore safely, though all were wet and several lost their shoes. They hastened along the bank toward Cincinnati, but it was now late in the night and daylight appeared before they reached the city.   Their plight was a most pitiable one.   They were cold, hungry and exhausted ; those who had lost their shoes in the mud suffered from bruised and lacerated feet, while to add to their discomfort a drizzling rain fell during the latter part of the night.   They could not enter the city for their appearance would at once proclaim them to be fugitives.   When they reached the outskirts of the city, below Mill Creek, John Fairfield hid them as well as he could, in ravines that had been washed in the sides of the steep hills, and told them not to move until he returned.   He then went directly to John Hatfield, a worthy colored man, a deacon in the Zion Baptist Church, and told his story.   He had applied to Hatfield before and knew him to be a great friend to the fugitives — one who had often sheltered them under his roof and aided them in every way he could.

. . . When he arrived, wet and muddy, at John Hatfield's house, he was scarcely recognized.   He soon made himself and his errand known, and Hatfield at once sent a messenger to me, requesting me to come to his house without delay, as there were fugitives in danger.   I went at once and met several prominent colored men who had also been sum-moned.   While dry clothes and a warm breakfast were furnished to John Fairfield, we anxiously discussed the situation of the twenty-eight fugitives who were lying, hungry and shivering, in the hills in sight of the city.

Several plans were suggested, but none seemed practicable.   At last I suggested that some one should go immediately to a certain German livery stable in the city and hire two coaches, and that several colored men should go out in buggies and take the women and children from

G

their hiding-places, then that the coaches and buggies should form a procession as if going to a funeral, and march solemnly along the road leading to Cumminsville, on the west side of Mill Creek. In the western part of Cumminsville was the Methodist Episcopal burying ground, where a certain lot of ground had been set apart for the use of the colored people. They should pass this and continue on the Colerain pike till they reached a right-hand road leading to College Hill. At the latter place they would find a few colored families, living in the outskirts of the village, and could take refuge among them. Jonathan Cable, a Presbyterian minister, who lived near Farmer's College, on the west side of the village, was a prominent abolitionist, and I knew that he would give prompt assistance to the fugitives.

I advised that one of the buggies should leave the procession at Cumminsville, after passing the burying-ground, and hasten to College Hill to apprise friend Cable of the coming of the fugitives, that he might make arrangements for their reception in suitable places. My suggestions and advice were agreed to, and acted upon as quickly as possible, John Hatfield agreeing to apprise friend Cable of the coming of the fugitives. We knew that we must act quickly and with discretion, for the fugitives were in a very unsafe position, and in great danger of being discovered and captured by the police, who were always on the alert for runaway slaves.

While the carriages and buggies were being procured, John Hatfield's wife and daughter, and other colored women of the neighborhood, busied themselves in preparing provisions to be sent to the fugitives. A large stone jug was filled with hot coffee, and this, together with a supply of bread and other provisions, was placed in a buggy and sent on ahead of the carriages, that the hungry fugitives might receive some nourishment before starting. The conductor of the party, accompanied by John Hatfield, went in the buggy, in order to apprise the fugitives of the arrangements that had been made, and have them in readiness to approach the road as soon as the carriages arrived. Several blankets were provided to wrap around the women and children, whom we knew must be chilled by their exposure to the rain and cold. The fugitives were very glad to get the supply of food, the hot coffee especially being a great treat to them, and felt much revived. About the time they finished their breakfast the carriages and buggies drove up and halted in the road, and the fugitives were quickly conducted to them and placed inside. The women in the tight carriages wrapped themselves in the blankets, and the woman who had a young babe muffled it closely to keep it warm, and to prevent its cries from being heard. The little thing seemed to be suffering much pain, having been exposed so long to the rain and cold.

All the arrangements were carried out, and the party reached College Hill in safety, and were kindly received and cared for. . . .

When it was known by some of the prominent ladies of the village that a large company of fugitives were in the neighborhood, they met together to prepare some clothing for them. Jonathan Cable ascertained the number and size of the shoes needed, and the clothes required to fit the fugitives for traveling, and came down in his carriage to my house, knowing that the Anti-Slavery Sewing Society had their depository there. I went with him to purchase the shoes that were needed, and my wife selected all the clothing we had that was suitable for the occasion ; the rest was furnished by the noble women of College Hill.

I requested friend Cable to keep the fugitives as secluded as possible until a way could be provided for safely forwarding them on their way to Canada. Friend Cable was a stockholder in the Underground Railroad, and we consulted together about the best route, finally deciding on the line by way of Hamilton, West Elkton, Eaton, Paris and Newport, Indiana. West Elkton, twenty-five or thirty miles from College Hill, was the first Underground Railroad depot. That line always had plenty of locomotives and cars in readiness. I agreed to send information to that point, and accordingly wrote to one of my particular friends at West Elkton, informing him that I had some valuable stock on hand which I wished to forward to Newport, and requested him to send three two-horse wagons — covered — to College Hill, where the stock was resting, in charge of Jonathan Cable. . . .

The three wagons arrived promptly at the time mentioned, and a little after dark took in the party, together with another fugitive, who had arrived the night before, and whom we added to the company. They went through to West Elkton safely that night, and the next night reached Newport, Indiana. With little delay they were forwarded on from station to station through Indiana and Michigan to Detroit, having fresh teams and conductors each night, and resting during the day. I had letters from different stations, as they progressed, giving accounts of the arrival and departure of the train, and I also heard of their safe arrival on the Canada shore.

Levi Coffin, *Reminiscences* (Cincinnati, [1876]), 304–311 *passim.*

30. "My Property I will Have" (1851)

BY WILLIAM PARKER

Parker was an escaped slave who had married another fugitive and settled at Christiana, in the southern part of Pennsylvania. The neighborhood was a favorite one for escaped slaves, and Parker was at the head of an organization for mutual protection against slaveholders and kidnappers. After the event here described he escaped to Canada. The affair caused much excitement, and there was an unsuccessful attempt to convict Hanway, mentioned in the text, of treason. The piece has apparently received a literary dress from a more practised hand than that of a fugitive slave. — Bibliography: McDougall, *Fugitive Slaves*, p. 127, No. 49.

THUS matters stood in Philadelphia on the 9th of September, 1851, when Mr. Gorsuch and his gang of Maryland kidnappers arrived there. Their presence was soon known to the little band of true men who were called "The Special Secret Committee." . . .

The trusty agent of this Special Committee, Mr. Samuel Williams, of Philadelphia, — a man true and faithful to his race, and courageous in the highest degree, — came to Christiana, travelling most of the way in company with the very men whom Gorsuch had employed to drag into slavery four as good men as ever trod the earth. . . .

The information brought by Mr. Williams spread through the vicinity like a fire in the prairies; and when I went home from my work in the evening, I found Pinckney (whom I should have said before was my brother-in-law), Abraham Johnson, Samuel Thompson, and Joshua Kite at my house, all of them excited about the rumor. I laughed at them, and said it was all talk. This was the 10th of September, 1851. They stopped for the night with us, and we went to bed as usual. Before day-light, Joshua Kite rose, and started for his home. Directly, he ran back to the house, burst open the door, crying, "O William! kidnappers! kidnappers!"

He said that, when he was just beyond the yard, two men crossed before him, as if to stop him, and others came up on either side. As he said this, they had reached the door. Joshua ran up stairs, (we slept up stairs,) and they followed him; but I met them at the landing, and asked, "Who are you?"

The leader, Kline, replied, "I am the United States Marshal."

I then told him to take another step, and I would break his neck.

He again said, "I am the United States Marshal."

I told him I did not care for him nor the United States. At that he turned and went down stairs. . . .

He then read the warrant, and said, — "Now, you see, we are commanded to take you, dead or alive; so you may as well give up at
once."

"Go up, Mr. Kline," then said Gorsuch, "you are the Marshal."

Kline started, and when a little way up said, "I am coming."

I said, "Well, come on."

But he was too cowardly to show his face. . . .

It was now about seven o'clock.

"You had better give up," said old Mr. Gorsuch, after another while,
"and come down, for I have come a long way this morning, and want
my breakfast; for my property I will have, or I'll breakfast in hell.
I will go up and get it."

He then started up stairs, and came far enough to see us all plainly.
We were just about to fire upon him, when Dickinson Gorsuch, who was
standing on the old oven, before the door, and could see into the up-
stairs room through the window, jumped down and caught his father,
saying, — "O father, do come down! do come down! They have guns,
swords, and all kinds of weapons! They'll kill you! Do come down!"

The old man turned and left. . . .

The whites, at this time, were coming from all quarters, and Kline was
enrolling them as fast as they came. . . .

. . . Elijah Lewis, a Quaker, also came along about this time; I
beckoned to him . . . but he came straight on, and was met by Kline,
who ordered him to assist him. Lewis asked for his authority, and
Kline handed him the warrant. While Lewis was reading, Castner
Hanway came up, and Lewis handed the warrant to him. Lewis asked
Kline what Parker said.

Kline replied, "He won't give up."

Then Lewis and Hanway both said to the Marshal, — "If Parker says
they will not give up, you had better let them alone, for he will kill some
of you. We are not going to risk our lives;" — and they turned to go
away.

While they were talking, I came down and stood in the doorway, my
men following behind. . . .

Kline now came running up, and entreated Gorsuch to come away.

"No," said the latter, "I will have my property, or go to hell."

"What do you intend to do?" said Kline to me.

"I intend to fight," said I. "I intend to try your strength."

"If you will withdraw your men," he replied, "I will withdraw mine."

I told him it was too late. "You would not withdraw when you had the chance, — you shall not now."

Kline then went back to Hanway and Lewis. Gorsuch made a signal to his men, and they all fell into line. I followed his example as well as I could; but as we were not more than ten paces apart, it was difficult to do so. At this time we numbered but ten, while there were between thirty and forty of the white men.

While I was talking to Gorsuch, his son said, "Father, will you take all this from a nigger?"

I answered him by saying that I respected old age; but that, if he would repeat that, I should knock his teeth down his throat. At this he fired upon me, and I ran up to him and knocked the pistol out of his hand, when he let the other one fall and ran in the field.

My brother-in-law, who was standing near, then said, "I can stop him;" — and with his double-barrel gun he fired.

Young Gorsuch fell, but rose and ran on again. Pinckney fired a second time, and again Gorsuch fell, but was soon up again, and, running into the cornfield, lay down in the fence corner.

I returned to my men, and found Samuel Thompson talking to old Mr. Gorsuch, his master. They were both angry.

"Old man, you had better go home to Maryland," said Samuel.

"You had better give up, and come home with me," said the old man.

Thompson took Pinckney's gun from him, struck Gorsuch, and brought him to his knees. Gorsuch rose and signalled to his men. Thompson then knocked him down again, and he again rose. At this time all the white men opened fire, and we rushed upon them; when they turned, threw down their guns, and ran away. We, being closely engaged, clubbed our rifles. We were too closely pressed to fire, but we found a good deal could be done with empty guns.

Old Mr. Gorsuch was the bravest of his party; he held on to his pistols until the last, while all the others threw away their weapons. I saw as many as three at a time fighting with him. Sometimes he was on his knees, then on his back, and again his feet would be where his head should be. He was a fine soldier and a brave man. Whenever he saw the least opportunity, he would take aim. . . .

Having driven the slavocrats off in every direction, our party now turned towards their several homes. Some of us, however, went back to my house, where we found several of the neighbors. . . .

The riot, so called, was now entirely ended. The elder Gorsuch was dead ; his son and nephew were both wounded, and I have reason to believe others were, — how many, it would be difficult to say. Of our party, only two were wounded. . . .

William Parker, *The Freedman's Story*, in *Atlantic Monthly*, March, 1866 (Boston), XVII, 281–288 *passim*.

---

31. Attack on a United States Court-House (1854)

BY RICHARD HENRY DANA

The attempted rescue of Burns was Boston's answer to the passage of the Kansas-Nebraska Act. Those who protested against, or attempted to prevent, the rendition of the fugitive were of high social position ; this fact, together with the national excitement caused by the case, made it the most important of the fugitive-slave episodes. Dana, who defended Burns, was one of Boston's most prominent lawyers. — For Dana, see No. 7 above. — Bibliography of Burns case : McDougall, *Fugitive Slaves*, p. 127, No. 57.

*M*AY 25 [1854]. *Thursday*. This morning, at a little before nine o'clock, as I was going past the court-house, a gentleman told me that there was a fugitive slave in custody in the United States court-room. I went up immediately, and saw a negro, sitting in the usual place for prisoners, guarded by a large corps of officers. . . . I offered to act as his counsel. . . .

The claimant, Colonel Suttle of Richmond or Alexandria, Va., was present, and sat in full sight of the poor negro all the time. . . .

[*May* 26.] To-night a great meeting is to be held at Faneuil Hall. There is a strong feeling in favor of a rescue, and some of the abolitionists talk quite freely about it. But the most remarkable exhibition is from the Whigs, the Hunker Whigs, the Compromise men of 1850 Men who would not speak to me in 1850 and 1851, and who enrolled themselves as special policemen in the Sims affair, stop me in the street and talk treason. This is all owing to the Nebraska bill. I cannot respect their feeling at all, except as a return to sanity. The Webster delusion is passing off. . . .

May 27. *Saturday*. Last night an attempt was made to rescue the slave. It was conducted by a few and failed for want of numbers, the greater part being opposed to an action then. They broke in a door of the court-house and a few of them entered, but they were not supported.

They killed one man, a truckman named Batchelder, who has volunteered three times to assist in catching and keeping slaves, and the officers retreated. But the men who entered were at first driven back, and the crowd thought themselves repulsed and retreated also. The men who went in first were wounded, and on being driven out, they found that the crowd outside had deserted them. The leader of this mob, I am surprised to hear, in secrecy, was Rev. T. W. Higginson of Worcester. I knew his ardor and courage, but I hardly expected a married man, a clergyman, and a man of education to lead the mob. But Theodore Parker offered to lead a mob to the rescue of Sims, if one hundred men could be got to enroll themselves, but they could not get thirty.

Robert Carter tells me that Dr. Samuel G. Howe offered to lead a mob of two hundred to storm the court-house, and that it would probably have been done had not Higginson's attempt led the marshal to call out the military.

Immediately after this mob, the marshal sent for a company of United States marines from Charlestown, and a company of artillery from Fort Independence. The mayor, too, ordered out two or three companies of volunteer militia to keep the peace, but not to aid in the return of the slave.

The hearing began at ten o'clock. The court-house was filled with hireling soldiers of the standing army of the United States, nearly all of whom are foreigners. The lazy hounds were lounging all day out of the windows, and hanging over the stairs, but ready to shoot down good men at a word of command. Some difficulties occurred between them and the citizens, but nothing very serious. . . .

The trial of the Burns case occupied all day of Monday, Tuesday and Wednesday, 29th, 30th and 31st of May. Each day the court-room was filled with the United States marshal's " guard " as he called them, a gang of about one hundred and twenty men, the lowest villains in the community, keepers of brothels, bullies, blacklegs, convicts, prizefighters, etc. Mr. Andrews, the ex-jailer, says that he finds forty-five men among them who have been under his charge at various times. . . . These are all armed with revolvers and other weapons and occupy the rows of seats behind the bar and the jury seats. A corps of marines from the navy yard, about sixty in number, commanded by Major Dulany, and two companies of United States Artillery, about one hundred and twenty men, commanded by Ridgely, occupy the court-house and guard all the passages with loaded guns and fixed bayonets. To reach the court-room one has to pass two or three cordons of police, and two of soldiers. Personally I have been well treated, and all whom I desire to have admitted have been admitted ; but there has been a great deal of rudeness and violence to others. . . . There were frequent instances of men prohibited from going into the courts of the state, and no one was permitted to enter the court-house, judges, jurors, witnesses or litigants, without satisfying the hirelings of the United States marshal that they had a right to be there. All this time there were, or attempted to be, in session in the building, the Supreme and Common Pleas Courts of Massachusetts, and the Justices' and Police Courts of Boston. . . . It was the clear duty of the court to summon before it the United States marshal to show cause why he should not be committed for contempt, and to commit him, if it required all the bayonets in Massachusetts to do it, unless he allowed free passage to all persons who desired to come into either of the courts of the State.

Beside the general " guard " which the marshal had to keep his prisoner, there was a special guard of Southern men, some of them law students from Cambridge, who sat round Colonel Suttle and went in and out with him. . . .

[*June*] 2. *Friday.* This was a day of intense excitement and deep feeling in the city, in the State and throughout New England, and indeed a great part of the Union. The hearts of millions of persons were beating high with hope, or indignation, or doubt. The mayor of Boston, who is a poor shoat, a physician of a timid, conceited, scatter-brain character, raised by accident to a mayoralty, has vacillated about for several days, and at last has done what a weak man almost always does, he has gone too far. He has ordered out the entire military force of the city, from 1,500 to 1,800 men, and undertaken to place full discretionary power in the hands of General Edmunds. These troops and the three companies of regulars fill the streets and squares from the court-house to the end of the wharf, where the revenue cutter lies, in which it is understood that Burns, if remanded, will be taken to Virginia. . . .

The decision was short. It took no notice of the objections to the admissibility or effect of the record, but simply declared it to be conclusive as to title and escape, and said that the only point before him was that of identity. On this, upon the evidence of witnesses, there was so much doubt that he could not decide the question, and would be obliged to discharge the prisoner. In this dilemma, he resorted to the testimony of Brent as to the admissions made by the prisoner to Colonel Suttle on the night of his arrest, which he considered as establishing the identity beyond a reasonable doubt, and on these admissions he was convicted. Convicted on an *ex parte* record, against the actual evidence, and on his own admissions made at the moment of arrest to his alleged master ! A tyrannical statute and a weak judge !

The decision was a grievous disappointment to us all, and chiefly to the poor prisoner. He looked the image of despair. . . .

Mr. Grimes and I walked to and fro in front of the court-house for an hour or so, the entire square being cleared of the people, and filled with troops. Every window was filled, and beyond the lines drawn by the police was an immense crowd. Whenever a body of troops passed to or fro, they were hissed and hooted by the people, with some attempts at applause from their favorers. Nearly all the shops in Court and State streets were closed and hung in black, and a huge coffin was suspended across State street and flags union down. A brass field-piece, belonging to the Fourth Artillery, was ostentatiously loaded in sight of all the people and carried by the men of that corps in rear of the hollow square in which Burns was placed. Some 1,500 or 1,800 men of the volunteer militia were under arms, all with their guns loaded and capped, and the officers with revolvers. These men were stationed at different posts in all the streets and lanes that led into Court or State streets, from the court-house to Long Wharf. The police forced the people back to a certain line, generally at the foot or middle of the lanes and streets leading into the main streets, and wherever there was a passage, there, a few paces behind the police, was a body of troops, from twenty or thirty to fifty or one hundred, according to the size and importance of the passage.

The mayor having given General Edmunds discretionary orders to preserve peace and enforce the laws, General Edmunds gave orders to each commander of a post to fire on the people whenever they passed the line marked by the police in a manner he should consider turbulent and disorderly. So, from nine o'clock in the morning until towards night, the city was really under martial law. The entire proceeding was illegal. The people were not treated as rioters or ordered to disperse. No civil officers were on the spot to direct the military or to give orders when and how to act. But the people were given their line, as on a parade day, and the troops were ordered, by a military commander, to fire upon them, at the discretion of the various commanders of posts. . . . It has been the greatest good fortune in the world that not a gun was fired by accident or design. No one could limit the consequences; and all concerned would have been in the eye of the law murderers.

Mr. Grimes and I remained in the court-house until the vile procession moved. Notwithstanding their numbers and the enormous military protection, the marshal's company were very much disturbed and excited. They were exceedingly apprehensive of some unknown and unforeseen violence.

The "guard" at length filed out and formed a hollow square. Each man was armed with a short Roman sword and one revolver hanging in his belt. In this square marched Burns with the marshal. The United States troops and the squadron of Boston light horse preceded and followed the square, with the field-piece. As the procession moved down, it was met with a perfect howl of Shame! Shame! and hisses.

I walked slowly down the streets at a considerable distance in the rear of the procession, and when I heard the news that it had safely reached the end of the wharf, and that the cutter was steaming out to sea, I returned to my office.

Charles Francis Adams, *Richard Henry Dana* (Boston, etc., 1890), I, 265–282 *passim*.

---◆---

32. Gratitude of Underground Railroad Passengers (1854–1856)

BY ESCAPED SLAVES

Of the various routes by which slaves escaped to the North, an important one through Philadelphia was under the management of William Still, himself a negro. Later he published an account of the operations of the "Road," including many letters from slaves whom he had assisted toward liberty. These letters were naturally from the more intelligent of the fugitives. — Bibliography as in No. 29 above.

ST. CATHARINES, C. W., MAY 15th, 1854.

MY DEAR FRIEND: — I receaved yours, Dated the 10th and the papers on the 13th, I also saw the pice that was in Miss Shadd's paper About me. I think Tolar is right About my being in A free State, I am and think A great del of it. Also I have no compassion on the penniless widow lady, I have Served her 25 yers 2 months, I think that is long Enough for me to live A Slave. Dear Sir, I am very sorry to hear of the Accadent that happened to our Friend Mr. Meakins, I have read the letter to all that lives in St. Catharines, that came from old Virginia, and then I Sented to Toronto to Mercer & Clayton to see, and to Farman to read fur themselves. Sir, you must write to me soon and let me know how Meakins gets on with his tryal, and you must pray for him, I have told all here to do the same for him. May God bless and protect him from prison, I have heard A great del of old Richmond and Norfolk. Dear Sir, if you see Mr. or Mrs. Gilbert Give my love to them and tell them to write to me, also give my respect to your Family and A part for yourself, love from the friends to you Soloman Brown, H. Atkins, Was. Johnson, Mrs Brooks, Mr. Dykes. Mr. Smith is better at presant. And do not forget to write the News of Meakin's tryal. I cannot say any more at this time; but remain yours and A true Friend ontell Death.

W. H. GILLIAM, the widow's Mite. . . .

NEW BEDFORD, August 26, 1855.

MR. STILL : — I avail my self to write you thes few lines hopeing they may find you and your family well as they leaves me very well and all the family well except my father he seams to be improveing with his shoulder he has been able to work a little   I received the papers   I was highly delighted to receive them   I was very glad to hear from you in the wheler case   I was very glad to hear that the persons ware safe   I was very sory to hear that mr Williamson was put in prison but I know if the praying part of the people will pray for him and if he will put his trust in the lord he will bring him out more than conquer please remember my Dear old farther and sisters and brothers to your family kiss the children for me I hear that the yellow fever is very bad down south now if the underground railroad could have free course the emergrant would cross the river of gordan rapidly   I hope it may continue to run and I hope the wheels of the car may be greesed with more substantial greese so they may run over swiftly   I would have wrote before but circumstances would not permit me   Miss Sanders and all the friends desired to be remembered to you and your family   I shall be pleased to hear from the underground rail road often   Yours respectfully,

MARY D. ARMSTEAD. . . .

HAVANA, August 11, 1856, Schuylkill Co., N. Y.

MR. WM. STILL — Dear Sir : — I came from Virginia in March, and was at your office the last of March. My object in writing you, is to inquire what I can do, or what can be done to help my wife to escape from the same bondage that I was in. You will know by your books that I was from Petersburg, Va., and that is where my wife now is. I have received two or three letters from a lady in that place, and the last one says, that my wife's mistress is dead, and that she expects to be sold. I am very anxious to do what I can for her before it is too late, and beg of you to devise some means to get her away. Capt. the man that brought me away, knows the colored agent at Petersburg, and knows he will do all he can to forward my wife. The Capt. promised, that when I could raise one hundred dollars for him that he would deliver her in Philadelphia. Tell him that I can now raise the money, and will forward it to you at any day that he thinks that he can bring her. Please see the Captain and find when he will undertake it, and then let me know when to forward the money to you. I am at work for the Hon. Charles Cook, and can send the money any day. My wife's name is Harriet Robertson, and the agent at Petersburg knows her.

Please direct your answer, with all necessary directions, to N. Coryell, of this village, and he will see that all is right.

Very respectfully,

DANIEL ROBERTSON.

William Still, *The Underground Railroad* (Philadelphia, 1872), 57–330 *passim.*

━━━━━◆━━━━━

33. A Personal-Liberty Act (1855)

BY THE COMMONWEALTH OF MASSACHUSETTS

This statute is a fair sample of those passed by nine other states in the North. They were not caused by the Fugitive-Slave Law itself so much as by the Kansas-Nebraska Act, but they approximated a nullification of the former law and helped to make it a dead letter. The personal-liberty laws were the most serious grievance of the South in 1861. In Massachusetts the measures of the personal-liberty law were intended especially to prevent a repetition of the Burns case (see No. 31 above). — Bibliography as in No. 29 above.

SECT. 1. All the provisions of the " Act further to protect Personal Liberty," passed the twenty-fourth day of March, in the year one thousand eight hundred and forty-three, shall apply to the act of congress, approved September eighteen, in the year one thousand eight hundred and fifty, entitled "An Act to amend, and supplementary to, the act entitled 'An Act respecting fugitives from justice and persons escaping from the service of their masters.'"

SECT. 2. The meaning of the one hundred and eleventh chapter of the Revised Statutes is hereby declared to be, that every person imprisoned or restrained of his liberty is entitled, as of right and of course, to the writ of *habeas corpus*, except in the cases mentioned in the second section of that chapter.

SECT. 3. The writ of *habeas corpus* may be issued by the supreme judicial court, the court of common pleas, by any justice's court or police court of any town or city, by any court of record, or by any justice of either of said courts, or by any judge of probate ; and it may be issued by any justice of the peace, if no magistrate above named is known to said justice of the peace to be within five miles of the place where the party is imprisoned or restrained, and it shall be returnable before the supreme judicial court, or any one of the justices thereof, whether the court may be in session or not, and in term time or vacation.

SECT. 4. The supreme judicial court, or any justice of said court before whom the writ of *habeas corpus* shall be made returnable, shall, on the application of any party to the proceeding, order a trial by jury as to any facts stated in the return of the officer, or as to any facts alleged, if it shall appear by the return of the officer or otherwise, that the person whose restraint or imprisonment is in question is claimed to be held to service or labor in another State, and to have escaped from such service or labor, and may admit said person to bail in a sum not exceeding two thousand dollars. . . .

SECT. 6. If any claimant shall appear to demand the custody or possession of the person for whose benefit said writ is sued out, such claimant shall state in writing the facts on which he relies, with precision and certainty ; and neither the claimant of the alleged fugitive, nor any person interested in his alleged obligation to service or labor, nor the alleged fugitive, shall be permitted to testify at the trial of the issue ; and no confessions, admissions or declarations of the alleged fugitive against himself shall be given in evidence. Upon every question of fact involved in the issue, the burden of proof shall be on the claimant, and the facts alleged and necessary to be established, must be proved by the testimony of at least two credible witnesses, or other legal evidence equivalent thereto, and by the rules of evidence known and secured by the common law ; and no *ex parte* deposition or affidavit shall be received in proof in behalf of the claimant, and no presumption shall arise in favor of the claimant from any proof that the alleged fugitive or any of his ancestors had been actually held as a slave, without proof that such holding was legal.

SECT. 7. If any person shall remove from the limits of this Commonwealth, or shall assist in removing therefrom, or shall come into the Commonwealth with the intention of removing or of assisting in the removing therefrom, or shall procure or assist in procuring to be so removed, any person being in the peace thereof who is not "held to service or labor " by the " party " making " claim," or who has not " escaped " from the " party " making " claim," or whose " service or labor " is not " due " to the " party " making " claim, " within the meaning of those words in the constitution of the United States, on the pretence that such person is so held or has so escaped, or that his " service or labor " is so " due," or with the intent to subject him to such " service or labor," he shall be punished by a fine not less than one thousand, nor more than five thousand dollars, and by imprisonment in the State Prison not less than one, nor more than five years. . . .

SECT. 9. No person, while holding any office of honor, trust, or emolument, under the laws of this Commonwealth, shall, in any capacity, issue any warrant or other process, or grant any certificate, under or by virtue of an act of congress, approved the twelfth day of February, in the year one thousand seven hundred and ninety-three, . . . or under or by virtue of an act of congress, approved the eighteenth day of September, in the year one thousand eight hundred and fifty, . . . or shall, in any capacity, serve any such warrant or other process.

SECT. 10. Any person who shall grant any certificate under or by virtue of the acts of congress, mentioned in the preceding section, shall be deemed to have resigned any commission from the Commonwealth which he may possess, his office shall be deemed vacant, and he shall be forever thereafter ineligible to any office of trust, honor or emolument, under the laws of this Commonwealth.

SECT. 11. Any person who shall act as counsel or attorney for any claimant of any alleged fugitive from service or labor, under or by virtue of the acts of congress mentioned in the ninth section of this act, shall be deemed to have resigned any commission from the Commonwealth that he may possess, and he shall be thereafter incapacitated from appearing as counsel or attorney in the courts of this Commonwealth. . . .

SECT. 14. Any person holding any judicial office under the constitution or laws of this Commonwealth, who shall continue, for ten days after the passage of this act, to hold the office of United States commissioner, or any office under the laws of the United States which qualifies him to issue any warrant or other process, or grant any certificate under the acts of congress named in the ninth section of this act, shall be deemed to have violated good behavior, to have given reason for loss of public confidence, and furnished sufficient ground either for impeachment or for removal by address.

SECT. 15. Any sheriff, deputy sheriff, jailer, coroner, constable or other officer of this Commonwealth, or the police of any city or town, or any district, county, city or town officer, or any officer or other member of the volunteer militia of this Commonwealth, who shall hereafter arrest, imprison, detain or return, or aid in arresting, imprisoning, detaining or returning, any person for the reason that he is claimed or adjudged to be a fugitive from service or labor, shall be punished by fine . . . and by imprisonment. . . .

SECT. 16. The volunteer militia of the Commonwealth shall not act in any manner in the seizure, detention or rendition of any person for the reason that he is claimed or adjudged to be a fugitive from service or labor. Any member of the same who shall offend against the provisions of this section shall be punished by fine . . . and by imprisonment. . . .

SECT. 19. No jail, prison, or other place of confinement belonging to, or used by, either the Commonwealth of Massachusetts or any county therein, shall be used for the detention or imprisonment of any person accused or convicted of any offence created by either of the said acts of congress mentioned in the ninth section of this act, or accused or convicted of obstructing or resisting any process, warrant, or order, issued under either of said acts, or of rescuing, or attempting to rescue, any person arrested or detained under any of the provisions of either of said acts, nor for the imprisonment of any person arrested on *mesne process*, or on execution in any suit for damages or penalties accruing, or being claimed to accrue, in consequence of any aid rendered to any escaping fugitive from service or labor.

Acts and Resolves passed by the General Court of Massachusetts in the Year 1855 (Boston, 1855), Chapter 489, pp. 924–929 *passim*.

PART III

CONTEST RENEWED

CHAPTER VI — "BLEEDING KANSAS"

34. Defence of the Kansas-Nebraska Bill (1854)

BY SENATOR STEPHEN ARNOLD DOUGLAS

(REPORTED BY JAMES MADISON CUTTS, 1866)

Douglas was a masterful man of great intellectual power, indomitable energy, shrewdness in forming political combinations, and little scruple. He was probably the only man in Congress who would have ventured or could have carried through the Kansas-Nebraska Bill, a voluntary offering to the South by a Northern Democrat. This extract is from a work intended by Douglas to be an indirect form of reminiscence ; it is of course a special plea. — For Douglas, see J. F. Rhodes, *History of the United States*, I, 493, note. — Bibliography : Channing and Hart, *Guide*, § 199.

AT the next meeting of Congress after the election of General Pierce, Mr. Douglas, as chairman of the Committee on Territories, reported the Kansas-Nebraska Bill, accompanied by a special report, in which he said, "that the object of the committee was to organize all Territories in the future upon the principles of the compromise measures of 1850. That these measures were intended to have a much broader and more enduring effect, than to merely adjust the disputed questions growing out of the acquisition of Mexican territory, *by prescribing certain great fundamental principles*, which, while they adjusted the existing difficulties, would prescribe rules of action in all future time, when new Territories were to be organized or new States to be admitted into the Union." The report then proceeded to show that the principle upon which the Territories of 1850 were organized was, that the slavery question should be banished from the halls of Congress and the political arena, and referred to the Territories and States who were immediately interested in the question, and alone responsible for its existence ; and concluded, by saying " that the bill reported by the committee proposed to carry into effect these principles *in the precise language of the compromise measures of* 1850." . . .

During the discussion of this measure it was suggested that the 8th section of the act of March 6, 1820, commonly called the Missouri Compromise, would deprive the people of the Territory, *while they remained in a Territorial condition* of the right to decide the slavery question, unless said 8th section should be repealed. In order to obviate this objection, and to allow the people the privilege of controlling this question, *while they remained in a Territorial condition*, the said restriction was declared inoperative and void, by an amendment which was incorporated into the bill, on the motion of Mr. Douglas, with these words in explanation of the object of the repeal : " *it being the true intent and meaning of this act, not to legislate slavery into any Territory or State, nor to exclude it therefrom, but to leave the people thereof perfectly free to form and regulate their domestic institutions in their own way, subject only to the Constitution of the United States.*" In this form, and with this intent, the Kansas-Nebraska Act became a law, by the approval of the President, on the 30th of May, 1854.

This bill and its author were principally *assailed* upon two points. First, that it was not necessary to renew slavery agitation, by the introduction of the measure ; and secondly, that there was no necessity for the repeal of the Missouri restriction.

To the first objection *it was replied*, that there was a necessity for the organization of the Territory, which could no longer be denied or resisted. That Mr. Douglas, as early as the session of 1843, had introduced a bill to organize the Territory of Nebraska . . . which was . . . renewed . . . each session of Congress, from 1844 to 1854, a period of ten years, and while he had failed to secure the passage of the act, in consequence of the Mexican war intervening, and the slavery agitation which ensued, *no one had objected to it upon the ground that there was no necessity for the organization of the Territory*. During the discussions upon our Territorial questions during this period, Mr. Douglas often called attention to the fact that a line of policy had been adopted many years ago, and was being executed each year, which was entirely incompatible with the growth and development of our country. It had originated as early as the administration of Mr. Monroe, and had been continued by Mr. Adams

General Jackson, Mr. Van Buren, Harrison, and by Tyler, by which treaties had been made with the Indians to the east of the Mississippi River,
for their removal to the country bordering upon the States west of the
Mississippi or Missouri Rivers, with guaranties in said treaties that the
country within which these Indians were located should never be embraced within any Territory or State, or subjected to the jurisdiction of
either, so long as grass should grow and water should run.   These Indian
settlements, thus secured by treaty, commenced upon the northern borders of Texas, or Red River, and were continued from year to year westward, until, when in 1844, Mr. Douglas introduced his first Nebraska
Bill, they had reached the Nebraska or Platte River, and the Secretary
of War was then engaged in the very act of removing Indians from Iowa,
and settling them in the valley of the Platte River, with similar guaranties of perpetuity, by which the road to Oregon was forever to be closed.
It was the avowed object of this Indian policy to form an Indian barrier
on the western borders of Arkansas, Missouri, and Iowa, by Indian settlements, secured in perpetuity by a compact, that the white settlements
should never extend westward of that line.   This policy originated in the
jealousy, on the part of the Atlantic States, of the growth and expansion
of the Mississippi Valley, which threatened in a few years to become the
controlling power of the nation.   Even Colonel Benton, of Missouri, who
always claimed to be the champion of the West, made a speech, in which
he erected the god Terminus upon the summit of the Rocky Mountains,
facing eastward, and with uplifted hand, saying to Civilization and Christianity, "Thus far mayest thou go, and no farther!" and General Cass,
while Secretary of War, was zealous in the execution of this policy.   This
restrictive system received its first check in 1844, by the introduction
of the Nebraska Bill, which was served on the Secretary of War, by its
author, on the day of its introduction, with a notice that Congress was
about to organize the Territory, and therefore he must not locate any
more Indians there.   In consequence of this notice, the Secretary (by
courtesy) suspended his operations until Congress should have an opportunity of acting upon the bill ; and inasmuch as Congress failed to act
that session, Mr. Douglas renewed his bill and notice to the Secretary
each year, and thus prevented action for ten years, and until he could
procure action on the bill.   In the mean time the passion of the Western
people for emigration had become so aroused, that they could be no
longer restrained ; and Colonel Benton, who was a candidate in Missouri
for re-election to the Senate in 1852 and 1853, so far yielded to the popu-

lar clamor, as to advise the emigrants, who had assembled, in a force of fifteen or twenty thousand, on the western border of Missouri, carrying their tents and wagons, to invade the Territory and take possession, in defiance of the Indian intercourse laws, and of the authority of the Federal Government, which, if executed, must inevitably have precipitated an Indian war with all those tribes.

When this movement on the part of Colonel Benton became known at Washington, the President of the United States despatched the Commissioner of Indian Affairs to the scene of excitement, with orders to the commanding officer at Fort Leavenworth to use the United States army in resisting the invasion, if he could not succeed in restraining the emigrants by persuasion and remonstrances. The Commissioner of Indian Affairs succeeded in procuring the agreement of the emigrants that they would encamp on the western borders of Missouri, until the end of the next session of Congress, in order to see if Congress would not in the mean time, by law, open the country to emigration. When Congress assembled at the session of 1853–'54, in view of this state of facts, Mr. Douglas renewed his Nebraska Act, which was modified, pending discussion, by dividing into two Territories, and became the Kansas-Nebraska Act. *From these facts you can draw your own conclusion, whether there was any necessity for the organization of the Territory and of Congressional action at that time.*

J. Madison Cutts, *A Brief Treatise upon Constitutional and Party Questions, and the History of Political Parties, as I received it orally from the late Senator Stephen A. Douglas, of Illinois* (New York, D. Appleton & Co., 1866), 84–91 *passim.*

---

35. Foundation of a New Party (1854–1856)

BY REPRESENTATIVE GEORGE WASHINGTON JULIAN (1883)

Julian was one of the leaders of the Free-Soil party, and in 1852 its candidate for vice-president. When a more extensive organization against the spread of slavery became possible, he was prominent in the founding of the Republican party. Since this extract is taken from his *Recollections*, caution is necessary in accepting it as authority in matters of detail. — Bibliography: Channing and Hart, *Guide*, § 201.

WHEN President Pierce was inaugurated, on the fourth of March, 1853, the pride and power of the Democratic party seemed to be at their flood. . . . In his annual message, in December following, he lauded the Compromise measures with great emphasis, and declared

that the repose which they had brought to the country should receive
no shock during his term of office if he could avert it. . . . In the beginning the session gave promise of a quiet one, but on the twenty-third
of January the precious repose of the country, to which the President
had so lovingly referred in his message, was rudely shocked by the proposition of Senator Douglas to repeal the Missouri compromise. . . .
The whole question of slavery was thus reopened, for the sacredness of
the compact of 1820 and the wickedness of its violation depended
largely upon the character of slavery itself, and our constitutional relations to it.

On all sides the situation was exceedingly critical and peculiar. The
Whigs, in their now practically disbanded condition, were free to act as
they saw fit, and were very indignant at this new demonstration in the
interest of slavery, while they were yet in no mood to countenance any
form of "abolitionism." Multitudes of Democrats were equally indignant, and were quite ready to join hands with the Whigs in branding
slavery with the violation of its plighted faith. Both made the sacredness of the bargain of 1820 and the crime of its violation the sole basis
of their hostility. . . .

The position of the Free Soilers was radically different. They opposed
slavery upon principle, and irrespective of any compact or compromise.
They did not demand the restoration of the Missouri compromise ; and
although they rejoiced at the popular condemnation of the perfidy which
had repealed it, they regarded it as a false issue. It was an instrument
on which different tunes could be played. To restore this compromise
would prevent the spread of slavery over soil that was free ; but it would
re-affirm the binding obligation of a compact that should never have
been made, and from which we were now offered a favorable opportunity
of deliverance. . . .

The situation was complicated by two other political elements. One
of these was Temperance, which now, for the first time, had become a
most absorbing political issue. . . .

The other element referred to made its appearance in the closing
months of 1853, and took the name of the Know-Nothing party. It
was a secret oath-bound political order, and its demand was the pro-
scription of Catholics and a probation of twenty-one years for the foreigner as a qualification for the right of suffrage. Its career was as
remarkable as it was disgraceful. . . .

Its birth, simultaneously with the repeal of the Missouri compromise,

was not an accident, as any one could see who had studied the tactics
of the slave-holders.   It was a well-timed scheme to divide the people
of the free States upon trifles and side issues, while the South remained
a unit in defense of its great interest.   It was the cunning attempt to
balk and divert the indignation aroused by the repeal of the Missouri
restriction, which else would spend its force upon the aggressions of
slavery ; for by thus kindling the Protestant jealousy of our people
against the Pope, and enlisting them in a crusade against the foreigner,
the South could all the more successfully push forward its schemes. . . .

Such were the elements which mingled and commingled in the political ferment of 1854, and out of which an anti-slavery party was to be
evolved capable of trying conclusions with the perfectly disciplined
power of slavery.   The problem was exceedingly difficult, and could not
be solved in a day.   The necessary conditions of progress could not be
slighted, and the element of time must necessarily be a large one in the
grand movement which was to come.   The dispersion of the old parties
was one thing, but the organization of their fragments into a new one on
a just basis was quite a different thing.   The honor of taking the first
step in the formation of the Republican party belongs to Michigan,
where the Whigs and Free Soilers met in State convention on the sixth
of July, formed a complete fusion into one party, and adopted the name
Republican.   This action was followed soon after by like movements
in the States of Wisconsin and Vermont.   In Indiana a State " fusion "
convention was held on the thirteenth of July, which adopted a platform,
nominated a ticket, and called the new movement the " People's Party."
The platform, however, was narrow and equivocal, and the ticket nominated had been agreed on the day before by the Know-Nothings, in
secret conclave, as the outside world afterward learned.   The ticket was
elected, but it was done by combining opposite and irreconcilable elements, and was not only barren of good fruits but prolific of bad ones,
through its demoralizing example ; for the same dishonest game was attempted the year following, and was overwhelmingly defeated by the
Democrats.   In New York the Whigs refused to disband, and the attempt to form a new party failed.   The same was true of Massachusetts
and Ohio.   The latter State, however, in 1855, fell into the Republican
column, and nominated Mr. Chase for Governor, who was elected by a
large majority.   A Republican movement was attempted this year in
Massachusetts, where conservative Whiggery and Know-Nothingism
blocked the way of progress, as they did also in the State of New York.

In November of the year 1854 the Know-Nothing party held a National Convention in Cincinnati, in which the hand of slavery was clearly revealed, and the "Third Degree," or pro-slavery obligation of the order, was adopted; and it was estimated that at least a million and a half of men afterward bound themselves by this obligation. In June of the following year another National Convention of the order was held in Philadelphia, and at this convention the party was finally disrupted on the issue of slavery, and its errand of mischief henceforward prosecuted by fragmentary and irregular methods; but even the Northern wing of this Order was untrustworthy on the slavery issue, having proposed, as a condition of union, to limit its anti-slavery demand to the restoration of the Missouri restriction and the admission of Kansas and Nebraska as free States.

. . . An unprecedented struggle for the Speakership began with the opening of the Thirty-fourth Congress, and lasted till the second day of February, when the free States finally achieved their first victory in the election of Banks. Northern manhood at last was at a premium, and this was largely the fruit of the "border ruffian" attempts to make Kansas a slave State, which had stirred the blood of the people during the year 1855. In the meantime, the arbitrary enforcement of the Fugitive Slave Act still further contributed to the growth of an anti-slavery opinion. The famous case of Anthony Burns in Boston, the prosecution of S. M. Booth in Wisconsin, and the decision of the Supreme Court of that State, the imprisonment of Passmore Williamson in Philadelphia, and the outrageous rulings of Judge Kane, and the case of Margaret Garner in Ohio, all played their part in preparing the people of the free States for organized political action against the aggressions of slavery.

Near the close of the year 1855, the chairmen of the Republican State Committees of Ohio, Massachusetts, Pennsylvania, Vermont, and Wisconsin, issued a call for a National Republican Convention to be held at Pittsburg, on the 22d of February, 1856, for the purpose of organizing a National Republican party, and making provision for a subsequent convention to nominate candidates for President and Vice President. . . . it was quite manifest that this was a *Republican* convention, and not a mere aggregation of Whigs, Know-Nothings, and dissatisfied Democrats. It contained a considerable Know-Nothing element, but it made no attempt at leadership. . . . The convention was in session two days, and was singularly harmonious throughout. . . . As chairman of the committee on organization, I had the honor to report the plan of action through which the new party took life, providing for the appointment of a National Executive Committee, the holding of a National Convention in Philadelphia on the 17th of June, for the nomination of candidates for President and Vice President, and the organization of the party in counties and districts throughout the States.

The Philadelphia convention was very large, and marked by unbounded enthusiasm. The spirit of liberty was up, and side issues forgotten. If Know-Nothingism was present, it prudently accepted an attitude of subordination. The platform reasserted the self-evident truths of the Declaration of Independence, and denied that Congress, the people of a Territory, or any other authority, could give legal existence to slavery in any Territory of the United States. It asserted the sovereign power of Congress over the Territories, and its right and duty to prohibit it therein. Know-Nothingism received no recognition, and the double-faced issue of the restoration of the Missouri compromise was disowned, while the freedom of Kansas was dealt with as a mere incident of the conflict between liberty and slavery. On this broad platform John C. Fremont was nominated for President on the first ballot, and Wm. L. Dayton was unanimously nominated for Vice President. . . .

George W. Julian, *Political Recollections*, 1840–1872 (Chicago, 1884), 134–150 *passim*. (Copyrighted; printed by permission of the Bowen-Merrill Co., Indianapolis.)

———◆———

36. Free-Soil Emigration to Kansas (1854–1855)

BY MRS. SARA TAPPAN DOOLITTLE ROBINSON

Mrs. Robinson was the wife of Charles Robinson, agent for the New England Emigrant Aid Company. As governor under the Topeka constitution, he was the special object of resentment of the "border ruffians" and pro-slavery party. He became first governor of the state in 1861. Mrs. Robinson shared the experiences of her husband. — Bibliography: Leverett W. Spring, *Kansas*, 323–327; Channing and Hart, *Guide*, § 200.

. . . IT was evident that a large emigration would naturally flow into Kansas from the North and East ; and, to enable the emigrant to reach his destination easily and cheaply, an association was formed, which completed its organization in July [1854]. The purpose of this association, as declared by themselves, was to "assist emigrants to settle in the West." Their objects were to induce emigrants to move westward in such large bodies, that arrangements might be made with boat lines and railroads for tickets at reduced rates ; to erect saw-mills and boarding-houses, and establish schools in different localities, that the people might gather around them, and not be obliged to wait years for the blessings and privileges of social life, as most early settlers in the West have done.   Transplanted into the wilderness, they hoped to bring to them the civilization and the comforts of their old homes.

Mr. Eli Thayer, of Worcester, Mass., was one of the first movers in the scheme.   To some suggestions of his the association owed its birth. He, with A. A. Lawrence of Boston, Mass., and J. M. F. Williams of Cambridge, Mass., acted as trustees of the Stock Company formed July 24, 1854.   They are all gentlemen of sterling integrity and noble purpose, and with untiring energy have devoted their labors and money to the cause of freedom. . . .

The first of August, 1854, a party of about thirty settlers, chiefly from New England, arrived in the territory, and settled at Lawrence. Mr. C. H. Branscomb, of Boston, on a tour in the territory a few weeks earlier in the summer, had selected this spot as one of peculiar loveliness for a town site.   A part of them pitched their tents upon the high hill south-west of the town site, and named it Mount Oread, after the Mount Oread School in Worcester, of which Mr. Thayer was founder and proprietor.

When the party arrived, one man only occupied the town site with his family.   His improvements were purchased, and he abandoned his claim for the town.   This party was met with insult and abuse on the Missouri river, and on their way into the territory.   After they arrived in Lawrence, bands of these Missourians gathered along the river bottoms, and wherever they put a stake they made a pretended claim. They invaded the meetings of the actual settlers in the neighborhood, and attempted to control them.   Attempts were also made to frighten and drive them from the territory by fomenting disputes about claims, and other quarrels. . . .

About the first of September, the second New England party arrived and settled at Lawrence.   As soon as it was known that a New England settlement was to be made at Lawrence, every means was resorted to, to break it up.

. . . The people however proceeded with their improvements, erecting a saw-mill, boarding-houses, and stores. . . .

The week came and went. . . . For some reason, the people of

Missouri, although urgently called upon, did not respond, and the belligerent parties concluded to postpone any warlike action. . . .

The buildings erected in Lawrence were of most primitive style, of pole and thatch. Most of the people for some weeks boarded in common, and, in such a dwelling, sleeping upon the ground on buffalo robes and blankets. . . .

The first Kansas party of the season left Boston, March 13, 1855, under the charge of Dr. C. Robinson. There were nearly two hundred in the party, men, women and children. We reached Kansas city March 24. . . .

[March] 25*th.* — Another boat came in with another party of Kansas passengers. . . . My husband made an arrangement to accompany a portion of our fellow-travellers into the country, to look for a pleasant location for a new settlement. . . .

[April] 17*th.* — We leave for Lawrence this morning. . . .

[18.] . . . Although the first work done upon the house was upon the Friday before, after taking supper down street, we preferred going to it to stopping elsewhere. One room was clapboarded within a foot of the chamber-floor, loose boards were laid over the joists above to keep out the rains or falling dews. The windows were also similarly protected upon each side, while at the front the glass was set. There were mattresses laid upon the floor and upon the lounge, while upon the table a candle was burning. . . . A broom had also been provided, and a brimming pail of cold water. Blessings on him who was thus thoughtful of our comfort ! By nailing a buffalo-robe at the door-way, and arranging some articles of bedding upon chairs, out of one room we made two for the night. . . .

21*st.* — The floor in the dining-room is laid. The windows are in. The door between the rooms is taken away, and the stove is set, with the pipe out of the window, after the true pioneer fashion. . . .

[May 17.] Take a walk down to the town, and call upon one of our fellow-travellers. We find her in a little cabin of mud walls, cottonwood roof, and with cloth covering the inside. It is tent-shaped, and very small. There is an earthy smell and a stifled feeling as I enter the low door ; and, as I at a glance see the want of comfort pervading all, I scarcely can find courage to ask how she likes Kansas. A bed, standing crosswise, fills up one entire end of the cabin, leaving only about eight feet square of space for the family, consisting of father, mother, and four little girls under six years. Two rough benches, about two

feet in length, and two rude tables, make up the furniture. The cooking is done out of doors, after camp fashion. The children have been
very ill, and the little one now tosses restlessly in its fevered dreams. . . .

24*th.* — The timbers are drawn for the kitchen. . . .

The roads for many days have been full of wagons — white-covered,
emigrant wagons. We cannot look out of the windows without seeing
a number, either upon the road through the prairie east of us, which
comes in from Kansas city, where most emigrants leave the boats and
buy wagons and provisions for the journey, or, going on the hill west,
on their way to Topeka, or other settlements above.

The prairie, too, is alive with people, coming and going. Some are
upon horseback, and others in carriages of eastern manufacture ; while
the busy teams, carrying stone for the hotel and other large buildings,
give to the whole town an appearance of unprecedented thrift which
renders the name of Yankee Town, bestowed upon it by the border
friends, richly merited. At night we see the camp-fires all about us,
on the prairies and in the ravines. The appearance of the men, preparing their evening meal, is singularly grotesque and gypsy-like. . . .

[June 12.] Large stone buildings, which would be an ornament to
any place, are fast being erected, while buildings of humble pretensions,
of wood and stone, are springing up with a rapidity almost equalling
the wonderful genius of Aladdin. We can count already fifty dwellings
erected since we came ; and the little city of less than a year's existence will, in intelligence, refinement, and moral worth, compare most
favorably with many New England towns of six times its number of
inhabitants. . . .

[August] 18*th.* — The quiet citizens of Lawrence are continually
annoyed by the street broils in our midst. . . . The border papers are
full of threats against the Yankees. An extract from the *Leavenworth
Herald* is a sample of all : " Dr. Robinson is sole agent for the underground railroad leading out of Western Missouri, and for the transportation of fugitive ' niggers.' His office is in Lawrence, K.T. Give him
a call." . . .

[September] 4*th.* — Emigration again begins to pour into the territory. During the last two months there has been little in this part of
the country. Cholera has raged on the river, and summer heats have
been too great for any comfort in travelling ; but now the prairies are
again dotted with white-covered wagons of the western emigrant. They
come bringing everything with them in their wagons, their furniture,

provisions, and their families.   Their stock, also, is driven with the teams.   Their wagons to them are a travelling home ; many of them having a stove set, with pipe running through the top.   They often travel far into the territory ; it matters to them little how far, so that they get a location which pleases them.   Then they build a cabin, and, with a fixed habitation, they will become the strength and sinew of the country. . . .

22*d*. . . . There are . . . continued rumors of new invasions, which disturb us but little. . . .

About this time the people of Lawrence entered into a self defensive organization.   The street broils and outrages were becoming so frequent their lives were in daily peril.   As soon as the organization was complete, and their badges gave evidence of a secret society, the outrages ceased. . . .

[November 18.] . . . There has been a good deal of sickness in the country this fall, — slow fever and chills.   They prevail mostly in the low grounds near the rivers.   We hear from some settlements, especially from those south on the Neosho, that sickness has laid its heavy hand on the strongest, and scarcely any have escaped the paralyzing blow. So far as we can learn, exposures, either necessary or unavoidable, have been the cause.

Sara T. L. Robinson, *Kansas ; its Interior and Exterior Life* (Boston, etc., 1856), 10–98 *passim*.

---

37. " Call to Kanzas " (1855)

BY LUCY LARCOM

The New England Emigrant Aid Company offered a prize for the song best suited to arouse Kansas immigrants, an offer characteristic of the methods of the association to kindle interest in the free-soil immigration to that territory.   Miss Larcom's lyric won the prize.   Later she enjoyed considerable reputation as a minor poet, and wrote several well-known patriotic poems during the Civil War. — Bibliography as in No. 36 above.

YEOMEN strong, hither throng !
  Nature's honest men,
We will make the wilderness
  Bud and bloom again.
Bring the sickle, speed the plough,
  Turn the ready soil !

Freedom is the noblest pay
    For the true man's toil.
Ho ! brothers ! come, brothers !
    Hasten all with me,
We'll sing upon the Kanzas plains
    A song of Liberty !

Father, haste ! o'er the waste
    Lies a pleasant land,
There your fire-side altar stones
    Fixed in truth shall stand.
There your sons, brave and good,
    Shall to freemen grow,
Clad in triple mail of Right,
    Wrong to overthrow.
Ho ! brothers ! come, brothers !
    Hasten all with me,
We'll sing upon the Kanzas plains
    A song of Liberty.

Mother, come ! here's a home
    In the waiting West.
Bring the seeds of love and peace
    You who sow them best.
Faithful hearts, holy prayers,
    Keep from taint the air,
Soil a mother's tears have wet,
    Golden crops shall bear.
Come, mother ! fond mother,
    List ! we call to thee,
We'll sing upon the Kanzas plains,
    A song of Liberty.

Brother brave, stem the wave !
    Firm the prairies tread !
Up the dark Missouri flood
    Be your canvas spread.
Sister true, join us too
    Where the Kanzas flows.

Let the Northern lily bloom
  With the Southern rose.
Brave brother, true sister,
  List ! we call to thee,
We'll sing upon the Kanzas plains,
  A song of Liberty.

One and all, hear our call
  Echo through the land !
Aid us with the willing heart
  And the strong right hand !
Feed the spark, the Pilgrims struck
  On old Plymouth Rock !
To the watch-fires of the free
  Millions glad shall flock.
Ho ! brothers ! come, brothers !
  Hasten all with me,
We'll sing upon the Kanzas plains,
  A song of Liberty.

Lucy Larcom, *Call to Kanzas* (published in one sheet by the New England
Emigrant Aid Company, [Boston, 1855]).

---

38. Pro-Slavery Emigration to Kansas (1855)

BY COLONEL JOHN SCOTT

Scott was a prominent citizen of St. Joseph, Missouri, and a militia officer.   He
went to Kansas for the elections of both November, 1854, and March, 1855, and presumably voted at both, although holding the office of city attorney in St. Joseph at the
time.   In the former election he was chosen judge of election by the crowd present
at the polls; and he considered himself qualified to accept, because the night before
he had engaged board at the settlement for a month. — Bibliography as in No. 36
above.

I WAS present at the election of March 30, 1855, in Burr Oak precinct in the 14th district, in this Territory.   I saw many Missourians
there.   There had been a good deal of talk about the settlement of
Kansas, and the interference of eastern people in the settlement of that
Territory, since the passage of the Kansas-Nebraska bill.   It was but
a short time after the passage of that act that we learned through the

papers about the forming of a society in the east for the purpose of promoting the settlement of Kansas Territory, with the view of making it a free State. Missouri, being a slave State, and believing that an effort of that kind, if successful, would injure her citizens in the enjoyment of their slave property, were indignant, and became determined to use all means in their power to counteract the efforts of eastern people upon that subject.

They were excited upon that subject, and have been so ever since. This rumor and excitement extended all over the State, and more particularly in the borders. The general rumor was that this eastern society was for no other purpose than making Kansas a free State. One great reason why we believed that was the only object of the society was, that we heard of and saw no efforts to settle Nebraska or the other Territories with free State men. The people of the south have always thought they have always been interfered with by the north, and the people of Missouri considered this the most open and bold movement the northern and eastern societies ever made. I am perfectly satisfied, and I have heard hundreds of Missourians lament that such a course had been pursued by the north, and gave it as their opinion that there would have been no excitement upon the subject of slavery, except for the extraordinary movement made by the north and east for the purpose of making Kansas a free State. Most of the slaves of the State of Missouri are in the western border counties, or the hemp growing portion of Missouri. The people of Missouri were a good deal excited just before the March election, because it had been so long postponed, and it was generally supposed that it was postponed in order to allow time for eastern emigrants to arrive here, that they might control the elections. Everybody that I heard speak of it expressed that belief, both in and out of the Territory. The same rumors were in the Territory as in Missouri. Immediately preceding that election, and even before the opening of navigation, we had rumors that hundreds of eastern people were in St. Louis, waiting for the navigation of the river to be opened, that they might get up to the Territory in time for the election, and the truth of these rumors was established by the accounts steamboat officers afterwards brought up of the emigrants they had landed at different places in and near the Territory, who had no families and very little property, except little oil cloth carpet sacks. For some two or three weeks before the election the rumor was prevalent that a good many eastern people were being sent here to be at the elections, and then were going back. There was a general expression of opinion that the people of Missouri should turn out and come to the Territory, and prevent this illegal voting by force, if necessary. We regarded this as invasion of the northern people of a Territory which was contiguous to Missouri, for the purpose of controlling the institutions of the Territory, and the defeat of the objects of the Kansas-Nebraska bill.

I do not recollect as I ever heard any Missourians advocate the policy of Missourians going over to that election and voting, in the absence of this eastern emigration about the time of the election, except, perhaps, General Stringfellow, who advocated the doctrine that the Missourians had the right to go there any time to vote, and, perhaps, urged them to come for that purpose. It was determined by the Missourians that if the eastern emigrants were allowed to vote, we would vote also, or we would destroy the poll books and break up the elections; and the determination is, that eastern people shall not be allowed to interfere and control the domestic institutions of Kansas, if the Union is dissolved in preventing it, though we are willing that all honest, well-meaning settlers shall come and be admitted to all the equality of the other citizens.

I went to the Burr Oak precinct with a company of other Missourians, with no arms myself, and I saw one gun in the party, and a few pistols and side arms. The determination of the people of Missouri was to interfere with no one except this boat load of eastern emigrants which was expected at that precinct, and if they arrived we determined, if strong enough, to march them back, to the tune of the Rogue's March, to the river, and make them get on the boat they got off. If we were not strong enough and they were allowed to vote, we were determined to vote too. . . . I did not see the slightest effort made on the 30th of March to interfere with the voters of the district, and there was no disturbance in regard to the election. . . .

I do not think the Missourians would ever have got excited about Kansas, but for the rumors concerning eastern emigrants. The [most] extraordinary efforts made by the eastern people, except these emigrant aid societies, that I have heard of, is the newspaper reports of men, rifles, and means being sent out here, as they say, to defend themselves, but, as we think, to control the elections here. If the Missouri compromise had not been repealed by the Kansas-Nebraska act, I think Kansas Territory would have been made a slave State, as most of the prominent men of Missouri considered that compromise repealed since 1850, and I have no doubt that the feeling in regard to Kansas then would have been the same as now.   The avowed object of making a free State by persons living remote from the Territory, and having no interest in it, and the raising of money and means for that purpose, is the obnoxious feature of these emigrant aid societies, though there is nothing illegal in that; but it is an extraordinary interference in a remote region of the country.   I think it is a new thing for free States to get up societies to make free States out of Territories.

The first extraordinary effort that the Missourians made to meet the action of these emigrant aid societies, was in the fall of 1854, or the early part of the winter, to form societies in Kansas and Missouri, in which each member pledged himself to use all honorable and legal means to make Kansas a slave State.   I cannot speak of but three counties, but I have heard that, in three counties there, societies existed. In our county I knew one society existed; it was a secret society.   I do not know that these societies are now in operation; I attended one up to the 30th March, 1855, and then stopped attending them, and do not know about them since.

I think, perhaps, through the influence of the members of these societies persons were induced to come over here to the election, but I do not think any who did come were members of this society.   The objects attempted to be affected by this society, was to hunt up and induce pro-slavery men to come to this Territory and become actual settlers.   I never heard of any fund; I deemed the society worthy, under the circumstances of the existing of the aid societies in the east. . . .   I consider it an unworthy object for persons who derive no pecuniary benefit from it, to undertake to make Kansas a free State, and thus injure Missouri.

But since the 30th of March, 1855, I think that society has been superseded by another society, which has a fund for the purpose, of sending pro-slavery emigration to this Territory, and is regularly organized for that purpose.   The fund is used in aiding emigrants, by loaning them money to get into the Territory, in providing claims, and entering the land.   It is a self-defensive organization, intended to have a bearing upon the political institutions of the Territory, as far as slavery is concerned.

So far as I know anything of the society, the means of the society is not to build up mills and hotels, but to aid individual settlers in their claims, and to do with the funds of the society for them what they indivi-dualy would do with their own money for themselves.   I think these

I

conversations have been formed pretty extensively over Missouri, and
I think persons have been selected in Missouri to go to other southern
States and build up similar societies there, but to what extent that has
been done I do not know. . . .

I do not think I would have suggested to any one in Missouri the
forming of societies in Missouri but for these eastern societies, and they
were formed but as a means of self-defence and to counteract the effect
of those eastern societies, and I think it is the general expression, and
I know it is the ardent hope of every man in Missouri that I have heard
express himself, that if the north would cease operating by these societies, Missouri would also cease to use those she has established.

All that Missourians asked was that the principles of the Kansas-
Nebraska act should be carried out, and the actual settlers of the Territory allowed to manage their own domestic institutions for themselves.

House Reports, 34 Cong., 1 sess. (Washington, 1856), II, No. 200, pp. 894-
897 *passim*.

---

39. Civil War in Kansas (1855–1856)

BY THOMAS H. GLADSTONE

Gladstone, a kinsman of William E. Gladstone, was an Englishman who came to
the United States as an ordinary traveller and after a tour through the South arrived
in Kansas at a critical period. His experience was to a large degree from the pro-
slavery side; and his account, first published in the London *Times*, is perhaps the
most impartial contemporary narrative that we have. — Bibliography as in No. 36
above.

THE autumn of 1854 witnessed the erection of the first log-huts of
Lawrence by a few families of New England settlers. During the
year 1855 its population increased rapidly, chiefly by the arrival of
emigrants from the Northern States. Its log-hut existence gave way to
a more advanced stage, in which buildings of brick and stone were introduced ; and the growing prosperity of the " Yankee town " early began
to excite the jealousy of the abettors of slavery. Viewed as the stronghold of the Free-state party, it was made the point of attack during what
was called " the Wakarusa war " in the winter of 1855. Before the termination of this its first siege, the necessity of some means of defence
being manifest, the inhabitants of Lawrence proceeded to fortify their
town by the erection of four or five circular earthworks, thrown up about
seven feet in height, and measuring a hundred feet in diameter. These

were connected with long lines of earthwork entrenchments, rifle-pits, and other means of fortification. Whilst these engineering operations were being carried on, the men might have been seen, day and night, working in the trenches, in haste to complete the defence of their Western Sebastopol. The inhabitants were also placed under arms, formed into companies, with their respective commanders, under the generalship of Robinson and Lane, had their daily drill, mounted guard day and night upon the forts, and sent out at night a horse-patrol to watch the outer posts, and give warning of approaching danger.

The pacification which followed the Wakarusa campaign in December, 1855, afforded only a temporary lull. Although war had ceased, the people did not cease to carry arms, and used them, when occasion offered, with fatal effect. The Missourians did not conceal that they were organizing another invasion, which should effectually "wipe out Lawrence," and win Kansas for slavery, "though they should wade to the knees in blood to obtain it." The Southern states were being appealed to far and wide, to aid by men and money in the extirpation of every Northern settler. . . .

The month of May arrived, and the state of parties continued as before. The pro-slavery, or, as it was commonly termed, the border-ruffian army, had, however, gained strength by large reinforcements from the States. Colonel Buford was there with his determined bands from Alabama, Colonel Titus from Florida, Colonel Wilkes and others with companies from South Carolina and Georgia, all of whom had sworn to fight the battles of the South in Kansas. The President, too, through his Secretary-at-War, had placed the federal troops at the command of Governor Shannon, and the Chief Justice Lecompte had declared, in a notable charge to a grand jury, that all who resisted the laws made by the fraudulently elected Legislature were to be found guilty of high treason. . . .

Meanwhile, Sheriff Jones rode about the country with a "posse" of United States troops, arresting whomsoever he pleased ; the grand jury declared the Free-state Hotel and the offices of the *Herald of Freedom* and *Kansas Free-State* newspapers in Lawrence to be nuisances, and as such to be removed ; Governor Robinson and several other men of influence in the Free-state cause were severally seized and held as prisoners ; Free-state men were daily molested in the highway, some robbed, and others killed ; and a constantly increasing army was encamping right and left of Lawrence, pressing daily more closely around it, and openly declaring that their intention was to " wipe out the traitorous city, and not to leave an abolitionist alive in the territory." . . .

At length the day approached when Lawrence was to fall. On the night previous to May 21st, could any one have taken a survey of the country around, he would have seen the old encampment at Franklin, four miles to the southeast of Lawrence, which was occupied during the Wakarusa war, again bristling with the arms of Colonel Buford's companies, brought from the States. This formed the lower division of the invading army. On the west of Lawrence, at twelve miles distance, he would have seen another encampment in the neighbourhood of Lecompton, occupied by the forces under Colonel Titus and Colonel Wilkes. These were reinforced by General Atchison, with his Platte County Rifles and two pieces of artillery; by Captain Dunn, heading the Kickapoo Rangers; by the Doniphan Tigers, and another company under General Clark, as well as by General Stringfellow, with his brother, the doctor, who had left for a time his editorship to take a military command, and other leaders, who brought up all the lawless rabble of the border-towns, to aid in the attack. These on the west of Lawrence formed the upper division. A large proportion were cavalry. The general control of the troops was in the hands of the United States Marshal, Donaldson, the whole body, of some six or eight hundred armed men, being regarded as a *posse comitatus* to aid this officer in the execution of his duties. . . .

During the forenoon Fain, the Deputy-Marshal, entered Lawrence with some assistants, to make arrests of its citizens. He failed, however, in provoking the resistance desired, on which to found a pretext for attacking the city; for the citizens permitted the arrests to be made, and responded to his demand for a " posse " to aid him. . . .

The United States Marshal had now, he stated, no more need of the troops; but, as Sheriff Jones had some processes to serve in Lawrence, he would hand them over to him as a *posse comitatus*.

Accordingly, in the afternoon, Jones rode into Lawrence at the head of twenty or more men, mounted and armed, and placed himself in front of the Free-state Hotel, demanding of General Pomeroy the surrender of all arms. He gave him five minutes for his decision, failing which the *posse* would be ordered to bombard the town. General Pomeroy gave up their brass howitzer and some small pieces, the only arms that were not private property. Jones then demanded the removal of the furniture from the hotel, stating that the District Court for Douglas

County had adjudged the hotel and the two free-state newspaper offices to be nuisances, and as nuisances to be removed, and that he was there as Sheriff to execute these indictments, and summarily remove the obnoxious buildings.

In the mean time the forces had left the hill, and were at the entrance of the town, under Titus and Buford, Atchison and Stringfellow. . . .

The newspaper offices were the first objects of attack. First that of the *Free State*, then that of the *Herald of Freedom*, underwent a thorough demolition. The presses were in each case broken to pieces, and the offending type carried away to the river. The papers and books were treated in like manner, until the soldiers became weary of carrying them to the Kaw, when they thrust them in piles into the street, and burnt, tore, or otherwise destroyed them.

From the printing offices they went to the hotel. . . .

As orders were given to remove the furniture, the wild mob threw the articles out of the windows, but shortly found more congenial employment in emptying the cellars. By this time four cannon had been brought opposite the hotel, and, under Atchison's command, they commenced to batter down the building. In this, however, they failed. The General's " Now, boys, let her rip ! " was answered by some of the shot missing the mark, although the breadth of Massachusetts-street alone intervened, and the remainder of some scores of rounds leaving the walls of the hotel unharmed. They then placed kegs of gunpowder in the lower parts of the building, and attempted to blow it up. The only result was, the shattering of some of the windows and other limited damage. At length, to complete the work which their own clumsiness or inebriety had rendered difficult hitherto, orders were given to fire the building in a number of places, and, as a consequence, it was soon encircled in a mass of flames. Before evening, all that remained of the Eldridge House was a portion of one wall standing erect, and for the rest a shapeless heap of ruins.

The firing of the cannon had been the signal for most of the women and children in Lawrence to leave the city. This they did, not knowing whither to turn their steps. The male portion of its citizens watched, without offering resistance, the destruction of the buildings named, and next had to see their own houses made the objects of unscrupulous plunder.

The sack of Lawrence occupied the remainder of the afternoon. Sheriff Jones, after gazing on the flames rising from the hotel, and saying that it was "the happiest day of his life," dismissed his "posse," and they immediately commenced their lawless pillage. In this officers and men all participated, and they did not terminate until they had rifled all the principal houses of whatever articles of value they could lay their hands upon, and had destroyed that which they could not carry away. Finally, Governor Robinson's house on Mount Oread was set fire to, after it had been searched for papers and valuables, and its burning walls lit up the evening sky as the army of desperadoes, now wild with plunder and excesses, and maddened with drink, retired from the pillaged city.

The value of the property stolen and destroyed during the day in Lawrence is estimated to have amounted to nearly thirty thousand pounds sterling.

Life was fortunately not taken, as the inhabitants of Lawrence disappointed their invaders of a fight, by offering no resistance. . . .

Among all the scenes of violence I witnessed, it is remarkable that the offending parties were invariably on the Pro-slavery side. The Free-state men appeared to me to be intimidated and overawed, in consequence, not merely of the determination and defiant boldness of their opponents, but still more through the sanction given to these acts by the Government.

I often heard the remark, that they would resist, but that they were resolved not to bring themselves into collision with the Federal power. . . .

Their later conduct, however, was different. In the hands of their oppressors all justice had been set at defiance. They had been driven out of house and home by an armed mob, acting under territorial authority. The Federal power had been appealed to in vain. The Free-state men were driven to desperation. It was but natural that some revulsion of feeling should be experienced. As it was, guerrilla parties were organized by some of the less passive spirits on the Free-state side, corresponding with those already existing amongst their opponents. These thought themselves justified in recovering stolen horses and other property. Other acts of retaliation occurred. In several instances the opposing parties came into collision, and violence ensued. For some time, therefore, after the attack upon Lawrence, an irregular strife was maintained, and a bitter remembrance filled each man's mind, and impelled to daily acts of hostility and not unfrequent bloodshed.

T. H. Gladstone, *The Englishman in Kansas ; or, Squatter Life and Border Warfare* (edited by F. L. Olmsted, New York, 1857), 22–66 *passim*.

40.　A Constitution made to Order (1857)

BY GOVERNOR ROBERT JOHN WALKER (1860)

Walker, a resident of Mississippi, is best known as Polk's secretary of the treasury, 1845–1849. He was an opponent of Calhoun's theories on the Constitution and on slavery. During the Civil War he was a financial agent of the United States abroad. As territorial governor of Kansas, a position which he accepted with reluctance, he gained distinction by refusing to lend himself to the scheme to force a pro-slavery constitution on an anti-slavery majority.— Bibliography as in No. 36 above.

FIRST, my instructions were drawn out, which, according to my judgment, fully confirmed the doctrine of the submission of the constitution to the vote of the people, and the President himself so regarded them. I then set about to draw up my inaugural address. . . . I prepared that inaugural address, and Mr. Buchanan, by appointment, met me at my house, where he spent many hours, which were devoted to that subject. That address was not then complete, except that portion of it that related to the question of the constitution being submitted to the vote of the people, and what I said on the subject of slavery in Kansas. What I said on the subject of submitting the constitution to the vote of the people Mr. Buchanan fully approved. . . .

When I first arrived in Kansas, every effort to make Kansas a slave State was apparently entirely abandoned. It was universally conceded that it could not be made a slave State by a fair vote of the people, which I thought was the only way in which it could be properly made either a slave State or a free State. . . .

Shortly before I arrived at Lecompton, the county of Douglas, of which Lecompton is the capital, had held a public democratic meeting, and nominated eight gentlemen, I think, as delegates to the Lecompton convention, of which John Calhoun, then the surveyor general of the Territory, was at the head. The resolutions of the meeting required them to sustain the submission of the constitution to the vote of the people. They published a written pledge to that effect. Rumors were circulated by their opponents that they would not submit the whole constitution to the people. They published a second circular a day or two before the election denouncing these rumors as falsehoods, and reaffirming their determination, if elected, to submit the constitution to the people. But for these assurances, it is universally conceded, they had no chance whatever of being elected, not the slightest. . . .

This attempt to make Kansas a slave State developed itself in the fall of 1857.　It first was fully developed by the terrible forgeries in the pretended returns — they were not legal returns — that were sent to me as governor of the Territory, and which I rejected, although that rejection gave a majority of the territorial legislature to my political opponents, the republicans, at which, I am free to say, I was deeply grieved. . . .

. . . at length it was fully developed that, contrary to all the pledges given, especially by Calhoun himself, the president of the convention, that they would submit the constitution to the vote of the people, another course was resolved upon.

Finally, a few days before the vote was taken upon the subject, Mr. Calhoun, the president of the convention, called upon me, and submitted substantially the programme as to slavery, which was subsequently adopted by the convention, and asked my concurrence.　He presented various prospects of the highest place from the people of this Union if I would concur, and assured me that that was the programme of the administration.　I said that that was impossible, and showed Mr. Calhoun this letter of Mr. Buchanan to me of the 12th of July, 1857.　He said that the administration had changed its policy.　I told him I did not believe it ; but let who would change their views on that question, with me the question of submitting the constitution to the vote of the people was fundamental, and I never would change or modify my views on that question in the slightest respect ; that I would fight it out to the end, be the consequences to me personally or politically what they might.　Mr. Calhoun continued to insist that I ought to go with the President upon this subject.　I denied that he had any right to speak for the President. . . . I asked him if he had any letter from the President.　He said he had not, but that the assurance came to him in such a manner as to be entirely reliable ; that this particular programme (which was finally adopted in Kansas) was the programme of the administration.　I stated that I never would assent to it, and I gave various reasons.　I stated, in the first place, that I had openly pledged myself to the people of Kansas — declaring that I was so authorized by the President — so far as my power and that of the government would avail, that this constitution should be submitted fairly to their vote for ratification or rejection ; that I had by these pledges (on which they relied) induced them to suspend putting the Topeka State government into operation, which otherwise undoubtedly would have been done ; and that it would be dishonorable in me to forfeit these pledges, and that I could not do it.　I stated that although I insisted that the Kansas and Nebraska bill required that the constitution itself should be submitted to the vote of the people, yet if they would make a good constitution, and submit the slavery question distinctly, by itself, to a fair vote of the people, although it did not correspond with my views, yet I would not interfere ; but that the particular programme which they proposed to adopt did not submit the question of slavery to the people of Kansas ; that it only submitted it to those constituting a small minority who were in favor of the constitution because the vote was limited to a vote "for the constitution with slavery," and "for the constitution without slavery," and those who were opposed to the constitution were not permitted to vote at all.   Therefore, I considered such a submission of the question a vile fraud, a base counterfeit, and a wretched device to prevent the people voting even on that question.   I said to him that not only would I not support it, but I would denounce it, no matter whether the administration sustained it or not ; and I always have denounced it, and shall ever continue to do so.

It is due to frankness to say, that when I came on here in November, 1857, the President himself distinctly and emphatically assured me that he had not authorized anybody to say that he had approved of that programme.   I told him that such being the case, I could not but believe that some member of the administration, or some person in high authority enjoying its confidence, must have given these assurances, or Mr. Calhoun would not have made the communication that he had to me, and also changed his own course upon the subject.   For Mr. Calhoun had been the distinguished and special leader of the Douglas party in Kansas, and was supposed to have been appointed surveyor general upon Judge Douglas's recommendation.   He, Judge Douglas, certainly requested me to have him, Calhoun, retained, assuring me that he would support the submission of the constitution to the vote of the people ; as he did, until a late period.

When Mr. Calhoun made this communication to me he requested me not to mention it to Mr. Stanton, the secretary of state of Kansas, and I believe I never have done so ; nor should I have communicated it to you now except as necessary to my vindication from the testimony you have shown me to-day.   It is also due to frankness to further say that I am fully impressed with the conviction that the President himself did not get up this programme, though I do believe it was gotten up by some of the administration, or others high in authority.

House Reports, 36 Cong., 1 sess. (Washington, 1860), V, No. 648, pp. 106–111 *passim.*

CHAPTER VII — THE CRISIS ARRIVES

41. Papers in the Dred Scott Case (1847–1848)

BY THE MISSOURI CIRCUIT COURT

These papers are introduced to show the process of claiming freedom, the succession of suits, and the original question at issue in the Missouri courts. The action for trespass here described was finally decided in Dred Scott's favor, but on appeal to the Supreme Court of Missouri the decision was reversed. Meanwhile Scott had brought action of trespass in the United States Circuit Court, as a citizen of Missouri suing Sandford, a citizen of New York. The court gave judgment for the defendant, and Dred Scott's counsel carried the case to the United States Supreme Court on a writ of error. After the decision, which is one of the most important opinions ever handed down by the court, Scott was at once set free by his titular master. — Bibliography: Channing and Hart, *Guide*, § 202.

A. DRED SCOTT'S FREEDOM SUIT

Dred Scott
vs.
Alex. Sandford,
Saml. Russel, and
Irene Emerson.

TO the Honorable, the Circuit Court within and for the County of St. Louis.

Your petitioner, Dred Scott, a man of color, respectfully represents that sometime in the year 1835 your petitioner was purchased as a slave by one John Emerson, since deceased, who afterwards, to-wit; about the year 1836 or 1837, conveyed your petitioner from the State of Missouri to Fort Snelling, a fort then occupied by the troops of the United States and under the jurisdiction of the United States, situated in the territory ceded by France to the United States under the name of Louisiana, lying north of 36 degrees and 30' North latitude, now included in the State of Missouri, and resided and continued to reside at Fort Snelling upwards of one year, and held your petitioner in slavery at such Fort during all that time in violation of the Act of Congress of 1806 and 1820, entitled An Act to Authorize the People of Missouri Territory to form a Constitution and State Government, and for the admission of such State

into the Union on an equal footing with the original states, and to Prohibit Slavery in Certain Territories.

Your petitioner avers that said Emerson has since departed this life,
leaving his widow Irene Emerson and an infant child whose name is
unknown to your petitioner ; and that one Alexander Sandford administered upon the estate of said Emerson and that your petitioner is now
unlawfully held in slavery by said Sandford and by said administrator,
and said Irene Emerson claims your petitioner as part of the estate of
said Emerson and by one Samuel Russell.

Your petitioner therefore prays your Honorable Court to grant him
leave to sue as a poor person, in order to establish his right to freedom,
and that the necessary orders may be made in the premises.

Dred Scott.

State of Missouri ⎫
County of St. Louis ⎰ ss.

This day personally came before me, the undersigned, a Justice of the
Peace, Dred Scott, the person whose name is affixed to the foregoing
petition, and made oath that the facts set forth in the above petition are
true to the best of his knowledge and belief, that he is entitled to his
freedom.

Witness my hand this 1st day of July, 1847.

his
Dred X Scott
mark.

Sworn to and subscribed before me this 1st day of July, 1847.

Peter W. Johnstone
Justice of the Peace.

Upon reading the above petition this day, it being the opinion of the
Judge of the Circuit Court, that the said petition contains sufficient
matter to authorize the commencement of a suit for his freedom, it is
hereby ordered that the said petitioner Dred Scott be allowed to sue on
giving security satisfactory to the Clerk of the Circuit Court for all costs
that may be adjudged against him, and that he have reasonable liberty
to attend to his counsel and the court as the occasion may require, and
that he be not subject to any severity on account of this application for
his freedom.

July 2d, 1847.   A. Hamilton

Judge of Circuit Court 8th Jud. Cir.

B. DRED SCOTT'S TRESPASS SUIT

Circuit Court of St. Louis County, November Term, 1847.

State of Missouri ⎱
County of St. Louis ⎰ ss.

Dred Scott, a man of color, by his attorneys, plaintiff in this suit, complains of Alexander Sandford, administrator of the estate of John Emerson, deceased, Irene Emerson and Samuel Russell defendants, of a plea of trespass that the said defendants, heretofore, to-wit, on the 1st day of July in the year 1846, at to-wit, the County of St. Louis aforesaid with force and arms assaulted said plaintiff, and then and there bruised and ill-treated him, and then and there put him in prison and kept and detained him in prison, and without any reason whatsoever for the space of one year, and then and there violating and contrary to law and against the will of said plaintiff; and said plaintiff avers that before and at the time of the committing of the grievance aforesaid, he, the said plaintiff, was then and there and still is a free person, and that the said defendants held and still hold him in slavery, and other wrongs to said plaintiff then and there did against the laws of the State of Missouri to the damage of the said plaintiff in the sum of $300, and therefore he sues.

C. VERDICT AGAINST SCOTT IN TRESPASS SUIT

April 30, 1847, April Term.   A. Hamilton, Judge.

Dred Scott of color ⎫
        vs.   ⎬ Trespass.
Irene Emmerson.   ⎭

This day come the parties by their attorney and comes also a jury . . . twelve good and lawful men, who being duly elected, tried and sworn the truth to speak upon the issue joined between the parties, upon their oaths, do find that the said defendant is not guilty in any manner and form as the plaintiff hath in his declaration complaint against her.   Therefore it is considered that the said defendant go hence without day and recover of the said plaintiff her costs in this behalf expended.   The plaintiff by his attorneys files a motion for a new trial herein.   Set aside. . . .

Dred Scott   ⎫
    vs.   ⎬ Freedom.
Irene Emmerson. ⎭

Dred Scott   ⎫
        vs.   ⎬ Freedom.
Alex. Sandford, Samuel
Russell, and Irene Emerson.   ⎭

It is ordered in this case that the plaintiff in these two suits make his election on or before the first day of the next term of this Court which of said suits he will continue to prosecute. . . .

D. NEW TRIAL ORDERED IN TRESPASS SUIT

Thursday December 2, 1847, November Term.

Dred Scott ⎫   On consideration of the motion of the plaintiff for
vs. ⎬ a new trial herein, it is ordered that the same be sus-
Irene Emmerson. ⎭ tained, and that the verdict and judgment herein rendered be set aside and a new trial had.

E. FREEDOM SUIT ABANDONED

Thursday Feby 29, 1848, Nov. Term.

Dred Scott ⎫   This day comes said plaintiff by his
vs. ⎪ attorneys and says that he will not fur-
Alex. Sandford, ⎬ Freedom. ther prosecute this suit. It is there-
Samuel Russell, ⎪ fore considered that said defendants go
Irene Emmerson. ⎭ hence without day and recover of said plaintiff their costs in this behalf, and have thereof execution.

F. DRED SCOTT HIRED OUT

Friday March 17th, 1848.

Dred Scott ⎫
vs. ⎬ Motion of Attorney for Defendant.
Irene Emmerson. ⎭

It is ordered that the Sheriff of St. Louis County take the said plaintiff into his possession and hire him out from time to time to the best advantage, during the pendency of this suit. And that he take bond from the hirer payable to the State of Missouri in the sum of $600 with good security conditioned that the said hirer shall not remove said plaintiff out of the jurisdiction of this Court ; that he will pay the hire to said Sheriff and return said plaintiff at the expiration of the term for which he is hired, or as soon as this action is ended.

From the MS. Court Records of St. Louis County.

42. Dred Scott Decision (1857)

BY CHIEF JUSTICE ROGER BROOKE TANEY

Taney succeeded Marshall as chief justice of the United States Supreme Court in 1835. Though earlier a decided partisan, he filled satisfactorily the difficult position of chief justice. Although inclined to a strict construction of the Constitution, he did little to weaken the theories of government set forth by Marshall. He was probably drawn into the delivery of the Dred Scott decision, a great *obiter dictum*, by the sincere hope that the great prestige of a Supreme Court decision would settle forever the slavery question. This is the first case of an act of Congress, not relating to the judiciary itself, which was held void by the Supreme Court. — For Taney, see Samuel Tyler, *Memoir of Roger Brooke Taney.* — Bibliography as in No. 41 above.

THE question is simply this : Can a negro, whose ancestors were imported into this country, and sold as slaves, become a member of the political community formed and brought into existence by the constitution of the United States, and as such become entitled to all the rights, and privileges, and immunities, guarantied by that instrument to the citizen? One of which rights is the privilege of suing in a court of the United States in the cases specified in the constitution.

It will be observed, that the plea applies to that class of persons only whose ancestors were negroes of the African race, and imported into this country, and sold and held as slaves. The only matter in issue before the court, therefore, is, whether the descendants of such slaves, when they shall be emancipated, or who are born of parents who had become free before their birth, are citizens of a State, in the sense in which the word citizen is used in the constitution of the United States. And this being the only matter in dispute on the pleadings, the court must be understood as speaking in this opinion of that class only, that is, of those persons who are the descendants of Africans who were imported into this country, and sold as slaves. . . .

The words " people of the United States " and " citizens " . . . mean the same thing. . . . The question before us is, whether the class of persons described in the plea in abatement compose a portion of this people, and are constituent members of this sovereignty? . . .

In discussing this question, we must not confound the rights of citizenship which a State may confer within its own limits, and the rights of citizenship as a member of the Union. It does not by any means follow, because he has all the rights and privileges of a citizen of a State, that he must be a citizen of the United States. . . .

It is very clear . . . that no State can, by any act or law of its own, passed since the adoption of the constitution, introduce a new member into the political community created by the constitution of the United States. It cannot make him a member of this community by making him a member of its own. And for the same reason it cannot introduce any person, or description of persons, who were not intended to be embraced in this new political family, which the constitution brought into existence, but were intended to be excluded from it. . . .

It is true, every person, and every class and description of persons, who were at the time of the adoption of the constitution recognized as citizens in the several States, became also citizens of this new political body; but none other; it was formed by them, and for them and their posterity, but for no one else. . . .

It becomes necessary, therefore, to determine who were citizens of the several States when the constitution was adopted. . . .

In the opinion of the court, the legislation and histories of the times, and the language used in the declaration of independence, show, that neither the class of persons who had been imported as slaves, nor their descendants, whether they had become free or not, were then acknowledged as a part of the people, nor intended to be included in the general words used in that memorable instrument.

It is difficult at this day to realize the state of public opinion in relation to that unfortunate race, which prevailed in the civilized and enlightened portions of the world at the time of the declaration of independence, and when the constitution of the United States was framed and adopted. But the public history of every European nation displays it in a manner too plain to be mistaken.

They had for more than a century before been regarded as beings of an inferior order, and altogether unfit to associate with the white race, either in social or political relations; and so far inferior, that they had no rights which the white man was bound to respect; and that the negro might justly and lawfully be reduced to slavery for his benefit. He was bought and sold, and treated as an ordinary article of merchandise and traffic, whenever a profit could be made by it. This opinion was at that time fixed and universal in the civilized portion of the white race. It was regarded as an axiom in morals as well as in politics, which no one thought of disputing, or supposed to be open to dispute; and men in every grade and position in society daily and habitually acted upon it in their private pursuits, as well as in matters of public concern, without doubting for a moment the correctness of this opinion.

And in no nation was this opinion more firmly fixed or more uniformly acted upon than by the English government and English people. They not only seized them on the coast of Africa, and sold them or held them in slavery for their own use; but they took them as ordinary articles of merchandise to every country where they could make a profit on them, and were far more extensively engaged in this commerce than any other nation in the world.

The opinion thus entertained and acted upon in England was naturally impressed upon the colonies they founded on this side of the Atlantic. And, accordingly, a negro of the African race was regarded by them as an article of property, and held, and bought and sold as such, in every one of the thirteen colonies which united in the declaration of independence, and afterwards formed the constitution of the United States. The slaves were more or less numerous in the different colonies, as slave labor was found more or less profitable. But no one seems to have doubted the correctness of the prevailing opinion of the time. . . .

The language of the declaration of independence is equally conclusive . . .

. . . "We hold these truths to be self-evident: that all men are created equal; that they are endowed by their Creator with certain unalienable rights; that among them is life, liberty, and the pursuit of happiness; that to secure these rights, governments are instituted, deriving their just powers from the consent of the governed."

The general words above quoted would seem to embrace the whole human family, and if they were used in a similar instrument at this day would be so understood. But it is too clear for dispute, that the enslaved African race were not intended to be included, and formed no part of the people who framed and adopted this declaration; for if the language, as understood in that day, would embrace them, the conduct of the distinguished men who framed the declaration of independence would have been utterly and flagrantly inconsistent with the principles they asserted; and instead of the sympathy of mankind, to which they so confidently appealed, they would have deserved and received universal rebuke and reprobation. . . .

But there are two clauses in the constitution which point directly and specifically to the negro race as a separate class of persons, and show clearly that they were not regarded as a portion of the people or citizens of the government then formed.

One of these clauses reserves to each of the thirteen States the right to import slaves until the year 1808, if it thinks proper. . . . And by the other provision the States pledge themselves to each other to maintain the right of property of the master, by delivering up to him any slave who may have escaped from his service, and be found within their respective territories. . . . And these two provisions show, conclusively, that neither the description of persons therein referred to, nor their descendants, were embraced in any of the other provisions of the constitution; for certainly these two clauses were not intended to confer on them or their posterity the blessings of liberty, or any of the personal rights so carefully provided for the citizen. . . .

The only two provisions which point to them and include them, treat them as property, and make it the duty of the government to protect it; no other power, in relation to this race, is to be found in the constitution; and as it is a government of special, delegated, powers, no authority beyond these two provisions can be constitutionally exercised. The government of the United States had no right to interfere for any other purpose but that of protecting the rights of the owner, leaving it altogether with the several States to deal with this race, whether emancipated or not, as each State may think justice, humanity, and the interests and safety of society, require. The States evidently intended to reserve this power exclusively to themselves.

. . . This court was not created by the constitution for such purposes. Higher and graver trusts have been confided to it, and it must not falter in the path of duty. . . .

And upon a full and careful consideration of the subject, the court is of opinion, that, upon the facts stated in the plea in abatement, Dred Scott was not a citizen of Missouri within the meaning of the constitution of the United States, and not entitled as such to sue in its courts; and, consequently, that the circuit court had no jurisdiction of the case, and that the judgment on the plea in abatement is erroneous.

. . . the plaintiff . . . admits that he and his wife were born slaves, but endeavors to make out his title to freedom and citizenship by showing that they were taken by their owner to certain places, hereinafter mentioned, where slavery could not by law exist, and that they thereby became free, and upon their return to Missouri became citizens of that State. . . .

The act of Congress, upon which the plaintiff relies, declares that slavery and involuntary servitude, except as a punishment for crime, shall be forever prohibited in all that part of the territory ceded by

K

France, under the name of Louisiana, which lies north of thirty-six degrees thirty minutes north latitude, and not included within the limits of Missouri. And the difficulty which meets us at the threshold of this part of the inquiry is, whether Congress was authorized to pass this law under any of the powers granted to it by the constitution; for if the authority is not given by that instrument, it is the duty of this court to declare it void and inoperative, and incapable of conferring freedom upon any one who is held as a slave under the laws of any one of the States.

The counsel for the plaintiff has laid much stress upon that article in the constitution which confers on congress the power " to dispose of and make all needful rules and regulations respecting the territory or other property belonging to the United States;" but, in the judgment of the court, that provision has no bearing on the present controversy, and the power there given, whatever it may be, is confined, and was intended to be confined, to the territory which at that time belonged to, or was claimed by, the United States, and was within their boundaries as settled by the treaty with Great Britain, and can have no influence upon a territory afterwards acquired from a foreign government. It was a special provision for a known and particular territory, and to meet a present emergency, and nothing more. . . .

. . . The form of government to be established necessarily rested in the discretion of congress. . . .

But the power of congress over the person or property of a citizen can never be a mere discretionary power under our constitution and form of government. The powers of the government and the rights and privileges of the citizen are regulated and plainly defined by the constitution itself. And when the territory becomes a part of the United States, the federal government enters into possession in the character impressed upon it by those who created it. It enters upon it with its powers over the citizen strictly defined, and limited by the constitution, from which it derives its own existence, and by virtue of which alone it continues to exist and act as a government and sovereignty. It has no power of any kind beyond it; and it cannot, when it enters a territory of the United States, put off its character, and assume discretionary or despotic powers which the constitution has denied to it. It cannot create for itself a new character separated from the citizens of the United States, and the duties it owes them under the provisions of the constitution. The territory being a part of the United States, the government and the citizen both enter it under the authority of the constitution, with their respective rights defined and marked out ; and the federal government can exercise no power over his person or property, beyond what that instrument confers, nor lawfully deny any right which it has reserved. . . .

. . . in considering the question before us, it must be borne in mind that there is no law of nations standing between the people of the United States and their government, and interfering with their relation to each other . . . if the constitution recognizes the right of property of tne master in a slave, and makes no distinction between that description of property and other property owned by a citizen, no tribunal, acting under the authority of the United States, whether it be legislative, executive, or judicial, has a right to draw such a distinction, or deny to it the benefit of the provisions and guarantees which have been provided for the protection of private property against the encroachments of the government.

Now, as we have already said in an earlier part of this opinion, upon a different point, the right of property in a slave is distinctly and expressly affirmed in the constitution. . . . This is done in plain words — too plain to be misunderstood. And no word can be found in the constitution which gives congress a greater power over slave property, or which entitles property of that kind to less protection than property of any other description. The only power conferred is the power coupled with the duty of guarding and protecting the owner in his rights.

Upon these considerations, it is the opinion of the court that the act of congress which prohibited a citizen from holding and owning property of this kind in the territory of the United States north of the line therein mentioned, is not warranted by the constitution, and is therefore void ; and that neither Dred Scott himself, nor any of his family, were made free by being carried into this territory ; even if they had been carried there by the owner, with the intention of becoming a permanent resident. . . .

. . . And it is contended, on the part of the plaintiff, that he is made free by being taken to Rock Island, in the State of Illinois. . . .

. . . As Scott was a slave when taken into the State of Illinois by his owner, and was there held as such, and brought back in that character, his *status*, as free or slave, depended on the laws of Missouri, and not of Illinois.

Dred Scott *v.* Sandford, 19 *Howard*, 403–452 *passim* ; in Samuel F. Miller, *Reports of Decisions in the Supreme Court of the United States* (Washington, 1875), II, 6–56 *passim*.

43. Dred Scott Decision Reviewed (1857)

BY THOMAS HART BENTON

Benton, after thirty years of continuous service as senator from Missouri (a state admitted by the Missouri Compromise), was dropped as not pliable enough for pro-slavery service. He was then in the House for two years, and fought the Kansas-Nebraska Bill. In 1857 he was in retirement, but he could not keep silent on what seemed to him a decision contrary to the facts of history and to the undisputed practice of the government. — For Benton, see Theodore Roosevelt, *Life of Thomas Hart Benton; Contemporaries*, III, No. 189. — Bibliography as in No. 41 above.

THE power of the Court is judicial — so declared in the Constitution; and so held in theory, if not in practice. · It is limited to cases *"in law and equity;"* and though sometimes encroaching upon political subjects, it is without right, without authority, and without the means of enforcing its decisions. It can issue no mandamus to Congress, or the people, nor punish them for disregarding its decisions, or even attacking them. Far from being bound by their decisions, Congress may proceed criminally against the judges for making them, when deemed criminally wrong — one house impeach and the other try : as done in the famous case of Judge Chase.

In assuming to decide these questions, — (Constitutionality of the Missouri Compromise, and the self-extension of the Constitution to Territories,) — it is believed the Court committed two great errors : *first*, in the assumption to try such questions : *secondly*, in deciding them as they did. And it is certain that the decisions are contrary to the uniform action of all the departments of the government — one of them for thirty-six years ; and the other for seventy years ; and in their effects upon each are equivalent to an alteration of the Constitution, by inserting new clauses in it, which could not have been put in it at the time that instrument was made, nor at any time since, nor now.

The Missouri Compromise act was a *"political enactment,"* made by the political power, for reasons founded in national policy, enlarged and liberal, of which it was the proper judge : and which was not to be reversed afterwards by judicial interpretation of words and phrases.

Doubtless the Court was actuated by the most laudable motives in undertaking, while settling an individual controversy, to pass from the private rights of an individual to the public rights of the whole body of the people ; and, in endeavoring to settle, by a judicial decision, a political question which engrosses and distracts the country : but the undertaking was beyond its competency, both legally and potentially.

It had no right to decide — no means to enforce the decision — no machinery to carry it into effect — no penalties of fines or jails to enforce
it : and the event has corresponded with these inabilities.   Far from
settling the question, the opinion itself has become a new question,
more virulent than the former ! has become the very watchword of parties ! has gone into party creeds and platforms — bringing the Court
itself into the political field — and condemning all future appointments
of federal judges, (and the elections of those who make the appointments, and of those who can multiply judges by creating new districts
and circuits,) to the test of these decisions.   This being the case, and the
evil now actually upon us, there is no resource but to face it — to face this
new question — examine its foundations — show its errors ; and rely upon
reason and intelligence to work out a safe deliverance for the country.

Repulsing jurisdiction of the original case, and dismissing it for want
of right to try it, there would certainly be a difficulty in getting at its
merits — at the merits of the dismissed case itself ; and, certainly, still
greater difficulty in getting at the merits of two great political questions
which lie so far beyond it.   The Court evidently felt this difficulty, and
worked sedulously to surmount it — sedulously, at building the bridge,
long and slender — upon which the majority of the judges crossed the
wide and deep gulf which separated the personal rights of Dred Scott
and his family from the political institutions and the political rights of
the whole body of the American people. . . .

. . . In the acquisition of Louisiana came the first new territory to
the United States, and over it Congress exercised the same power
that it had done over the original territory.   It saw no difference
between the old and new, as the Court has done, and governed both,
independently of the Constitution, and incompatibly with it, and by
virtue of the same right — Sovereignty and Proprietorship ! the right
converted into a duty, and only limited by the terms of the grant in
each case.

Louisiana was acquired in the spring of 1803 : an extra session of
Congress . . . in October . . . passed an act . . . providing for a
temporary government : and which was in these words : —

"That until the expiration of the present session of Congress, unless provision for
the temporary government of the said territories be sooner made by Congress, all the
military, civil and judicial powers exercised by the officers of the existing government
of the same, shall be vested in such persons, and shall be exercised in such manner,
as the President of the United States shall direct for maintaining and protecting the
inhabitants of Louisiana in the free enjoyment of their liberty, property and religion."

. . . Nothing could be more incompatible with our Constitution than such a government — a mere emanation of Spanish despotism. . . .

. . . It was a royal despotic Government, and every body knew it; and no one thought of testing it by the Constitution (some few new members in the House excepted) than by the Koran. . . .

As early as November 28th, Mr. Breckenridge, always a coadjutor of Mr. Jefferson, submitted a resolution in the Senate to raise a committee to prepare a form of government for Louisiana. . . . This [bill] contains three provisions on the subject of slaves: 1. That no one shall be imported into the Territory from foreign parts. 2. That no one shall be carried into it who had been imported into the United States since the first day of May, 1798. 3. That no one shall be carried into it except by the owner, and for his own use as a settler; the penalty in every instance being a fine upon the violator of the law, and freedom to the slave. . . .

These three prohibitions certainly amount to legislating upon slavery in a Territory, and that a new Territory, acquired since the formation of the Constitution, and without the aid of compacts with any State. . . .

. . . The Supreme Court makes a great difference between these two classes of territories, and a corresponding difference in the power of Congress with respect to them, and to the prejudice of the new Territory. The Congress of 1803-'4 did not see this difference; and acting upon a sense of plenary authority, it extended the ordinance across the Mississippi — sent the governor and judges of Indiana (for Indiana had then become a Territory) — sent this governor (William Henry Harrison) and the three Indiana judges across the Mississippi river, to administer the ordinance of '87 in that upper half of Louisiana. . . .

Strong as was the course of Congress in the act taking possession of Louisiana, and continuing therein the Spanish government under American officers, it was repeated, in all its extent, sixteen years afterwards, on the acquisition of Florida. . . .

. . . It was at the session of 1818-'19 that the Missouri Territory . . . applied through her Territorial Legislature for an Act of Congress to enable her to hold a convention for the formation of a State Constitution, preparatory to the formal application for admission into the Union. The bill had been perfected, its details adjusted, and was upon its last reading, when a motion was made by Mr. James Tallmadge, of New York, to impose a restriction on the State in relation to slavery, to restrain her from the future admission of slavery within her borders. . . .

. . . the eventful question was called, and resulted 134 for the compromise to 42 against it — a majority of three to one, and eight over. Such a vote was a real compromise ! a surrender on the part of the restrictionists, of strong feeling to a sense of duty to the country ! a settlement of a distracting territorial question upon the basis of mutual concession, and according to the principles of the ordinance of 1787. Such a measure may appear on the statute book as a mere act of Congress ; and lawyers may plead its repealability : but to those who were cotemporary with the event, and saw the sacrifice of feeling, or prejudice, which was made, and the loss of popularity incurred, and how great was the danger of the country from which it saved us, it becomes a national compact, founded on considerations higher than money : and which good faith and the harmony and stability of the Union deserved to be cherished next after the Constitution.

Of the 42 who voted against the compromise, there was not one who stated a constitutional objection : all that stated reasons for their votes, gave those of expediency — among others that it was an unequal division, which was true, but the fault of the South ; for, while contending for their share in Louisiana, they were giving away nearly all below 36° 30' to the King of Spain. There being no tie, the speaker (Mr. Clay) could not vote ; but his exertions were as zealous and active in support of it, as indispensable to the pacification of the country.

From Congress the bill went to the President for his approval ; and there it underwent a scrutiny which brought out the sense both of the President and his cabinet upon the precise point which has received the condemnation of the Supreme Court, and exactly contrary to the Court's decision. There was a word in the restrictive clause which, taken by itself and without reference to its context, might be construed as extending the slavery prohibition beyond the territorial condition of the country to which it attached — might be understood to extend it to the State form. It was the word " forever." Mr. Monroe took the opinion of his cabinet upon the import of this word, dividing his inquiry into two questions — whether the word would apply the restriction to Territories after they became States ? and whether Congress had a right to impose the restriction upon a Territory ? Upon these two questions, the opinion of the cabinet was unanimous — negatively, on the first ; affirmatively, on the other. . . .

[Thomas H. Benton], *Historical and Legal Examination . . . of the Decision of the Supreme Court of the United States in the Dred Scott Case* (New York, 1857), 4–96 *passim.*

44. "A House Divided against Itself cannot Stand" (1858)

BY ABRAHAM LINCOLN

Lincoln was scarcely known outside of Illinois when he delivered the oration from which this extract is taken. The occasion was his nomination to the United States Senate by the Republican state convention. The simplicity, cogency, and fitness of this speech, and of his speeches in the joint debates with Douglas, made him not only a national character but a candidate for the Republican nomination for president. Of all the party leaders in 1858 he saw most clearly the inevitable trend of events, and gave it expression in a radical doctrine. — For Lincoln, see Henry Matson, *References for Literary Workers*, 116–117. — Bibliography: Channing and Hart, *Guide*, § 203.

. . . IF we could first know where we are, and whither we are tending, we could better judge what to do, and how to do it. We are now far into the fifth year since a policy was initiated with the avowed object and confident promise of putting an end to slavery agitation. Under the operation of that policy, that agitation has not only not ceased, but has constantly augmented. In my opinion, it will not cease until a crisis shall have been reached and passed. "A house divided against itself cannot stand." I believe this government cannot endure permanently half slave and half free. I do not expect the Union to be dissolved — I do not expect the house to fall — but I do expect it will cease to be divided. It will become all one thing, or all the other. Either the opponents of slavery will arrest the further spread of it, and place it where the public mind shall rest in the belief that it is in the course of ultimate extinction; or its advocates will push it forward till it shall become alike lawful in all the States, old as well as new, North as well as South.

Have we no tendency to the latter condition?

Let any one who doubts carefully contemplate that now almost complete legal combination — piece of machinery, so to speak — compounded of the Nebraska doctrine and the Dred Scott decision. Let him consider not only what work the machinery is adapted to do, and how well adapted; but also let him study the history of its construction, and trace, if he can, or rather fail, if he can, to trace the evidences of design and concert of action among its chief architects, from the beginning.

The new year of 1854 found slavery excluded from more than half the States by State constitutions, and from most of the national territory by congressional prohibition. Four days later commenced the struggle which ended in repealing that congressional prohibition. This opened all the national territory to slavery, and was the first point gained.

But, so far, Congress only had acted; and an indorsement by the people, real or apparent, was indispensable to save the point already gained and give chance for more.

This necessity had not been overlooked, but had been provided for, as well as might be, in the notable argument of " squatter sovereignty," otherwise called " sacred right of self-government," which latter phrase, though expressive of the only rightful basis of any government, was so perverted in this attempted use of it as to amount to just this : That if any one man choose to enslave another, no third man shall be allowed to object. . . . Then opened the roar of loose declamation in favor of " squatter sovereignty " and " sacred right of self-government." " But," said opposition members, " let us amend the bill so as to expressly declare that the people of the Territory may exclude slavery." " Not we," said the friends of the measure ; and down they voted the amendment.

While the Nebraska bill was passing through Congress, a law case involving the question of a negro's freedom . . . was passing through the United States Circuit Court for the District of Missouri. . . . Before the then next presidential election, the law case came to and was argued in the Supreme Court of the United States. . . .

The election came. Mr. Buchanan was elected, and the indorsement, such as it was, secured. That was the second point gained. . . . The Supreme Court met again ; did not announce their decision, but ordered a reargument. The presidential inauguration came, and still no decision of the court ; but the incoming President in his inaugural address fervently exhorted the people to abide by the forthcoming decision, whatever it might be. Then, in a few days, came the decision.

The reputed author of the Nebraska bill finds an early occasion to make a speech at this capital indorsing the Dred Scott decision, and vehemently denouncing all opposition to it. The new President, too, seizes the early occasion of the Silliman letter to indorse and strongly construe that decision, and to express his astonishment that any different view had ever been entertained !

At length a squabble springs up between the President and the author of the Nebraska bill, on the mere question of fact, whether the Lecompton constitution was or was not, in any just sense, made by the people of Kansas ; and in that quarrel the latter declares that all he wants is a fair vote for the people, and that he cares not whether slavery be voted down or voted up. I do not understand his declaration that he cares not whether slavery be voted down or voted up to be intended by him other than as an apt definition of the policy he would impress upon the public mind — the principle for which he declares he has suffered so much, and is ready to suffer to the end. And well may he cling to that principle. If he has any parental feeling, well may he cling to it. That principle is the only shred left of his original Nebraska doctrine. Under the Dred Scott decision " squatter sovereignty " squatted out of existence, tumbled down like temporary scaffolding, — like the mold at the foundry, served through one blast and fell back into loose sand, — helped to carry an election, and then was kicked to the winds. . . .

We cannot absolutely know that all these exact adaptations are the result of preconcert. But when we see a lot of framed timbers, different portions of which we know have been gotten out at different times and places and by different workmen, — Stephen, Franklin, Roger, and James, for instance, — and we see these timbers joined together, and see they exactly make the frame of a house or a mill, all the tenons and mortises exactly fitting, and all the lengths and proportions of the different pieces exactly adapted to their respective places, and not a piece too many or too few, not omitting even scaffolding — or, if a single piece be lacking, we see the place in the frame exactly fitted and prepared yet to bring such piece in — in such a case we find it impossible not to believe that Stephen and Franklin and Roger and James all understood one another from the beginning, and all worked upon a common plan or draft drawn up before the first blow was struck.

Abraham Lincoln, *Complete Works* (edited by John G. Nicolay and John Hay, New York, 1894), I, 240–243 *passim*.

———◆———

45. "The Irrepressible Conflict" (1858)

BY SENATOR WILLIAM HENRY SEWARD

Seward's term, " irrepressible conflict," was another way of expressing Lincoln's idea of " a house divided against itself " (see No. 44 above); but Seward was a man of national prominence and a representative Republican, and his phrase exerted an immediate and a lasting influence. — For Seward, see No. 22 above. — Bibliography as No. 44 above.

OUR country is a theatre, which exhibits, in full operation, two radically different political systems; the one resting on the basis of servile or slave labor, the other on the basis of voluntary labor of freemen. . . .

. . . The two systems are at once perceived to be incongruous. But they are more than incongruous — they are incompatible. They never have permanently existed together in one country, and they never can. It would be easy to demonstrate this impossibility, from the irreconcilable contrast between their great principles and characteristics. But the experience of mankind has conclusively established it. . . .

Hitherto, the two systems have existed in different States, but side by side within the American Union. This has happened because the Union is a confederation of States. But in another aspect the United States constitute only one nation. Increase of population, which is filling the States out to their very borders, together with a new and extended network of railroads and other avenues, and an internal commerce which daily becomes more intimate, is rapidly bringing the States into a higher and more perfect social unity or consolidation. Thus, these antagonistic systems are continually coming into closer contact, and collision results.

Shall I tell you what this collision means? They who think that it is accidental, unnecessary, the work of interested or fanatical agitators, and therefore ephemeral, mistake the case altogether. It is an irrepressible conflict between opposing and enduring forces, and it means that the United States must and will, sooner or later, become either entirely a slave-holding nation, or entirely a free-labor nation. Either the cotton and rice fields of South Carolina and the sugar plantations of Louisiana will ultimately be tilled by free labor, and Charleston and New Orleans become marts for legitimate merchandise alone, or else the rye-fields and wheat-fields of Massachusetts and New York must again be surrendered by their farmers to slave culture and to the production of slaves, and Boston and New York become once more markets for trade in the bodies and souls of men. It is the failure to apprehend this great truth that induces so many unsuccessful attempts at final compromise between the slave and free States, and it is the existence of this great fact that renders all such pretended compromises, when made, vain and ephemeral. Startling as this saying may appear to you, fellow-citizens, it is by no means an original or even a modern one. Our forefathers knew it to be true, and unanimously acted upon it when they framed the Constitution of the United States. They regarded the existence of the servile system in so many of the States with sorrow and shame, which they openly confessed, and they looked upon the collision between them, which was then just revealing itself, and which we are now accustomed to deplore, with favor and hope. They knew that either the one or the other system must exclusively prevail.

Unlike too many of those who in modern time invoke their authority, they had a choice between the two. They preferred the system of free labor, and they determined to organize the Government, and so to direct its activity, that that system should surely and certainly prevail. For this purpose, and no other, they based the whole structure of Government broadly on the principle that all men are created equal, and therefore free — little dreaming that, within the short period of one hundred years, their descendants would bear to be told by any orator, however popular, that the utterance of that principle was merely a rhetorical rhapsody ; or by any judge, however venerated, that it was attended by mental reservations, which rendered it hypocritical and false. By the Ordinance of 1787, they dedicated all of the national domain not yet polluted by Slavery to free labor immediately, thenceforth and forever ; while by the new Constitution and laws they invited foreign free labor from all lands under the sun, and interdicted the importation of African slave labor, at all times, in all places, and under all circumstances whatsoever. It is true that they necessarily and wisely modified this policy of Freedom, by leaving it to the several States, affected as they were by differing circumstances, to abolish Slavery in their own way and at their own pleasure, instead of confiding that duty to Congress, and that they secured to the Slave States, while yet retaining the system of Slavery, a three-fifths representation of slaves in the Federal Government, until they should find themselves able to relinquish it with safety. But the very nature of these modifications fortifies my position that the fathers knew that the two systems could not endure within the Union, and expected that within a short period Slavery would disappear forever. Moreover, in order that these modifications might not altogether defeat their grand design of a Republic maintaining universal equality, they provided that two-thirds of the States might amend the Constitution.

It remains to say on this point only one word, to guard against misapprehension. If these States are to again become universally slaveholding, I do not pretend to say with what violations of the Constitution that end shall be accomplished. On the other hand, while I do confidently believe and hope that my country will yet become a land of universal Freedom, I do not expect that it will be made so otherwise than through the action of the several States coöperating with the Federal Government, and all acting in strict conformity with their respective Constitutions.

The strife and contentions concerning Slavery, which gently-disposed persons so habitually deprecate, are nothing more than the ripening of the conflict which the fathers themselves not only thus regarded with favor, but which they may be said to have instituted.

It is not to be denied, however, that thus far the course of that contest has not been according to their humane anticipations and wishes. . . .

. . . At last, the Republican party has appeared. It avows now, as the Republican party of 1800 did, in one word, its faith and its works, " Equal and exact justice to all men." Even when it first entered the field, only half organized, it struck a blow which only just failed to secure complete and triumphant victory. In this, its second campaign, it has already won advantages which render that triumph now both easy and certain.

The secret of its assured success lies in that very characteristic which, in the mouth of scoffers, constitutes its great and lasting imbecility and reproach. It lies in the fact that it is a party of one idea ; but that idea is a noble one — an idea that fills and expands all generous souls; the idea of equality — the equality of all men before human tribunals and human laws, as they all are equal before the Divine tribunal and Divine laws.

I know, and you know, that a revolution has begun. I know, and all the world knows, that revolutions never go backward. Twenty Senators and a hundred Representatives proclaim boldly in Congress to-day sentiments and opinions and principles of Freedom which hardly so many men, even in this free State, dared to utter in their own homes twenty years ago. While the Government of the United States, under the conduct of the Democratic party, has been all that time surrendering one plain and castle after another to Slavery, the people of the United States have been no less steadily and perseveringly gathering together the forces with which to recover back again all the fields and all the castles which have been lost, and to confound and overthrow, by one decisive blow, the betrayers of the Constitution and Freedom forever.

William H. Seward, *The Irrepressible Conflict : a Speech delivered at Rochester*, October 25, 1858 (no title-page, New York, 1858), 1–7 *passim*.

46. "Niggers to the Niggerless" (1859)

BY SENATOR BENJAMIN FRANKLIN WADE

Wade was a typical self-made man, a true representative of the vigorous farmers of Connecticut stock in northern Ohio. His fearlessness in opposing slavery made him prominent in the Senate, where his rugged style of oratory and his disinclination to mince his words often led to an exchange of pertinent remarks with prominent defenders of slavery. This speech is in reply to an equally sharp harangue by Toombs, the question at issue being one of precedence between the homestead bill and a bill to appropriate money with which to purchase Cuba. The burden of Toombs's remarks had been a sneer at the "land to the landless" bill. — For Wade, see A. G. Riddle, *Life of Benjamin F. Wade.* — Bibliography as in No. 44 above.

. . . I AM very glad that this question has at length come up : I am glad, too, that it has antagonized with this nigger question. We are "shivering in the wind," are we, sir, over your Cuba question? You may have occasion to shiver on that question before you are through with it.   Now, sir, I have been trying here for nearly a month to get a straight forward vote upon this great measure of land to the landless.   I glory in that measure.   It is the greatest that has ever come before the American Senate, and it has now come so that there is no dodging it. The question will be, shall we give niggers to the niggerless, or land to the landless ? . . .

. . . I will meet that measure.   I do not tremble before them or their owners, or anybody else ; and it does not become gentlemen of the Senate to tremble over a measure.   Sir, it is not very senatorial language. God knows, I never tremble before anybody.   I do not expect to tremble before anybody.   I do not expect to use language that ought to be offensive to anybody here, and I will not submit to it from anybody.

I moved some days ago to take up this subject.   It was said then that there was an appropriation bill that stood in the way of this great question being settled.   The Senator from Virginia had his appropriation bills.   It was important, then, that they should be settled at once ; there was danger that they would be lost, and the Government would stop in consequence, and an appeal was made to gentlemen to give this bill the go-by for the time being, at all events, and the appeal was successful. Gentlemen said the appropriation bills must be passed ; and, although they were anxious for the passage of this bill, nevertheless it must be postponed for the appropriation bills.   The appropriation bills lie very easy now behind this nigger operation.   When you come to niggers for the niggerless, all other questions sink into perfect insignificance.   But.

sir, we will antagonize these measures. I appeal to the country upon them. I ask the people do you choose that we should go through the earth hunting for niggers, for really that is the whole purpose of the Democratic party? They can no more run their party without niggers than you could run a steam engine without fuel. That is all there is of Democracy; and when you cannot raise niggers enough for the market, then you must go abroad fishing for niggers through the whole world. Are you going to buy Cuba for land for the landless? What is there? You will find three quarters of a million of niggers, but you will not find any land; not one foot, not an inch. I am exceedingly glad that the question has come up. Let us now see who are the friends of this land measure; let us vote it through; and then, without fear or trembling, take up the nigger bill.

I say there is no excuse for gentlemen who are really in favor of this measure. Tell, me, sir, that you skulked behind this Cuba bill? It would be a very poor story to tell those landless men of whom the gentleman speaks. These lacklanders will say to you: " When we lacked land, and you had it in your power to give it to us, you went off fishing for niggers." Will that satisfy them? It may, and it may not. I fear that there will be trembling in some quarters over this question. I hope the vote will be taken, and I warn every man who is a friend of this bill that now is the time; now or never. Give this homestead bill the go-by now, and it dies, and every man knows it. Therefore it is idle to tell me that any man is a friend of the homestead bill who will not give it his support now.

Mr. President, I do not like these taunts and threats about fearing one question or another. I do not very much fear anybody or anything. It would be a very uncomfortable state of mind, I should think. But, sir, I am in favor of this measure. The merits of it, I suppose, are open to discussion. I think it would be easy to show that there has not been, at any time, a measure so fraught with benefit to the people all over the country, as this great measure—the homestead bill. If gentlemen see fit, they can pass it in ten minutes; and then we can go back to the nigger bill, and take that up, and make the best headway we can with that. You need not be ten minutes in passing the bill, if you are true to yourselves, true to your constituents, and faithful to those who have asked at the hands of every honest man that this measure should pass. I say, again, there is no reason to skulk it now. It is fairly up. It is in contrast with the other measure; and no man can fail to see that he who votes and prefers one to the other, has done it because his soul was steeped in the nigger bill.

Congressional Globe, 35 Cong., 2 sess. (John C. Rives, Washington, 1859), 1354 *passim*, February 25, 1859.

---

47. Capture of the Engine-House (1859)

BY COLONEL ROBERT EDWARD LEE

Robert E. Lee, son of "Light-Horse Harry" Lee of Revolutionary fame, and one of the most prominent of the younger officers in the army, had served with distinction during the Mexican War. Later, when the Civil War threatened, he refused the suggestion of high rank in the Union army, and followed his state, Virginia, in her secession; later he accepted a command in the Confederate army, and showed himself the greatest soldier on his side. — For Lee, see W. P. Trent, *Robert E. Lee*, 132–135. — Bibliography of Harper's Ferry Raid as in No. 41 above.

HEADQUARTERS HARPER'S FERRY,
October 19, 1859.

. . . I HAVE the honor to report, for the information of the Secretary of War, that on arriving here on the night of the 17th instant, in obedience to Special Orders No. 194 of that date from your office, I learn that a party of insurgents, about 11 p. m. on the 16th, had seized the watchmen stationed at the armory, arsenal, rifle factory, and bridge across the Potomac, and taken possession of those points. They then dispatched six men, under one of their party, called Captain Aaron C. Stevens, to arrest the principal citizens in the neighborhood and incite the negroes to join in the insurrection. The party took Colonel L. W. Washington from his bed about 1½ a. m. on the 17th, and brought him, with four of his servants, to this place. Mr. J. H. Allstadt and six of his servants were in the same manner seized about 3 a. m., and arms placed in the hands of the negroes. Upon their return here, John E. Cook, one of the party sent to Mr. Washington's, was dispatched to Maryland, with Mr. Washington's wagon, two of his servants, and three of Mr. Allstadt's, for arms and ammunition, &c. As day advanced, and the citizens of Harper's Ferry commenced their usual avocations, they were separately captured, to the number of forty, as well as I could learn, and confined in one room of the fire-engine house of the armory, which seems early to have been selected as a point of defense. About 11 a. m. the volunteer companies from Virginia began to arrive, and the Jefferson

Guards and volunteers from Charlestown, under Captain J. W. Rowen, I understood, were first on the ground. The Hamtramck Guards, Captain V. M. Butler; the Shepherdstown troop, Captain Jacob Rienahart; and Captain Alburtis's company from Martinsburg arrived in the afternoon. These companies, under the direction of Colonels R. W. Baylor and John T. Gibson, forced the insurgents to abandon their positions at the bridge and in the village, and to withdraw within the armory inclosure, where they fortified themselves in the fire-engine house, and carried ten of their prisoners for the purpose of insuring their safety and facilitating their escape, whom they termed hostages. . . . After sunset more troops arrived. Captain B. B. Washington's company from Winchester, and three companies from Fredericktown, Maryland, under Colonel Shriver. Later in the evening the companies from Baltimore, under General Charles C. Edgerton, second light brigade, and a detachment of marines, commanded by Lieutenant J. Green accompanied by Major Russell, of that corps, reached Sandy Hook, about one and a half mile east of Harper's Ferry. At this point I came up with these last-named troops, and leaving General Edgerton and his command on the Maryland side of the river for the night, caused the marines to proceed to Harper's Ferry, and placed them within the armory grounds to prevent the possibility of the escape of the insurgents. Having taken measures to halt, in Baltimore, the artillery companies ordered from Fort Monroe, I made preparations to attack the insurgents at daylight. But for the fear of sacrificing the lives of some of the gentlemen held by them as prisoners in a midnight assault, I should have ordered the attack at once.

Their safety was the subject of painful consideration, and to prevent, if possible, jeopardizing their lives, I determined to summon the insurgents to surrender. As soon after daylight as the arrangements were made Lieutenant J. E. B. Stewart, 1st cavalry, who had accompanied me from Washington as staff officer, was dispatched, under a flag, with a written summons. . . . Knowing the character of the leader of the insurgents, I did not expect it would be accepted. I had therefore directed that the volunteer troops, under their respective commanders, should be paraded on the lines assigned them outside the armory, and had prepared a storming party of twelve marines, under their commander, Lieutenant Green, and had placed them close to the engine-house, and secure from its fire. Three marines were furnished with sledge-hammers to break in the doors, and the men were instructed how to distinguish our citizens from the insurgents; to attack with the bayo-

L

net, and not to injure the blacks detained in custody unless they resisted. Lieutenant Stewart was also directed not to receive from the insurgents any counter propositions. If they accepted the terms offered, they must immediately deliver up their arms and release their prisoners. If they did not, he must, on leaving the engine-house, give me the signal. My object was, with a view of saving our citizens, to have as short an inter-val as possible between the summons and attack. The summons, as I had anticipated, was rejected. At the concerted signal the storming party moved quickly to the door and commenced the attack. The fire-engines within the house had been placed by the besieged close to the doors. The doors were fastened by ropes, the spring of which prevented their being broken by the blows of the hammers. The men were there-fore ordered to drop the hammers, and, with a portion of the reserve, to use as a battering-ram a heavy ladder, with which they dashed in a part of the door and gave admittance to the storming party. The fire of the insurgents up to this time had been harmless. At the threshold one marine fell mortally wounded. The rest, led by Lieutenant Green and Major Russell, quickly ended the contest. The insurgents that resisted were bayoneted. Their leader, John Brown, was cut down by the sword of Lieutenant Green, and our citizens were protected by both officers and men. The whole was over in a few minutes. . . .

From the information derived from the papers found upon the persons and among the baggage of the insurgents, and the statement of those now in custody, it appears that the party consisted of nineteen men — four-teen white and five black. That they were headed by John Brown, of some notoriety in Kansas, who in June last located himself in Maryland, at the Kennedy farm, where he has been engaged in preparing to capture the United States works at Harper's Ferry. He avows that his object was the liberation of the slaves of Virginia, and of the whole South ; and acknowledges that he has been disappointed in his expectations of aid from the black as well as white population, both in the Southern and Northern States. The blacks whom he forced from their homes in this neighborhood, as far as I could learn, gave him no voluntary assistance. . . . The result proves that the plan was the attempt of a fanatic or mad-man, which could only end in failure ; and its temporary success was owing to the panic and confusion he succeeded in creating by magnify-ing his numbers. . . .

Senate Reports, 36 Cong., 1 sess. (Washington, 1860), II, No. 278, pp. 40–4? *passim*.

48. Why John Brown Broke the Laws (1859)

BY JOHN BROWN

John Brown, "of Ossawatomie," was an abolitionist of that stern puritanical spirit and narrow-mindedness that feeds upon the Old Testament. In himself he saw a chosen instrument for visiting the iniquity of slavery upon its advocates. In Kansas he began retaliation upon pro-slavery settlers, and his desire for action in the anti-slavery cause culminated in his ill-planned raid on Harper's Ferry; but in defeat he showed himself such a man that he won the admiration of his enemies. This extract is from an interview, after his capture, with Senator Mason, Congressman Vallandigham, and others. — For Brown, see J. E. Chamberlin, *John Brown*, 135-138. — Bibliography as in No. 41 above.

MR. MASON — If you would tell us who sent you here — who provided the means — that would be information of some value.

Mr. BROWN — I will answer freely and faithfully about what concerns myself — I will answer anything I can with honor — but not about others.

Mr. VALLANDIGHAM (member of Congress from Ohio, who had just entered) — Mr. Brown, who sent you here?

Mr. BROWN — No man sent me here ; it was my own prompting and that of my Maker, or that of the devil, which ever you please to ascribe it to. I acknowledge no man [master] in human form.

Mr. VALLANDIGHAM — Did you get up the expedition yourself?

Mr. BROWN — I did. . . .

Mr. MASON — How many are engaged with you in this movement? I ask those questions for our own safety.

Mr. BROWN — Any questions that I can honorably answer I will, not otherwise. So far as I am myself concerned I have told everything truthfully. I value my word, sir.

Mr. MASON — What was your object in coming ?

Mr. BROWN — We came to free the slaves, and only that.

A YOUNG MAN (in the uniform of a volunteer company) —How many men in all had you?

Mr. BROWN — I came to Virginia with eighteen men only, besides myself.

VOLUNTEER — What in the world did you suppose you could do here in Virginia with that amount of men?

Mr. BROWN — Young man, I don't wish to discuss that question here.

VOLUNTEER — You could not do anything.

Mr. BROWN — Well, perhaps your ideas and mine on military subjects would differ materially.

Mr. MASON — How do you justify your acts?

Mr. BROWN — I think, my friend, you are guilty of a great wrong against God and humanity — I say it without wishing to be offensive — and it would be perfectly right for any one to interfere with you so far as to free those you wilfully and wickedly hold in bondage. I do not say this insultingly.

Mr. MASON — I understand that.

Mr. BROWN — I think I did right, and that others will do right who interfere with you at any time and all times. I hold that the golden rule, " Do unto others as you would that others should do unto you," applies to all who would help others to gain their liberty.

Lieut. STEWART — But you don't believe in the Bible.

Mr. BROWN — Certainly I do. . . .

Mr. VALLANDIGHAM — When in Cleveland did you attend the Fugitive Slave Law Convention there?

Mr. BROWN — No. I was there about the time of the sitting of the court to try the Oberlin rescuers. . . .

Mr. VALLANDIGHAM — Did you see anything of Joshau [Joshua] R. Giddings there?

Mr. BROWN — I did meet him. . .

Mr. VALLANDIGHAM — Will you answer this : Did you talk with Giddings about your expedition here?

Mr. BROWN — No, I won't answer that, because a denial of it I would not make, and to make any affirmation of it I should be a great dunce.

Mr. VALLANDIGHAM — Have you had any correspondenc[e] with parties at the North on the subject of this movement?

Mr. BROWN — I have had correspondence.

A BYSTANDER — Do you consider this a religious movement?

Mr. BROWN — It is, in my opinion, the greatest service a man can render to God.

BYSTANDER — Do you consider yourself an instrument in the hands of Providence?

Mr. BROWN — I do.

BYSTANDER — Upon what principle do you justify your acts?

Mr. BROWN — Upon the golden rule. I pity the poor in bondage that have none to help them ; that is why I am here ; not to gratify any personal animosity, revenge or vindictive spirit. It is my sympathy with the oppressed and the wronged, that are as good as you and as precious in the sight of God.

BYSTANDER — Certainly.   But why take the slaves against their will?

Mr. BROWN — I never did. . . .

. . . I want you to understand gentlemen — (and to the reporter of the Herald) you may report that — I want you to understand that I respect the rights of the poorest and weakest of colored people, oppressed by the slave system, just as much as I do those of the most wealthy and powerful.   That is the idea that has moved me, and that alone.   We expected no reward except the satisfaction of endeavoring to do for those in distress and greatly oppressed as we would be done by.   The cry of distress of the oppressed is my reason, and the only thing that prompted me to come here.

A BYSTANDER — Why did you do it secretly?

Mr. BROWN — Because I thought tht [that] necessary to success ; no other reason.

BYSTANDER — And you think that honorable?   Have you read Gerritt Smith's last letter?

Mr. BROWN — What letter do you mean ?

BYSTANDER — The NEW YORK HERALD of yesterday in speaking of this affair mentions a letter in this way : —

Apropos of this exciting news, we recollect a very significant passage in one of Gerrit Smith's letters, published a month or two ago, in which he speaks of the folly of attempting to strike the shackles off the slaves by the force of moral suasion or legal agitation, and predicts that the next movement made in the direction of negro emancipation would be an insurrection in the South.

Mr. BROWN — I have not seen the NEW YORK HERALD for some days past ; but I presume, from your remark about the gist of the letter, that I should concur with it.   I agree with Mr. Smith that moral suasion is hopeless.   I don't think the people of the slave States will ever consider the subject of slavery in its true light till some other argument is resorted to than moral suasion.

Mr. VALLANDIGHAM — Did you expect a general rising of the slaves in case of your success?

Mr. BROWN — No, sir ; nor did I wish it ; I expected to gather them up from time to time and set them free.

Mr. VALLANDIGHAM — Did you expect to hold possession here till then?

Mr. BROWN — Well, probably I had quite a different idea.   I do not know that I ought to reveal my plans.   I am here a prisoner and wounded, because I foolishly allowed myself to be so. You overrate your strength in supposing I could have been taken if I had not allowed it. I was too tardy after commencing the open attack — in delaying my movements through Monday night, and up to the time I was attacked by the government troops. It was all occasioned by my desire to spare the feelings of my prisoners and their families and the community at large. I had no knowledge of the shooting of the negro (Heywood). . . .

Q. Where did you get arms to obtain possession of the armory? A. I bought them.

Q. In what State? A. That I would not state. . . .

REPORTER OF THE HERALD — I do not wish to annoy you ; but if you have anything further you would like to say I will report it.

Mr. BROWN — I have nothing to say, only that I claim to be here in carrying out a measure I believe perfectly justifiable, and not to act the part of an incendiary or ruffian, but to aid those suffering great wrong. *I wish to say, furthermore, that you had better — all you people at the South — prepare yourselves for a settlement of that question that must come up for settlement sooner than you are prepared for it.* The sooner you are prepared the better. You may dispose of me very easily. I am nearly disposed of now ; but this question is still to be settled — this negro question I mean ; the end of that is not yet. . . .

Q. Brown, suppose you had every nigger in the United States, what would you do with them? A. Set them free.

Q. Your intention was to carry them off and free them? A. Not at all.

A BYSTANDER — To set them free would sacrifice the life of every man in this community.

Mr. BROWN — I do not think so.

BYSTANDER — I know it. I think you are fanatical.

Mr. BROWN — And I think you are fanatical. "Whom the gods would destroy they first made mad," and you are mad.

Q. Was it your only object to free the negroes? A. Absolutely our only object.

Q. But you demanded and took Col. Washington's silver and watch? A. Yes ; *we intended freely to appropriate the property of slaveholders to carry out our object.* It was for that, and only that, and with no design to enrich ourselves with any plunder whatever.

New York Herald, October 21, 1859.

PART IV

CAUSES OF CIVIL WAR

CHAPTER VIII—ELECTION OF 1860

49. Split in the Democratic Party (1860)

Halstead, ever since that time a journalist of national reputation, made the circuit of the political conventions in 1860, acting as correspondent of the *Cincinnati Commercial*. Later these letters were collected. — Bibliography: J. F. Rhodes, *History of the United States*, II, 440–454, notes; Channing and Hart, *Guide*, § 203.

[April 27, 1860.] . . . MR. AVERY of North Carolina presented the following from a majority of the committee on Resolutions . . .

Resolved, That the platform adopted at Cincinnati be affirmed, with the following resolutions:

1. *Resolved*, That the Democracy of the United States hold these cardinal principles on the subject of slavery in the Territories: First, That Congress has no power to abolish slavery in the Territories. Second, That the Territorial Legislature has no power to abolish slavery in any Territory, nor to prohibit the introduction of slaves therein, nor any power to exclude slavery therefrom, nor any right to destroy or impair the right of property in slaves by any legislation whatever. . . .

3. *Resolved*, That it is the duty of the Federal Government to protect, when necessary, the rights of persons and property on the high-seas, in the Territories, or wherever else its constitutional authority extends. . . .

. . . The resolutions of the minority . . . are as follows:

1. *Resolved*, That we, the Democracy of the Union, in Convention assembled, hereby declare our affirmance of the resolutions unanimously adopted and declared as a platform of principles by the Democratic Convention at Cincinnati in the year 1856, believing that Democratic principles are unchangeable in their nature when applied to the same subject-matters; and we recommend, as the only further resolutions, the following:

2. *Resolved*, That all questions in regard to the rights of property in States or Territories arising under the Constitution of the United States are judicial in their character, and the Democratic party is pledged to abide by and faithfully carry out such determination of these questions as has been or may be made by the Supreme Court of the United States. . . .

Mr. Yancey of Alabama rose . . . and received a perfect ovation. The hall for several minutes rang with applause. It appeared at once that the outside pressure was with the fire-eaters.

. . . He filled up his time (an hour and a half) with great effect. There was no question after he had been upon the platform a few minutes, that he was a man of remarkable gifts of intellect and captivating powers as a speaker. He reviewed the differences on the slavery question of the Democracy. He charged that the defeats of the Democracy in the North were to be traced to the pandering by the party in the free States to anti-slavery sentiments ; they had not come up to the high ground which must be taken on the subject, in order to defend the South — namely, that slavery was right. . . . He traced the history of Northern aggression and Southern concession as he understood it. He spoke of the deep distrust the South had begun to entertain of the Northern Democracy, and urged the propriety of the demand of the South, that the Democratic party should now take clear and high ground upon a constitutional basis. He pronounced false all charges that the State of Alabama, himself or his colleagues, were in favor of a dissolution of the Union *per se*. But he told the Democracy of the North that they must, in taking high constitutional ground, go before the people of the North and tell them of the inevitable dissolution of the Union if constitutional principles did not prevail at the ballot-boxes. He spoke of the Democratic indorsement which the majority platform had received, saying that not one State which had voted against it, in committee, could be certainly relied upon to cast Democratic electoral votes, while every State that had supported that platform, with but one exception (Maryland) could, upon that platform, be counted absolutely certain in the electoral college for the Democratic candidate. He spoke directly to Southern men and appealed to them to present a united front in favor of a platform that recognized their rights and guaranteed their honor. He said defeat upon principle was better than a mere victory gained by presenting ambiguous issues and cheating the people. . . . The Southerners in the hall were thoroughly warmed up by his speech, and applauded with rapturous enthusiasm. Several of his points were received with outbursts of applause that rung around the hall as if his hearers had been made to shout and stamp by the simultaneous action of electricity. One of his most effective points was in relation to the Dred Scott decision and the plea made by Douglas and others that almost all of it was mere *obiter dicta*. This plea was disrespectful to the venerable man, who, clothed in the supreme ermine, had made an exposition of constitutional law, which had rolled in silvery cadence from the dark forests of the North to the glittering waters of the Gulf.

He distinctly admitted that the South did ask of the Northern Democracy an advanced step in vindication of Southern rights ; and Mr. Yancey's hour and a half closed while he was in the midst of a series of lofty periods, and Mr. Pugh of Ohio sprung to his feet. . . .

Mr. Pugh took the platform in a condition of considerable warmth. There was an effort made to adjourn, but the crowd was eager for the fray, and insisted that Pugh should go on. He did so, thanking God that a bold and honest man from the South had at last spoken, and told the whole truth of the demands of the South. It was now before the Convention and the country, that the South did demand an advanced step from the Democratic party. . . . He then traced the downfall of the Northern Democracy, and the causes of that fall, charging the South with it. And now the Northern Democracy were taunted by the South with weakness. And here, it seemed, the Northern Democracy, because they were in the minority, were thrust back and told in effect they must put their hands on their mouths, and their mouths in the dust. "Gentlemen of the South," said Mr. Pugh, "you mistake us — you mistake us — we will not do it." . . .

He spoke of the sacrifice of the Northern Democrats of their political lives, battling for the doctrine of the South, now scornfully repudiated ; and pointed out among the delegates, men who had been Senators and Representatives, and who had fallen in the fight. In conclusion, he stated [that] the Democracy, who were prepared to stand by the old faith, would be sorry to part with their Southern friends, but if the gentlemen from the South could only stay on the terms proposed, they must go. The Democracy of the North-west would make itself heard and felt. The Northern Democrats were not children under the pupilage of the South, and to be told to stand here and there, and moved at the beck and bidding of the South. . . .

[April 30.] . . . Yesterday there was a report current that the South, discovering the total impossibility of the nomination of Douglas while the Convention remained consolidated, his full strength having been shown, and amounting to a bare majority, would find some excuse for staying in the Convention even after the adoption of the minority report, and would slaughter Douglas under the two-thirds rule. . . . This morning, however, it became apparent that the Douglas majority was firm, and the South desperate. It was not long before every observer saw that the long-looked for explosion was at hand. The South would not stay in the Convention, even to defeat Douglas, if the double-shuffle platform were adopted. . . .

The minority resolutions were . . . carried as a substitute for the majority resolutions, by a vote of 165 to 138 — this 138 is the solid anti-Douglas strength. Now the question came on the *adoption* of the substituted report — the definite, irrevocable vote of the Convention upon the Douglas Platform, was divided into its substantive propositions. The resolution reaffirming the Cincinnati Platform, believing Democratic principles to be unchangeable in their nature, was first voted upon, and it was carried by 237½ to 65. . . . Now the question arose upon the adoption of the Squatter Sovereignty part of the platform — that part wherein it is stated that, " inasmuch as differences of opinion exist in the Democratic party," it will abide by the Supreme Court. . . .

Mr. William A. Richardson of Illinois wished to speak. . . . There were cries of " Hear Richardson." A thrill of excitement passed around the hall, and every body leaned forward or stood up to see and hear the right-hand man of the Little Giant on the crisis. . . . But . . . Mr. Hooper of Mississippi objected peremptorily, and . . . would not let him be heard. . . .

. . . He had desired to say, that Illinois and the North-west in general, had not been anxious to have any thing but the Cincinnati Platform, and would be content with that, if the others would. This was to have been his peace-offering — his olive-branch. . . . It took some minutes for the new tactics of Richardson to get circulation, and in the mean time, as one delegation after another understood the point, the votes of States were counted, and finally, with a general rush, the only resolution having the slightest significance in the minority report, was stricken out. . . . By a flank movement, they had placed themselves upon the Cincinnati Platform, pure and simple. . . .

And now commenced the regular stampede. Alabama led the Southern column. . . . Mississippi went next, with less formality but more vim. . . . Mr. Glenn of Mississippi mounted a chair, and facing the Ohio delegation, which sat directly behind Mississippi, made one of the most impassioned and thrilling twenty-minute speeches to which I have ever listened. It was evident that every word was from his deepest convictions. He was pale as ashes, and his eyes rolled and glared, as he told the gentlemen from Ohio how far they were from doing their duty now, and how kindly he felt toward them, and how they would have to take position yet upon the high ground of the South, or it would be all in vain that they would attempt to arrest the march of Black Republicanism. For the present, they must go their ways, and the South must go her ways. He declared, too, with piercing emphasis, that in less than sixty days there would be an United South ; and at this declaration there was the most enthusiastic shouting yet heard in the Convention. . . .

. . . as the spokesman of Mississippi concluded what he had to say, Alexander Mouton of Louisiana, and Col. Simmons of South Carolina . . . were claiming the floor, each to give warning that his State was going. . . .

. . . Florida was the next to go, and then Arkansas. . . .

M[urat] Halstead, *Caucuses of 1860: a History of the National Political Conventions of the Current Presidential Campaign* (Columbus, 1860), 43–74, *passim.*

---

50. Nomination of Lincoln (1860)

BY MURAT HALSTEAD

The convention here described was the first of those conducted on the plan of nomination by enthusiasm. — For Halstead, see No. 49 above. — Bibliography : J. F. Rhodes, *History of the United States*, II, 456–473, notes ; Channing and Hart, *Guide*, § 203.

[May 18, 1860.] AFTER adjournment on Thursday (the second day), there were few men in Chicago who believed it possible to prevent the nomination of Seward. . . .

But there was much done after midnight and before the Convention assembled on Friday morning. There were hundreds of Pennsylvanians, Indianians and Illinoisans, who never closed their eyes that night. . . .

The Seward men generally abounded in confidence Friday morning. The air was full of rumors of the caucusing the night before, but the opposition of the doubtful States to Seward was an old story ; and after the distress of Pennsylvania, Indiana & Co., on the subject of Seward's availability, had been so freely and ineffectually expressed from the start, it was not imagined their protests would suddenly become effective. The Sewardites marched as usual from their head-quarters at the Richmond House after their magnificent band, which was brilliantly uniformed — epaulets shining on their shoulders, and white and scarlet feathers waving from their caps — marched under the orders of recognized leaders, in a style that would have done credit to many volunteer military companies. They were about a thousand strong, and protracting their march a little too far, were not all able to get into the wigwam. This was their first misfortune. They were not where they could scream with the best effect in responding to the mention of the name of William H. Seward.

When the Convention was called to order, breathless attention was given the proceedings. There was not a space a foot square in the wigwam unoccupied. There were tens of thousands still outside, and torrents of men had rushed in at the three broad doors until not another one could squeeze in. . . .

The applause, when Mr. Evarts named Seward, was enthusiastic. When Mr. Judd named Lincoln, the response was prodigious, rising and raging far beyond the Seward shriek. Presently, upon Caleb B. Smith seconding the nomination of Lincoln, the response was absolutely terrific. It now became the Seward men to make another effort, and when Blair of Michigan seconded his nomination,

> "At once there rose so wild a yell,
> Within that dark and narrow dell;
> As all the fiends from heaven that fell
> Had pealed the banner cry of hell."

The effect was startling. Hundreds of persons stopped their ears in pain. The shouting was absolutely frantic, shrill and wild. No Camanches, no panthers ever struck a higher note, or gave screams with more infernal intensity. Looking from the stage over the vast amphitheatre, nothing was to be seen below but thousands of hats — a black, mighty swarm of hats — flying with the velocity of hornets over a mass of human heads, most of the mouths of which were open. Above, all around the galleries, hats and handkerchiefs were flying in the tempest together. The wonder of the thing was, that the Seward outside pressure should, so far from New York, be so powerful.

Now the Lincoln men had to try it again, and as Mr. Delano of Ohio, on behalf " of a portion of the delegation of that State," seconded

the nomination of Lincoln, the uproar was beyond description. . . .
I thought the Seward yell could not be surpassed ; but the Lincoln boys
were clearly ahead, and feeling their victory, as there was a lull in the
storm, took deep breaths all round, and gave a concentrated shriek that
was positively awful, and accompanied it with stamping that made every
plank and pillar in the building quiver. . . .

. . . The division of the first vote caused a fall in Seward stock. It
was seen that Lincoln, Cameron and Bates had the strength to defeat
Seward, and it was known that the greater part of the Chase vote would
go for Lincoln. . . .

The Convention proceeded to a second ballot. . . .   The first gain
for Lincoln was in New Hampshire.   The Chase and the Fremont vote
from that State were given him.   His next gain was the whole vote of
Vermont.   This was a blighting blow upon the Seward interest.   The
New Yorkers started as if an Orsini bomb had exploded.   And presently
the Cameron vote of Pennsylvania was thrown for Lincoln, increasing
his strength forty-four votes.   The fate of the day was now determined.
New York saw " checkmate " next move, and sullenly proceeded with
the game, assuming unconsciousness of her inevitable doom.   On this
ballot Lincoln gained seventy-nine votes ! Seward had $184\frac{1}{2}$ votes ;
Lincoln, 181. . . .

While this [the third] ballot was taken amid excitement that tested
the nerves, the fatal defection from Seward in New England still further
appeared — four votes going over from Seward to Lincoln in Massachusetts.   The latter received four additional votes from Pennsylvania and
fifteen additional votes from Ohio. . . .   The number of votes necessary
to a choice were two hundred and thirty-three, and I saw under my
pencil, as the Lincoln column was completed, the figures $231\frac{1}{2}$ — one
vote and a half to give him the nomination.   In a moment the fact was
whispered about.   A hundred pencils had told the same story.   The
news went over the house wonderfully, and there was a pause.   There
are always men anxious to distinguish themselves on such occasions.
There is nothing that politicians like better than a crisis.   I looked up
to see who would be the man to give the decisive vote. . . .   In about
ten ticks of a watch, Cartter of Ohio was up.   I had imagined Ohio
would be slippery enough for the crisis.   And sure enough ! Every
eye was on Cartter, and every body who understood the matter at all,
knew what he was about to do. . . .   He said, " I rise (eh), Mr. Chairman (eh), to announce the change of four votes of Ohio from Mr.

Chase to Mr. Lincoln." The deed was done. There was a moment's silence. The nerves of the thousands, which through the hours of suspense had been subjected to terrible tension, relaxed, and as deep breaths of relief were taken, there was a noise in the wigwam like the rush of a great wind, in the van of a storm — and in another breath, the storm was there. There were thousands cheering with the energy of insanity.

A man who had been on the roof, and was engaged in communicating the results of the ballotings to the mighty mass of outsiders, now demanded by gestures at the sky-light over the stage, to know what had happened. One of the secretaries, with a tally sheet in his hands, shouted — " Fire the salute ! Abe Lincoln is nominated ! " As the cheering inside the wigwam subsided, we could hear that outside, where the news of the nomination had just been announced. And the roar, like the breaking up of the fountains of the great deep, that was heard, gave a new impulse to the enthusiasm inside. Then the thunder of the salute rose above the din, and the shouting was repeated with such tremendous fury that some discharges of the cannon were absolutely not heard by those on the stage. Puffs of smoke, drifting by the open doors, and the smell of gunpowder, told what was going on.

The moment that half a dozen men who were on their chairs making motions at the President could be heard, they changed the votes of their States to Mr. Lincoln. . . .

While these votes were being given, the applause continued, and a photograph of Abe Lincoln which had hung in one of the side rooms was brought in, and held up before the surging and screaming masses. The places of the various delegations were indicated by staffs, to which were attached the names of the States, printed in large black letters on pasteboard. As the Lincoln enthusiasm increased, delegates tore these standards of the States from their places and swung them about their heads. A rush was made to get the New York standard and swing it with the rest, but the New Yorkers would not allow it to be moved, and were wrathful at the suggestion.

When the vote was declared, Mr. Evarts, the New York spokesman, mounted the Secretaries' table and handsomely and impressively expressed his grief at the failure of the Convention to nominate Seward — and in melancholy tones, moved that the nomination be made unanimous. . . .

. . . The town was full of the news of Lincoln's nomination, and could hardly contain itself. . . . hundreds of men who had been in the wigwam were so prostrated by the excitement they had endured, and their exertions in shrieking for Seward or Lincoln, that they were hardly able to walk to their hotels. There were men who had not tasted liquor, who staggered about like drunkards, unable to manage themselves. The Seward men were terribly stricken down. They were mortified beyond all expression, and walked thoughtfully and silently away from the slaughter-house, more ashamed than embittered. They acquiesced in the nomination, but did not pretend to be pleased with it ; and the tone of their conversations, as to the prospect of electing the candidate, was not hopeful. It was their funeral, and they would not make merry. . . .

I left the city on the night train on the Fort Wayne and Chicago road. The train consisted of eleven cars, every seat full and people standing in the aisles and corners. . . . At every station where there was a village, until after two o'clock, there were tar barrels burning, drums beating, boys carrying rails ; and guns, great and small, banging away. The weary passengers were allowed no rest, but plagued by the thundering jar of cannon, the clamor of drums, the glare of bonfires, and the whooping of the boys, who were delighted with the idea of a candidate for the Presidency, who thirty years ago split rails on the Sangamon River — classic stream now and for evermore — and whose neighbors named him " honest."

M[urat] Halstead, *Caucuses of 1860 : a History of the National Political Conventions of the Current Presidential Campaign* (Columbus, 1860), 141–154 *passim*.

———◆———

51. Threats of Secession (1860)

BY "COMMON SENSE"

The *Charleston Mercury*, edited by R. B. Rhett, had for a long time held advanced views on the question of secession, but the communication here given is one of many indications that public opinion in South Carolina was rapidly approaching the position taken by that paper. This is a good example of the southern journalism of the time. — Bibliography : Channing and Hart, *Guide*, § 205.

THAT the time has come for the South to look to her interests, when considered in connection with the great political strife now existing between the two sections of this country, I think no true Southerner, who loves liberty and hates oppression, will attempt to deny. If there are any who think that the time has not yet arrived "when patience ceases to be a virtue," and when we, as a free people, should not cry out against the insults and impositions of the North, and declare our independence to the world, they must indeed have charitable and forgiving souls. Isn't it enough that the rights of the South, in the sovereign capacity of her several States, have been most persistently denied her for forty years? Have we not, as a section, been insulted and oppressed, not only at home, but in every Foreign Court in Christendom, by abolition fanatics, who should, as citizens of the same Government, regard us as brothers? The leaders and oracles of the most powerful party in the United States have denounced us as tyrants and unprincipled heathens, through the whole civilized world. They have preached it from their pulpits. They have declared it in the halls of Congress and in their newspapers. In their school-houses they have taught their children (who are to rule this Government in the next generation) to look upon the slaveholder as the especial disciple of the devil himself. They have published books and pamphlets in which the institution of slavery is held up to the world as a blot and a stain upon the escutcheon of America's honor as a nation. They have established Abolition Societies among them for the purpose of raising funds — first to send troops to Kansas to cut the throats of all the slaveholders there, and now to send emissaries among us to incite our slaves to rebellion against the authority of their masters, and thereby endanger the lives of our people and the destruction of our property. They have brought forth an open and avowed enemy to the most cherished and important institution of the South, as candidate for election to the Chief Magistracy of this Government — the very basis of whose political principles is an uncompromising hostility to the institution of slavery under all circumstances. They have virtually repealed the Fugitive Slave Law, and declare their determination not to abide by the decision of the Supreme Court, guaranteeing to us the right to claim our property wherever found in the United States. And, in every conceivable way, the whole Northern people, as a mass, have shown a most implacable hostility to us and our most sacred rights ; and this, too, without the slightest provocation on the part of the South. Never, in a single instance, has the South, in any shape or form, interfered with the North in her municipal regulations ; but, on the contrary, has tamely submitted to paying tribute to the support of her manufactures, and the establishment of her commercial greatness ; yet, like the " serpent warmed in the husbandman's bosom," she turns upon us and stings us to the heart.   If Great Britain, or *any* foreign power, had heaped upon us the long catalogue of insult and abuses that the North has, there is not a man in the whole South who would not have long since shouldered his musket, and, if necessary, spilt his heart's blood to have avenged them.   But because we are members of the same political family it is contended we must not quarrel, but suffer all the impositions at their hands that in their fanatical spleen they may choose to heap on us.   Has a man's own brother, born of the same parents, a right to invade the sacred precincts of his fireside, to wage war upon him and his family, and deprive him of his property?   And if he should do so, the aggrieved brother has not only a right, but it is his duty, sanctioned by every principle of right, to cut off all communication with that unnatural brother, to drive him from the sanctuary of his threshold, and treat him as an enemy and a stranger.   Then why should we any longer submit to the galling yoke of our tyrant brother — the usurping, domineering, abolition North !

The political policy of the South demands that we should not hesitate, but rise up with a single voice and proclaim to the world that we will be subservient to the North no longer, but that we *will* be a free and an independent people.   Here, then, would be an end to all political dissensions among us, because our interests, feelings, institutions, wants and pursuits, would be identical.   Manufactures would be encouraged at home, our commercial interests enhanced, and our national importance established.   Our towns would grow into cities, and our cities soon grow to be respected among the great commercial emporiums of the world.   We should then have a *national right to demand respect* from the North, and the restoration of our property when it is abducted by them, or escapes into their territory.   And we should no longer be compelled to pay tribute to the support of a corrupt predominant power, whose boasted principles are based upon an opposition to our interests.

All admit that an ultimate dissolution of the Union is inevitable, and we believe the crisis is not far off.   Then let it come now ; the better for the South that it should be to-day ; *she* cannot afford to wait.   With the North it is different.   Every day adds to her sectional strength, and every day the balance of power becomes less proportionate between the two sections.   In a few more years (unless this course is speedily adopted by us) there will not be an inch of territorial ground for the Southern emigrant to place his foot on.   Our doom will be sealed ; the decree shall have gone forth : " Thus far shalt thou go and no farther."

M

But the territories are now the common property of the Government, and in a division of the Union, we should be entitled to our legitimate share in the division, over which, thenceforth, the South would have exclusive jurisdiction, to the exclusion of the meddlesome and power-loving North.

COMMON SENSE.

Charleston Mercury, September 18, 1860.

---

52. Result of the Election (1860)

BY REPRESENTATIVE JOHN SHERMAN

As representative, senator, and cabinet officer, Sherman enjoyed an unbroken political career of forty-three years. The letter from which this extract is taken was addressed to his brother, W. T. Sherman, then in Louisiana. It shows the views of a young, but prominent, Republican statesman. — For Sherman, see *John Sherman's Recollections.* — Bibliography: Channing and Hart, *Guide*, § 207. — For the views of an older Republican statesman, see No. 65 below.

MANSFIELD, OHIO, Nov. 26, 1860.

. . . WELL, Lincoln is elected. No doubt, a large portion of the citizens of Louisiana consider this a calamity. If they believe their own newspapers, what is far worse, the lying organs of the Democratic party in the free States, they have just cause to think so. But you were long enough in Ohio and heard enough of the ideas of the Republican leaders to know that the Republican party is not likely to interfere directly or indirectly with slavery in the States or with the laws relating to slavery ; that, so far as the slavery question is concerned, the contest was for the possession of Kansas and perhaps New Mexico, and that the chief virtue of the Republican success was in its condemnation of the narrow sectionalism of Buchanan's administration and the corruptions by which he attempted to sustain his policy. Who doubts but that, if he had been true to his promises in submitting the controversy in Kansas to its own people, and had closed it by admitting Kansas as a free State, that the Democratic party would have retained its power? It was his infernal policy in Kansas (I can hardly think of the mean and bad things he allowed there without swearing) that drove off Douglas, and led to the division of the Democratic party and the consequent election of Lincoln.

As a matter of course, I rejoice in the result, for in my judgment the administration of Lincoln will do much to dissipate the feeling in the South against the North by showing what are the real purposes of the Republican party. In the meantime, it is evident we have to meet in a serious form the movements of South Carolinian Disunionists. These men have for years desired this disunion; they have plotted for it. They drove Buchanan into his Kansas policy; they got up this new dogma about slave protection; they broke up the Charleston Convention merely to advance secession; they are now hurrying forward excited men into acts of treason without giving time for passion to cool or reason to resume its sway. God knows what will be the result. If by a successful revolution they can go out of the Union, they establish a principle that will break up the government into fragments. Some local disaffection or temporary excitement will lead one State after another out of the Union. We will have the Mexican Republic over again, with a fiercer race of men to fight with each other. Secession is revolution. They seem bent upon attempting it. If so, shall the government resist? If so, then comes civil war, a fearful subject for Americans to think of.

. . . I know we will have trouble this winter, but I intend to be true to the moderate conservative course I think I have hitherto undertaken. Whatever may be the consequences, I will insist on preserving the unity of the States, and all the States without exception and without regard to consequences. If any Southern State has really suffered any injury or is deprived of any right, I will help redress the injury and secure the right. They must not, merely because they are beaten in an election, or have failed in establishing slavery where it was prohibited by compromise, attempt to break up the government. If they will hold on a little while, they will find no injury can come to them unless, by their repeated misrepresentation of us, they stir up their slaves to insurrection. I still hope that no State will follow in the wake of South Carolina. If so, the weakness of her position will soon bring her back again or subject her to ridicule and insignificance.

It may be supposed by some that the excitement in the South has produced a corresponding excitement in the North. This is true in financial matters, especially in the cities. In political circles, it only strengthens the Republican party. Even Democrats of all shades say, The election is against us; we will submit and all must submit. . . .

The Sherman Letters, 1837–1891 (edited by Rachel Sherman Thorndike, New York, 1894), 85–88 *passim.*

CHAPTER IX—DOCTRINE OF SECESSION

53. A Southern Opponent of Secession (1860)

BY ALEXANDER HAMILTON STEPHENS

Down to the Rebellion, Stephens's political career was nominally that of a Whig, but he usually advocated or voted for such measures as harmonized with his own doctrine of pro-slavery and states'-rights. He believed in the abstract right of secession, but declaimed against the expediency of nullification in 1832 and of secession in 1860. When his state seceded in 1861 he followed, and became vice-president of the Confederacy. This extract is from an extemporaneous speech delivered before the Georgia legislature. — For Stephens, see Johnston and Browne, *Life of Alexander H. Stephens;* on Lincoln's interest in the speech, Nicolay and Hay, *Abraham Lincoln,* III, 270–273. — Bibliography: Channing and Hart, *Guide,* § 205.

FELLOW CITIZENS : I appear before you to-night at the request of Members of the Legislature and others, to speak of matters of the deepest interest that can possibly concern us all, of an earthly character. . . . Had I consulted my personal ease and pleasure, I should not be before you ; but believing that it is the duty of every good citizen, when called on, to give his counsels and views whenever the country is in danger, as to the best policy to be pursued, I am here. For these reasons, and these only, do I bespeak a calm, patient, and attentive hearing.

My object is not to stir up strife, but to allay it ; not to appeal to your passions, but to your reason. Let us, therefore, reason together. It is not my purpose to say aught to wound the feelings of any individual who may be present ; and if in the ardency with which I shall express my opinions, I shall say anything which may be deemed too strong, let it be set down to the zeal with which I advocate my own convictions. There is with me no intention to irritate or offend. . . .

The first question that presents itself is, shall the people of Georgia secede from the Union in consequence of the election of Mr. Lincoln to the Presidency of the United States? My countrymen, I tell you frankly, candidly, and earnestly, that I do not think that they ought. In my judgment, the election of no man, constitutionally chosen to that high office, is sufficient cause to justify any State to separate from the Union. It ought to stand by and aid still in maintaining the Constitution of the country. To make a point of resistance to the Government, to withdraw from it because any man has been elected, would put us in the wrong. We are pledged to maintain the Constitution. Many of us have sworn to support it. Can we, therefore, for the mere election of any man to the Presidency, and that, too, in accordance with the prescribed forms of the Constitution, make a point of resistance to the Government, without becoming the breakers of that sacred instrument ourselves, by withdrawing ourselves from it? Would we not be in the wrong? Whatever fate is to befall this country, let it never be laid to the charge of the people of the South, and especially to the people of Georgia, that we were untrue to our national engagements. Let the fault and the wrong rest upon others. If all our hopes are to be blasted, if the Republic is to go down, let us be found to the last moment standing on the deck with the Constitution of the United States waving over our heads. Let the fanatics of the North break the Constitution, if such is their fell purpose. Let the responsibility be upon them. I shall speak presently more of their acts ; but let not the South, let us not be the ones to commit the aggression. We went into the election with this people. The result was different from what we wished ; but the election has been constitutionally held. Were we to make a point of resistance to the Government and go out of the Union merely on that account, the record would be made up hereafter against us.

But it is said Mr. Lincoln's policy and principles are against the Constitution, and that, if he carries them out, it will be destructive of our rights. Let us not anticipate a threatened evil. If he violates the Constitution, then will come our time to act. Do not let us break it because, forsooth, he may. If he does, that is the time for us to act. I think it would be injudicious and unwise to do this sooner. I do not anticipate that Mr. Lincoln will do anything, to jeopard our safety or security, whatever may be his spirit to do it ; for he is bound by the Constitutional checks which are thrown around him, which at this time render him powerless to do any great mischief. This shows the wisdom of our system. The President of the United States is no Emperor, no Dictator — he is clothed with no absolute power. He can do nothing, unless he is backed by power in Congress. The House of Representatives is largely in a majority against him. . . . Is this the time, then, to apprehend that Mr. Lincoln, with this large majority in the House of Representatives against him, can carry out any of his unconstitutional principles in that body?

In the Senate he will also be powerless. There will be a majority of four against him. . . .

My countrymen, I am not of those who believe this Union has been a curse up to this time. . . . There is nothing perfect in this world of human origin; nothing connected with human nature, from man himself to any of his works. . . . And it is so in our Government. But that this Government of our Fathers, with all its defects, comes nearer the objects of all good Governments than any other on the face of the earth, is my settled conviction. . . .

. . . Have we not at the South, as well as the North, grown great, prosperous and happy under its operation? Has any part of the world ever shown such rapid progress in the development of wealth, and all the material resources of national power and greatness, as the Southern States have under the General Government, notwithstanding all its defects?

Mr. Toombs. In spite of it!

Mr. Stephens. My honorable friend says we have, in spite of the General Government; that without it I suppose he thinks we might have done as well, or perhaps better than we have done. This grand result is in spite of the Government! That may be, and it may not be; but the great fact that we have grown great and powerful under the Government, as it exists, is admitted. . . .

. . . It is true, there is no equal part of the earth with natural resources superior, perhaps, to ours. That portion of this country known as the Southern States, stretching from the Chesapeake to the Rio Grande, is fully equal to the picture drawn by the honorable and eloquent Senator, last night, in all natural capacities. But how many ages, centuries, passed before these capacities were developed to reach this advanced stage of civilization? . . .

It was only under our Institutions as they are, that they were developed. Their development is the result of the enterprise of our people under operations of the Government and Institutions under which we have lived. Even our people, without these, never would have done it. The organization of society has much to do with the development of the natural resources of any country or any land. . . . Look at Greece! There is the same fertile soil, the same blue sky, the same inlets and harbors, the same Ægean, the same Olympus — there is the same land where Homer sung, where Pericles spoke — it is, in nature, the same old Greece ; but it is " living Greece no more ! "

Descendants of the same people inhabit the country ; yet what is the reason of this mighty difference? . . . I answer this, their Institutions have been destroyed. . . . And, my countrymen, if we shall, in an evil hour, rashly pull down and destroy those Institutions, which the patriotic hand of our Fathers labored so long and so hard to build up, and which have done so much for us, and for the world ; who can venture the prediction that similar results will not ensue? Let us avoid them if we can. I trust the spirit is amongst us that will enable us to do it. Let us not rashly try the experiment of change, of pulling down and destroying ; for, as in Greece and Italy, and the South American Republics, and in every other place, whenever our liberty is once lost, it may never be restored to us again. . . .

I look upon this country with our Institutions as the Eden of the world, the Paradise of the Universe. It may be that out of it we may become greater and more prosperous, but I am candid and sincere in telling you that I fear if we yield to passion, and without sufficient cause shall take that step, that instead of becoming greater or more peaceful, prosperous, and happy — instead of becoming Gods, we will become demons, and at no distant day commence cutting one another's throats. This is my apprehension. Let us, therefore, whatever we do, meet these difficulties, great as they are, like wise and sensible men, and consider them in the light of all the consequences which may attend our action. Let us see first, clearly, where the path of duty leads, and then we may not fear to tread therein.

Now, upon another point, and that the most difficult, and deserving your most serious consideration, I will speak. That is, the course which this State should pursue toward those Northern States which, by their legislative acts, have attempted to nullify the Fugitive Slave Law.

. . . They have violated their plighted faith. What ought we to do in view of this? That is the question. What is to be done? By the law of nations, you would have a right to demand the carrying out of this article of agreement, and I do not see that it should be otherwise with respect to the States of this Union ; and in case it be not done, we would, by these principles, have the right to commit acts of reprisal on these faithless Governments, and seize upon their property, or that of their citizens, wherever found. The States of this Union stand upon the same footing with foreign Nations in this respect.

. . . Let your Committee on the state of the Republic make out a bill of grievances; let it be sent by the Governor to those faithless States; and if reason and argument shall be tried in vain — if all shall fail to induce them to return to their Constitutional obligations, I would be for retaliatory measures, such as the Governor has suggested to you. This mode of resistance in the Union is in our power.

Now, then, my recommendation to you would be this : In view of all these questions of difficulty, let a Convention of the people of Georgia be called, to which they may be all referred. Let the Sovereignty of the people speak. . . . I have no hesitancy in saying that the Legislature is not the proper body to sever our Federal relations, if that necessity should arise.

. . . Sovereignty is not in the Legislature. We, the People, are Sovereign ! I am one of them, and have a right to be heard ; and so has every other citizen of the State. . . . Our Constitutions, State and Federal, came from the people. They made both, and they alone can rightfully unmake either.

Should Georgia determine to go out of the Union, I speak for one, though my views might not agree with them, whatever the result may be, I shall bow to the will of her people. Their cause is my cause, and their destiny is my destiny; and I trust this will be the ultimate course of all. The greatest curse that can befall a free people, is civil war.

. . . Before making reprisals, we should exhaust every means of bringing about a peaceful settlement of the controversy. . . . At least, let these offending and derelict States know what your grievances are, and if they refuse, as I said, to give us our rights under the Constitution, I should be willing, as a last resort, to sever the ties of our Union with them.

My own opinion is, that if this course be pursued, and they are informed of the consequences of refusal, these States will recede, will repeal their nullifying acts ; but if they should not, then let the consequences be with them, and the responsibility of the consequences rest upon them. . . .

I am for exhausting all that patriotism demands, before taking the last step. I would invite, therefore, South Carolina to a conference. I would ask the same of all the other Southern States, so that if the evil has got beyond our control, which God in his mercy grant may not be the case, we may not be divided among ourselves; but if possible, secure the united co-operation of all the Southern States, and then, in the face of the civilized world, we may justify our action, and, with the wrong all on the other side, we can appeal to the God of Battles, if it comes to that, to aid us in our cause.   But do nothing, in which any portion of our people, may charge you with rash or hasty action.   It is certainly a matter of great importance, to tear this Government asunder.   You were not sent here for that purpose.   I would wish the whole South to be united, if this is to be done; and I believe if we pursue the policy which I have indicated, this can be effected. . . .

. . . I am, as you clearly perceive, for maintaining the Union as it is, if possible.   I will exhaust every means, thus, to maintain it with an equality in it.   My position, then, in conclusion, is for the maintenance of the honor, the rights, the equality, the security, and the glory of my native State in the Union, if possible; but if these cannot be maintained in the Union, then I am for their maintenance, at all hazards, out of it. Next to the honor and glory of Georgia, the land of my birth, I hold the honor and glory of our common country. . . .

Alexander H. Stephens, *A Constitutional View of the late War between the States* (Philadelphia, etc., [1870]), II, 279–299 *passim*.

---

54. Constitutional Doctrine of Secession (1861)

BY SENATOR ROBERT TOOMBS

This extract is from the constitutional exposition of one who as an old-time Whig sincerely loved the Union, and as an able lawyer understood the advantages of it; but who as a representative of slaveholders and an advocate of states' rights was willing to go to extremes rather than submit to any derogation of southern principles. The speech was delivered in the Senate a short time before his withdrawal.   In the Civil War Toombs took a prominent part on the southern side, and remained irreconcilable throughout his life. — For Toombs, see P. A. Stovall, *Robert Toombs*. — Bibliography as in No. 53 above. — For earlier expositions of this doctrine, see *Contemporaries*, III, No. 161; IV, No. 19.

THESE thirteen colonies originally had no bond of union whatever; no more than Jamaica and Australia have to-day.   They were wholly separate communities, independent of each other, and dependent on the Crown of Great Britain.   All the union between them that was ever made is in writing.   They made two written compacts. . . .

Senators, the Constitution is a compact. It contains all our obligations and duties of the Federal Government. . . . All the obligations, all the chains that fetter the limbs of my people, are nominated in the bond, and they wisely excluded any conclusion against them, by declaring that the powers not granted by the Constitution to the United States, or forbidden by it to the States, belonged to the States respectively or the people. Now I will try it by that standard; I will subject it to that test. The law of nature, the law of justice, would say — and it is so expounded by the publicists — that equal rights in the common property shall be enjoyed. . . . This right of equality being, then, according to justice and natural equity, a right belonging to all States, when did we give it up? You say Congress has a right to pass rules and regulations concerning the Territory and other property of the United States. Very well. Does that exclude those whose blood and money paid for it? Does "dispose of" mean to rob the rightful owners? You must show a better title than that, or a better sword than we have.

But, you say, try the right. I agree to it. But how? By our judgment? No, not until the last resort. What then; by yours? No, not until the same time. How then try it? The South has always said, by the Supreme Court. But that is in our favor, and Lincoln says he will not stand that judgment. Then each must judge for himself of the mode and manner of redress. But you deny us that privilege, and finally reduce us to accepting your judgment. We decline it. You say you will enforce it by executing laws; that means your judgment of what the laws ought to be. Perhaps you will have a good time of executing your judgment. The Senator from Kentucky comes to your aid, and says he can find no constitutional right of secession. Perhaps not; but the Constitution is not the place to look for State rights. If that right belongs to independent States, and they did not cede it to the Federal Government, it is reserved to the States, or to the people. Ask your new commentator where he gets your right to judge for us. Is it in the bond? . . .

. . . In a compact where there is no common arbiter, where the parties finally decide for themselves, the sword alone at last becomes the real, if not the constitutional, arbiter. Your party says that you will not take the decision of the Supreme Court. You said so at Chicago; you said so in committee; every man of you in both Houses says so. What are you going to do? You say *we shall submit to your construction.* We shall do it, if you can make us; but not otherwise, or in any other manner. That is settled. You may call it secession, or you may call it revolution; but there is a big fact standing before you, ready to oppose you — that fact is, freemen with arms in their hands. The cry of the Union will not disperse them; we have passed that point; they demand equal rights : you had better heed the demand. . . .

I have, then, established the proposition — it is admitted — that you seek to outlaw $4,000,000,000 of property of our people in the Territories of the United States. Is not that a cause of war ? Is it a grievance that $4,000,000,000 of the property of the people should be outlawed in the Territories of the United States by the common Government? . . . Then you have declared, Lincoln declares, your platform declares, your people declare, your Legislatures declare — there is one voice running through your entire phalanx — that we shall be outlawed in the Territories of the United States. I say we will not be ; and we are willing to meet the issue ; and rather than submit to such an outlawry, we will defend our territorial rights as we would our household gods. . . .

You will not regard confederate obligations ; you will not regard constitutional obligations ; you will not regard your oaths. What, then, am I to do? Am I a freeman? Is my State, a free State, to lie down and submit because political fossils raise the cry of the glorious Union? Too long already have we listened to this delusive song. We are freemen. We have rights ; I have stated them. We have wrongs ; I have recounted them. I have demonstrated that the party now coming into power has declared us outlaws, and is determined to exclude four thousand million of our property from the common Territories ; that it has declared us under the ban of the Empire, and out of the protection of the laws of the United States everywhere. They have refused to protect us from invasion and insurrection by the Federal Power, and the Constitution denies to us in the Union the right either to raise fleets or armies for our own defense. All these charges I have proven by the record ; and I put them before the civilized world, and demand the judgment of to-day, of to-morrow, of distant ages, and of Heaven itself, upon the justice of these causes. I am content, whatever it be, to peril all in so noble, so holy a cause. We have appealed, time and time again, for these constitutional rights. You have refused them. We appeal again. Restore us these rights as we had them, as your court adjudges them to be, just as all our people have said they are ; redress these flagrant wrongs, seen of all men, and it will restore fraternity, and peace, and unity, to all of us. Refuse them, and what then? We shall then ask you, " let us depart in peace." Refuse that, and you present us war. We accept it; and inscribing upon our banners the glorious words, " liberty and equality," we will trust to the blood of the brave and the God of battles for security and tranquillity.

Congressional Globe, 36 Cong., 2 sess. (John C. Rives, Washington, 1861), 269–271 *passim*, January 7, 1861.

———◆———

55. A Fire-Eater (1861)

BY SENATOR LOUIS TREZEVANT WIGFALL

Wigfall did not enter the United States Senate until 1860, but during his brief service he became prominent as an uncompromising advocate of the rights of slavery. The speech from which this extract is taken is characteristic of the air of indifference to the war assumed by many of the southern statesmen. Wigfall took part in the bombardment of Sumter, and demanded the surrender of the fort (see No. 72 below). — Bibliography as in No. 53 above.

. . . THIS Federal Government is dead. The only question is, whether we will give it a decent, peaceable, Protestant burial, or whether we shall have an Irish wake at the grave. . . . I think myself it would be for the benefit of both sections that we should not have an Irish wake at our funeral; but that is for the North to decide, and not for us. Believing — no, sir, not believing, but knowing — that this Union is dissolved, never, never to be reconstructed upon any terms — not if you were to hand us blank paper, and ask us to write a constitution, would we ever again be confederated with you. . . . Then, knowing that the Union is dissolved, that reconstruction is impossible, I would, myself, had I been consulted by the Union-savers, have told them that Union-saving was impracticable, but that peaceable separation was practicable. . . . I suppose commissioners, in a few days, will be here from the confederate States. . . . Turn your backs upon these commissioners, attempt to reinforce the forts and retake those which we now have; attempt to collect the revenues, or do any other manner or matter of thing that denies to the free white men, living in those seven sovereign States, the right which they have asserted of self-government, and you will have war, and it will be war in all its stern realities. I say this not in bravado, but I say it because I know it and you know it. . . .

. . . The Senator from Illinois seemed to be shocked at my speaking with a feeling of gratification at the flag of what he chooses to call my country being insulted. It is not the flag of my country, I hope and believe; but I have not official information on that point. That flag was never insulted with impunity until it floated over a cargo of Black Republican hirelings, sent to one of the sovereign States of this Union to coerce them to obedience to a Government that was distasteful to them. . . .

. . . I was speaking of this parenthesis that is now incumbent in the War office. Without allowing even the President to know it, as it is said in the newspapers — I am not in the confidence of the last Cabinet, and I suspect will not be in the new one, — it is said that, without allowing even the President to know it, he surreptitiously, in the dead of night, sneaked a merchant vessel out of the harbor of New York, intending to sneak it into Charleston harbor; but they had put out the lights and blocked up the channel, and she was obliged to come up in broad daylight. A shot was thrown athwart the bow of this vessel containing armed men; they displayed a flag and it was fired at. I did say that that vessel had swaggered into Charleston harbor, had received a blow in the face, and had staggered out; and that this Secretary of War, who had brought the flag of this country in a condition to be fired at, had never dared, from that time to this, to resent the injury and insult; and in consequence of that, the State to which I owe my allegiance has withdrawn and cut loose from all connection with a Government that allows its flag to be so insulted. She has plucked her bright star from a bunting that can be fired at with impunity. If your President elect has recovered from that artificial fright, see if you cannot induce him to try and wipe out the insult; but I predicted last night that he would not; and I predict again that he will not. You fear to pass your force bills; you abandon them in both Houses. If you can get a Cabinet properly organized, with fire-eaters enough in it, the Cabinet may precipitate the country into a war, and then call upon what is denominated the conservative elements of your party to sustain the country in a war in which you have already involved it; but I know, and you know, that those men whom you represent are not in favor of war, and that their representatives here, a large number of them, fear it. What will be the result, I do not know; and to be very frank, I do not care.

Now, having explained why it was that I felt rejoiced at this insult to the flag of your country, I shall take up very little more time. The country is composed of States; and when that Government which was established by those States, and that flag which bears upon its broad folds the stars representing those States, is used for the purpose of making war upon some of those States, I say that it has already been degraded, and that it ought to be fired at, and it should be torn down and trampled upon. These are my feelings upon the subject; and "if this be treason, make the most of it." I owe my allegiance — and Senators are not mistaken about that, for I have said it frequently — to the State which I here represent. I do not owe my allegiance to this Government. The Senator from Illinois spoke of the necessity of coercing these States, or not entertaining propositions from them, and likened it to the case of a Government in which there were revolted provinces. Your President elect, a short time ago, in a speech, asked the question gravely, what is the difference between a State and a county? And he seemed to be really in quest of information. Now, I was not astonished at that, for I did not expect anything better of him. From a man who is taken up because he is an ex-rail splitter, an ex-grocery keeper, an ex-flatboat captain, and an ex-Abolition lecturer, and is run upon that question, I would not expect any great information as to the Government which he was to administer. But I was surprised to hear a Senator — a Senator of education and ability, such as the Senator from Illinois is — compare the States of this Union, the States that formed this Government, the States without the consent of which this Government could not originally have had existence, and without the consent of which this Government cannot exist a day. To hear him talk about those States as revolted provinces, did surprise and shock me.

Then, briefly, a party has come into power that represents the antagonism to my own section of the country. It represents two million men who hate us, and who, by their votes for such a man as they have elected, have committed an overt act of hostility. That they have done. You have won the Presidency, and you are now in the situation of the man who had won the elephant at a raffle. You do not know what to do with the beast now that you have it; and one half of you to-day would give your right arms if you had been defeated. But you succeeded, and you have to deal with facts. Our objection to living in this Union, and therefore the difficulty of reconstructing it, is not your personal liberty bill, not the territorial question, but that you utterly and wholly misapprehend the form of government. You deny the sovereignty of the States; you deny the right of self-government in the people; you insist upon negro equality; your people interfere impertinently with our institutions and attempt to subvert them; you publish newspapers; you deliver lectures; you print pamphlets, and you send them among us, first, to excite our slaves to insurrection against their masters, and next, to array one class of citizens against the other; and I say to you that we cannot live in peace, either in the Union or out of it, until you have abolished your Abolition societies; not, as I have been misquoted, abolish or destroy your school-houses; but until you have ceased in your school-houses teaching your children to hate us; until you have ceased to convert your pulpits into hustings; until you content yourselves with preaching Christ, and Him crucified, and not delivering political harangues on the Sabbath; until you have ceased inciting your own citizens to make raids and commit robberies; until you have done these things we cannot live in the same Union with you. Until you do these things, we cannot live out of the Union at peace. . . .

Now, having made these few, little, conciliatory, peace-preserving remarks, I am not disposed to take up more time, and am willing that there should be a vote.

Congressional Globe, 36 Cong., 2 sess. (John C. Rives, Washington, 1861), 1399–1400 *passim*, March 2, 1861.

———◆———

56. The Wrong of Secession (1861)

BY PROFESSOR JOEL PARKER

When the lecture from which this extract is taken was delivered, Parker was a professor in the Harvard Law School. Formerly he had been chief justice of the superior court of New Hampshire. As a constitutional lawyer he was not a strict constructionist, but his veneration for the Constitution itself was such that he was outspoken against the efforts of the South to destroy it, and later against any departures from it on the Union side. — Bibliography as in No. 53 above. — For an earlier refutation of states' rights see *Contemporaries*, III, No. 159.

THE right of secession is asserted as a *State right*, consistent with the Constitution, and founded upon it, or upon the history preceding it, and the circumstances attending its formation and adoption; — a right to be exercised only through State action, and to be made effectual by a peaceful declaration of the fact of secession, which of itself accomplishes the separation of the State from the Union; any forcible opposition to it on the part of the United States being usurpation and oppression. . . .

In determining whether such a right exists, we naturally turn in the first instance to the Constitution itself. But it is clear that this instrument contains no provision to that effect, in terms, nor any one which suggests such a result by any direct implication. It purports to be an organic and supreme law, limited as to its objects, and of course in its powers. . . . The government organized under it is formed through the instrumentality of the Constitution itself, as a fundamental law enacted by " We, the people of the United States ; " and not one formed by the States, or one which when formed represents the States ; although from the previous existence of the States, as sovereign communities, except so far as they were bound by the Articles of Confederation, the Constitution could not be adopted without the assent and sanction of the several States ; — for which reason, and because the States were still to exist, the ratifications were by " the people " of each State. In no instance was it supposed that the existing State government could make the necessary ratification as a State act. . . . The powers of the government organized under it usually act directly upon the people of the whole country, as the powers of the State government act upon all the people of the State ; sometimes with reference to geographical or State lines, as the powers of the State government act with regard to county, town, or city limits. . . . It is none the less true, that the States have no control over any of the departments of the general government. They do not direct their action, in the first instance, nor is there, by the Constitution, any appeal to State judgment, or State sanction, through which errors are corrected, or the action of the departments is affirmed or reversed. . . .

The Constitution declares that itself, the laws of the United States made in pursuance of it, and treaties made under its authority, shall be the supreme law of the land, by which the judges of every State shall be bound, anything in the laws or constitution of the State to the contrary notwithstanding. It is a perversion of terms to call the " supreme law of the land " a compact between the States, which any State may rescind at pleasure. It is not itself an agreement, but is the result of an agreement. And in the absence of an express declaration, or reservation, it is an entire subversion of all legal principles to maintain that the subordinate may at pleasure set itself free from the restrictions imposed upon it by the fundamental law constituting the superior, even if the subordinate have in other particulars an uncontrolled authority. The judges of each State being expressly bound by the Constitution and laws of the United States, anything in the constitution or laws of the State to the contrary, how can a State law (or ordinance, which is but another name for a law) relieve them from the obligation?   And if they are bound, the State and the people are bound also.   The judges are expressly named, the more surely to prevent a conflict of jurisdiction and decision.   —

The clause of the Constitution providing for amendments adds another to the arguments which show it to have the character of an organic law, and not of a compact.   Whether regarded as the one or the other, it is clear that it could not become obligatory upon a State, or the people of a State, until adopted by them.   The people of one State could not ratify and adopt it for the people of another State.   But, being adopted by all, it contains a clause binding upon all, providing that " the Congress, whenever two thirds of both houses shall deem it necessary, shall propose amendments to the Constitution, or, on application of the legislatures of two thirds of the several States, shall call a convention for proposing amendments, which, in either case, shall be valid to all intents and purposes, when ratified by the legislatures of three fourths of the several States, or by conventions in three fourths thereof, as the one or the other mode of ratification may be proposed by the Congress."

Now, considered as an organic law, the Constitution may be altered and amended in any mode which may be agreed upon and prescribed by the instrument itself. . . .

But if the Constitution is a compact between the States, any amendment which becomes a part of the Constitution is also a compact between the States, and the question arises, How is it that three fourths of the States, voting in favor of an amendment, are to make a compact with the other fourth, voting at the same time against it, and thus refusing to enter into the compact?   How is it that the States voting to adopt, represent the States refusing to adopt, so that, by the vote of adoption, they make a compact between themselves and the others, against the will of the others expressed at the same time.   Those voting to adopt act in their own behalf, thereby being one party to the bargain, and thus far it is well ; but, on the compact theory, they must at the same time represent those who vote against the adoption, and thus make them another party to the bargain ; when the others at the same time represent themselves, and refuse to make the bargain. . . .

Will the advocate of the compact theory say that the provision relative to amendments, in the Constitution as first adopted, constitutes the States *agents* of one another, so that three fourths of the whole number may thus make an agreement for all, against the will of their principals.

N

acting at the same time and dissenting? If this is so, we must add a new chapter to the law of Agency. . . .

The Articles of Confederation expressly, explicitly, and in the most emphatic manner, established a " Perpetual Union" between the States. . . .

The Articles of Confederation which established this "perpetual," "permanent," "indissoluble" Union, proved to be inadequate to the purpose for which they were adopted. . . . The history of the change by which a Union under the Constitution was substituted for that under the Articles of Confederation, need not be set forth at this time. . . . The reasons for its adoption, summarily set forth in the preamble of the instrument itself, are "*to form a more perfect Union*, establish justice, insure domestic tranquillity, promote the general welfare, and secure the blessings of liberty to ourselves *and our posterity*."

Now it appears to be preposterous to contend that this more perfect Union, established for posterity as well as for the existing generation, and thus substituted for the perpetual, indissoluble Union under the Articles, is one which was to exist only at the pleasure of each and every State, and to be dissolved when any State shall assert that it is aggrieved, and repeal the act of ratification. The Union could not be made "more perfect" in relation to its endurance. It certainly was not intended to be made less perfect in that particular.

[Joel Parker], *The Right of Secession*, in *North American Review*, July, 1861 (Boston), XCIII, 221–244 *passim*.

---

57. "Let Us Alone" (1861)

BY HENRY HOWARD BROWNELL

Brownell abandoned the law for literature, and wrote popular histories and war lyrics. The title of the verses given below was derived from Jefferson Davis's first message to the Confederate Congress. — Bibliography as in No. 53 above.

AS vonce I valked by a dismal svamp,
  There sot an Old Cove in the dark and damp,
And at everybody as passed that road
A stick or a stone this Old Cove throwed.
And venever he flung his stick or his stone,
He'd set up a song of " Let me alone."

"Let me alone, for I loves to shy
These bits of things at the passers by —
Let me alone, for I've got your tin
And lots of other traps snugly in —
Let me alone, I'm riggin a boat
To grab votever you've got afloat —
In a veek or so I expects to come
And turn you out of your 'ouse and 'ome —
I'm a quiet Old Cove," says he, vith a groan:
"All I axes is — Let me alone."

Just then came along, on the self-same vay,
Another Old Cove, and began for to say —
"Let you alone!   That's comin' it strong! —
You've *ben* let alone — a darned sight too long —
Of all the sarce that ever I heerd!
Put down that stick!   (You may well look skeered.)
Let go that stone!   If you once show fight,
I'll knock you higher than ary kite.

You must hev a lesson to stop your tricks,
And cure you of shying them stones and sticks —
And I'll hev my hardware back and my cash,
And knock your scow into tarnal smash,
And if ever I catches you 'round my ranch,
I'll string you up to the nearest branch.
The best you can do is to go to bed,
And keep a decent tongue in your head;
For I reckon, before you and I are done,
You'll wish you had let honest folks alone."

The Old Cove stopped, and the t'other Old Cove
He sot quite still in his cypress grove,
And he looked at his stick, revolvin' slow
Vether t'were safe to shy it or no —
And he grumbled on, in an injured tone
All that I axed vos, *let me alone.*

[Henry Howard Brownell], *Lyrics of a Day* (Hartford, 1863), 16–17.

CHAPTER X — PRACTICE OF SECESSION

58. Secession Spirit in Mississippi (1860)

BY REPRESENTATIVE REUBEN DAVIS (1889)

Davis was a member of Congress from 1857 to 1861, and later a member of the Confederate Congress ; but his life was spent chiefly in Mississippi, where both before and after the Civil War he was very prominent as a lawyer. This extract is from his recollections, written over twenty-five years after the event. — Bibliography : Channing and Hart, *Guide*, § 206.

TO say that the nomination and election of Lincoln caused the war is to make a mistake. It was the signal for battle, but the troops were marshalled and war declared, long before. During the long contest for speaker, passion on both sides had been intensified, and the excitement and danger of collision continued to increase until the last hour of the session.

Lincoln's nomination took place about two weeks before adjournment. The intelligence came like a thunderbolt. Members from the South purchased long-range guns to take home with them. The unthinking among them rejoiced that the end was in sight, but those who considered more deeply were dismayed by the prospect.

It was regarded almost certain that Lincoln would be elected, unless Breckenridge or Douglas could be withdrawn from the field, and it was idle to hope that this could be done. . . .

The presidential campaign was, as was inevitable, one of extraordinary violence. In all my speeches in Mississippi, I broadly asserted that war was unavoidable. For this I was often blamed, but I replied that it was our duty to deal frankly with the people, who had confided such vast interests to our hands.

Governor John J. Pettus issued a proclamation, by which he called upon the legislature to meet, in extra session, upon the third Monday in November, 1860. He also invited the senators and representatives to meet him in Jackson, some days before the meeting of the legislature.

in order that he might counsel with them in regard to his message and what he should say upon the subject of secession.

We met there upon this invitation. Congressman John J. McRae was not present. There was much discussion, in which divers opinions were maintained. Some opposed separate state action in secession. Some were opposed to secession, unless eight other States would consent to go out at the same time.

As these discussions were prolonged without seeming to lead to anything definite, I at last proposed a resolution that the governor should recommend the legislature to call a convention to secede the State of Mississippi, by separate action, such action to take effect *eo instanti*.

This resolution was voted for by Governor Pettus, O. R. Singleton, William Barksdale, and myself. It was practically a declaration of war.

Governor Pettus then showed us a telegram which he had received from the governor of South Carolina, requesting his opinion whether the South Carolina secession convention, which was then about to meet, should make their ordinance of secession take effect instantly, or on the 4th of March.

Being called upon for a resolution upon this point, I offered one that the reply should advise the ordinance to take effect instantly. The same four votes adopted this resolution also, and our work was done. If a convention was called, and delegates in favor of secession elected, there would be no pause or tarrying.

Hon. L. Q. C. Lamar and General Ethel Barksdale were invited by the people of Brandon to make addresses at that place, the day after these resolutions had been adopted.

Returning home, it was necessary for me to pass immediately through Brandon, and Lamar and Barksdale, with their accustomed courtesy, sent me an invitation to arrange my journey with reference to joining them. It was with great pleasure that I accepted this invitation, knowing that I should hear from both gentlemen speeches of unusual eloquence.

Mr. Lamar made the opening address, speaking with even more than his wonted fluency and beauty. It is useless to attempt to describe his peculiar style. His fame is national, and he stands upon a pedestal wrought out by his own great gift of words. It was remarked that in this speech he made no reference to the possibilities of war, or the horrors that must result from disunion.

As soon as the applause which greeted the conclusion of Lamar's address had subsided, General Barksdale invited me to speak. I had made no preparation, but the subject to be handled had occupied my mind exclusively for many weeks, and had become so much a part of my consciousness that I had but to look at a crowd and open my mouth, and speech flowed spontaneously. I was, so to speak, so saturated with the thoughts and passions of the time, that the difficulty was not so much how to speak as how to leave off.

After stating the issues between the two sections, I informed the people how far, and in what spirit, the struggle had been carried on, telling them frankly that we had reached a point where to turn back would be dishonor. . . .

As we came down from the stand, some of the principal citizens in the crowd came to me, and said, "Your boldness startled us. Is it your sober judgment that we are in such peril as you have described?" I replied that by the first of January they would see for themselves.

A gentleman then said, "I believe your opinions are correct, but do you not doubt the propriety of saying these things in public? Would it not be wiser to preserve a discreet silence until everything is ready?" To this I made answer that it was the people's right to know where they were going, and our duty to give them fair warning. Otherwise, they might justly utter the reproach that they had been led blindfold to the very brink of a precipice, and their representatives had given them no warning. The gentleman looked at me for a moment as if in doubt, and then said, "Well, that's honest, any way."

Reuben Davis, *Recollections of Mississippi and Mississippians* (Boston, etc., 1891), 389–394 *passim.*

———◆———

59. Crisis in South Carolina (1860)

BY ASSISTANT-SURGEON SAMUEL WYLIE CRAWFORD (1887)

Crawford was sent in 1860 to act as surgeon for the troops stationed at Charleston, and remained with them there until the surrender of Fort Sumter. His description is that of an eye-witness, and, although a reminiscence, it is accurate. Later, during the war, Crawford entered the infantry and rose to high rank through his distinguished bravery. — Bibliography as in No. 58 above.

HARDLY had the Convention assembled at Columbia when a resolution was introduced by Chancellor J. A. Inglis to the effect that "it is the opinion of the Convention that the State should forthwith secede from the Federal Union known as the United States of America, and that a committee be appointed to draft an ordinance to be adopted by the Convention in order to accomplish this purpose of secession." . . . It passed without a dissenting voice.

Meantime, a contagious disease having broken out in the city, the Convention resolved to change its session to Charleston, and it reassembled in that city on the 18th. . . .

In the large room of Institute Hall, the Convention reassembled at 4 o'clock on the afternoon of the 18th of December. Crowds of excited people thronged the streets and open squares of the city, and filled the passage and stairways of the hall. Congratulations were exchanged on every side, while earnest dissatisfaction was freely expressed that the passage of the Secession Ordinance had been delayed.

Blue cockades and cockades of palmetto appeared in almost every hat; flags of all descriptions, except the National colors, were everywhere displayed. Upon the gavel that lay upon the Speaker's table, the word "Secession" had been cut in deep black characters. The enthusiasm spread to the more practical walks of trade, and the business streets were gay with bunting and flags, as the tradespeople, many of whom were Northern men, commended themselves to the popular clamor by a display of coarse representations on canvas of the public men, and of the incidents daily presenting themselves, and of the brilliant future in store for them. . . .

On the 19th the Convention reassembled at St. Andrews Hall. . . .

The special order of the day being the resolution in reference to that part of the message of the President of the United States which refers to the property of the United States in South Carolina, it was considered, and a committee of thirteen was appointed, at the head of which was A. G. Magrath, to report to the Convention upon the resolution.

It was resolved, also, to send three commissioners, bearing an authenticated copy of the Secession Ordinance to Washington to be laid before the President and Congress. And, also, that these commissioners should be empowered to treat for the delivery of the forts, magazines, and other "real estate;" and they were authorized to treat of the public debt, and for a division of all the property held by the United States as the agents of the States, and until a new Confederacy should be formed. This latter resolution was referred to the "Committee on Foreign Relations." . . .

Early on the morning of the 20th knots of men were seen gathered here and there through the main streets and squares of Charleston. The Convention was not to meet until 12 o'clock, but it was understood that the Committee were ready to report the Ordinance of Secession, and that it would certainly pass the Convention that day. The report soon spread. Although this action had been fully anticipated, there was a feverish anxiety to know that the secession of the State was really accomplished, and as the hour of noon approached, crowds of people streamed along the avenues towards St. Andrew's Hall and filled the approaches. A stranger passing from the excited throng outside into the hall of the Convention would be struck with the contrast. Ordinary business was quietly disposed of; the Mayor and Governor and the officials of the Legislature were invited to seats upon the floor; committees authorized by previous resolutions were announced by the President, the more noticeable being that of the late United States Judge Magrath, to head the Committee on so much of the President's message as related to the property in the harbor, and W. P. Miles on Foreign Relations looking to the ordeal in Washington. Quietly the Convention had met, and had been opened with prayer to God. There was no excitement. There was no visible sign that the Commonwealth of South Carolina was about to take a step more momentous for weal or woe than had yet been known in her history.

Then followed the introduction of a resolution by Mr. R. B. Rhett, that a committee of thirteen be appointed to report an ordinance providing for a convention to form a Southern Confederacy, as important a step as the secession of the State itself. It was referred to the appropriate committee, when Chancellor Inglis of Chesterfield, the Chairman of the Committee to report an ordinance proper of secession, arose and called the attention of the President.

An immediate silence pervaded the whole assemblage as every eye turned upon the speaker. Addressing the chair, he said that the Committee appointed to prepare a draft of an ordinance proper, to be adopted by the Convention in order to effect the secession of South Carolina from the Federal Union, respectfully report that they have had the matter under consideration, and believe that they would best meet the exigencies of the occasion by expressing in the fewest and simplest words all that was necessary to effect the end proposed, and so to exclude everything which was not a necessary part of the " solemn act of secession." They therefore submitted the following :

ORDINANCE

to dissolve the Union from [between] the State of South Carolina and other States united with her under the compact entitled "The Constitution of the United States of America."

We, the people of the State of South Carolina, in convention assembled, do declare and ordain, and it is hereby declared and ordained, that the Ordinance adopted by us in convention, on the 23d day of May, in the year of our Lord, seventeen hundred and eighty-eight, whereby the Constitution of the United States was ratified, and also all the acts and part of acts of the General Assembly of this State ratifying amendments of the said Constitution, are hereby repealed, and that the union now subsisting between South Carolina and other States under the name of "United States of America" is hereby dissolved.

A proposition that business be suspended for fifteen minutes was not agreed to, and the question was at once put, with the result of a unanimous vote, at 1:30 P.M., of 169 yeas, nays none. An immediate struggle for the floor ensued. Mr. W. Porcher Miles moved that an immediate telegram be sent to the Members of Congress, at Washington, announcing the result of the vote and the Ordinance of Secession. It was then resolved to invite the Governor and both branches of the Legislature to Institute Hall, at seven o'clock in the evening, and that the Convention should move in procession to that hall, and there, in the presence of the constituted authorities of the State and the people, sign the Ordinance of Secession. That a clergyman of the city should be invited to attend, and upon the completion of the signing of the Ordinance, he should "return thanks to Almighty God in behalf of the people of this State and to invoke His blessings upon our proceedings." The Ordinance was then turned over to the Attorney-General and solicitors to be engrossed.

The invitations to the Senate and House of Representatives having been accepted, the Convention moved in procession at the hour indicated to Institute Hall, amid the crowds of citizens that thronged the streets, cheering loudly as it passed. The galleries of the hall were crowded with ladies, who waved their handkerchiefs to the Convention as it entered, with marked demonstration. On either side of the President's chair were two large palmetto trees. The Hall was densely crowded. The Ordinance, having been returned engrossed and with the great seal of the State, attached by the Attorney-General, was presented and was signed by every member of the Convention, special favorites being received with loud applause. Two hours were thus occupied. The President then announced that "the Ordinance of Secession has been signed and ratified, and I proclaim the State of South Carolina," said he, "an independent Commonwealth."

At once the whole audience broke out into a storm of cheers; the ladies again joined in the demonstration; a rush was made for the palmetto trees, which were torn to pieces in the effort to secure mementos of the occasion. As soon as the passage of the Secession Ordinance at St. Andrews Hall was accomplished, a messenger left the house and rode with the greatest speed to the camp of the First Regiment of Rifles, South Carolina Militia, Colonel Pettigrew, one mile distant, where in front of the paraded regiment the Ordinance was read amid the loud acclamations of the men.

The adjournment of the Convention was characterized by the same dignity that had marked its sessions. Outside, the whole city was wild with excitement as the news spread like wild-fire through its streets. Business was suspended everywhere; the peals of the church bells mingling with salvos of artillery from the citadel. Old men ran shouting down the street. Every one entitled to it, appeared at once in uniform. In less then [than] fifteen minutes after its passage, the principal newspaper of Charleston had placed in the hands of the eager multitude a copy of the Ordinance of Secession. Private residences were illuminated, while military organizations marched in every direction, the music of their bands lost amid the shouts of the people. The whole heart of the people had spoken. . . .

Samuel Wylie Crawford, *The Genesis of the Civil War* (New York, 1887), 47–55 *passim*.

———◆———

60. "Brother Jonathan's Lament" (1861)

BY OLIVER WENDELL HOLMES

As physician, poet, essayist, and humorist, Holmes gained fame in many fields, but he was especially noted for his ability to write occasional poems. The verses below show the position of a large and influential class in the North up to the time of the firing upon Sumter. — For Holmes, see Providence Public Library, *Monthly Bulletins,* I, 3–4. — Bibliography: Channing and Hart, *Guide,* §§ 206, 207.

SHE has gone, — she has left us in passion and pride, —
  Our stormy-browed sister, so long at our side!
She has torn her own star from our firmament's glow,
And turned on her brother the face of a foe!

O Caroline, Caroline, child of the sun,
We can never forget that our hearts have been one, —
Our foreheads both sprinkled in Liberty's name,
From the fountain of blood with the finger of flame !

You were always too ready to fire at a touch ;
But we said, " She is hasty, — she does not mean much."
We have scowled, when you uttered some turbulent threat ;
But Friendship still whispered, " Forgive and forget ! "

Has our love all died out?   Have its altars grown cold?
Has the curse come at last which the fathers foretold?
Then Nature must teach us the strength of the chain
That her petulant children would sever in vain.

They may fight till the buzzards are gorged with their spoil,
Till the harvest grows black as it rots in the soil,
Till the wolves and the catamounts troop from their caves,
And the shark tracks the pirate, the lord of the waves :

In vain is the strife !   When its fury is past,
Their fortunes must flow in one channel at last,
As the torrents that rush from the mountains of snow
Roll mingled in peace through the valleys below.

Our Union is river, lake, ocean, and sky :
Man breaks not the medal, when God cuts the die !
Though darkened with sulphur, though cloven with steel,
The blue arch will brighten, the waters will heal !

O Caroline, Caroline, child of the sun,
There are battles with Fate that can never be won !
The star-flowering banner must never be furled,
For its blossoms of light are the hope of the world !

Go, then, our rash sister ! afar and aloof,
Run wild in the sunshine away from our roof ;
But when your heart aches and your feet have grown sore,
Remember the pathway that leads to our door !

Oliver Wendell Holmes, *Songs in Many Keys* (Boston, 1862), 282-284.

61. An Ordinance of Secession (1861)

BY THE CONVENTION OF ALABAMA

Alabama was the fourth state to secede. Her ordinance was the only one that declared Lincoln's election to be the cause of the secession, though other ordinances made general statements to the same effect. Only three of the states — Texas, Tennessee, and Virginia — submitted the ordinance to the people for ratification. — For the several ordinances of secession, see *American History Leaflets*, No. 12.

A N ordinance *to dissolve the Union between the State of Alabama and other States united under the compact styled " the Constitution of the United States of America."*

Whereas the election of Abraham Lincoln and Hannibal Hamlin to the offices of President and Vice-President of the United States of America, by a sectional party, avowedly hostile to the domestic institutions and to the peace and security of the people of the State of Alabama, preceded by many and dangerous infractions of the Constitution of the United States by many of the States and people of the Northern section, is a political wrong of so insulting and menacing a character as to justify the people of the State of Alabama in the adoption of prompt and decided measures for their future peace and security : Therefore,

Be it declared and ordained by the people of the State of Alabama in convention assembled, That the State of Alabama now withdraws, and is hereby withdrawn, from the Union known as "the United States of America," and henceforth ceases to be one of said United States, and is, and of right ought to be, a sovereign and independent State.

SEC. 2. *Be it further declared and ordained by the people of the State of Alabama in convention assembled,* That all the powers over the territory of said State, and over the people thereof, heretofore delegated to the Government of the United States of America be, and they are hereby, withdrawn from said Government, and are hereby resumed and vested in the people of the State of Alabama.

And as it is the desire and purpose of the State of Alabama to meet the slaveholding States of the South who may approve such purpose, in order to frame a provisional as well as permanent government, upon the principles of the Constitution of the United States,

Be it resolved by the people of Alabama in convention assembled, That the people of the States of Delaware, Maryland, Virginia, North Carolina, South Carolina, Florida, Georgia, Mississippi, Louisiana, Texas, Arkansas, Tennessee, Kentucky, and Missouri, be, and are hereby, invited to meet the people of the State of Alabama, by their delegates, in convention, on the 4th day of February, A.D. 1861, at the city of Montgomery, in the State of Alabama, for the purpose of consulting with each other as to the most effectual mode of securing concerted and harmonious action in whatever measures may be deemed most desirable for our common peace and security.

And be it further resolved, That the President of this convention be, and is hereby, instructed to transmit forthwith a copy of the foregoing preamble, ordinance, and resolutions, to the Governors of the several States named in said resolutions.

Done by the people of the State of Alabama in convention assembled, at Montgomery, on this, the 11th day of January, A.D. 1861.

From one of the original copies printed by order of the Convention, 1861.

---

62. Principles of the Confederacy (1861)

BY PRESIDENT JEFFERSON DAVIS

After Calhoun's death Davis became the recognized leader of the extreme pro-slavery and states'-rights school of statesmen. He attempted to carry into practice Calhoun's theories; but when secession was accomplished and he found himself at the head of a government founded on these theories, his administration soon displayed tendencies toward centralization which provoked much opposition. This extract is from his inaugural address under the provisional constitution of the Confederacy. — For Davis, see Channing and Hart, *Guide*, § 25. — Bibliography as in No. 58 above.

GENTLEMEN of the Congress of the Confederate States of America:

FRIENDS AND FELLOW-CITIZENS: Called to the difficult and responsible station of Chief Executive of the Provisional Government which you have instituted, I approach the discharge of the duties assigned to me with an humble distrust of my abilities, but with a sustaining confidence in the wisdom of those who are to guide and to aid me in the administration of public affairs, and an abiding faith in the virtue and patriotism of the people. Looking forward to the speedy establishment of a permanent government to take the place of this, and which, by its greater moral and physical power, will be better able to combat with the many difficulties which arise from the conflicting interests of separate nations, I enter upon the duties of the office to which I have been chosen with a hope that the beginning of our career as a confederacy may not be obstructed by hostile opposition to our enjoyment of the separate existence and independence which we have asserted, and, with the blessing of Providence, intend to maintain. Our present condition, achieved in a manner unprecedented in the history of nations, illustrates the American idea that governments rest upon the consent of the governed, and that it is the right of the people to alter or abolish governments whenever they become destructive of the ends for which they were established. The declared purpose of the compact of the Union from which we have withdrawn was " to establish justice, insure domestic tranquillity, provide for the common defense, promote the general welfare, and secure the blessings of liberty to ourselves and our posterity ; " and when, in the judgment of the sovereign States now composing this Confederacy, it had been perverted from the purposes for which it was ordained, and had ceased to answer the ends for which it was established, a peaceful appeal to the ballot box declared that, so far as they were concerned, the Government created by that compact should cease to exist. In this they merely asserted a right which the Declaration of Independence of 1776 had defined to be inalienable ; of the time and occasion for its exercise they, as sovereigns, were the final judges, each for itself. The impartial and enlightened verdict of mankind will vindicate the rectitude of our conduct, and He who knows the hearts of men, will judge of the sincerity with which we labored to preserve the Government of our fathers in its spirit. The right solemnly proclaimed at the birth of the States, and which has been affirmed and reaffirmed in the bills of rights of States subsequently admitted into the Union of 1789, undeniably recognize[s] in the people the power to resume the authority delegated for the purposes of government. Thus the sovereign States here represented proceeded to form this Confederacy, and it is by abuse of language that their act has been denominated a revolution. They formed a new alliance, but within each State its government has remained ; the rights of person and property have not been disturbed. The agent through whom they communicated with foreign nations is changed, but this does not necessarily interrupt their international relations.

Sustained by the consciousness that the transition from the former Union to the present Confederacy has not proceeded from a disregard on our part of just obligations or any failure to perform every constitutional duty ; moved by no interest or passion to invade the rights of others; anxious to cultivate peace and commerce with all nations, if we may not hope to avoid war, we may at least expect that posterity will acquit us of having needlessly engaged in it.} Doubly justified by the absence of wrong on our part, and by wanton aggression on the part of others, there can be no cause to doubt that the courage and patriotism of the people of the Confederate States will be found equal to any measures of defense which honor and security may require.

An agricultural people, whose chief interest is the export of a commodity required in every manufacturing country, our true policy is peace, and the freest trade which our necessities will permit. It is alike our interest and that of all those to whom we would sell and from whom we would buy that there should be the fewest practicable restrictions upon the interchange of commodities. There can be but little rivalry between ours and any manufacturing or navigating community, such as the Northeastern States of the American Union. It must follow, therefore, that a mutual interest would invite good will and kind offices. If, however, passion or the lust of dominion should cloud the judgment or inflame the ambition of those States, we must prepare to meet the emergency and to maintain by the final arbitrament of the sword the position which we have assumed among the nations of the earth. We have entered upon the career of independence, and it must be inflexibly pursued. Through many years of controversy with our late associates, the Northern States, we have vainly endeavored to secure tranquillity and to obtain respect for the rights to which we were entitled. As a necessity, not a choice, we have resorted to the remedy of separation ; and henceforth our energies must be directed to the conduct of our own affairs and the perpetuity of the confederacy which we have formed. If a just perception of a mutual interest shall permit us peaceably to pursue our separate political career, my most earnest desire will have been fulfilled. But if this be denied to us, and the integrity of our territory and jurisdiction be assailed, it will but remain for us, with firm resolve, to appeal to arms and invoke the blessings of Providence on a just cause. . . .

With a Constitution differing only from that of our fathers in so far as it is explanatory of their well-known intent, freed from the sectional conflicts which have interfered with the pursuit of the general welfare, it is not unreasonable to expect that States from which we have recently parted may seek to unite their fortunes with ours under the Government which we have instituted. For this your Constitution makes adequate provision ; but beyond this, if I mistake not the judgment and will of the people, a reunion with the States from which we have separated is neither practicable nor desirable. To increase the power, develop the resources, and promote the happiness of a confederacy, it is requisite that there should be so much of homogeneity that the welfare of every portion shall be the aim of the whole. Where this does not exist antagonisms are engendered, which must and should result in separation.

Actuated solely by the desire to preserve our own rights and promote our own welfare, the separation of the Confederate States has been marked by no aggression upon others, and followed by no domestic convulsion. Our industrial pursuits have received no check, the cultivation of our fields has progressed as heretofore, and even should we be involved in war, there would be no considerable diminution in the production of the staples which have constituted our exports, and in which the commercial world has an interest scarcely less than our own. This common interest of the producer and consumer can only be interrupted by an exterior force which should obstruct its transmission to foreign markets — a course of conduct which would be as unjust toward us as it would be detrimental to manufacturing and commercial interests abroad. Should reason guide the action of the Government from which we have separated, a policy so detrimental to the civilized world, the Northern States included, could not be dictated by even the strongest desire to inflict injury upon us ; but otherwise a terrible responsibility will rest upon it, and the suffering of millions will bear testimony to the folly and wickedness of our aggressors. In the meantime there will remain to us, besides the ordinary means before suggested, the well-known resources for retaliation upon the commerce of the enemy. . . .

It is joyous, in the midst of perilous times, to look around upon a people united in heart, where one purpose of high resolve animates and actuates the whole ; where the sacrifices to be made are not weighed in the balance against honor, and right, and liberty, and equality. Obstacles may retard, they cannot long prevent, the progress of a movement sanctified by its justice and sustained by a virtuous people. Reverently let us invoke the God of our fathers to guide and protect us in our efforts to perpetuate the principles which, by His blessing, they were able to vindicate, establish, and transmit to their posterity, and with a continuance of His favor ever gratefully acknowledged, we may hopefully look forward to success, to peace, and to prosperity.

The War of the Rebellion: Official Records of the Union and Confederate Armies, Fourth Series (Washington, 1900), I, 104–106 *passim*.

CHAPTER XI — QUESTION OF COMPROMISE

63. A Basis of Reconciliation (1860)

BY THURLOW WEED

As a journalist and politician Weed exerted great influence in the Whig and Republican parties, especially in New York. He was Seward's warmest supporter and friend throughout the political career of the latter, and this utterance was supposed to reflect Seward's opinion. During the Civil War he was able, in an unofficial capacity, to perform valuable services for the Union cause, both at home and abroad. These extracts are from editorials in his paper, the *Albany Evening Journal*, under dates November 24 and 30, 1860. — For Weed, see T. W. Barnes, *Memoir of Thurlow Weed*; F. Bancroft, *William H. Seward, passim.* — Bibliography: Channing and Hart, *Guide*, § 207.

Augusta, Nov. 23, [1860].

A RESOLUTION was offered in the Georgia Legislature, demanding the repeal, by Northern States, of laws obstructing the rendition of fugitive slaves; also, an enactment of Congress for removing obstructions by Territories in the introduction of all property; such action being contingent on Georgia remaining in the Union.

Here is something tangible. It suggests a basis on which negotiations can be inaugurated. South Carolina goes ahead without "rhyme or reason." There, it is not Disunion for cause, but Disunion *per se.*

Assuming the possibility of coming together in a fraternal spirit for the purpose of effecting "a more perfect union among the states," we are not without hopes that the result may prove auspicious. With a mutual desire to harmonize differences, let us suppose that in the place of a *vindictive* Fugitive Slave Law — a Law repugnant to manhood and honor — one should be enacted which arms the Federal Authorities with all needful power for its execution, together with a provision making Counties where Fugitives are rescued by violence, from Officers who have them in charge, liable for the value of the Slaves so rescued.

And in regard to the other vexed question, viz : the right of going into the Territories with Slaves, why not restore the Missouri Compromise Line? That secured to the South all Territory adapted, by soil and climate, to its "peculiar institution." . . .

The suggestions, in a recent number of *The Journal,* of a basis of settlement of differences between the North and the South, have, in awakening attention and discussion, accomplished their purpose. We knew that in no quarter would these suggestions be more distasteful than with our own most valued friends. . . .

To our dissenting friends, who will not question our devotion to freedom, however much they may mistrust our judgment, we submit a few earnest admonitions :

1. There is imminent danger of a dissolution of the Union.

2. This danger originated in the ambition and cupidity of men who desire a Southern despotism ; and in the fanatic zeal of Northern Abolitionists, who seek the emancipation of slaves regardless of consequences.

3. The danger can only be averted by such moderation and forbearance as will draw out, strengthen, and combine the Union sentiment of the whole country.

The Disunion sentiment is paramount in at least seven States ; while it divides and distracts as many more. Nor is it wise to deceive ourselves with the impression that the South is not in earnest. It *is* in earnest ; and the sentiment has taken hold of all classes with such blind vehemence as to " crush out " the Union sentiment.

Now, while, as has been said, it is easy to prove all this unjust and wrong, we have to deal with things as they are — with facts as they exist — with people blinded by passion. Peaceable Secession is not intended ; nor is it practicable, even if such were its object. Mad, however, as the South is, there is a Union sentiment there worth cherishing. It will develop and expand as fast as the darkness and delusion, in relation to the feelings of the North, can be dispelled. This calls for moderation and forbearance. We do not, when our dwelling is in flames, stop to ascertain whether it was the work of an incendiary before we extinguish the fire. Hence our suggestions of a basis of adjustment, without the expectation that they would be accepted, in terms, by either section, but that they might possibly inaugurate a movement in that direction. The Union is worth preserving. And, if worth preserving, suggestions in its behalf, however crude, will not be contemned. A victorious party can afford to be tolerant — not, as our friends assume, in the abandonment or abasement of its principles or character — but in efforts to correct and disabuse the minds of those who misunderstand both.

Before a final appeal — before a resort to the " rough frown of war " —

we should like to see a Convention of the People, consisting of delegates appointed by the States. . . .

It will be said that we have done nothing wrong, and have nothing to offer. This, supposing it true, is precisely the reason why we should both propose and offer whatever may, by possibility, avert the evils of civil war, and prevent the destruction of our, hitherto, unexampled blessings of Union.

Many suppose that the North has nothing to lose by a division of the Union. Some even say that we must be gainers by it. We do not, for obvious reasons, intend to discuss this aspect of the question. But it is a mistake — a serious and expensive mistake. The North and South were wisely and by a good Providence united. Their interests, their welfare, their happiness, their glory, their destiny, is one. Separated, while the North languishes, the South becomes, first, a despotism, running riot, for a season, with unrestrained African Slavery, to share in time the fate of every tropical nation, whether despotism, monarchy, or republic. That fate, induced by the indolence, luxury, and laxity of the privileged few over the oppressed, degraded, and enslaved many, is anarchy and destruction. That fate is written in the history of all enslaved nations — its ancient, seared, and crumbling, but instructive, monuments are seen in Egypt, in Italy, in Central America, and in Mexico.

These are the evils — and they are not imaginary — that we desire to avert. But, conscious of the feebleness of a single voice in such a tempest, there is little to expect but to abide its peltings. The Republican party now represents one side of a controversy fraught with the safety and welfare of this Government and nation. As an individual, we shall endeavor to do our duty ; and, as we understand it, that duty does not consist in folded arms, or sealed ears, or closed eyes. Even if . . . the North stands, in all respects, blameless in this controversy, much is needed to correct the impression of the Southern people ; many of whom, truly informed, would join us in defending the Union. We do not mistake the mission of the Republican party in assuming that, while defending free territory from aggression, it maintains and upholds the supremacy of the Constitution and laws. The people have intrusted the Government to our keeping ; and we must not abuse their confidence or disappoint their expectations.

Albany Evening Journal, November 24 and 30, 1860; reprinted (in part) in Horace Greeley, *The American Conflict* (Hartford, etc., 1864), I, 360–361.

64. Helplessness of the Administration (1860)

BY PRESIDENT JAMES BUCHANAN

Buchanan held many honorable positions under the United States government. When president, his subservience to the radical southern faction was early shown and extremely marked. Hence, when the crisis came, he found himself isolated and helpless, and sent the timid annual message to Congress from which this extract is taken. — For Buchanan, see G. T. Curtis, *Life of James Buchanan.* — Bibliography as in No. 63 above.

WHY is it . . . that discontent now so extensively prevails, and the union of the States, which is the source of all these blessings is threatened with destruction?

The long continued and intemperate interference of the northern people with the question of slavery in the southern States has at length produced its natural effects. . . .

Self-preservation is the first law of nature, and has been implanted in the heart of man by his Creator, for the wisest purpose ; and no political union, however fraught with blessings and benefits in all other respects, can long continue, if the necessary consequence be to render the homes and the firesides of nearly half the parties to it habitually and hopelessly insecure. Sooner or later the bonds of such a Union must be severed. It is my conviction that this fatal period has not yet arrived ; and my prayer to God is, that he would preserve the Constitution and the Union throughout all generations.

But let us take warning in time, and remove the cause of danger. It cannot be denied that for five and twenty years the agitation at the North against slavery has been incessant. . . .

How easy would it be for the American people to settle the slavery question forever, and to restore peace and harmony to this distracted country ! They, and they alone, can do it. All that is necessary to accomplish the object, and all for which the slave States have ever contended, is to be let alone and permitted to manage their domestic institutions in their own way. As sovereign States, they and they alone are responsible before God and the world for the slavery existing among them. For this the people of the North are not more responsible, and have no more right to interfere, than with similar institutions in Russia or in Brazil.

Upon their good sense and patriotic forbearance, I confess, I still greatly rely. Without their aid it is beyond the power of any President, no matter what may be his own political proclivities, to restore peace and harmony among the States. Wisely limited and restrained as is his power under our Constitution and laws, he alone can accomplish but little for good or for evil on such a momentous question. . . .

. . . secession is neither more nor less than revolution. It may or it may not be a justifiable revolution ; but still it is revolution.

What, in the meantime, is the responsibility and true position of the Executive? He is bound by solemn oath, before God and the country, " to take care that the laws be faithfully executed," and from this obligation he cannot be absolved by any human power. But what if the performance of this duty, in whole or in part, has been rendered impracticable by events over which he could have exercised no control? Such, at the present moment, is the case throughout the State of South Carolina, so far as the laws of the United States to secure the administration of justice by means of the federal judiciary are concerned. All the federal officers within its limits, through whose agency alone these laws can be carried into execution, have already resigned. We no longer have a district judge, a district attorney, or a marshal in South Carolina. In fact, the whole machinery of the federal government necessary for the distribution of remedial justice among the people has been demolished, and it would be difficult, if not impossible, to replace it. . . .

Then, in regard to the property of the United States in South Carolina. This has been purchased for a fair equivalent, " by the consent of the legislature of the State," " for the erection of forts, magazines, arsenals," &c., and over these the authority " to exercise exclusive legislation," has been expressly granted by the Constitution to Congress. It is not believed that any attempt will be made to expel the United States from this property by force ; but if in this I should prove to be mistaken, the officer in command of the forts has received orders to act strictly on the defensive. In such a contingency the responsibility for consequences would rightfully rest upon the heads of the assailants.

Apart from the execution of the laws, so far as this may be practicable, the Executive has no authority to decide what shall be the relations between the federal government and South Carolina. He has been invested with no such discretion. He possesses no power to change the relations heretofore existing between them, much less to acknowledge the independence of that State. This would be to invest a mere executive officer with the power of recognizing the dissolution of the Confederacy among our thirty-three sovereign States. It bears no resemblance to the recognition of a foreign *de facto* government, involving no such responsibility. Any attempt to do this would, on his part, be a naked act of usurpation. It is, therefore, my duty to submit to Congress the whole question in all its bearings. The course of events is so rapidly hastening forward that the emergency may soon arise when you may be called upon to decide the momentous question whether you possess the power, by force of arms, to compel a State to remain in the Union. I should feel myself recreant to my duty were I not to express an opinion on this important subject.

The question fairly stated is: Has the Constitution delegated to Congress the power to coerce a State into submission which is attempting to withdraw or has actually withdrawn from the Confederacy? If answered in the affirmative, it must be on the principle that the power has been conferred upon Congress to declare and to make war against a State. After much serious reflection, I have arrived at the conclusion that no such power has been delegated to Congress or to any other department of the federal government. It is manifest, upon an inspection of the Constitution, that this is not among the specific and enumerated powers granted to Congress ; and it is equally apparent that its exercise is not " necessary and proper for carrying into execution " any one of these powers. So far from this power having been delegated to Congress, it was expressly refused by the convention which framed the Constitution. . . .

But, if we possessed this power, would it be wise to exercise it under existing circumstances? The object would doubtless be to preserve the Union. War would not only present the most effectual means of destroying it, but would banish all hope of its peaceable reconstruction. Besides, in the fraternal conflict a vast amount of blood and treasure would be expended, rendering future reconciliation between the States impossible. In the meantime, who can foretell what would be the sufferings and privations of the people during its existence?

The fact is, that our Union rests upon public opinion, and can never be cemented by the blood of its citizens shed in civil war. If it cannot live in the affections of the people, it must one day perish. Congress possesses many means of preserving it by conciliation ; but the sword was not placed in their hand to preserve it by force.

But may I be permitted solemnly to invoke my countrymen to pause and deliberate, before they determine to destroy this, the grandest temple which has ever been dedicated to human freedom since the world began. . . .

It is not every wrong — nay, it is not every grievous wrong — which can justify a resort to such a fearful alternative.   This ought to be the last desperate remedy of a despairing people, after every other constitutional means of conciliation had been exhausted.   We should reflect that, under this free government, there is an incessant ebb and flow in public opinion.   The slavery question, like everything human, will have its day. I firmly believe that it has reached and passed the culminating point. But if, in the midst of the existing excitement, the Union shall perish, the evil may then become irreparable.

Congress can contribute much to avert it, by proposing and recommending to the legislatures of the several States the remedy for existing evils which the Constitution has itself provided for its own preservation. . . .

Senate Journal, 36 Cong., 2 sess. (Washington, 1860–1861), 7–17 *passim.*

---

65. Objections to Compromise (1860)

BY SENATOR BENJAMIN FRANKLIN WADE

The speech from which this excerpt is taken was delivered in the Senate, and represents the radical Republican feeling of the time. — For Wade, see No. 46 above. — Bibliography as in No. 63 above.

WELL, Mr. President, I have disavowed all intention on the part of the Republican party to harm a hair of your heads anywhere. We hold to no doctrine that can possibly work you an inconvenience. We have been faithful to the execution of all the laws in which you have any interest, as stands confessed on this floor by your own party, and as is known to me without their confessions.   It is not, then, that Mr. Lincoln is expected to do any overt act by which you may be injured ; you will not wait for any ; but anticipating that the Government may work an injury, you say you will put an end to it, which means simply, that you intend either to rule or ruin this Government. . . .

This brings me, sir, to the question of compromises.   On the first day of this session, a Senator rose in his place and offered a resolution for the appointment of a committee to inquire into the evils that exist between the different sections, and to ascertain what can be done to settle this great difficulty !   That is the proposition, substantially.   I tell the Senator that I know of no difficulty ; and as to compromises, I had

supposed that we were all agreed that the day of compromises was at
an end.   The most solemn compromises we have ever made have been
violated without a whereas. . . .

But what have we to compromise?   Sir, I am one of those who went
forth with zeal to maintain the principles of the great Republican party.
In a constitutional way we met, as you met.   We nominated our candidates for President and Vice President, and you did the same for yourselves.   The issue was made up ; and we went to the people upon it.
Although we have been usually in the minority ; although we have been
generally beaten, yet, this time, the justice of our principles, and the
maladministration of the Government in your hands, convinced the
people that a change ought to be wrought ; and after you had tried
your utmost, and we had tried our utmost, we beat you ; and we beat
you upon the plainest and most palpable issue that ever was presented
to the American people, and one that they understood the best.   There
is no mistaking it ; and now, when we come to the Capitol, I tell you
that our President and our Vice President must be inaugurated, and
administer the Government as all their predecessors have done.   Sir,
it would be humiliating and dishonorable to us if we were to listen to
a compromise by which he who has the verdict of the people in his
pocket, should make his way to the presidential chair.   When it comes
to that, you have no Government ; anarchy intervenes ; civil war may
follow it ; all the evils that may come to the human imagination may
be consequent upon such a course as that. . . .   Sir, I know not what
others may do ; but I tell you that, with the verdict of the people given
in favor of the platform upon which our candidates have been elected,
so far as I am concerned, I would suffer anything to come before I
would compromise that away.   I regard it as a case where I have no
right to extend comity or generosity.   A right, an absolute right, the
most sacred that a free people can ever bestow on any man, is their
undisguised, fair verdict, that gives him a title to the office that he is
chosen to fill ; and he is recreant to the principle of free government
who will ask a question beyond the fact whether a man has the verdict
of the people, or if he will entertain for a moment a proposition in addition to that.   It is all I want.   If we cannot stand there, we cannot
stand anywhere.   Any other principle than that would be as fatal to you,
my friends, as to us. . . .

. . . Sir, I do not believe there is a man on the other side who will
not do us more credit than to suppose that if the case were reversed,

there would be any complaint on our side. There never has been any from us under similar circumstances, and there would not be now. Sir, I think we have patriotism enough to overcome the pride and the prejudice of the canvass, and submit gracefully to the unmistakable verdict of the people; and as I have shown that you have nothing else to complain of, I take it that this is your complaint. Some of you have said that the election of Mr. Lincoln showed hostility to you and your institution. Sir, it is the common fate of parties to differ, and one does not intend to follow exactly the course of policy of the other; but when you talk of constitutional rights and duties, honest men will observe them alike, no matter to what party they belong.

I say, then, that so far as I am concerned, I will yield to no compromise. I do not come here begging, either. It would be an indignity to the people that I represent if I were to stand here parleying as to the rights of the party to which I belong. We have won our right to the Chief Magistracy of this nation in the way that you have always won your predominance; and if you are as willing to do justice to others as to exact it from them, you would never raise an inquiry as to a committee for compromises. . . . in my judgment, this long, chronic controversy that has existed between us must be met, and met upon the principles of the Constitution and laws, and met now. I hope it may be adjusted to the satisfaction of all; and I know no other way to adjust it, except that way which is laid down by the Constitution of the United States. Whenever we go astray from that, we are sure to plunge ourselves into difficulties. The old Constitution of the United States, although commonly and frequently in direct opposition to what I could wish, nevertheless, in my judgment, is the wisest and best Constitution that ever yet organized a free Government; and by its provisions I am willing, and intend, to stand or fall. Like the Senator from Mississippi, I ask nothing more. I ask no ingrafting upon it. I ask nothing to be taken away from it. Under its provisions a nation has grown faster than any other in the history of the world ever did before in prosperity, in power, and in all that makes a nation great and glorious. It has ministered to the advantages of this people; and now I am unwilling to add or take away anything till I can see much clearer than I can now that it wants either any addition or lopping off.

Congressional Globe, 36 Cong., 2 sess. (John C. Rives, Washington, 1861), 102–103 *passim*, December 17, 1860.

66. No Extension of Slavery (1860–1861)

BY PRESIDENT-ELECT ABRAHAM LINCOLN

After his election in November, 1860, Lincoln had to be consulted by those who were to be the Republican leaders in the next cabinet and Congress; and he repeatedly gave such cautions as appear in this piece. His influence probably prevented the adoption of the Crittenden Compromise, which he opposed because he thought it an unreasonable concession which could not permanently reconcile the two sections. — For Lincoln, see No. 44 above. — Bibliography: Channing and Hart, *Guide*, §§ 207, 208.

A. TO WILLIAM KELLOGG

[December 11, 1860.] ENTERTAIN no proposition for a compromise in regard to the extension of slavery. The instant you do they have us under again : all our labor is lost, and sooner or later must be done over. Douglas is sure to be again trying to bring in his "popular sovereignty." Have none of it. The tug has to come, and better now than later. You know I think the fugitive-slave clause of the Constitution ought to be enforced — to put it in its mildest form, ought not to be resisted.

B. TO GENERAL DUFF GREEN

[December 28, 1860.] MY *dear Sir:* I do not desire any amendment of the Constitution. Recognizing, however, that questions of such amendment rightfully belong to the American people, I should not feel justified nor inclined to withhold from them, if I could, a fair opportunity of expressing their will thereon through either of the modes prescribed in the instrument.

In addition I declare that the maintenance inviolate of the rights of the States, and especially the right of each State to order and control its own domestic institutions according to its own judgment exclusively, is essential to that balance of powers on which the perfection and endurance of our political fabric depend ; and I denounce the lawless invasion by armed force of the soil of any State or Territory, no matter under what pretext, as the gravest of crimes.

I am greatly averse to writing anything for the public at this time ; and I consent to the publication of this only upon the condition that six of the twelve United States senators for the States of Georgia, Alabama, Mississippi, Louisiana, Florida, and Texas shall sign their names to what is written on this sheet below my name, and allow the whole to be published together.

            Yours truly,   A. LINCOLN.

We recommend to the people of the States we represent respectively, to suspend all action for dismemberment of the Union, at least until some act deemed to be violative of our rights shall be done by the incoming administration.

C. TO WILLIAM H. SEWARD

[February 1, 1861.] . . . ON the 21st ult. Hon. W. Kellogg, a Republican member of Congress of this State, whom you probably know, was here in a good deal of anxiety seeking to ascertain to what extent I would be consenting for our friends to go in the way of compromise on the now vexed question. While he was with me I received a despatch from Senator Trumbull, at Washington, alluding to the same question and telling me to await letters. I therefore told Mr. Kellogg that when I should receive these letters posting me as to the state of affairs at Washington, I would write to you, requesting you to let him see my letter. To my surprise, when the letters mentioned by Judge Trumbull came they made no allusion to the "vexed question." This baffled me so much that I was near not writing you at all, in compliance to what I have said to Judge Kellogg. I say now, however, as I have all the while said, that on the territorial question — that is, the question of extending slavery under the national auspices — I am inflexible. I am for no compromise which assists or permits the extension of the institution on soil owned by the nation. And any trick by which the nation is to acquire territory, and then allow some local authority to spread slavery over it, is as obnoxious as any other. I take it that to effect some such result as this, and to put us again on the highroad to a slave empire, is the object of all these proposed compromises. I am against it. As to fugitive slaves, District of Columbia, slave-trade among the slave States, and whatever springs of necessity from the fact that the institution is amongst us, I care but little, so that what is done be comely and not altogether outrageous. Nor do I care much about New Mexico, if further extension were hedged against.

Abraham Lincoln, *Complete Works* (edited by John G. Nicolay and John Hay, New York, 1894), I, 657–669 *passim*.

67. "If Any One Attempts to Haul down the American Flag" (1861)

BY SECRETARY JOHN ADAMS DIX

Dix began his career as a young army officer in the War of 1812. Later he entered politics and became a member of the Albany Regency. For four years he held a seat in the United States Senate as a Democrat. When Buchanan's cabinet broke up in January, 1861, Dix became secretary of the treasury as a Union Democrat, and he sent this memorable telegram for the benefit of the captain of a revenue cutter who refused to obey his orders. When the war broke out, Dix accepted a major-general's commission and did good service. — For Dix, see Morgan Dix, *Memoirs of J. A. Dix.* — Bibliography as in No. 63 above.

Treasury Department, January 29, 1861.

TELL Lieutenant Caldwell to arrest Captain Breshwood, assume command of the cutter, and obey the order I gave through you. If Captain Breshwood, after arrest, undertakes to interfere with the command of the cutter, tell Lieutenant Caldwell to consider him as a mutineer, and treat him accordingly. If any one attempts to haul down the American flag, shoot him on the spot. JOHN A. DIX,
Secretary of the Treasury.

Morgan Dix, *Memoirs of John Adams Dix* (New York, 1883), I, 371.

◆

68. Last Effort at Compromise (1861)

REPORTED BY DELEGATE LUCIUS EUGENE CHITTENDEN

Chittenden was a delegate from Vermont to the peace conference, called by Virginia and attended by delegates from twenty-one states, including all the border states. This was a last attempt by the border states to recall the seceded states and restore the Union with slavery. An amendment on the slavery question, a proposed modification of which is described in the extract, was adopted by the convention by a narrow and inconclusive majority; it differed little from Crittenden's Compromise, and was not accepted by Congress. — Bibliography as in No. 63 above.

MR. FIELD . . . I will modify my motion, and state it in this way . . .

" It is declared to be the true intent and meaning of the present Constitution, that the Union of the States under it is indissoluble." . . .

Mr. COALTER : — We have not met here for any such purpose as that indicated in the present amendment. We are not here to discuss the question of secession. We are here because the Border States are alarmed for their own safety. We wish them to remain in the Union.

The purpose of our consultations is to make an arrangement under which they can stay in the Union.   If we do not confine ourselves to that purpose, and leave these questions alone, our differences may be submitted to a greater than any human judge.   I hope, in Heaven's name, they will not be submitted to the arbitrament of battle. . . .

Mr. PRICE . . . I believe in the doctrine of the gentleman from New York.   That is the doctrine of my State; but I believe in a great many other things which it is not necessary to insert in the Constitution. We came here to treat a fact, a great fact.   There is a Southern Confederacy — there is a President DAVIS — there is a Government organized within the Union hostile to the United States. . . .

. . . Shall we sit here debating abstract questions when State after State is seceding?   I hope not. . . .   We all agree to the principle contained in this amendment; but if we adopt it and make it a part of the Constitution, we could never, under it, bring back the seceded States.   They will not admit the principle.   What is to be gained, then, by adopting it? . . .

[Mr. KING.]   Myself and the majority of my colleagues differ from the majority of the Conference. . . .   We do not intend to be driven from our position by threats or by intimidation.   We believe that it is eminently proper for this Conference to express its decided convictions upon the question of secession.   We are told here that secession is a fact.   Then let us deal with it as such.   I go for the enforcement of the laws passed in pursuance of the Constitution.   I will never give up the idea that this is a Government of the people, and possessing within itself the power of enforcing its own decrees.   This I shall never do.   This Conference could perform no nobler act than that of sending to the country the announcement that the union of the States under the Constitution is indissoluble, and that secession is but another term for rebellion. . . .

I will occupy no farther time.   I wish to live in peace and harmony with our brethren in the slave States.   But I wish to put upon the record here a statement of the fact that this is a Government of the people, and not a compact of States.

Mr. PALMER . . . Are we to be gravely told that secession and treason are not proper subjects for our consideration?   To be told this when every mail that comes to us from the South is loaded with both these crimes?   Sir, we have commenced wrong.   The first thing we ought to have done was to declare that these were crimes, and that we would not negotiate with those who denied the authority of the Government, and claimed to have thrown off their allegiance to it. Far better would it be for the country if, instead of debating the question of slavery in reference to our Territories, we had set to work to strengthen the hands of the Government, and to put down the treason which threatens its existence.

You, gentlemen of the slave States, say that we of the North use fair words, that we promise fairly, but you insist that you will not rely upon our promises, and you demand our bond as security that we will keep them. I return the statement to you with interest. You, gentlemen, talk fairly also — give us your bond! You have been talking fairly for the last dozen or twenty years, and yet this treason, black as night, has been plotted among you, and twelve years ago one of your statesmen predicted the very state of things which now exists. I am willing to give bonds, but I want our action in this respect to be reciprocal. I want your bond against secession, and I ask it because seven States in sympathy with you have undertaken to set up an independent Government — have placed over it a military chieftain who asserts that we, the people of the United States, are foreigners, and must be treated with as a foreign nation.

. . . Will you, gentlemen of the South, declare that you will stand by the Union, and brand secession as treasonable? If you will, you must vote for this amendment.

Mr. HOWARD : — I am sure no member of this Conference could have listened to the remarks of the two gentlemen who have last spoken without the deepest regret. It has been intimated here that Maryland will secede unless she secures these guarantees. I do not know whether she will or not. I know there is danger that she will. . . .

Yes, gentlemen, we are all in danger. The storm is raging ; Virginia has hung her flag at half-mast as a signal of distress. If Virginia secedes our State will go with her, hand in hand, with Providence as our guide. This is not intended as a threat. GOD forbid ! It is a truth which we cannot and ought not to conceal.

Why will not New York and Massachusetts for once be magnanimous ? Why will they not follow the glorious example of Rhode Island? If they will, I should still have hope. But if those two great States are against us, I can see nothing but gloom in the future. . . .

The PRESIDENT : — The question now recurs on the amendment offered by the gentleman from New York — Mr. FIELD. . . .

. . . the amendment was disagreed to. . . .

Mr. WICKLIFFE : — I hope now that we may be permitted to take the vote at once upon the report of the majority.

Mr. REID : — Before this vote is taken, I deem it my duty to myself and my State to make a remark.

I came here disposed to agree upon terms that would be mutually satisfactory to both sections of the Union. I would agree to any fair terms now, but the propositions contained in the report of the majority, as that report now stands, can never receive my assent. I cannot recommend them to Congress or to the people of my own State. They do not settle the material questions involved ; they contain no sufficient guarantees for the rights of the South. Therefore, in good faith to the Conference and to the country, I here state that I cannot and will not agree to them.

Mr. CLEVELAND : — If the gentlemen from the South, after we have yielded so much as we have, assert that these propositions will not be satisfactory to the slave States, I, for one, will not degrade myself by voting for them. . . .

Mr. BARRINGER . . . I know the people of the South, and I tell you this hollow compromise will never satisfy them, nor will it bring back the seceded States. We are acting for the people who are not here. We are their delegates that have come here, not to demand indemnity for the past, but security for the future. . . .

Mr. STOCKTON . . . I have heard these discussions with pain from the commencement. Shall we deliberate over any proposition which shall save the Union? The country is in jeopardy. We are called upon to save it. New Jersey and Delaware came here for that purpose, and no other. They have laid aside every other motive ; they have yielded every thing to the general good of the country.

The report of the majority of the committee meets their concurrence. Republicans and Democrats alike, have dropped their opinions, for politics should always disappear in the presence of a great question like this. Politics should not be thought of in view of the question of disunion. By what measure of execration will posterity judge a man who contributed toward the dissolution of the Union? Shall we stand here and higgle about terms when the roar of the tornado is heard that threatens to sweep our Government from the face of the earth? Believe me, sir, this is a question of peace or war. . . .

The PRESIDENT . . . the question will be taken on the motion of the gentleman from Kentucky for the adoption of the first section, which the Secretary will now read.

SECTION I. In all the present territory of the United States north of the parallel of 36° 30′ of north latitude, involuntary servitude, except in punishment of crime, is prohibited. In all the present territory south of that line, the status of persons held to involuntary service or labor, as it now exists, shall not be changed; nor shall any law be passed by Congress or the Territorial Legislature to hinder or prevent the taking of such persons from any of the States of this Union to said territory, nor to impair the rights arising from said relation; but the same shall be subject to judicial cognizance in the Federal courts, according to the course of the common law. When any Territory north or south of said line, within such boundary as Congress may pre-scribe, shall contain a population equal to that required for a member of Congress, it shall, if its form of government be republican, be admitted into the Union on an equal footing with the original States, with or without involuntary servitude, as the Consti-tution of such State may provide.

The question on agreeing to said section resulted as follows — Indiana declining to vote :

AYES. — Delaware, Kentucky, Maryland, New Jersey, Ohio, Pennsylvania, Rhode Island, and Tennessee — 8.

NOES. — Connecticut, Illinois, Iowa, Maine, Massachusetts, Missouri, New York, North Carolina, New Hampshire, Vermont, and Virginia — 11.

And the section was not agreed to. . . .

The vote was taken in the midst of much partially suppressed excite-ment, and the announcement of the vote of different States occasioned many sharp remarks of dissent or approval. After the vote was an-nounced, for some minutes no motion was made, and the delegates engaged in an informal conversation.

Mr. TURNER finally moved a reconsideration of the vote.

Mr. GRANGER : — To say that I am disappointed by the result of this vote, would fail to do justice to my feelings. I move that the Con-ference adjourn until half-past seven o'clock this evening. I think it well for those gentlemen from the slave States especially, who have by their votes defeated the compromise we have labored so long and so earnestly to secure, to take a little time for consideration. Gentlemen we have yielded much to your fears, much to your apprehensions ; we have gone to the very verge of propriety in giving our assent to the committee's report. We have incurred the censure of some of our own people, but we were willing to take the risk of all this censure in order to allay your apprehensions. We expected you to meet us in the path of compromise. Instead of that you reject and spurn our propositions. Take time, gentlemen, for reflection. Beware how you spurn this report, and incur the awful responsibility which will follow. Reject it, and if the country is plunged in war, and the Union endangered, you are the men who will be held responsible. . . .

The motion to reconsider was then adopted by a vote of 14 ayes to 5 noes, and the Conference adjourned to seven o'clock and thirty minutes this evening.

L. E. Chittenden, *A Report of the Debates and Proceedings in the Secret Sessions of the Conference Convention, for proposing Amendments to the Constitution of the United States* (New York, 1864), 398–439 *passim*.

---

69. Explanation of the Crittenden Compromise (1861)

BY SENATOR JOHN JORDAN CRITTENDEN

Crittenden sat for many years in the Senate as a Whig, and was attorney-general in the cabinets of Harrison and Fillmore. As he came from Kentucky and shared most of Henry Clay's political beliefs, his love for the Union suggested compromises; when that hope failed, he adhered loyally to the Union. He supported Lincoln's administration, and did much to keep Kentucky in the Union; but his was a "house divided against itself," for one son served in the Union army and another in the Confederate army. This is an extract from a letter to Larz Anderson, of Cincinnati, March 29. — For Crittenden, see Ann M. Coleman, *Life of John J. Crittenden*. — Bibliography as in No. 63 above.

THE resolutions were proposed in the pure spirit of compromise, and with the hopes of preserving or restoring to the country peace and union. They were the result of the joint labors of, and consultation with, friends having the same object in view; and I believe if those measures thus offered had been at a suitable time promptly adopted by the Congress of the United States, it would have checked the progress of the rebellion and revolution, and saved the Union.

For myself, I had no objection to including in their scope all after-acquired territory, *because that made a final settlement of the distracting question of slavery in all time to come,* and because I hoped that such a provision — by prohibiting slavery in all the acquired territory north of the line of 36° 30' of north latitude, and allowing it in all south of that line — would have the effect of preventing any further acquisition of territory, as the Northern States would be unwilling to make any southern acquisitions, on which slavery was to be allowed, and the Southern States would not be inclined to increase the preponderance of the North by

P

northern acquisitions. And thus I hoped that the provision respecting future territory would prevent any further acquisitions of territory, and I did not desire that any more should be made.

These were my reasons for submitting the proposition in relation to future acquired territory. But my great object *was compromise*, — compromise on terms *satisfactory*, *as far as possible*, to all parties and all sections ; and when I found that this provision in my resolutions was much and particularly objected to, and might prove an obstacle to their adoption, I determined, in my anxiety for compromise, that I would not insist upon it, but would consent to have it stricken out.

To accomplish the great object I had in view, the peace and union of the country, I would, rather than have witnessed their total failure, have yielded to any modification of my resolutions that would not, in my judgment, have destroyed their essential character and their pacifying effect. Indeed, I intended, if opportunity had been afforded me, to make several amendments in the *phraseology* of those resolutions, in order to render their language as little offensive as possible.

I wish to see reconciliation and union established. It was of no importance by whose resolutions or by whose measures it was brought about, so that the great end was accomplished.

It was in that spirit, that when the Peace Conference or Convention, that met at Washington upon the invitation of the State of Virginia, made a report to Congress of the resolutions or measures recommended by them for the restoration of peace and union, I at once determined to support their measures rather than those I had before proposed. I did this, not only because their propositions contained, as I thought, the substance of my own, but because they came with the high sanction of a convention of twenty-one States, and would, therefore, be more likely to be acceptable to Congress and the country. Besides that, I felt myself somewhat bound to act with this deference to a convention so distinguished. I had ascertained to my satisfaction that the resolutions would not be adopted in the Senate.

Mrs. Chapman [Ann M.] Coleman, *The Life of John J. Crittenden, with Selections from his Correspondence and Speeches* (Philadelphia, 1871), II, 296-297.

CHAPTER XII — CRISIS OF FORT SUMTER

70. Shall Sumter be Relieved? (1861)

BY THE MEMBERS OF THE CABINET

On March 16 President Lincoln obtained written opinions from every member of his cabinet, and found that only two favored an attempt to relieve Fort Sumter. On March 29 he obtained a second set of opinions, which are printed in this extract. The question was complicated, depending upon both military and political considerations. On April 4 the President finally decided to send provisions to Anderson, and the Confederacy thereupon cut the Gordian knot by firing upon Sumter. — Bibliography: Nicolay and Hay, *Abraham Lincoln*, IV, ch. ii ; Channing and Hart, *Guide*, § 208.

MR. SEWARD, Secretary of State, wrote :

First. The despatch of an expedition to supply or reinforce Sumter would provoke an attack, and so involve a war at that point.

The fact of preparation for such an expedition would inevitably transpire, and would therefore precipitate the war, and probably defeat the object. I do not think it wise to provoke a civil war beginning at Charleston, and in rescue of an untenable position.

Therefore I advise against the expedition in every view.

Second. I would call in Captain M. C. Meigs forthwith. Aided by his counsel, I would at once, and at every cost, prepare for a war at Pensacola and Texas : to be taken, however, only as a consequence of maintaining the possessions and authority of the United States.

Third. I would instruct Major Anderson to retire from Sumter forthwith.

Mr. Chase, Secretary of the Treasury, wrote :

If war is to be the consequence of an attempt to provision Fort Sumter, war will just as certainly result from the attempt to maintain possession of Fort Pickens.

I am clearly in favor of maintaining Fort Pickens, and just as clearly in favor of provisioning Fort Sumter.

If that attempt be resisted by military force, Fort Sumter should, in my judgment, be reinforced.

If war is to be the result, I perceive no reason why it may not be best begun in consequence of military resistance to the efforts of the administration to sustain troops of the Union, stationed under the authority of the government, in a fort of the Union, in the ordinary course of service.

Mr. Welles, Secretary of the Navy, wrote :

I concur in the proposition to send an armed force off Charleston with supplies of provisions and reinforcements for the garrison at Fort Sumter, and of communicating at the proper time the intentions of the government to provision the fort peaceably if unmolested. There is little probability that this will be permitted if the opposing forces can prevent it. An attempt to force in provisions without reinforcing the garrison at the same time might not be advisable; but armed resistance to a peaceable attempt to send provisions to one of our own forts will justify the government in using all the power at its command to reinforce the garrison and furnish the necessary supplies.

Fort Pickens and other places retained should be strengthened by additional troops, and, if possible, made impregnable.

The naval force in the gulf and on the southern coast should be increased. Accounts are published that vessels having on board marketable products for the crews of the squadron at Pensacola are seized — the inhabitants we know are prohibited from furnishing the ships with provisions or water; and the time has arrived when it is the duty of the government to assert and maintain its authority.

Mr. Smith, Secretary of the Interior, wrote :

Viewing the question whether Fort Sumter shall be evacuated as a political one, I remark that the effect of its evacuation upon the public mind will depend upon the concurrent and subsequent action of the government. If it shall be understood that by its evacuation we intend to acknowledge our inability to enforce the laws, and our intention to allow treason and rebellion to run their course, the measure will be extremely disastrous and the administration will become very unpopular. If, however, the country can be made to understand that the fort is abandoned from necessity, and at the same time Fort Pickens and other forts in our possession shall be defended, and the power of the government vindicated, the measure will be popular and the country will sustain the administration.

Believing that Fort Sumter cannot be successfully defended, I regard its evacuation as a necessity, and I advise that Major Anderson's command shall be unconditionally withdrawn.

At the same time I would adopt the most vigorous measures for the defense of the other forts, and if we have the power I would blockade the Southern ports, and enforce the collection of the revenue with all the power of the government.

Mr. Blair, Postmaster-General, wrote . . .

Second. It is acknowledged to be possible to relieve Fort Sumter. It ought to be relieved without reference to Pickens or any other possession. South Carolina is the head and front of this rebellion, and when that State is safely delivered from the authority of the United States it will strike a blow against our authority from which it will take us years of bloody strife to recover.

Third. For my own part, I am unwilling to share in the responsibility of such a policy.

Mr. Bates, Attorney-General, wrote :

It is my decided opinion that Fort Pickens and Key West ought to be reinforced and supplied, so as to look down opposition at all hazards — and this whether Fort Sumter be or be not evacuated.

It is also my opinion that there ought to be a naval force kept upon the southern coast sufficient to command it and, if need be, actually close any port that practically ought to be closed, whatever other station is left unoccupied.

It is also my opinion that there ought to be immediately established a line of light, fast-running vessels, to pass as rapidly as possible between New York or Norfolk at the North and Key West or other point in the gulf at the South.

As to Fort Sumter, I think the time is come either to evacuate or relieve it.

Abraham Lincoln, *Complete Works* (edited by John G. Nicolay and John Hay, New York, 1894), II, 26–28 *passim.*

71. Breaking of the Storm (1861)

BY SECRETARY LEROY POPE WALKER, BRIGADIER-GENERAL
PIERRE GUSTAVE TOUTANT BEAUREGARD, AND
MAJOR ROBERT ANDERSON

Walker served as Confederate secretary of war during the first year of the Rebellion, but was not otherwise eminent. Beauregard had been an officer in the
United States army, but resigned to take charge of the Confederate defences of
Charleston: during the war he rose to the rank of general, and served with distinction in different parts of the Confederacy. Anderson was of southern birth, and a
veteran of thirty-five years' service in the United States army; his firm stand for the
Union and his sagacious operations in Charleston harbor, together with his sturdy
defence of Sumter, give him a just claim to remembrance among the preservers of the
Union. The attack on Sumter placed on the South the onus of aggression. — Bibliography as in No. 70 above.

CHARLESTON, *April* 8, 1861.
L. P. WALKER:

AUTHORIZED messenger from Lincoln just informed Governor
Pickens and myself that provisions would be sent to Sumter peaceably, otherwise by force.

G. T. BEAUREGARD. . . .

MONTGOMERY, *April* 10, 1861.

General BEAUREGARD, *Charleston:*

If you have no doubt of the authorized character of the agent who
communicated to you the intention of the Washington Government to
supply Fort Sumter by force you will at once demand its evacuation,
and if this is refused proceed, in such manner as you may determine, to
reduce it. Answer.

L. P. WALKER.

CHARLESTON, *April* 10, 1861.
L. P. WALKER:

The demand will be made to-morrow at 12 o'clock.

G. T. BEAUREGARD,
Brigadier-General. . . .

HEADQUARTERS PROVISIONAL ARMY, C. S. A.,
Charleston, S. C., April 11, 1861.

SIR: The Government of the Confederate States has hitherto forborne
from any hostile demonstration against Fort Sumter, in the hope that
the Government of the United States, with a view to the amicable

adjustment of all questions between the two Governments, and to avert the calamities of war, would voluntarily evacuate it.

There was reason at one time to believe that such would be the course pursued by the Government of the United States, and under that impression my Government has refrained from making any demand for the surrender of the fort. But the Confederate States can no longer delay assuming actual possession of a fortification commanding the entrance of one of their harbors, and necessary to its defense and security.

I am ordered by the Government of the Confederate States to demand the evacuation of Fort Sumter. My aides, Colonel Chesnut and Captain Lee, are authorized to make such demand of you. All proper facilities will be afforded for the removal of yourself and command, together with company arms and property, and all private property, to any post in the United States which you may select. The flag which you have upheld so long and with so much fortitude, under the most trying circumstances, may be saluted by you on taking it down.

Colonel Chesnut and Captain Lee will, for a reasonable time, await your answer.

I am, sir, very respectfully, your obedient servant,

G. T. BEAUREGARD,
Brigadier-General, Commanding.

Maj. ROBERT ANDERSON,
Commanding at Fort Sumter, Charleston Harbor, S. C.

FORT SUMTER, S. C., *April* 11, 1861.

GENERAL: I have the honor to acknowledge the receipt of your communication demanding the evacuation of this fort, and to say, in reply thereto, that it is a demand with which I regret that my sense of honor, and of my obligations to my Government, prevent my compliance. Thanking you for the fair, manly, and courteous terms proposed, and for the high compliment paid me,

I am, general, very respectfully, your obedient servant,

ROBERT ANDERSON,
Major, First Artillery, Commanding.

Brig. Gen. BEAUREGARD,
Commanding Provisional Army. . . .

MONTGOMERY, *April* 11, 1861.

General BEAUREGARD, *Charleston :*

Do not desire needlessly to bombard Fort Sumter. If Major Ander-son will state the time at which, as indicated by him, he will evacuate, and agree that in the mean time he will not use his guns against us unless ours should be employed against Fort Sumter, you are authorized thus to avoid the effusion of blood. If this or its equivalent be refused, reduce the fort as your judgment decides to be most practicable.

L. P. WALKER. . . .

HEADQUARTERS PROVISIONAL ARMY, C. S. A.,
Charleston, S. C., April 11, 1861.

MAJOR : In consequence of the verbal observation made by you to my aides, Messrs. Chesnut and Lee, in relation to the condition of your supplies, and that you would in a few days be starved out if our guns did not batter you to pieces, or words to that effect, and desiring no useless effusion of blood, I communicated both the verbal observations and your written answer to my communications to my Government.

If you will state the time at which you will evacuate Fort Sumter, and agree that in the mean time you will not use your guns against us unless ours shall be employed against Fort Sumter, we will abstain from open-ing fire upon you. Colonel Chesnut and Captain Lee are authorized by me to enter into such an agreement with you. You are, therefore, requested to communicate to them an open answer.

I remain, major, very respectfully, your obedient servant,

G. T. BEAUREGARD,
Brigadier-General, Commanding.

Maj. ROBERT ANDERSON,
Commanding Fort Sumter, Charleston Harbor, S. C.

FORT SUMTER, S.C., *April* 12, 1861.

GENERAL : I have the honor to acknowledge the receipt by Colonel Chesnut of your second communication of the 11th instant, and to state in reply that, cordially uniting with you in the desire to avoid the useless effusion of blood, I will, if provided with the proper and necessary means of transportation, evacuate Fort Sumter by noon on the 15th instant, and that I will not in the mean time open my fires upon your forces unless compelled to do so by some hostile act against this fort or the flag of my Government by the forces under your command, or by some portion of them, or by the perpetration of some act showing a hostile intention on your part against this fort or the flag it bears, should I not receive prior to that time controlling instructions from my Government or additional supplies.

I am, general, very respectfully, your obedient servant,

ROBERT ANDERSON,
Major, First Artillery, Commanding.

Brig. Gen. BEAUREGARD, *Commanding.*

FORT SUMTER, S. C., *April 12*, 1861—3.20 a. m.

SIR : By authority of Brigadier-General Beauregard, commanding the Provisional Forces of the Confederate States, we have the honor to notify you that he will open the fire of his batteries on Fort Sumter in one hour from this time.

We have the honor to be, very respectfully, your obedient servants,

JAMES CHESNUT, JR.,
Aide-de-Camp.

STEPHEN D. LEE,
Captain, C. S. Army, Aide-de-Camp.

Maj. ROBERT ANDERSON,
U. S. Army, Commanding Fort Sumter.

The War of the Rebellion: Official Records of the Union and Confederate Armies, First Series, (Washington, 1880) I, 13–301 *passim.*

---

72. Surrender of Fort Sumter (1861)

BY MAJOR JOHN GRAY FOSTER AND MAJOR ROBERT ANDERSON

Foster was in charge of the engineering operations of the United States troops at Charleston, and he had superintended the successful transfer from Fort Moultrie to Fort Sumter. During the war he rose to the command of departments. — For Anderson, see No. 71 above. — Bibliography as in No. 70 above.

A. FOSTER'S ACCOUNT

[April 12, 1861.] AT $4\frac{1}{2}$ a.m. a signal shell was thrown from the mortar battery on James Island ; after which the fire soon became general from all the hostile batteries. . . .

At 7 a.m. the guns of Fort Sumter replied, the first shot being fired

from the battery at the right gorge angle, in charge of Captain Doubleday. . . .

The supply of cartridges, 700 in number, with which the engagement
commenced, became so much reduced by the middle of the day, although
the six needles in the fort were kept steadily employed, that the firing
was forced to slacken, and to be confined to six guns — two firing towards
Morris Island, two towards Fort Moultrie, and two towards the batteries
on the west end of Sullivan's Island.

At 1 o'clock two United States men-of-war were seen off the bar, and
soon after a third appeared.

The fire of our batteries continued steadily until dark. The effect
of the fire was not very good, owing to the insufficient caliber of the
guns for the long range, and not much damage appeared to be done to
any of the batteries, except those of Fort Moultrie, where our two 42-
pounders appeared to have silenced one gun for a time, to have injured
the embrasures considerably, riddled the barracks and quarters, and torn
three holes through their flag. . . .

The effect of the enemy's fire upon Fort Sumter during the day was
very marked in respect to the vertical fire. This was so well directed
and so well sustained, that from the seventeen mortars engaged in firing
10-inch shells, one-half of the shells came within or exploded above the
parapet of the fort, and only about ten buried themselves in the soft
earth of the parade without exploding. In consequence of this precision
of vertical fire, Major Anderson decided not to man the upper tier of
guns, as by doing so the loss of men, notwithstanding the traverses and
bomb-proof shelters that I had constructed, must have been great. . . .

. . . The effect of the direct fire from the enemy's guns was not so
marked as the vertical. For several hours firing from the commencement a large proportion of their shot missed the fort. Subsequently it
improved, and did considerable damage to the roof and upper story
of the barracks and quarters, and to the tops of the chimneys on the
gorge. . . .

The night was very stormy, with high wind and tide. . . . The enemy
threw shells every ten or fifteen minutes during the night. The making
of cartridge bags was continued by the men, under Lieutenant Meade's
directions, until 12 o'clock, when they were ordered to stop by Major
Anderson. To obtain materials for the bags all the extra clothing of the
companies was cut up, and all coarse paper and extra hospital sheets
used.

April 13.— At daybreak no material alteration was observed in the enemy's batteries. The three U. S. men-of-war were still off the bar. The last of the rice was cooked this morning, and served with the pork — the only other article of food left in the engineer mess-room, where the whole command has messed since the opening of the fire. After this the fire was reopened, and continued very briskly as long as the increased supply of cartridges lasted. The enemy reopened fire at daylight, and continued it with rapidity. The aim of the enemy's gunners was better than yesterday. . . .

It soon became evident that they were firing hot shot from a large number of their guns, especially from those in Fort Moultrie, and at nine o'clock I saw volumes of smoke issuing from the roof of the officers' quarters, where a shot had just penetrated. From the exposed position it was utterly impossible to extinguish the flames, and I therefore immediately notified the commanding officer of the fact, and obtained his permission to remove as much powder from the magazine as was possible before the flames, which were only one set of quarters distant, should encircle the magazine and make it necessary to close it. All the men and officers not engaged at the guns worked rapidly and zealously at this, but so rapid was the spread of the flames that only fifty barrels of powder could be taken out and distributed around in the casemates before the fire and heat made it necessary to close the magazine doors and pack earth against them. . . . The whole range of officers' quarters was soon in flames. The wind being from the southward, communicated fire to the roof of the barracks, and this being aided by the hot shot constantly lodging there, spread to the entire roofs of both barracks, so that by twelve o'clock all the woodwork of quarters and of upper story of barracks was in flames. Although the floors of the barracks were fire-proof, the utmost exertions of the officers and men were often required to prevent the fire communicating down the stairways, and from the exterior, to the doors, window frames, and other woodwork of the east barrack, in which the officers and men had taken their quarters. All the woodwork in the west barrack was burned. The clouds of smoke and cinders which were sent into the casemates by the wind set on fire many boxes, beds, and other articles belonging to the men, and made it dangerous to retain the powder which had been saved from the magazine. The commanding officer accordingly gave orders to have all but five barrels thrown out of the embrasures into the water, which was done.

The small stock of cartridges now only allowed a gun to be fired at intervals of ten minutes. . . .

At 1 o'clock the flagstaff, having been struck twice before this morning, fell. The flag was immediately secured by Lieutenant Hall, and as soon as it could be attached to a temporary staff, hoisted again upon the parapet at the middle of the right face by Lieutenant Snyder, Corps of Engineers, assisted by Hart, and Davey, a laborer.

About this time information was brought to the commanding officer that Mr. Wigfall, bearing a white flag, was on the outside, and wished to see him. He accordingly went out to meet Mr. Wigfall, passing through the blazing gateway, accompanied by Lieutenant Snyder. In the mean time, however, Mr. Wigfall had passed to an embrasure on the left flank, where, upon showing the white flag upon his sword, he was permitted to enter, and Lieutenant Snyder entering immediately after, accompanied him down the batteries to where some other officers were posted, to whom Mr. Wigfall commenced to address himself, to the effect that he came from General Beauregard to desire that, inasmuch as the flag of the fort was shot down, a fire raging in the quarters, and the garrison in a great strait, hostilities be suspended, and the white flag raised for this object. He was replied to that our flag was again hoisted on the parapet, that the white flag would not be hoisted except by order of the commanding officer, and that his own batteries should set the example of suspending fire. He then referred to the fact of the batteries on Cummings Point, from which he came, having stopped firing, and asked that his own white flag might be waved to indicate to the batteries on Sullivan's Island to cease also. This was refused; but he was permitted to wave the white flag himself. . . .

At this moment the commanding officer, having re-entered through an embrasure, came up. To him Mr. Wigfall addressed nearly the same remarks that he had used on entering, adding some complimentary things about the manner in which the defense had been made, and ending by renewing the request to suspend hostilities in order to arrange terms of evacuation. The commanding officer desiring to know what terms he came to offer, Mr. Wigfall replied, " Any terms that you may desire — your own terms — the precise nature of which General Beauregard will arrange with you."

The commanding officer then accepted the conditions, saying that the terms he accepted were those proposed by General Beauregard on the 11th, namely: To evacuate the fort with his command, taking arms and all private and company property, saluting the United States flag as it was lowered, and being conveyed, if he desired it, to any northern port. With this understanding Mr. Wigfall left, and the white flag was raised and the United States flag lowered by order of the commanding officer.

Very soon after a boat arrived from the city, containing three aides of General Beauregard, with a message to the effect that, observing the white flag hoisted, General B. sent to inquire what aid he could lend in extinguishing the flames, &c. Being made acquainted with the condition of affairs and Mr. Wigfall's visit, they stated that the latter, although an aid of General Beauregard, had not seen him for two days.

The commanding officer then stated that the United States flag would be raised again, but yielded to the request of the aides for time to report to their chief and obtain his instructions. They soon returned, with the approval of all the conditions desired except the saluting of the flag as it was lowered, and this exception was subsequently removed after correspondence. In the morning communication was had with the fleet, and Captain Gillis paid a visit to the fort. . . .

B. ANDERSON'S REPORT

STEAMSHIP BALTIC, OFF SANDY HOOK,
April 18, [1861] — 10.30 a.m. — via New York.

HAVING defended Fort Sumter for thirty-four hours, until the quarters were entirely burned, the main gates destroyed by fire, the gorge walls seriously injured, the magazine surrounded by flames, and its door closed from the effects of heat, four barrels and three cartridges of powder only being available, and no provisions remaining but pork, I accepted terms of evacuation offered by General Beauregard, being the same offered by him on the 11th instant, prior to the commencement of hostilities, and marched out of the fort Sunday afternoon, the 14th instant, with colors flying and drums beating, bringing away company and private property, and saluting my flag with fifty guns.

ROBERT ANDERSON,
Major, First Artillery, Commanding.

Hon. S. CAMERON,
Secretary of War, Washington.

The War of the Rebellion: Official Records of the Union and Confederate Armies, First Series, (Washington, 1880) I, 12–24 *passim.*

73. Rising of the People (1861)

BY MRS. MARY ASHTON LIVERMORE (1887)

During the Civil War Mrs. Livermore was very prominent in the service of the
Sanitary Commission ; later she became noted as a lecturer and reformer. She is
still living in 1900. This extract describes a scene in Boston which was duplicated
throughout the whole North in a spontaneous movement that has no equal in American
history, and few parallels in the history of the world. — Bibliography as in No. 70 above.

THE day after my arrival, came the news that Fort Sumter was
attacked, which increased the feverish anxiety. The threats of
its bombardment had been discredited, for the North believed the
South to be as deeply rooted in attachment to the Union as it knew
itself to be. All its high-sounding talk of war was obstinately regarded
as empty gasconade, and its military preparations, as the idle bluster of
angry disappointment. When, therefore, the telegraph, which had registered for the astounded nation the hourly progress of the bombardment,
announced the lowering of the stars and stripes, and the surrender of the
beleaguered garrison, the news fell on the land like a thunderbolt. . . .

The next day, April 14, was Sunday. The pulpits thundered with
denunciations of the rebellion. Congregations applauded sermons such
as were never before heard in Boston, not even from radical preachers.
Many of the clergy saw with clear vision, at the very outset, that the
real contest was between slavery and freedom ; and, with the prophetic
instinct of the seer, they predicted the death of slavery as the outcome
of the war. . . .

Monday dawned, April 15. Who that saw that day will ever forget it !
For now, drowning the exultations of the triumphant South, louder than
their boom of cannon, heard above their clang of bells and blare of
trumpets, there rang out the voice of Abraham Lincoln calling for
seventy-five thousand volunteers for three months. They were for the
protection of Washington and the property of the government. All who
were in arms against the country were commanded to return home in
twenty days, and Congress was summoned to meet on the 4th of July.

This proclamation was like the first peal of a surcharged thunder-
cloud, clearing the murky air. The South received it as a declaration of
war, the North as a confession that civil war had begun ; and the whole
North arose as one man. The Union was not to be destroyed without
a struggle that would deluge the land with blood. The calls of the governors of the loyal states were met with a response so generous, that ten

times seventy-five thousand volunteers could have been furnished had they been asked. All the large cities and towns raised money for the volunteers and their families, and it was believed that abundant means were placed at the disposal of the general government for a speedy quelling of the rebellion.

Everywhere the drum and fife thrilled the air with their stirring call. Recruiting offices were opened in every city, town, and village. No stimulus was needed. The plough was left in the furrow ; the carpenter turned from the bench ; the student closed his books ; the clerk abandoned the counting-room ; the lawyer forsook his clients ; and even the clergyman exchanged his pulpit for the camp and the tented field, preaching no longer the gospel of peace, but the duty of war. Hastily formed companies marched to camps of rendezvous, the sunlight flashing from gun-barrel and bayonet, and the streets echoing the measured tread of soldiers. Flags floated from the roofs of houses, were flung to the breeze from chambers of commerce and boards of trade, spanned the surging streets, decorated the private parlor, glorified the schoolroom, festooned the church walls and pulpit, and blossomed everywhere. All normal habits of life were suspended, and business and pleasure alike were forgotten.

. . . When, on the morning of Tuesday, volunteers began to arrive in Boston . . . they were escorted by crowds cheering vociferously. Merchants and clerks rushed out from stores, bareheaded, saluting them as they passed. Windows were flung up ; and women leaned out into the rain, waving flags and handkerchiefs. Horse-cars and omnibuses halted for the passage of the soldiers, and cheer upon cheer leaped forth from the thronged doors and windows. The multitudes that followed after, and surged along on either side, and ran before in dense and palpitating masses, rent the air with prolonged acclamations.

As the men filed into Faneuil Hall, in solid columns, the enthusiasm knew no bounds. Men, women, and children seethed in a fervid excitement. " God bless it ! " uttered my father in tender and devout tone, as he sat beside me in the carriage, leaning heavily forward on his staff with clasped hands. And following the direction of his streaming eyes, and those of the thousands surrounding us, I saw the dear banner of my country, rising higher and higher to the top of the flagstaff, fling out fold after fold to the damp air, and float proudly over the hallowed edifice. Oh, the roar that rang out from ten thousand throats ! Old men, with white hair and tearful faces, lifted their hats to the national ensign, and reverently saluted it.   Young men greeted it with fierce and wild hurrahs, talking the while in terse Saxon of the traitors of the Confederate States, who had dragged in the dirt this flag of their country, never before dishonored. . . .

That day cartridges were made for the regiments by the hundred thousand.   Army rifles were ordered from the Springfield Armory. Fifteen hundred workmen were engaged for the Charlestown Navy Yard.   Enlistments of hardy-looking men went on vigorously, and hundreds of wealthy citizens pledged pecuniary aid to the families of the soldiers.   Military and professional men tendered their services to the government in its present emergency.   The Boston banks offered to loan the state three million six hundred thousand dollars without security, while banks outside the city, throughout the state, were equally generous in their offers.   By six o'clock on the afternoon of Tuesday, April 16, three regiments were ready to start for Washington, and new companies were being raised in all parts of the state.   On the afternoon of the next day, the Sixth Massachusetts, a full regiment one thousand strong, started from Boston by rail, leaving the Fourth Massachusetts to follow.

An immense concourse of people gathered in the neighborhood of the Boston and Albany railroad station to witness their departure.   The great crowd was evidently under the influence of deep feeling, but it was repressed, and the demonstrations were not noisy.   In all hands were evening editions of the daily papers ; and as the record of the disloyal behavior of Maryland and Virginia was read aloud, the comments were emphatic in disapproval.   With the arrival of the uniformed troops, the excitement burst out into a frenzy of shouts, cheers, and ringing acclamation.   Tears ran down not only the cheeks of women, but those of men ; but there was no faltering.   A clergyman mounted an extemporized platform, to offer prayer, where he could be seen and heard by all, and a solemn hush fell on the excited multitude, as if we were inside a church.   His voice rang out to the remotest auditor.   The long train backed down where the soldiers were scattered among mothers, wives, sweethearts, and friends uttering last words of farewell.

" Fall into line ! " was the unfamiliar order that rang out, clear and distinct, with a tone of authority.   The blue-coated soldiers released themselves tenderly from the clinging arms of affection, kissed again, and again, and again, the faces upturned to theirs, white with the agony of parting, formed in long lines, company by company, and were marched into the cars.   The two locomotives, drawing the long train slowly out of the station, whistled a shrill "good-bye"—every engine in the neighborhood shrieked back an answering farewell—from the crowded streets, the densely packed station, the roofs of houses, the thronged windows, and the solid mass of human beings lining both sides of the track, further than the eye could see, there rang out a roar of good wishes, and parting words, accompanied with tears and sobs, and the waving of hats and handkerchiefs—and the Sixth Massachusetts was on its way to Washington. Ah, how little they, or we, foresaw the reception awaiting them in the streets of Baltimore!

Mary A. Livermore. *My Story of the War* (Hartford, A. D. Worthington & Co., 1889), 86–96 *passim*.

---

74. "It Came to Pass that there was War" (1861)

BY RICHARD GRANT WHITE (1863)

White was a prominent journalist, author, and scholar, ranking among the most learned of Shakesperian commentators. He had a fancy for anonymous publication; and his political satire, *The New Gospel of Peace*, from which this excerpt is taken, was so published. The book was of influence in crystallizing the spirit of loyalty in the North. The characters in the drama are easily recognizable: James Buchanan; the fire-eaters; Stephens of Georgia; Kennedy, chief of police in New York City; Robert Toombs; and Fernando Wood, mayor of New York. — Bibliography: Channing and Hart, *Guide*, §§ 207, 208.

1. NOW the time drew nigh when James should cease to rule in the land of Unculpsalm.

2. And the men of the North, save the Dimmichrats, among whom were the Pahdees, strove to have Abraham, who was surnamed the honest, made ruler in the place of James Facing-both-ways.

3. But the Phiretahs of the South said, Let us choose, and let the voices be numbered, and if our man be chosen, it is well, but if Abraham, we will destroy the nation.

4. But the men of the North believed them not, because of the Great Covenant, and because they trusted them to be of good faith in this matter. For among the men of the North, even those who lived by casting lots for gold, stood by the lot when it was cast. And the men of the North believed not that men of their own blood, whose sons were married unto their daughters, and whose daughters unto their sons, would faithlessly do this thing which they threatened.

5. But the men of the North knew not how the Niggah had driven out all other thoughts from the hearts of the men of the South, even so

that they would violate the Great Covenant, and set at naught the election according thereunto if it went against them.

6. And there were throughout the provinces of the land of Unculpsalm at the North great multitudes, Dimmichrats, of whom were the Pahdees, who were friends of the Phiretahs of the South, and wished them well, and labored with them ; for they said, It is by the alliance of the men of the South, and by reason of the everlasting Niggah, that we rule the land.

7. But they deceived themselves ; for it was the Phiretahs which ruled the land, using the Dimmichrats, and by the one thought of the everlasting Niggah.

8. Yet it came to pass that when the voices of the people were numbered, according to the Great Covenant, Abraham was chosen.

9. Then the Phiretahs of the South began to do as they had threatened ; and they gathered together in their provinces, and said, Our provinces shall no longer be a part of the land of Unculpsalm, for we will not have this man Abraham to rule over us.

10. Yet there were men of the South, a great multitude, among whom was Stephen, of Joarji, who said, Not so. Why will ye do this great evil and destroy the nation? It is right for us to respect the Great Covenant. If the man who had our voices had been chosen, the men of the North would have received him, and obeyed him as the chief ruler in the land of Unculpsalm ; and it is meet and right that we should do likewise, even according to the Great Covenant. Moreover, we have suffered no wrong at the hands of the new rulers ; and the old were men of our own choosing. Will ye make this land like unto Mecsicho?

11. But the Phiretahs would not hearken unto these men, and went on their way, and beat some of them, and hanged others, and threatened noisily, and gathering unto them all the people of the baser sort, and inflaming them with hate and strong drink, they set up a rule of terror throughout their provinces. For the Phiretahs were men of blood. So the Phiretahs prevailed over the men who would have respected the Great Covenant.

12. And the men of the North, both they who had given their voices for Abraham and they who had given their voices with the men of the South against him, were amazed and stood astounded. And they said among themselves, This is vain boasting and vaunting, such as we have seen aforetime, done for the sake of more compromise.

Q

13. (Now in the land of Unculpsalm, when a man humbled himself before another which threatened him, he was said to compromise.)

14. And the Dimmichrats, save those who had hearkened unto the ministers of Belial, said, Let us compromise ourselves again unto our Southern brethren, and it shall be well with us.

15. For they said among themselves, If the men of the South go, they and their provinces, there will be no more everlasting Niggah; and we shall cease to rule the land. And if they go not, behold then they will remember that we have compromised unto them, and they will again be gracious unto their servants, and will admit us unto a share in the government, and we shall rule the land as aforetime.

16. But the Phiretahs were wise in their generation, and they saw that the Dimmichrats were of no more use unto them, and that because the men of Belial had prevailed against the Dimmichrats, their power was gone in their provinces; and so as they could no more use the Dimmichrats, they would not listen to them, and spurned their compromising, and spat upon it, and went on to destroy the nation, and prepared to make war against Abraham if he should begin to rule over them.

17. Now in those days there was a man in Gotham named Ken Edee, who was chief captain of the watchmen of the city and the region round about; and in Joarji was a man named Robert, who dwelt among the tombs, and who was possessed of an evil spirit whose name was Blustah. And Robert was a Phiretah.

18. And Ken Edee, chief captain of the watch in Gotham, found arms going from Gotham to the Phiretahs in Joarji, and he seized them. For he said, Lest they be used to destroy the nation, and against the Great Covenant, which is the supreme law in the land of Unculpsalm, to which first belongeth my obedience.

19. Then Robert, who dwelt among the tombs, being seized upon by his demon Blustah, sent a threatening message unto Phernandiwud.

20. (For at this time Phernandiwud was chief ruler in the city of Gotham.)

21. Saying, Wherefore keep ye the arms of the Phiretahs? Give them unto us that we may make war against you, or it shall be worse for you.

22. Then Phernandiwud, because he hated the chief of the watchmen of Gotham, and because he hoped for the good success of the Phiretahs, compromised himself unto Robert, and crawled on his belly before him in the dust, and said, Is thy servant a man that he should

do this thing? Thy servant kept no arms, neither would he do so. Let them who have the evil spirit Bak Bohn do thus unto my lords the Phiretahs.   Behold, thy servant is no man, but a Phlunkee.

23. (Now the Phlunkees were men who had never had the spirit Bak Bohn, or who had had it cast out of them, because when they would have prostrated themselves and humbled themselves in the dust and compromised to their profit, the spirit rent them sore.   So they had each of them his Bak Bohn cast out of him.)

24. And the Phiretahs went on their way without hindrance.   For James, by facing both ways, faced neither ; and both of the men of the South and the men of the North he was not regarded.   And the nation spued him out of its mouth.

25. And Abraham ruled the land.   But the Phiretahs withstood him, and made war upon him, and drove his captains out of the strongholds which were in their provinces, and humbled the banner of Unculpsalm.

26. Then all the men of the North, even the Dimmichrats, of whom were the Pahdees, were exceeding wroth ; and they rose up against the Phiretahs of the South, and marched against them to drive them out of the strong places which they had seized, and to plant thereon again the banner of Unculpsalm.

27. For they all had exceeding reverence for the Great Covenant, and they were filled with pride of their nation, its might, and its wealth, and its vastness, and chiefly that its people were more free than any other people, and that its tillers of the soil and its wayfaring men could read and understand, and that there each man sat under his own vine and under his own fig tree with none to molest him or make him afraid. And they worshipped the banner of Unculpsalm, and its folds were unto them as the wings of a protecting angel.

28. Moreover, the Dimmichrats said, We have striven for our brethren of the South against the men of Belial, who teach that it is wrong to oppress the Niggah by the power of Unculpsalm, and now they can no longer use us they cast us off.   Behold, we will fight against them, lest, also, they make good their threats, and sever their provinces from our provinces, and there be no more everlasting Niggah, and our occupation be departed forever.

29. And thus it came to pass that there was war in the land of Unculpsalm.

[Richard Grant White], *The New Gospel of Peace according to St. Benjamin* (New York, [1863]), Book I, 17–21.

PART V

CONDITIONS OF WAR

CHAPTER XIII — THE NORTHERN PEOPLE

75. Good Advice to J. Davis (1861)

BY CHARLES FARRAR BROWNE (ARTEMUS WARD)

Under the *nom de plume* of " Artemus Ward," Mr. Browne, originally a journalist in Cleveland, became, during his brief career, the most famous and original of American humorists; and his satires on the causes and objects of the war were widely read. Lincoln much enjoyed his writings. — Bibliography of the conditions of the war : Channing and Hart, *Guide*, § 213.

. . . IN my travels threw the Sonny South I heared a heap of talk about Seceshon and bustin up the Union, but I didn't think it mounted to nothin. The politicians in all the villages was swearin that Old Abe (sometimes called the Prahayrie flower) shouldn't never be noggerated. They also made fools of theirselves in varis ways, but as they was used to that I didn't let it worry me much, and the Stars and Stripes continued for to wave over my little tent. Moor over, I was a Son of Malty and a member of several other Temperance Societies, and my wife she was a Dawter of Malty, an I sposed these fax would secoor me the infloonz and pertectiun of all the fust families. Alas ! I was dispinted. State arter State seseshed and it growed hotter and hotter for the undersined Things came to a climbmacks in a small town in Alabamy, where I was premtorally ordered to haul down the Stars & Stripes. A deppytashun of red-faced men cum up to the door of my tent ware I was standin takin money (the arternoon exhibishun had commenst, an' my Italyun organist was jerkin his sole-stirrin chimes.) "We air cum, Sir," said a millingtary man in a cockt hat, "upon a hi and holy mishun. The Southern Eagle is screamin threwout this sunny land — proudly and defiantly screamin, Sir ! "

" What's the matter with him," sez I, " don't his vittles sit well on his stummick ? "

" That Eagle, Sir, will continner to scream all over this Brite and tremenjus land ! "

" Wall, let him *scream*. If your Eagle can amuse hisself by screamin, let him went ! " The men annoyed me for I was Bizzy makin change.

" We are cum, Sir, upon a matter of dooty —— "

" You're right, Capting. It's every man's dooty to visit my show," sed I.

" We air cum —— "

" And that's the reason you are here ! " sez I, larfin one of my silvery larfs. I thawt if he wanted to goak I'd giv him sum of my sparklin eppygrams.

" Sir, you're inserlent. The plain question is, will you haul down the Star-Spangled Banner, and hist the Southern flag ! "

" Nary hist ! " Those was my reply.

" Your wax works and beests is then confisticated, & you air arrested as a Spy ! " . . .

I was carrid to Montgomry in iuns and placed in durans vial. The jail was a ornery edifiss, but the table was librally surplied with Bakin an Cabbidge. This was a good variety, for when I didn't hanker after Bakin I could help myself to the cabbige.

I had nobody to talk to nor nothing to talk about, howsever, and I was very lonely, specially on the first day ; so when the jailer parst my lonely sell I put the few stray hairs on the back part of my hed (I'm bald now, but thare was a time when I wore sweet auburn ringlets) into as dish-hevild a state as possible, & rollin my eyes like a manyyuck, I cride : "Stay, jaler, stay ! I am not mad but soon shall be if you don't bring me suthing to Talk ! " He brung me sum noospapers, for which I thanked him kindly.

At larst I got a interview with Jefferson Davis, the President of the Southern Conthieveracy. He was quite perlite, and axed me to sit down and state my case. I did it, when he larfed and said his gallunt men had been a little 2 enthoosiastic in confisticatin my show.

" Yes," sez I, " they confisticated me too muchly. I had sum hosses confisticated in the same way onct, but the confisticaters air now poundin stun in the States Prison in Injinnapylus."

" Wall, wall, Mister Ward, you air at liberty to depart ; you air frendly to the South, I know.   Even now we hav many frens in the North, who sympathise with us, and won't mingle with this fight."

"J. Davis, there's your grate mistaik.   Many of us was your sincere frends, and thought certin parties amung us was fussin about you and meddlin with your consarns intirely too much.   But J. Davis, the minit you fire a gun at the piece of dry-goods called the Star-Spangled Banner, the North gits up and rises en massy, in defence of that banner. Not agin you as individooals, — not agin the South even — but to save the flag.   We should indeed be weak in the knees, unsound in the heart, milk-white in the liver, and soft in the hed, if we stood quietly by and saw this glorus Govyment smashed to pieces, either by a furrin or a intestine foe   The gentle-harted mother hates to take her naughty child across her knee, but she knows it is her dooty to do it.   So we shall hate to whip the naughty South, but we must do it if you don't make back tracks at onct, and we shall wallup you out of your boots ! J. Davis, it is my decided opinion that the Sonny South is making a egrejus mutton-hed of herself ! "

"Go on, sir, you're safe enuff.   You're too small powder for me ! " sed the President of the Southern Conthieveracy.

"Wait till I go home and start out the Baldinsvill Mounted Hoss Cavalry !   I'm Capting of that Corpse, I am, and J. Davis, beware ! Jefferson D., I now leave you !   Farewell my gay Saler Boy !   Good bye, my bold buccaneer !   Pirut of the deep blue sea, adoo ! adoo ! "

[Charles Farrar Browne], *Artemus Ward his Book* (New York, 1865), 162–169 *passim*.

---

76.   " Our Country's Call "   (1861)

BY WILLIAM CULLEN BRYANT

Bryant was the oldest of the greater American poets at the outbreak of the Civil War.   He was also a journalist, and as editor of the New York *Evening Post* had for many years been prominent as a fearless advocate of numerous good causes, including that of anti-slavery. — For Bryant, see Henry Matson, *References for Literary Workers*, 322–324. — Bibliography in No. 75 above.

LAY down the axe ; fling by the spade ;
    Leave in its track the toiling plough ;
The rifle and the bayonet blade
    For arms like yours were fitter now ;

And let the hands that ply the pen
　　Quit the light task, and learn to wield
The horseman's crooked brand, and rein
　　The charger on the battle field.

Our country calls; away! away!
　　To where the blood-stream blots the green.
Strike to defend the gentlest sway
　　That Time in all his course has seen.
See, from a thousand coverts — see,
　　Spring the armed foes that haunt her track;
They rush to smite her down, and we
　　Must beat the banded traitors back.

Ho! sturdy as the oaks ye cleave,
　　And moved as soon to fear and flight,
Men of the glade and forest! leave
　　Your woodcraft for the field of fight.
The arms that wield the axe must pour
　　An iron tempest on the foe;
His serried ranks shall reel before
　　The arm that lays the panther low.

And ye, who breast the mountain storm
　　By grassy steep or highland lake,
Come, for the land ye love, to form
　　A bulwark that no foe can break.
Stand, like your own gray cliffs that mock
　　The whirlwind, stand in her defence;
The blast as soon shall move the rock
　　As rushing squadrons bear ye thence.

And ye, whose homes are by her grand
　　Swift rivers, rising far away,
Come from the depth of her green land,
　　As mighty in your march as they;
As terrible as when the rains
　　Have swelled them over bank and bourne,
With sudden floods to drown the plains
　　And sweep along the woods uptorn.

And ye, who throng, beside the deep,
  Her ports and hamlets of the strand,
In number like the waves that leap
  On his long murmuring marge of sand,
Come, like that deep, when, o'er his brim,
  He rises, all his floods to pour,
And flings the proudest barks that swim,
  A helpless wreck, against his shore.

Few, few were they whose swords of old
  Won the fair land in which we dwell;
But we are many, we who hold
  The grim resolve to guard it well.
Strike, for that broad and goodly land,
  Blow after blow, till men shall see
That Might and Right move hand in hand,
  And glorious must their triumph be.

William Cullen Bryant, *Thirty Poems* (New York, D. Appleton & Co., 1864),
  104–107.

---

77. A War Meeting (1862)

FROM THE CHICAGO TRIBUNE

Under the editorship of Joseph Medill, the *Chicago Tribune* became one of the most prominent Republican papers in the West and a firm supporter of Lincoln's administration. The meeting described in this extract is typical of those held in all the larger cities of the North in answer to the president's call, on July 1, 1862, for three hundred thousand more volunteers. — Bibliography as in No. 75 above.

SATURDAY night was a night long to be remembered in the municipal annals of Chicago, as well as in the history of the State of Illinois. One occasion only has furnished its parallel — the public gatherings at the fall of Sumter. . . .

Bryan Hall was jammed to overflowing; Metropolitan Hall was full; five thousand people were in the Court House square. Earnest, able and eloquent speakers addressed them; patriotic songs were sung; voluntary contributions poured in; by unanimous vote men asked to be taxed to meet the present emergency. The vast assemblages were moved by one common impulse.

Perhaps the most gratifying feature of these meetings was the fixed determination that Chicago traitors must be rooted out.   Let it be done, root and branch.   Spare none of them, males or females.   They must leave this city instantly, every traitor and every sympathizer with a traitor. . . .

A prevailing characteristic of all the meetings was the unanimous and hearty approval of every sentiment favorable to the confiscation of rebel property, foraging upon the enemy, and the employment of the blacks in fighting against the rebels.   Every allusion to either of the measures was greeted with thunders of applause.   Every man was in favor of employing the negro upon the trenches, of arming him to fight, if necessary, and of giving him his freedom for it.   These sentiments most eloquently urged by noted speakers, spoken in plain terms by common men, found a lodgment in the great popular heart, and that heart gave back a response with no uncertain sound. . . . *Vox populi, vox Dei* was never better exemplified.   The people always loyal, always true, have indeed risen to the full appreciation of the crisis and now demand in thunder tones that *every* means God has placed in our hands [are] to be used for the vigorous prosecution of this war, the swift and terrible retribution of its authors. . . .

Precisely at the ringing of the bells and firing of cannon, the doors of Bryan Hall were thrown open, and the immense crowd surging around the entrance rapidly poured in and filled up the hall, until every available inch of standing or sitting room was occupied.   The stage, which had been handsomely decorated with flags, was reserved for the speakers, prominent citizens, the committees and the band—Barnard's Light Guard Band.

About eight o'clock the band came forward and played Hail Columbia, Star Spangled Banner, and Yankee Doodle in a manner which appealed to the patriotism of the assemblage and called out the most enthusiastic applause.

After the close of the music, Eliphalet Wood, Esq., announced the . . . officers of the evening, who were elected. . . .

The meeting was then opened with a solemn and impressive prayer by Rev. Wm. H. Ryder, delivered amid profound silence. . . .

Dr. O. H. Tiffany came forward amid the most prolonged applause, which continued for several minutes.   He congratulated his fellow-citizens upon the character of the gathering. . . .

They were here to-night not for talk, but to provide for the removal of traitors from our homes, as well as the South ; to provide means for action. . . .

We first sent 70,000 men. The South sneered at us and said, "Send five to our one and you will not have enough." We would have been wise had we done so. Then we sent 500,000 men. With the first enlistment we taught them to skedaddle, with the second the Virginia reel, and with both the "Rogue's March." Now we propose to send 300,000 to teach them to keep step to the music of the Union. Will you do it? (Cries "We will.") Casting the horoscope of the nation's future, I dare believe when the hour of victory strikes in the hearing of the nations, it will ring out the same old note the first bell of liberty sounded, proclaiming "liberty throughout the land and to all the inhabitants." Our first struggle was for existence ; our second is for carrying liberty to all the earth. Southrons, your doom comes swiftly ! A gloom of settled resolution and determination rests on every countenance in the whole land. Men think as they never thought, feel as they never felt before, and will carry out their purposes with a fearful daring. The Southern almanacs are predicting an eclipse. That eclipse will come soon enough. God has made their sun so dark that they can see our stars in day time. Lay the stripes of our flag about traitors till they revere our stars. Say, brothers, you will be with our brave volunteers now in the field, and never lay down your arms till our flag waves triumphantly over every city and citadel in this country. (Tremendous applause.) . . .

Hon. Robert S. Wilson was introduced amidst great cheering. . . . It is well known that we all cannot fight and will not fight. He had a practical proposition to make to his friends Steele, Scammon and Kinzie. They had made a great deal of money under this government.

. . . His proposition to his friends who could not fight, was substantially this : He would furnish a list of all the property he had got, and he wanted the rest to do it. He would then give a deed of $200 worth of land to each of two men — two straightforward, honest, sober, straight-haired men who would volunteer. He would say to all these men, your property is good for nothing if the Republic is gone. If these men who have made their thousands can't contribute, they don't deserve the protection of the government. We have lived so long prosperously that we have forgotten our benefits. If you don't give down, I don't care how much the Southerners take from you if they ever get up here.

Hon. J. Y. Scammon being called for, said : This war had already cost him $50,000, and he was willing to give $50,000 more if it was necessary. He had given his only son. He would give $1,000 to the volunteers if it was necessary. . . .

Geo. C. Cook, Esq., in behalf of his firm offered $200 additional bounty to the first two men who would enlist. . . .

J. H. McVicker, Esq., had no land except that covered by mortgages. He wanted two good men to come to him Sunday or Monday and he would give them $100 a piece, green backs.

Judge Manierre, Chairman of the Committee on Resolutions, then read the following:

RESOLUTIONS. . . .

Resolved, That the people of Chicago reviewing the present position of our national struggle to put down this infamous " Hell born " rebellion, against the mildest, most beneficent government, vouchsafed to man, see nothing to discourage or dampen our hopes of the ultimate triumph of our arms, and the restoration and firm establishment of our glorious constitution in every part of our country.

Resolved, That the people of Chicago having entire confidence in the ability, integrity and patriotism of our chief magistrate, do most heartily approve of his call for 300,000 men, and relying with firm and unshaken confidence in the valor and patriotism of our young men, we here solemnly pledge our city to the State, and to the nation, for our full quota of men to share with our brothers already in the field, the perils and the glory of this terrible war, waged by ambitious traitors and the dupes of their perfidy, so long as a rebel hand shall dare to desecrate our flag, the emblem of our Union, or to resist the constitutional power of the government.

Resolved, That this assembly hail with delight and satisfaction, the omens of a more energetic and vigorous policy in the prosecution of the war, and that our soldiers are to be relieved from the fatigues, exposures and privations incident to the situation, as far as possible, by the use and application of every species of property claimed by rebels, which can be made to contribute to the comfort and efficiency of our soldiers or weaken the power of our enemies ; that we are firmly convinced such policy will arouse new energies and hopes in the hearts of our loyal people, and spread terror and dismay in the ranks of traitors, and will receive the approval of that God who ever giveth victory to the cause of truth and justice, without whose countenance no people can prosper, no government can stand. . . .

The President announced that J. G. Lumbard, Esq., would give a song. Mr. L. came forward and sang the Marseillaise in splendid style, the audience joining in the chorus. . . .

The . . . poem, entitled " Three Hundred Thousand More," was read amid great enthusiasm. . . .

Col. Hough read the following resolution :

Resolved, That this meeting in mass assembled instruct the Board of Supervisors of Cook county to meet at once and vote a tax of $200,000 to be used as a bounty for the first two regiments raised in this county, and the same be paid on his enlistment and being mustered into service at the rate of $100 to each man.

Upon motion the resolution was unanimously adopted. . . .

T. J. Sloan of Sloan's Commercial College, then took the floor, and said that he and others had already planned a regiment, and as the spokesman he offered convertible collaterals to the amount of $25,000. He stated that two full companies were already organized and had offered themselves for the regiment, and asked all the fighting young men present to call at his commercial hall and enroll forthwith. . . .

. . . Mr. Prior, the "heavy" man of McVicker's theatre, was called for, and made a brief, business like appeal to the young men to join his company.

Chicago Daily Tribune, July 21, 1862.

78.　"Voice of the Northern Women" (1861?)

BY PHŒBE CARY

Phœbe Cary and her sister Alice both attained distinction as writers. Phœbe, the younger sister, is remembered chiefly for her lyrics. The intense patriotism engendered by the crisis of civil war found voice in many passionate verses both north and south. — For the Cary sisters, see Mrs. M. C. (Ames) Hudson, *Memorial of Alice and Phœbe Cary.* — Bibliography as in No. 75 above.

ROUSE, freemen, the foe has arisen,
　　His hosts are abroad on the plain;
And, under the stars of your banner,
　　Swear never to strike it again!

O, fathers, who sit with your children,
　　Would you leave them a land that is free?
Turn now from their tender caresses,
　　And put them away from your knee.

O, brothers, we played with in childhood,
　　On hills where the clover bloomed sweet;
See to it, that never a traitor
　　Shall trample them under his feet.

O, lovers, awake to your duty
　　From visions that fancy has nursed;
Look not in the eyes that would keep you;
　　Our country has need of you first.

And we, whom your lives have made blessed,
  Will pray for your souls in the fight;
That you may be strong to do battle
  For Freedom, for God, and the Right.

We are daughters of men who were heroes;
  We can smile as we bid you depart;
But never a coward or traitor
  Shall have room for a place in our heart.

Then quit you like men in the conflict,
  Who fight for their home and their land;
Smite deep, in the name of Jehovah,
  And conquer, or die where you stand.

Lyrics of Loyalty (edited by Frank Moore, New York, 1864), 325–326

---

79.   Stand for the Union (1863)

BY EDWARD EVERETT

Edward Everett, type of the trained and polished public man, was at different times clergyman, educator, editor, orator, statesman, and diplomatist. In 1861 Everett advocated the policy of compromise, but when compromises failed he devoted his waning strength to appeals to crush the rebellion. This speech was delivered at the inauguration of the Union Club in Boston. — For Everett, see Massachusetts Historical Society, *Proceedings*, 1864–1865, pp. 101–170. — Bibliography as in No. 75 above.

AND now the great question which we have to settle is, Shall this mighty aggregate of prosperity perish, or shall it endure? Shall this imperial heritage of blessings descend unimpaired to our posterity, or shall it be ignominiously, profligately, thrown away? Shall the territory of the Union, late so happy under the control and adjustment of the National and State governments, be broken up into miserable fragments, sure to be engaged in constantly recurring border wars, and all lying at the mercy of foreign powers, or shall it preserve its noble integrity under the ægis of the National government? . . . Better at whatever cost, by whatever sacrifice, settle the question at once, and settle it forever.

For remember, my friends, that, in this desolating war, the government and loyal people of the country are the party assailed, and that they are clad in the triple armor of a just cause. . . .

We often hear it said that measures of compromise . . . would, in the winter of 1860–1861, have been accepted by the South, and would have prevented the war, and that similar measures, if now tendered, would restore the Union. I have no belief of either. Never since the war broke out has there been the slightest intimation that the South would treat with the United States, on any other basis than the recognition of the Confederacy and the dismemberment of the Union. . . .

. . . War is justly regarded as *one* of the greatest evils that can befall a nation, though it is not *the* greatest, and of this great evil civil war is the most deplorable form. . . . I want words to express the sorrow with which from the first I have contemplated, and unceasingly contemplate, the necessity laid upon us, to wage this war for the integrity of the Nation. I recoiled from it to the last. Few persons, I think, have entertained visions more glowing of the amount of blessings stored up for the latest posterity in the perpetual Union of the States. I had seen them already expanded from sixteen States and four million inhabitants, which were the numbers at the time of my birth, to a family of thirty-four States and a population augmented eightfold; and reason and imagination were alike tasked to find a limit to the natural growth of the country. But numbers and space are but the relation of material things. I saw exemplified in this Western world, long hidden, and late revealed, the idea of a form of government as nearly perfect as our frail nature admits, — prodigal of blessings to the millions now on the stage, and promising a share in the same rich inheritance to the millions on millions that should follow us. I grew up beneath the shadow of our beautiful flag, and often, when I have seen it floating on distant seas, my heart has melted at the thought of the beloved and happy land whose union was emblazoned on its streaming folds. On a hundred festive and patriotic occasions my voice has dwelt — would it had been more worthily — on the grateful theme; and my prayer to Heaven has been, that it might be hushed in death, rather than it should be compelled to abandon that auspicious strain. Not without deep solicitude I saw the angry clouds gathering in the horizon North and South; and I devoted the declining years of my life, with a kind of religious consecration, to the attempt to freshen the sacred memories that cluster round that dear and venerated name which I need not repeat, — memories which had survived the multiplying causes of alienation, and were so well calculated to strengthen the cords of the Union. To these humble efforts, and the time and labor expended upon them, — truly a labor of love, — I would, as Heaven is my witness, have cheerfully added the sacrifice of my life, if by so doing I could have averted the catastrophe. For that cause, I should have thought a few care-worn and weary years cheaply laid on the altar of my country.

But it could not be. A righteous Providence in its wisdom has laid upon us — even upon us — the performance of this great and solemn duty. It is now plain to the dullest perception, that the hour of trial could not be much longer delayed. The leaders of the Rebellion tell us themselves that they had plotted and planned it for an entire generation. It might have been postponed for four years or for eight years, but it was sure in no long time to come ; and if, by base compliance, we could have turned the blow from ourselves, it would have fallen with redoubled violence on our children.

Let us, then, meet it like men. It must needs be that offences shall come, but woe unto that man by whom the offence cometh. Let us show ourselves equal to the duty imposed upon us, and faithful to the trust to which we are called. The cause in which we are engaged is the cause of the Constitution and the Law, of civilization and freedom, of man and of God. Let us engage in it with a steadiness and fortitude, a courage and a zeal, a patience and a resolution, a hope and a cheer, worthy of the fathers from whom we are descended, of the country we defend, and of the privileges we inherit. There is a call and a duty, a work and a place, for all ; — for man and for woman, for rich and for poor, for old and for young, for the stout-hearted and strong-handed, for all who enjoy and all who deserve to enjoy the priceless blessings at stake. Let the venerable forms of the Pilgrim Fathers, the majestic images of our Revolutionary sires, and of the sages that gave us this glorious Union ; let the anxious expectation of the Friends of Liberty abroad, awakened at last to the true cause and the great issues of this contest ; let the hardships and perils of our brethren in the field, and the fresh-made graves of the dear ones who have fallen ; let every memory of the past and every hope of the future, every thought and every feeling, that can nerve the arm, or fire the heart, or elevate and purify the soul of a patriot, — rouse and guide and cheer and inspire us to do, and, if need be, to die, for our Country !

Edward Everett, *Orations and Speeches on Various Occasions* (Boston, 1868), IV, 557–588 *passim*.

CHAPTER XIV — THE SOUTHERN PEOPLE

80. In the Confederate Congress (1862–1863)

BY REPRESENTATIVE REUBEN DAVIS (1889)

For Davis, see No. 58 above. — Bibliography : Channing and Hart, *Guide*, §§ 204, 209.

THUS dawned upon Richmond and the South the morning of the 22d of February [1862], appointed for the ceremonial of inauguration and the meeting of the two houses of Congress. . . .

I have been often spoken of as a man of an over-sanguine temperament, prone to see things through the medium of my hopes rather than of my fears, but I will confess that at this time I could not be accused of any undue cheerfulness of spirit. Every step taken up to that time had been, as I thought, defeated by tardiness of movement and inadequate preparation, and I could discover no indications of an improved system for the future.

In a conversation which I had about this time with Mr. Benjamin, the secretary of war, he said to me, " There is no doubt that the Southern Confederacy will be recognized by England in ninety days, and that ends the war." I asked him if he would not, in the mean time, make vigorous preparations, and endeavor to drive the enemy out of Tennessee.

He replied that it was wholly unnecessary. I then said that even if recognition by England was certain, and that it would certainly end the war, there might be grave questions to be considered, and grave consequences to be provided for. As for example, if the peace should be declared, each party would, of course, claim all the territory held when the war closed. Was Mr. Benjamin prepared to give up Tennessee and Kentucky?

His answer was, " We shall hold from the Memphis and Charleston Road south, and the Northern States can keep what is north of that line." I was astonished by this reply, and told him plainly that if we could hope for no better result than he promised, I, for one, would rather go back in the Union without further bloodshed.

Speaker Bocock was prompt in reporting committees, and I was put upon the military committee. . . . After a few days, I discovered, with sincere regret, that I could not honestly declare myself in harmony with the other members of the committee or with the administration. There was a radical and irreconcilable difference in our views upon all the questions and measures of the war. This sprang from the fact that I was for a bold, aggressive policy, while they advocated caution and delay.

I believed that our only hope was to concentrate all the forces we could raise into two great invading columns, and then boldly carry the war into the enemy's country. I argued that it depended largely upon which side took the initiative steps, which section should be invaded, wasted, and destroyed.

Other members of the committee were confident that the war would be ended in ninety days, and they were opposed to what they considered useless expense. The cry of the demagogue rang long and loud, "The poor people must not be taxed." This is a favorite watchword for those who court popularity, and I have heard it used with some success both before and since that time.

Realizing this condition of affairs, I made application to the House to be relieved from further connection with the committee, upon the ground that I was an obstacle to its progress. I was excused, and had not afterwards any connection with any committee. . . .

. . . In the fall of 1863 [1862] a bill was introduced into the House, exempting from military service any man who owned twenty negroes. It was referred to a committee, and reported back favorably, and a speech of half an hour in length made in support of the bill.

I replied in a speech of the same length in opposition.

I then called for the ayes and noes. The call was granted as a favor to me, and, perhaps, in some derision of the foreseen result. I was very earnest in my opposition to the bill, and warned the House that to pass such a measure would be to disband the army. My vote was the only one cast against it, the House voting for it with some clamor and vociferation. There was some laughter over my isolated stand-point, but I said, "Laugh on, my merry gentlemen, in a short time you will laugh on the wrong side of your faces!"

A few members afterwards changed their votes to " No." The effect of the bill was just what might have been anticipated. No sooner was the news carried to the army than the soldiers became infuriated. The officers had great difficulty in keeping the army together until Congress could meet and repeal the obnoxious law.

I remember well what a scene we had when Congress met, and the Speaker announced the House ready for business. Fifty members sprang to their feet, and offered resolutions to repeal this law, each eager to be before all others in his recantation. The Speaker recognized Mr. Dowdle, of Alabama, sent from some point on the Coosa River. The rules were suspended, and the resolution hastily passed.

It was my turn to laugh then. . . .

After the fall of Fort Donelson, and the surrender of the troops under command of General Floyd, General Sidney Johnston fell back from Bowling Green to Nashville, pursued by the large force under General Buell.

General Johnston reached Nashville successfully, but was so over-matched that he continued his retreat to Murfreesboro. The Tennessee delegations, at this intelligence, became so wild with rage that they demanded the instant removal of General Johnston. They were frantic with grief and rage, and would listen to no reason.

The President stood firm. He declared that if General Johnston was not an able general, not one could be found in the Confederacy. The most violent attacks and savage denunciations were made against him.

Now I had been at Bowling Green for two months, and had learned there not only to feel confidence in General Johnston's ability and devotion to the cause, but to understand something of the difficulties of his position. I knew how small his army was, and how unwilling the war department had been to allow him reinforcements. He had stood for months with a mere handful of men, badly armed and equipped, and so poorly fed that the men were hardly fit for duty, before a large force, splendidly appointed and furnished with abundant supplies.

Knowing all this, I felt bound to defend General Johnston to the extent of my ability. In my speech I denounced the whole policy of the war, and the stupendous folly of the provisional Congress in entering upon a gigantic conflict with such puerile and inadequate preparation.

This speech gave great offence to the administration, so that I had afterwards no influence, nor indeed much personal intercourse, with heads of government.   I felt from that time that I was a mere spectator in the final acts of our tragedy.

In May, 1864 [1863], I became satisfied that the immense augmentation of the enemy's military resources, already so disproportioned to our own, took away almost every hope of success still remaining in our hearts.

The only hope I could see — and it was born of desperation — was in concentrating our entire forces into two invading columns ; one under General R. E. Lee in Virginia, and the other at Tullahoma in Tennessee.   I went to the adjutant-general's department, and was informed that it would be possible to supply General Lee with two hundred and fifty thousand efficient soldiers.   This would necessitate the abandonment of every defensive point in Georgia, South Carolina, North Carolina, and Virginia, and the calling in of quartermasters, commissioners, and their laborers.   It was also stated that a force of equal magnitude could be furnished General Johnston at Tullahoma.   This would require the abandonment of Vicksburg, Fort Hudson, Mobile, and other points in Mississippi and elsewhere.

For this purpose I prepared a bill, providing that these measures should be carried out, and that General Lee should move, as soon as the result was accomplished, upon some point on the Potomac, and carry out the scheme of invasion.   Also that General Johnston should advance upon General Buell, then near Nashville, driving him, if possible, across the Ohio River, and making every effort to invade the enemy's country.   I endeavored to show that this movement by General Johnston would force General Grant to abandon Vicksburg and the whole South, and put himself upon his own territory to repel invasion. Two such armies on the Potomac and Ohio rivers would have driven the enemy to divide their forces into several grand divisions to defend important points, and left Lee and Johns[t]on to choose their points of attack, or to remain in camp until some adjustment of difficulties could be negotiated.   I urged these measures with what little force of argument I possessed, though with small hope of success.   The bill received but two votes besides my own.

Upon the announcement of this result, I sat down at my desk and wrote out my resignation, and sent a copy to the speaker, and one to the governor.

Reuben Davis, *Recollections of Mississippi and Mississippians* (Boston, etc., 1891), 429–437 *passim*.

81. Home Life of a Southern Lady (1862–1865)

BY MRS. VICTORIA VIRGINIA CLAYTON (1899)

Mrs. Clayton was the wife of a prominent lawyer and planter in Alabama before the Civil War. During the war her husband rose to the rank of major-general in the Confederate army; on the restoration of peace he became a state judge, and later president of the University of Alabama. — Bibliography as in No. 80 above.

WHILE my husband was at the front doing active service, suffering fatigue, privations, and the many ills attendant on a soldier's life, I was at home struggling to keep the family comfortable.

We were blockaded on every side, could get nothing from without, so had to make everything at home ; and having been heretofore only an agricultural people, it became necessary for every home to be supplied with spinning wheels and the old-fashioned loom, in order to manufacture clothing for the members of the family. This was no small undertaking. I knew nothing about spinning and weaving cloth. I had to learn myself, and then to teach the negroes. Fortunately for me, most of the negroes knew how to spin thread, the first step towards clothmaking. Our work was hard and continuous. To this we did not object, but our hearts sorrowed for our loved ones in the field.

Our home was situated a mile from the town of Clayton. On going to town one day I discovered a small bridge over which we had to pass that needed repairing. It was almost impassable. I went home, called some of our men, and gave them instructions to get up the necessary articles and put the bridge in condition to be passed over safely. I was there giving instructions about the work, when an old gentleman, our Probate Judge, came along. He stopped to see what we were doing. When satisfied, he said to me :

"Madam, I think we will never be conquered, possessing such noble women as we do." . . .

There was no white person on the plantation beside myself and children, the oldest of whom was attending school in Eufaula, as our Clayton schools were closed, and my time was so occupied that it was impossible for me to teach my children. Four small children and myself constituted the white family at home.

I entrusted the planting and cultivation of the various crops to old Joe. He had been my husband's nurse in infancy, and we always loved and trusted him. I kept a gentle saddle horse, and occasionally, accompanied by Joe, would ride over the entire plantation on a tour of inspection. Each night, when the day's work was done, Joe came in to make a report of everything that had been done on the plantation that day. When Mr. Clayton was where he could receive my letters, I wrote him a letter every night before retiring, and in this way he, being kept informed about the work at home, could write and make suggestions about various things to help me manage successfully.

We made good crops every year, but after the second year we planted provision crops entirely, except enough cotton for home use.

All the coloring matter for cloth had to be gathered from the forest. We would get roots and herbs and experiment with them until we found the color desired, or a near approach to it. We also found out what would dye cotton and what woolen fabrics. We had about one hundred head of sheep ; and the wool yielded by these sheep and the cotton grown in the fields furnished us the material for our looms. After much hard work and experience we learned to make very comfortable clothing, some of our cloth being really pretty.

Our ladies would attend services in the church of God, dressed in their home-spun goods, and felt well pleased with their appearances ; indeed, better pleased than if they had been dressed in silk of the finest fabric.

We made good warm flannels and other articles of apparel for our soldiers, and every woman learned to knit socks and stockings for her household, and many of the former were sent to the army.

In these dark days the Southern matron, when she sat down at night feeling that the day's work was over, took her knitting in her hands as a pastime, instead of the fancy work which ladies so frequently indulge in now.

I kept one woman at the loom weaving, and several spinning all the time, but found that I could not get sufficient cloth made at home ; consequently I gave employment to many a poor woman whose husband was far away. Many a time have I gone ten miles in the country with my buggy filled with thread, to get one of these ladies to weave a piece of cloth for me, and then in return for her labor sent her syrup, sugar, or any of our home produce she wished.

We always planted and raised large crops of wheat, rice, sugar cane, and potatoes. In fact, we grew almost everything that would make food for man or beast. Our land is particularly blessed in this respect. I venture to say there is no land under the sun that will grow a greater variety of products than the land in these Southern states.

Being blockaded, we were obliged to put our ingenuity to work to meet the demands on us as heads of families. Some things we could not raise ; for instance, the accustomed necessary luxury of every home — coffee. So we went to work to hunt up a substitute. Various articles were tried, but the best of all was the sweet potato. The potatoes were peeled, sliced, and cut into pieces as large as a coffee bean, dried, and then roasted just as we prepared coffee. This substitute, mixed with genuine coffee, makes a very palatable drink for breakfast. . . .

Another accustomed luxury of which we were deprived was white sugar. We had, however, a good substitute with which we soon became satisfied ; our home-made brown sugar, from the sugar cane. It had the redeeming quality of being pure. . . .

We made many gallons of wine from the scuppernong and other grapes every year. One year I remember particularly. Sheets were spread under the long scuppernong arbors, little negro boys put on top to throw the grapes down, and grown men underneath to gather them in baskets as they fell. When brought to the house they measured thirty-two bushels, and made one hundred and twenty gallons of wine. I did not make so large a quantity from the other varieties of grapes. This wine was kept in the cellar and used for the common benefit. When the negroes would get caught out in the rain, and come to the house wet, they did not hesitate to say, " Mistus, please give me a little wine to keep cold away ; " and they always received it. There never was any ill result from the use of domestic wine. We were a temperate family and the use was invariably beneficial.

Closed in as we were on every side, with nearly every white man of proper age and health enlisted in the army, with the country filled with white women, children, and old, infirm men, with thousands of slaves to be controlled, and caused through their systematic labor to feed and clothe the people at home, and to provide for our army, I often wonder, as I contemplate those by-gone days of labor and sorrow, and recall how peacefully we moved on and accomplished what we did.

We were required to give one-tenth of all that was raised, to the government. There being no educated white person on the plantation except myself, it was necessary that I should attend to the gathering and measuring of every crop and the delivery of the tenth to the government authorities. This one-tenth we gave cheerfully and often wished we had more to give.

My duties, as will be seen, were numerous and often laborious ; the family on the increase continually, and every one added increased labor and responsibility.   And this was the case with the typical Southern woman.

Victoria V. Clayton, *White and Black under the Old Régime* (Milwaukee, etc., [1899]), 113–124 *passim*.

* * *

82. "When Money was Easy" (1862–1865)

BY GEORGE CARY EGGLESTON (1874)

Eggleston (who is not to be confused with his brother Edward Eggleston) served during the Civil War as a private and subaltern in the Confederate army.   Since the war he has engaged in various literary pursuits, and has attained eminence as a newspaper editor. — Bibliography as in No. 80 above.

THE financial system adopted by the Confederate government was singularly simple and free from technicalities.   It consisted chiefly in the issue of treasury notes enough to meet all the expenses of the government, and in the present advanced state of the art of printing there was but one difficulty incident to this process ; namely, the impossibility of having the notes signed in the Treasury Department, as fast as they were needed.   There happened, however, to be several thousand young ladies in Richmond willing to accept light and remunerative employment at their homes, and as it was really a matter of small moment whose name the notes bore, they were given out in sheets to these young ladies, who signed and returned them for a consideration.   I shall not undertake to guess how many Confederate treasury notes were issued.   Indeed, I am credibly informed by a gentleman who was high in office in the Treasury Department, that even the secretary himself did not certainly know.   The acts of Congress authorizing issues of currency were the hastily formulated thought of a not very wise body of men, and my informant tells me they were frequently susceptible of widely different construction by different officials.   However that may be, it was clearly out of the power of the government ever to redeem the notes, and whatever may have been the state of affairs within the treasury, nobody outside its precincts ever cared to muddle his head in an attempt to get at exact figures.

We knew only that money was astonishingly abundant.   Provisions fell short sometimes, and the supply of clothing was not always as large as we should have liked, but nobody found it difficult to get money enough.   It was to be had almost for the asking.   And to some extent the abundance of the currency really seemed to atone for its extreme badness. . . .

. . . Money was so easily got, and its value was so utterly uncertain, that we were never able to determine what was a fair price for anything. We fell into the habit of paying whatever was asked, knowing that to-morrow we should have to pay more.   Speculation became the easiest and surest thing imaginable.   The speculator saw no risks of loss. Every article of merchandise rose in value every day, and to buy anything this week and sell it next was to make an enormous profit quite as a matter of course. . . .

Naturally enough, speculation soon fell into very bad repute, and the epithet " speculator " came to be considered the most opprobrious in the whole vocabulary of invective.   The feeling was universal that the speculators were fattening upon the necessities of the country and the sufferings of the people.   Nearly all mercantile business was regarded at least with suspicion, and much of it fell into the hands of people with no reputations to lose, a fact which certainly did not tend to relieve the community in the matter of high prices.

The prices which obtained were almost fabulous, and singularly enough there seemed to be no sort of ratio existing between the values of different articles.   I bought coffee at forty dollars and tea at thirty dollars a pound on the same day.

My dinner at a hotel cost me twenty dollars, while five dollars gained me a seat in the dress circle of the theatre.   I paid one dollar the next morning for a copy of the Examiner, but I might have got the Whig, Dispatch, Enquirer, or Sentinel, for half that sum.   For some wretched tallow candles I paid ten dollars a pound.   The utter absence of proportion between these several prices is apparent, and I know of no way of explaining it except upon the theory that the unstable character of the money had superinduced a reckless disregard of all value on the part of both buyers and sellers.   A facetious friend used to say prices were so high that nobody could see them, and that they " got mixed for want of supervision."   He held, however, that the difference between the old and the new order of things was a trifling one.   " Before the war," he said, " I went to market with the money in my pocket, and brought back my purchases in a basket ; now I take the money in the basket, and bring the things home in my pocket." . . .

. . . Everybody knew, long before the surrender, that these notes never could be redeemed. There was little reason to hope, during the last two years of the war, that the " ratification of a treaty of peace between the Confederate States and the United States," on which the payment was conditioned, would ever come. We knew the paper was worthless, and yet it continued to circulate. It professed to be money, and on the strength of that profession people continued to take it in payment for goods. The amount of it for which the owner of any article would part with his possession was always uncertain. Prices were regulated largely by accident, and were therefore wholly incongruous. . . .

In the winter of 1863–64 Congress became aware of the fact that prices were higher than they should be under a sound currency. If Congress suspected this at any earlier date, there is nothing in the proceedings of that body to indicate it. Now, however, the newspapers were calling attention to an uncommonly ugly phase of the matter, and reminding Congress that what the government bought with a currency depreciated to less than one per cent. of its face, the government must some day pay for in gold at par. The lawgivers took the alarm and sat themselves down to devise a remedy for the evil condition of affairs. With that infantile simplicity which characterized nearly all the doings and quite all the financial legislation of the Richmond Congress, it was decided that the very best way to enhance the value of the currency was to depreciate it still further by a declaratory statute, and then to issue a good deal more of it. The act set a day, after which the currency already in circulation should be worth only two thirds of its face, at which rate it was made convertible into notes of the new issue, which some, at least, of the members of Congress were innocent enough to believe would be worth very nearly their par value. This measure was intended, of course, to compel the funding of the currency, and it had that effect to some extent, without doubt. Much of the old currency remained in circulation, however, even after the new notes were issued. For a time people calculated the discount, in passing and receiving the old paper, but as the new notes showed an undiminished tendency to still further depreciation, there were people, not a few, who spared themselves the trouble of making the distinction. . . .

The government's course in levying a tax in kind, as the only possible way of making the taxation amount to anything, led speedily to the adoption of a similar plan, as far as possible, by the people. A physician would order from his planter friend ten or twenty visits' worth of corn, and the transaction was a perfectly intelligible one to both. The visits would be counted at ante-war rates, and the corn estimated by the same standard. . . .

How did people manage to live during such a time? I am often asked; and as I look back at the history of those years, I can hardly persuade myself that the problem was solved at all. A large part of the people, however, was in the army, and drew rations from the government. During the early years of the war, officers were not given rations, but were allowed to buy provisions from the commissaries at government prices. Subsequently, however, when provisions became so scarce that it was necessary to limit the amount consumed by officers as well as that eaten by the men, the purchase system was abolished, and the whole army was fed upon daily rations. The country people raised upon their plantations all the necessaries of life, and were generally allowed to keep enough of them to live on, the remainder being taken by the subsistence officers for army use. The problem of a salt supply, on which depended the production of meat, was solved in part by the establishment of small salt factories along the coast, and in part by Governor Letcher's vigorous management of the works in southwestern Virginia, and his wise distribution of the product along the various lines of railroad.

In the cities, living was not by any means so easy as in the country. Business was paralyzed, and abundant as money was, it seems almost incredible that city people got enough of it to live on. Very many of them were employed, however, in various capacities, in the arsenals, departments, bureaus, etc., and these were allowed to buy rations at fixed rates, after the post-office clerks in Richmond had brought matters to a crisis by resigning their clerkships to go into the army, because they could not support life on their salaries of nine thousand dollars a year. For the rest, if people had anything to sell, they got enormous prices for it, and could live a while on the proceeds. Above all, a kindly, helpful spirit was developed by the common suffering, and this, without doubt, kept many thousands of people from starvation. Those who had anything shared it freely with those who had nothing. There was no selfish looking forward, and no hoarding for the time to come. During those terrible last years, the future had nothing of pleasantness in its face, and people learned not to think of it at all. To get through to-day was the only care. Nobody formed any plans or laid by any money for to-morrow or next week or next year, and indeed to most of us there really seemed to be no future. . . .

Towards the last, as I have already said, resort was had frequently to

first principles, and bartering, or " payment in kind," as it was called,
became common, especially in those cases in which it was necessary to
announce prices in advance.   To fix a price for the future in Confederate money when it was daily becoming more and more exaggeratedly
worthless, would have been sheer folly ; and so educational institutions,
country boarding-houses, etc., advertised for patronage at certain prices,
payment to be made in provisions at the rates prevailing in September,
1860.   In the advertisement of Hampden Sidney College, in the Examiner for October 4, 1864, I find it stated that students may get
board in private families at about eight dollars a month, payable in this
way. The strong contrast between the prices of 1860 and those of 1864
is shown by a statement, in the same advertisement, that the students
who may get board at eight dollars a month in provisions, can buy wood
at twenty-five dollars a cord and get their washing done for seven
dollars and fifty cents a dozen pieces.

George Cary Eggleston, *A Rebel's Recollections* (New York, 1875), 78–105
passim.

------◆------

83. Life in the Confederate Capital (1865)

BY JOHN B. JONES

Jones was an author of various works in light literature, and a man who enjoyed
the close acquaintance of some prominent ante-bellum southern statesmen.   When
the Civil War began he accepted a clerkship in the war department of the Confederate government, in order that he might have " facilities to preserve interesting facts
for future publication."   This extract is from the diary in which he carried out
the purpose indicated. — Bibliography as in No. 80 above.

[January 9, 1865.]   WE have Hood's acknowledgment of defeat, and loss of 50 guns before
Nashville.

The papers contain the proceedings of a meeting in Savannah, over
which the Mayor presided, embracing the terms of submission offered
in President Lincoln's message.   They have sent North for provisions —
indicating that the city was in a famishing condition.   Our government
is to blame for this !   The proceedings will be used as a " form,"
probably, by other cities — thanks to the press !

The *Examiner* is out this morning for a convention of all the (Confederate) States, and denouncing the President.   I presume the object
is to put Lee at the head of military affairs. . . .

The Piedmont Railroad has been impressed.   A *secret* act of Congress authorizes it.

Miers W. Fisher writes that if the cabinet indorses the newspaper suggestions of giving up slavery and going under true monarchies, it is an invitation to refugees like himself to return to their homes, and probably some of the States will elect to return to the Union for the sake of being under a republican government, etc. . . .

Flour is $700 per barrel to-day; meal, $80 per bushel; coal and wood, $100 per load.   Does the government (alone to blame) mean to allow the rich speculators, the quartermasters, etc. to starve honest men into the Union? . . .

[January 10.]   We have nothing new in the papers this morning.   It is said with more confidence, however, that Butler's canal is not yet a success.   Daily and nightly our cannon play upon the works, and the deep sounds in this moist weather are distinctly heard in the city.

The amount of requisition for the War Department for 1865 is $670,000,000, and a deficiency of $400,000,000! . . .

A Mr. Lehman, a burly Jew, about thirty-five years old, got a passport to-day on the recommendation of the Secretary of the Treasury, to arrange as (agent, no doubt) for the shipment of several thousand bales of cotton, for which sterling funds are to be paid.   No doubt it is important to keep the government cotton out of the hands of the enemy; and this operation seems to indicate that some fear of its loss exists.

Some 40,000 bushels of corn, etc. were consumed at Charlotte, N. C., the other day.   A heavy loss !   Both the army and the people will feel it. There seems already to exist the preliminary symptoms of panic and anarchy in the government.   All the dignitaries wear gloomy faces; and this is a gloomy day — raining incessantly.   A blue day — a miserable day ! The city council put up the price of gas yesterday to $50 per 1000 feet. . . .

[January 11.]   Mr. E. A. Pollard, taken by the Federals in an attempt to run the blockade last spring, has returned, and reports that Gen. Butler has been relieved of his command — probably for his failure to capture Wilmington.   Mr. Pollard says that during his captivity he was permitted, on parole, to visit the Northern cities, and he thinks the Northern conscription will ruin the war party.

But, alas ! the lax policy inaugurated by Mr. Benjamin, and continued by every succeeding Secretary of War, enables the enemy to obtain information of all our troubles and all our vulnerable points.   The United

States can get recruits under the conviction that there will be little or no more fighting.

Some $40,000 worth of provisions, belonging to speculators, but marked for a naval bureau and the Mining and Niter Bureau, have been seized at Danville. This is well — if it be not too late.

A letter from Mr. Trenholm, Secretary of the Treasury, to Mr. Wagner, Charleston, S. C. (sent over for approval), appoints him agent to proceed to Augusta, etc., with authority to buy all the cotton for the government, at $1 to $1.25 per pound ; and then sell it for sterling bills of exchange to certain parties, giving them permission *to remove it within the enemy's lines;* or "better still," to have it shipped abroad on government account by *reliable* parties. This indicates a purpose to die "full-handed," if the government *must* die, and to defeat the plans of the enemy to get the cotton. Is the Federal *Government* a party to this arrangement? Gold was $60 for one yesterday. I suppose there is no change to-day . . .

Col. Sale, Gen. Bragg's military secretary, told me to-day that the general would probably return from Wilmington soon. His plan for filling the ranks by renovating the whole conscription system, will, he fears, slumber until it is too late, when ruin will overtake us ! If the President would only put Bragg at the head of the conscription business — *and in time* — we might be saved.

JANUARY 12TH. . . . Gold at $66 for one yesterday, at auction.

Major R. J. Echols, Quartermaster, Charlotte, N. C., says the fire there destroyed 70,000 bushels of grain, a large amount of sugar, molasses, clothing, blankets, etc. He knows not whether it was the result of design or accident. All his papers were consumed. A part of Conner's brigade on the way to South Carolina, 500 men, under Lieut.-Col. Wallace, refused to aid in saving property, but plundered it ! This proves that the soldiers were all poor men, the rich having bought exemptions or details ! . . .

Mr. Ould, to whom it appears the Secretary has written for his opinion . . . gives a very bad one on the condition of affairs. He says the people have confidence in Mr. *Seddon,* but not in President *Davis,* and a strong reconstruction party will spring up in Virginia rather than adopt the President's ideas about the slaves, etc. . . .

Mr. Miles introduced a resolution yesterday (in Congress) affirming that for any State to negotiate peace is *revolutionary. Ill timed, because self-evident.*

Gen. Bradley T. Johnson writes from Salisbury, N. C., that because the travel hither has been suspended by the government, the Central Railroad Company of that State *refuse* to send the full amount of trains for the transportation of soldiers.   It must be impressed too.

I am assured by one of the President's special detectives that Francis P. Blair, Sr. is truly in this city.   What for?   A rumor spreads that Richmond is to be evacuated.

Gen. Lee writes for the Secretary's sanction to send officers everywhere in Virginia and North Carolina, to collect provisions and to control railroads, etc.   The Secretary is sending orders to different commanders, and says *he* would rather have the odium than that it should fall on Lee ! The Commissary-General approves Lee's measure.

Gen. Lee's dispatch was dated last night.   He says he has not *two days'* rations for his army !

Commissary-General Northrop writes to the Secretary that the hour of emergency is upon us, and that Gen. Lee's name may "save the cause," if he proclaims the necessity of indiscriminate impressment, etc.

JANUARY 13TH. . . . Beef (what little there is in market) sells to-day at $6 per pound ; meal, $80 per bushel ; white beans, $5 per quart, or $160 per bushel.   And yet Congress is fiddling over stupid abstractions !

The government will awake speedily, however ; and after Congress hurries through its business (when roused), the adjournment of that body will speedily ensue.   But will the President dismiss his cabinet in time to save Richmond, Virginia, and the cause?   That is the question. He can easily manage Congress, by a few letters from Gen. Lee.   But will the potency of his cabinet feed Lee's army?

A great panic still prevails in the city, arising from rumors of contemplated evacuation.   If it should be evacuated, the greater portion of the inhabitants will remain, besides many of the employees of government and others liable to military service, unless they be forced away. But how can they be fed?   The government cannot feed, sufficiently, the men already in the field. . . .

I believe there is a project on foot to borrow flour, etc. from citizens for Gen. Lee's army.   Many officers and men from the army are in the city to-day, confirming the reports of suffering for food in the field. . . .

Mr. Secretary Seddon is appointing men in the various districts of the city to hunt up speculators and flour ; appointing such men as W. H. McFarland and others, who aspire to office by the suffrages of the people.   *They* will not offend the speculators and hoarders by taking much flour from them.   No — domiciliary visits with *bayonets* alone will suffice. . . .

It is understood that the President announced to Congress to-day the arrest of the Hon. H. S. Foote, member of that body, near Fredericksburg, while attempting to pass into the enemy's lines.   This, then, may have been Capt. Norton's secret mission ; and I believe the government had traps set for him at other places of egress.   Meantime the enemy *came in* at Savannah.   This is considered the President's foible — a triumph over a political or personal enemy will occupy his attention and afford more delight than an ordinary victory over the common enemy. Most men will say Mr. Foote should have been permitted to go — if he desired it.

JANUARY 14TH. . . . The news that Goldsborough, N. C., had been taken is not confirmed.   Nor have we intelligence of the renewal of the assault on Fort Fisher — but no one doubts it.

The government sent pork, butchered and salted a few weeks ago, to the army.   An order has been issued to borrow, buy, or impress flour, wherever found ; but our *political* functionaries will see that it be not executed.   The rich hoarders may control votes hereafter, when they may be candidates, etc.   If domiciliary visits were made, many thousands of barrels of flour would be found.   The speculators have not only escaped hitherto, but they have been exempted besides.

The Assembly of Virginia passed a resolution yesterday, calling upon the President to have revoked any orders placing restrictions upon the transportation of provisions to Richmond and Petersburg.   The President sends this to the Secretary, asking a copy of any orders *preventing carts from coming to market.*

Flour is $1,000 per barrel to-day ! . .

If Richmond be relinquished, it ought to be by convention and capitulation, getting the best possible terms for the citizens ; and not by evacuation, leaving them at the mercy of the invaders.   Will our authorities think of this?   Doubtful.

J. B. Jones, *A Rebel War Clerk's Diary at the Confederate States Capital* (Philadelphia, 1866), II, 381–386 *passim.*

CHAPTER XV — THE NORTHERN ARMIES

84. Enlisting (1861–1864)

BY JOHN DAVIS BILLINGS (1888)

Billings was a member of the Tenth Massachusetts battery of light artillery, which was mustered in September, 1862, and remained in service until the end of the war, during most of the period forming a part of the Army of the Potomac. — Bibliography : Channing and Hart, *Guide*, §§ 204, 210.

THE methods by which these regiments were raised were various. In 1861 a common way was for some one who had been in the regular army, or perhaps who had been prominent in the militia, to take the initiative and circulate an enlistment paper for signatures. His chances were pretty good for obtaining a commission as its captain, for his active interest, and men who had been prominent in assisting him, if they were popular, would secure the lieutenancies. On the return of the "Three months" troops many of the companies immediately re-enlisted in a body for three years, sometimes under their old officers. A large number of these short-term veterans, through influence at the various State capitals, secured commissions in new regiments that were organizing. In country towns too small to furnish a company, the men would post off to a neighboring town or city, and there enlist.

In 1862, men who had seen a year's active service were selected to receive a part of the commissions issued to new organizations, and should in justice have received *all* within the bestowal of governors. But the recruiting of troops soon resolved itself into individual enlistments or [on?] this programme ; — twenty, thirty, fifty or more men would go in a body to some recruiting station, and signify their readiness to enlist in a certain regiment *provided* a certain specified member of their number should be commissioned captain. Sometimes they would compromise, if the outlook was not promising, and take a lieutenancy, but equally often it was necessary to accept their terms, or count them out. In the rivalry for men to fill up regiments, the result often was officers who were diamonds in the rough, but liberally intermingled with *veritable clod-hoppers* whom a brief experience in active service soon sent to the rear.

This year the War Department was working on a more systematic basis, and when a call was made for additional troops each State was immediately assigned its quota, and with marked promptness each city and town was informed by the State authorities how many men it was to furnish under that call. . . .

The flaming advertisements with which the newspapers of the day teemed, and the posters pasted on the bill-boards or the country fence, were the decoys which brought patronage to these fishers of men. Here is a sample : —

More Massachusetts Volunteers Accepted ! ! !

Three Regiments to be Immediately Recruited !

GEN. WILSON'S REGIMENT,
To which CAPT. FOLLETT'S BATTERY is attached;
COL. JONES' GALLANT SIXTH REGIMENT,
WHICH WENT "THROUGH BALTIMORE";

THE N. E. GUARDS REGIMENT, commanded by that excellent officer, MAJOR J. T. STEVENSON.

The undersigned has this day been authorized and directed to fill up the ranks of these regiments forthwith. A grand opportunity is afforded for patriotic persons to enlist in the service of their country under the command of as able officers as the country has yet furnished. Pay and rations will begin immediately on enlistment.

UNIFORMS ALSO PROVIDED !

Citizens of Massachusetts should feel pride in attaching themselves to regiments from their own State, in order to maintain the proud supremacy which the Old Bay State now enjoys in the contest for the Union and the Constitution. The people of many of the towns and cities of the Commonwealth have made ample provision for those joining the ranks of the army. If any person enlists in a Company or Regiment out of the Commonwealth, he cannot share in the bounty which has been thus liberally voted. Wherever any town or city has assumed the privilege of supporting the families of Volunteers, the Commonwealth reimburses such place to the amount of $12 per month for families of three persons.

Patriots desiring to serve the country will bear in mind that

THE GENERAL RECRUITING STATION
IS AT
No. 14 PITTS STREET, BOSTON !

WILLIAM W. BULLOCK,
General Recruiting Officer, Massachusetts Volunteers.

(*Boston Journal* of Sept. 12, 1861.)

S

Here is a call to a war meeting held out-of-doors : —

TO ARMS!   TO ARMS!!

GREAT WAR MEETING
IN ROXBURY.

Another meeting of the citizens of Roxbury, to re-enforce their brothers in the field, will be held in

ELIOT SQUARE, ROXBURY,

THIS EVENING AT EIGHT O'CLOCK.

SPEECHES FROM

Paul Willard, Rev. J. O. Means, Judge Russell,

And other eloquent advocates.

The Brigade Band will be on hand early.   **Come one, come all!**

God and your Country Call!!

Per Order.

(*Boston Journal* of July 30, 1862.) . .

War meetings similar to the one called in Roxbury were designed to stir lagging enthusiasm.   Musicians and orators blew themselves red in the face with their windy efforts.   Choirs improvised for the occasion, sang "Red, White, and Blue" and "Rallied 'Round the Flag" till too hoarse for further endeavor.   The old veteran soldier of 1812 was trotted out, and worked for all he was worth, and an occasional Mexican War veteran would air his nonchalance at grim-visaged war.   At proper intervals the enlistment roll would be presented for signatures.   There was generally one old fellow present who upon slight provocation would yell like a hyena, and declare his readiness to shoulder his musket and go, if he wasn't so old, while his staid and half-fearful consort would pull violently at his coat-tails to repress his unseasonable effervescence ere it assumed more dangerous proportions.   Then there was a patriotic maiden lady who kept a flag or a handkerchief waving with only the rarest and briefest of intervals, who "would go in a minute if she was a man."   Besides these there was usually a man who would make one of fifty (or some other safe number) to enlist, when he well understood that such a number could not be obtained.   And there was one more often found present who when challenged to sign would agree to, *provided* that A or B (men of wealth) would put down *their* names. . . .

Sometimes the patriotism of such a gathering would be wrought up so intensely by waving banners, martial and vocal music, and burning eloquence, that a town's quota would be filled in less than an hour. It needed only the first man to step forward, put down his name, be patted on the back, placed upon the platform, and cheered to the echo as the hero of the hour, when a second, a third, a fourth would follow, and at last a perfect stampede set in to sign the enlistment roll, and a frenzy of enthusiasm would take possession of the meeting. The complete intoxication of such excitement, like intoxication from liquor, left some of its victims on the following day, especially if the fathers of families, with the sober second thought to wrestle with ; but Pride, that tyrannical master, rarely let them turn back.

John D. Billings, *Hardtack and Coffee, or The Unwritten Story of Army Life* (Boston, etc., 1888), 34–41 *passim*.

---

85. War Songs (1861–1864)

BY NORTHERN POETS

The Civil War was a people's war; and the camp, the march, the public meetings at home, and even the hospital were enlivened by patriotic songs. The northern songs given below include some often sung, chiefly of little poetic value, and one of less popularity but more literary merit. — For southern songs, see No. 91 below. — Bibliography as in No. 84 above.

A. "JOHN BROWN'S BODY"

(ANONYMOUS)

JOHN BROWN'S body lies a-mould'ring in the grave,
John Brown's body lies a-mould'ring in the grave,
John Brown's body lies a-mould'ring in the grave,
    His soul is marching on !

> *Chorus.* — Glory ! Glory Hallelujah !
>   Glory ! Glory Hallelujah !
>   Glory ! Glory Hallelujah !
>   His soul is marching on.

He's gone to be a soldier in the army of the Lord !
He's gone to be a soldier in the army of the Lord !

He's gone to be a soldier in the army of the Lord !
    His soul is marching on. — *Chorus.*

John Brown's knapsack is strapped upon his back.
    His soul is marching on. — *Chorus.*

His pet lambs will meet him on the way,
    And they'll go marching on. — *Chorus.*

They'll hang Jeff Davis on a sour apple tree,
    As they go marching on. — *Chorus.*

Now for the Union let's give three rousing cheers,
    As we go marching on.
        Hip, hip, hip, hip, Hurrah !

B. "THREE HUNDRED THOUSAND MORE"

By James Sloan Gibbons

WE are coming, Father Abraham, three hundred thousand more,
    From Mississippi's winding stream and from New England's
        shore ;
We leave our ploughs and workshops, our wives and children dear,
With hearts too full for utterance, with but a silent tear ;
We dare not look behind us, but steadfastly before :
We are coming, Father Abraham, three hundred thousand more !

If you look across the hilltops that meet the northern sky,
Long moving lines of rising dust your vision may descry ;
And now the wind, an instant, tears the cloudy veil aside,
And floats aloft our spangled flag in glory and in pride,
And bayonets in the sunlight gleam, and bands brave music pour :
We are coming, Father Abraham, three hundred thousand more !

If you look all up our valleys where the growing harvests shine,
You may see our sturdy farmer boys fast forming into line ;
And children from their mother's knees are pulling at the weeds,
And learning how to reap and sow against their country's needs ;
And a farewell group stands weeping at every cottage door :
We are coming, Father Abraham, three hundred thousand more !

You have called us, and we're coming, by Richmond's bloody tide
To lay us down, for Freedom's sake, our brothers' bones beside,
Or from foul treason's savage grasp to wrench the murderous blade,
And in the face of foreign foes its fragments to parade.
Six hundred thousand loyal men and true have gone before:
We are coming, Father Abraham, three hundred thousand more!

C. "WAR SONG"

BY WILLIAM WETMORE STORY

UP with the Flag of the Stripes and the Stars !
   Gather together from plough and from loom !
  Hark to the signal ! — the music of wars
Sounding for tyrants and traitors their doom.
     March, march, march, march !
    Brothers unite — rouse in your might,
     For Justice and Freedom, for God and the Right !

  Down with the foe to the Land and the Laws !
Marching together, our country to save,
  God shall be with us to strengthen our cause,
Nerving the heart and the hand of the brave.
     March, march, march, march !
    Brothers unite — rouse in your might,
     For Justice and Freedom, for God and the Right !

  Flag of the Free ! under thee we will fight,
Shoulder to shoulder, our face to the foe ;
  Death to all traitors, and God for the Right !
Singing this song as to battle we go :
     March, march, march, march !
    Freemen unite — rouse in your might,
     For Justice and Freedom, for God and the Right !

  Land of the Free — that our fathers of old,
Bleeding together, cemented in blood —
  Give us thy blessing, as brave and as bold,
Standing like one, as our ancestors stood —
     We march, march, march, march !

Conquer or fall !　Hark to the call :
Justice and Freedom for one and for all !

Chain of the slave we have suffered so long —
Striving together, thy links we will break !
Hark ! for God hears us, as echoes our song,
Sounding the cry to make Tyranny quake :
　　　March, march, march, march !
　　Conquer or fall !　Rouse to the call —
　Justice and Freedom for one and for all !

Workmen arise !　There is work for us now ;
Ours the red ledger for bayonet pen ;
　Sword be our hammer, and cannon our plough ;
Liberty's loom must be driven by men !
　　　March, march, march, march !
　　Freemen ! we fight, roused in our might,
　For Justice and Freedom, for God and the Right !

D.　"THE BATTLE-CRY OF FREEDOM"

By George Frederick Root

YES, we'll rally round the flag, boys, we'll rally once again,
　　Shouting the battle-cry of freedom,
We will rally from the hill-side, we'll gather from the plain,
　Shouting the battle-cry of freedom.

Chorus. — The Union forever, hurrah ! boys, hurrah,
　　　　Down with the traitor, up with the star,
　　　　While we rally round the flag, boys, rally once again,
　　　　Shouting the battle-cry of freedom.

We are springing to the call of our brothers gone before,
　　Shouting the battle-cry of freedom,
And we'll fill the vacant ranks with a million freemen more,
　Shouting the battle-cry of freedom. — *Chorus.*

We will welcome to our numbers the loyal, true, and brave,
　　Shouting the battle-cry of freedom,
And altho' they may be poor, not a man shall be a slave,
　Shouting the battle-cry of freedom. — *Chorus.*

So we're springing to the call from the East and from the West,
 Shouting the battle-cry of freedom,
And we'll hurl the rebel crew from the land we love the best,
 Shouting the battle-cry of freedom. — *Chorus.*

From reprints in *Lyrics of Loyalty* (edited by Frank Moore, New York, 1864),
78 ; *American War Ballads and Lyrics* (edited by George Cary Eggleston,
New York, etc., [1889]), II, 160, 271, 275.

———◆———

86. The Rough Side of Campaigning (1862)

BY MAJOR WILDER DWIGHT

Dwight, a member of a prominent Massachusetts family, is a good example of the
young volunteer officers of good birth and college education who were numerous in
both armies during the war. — Bibliography of the campaign : J. C. Ropes, *Story of
the Civil War*, II, vii–xii ; Channing and Hart, *Guide*, § 210.

CAMP NEAR EDINBURG, April 9, 1862.

*S*CENE, camp, snowing and raining, and blowing angrily ; *Time*,
 Tuesday morning. The Major Second Massachusetts Regiment
enters his tent, shaking the dripping oil-skin cap and India-rubber clothing. He discovers John, his John, surnamed Strong i' the arm, or Arm-
strong, digging a hole within the damp tent to receive some coals from
the hickory fire that is trying to blaze without. *John* (*loquitur*). Soger-
ing is queer business, sir. *M.* Yes, John. *J.* But it 's hard, too, sir,
on them that follers it. *M.* Yes, John. *J.* It 's asy for them as sits to
home, sir, by the fire, and talks about sogers and victories, very fine and
asy like. It 's little they know of the raal work, sir. *M.* Yes, John.
J. 'T would n't be quite the same, sir, if they was out here theirselves
trying to warm theirselves at a hole in the ground, sir. *M.* No, John.
Then the coals are brought on, and a feeble comfort is attained. The
woods are heavy without with snow and ice. In the afternoon I visit
the pickets, and spend a chilly and wearisome day. This morning is
again like yesterday. ———, who has shown himself a trump in our
recent exigencies, but who has certain eccentricities of manner and
speech, came to breakfast this morning, rubbing his hands and saying,
" You would n't hardly know that this was the South if you did n't keep
looking on the map, would you ? hey ? What say ? "

Since I wrote the above I have spent two hours in the hail-storm
visiting pickets. This, then, is an invasion of the South, query ? . . .

BIVOUAC NEAR NEW MARKET, VIRGINIA,
Raining from the East. Easter Sunday, April 20, 1862. . . .

After a short halt at Mount Jackson, which is a town, and filled with evidences of Rebel occupation, such as large hospitals, one of them unfinished, we were ordered to march round to " turn the enemy's left."

Our path was a rough one, through a river, over rocks, and through deep mud, on, on, on. We heard occasional cannonading over toward the centre, where Shields's force remained drawn up in line of battle, to await our tedious circuit. The day was long and hot; the artillery labored over the almost impassable road. I went on in advance, with some pioneers to aid a little by removing obstacles. As we passed through the little village of Forrestville, a party of young girls sang Dixie to us. . . . On we go. We have got round the enemy's position. It is dark; too late to ford the North Fork of the Shenandoah to rejoin the rest of the army, who have now entered New Market, which Ashby even has left. Tired and foot-sore, we lay down to sleep in the woods. Marching for eighteen hours, and such marching! the bivouac, in the warm, pleasant night is a luxury. The next morning we start again, and ford the Shenandoah, and get on to the turnpike at New Market which we had left at Mount Jackson. The Shenandoah is swift, and up to one's middle. Fording is an exciting, amusing, long task. It is finished at last, and the brigade, led by our regiment, moves through the town of New Market to the saucy strains of Yankee Doodle. We move two miles beyond the town, and bivouac on a hillside. Our tents and baggage are all sixteen miles back, at Edinburg.

It is late Friday evening before we get bivouacked. Many of the men are barefoot and without rations. Saturday morning it begins early to rain, and ever since we have been dripping under this easterly storm. . . .

Aha! the clouds begin to break. I wish you a pleasant Easter Sunday. One thing at least we may hope for, that before another Easter day we may be at home again; for this Rebellion will die rapidly when we hit its vitals. They have not been hit yet, however.

I wish you could look at our regiment under rude shelters of rails and straw, and dripping in this cold storm. Our shoes and clothing came up yesterday, and this morning we are giving them out. So we are not wholly helpless yet. . . .

CAMP NEAR HARRISONBURG, April 26, 1862, Saturday.

Rain ! rain ! rain ! March ! march ! march ! What a life ! We marched fifteen miles yesterday, in mud and rain, to this point, and got into camp at night in reasonable comfort, but almost without rations, and now we are busy with the miserable interrogatory of what to eat ?

Such is our experience. Colonel Andrews is again on detached duty, and, for the past few days, I have been in command. It is impossible to exaggerate the difficulty of taking care of a regiment when the whole Quartermaster and Commissary Departments of the army corps are in such hopeless confusion and debility.

No other army corps has the obstacles to contend against of this kind that we have. At Yorktown they have the sea, and the Western rivers bear supplies as well as gunboats. Here our wagons cannot bring supplies enough to last until they return from a second trip. We shall be driven to forage from the country ; and I do not see any system adopted wise enough and prompt enough for that effort. But there is no use in croaking ; we shall get out of the woods somehow, I suppose.

Among other short supplies, we are wholly without newspapers since a week ago. What is the news? I hope McClellan is silencing his opponents by silencing the enemy's batteries. That 's his best answer.

[Mrs. E. A. W. Dwight], *Life and Letters of Wilder Dwight* (Boston, 1868), 230-241 *passim*.

---

87. On the Firing Line (1863)

BY CORPORAL JAMES KENDALL HOSMER

Hosmer, then a minister, now librarian in Minneapolis, served as a private and corporal in a Massachusetts regiment, and was one of the color-guard. After the war he became prominent as a college professor and author. The battle here described was a futile attack on Port Hudson. — Bibliography of the campaign : J. F. Rhodes, *History of the United States*, IV, 319, note; Channing and Hart, *Guide*, § 210.

[June 16, 1863.] WE have had a battle. Not quite a week ago, we began to hear of it. . . . We knew nothing certain, however, until Saturday. (It is now Tuesday.) Toward the end of that afternoon, the explicit orders came. The assault was to be made the next morning, and our regiment was to have a share in it. We were not to go home without the baptism of fire and blood.

Before dark, we were ordered into line, and stacked our arms. Each captain made a little speech. " No talking in the ranks ; no flinching.

Let every one see that his canteen is full, and that he has hard bread enough for a day. That is all you will carry beside gun and equipments." We left the guns in stack, polished, and ready to be caught on the instant; and lay down under the trees. At midnight came the cooks with coffee and warm food. Soon after came the order to move; then, slowly and with many halts, nearly four hundred strong, we took up our route along the wood-paths. Many other regiments were also in motion. The forest was full of Rembrandt pictures, — a bright blaze under a tree, the faces and arms of soldiers all aglow about it; the wheel of an army-wagon, or the brass of a cannon, lit up; then the gloom of the wood, and the night shutting down about it.

At length, it was daybreak. . . . We were now only screened from the rebel works by a thin hedge. Here the rifle-balls began to cut keen and sharp through the air about us; and the cannonade, as the east now began to redden, reached its height, — a continual deafening uproar, hurling the air against one in great waves, till it felt almost like a wall of rubber, bounding and rebounding from the body, — the great guns of the " Richmond," the siege-Parrotts, the smaller field-batteries; and, through all, the bursting of the shells within the rebel lines, and the keen, deadly whistle of well-aimed bullets. A few rods down the military road, the column paused. . . . The banks of the ravine rose on either side of the road in which we had halted : but just here the trench made a turn; and in front, at the distance of five or six hundred yards, we could plainly see the rebel rampart, red in the morning-light as with blood, and shrouded in white vapor along the edge as the sharpshooters behind kept up an incessant discharge. I believe I felt no sensation of fear, nor do I think those about me did. . . .

. . . We climb up the path. I go with my rifle between Wilson and Hardiker; keeping nearest the former, who carries the national flag. In a minute or two, the column has ascended, and is deploying in a long line, under the colonel's eye, on the open ground. The rebel engineers are most skilful fellows. Between us and the brown earth-heap which we are to try to gain to-day, the space is not wide; but it is cut up in every direction with ravines and gullies. These were covered, until the parapet was raised, with a heavy growth of timber; but now it has all been cut down, so that in every direction the fallen tops of large trees interlace, trunks block up every passage, and brambles are growing over the whole. It is out of the question to advance here in line of battle it seems almost out of the question to advance in any order : but the word is given, " Forward ! " and on we go.   Know that this whole space is swept by a constant patter of balls : it is really a " leaden rain."   We go crawling and stooping : but now and then before us rises in plain view the line of earth-works, smoky and sulphurous with volleys ; while all about us fall the balls, now sending a lot of little splinters from a stump, now knocking the dead wood out of the old tree-trunk that is sheltering me, now driving up a cloud of dust from a little knoll, or cutting off the head of a weed just under the hand as with an invisible knife. . . . " Forward ! " is the order.   We all stoop ; but the colonel does not stoop : he is as cool as he was in his tent last night, when I saw him drink iced lemonade.   He turns now to examine the ground, then faces back again to direct the advance of this or that flank.   Wilson springs on from cover to cover, and I follow close after him.   It is hard work to get the flag along : it cannot be carried in the air ; and we drag it and pass it from hand to hand among the brambles, much to the detriment of its folds.   The line pauses a moment.   Capt. Morton, who has risen from a sick-bed to be with his command, is coolly cautioning his company.   The right wing is to remain in reserve, while the left pushes still farther forward.   The major is out in front of us now.   He stands upon a log which bridges a ravine, — a plain mark for the sharp-shooters, who overlook the position, not only from the parapet, but from the tall trees within the rebel works.   Presently we move on again, through brambles and under charred trunks, tearing our way, and pulling after us the colors ; creeping on our bellies across exposed ridges, where bullets hum and sing like stinging bees ; and, right in plain view, the ridge of earth, its brow white with incessant volleys. . . .

. . . Down into our little nook now come tumbling a crowd of disorganized, panting men.   They are part of a New-York regiment, who, on the crest just over us, have been meeting with very severe loss.   They say their dead and dying are heaped up there.   We believe it ; for we can hear them, they are so near : indeed, some of those who come tumbling down are wounded ; some have their gun-stocks broken by shot, and the barrels bent, while they are unharmed.   They are frightened and exhausted, and stop to recover themselves ; but presently their officers come up, and order them forward again.   From time to time, afterwards, wounded men crawl back from their position a few yards in front of where we are. . . .

. . . We begin to know that the attack has failed. . . . We know nothing certainly.   There are rumors, thick as the rifle-balls, of this gen eral killed, that regiment destroyed, and successful attempts elsewhere. The sun goes down on this day of blood. We have lost several killed. . . .

At dusk, I creep back to the ravine, where I am to sleep. . . . For food to-day, I have had two or three hard crackers and cold potatoes. We have no blankets : so down I lie to sleep as I can on the earth, without covering ; and, before morning, am chilled through with the dew and coldness of the air.

James K. Hosmer, *The Color-Guard* (Boston, 1864), 187–195 *passim*.

——————◆——————

88. The Bummers (1863)

BY REVEREND GEORGE HUGHES HEPWORTH

Hepworth was a clergyman who was with the Union army in Louisiana in 1862 and 1863, first as chaplain of a Massachusetts regiment and later as a member of General Banks's staff. The piece is inserted to show a very common and depressing side of the war — the demoralized soldier. — Bibliography as in No. 84 above.

AFTER our column reached Opelousas, I left it, intending to go on with my work in the labor system ; and I found but one thing, that, to my mind, marred the glory of our march through the Têche. That was the extensive system of plundering and pillaging which was carried on by the stragglers, — a class of men sufficiently large to attract attention. I afterwards found that their practices had been made known to the general, and that several of the offenders had been condemned to be shot. I am not one of those who would have mercy on a rebel ; but even war is not exactly barbarism : it does not give a soldier license to do as he chooses with what does not belong to him. . . .

What made me more indignant was the fact, that the men who were bearing the brunt of the battle were not the ones who were enriching themselves. They simply hewed a way, through which otners, less worthy, came at their leisure. The stragglers numbered not more than five hundred in all. These did all the mischief. One of these we found in the Newtown jail, with a thousand dollars in gold and silver on his person. If you should go up to any cottage within fifty miles of the rear, you would probably find some five or six of these fellows sitting in the gallery, smoking, sleeping, or boasting of their exploits. If you should take the trouble to empty their pockets, you would find an assortment of articles sufficiently large for a Jew to commence business with. They would show you gold pencils, silver spoons, and large rolls of

Confederate bills, and offer to sell you relics enough to fill a good-sized museum. There was an independence or an audacity about these fellows which was very striking. They would enter a house with the air of one who owned the place, and order the landlord to prepare dinner for two or three, as the case might be ; and, while the frightened Creole was hurrying and bustling to do their bidding, they were quietly opening all his drawers, looking under his beds, unlocking his trunks, and making whatever discoveries they could. Perhaps, by the time dinner was announced, the whole party would have donned a new suit of clothes ; and, not satisfied with eating the best the poor man had, would proceed to fill their pockets with his watches, his wife's jewelry, and all the little articles of *vertu* which could be found. At Franklin, Mr. Secesh and his family were quietly seated at the breakfast-table. Upon congratulating himself, that, so far, his property had remained intact, he saw half a dozen soldiers just entering his gate. They came very leisurely into the room where he sat with his wife and children, and politely requested them to rise from the table, and make room for Uncle Sam's boys : then, after having satisfied their hunger with what the planter had supplied for himself, they pocketed every silver fork and spoon, and as leisurely took their departure. I confess, that, in this particular instance, I heard Mr. Secesh whine about his trouble, with a great deal of inward chuckling. He was a bad man, a Northern man, an adventurer, who had married a large plantation, and out-Heroded Herod in his virulence against the Yankees.

But the practice I most deeply deplore. Once I came near getting into difficulty by trying to check it. I remained all night with a man who had suffered severely from these military thieves. About five o'clock in the morning, I was roused by a tremendous noise down stairs. Dressing myself with all due haste, I went to the window, and, looking down, saw one of the gang just emerging from the cellar window below, his arms and pockets full of plunder. Presenting my pistol to his *caput*, I demanded what he was doing. He turned suddenly, caught sight of the ugly little revolver close to his brains, and, with a rapidity only equalled by a turtle drawing in his head when struck, he tumbled back into the room, greatly surprised. I went to the door to find the rest of the gang, when I was met by the roundest and most complete cursing it has ever been my fortune to receive. Expletives which I had supposed were long since obsolete, and all the most damnatory phrases in our language, were used with refreshing license. The men had screened themselves on the other side of a bayou ; and, when I drew my weapon on them, they dodged behind the levee, and made good their escape.   Just then, I recollected that I was in my shirt-sleeves, and without any insignia of rank, and started for the house to get my coat.   I had proceeded but a few steps, however, when I found myself surrounded by five of the gang, each with his musket.   A pretty fix to be in, surely !   The rascals might shoot me, and then swear that I was a planter who had offered them violence.   Nothing but the most unadulterated bravado would clear me.   So, just as I was pondering what it was best to do, the fellow who had played the turtle so beauti-fully, quietly cocked his musket, and said, —

" Throw down your pistol, or I will shoot ! "

This, of course, was unendurable.   My pistol had on it the name of the friend who gave it to me, and it was one of the last things to be given up.

He repeated his very praiseworthy determination to shoot me ; when I rather took him by surprise by bellowing in my loudest tones, —

" Sirrah, I place you under arrest ; and, if you budge an inch, you shall become intimately acquainted with that " (displaying my pistol to the best possible advantage).   " Shoulder arms ! " I repeated, as loud as I could bawl.

The fellow was completely disconcerted, and actually came to the shoulder arms ; when I put on the coat I had sent for (having on shoulder-straps, of course), and placed the fellow under arrest.   But I never preferred charges against him, and so the matter ended as a joke.

George H. Hepworth, *The Whip, Hoe, and Sword, or The Gulf-Depart-ment in '63* (Boston, 1864), 278–283 *passim*.

---

89. The Sanitary Commission (1863)

BY REVEREND FREDERICK NEWMAN KNAPP

Knapp, previously a minister, joined the Sanitary Commission in 1861, and became the superintendent of the special relief department; he furnished aid to some fifty thousand sick and wounded soldiers.   He was a personal friend of Lincoln and Grant.   The extract below gives information about only one of the many duties under-taken by the Sanitary Commission in its noble work of mitigating the horrors of war. — Bibliography as in No. 84 above.

WASHINGTON, D. C.,
CENTRAL OFFICE, U. S. SANITARY COM'N, *October 1st*, 1863. . . .

THE main purpose kept in view in this work of Special Relief for the past two years has been . . .

First. To supply to the sick men of the newly arrived regiments such medicines, food, and care as it is impossible for them to receive, in the midst of the confusion, and with the unavoidable lack of facilities, from their own officers. The men to be thus aided are those who are not so sick as to have a claim upon a general hospital, and yet need immediate care to guard them against serious sickness.

Second. To furnish suitable food, lodging, care and assistance to men who are honorably discharged from service, sent from general hospitals, or from their regiments, but who are often delayed a day or more in the city, sometimes many days before they obtain their papers and pay.

Third. To communicate with distant regiments in behalf of discharged men whose certificates of disability or descriptive lists on which to draw their pay prove to be defective — the invalid soldiers meantime being cared for, and not exposed to the fatigue and risk of going in person to their regiments to have their papers corrected.

Fourth. To act as the unpaid agent or attorney of discharged soldiers who are too feeble or too utterly disabled to present their own claim at the paymaster's office.

Fifth. To look into the condition of discharged men who assume to be without means to pay the expense of going to their homes; and to furnish the necessary means where we find the man is true and the need real.

Sixth. To secure to disabled soldiers railroad tickets at reduced rates, and, through an agent at the railroad station, see that these men are not robbed or imposed upon by sharpers.

Seventh. To see that all men who are discharged and paid off do at once leave the city for their homes; or, in cases where they have been induced by evil companions to remain behind, to endeavor to rescue them, and see them started with through-tickets to their own towns.

Eighth. To make reasonably clean and comfortable before they leave the city, such discharged men as are deficient in cleanliness and clothes.

Ninth. To be prepared to meet at once with food or other aid, such immediate necessities as arise when sick men arrive in the city in large numbers from battle-fields or distant hospitals.

Tenth. To keep a watchful eye upon all soldiers who are out of hospitals, yet not in service; and give information to the proper authorities of such soldiers as seem endeavoring to avoid duty or to desert from the ranks. . . .

Having made these general statements, I will now report, in detail, but briefly as may be, upon the several branches of Relief; — and first, at Washington :

1st. "*The Home,*" 374 *North Capitol Street.* — Increased accommodations for securing room and comfort at the Home, referred to in my
last report, have been obtained ; and now, instead of 140 beds, we have
at the Home 320, besides a large baggage-room, a convenient washroom,
a bath-house, &c. . . . The third building . . . for a "Hospital." . . .
The necessity for this building, devoted exclusively to Hospital purposes,
is found in the fact, that although the men who come under the care of
the Commission are mostly on their way to their homes, and might therefore be supposed to be not so very feeble as to need specially "Hospital" treatment, yet, as a matter of fact, many of them are weakened to
such a degree by disease, that by the time they reach Washington, or
the railway station from the front, or from the various hospitals, their
strength is nearly exhausted, and they are only restored, if at all, by
such care as hospital treatment affords; and frequently they are too far
gone to make even that available. . . . These were nearly all men having their discharge papers with them, and they had, consequently, given
up their claim upon the General or Regimental Hospitals, and had taken
the first stage of their journey towards their homes. If they had not
found the care which the Commission thus offered to them, these same
men must have died in the cars along the way, or at some stopping-
point on their journey. . . .

"The doors of the 'Home' are open night and day ; yet vigilant watch
is kept, not to harbor any man who ought to be with his regiment, or
reporting to some Medical Officer. Otherwise, the 'Home' would
quickly become what of course there is, as we are ready to acknowledge, apparent and real danger of its becoming, unless wisely managed,
viz., *a philanthropic interference* with Army discipline, pleading its humanity as an excuse for its intrusion. . . ." . . .

Lodge No. 4, in "H" Street. This is the new Lodge with large
accommodations, immediately connected with the office of the Paymaster for discharged soldiers. . . .

This relief station consists of six buildings. A dormatory of a hundred beds : a dining-room, seating about one hundred, with a large
kitchen attached : a baggage-room, where all the discharged men coming in to be paid off can deposit their baggage, receiving a check for
it : a storehouse : quarters for the guard : and a building containing the
office of the Free Pension Agency, office of the Medical Examiner for
pensions, and ticket office for the Railroad agent, selling through-tickets
to soldiers at reduced rates of fare.

All disabled soldiers discharged directly from the Army of the Potomac or from the Hospitals in this vicinity come to the Paymaster's office, which is within this same inclosure, to be paid off. Government can no longer hold itself directly responsible for these men, and here is where we take them up. Yet Government cordially co-operates in our work, furnishing to the Commission part of these very buildings, and giving such army rations at this Lodge as we can use for these men advantageously with our other supplies.

The object of the whole thing at this Lodge is this, viz. : so to supply to the discharged soldier close at his hand and without a cent of cost, all that he needs — food, lodging, assistance in correcting his papers, aid in looking up his claims, help in obtaining his pension and his bounty — such that there can be no excuse or opportunity for the soldier to put himself or be put into the hands of claim agents and sharpers, or to go out and expose himself to the temptations of the city. . . .

But for the gratuitous aid thus afforded these soldiers discharged from the service, disabled by wounds or worn down by long marches and exposure in the field, or enfeebled by disease, anxious to get home, would have applied to " Claim Agents " for aid in obtaining speedily their dues from the Government, submitting willingly to pay a commission ranging from 10 to 40 per cent. These agents, with some rare and admirable exceptions, in four cases out of every five, impede the settlement of accounts instead of facilitating them.

The Sanitary Commission Bulletin, November 1, 1863 (New York), I, 11–16 *passim.*

---

90. A Night Attack (1863)

BY SURGEON ALBERT GAILLARD HART

Dr. Hart was a practising physician in western Pennsylvania who was commissioned in the Forty-First Ohio Regiment in 1861 and served as assistant surgeon and surgeon in the western campaigns from 1861 to 1864. He is still a practising physician. The attack described in this letter was Grant's first movement toward the relief of Chattanooga. — Bibliography of the campaign as in No. 122 below.

41st Regiment, O. V. I., Tennessee River, nine miles below
Chattanooga, Tuesday Morning, October 27th, 1863.

My Dear Boys : —

I WRITE you from the river bank, with my hospital knapsack my writing-desk. But this morning is the fastest in military matters

T

which I have ever known since I have been in the army, and I must sketch it to you just as it is before me. . . .

About 5 o'clock yesterday afternoon I received an order from Brigade Headquarters, that "one surgeon or assistant surgeon will accompany each regiment in the march to-night." . . . It was dark when 175 men out of our regiment, who on some pretense had been previously detailed, and ordered to have cartridge boxes filled up to sixty rounds, were ordered to be ready to go on a march, without blankets. No intimation was given as to the nature of the service. As the night wore on, it became known that a boat expedition was on foot. . . .

I was called up at 1 o'clock A.M., and found a detail from each regiment in our brigade waiting to march. It was 2 o'clock A.M. when we got down to the river. Here a flotilla of fifty pontoon boats awaited us, and slowly we got on board. The boats were twenty-five to thirty feet long, and about seven feet wide, but shallow. On board of each twenty-five men embarked, with five rowers and a steersman to each boat. . . .

It is a moonlight night, but fortunately cloudy, and we gladly see the fog which hangs over the river, thicken, and the dark shadow of the forest skirting the right or north bank of the river, widening and throwing its friendly protection out to shield us even partially from observation. We are 1,300 strong, bold, resolute, daring men, with enough of the electric fire among officers and men to kindle enthusiasm for any required deed of danger or daring. But night attacks are notoriously uncertain, and ours is no exception. I think it all over in quiet reflection as we float down, and make up my mind that some of us are pretty sure to sink in the waters of the Tennessee before the expedition is over. . . .

It is understood that after we have descended two miles, or two and a half, the rebels hold the south side of the river, with their pickets, and that we are liable to be fired upon at any point below that. Perfect silence is enjoined. I sit beside one of our Captains, facing the south bank and waiting for the first gun from the enemy. After two miles our oarsmen ceased rowing, and we floated still and silent down the rapid stream. . . .

Gen. Hazen is in the van, directing in barely intelligible voice, and calling out clear and low, "close up! close up!" For the boats are straggling as they move at different speed, and when we make our landing our boats should be together, that we may not be beaten in detail. My head drops down upon my arm; I find room between the legs of the oarsmen, drop upon the bottom of the boat, and sleep sweetly and soundly. We have floated miles while I slept. We have descended nine miles by the river in just two hours. There is the sharp rattle of musketry as we turn toward the left bank. I fully awaken only after several shots are fired from the shore, to find the balls whizzing over and around, and striking the water close to our boat. "Push for the shore! Push for the shore!" The oarsmen pull heavily at the oars. Our boats have dropped a little below our intended landing, but we reach the bank and leap ashore as we may. The Company in our boat is formed instantly, and rushes up along the bank to reach our proper position. Day is just beginning to break, but objects are confused at a short distance.

We are at Brown's Ferry. A few feet above the water there is a narrow bench of level ground 100 to 150 feet wide, above which towers a hill ascending at an angle of forty-five degrees. . . . At this landing a ravine terminates, which cuts through the ridge I have described, and a road comes down along it to the water's edge. On each side of this road is the high hill. In going back along this road 500 yards you come out upon the broad valley beyond. Stopping to dress a wounded man I got behind the regiment. . . . I had not gone up more than 200 yards when I came upon a squad of sixty men of the 23rd Kentucky holding the road, and although ten minutes had hardly elapsed since the landing, they were already cutting down trees to build a breastwork. . . . I had only ascended a little distance when a fierce fight began at the point I had just left. I could not see it in the gloom, but I could hear the sharp, shrill *yells* of the rebs, so different from the cheer which our men use. Crack upon crack came the musketry! I could hear our men falling rapidly back; the rebels had got upon the opposite hill, and as our men retreated, the rebel shots crossed the road and came thick and fast around us. . . . Our men threw out skirmishers to the right along the precipitous side of the hill to the right of the ravine, and the whole force pressed forward with furious cheers, and moved up over rocks, and up the almost perpendicular hill down which the rebels in the same order were advancing but a moment before. No man could guess what force the rebels had, or how soon we might run upon a line of battle which would sweep us down the hill like chaff. But the officers, who had been made fully aware of the ground to be gone over, pressed on at the best speed they could make, and in a few minutes more they reached the top of the ridge on this hill. Meanwhile our detachment of 600 men with which I had landed had moved up the precipitous path and reached the top of the hill on the left. The perpendicular ascent was not less than 300 feet. Great boulders, rocks, rubbish, and underbrush were in their way. Along this ridge or razor-back, a few feet wide, our men were posted when I reached them. Of course, our regiment with Col. Wiley is in the advance ; the 6th and 24th O. V. I. and 5th Kentucky follow. The top is scarcely two yards wide, and in front again descends rapidly, but is not so steep as on the river side. Our skirmishers form and push down the hill through trees and under-brush. . . . The rebels form rapidly, and probably imagining our force to be small, make a furious effort to take back from us the ground we have gained. Our skirmishers fall back for a moment, but soon drive back the enemy, who, as the daylight advances, are to be plainly seen in the broad valley below, and can be heard giving orders for a rapid retreat. The day is won ! But to secure ourselves in our position our men throw up quickly a breastwork of small trees hastily cut down, loose stones, and earth scratched up with their tin plates. . . .

As soon as the position was secured another act began. As I sat fronting the ferry, a cloud of men appeared on the opposite shore. At half-past eight A.M. a pontoon bridge, made with the boats which carried us down, started from the bank. As it was pushed into the river, straight as an arrow, I thought how savage Indians of the olden time, watching its progress from the shore, would have thought it some wondrous animal, pushing itself across the water, and bearing upon its broad back a thousand strange and unknown men, coming to drive them from their hunting grounds. At 4 P.M. I crossed the river upon this bridge, capable of ferrying over a great army. And over it, a day or two later, Hooker, coming up from Bridgeport with the Eleventh and Twelfth Army Corps, would reëstablish our " cracker line," and bring hope and relief to our starving army in Chattanooga.

From a MS. letter communicated for this volume to his son by Dr. Hart.

CHAPTER XVI — THE SOUTHERN ARMIES

91. War Songs (1861 ?)

BY SOUTHERN POETS

Pike, the author of "Dixie," was of New England birth and education, but he settled in the South, where he gained a reputation as a lawyer and author. During the Civil War he was Confederate Indian commissioner. Macarthy was a light comedian who appeared at most of the theatres in the South during the war, making a specialty of this and other patriotic ballads. — Bibliography as in No. 80 above.

A. "DIXIE"

BY ALBERT PIKE

SOUTHRONS, hear your Country call you !
Up ! lest worse than death befall you !
   To arms ! To arms ! To arms ! in Dixie !
Lo ! all the beacon-fires are lighted,
Let all hearts be now united !
   To arms ! To arms ! To arms ! in Dixie !
    Advance the flag of Dixie !
        Hurrah ! hurrah !
  For Dixie's land we take our stand,
   And live or die for Dixie !
     To arms ! To arms !
      And conquer peace for Dixie !
     To arms ! To arms !
      And conquer peace for Dixie !

Hear the Northern thunders mutter !
Northern flags in South wind flutter ;
    [To arms, etc.
Send them back your fierce defiance !
Stamp upon the accursed alliance !]
    To arms, etc.
      Advance the flag of Dixie ! etc.

Fear no danger !　Shun no labor !
Lift up rifle, pike, and sabre !
　　　To arms, etc.
Shoulder pressing close to shoulder,
Let the odds make each heart bolder !
　　　To arms, etc.
　　　　　Advance the flag of Dixie ! etc.

How the South's great heart rejoices,
At your cannons' ringing voices ;
　　　To arms ! etc.
For faith betrayed and pledges broken,
Wrongs inflicted, insults spoken ;
　　　To arms ! etc.
　　　　　Advance the flag of Dixie ! etc.

Strong as lions, swift as eagles,
Back to their kennels hunt these beagles ;
　　　To arms ! etc.
Cut the unequal words [bonds ?] asunder !
Let them then each other plunder !
　　　To arms ! etc.
　　　　　Advance the flag of Dixie ! etc.

Swear upon your Country's altar,
Never to submit or falter ;
　　　To arms ! etc.
Till the spoilers are defeated,
Till the Lord's work is completed.
　　　To arms ! etc.
　　　　　Advance the flag of Dixie ! etc.

Halt not, till our Federation
Secures among Earth's Powers its station !
　　　To arms ! etc.
Then at peace, and crowned with glory,
Hear your children tell the story !
　　　To arms ! etc.
　　　　　Advance the flag of Dixie ! etc.

If the loved ones weep in sadness,
Victory soon shall bring them gladness:
    To arms! etc.
Exultant pride soon banish sorrow;
Smiles chase tears away to-morrow.
    To arms! etc.
        Advance the flag of Dixie! etc.

B. "THE BONNIE BLUE FLAG"

BY HARRY MACARTHY

WE are a band of brothers, and natives to the soil,
    Fighting for the property we gained by honest toil;
And when our rights were threatened, the cry rose near and far:
Hurrah for the bonnie Blue Flag that bears a single star!
    Chorus — Hurrah! hurrah! for the bonnie Blue Flag
            That bears a single star.

As long as the Union was faithful to her trust,
Like friends and like brothers, kind were we and just;
But now when Northern treachery attempts our rights to mar,
We hoist on high the bonnie Blue Flag that bears a single star.

First, gallant South Carolina nobly made the stand;
Then came Alabama, who took her by the hand;
Next, quickly, Mississippi, Georgia, and Florida —
All raised the flag, the bonnie Blue Flag that bears a single star.

Ye men of valor, gather round the banner of the right;
Texas and fair Louisiana join us in the fight.
Davis, our loved President, and Stephens, statesmen are;
Now rally round the bonnie Blue Flag that bears a single star.

And here's to brave Virginia! the Old Dominion State
With the young Confederacy at length has linked her fate.
Impelled by her example, now other States prepare
To hoist on high the bonnie Blue Flag that bears a single star

Then here's to our Confederacy; strong we are and brave,
Like patriots of old we'll fight, our heritage to save;

And rather than submit to shame, to die we would prefer;
So cheer for the bonnie Blue Flag that bears a single star.

Then cheer, boys, cheer, raise the joyous shout,
For Arkansas and North Carolina now have both gone out;
And let another rousing cheer for Tennessee be given,
The single star of the bonnie Blue Flag has grown to be eleven!

From reprints in *Rebel Rhymes and Rhapsodies* (edited by Frank Moore, New York, 1864), 20–23, 120–122.

———◆———

92. Horrors of War (1862)

BY LIEUTENANT WILLIAM GEORGE STEVENSON

Stevenson was a young New York man residing in Arkansas at the outbreak of the war. He "volunteered" in the Confederate army at the advice of a vigilance committee, and rose to the rank of lieutenant. At the battle of Shiloh, or Pittsburg Landing, he saw the scenes which are described in this extract. After the battle he acted as civilian assistant-surgeon until he succeeded in escaping to the Union lines some months later. — Bibliography of the campaign as in No. 107 below.

ABOUT three o'clock I was sent to the rear with dispatches of the progress of the battle, and asking reinforcements. When about half way to Beauregard's staff, riding at full gallop, my first serious accident occurred, my life being saved by but a hair's breadth. As my horse rose in a long leap, his fore-feet in the air and his head about as high as my shoulder, a cannon-ball struck him above the eye and carried away the upper part of his head. Of course the momentum carried his lifeless body some ten feet ahead, and hurled me some distance further, — saber, pistols, and all. . . .

. . . When I had reached the camp of the 71st Ohio Volunteers, my strength failed, and after getting something to eat for myself and horse, and a bucket of water to bathe my side during the night, I tied my horse near the door of a tent, and crept in to try to sleep. But the shells from the gunboats, which made night hideous, the groans of the wounded, and the pleadings of the dying, for a time prevented. Weariness at length overcame me, and sleep followed more refreshing and sound than I hoped for under the circumstances. . . .

. . . At five A.M. I was in the saddle, though scarcely able to mount, from the pain in knee and side; and in making my way to General Beauregard's staff, my head reeled and my heart grew sick at the scenes through which I passed. I record but one. In crossing a small ravine, my horse hesitated to step over the stream, and I glanced down to detect the cause. The slight rain during the night had washed the leaves out of a narrow channel down the gully some six inches wide, leaving the hard clay exposed. Down this pathway ran sluggishly a band of blood nearly an inch thick, filling the channel. For a minute I looked and reflected, how many human lives are flowing past me, and who shall account for such butchery ! Striking my rowels into the horse to escape from the horrible sight, he plunged his foot into the stream of blood, and threw the already thickening mass in ropy folds upon the dead leaves on the bank ! The only relief to my feelings was the reflection that I had not shed one drop of that blood. . . .

At three o'clock P.M. the Confederates decided on a retreat to Corinth. . . .

About five o'clock I requested permission to ride on toward Corinth, as I was faint and weary, and, from the pain in my side and knee, would not be able to keep the saddle much longer. This was granted, and I made a *détour* from the road on which the army was retreating, that I might travel faster and get ahead of the main body. In this ride of twelve miles alongside of the routed army, I saw more of human agony and woe than I trust I will ever again be called on to witness. The retreating host wound along a narrow and almost impassable road, extending some seven or eight miles in length. Here was a long line of wagons loaded with wounded, piled in like bags of grain, groaning and cursing, while the mules plunged on in mud and water belly-deep, the water sometimes coming into the wagons. Next came a straggling regiment of infantry pressing on past the train of wagons, then a stretcher borne upon the shoulders of four men, carrying a wounded officer, then soldiers staggering along, with an arm broken and hanging down, or other fearful wounds which were enough to destroy life. And to add to the horrors of the scene, the elements of heaven marshaled their forces, — a fitting accompaniment of the tempest of human desolation and passion which was raging. A cold, drizzling rain commenced about nightfall, and soon came harder and faster, then turned to pitiless blinding hail. This storm raged with unrelenting violence for three hours. I passed long wagon trains filled with wounded and dying soldiers, without even a blanket to shield them from the driving sleet and hail, which fell in stones as large as partridge eggs, until it lay on the ground two inches deep.

Some three hundred men died during that awful retreat, and their bodies were thrown out to make room for others who, although wounded, had struggled on through the storm, hoping to find shelter, rest, and medical care.

By eight o'clock at night I had passed the whole retreating column. . . . But my powers of endurance . . . were exhausted, and I dismounted at a deserted cabin by the wayside, scarce able to drag myself to the doorway. . . . Procuring two hard crackers and a cup of rye coffee, I made a better meal than I had eaten in three days, and then lay down in a vacant room and slept.

[W. G. Stevenson], *Thirteen Months in the Rebel Army. By an Impressed New Yorker* (New York, A. S. Barnes & Co., 1862), 155-172 *passim.*

---

93. "Stonewall Jackson's Way" (1862)

BY JOHN WILLIAMSON PALMER

Palmer was born in Maryland and educated as a physician. During the latter half of the war he was a Confederate correspondent for the *New York Tribune.* Since the war he has gained prominence as an author and editor. This ballad was one of the most popular lyrics in the South. — For Jackson, see No. 113 below. — Bibliography as in No. 80 above.

COME, stack arms, men ! Pile on the rails,
  Stir up the camp-fire bright ;
No matter if the canteen fails,
  We 'll make a roaring night.
Here Shenandoah brawls along,
There burly Blue Ridge echoes strong,
To swell the brigade's rousing song
  Of "Stonewall Jackson's Way."

We see him now — the old slouched hat
  Cocked o'er his eye askew,
The shrewd, dry smile, the speech so pat,
  So calm, so blunt, so true.
The "Blue-Light Elder" knows 'em well ;
Says he, "That 's Banks — he 's fond of shell ;
Lord save his soul ! we 'll give him —— " well,
  That 's "Stonewall Jackson's way."

Silence ! ground arms ! kneel all ! caps off !
    Old Blue-Light's going to pray.
Strangle the fool that dares to scoff !
    Attention ! it's his way.
Appealing from his native sod,
In *forma pauperis* to God —
" Lay bare thine arm, stretch forth thy rod !
    Amen ! "   That's " Stonewall's way."

He's in the saddle now.   Fall in !
    Steady ! the whole brigade !
Hill's at the ford, cut off — we 'll win
    His way out, ball and blade !
What matter if our shoes are worn ?
What matter if our feet are torn ?
" Quick-step ! we 're with him before dawn ! "
    That 's " Stonewall Jackson's way."

The sun's bright lances rout the mists
    Of morning, and by George !
Here's Longstreet struggling in the lists,
    Hemmed in an ugly gorge.
Pope and his Yankees, whipped before,
" Bay'nets and grape ! " near [hear ?] Stonewall roar ;
" Charge, Stuart !   Pay off Ashby's score ! "
    Is " Stonewall Jackson's way."

Ah ! maiden, wait and watch and yearn
    For news of Stonewall's band !
Ah ! widow, read with eyes that burn
    That ring upon thy hand.
Ah ! wife, sew on, pray on, hope on !
Thy life shall not be all forlorn.
The foe had better ne'er been born
    That gets in " Stonewall's way."

Rebel Rhymes and Rhapsodies (edited by Frank Moore. New York, 1864)
185–186.

94. Behind the Confederate Lines (1863)

BY LIEUTENANT-COLONEL ARTHUR JAMES LYON FREMANTLE

Fremantle was a young officer in the English army who, according to his own statement, was strongly affected by the "gallantry and determination of the southerners," and was unable to repress a desire to see something of the struggle. He entered the Confederacy from Mexico, spent three months with the different armies of the South, and was present at Gettysburg. — Bibliography as in No. 80 above.

[May 20, 1863.] GENERAL JOHNSTON received me with much kindness, when I presented my letters of introduction, and stated my object in visiting the Confederate armies.

In appearance General Joseph E. Johnston (commonly called Joe Johnston) is rather below the middle height, spare, soldierlike, and well set up ; his features are good, and he has lately taken to wear a greyish beard. He is a Virginian by birth, and appears to be about fifty-seven years old. He talks in a calm, deliberate, and confident manner ; to me he was extremely affable, but he certainly possesses the power of keeping people at a distance when he chooses, and his officers evidently stand in great awe of him. He lives very plainly, and at present his only cooking-utensils consisted of an old coffee-pot and frying-pan — both very inferior articles. There was only one fork (one prong deficient) between himself and Staff, and this was handed to me ceremoniously as the "guest."

He has undoubtedly acquired the entire confidence of all the officers and soldiers under him. Many of the officers told me they did not consider him inferior as a general to Lee or any one else.

He told me that Vicksburg was certainly in a critical situation, and was now closely invested by Grant. He said that he (Johnston) had 11,000 men with him (which includes Gist's), hardly any cavalry, and only sixteen pieces of cannon ; but if he could get adequate reinforcements, he stated his intention of endeavouring to relieve Vicksburg.

I also made the acquaintance of the Georgian General Walker, a fierce and very warlike fire-eater, who was furious at having been obliged to evacuate Jackson after having only destroyed four hundred Yankees. He told me, "I know I couldn't hold the place, but I did want to kill a few more of the rascals."

At 9 P.M. I returned with General Gist to his camp, as my baggage was there. On the road we were met by several natives, who complained that soldiers were quartering themselves upon them and eating everything.

The bivouacs are extremely pretty at night, the dense woods being lit up by innumerable camp fires.

21st May (Thursday). — I rejoined General Johnston at 9 A. M., and was received into his mess. . . .

I was presented to Captain Henderson, who commanded a corps of about fifty "scouts." These are employed on the hazardous duty of hanging about the enemy's camps, collecting information, and communicating with Pemberton in Vicksburg. They are a fine-looking lot of men, wild, and very picturesque in appearance. . . .

Whilst seated round the camp fire in the evening, one of the officers remarked to me, " I can assure you, colonel, that nine men out of ten in the South would sooner become subjects of Queen Victoria than return to the Union." "Nine men out of ten!" said General Johnston — " ninety-nine out of a hundred ; I consider that few people in the world can be more fortunate in their government than the British colonies of North America." But the effect of these compliments was rather spoilt when some one else said they would prefer to serve under the Emperor of the French or the Emperor of Japan to returning to the dominion of Uncle Abe ; and it was still more damaged when another officer alluded in an undertone to the infernal regions as a more agreeable alternative than reunion with the Yankees.

22d May (Friday). — The bombardment at Vicksburg was very heavy and continuous this morning.

I had a long conversation with General Johnston, who told me that the principal evils which a Confederate general had to contend against consisted in the difficulty of making combinations, owing to uncertainty about the time which the troops would take to march a certain distance, on account of their straggling propensities.

But from what I have seen and heard *as yet*, it appears to me that the Confederates possess certain great qualities as soldiers, such as individual bravery and natural aptitude in the use of firearms, strong, determined patriotism, and boundless confidence in their favourite generals, and in themselves. They are sober of necessity, as there is literally no liquor to be got. They have sufficient good sense to know that a certain amount of discipline is absolutely necessary ; and I believe that instances of insubordination are extremely rare. They possess the great advantage of being led by men of talent and education as soldiers who thoroughly understand the people they have to lead, as well as those they have to beat. These generals, such as Lee, Johnston, Beauregard, or Longstreet, they would follow anywhere, and obey implicitly. But, on the other hand, many of their officers, looking forward to future political advancement, owing to their present military rank, will not punish their men, or are afraid of making themselves obnoxious by enforcing rigid discipline. The men are constantly in the habit of throwing away their knapsacks and blankets on a long march, if not carried for them, and though actuated by the strongest and purest patriotism, can often not be got to consider their obligations as soldiers. In the early part of the war they were often, when victorious, nearly as disorganised as the beaten, and many would coolly walk off home, under the impression that they had performed their share. But they are becoming better in these respects as the war goes on.

All this would account for the trifling benefits derived by the Confederates from their numerous victories.

General Johnston told me that Grant had displayed more vigour than he had expected, by crossing the river below Vicksburg, seizing Jackson by vastly superior force, and, after cutting off communications, investing the fortress thoroughly, so as to take it if possible before a sufficient force could be got to relieve it. His army is estimated at 75,000 men, and General Johnston has very little opinion of the defences of Vicksburg on the land side. He said the garrison consisted of about 20,000 men. . . .

One of Henderson's scouts caused much hilarity amongst the General's Staff this afternoon. He had brought in a Yankee prisoner, and *apologised* to General Johnston for doing so, saying, "I found him in a negro quarter, and *he surrendered so quick, I couldn't kill him.*" There can be no doubt that the conduct of the Federals in captured cities tends to create a strong indisposition on the part of the Confederates to take prisoners, particularly amongst these wild Mississippians.

General Johnston told me this evening that altogether he had been wounded ten times. He was the senior officer of the old army who joined the Confederates. . . .

. . . I shall be much surprised if he is not heard of before long. That portion of his troops which I saw, though they had been beaten and forced to retreat, were in excellent spirits, full of confidence, and clamouring to be led against *only* double their numbers.

Lieut. Col. [A. J. L.] Fremantle, *Three Months in the Southern States* (Edinburgh, etc., 1863), 116–126 *passim*.

95. Guerrilla Warfare (1863)

BY COLONEL JOHN SINGLETON MOSBY (1888)

Mosby enlisted as a private in the Confederate army before the battle of Bull Run, and later became one of the most daring and successful partisan leaders. His rangers were considered by the Confederate authorities as regular soldiers; but Mosby's connection with his superior officers was very loose. — Bibliography as in No. 80 above.

. . . ON June 16 [1863] Stuart crossed the Rappahannock, and bivouacked near Piedmont station in Farquier that night. On the same day I went with a few men on a scout in the neighborhood of Thoroughfare, to find out which way Hooker was moving. . . .

. . . From a commanding position on the mountain, which we reached in a few minutes, I could see clouds of dust rising on every road, which showed that Hooker was marching for the Potomac. After going a little farther, we captured a number of prisoners, and I immediately sent a despatch to Stuart, with the information I got from them. I could not now get to Seneca without passing through Hooker's infantry, so I concluded to go down on the Little River turnpike, and operate on the line of communication between Pleasanton's cavalry and the general headquarters. I knew I could gather some prizes there, and probably keep Stahel's cavalry from coming to the front, by giving them plenty to do in their rear. So we kept ourselves concealed, like Robin Hood and his merry men, in the green wood until night, and then sallied out in quest of game. After it was dark, we moved to a point about four miles below Aldie, where Pleasanton and Rosser had been fighting, and on the pike leading to Fairfax Court House, near which Hooker's headquarters were established that evening. My command was now inside of Hooker's lines, and environed on all sides by the camps of his different corps. Along the pike a continuous stream of troops, with all the impedimenta of war, poured along. Taking three men with me — Joe Nelson, Charlie Hall, and Norman Smith — I rode out into the column of Union troops as they passed along. As it was dark, they had no suspicion who we were, although we were all dressed in full Confederate uniform. A man by the name of Birch lived in a house near the roadside, and I discovered three horses standing at his front gate, with a man holding them by their bridles. I was sure that he was an orderly, and that they were officers' horses. We rode up, and asked him to whom they belonged. He replied that they were Maj. Stirling's and Capt. Fisher's, and that they were just from Gen. Hooker's headquarters. I then called him up to me and took him by the collar, and leaning down, whispered in his ear : "You are my prisoner. My name is Mosby." . . .

In a few minutes the officers came out of the house. I saluted them, and asked which way they were going and where they were from. As we seemed to be in such friendly relations with their orderly, they never suspected our hostile character, and promptly answered that they were from Gen. Hooker's headquarters, and were carrying despatches to Pleasanton. Capt. Fisher was his chief signal officer, going up to establish a signal station at Snicker's gap — if he could get there. By this time my men had dismounted, and as I was talking to Maj. Stirling, Joe Nelson walked up, and, politely extending his hand, asked for his pistol. Charlie Hall, not to be outdone in courtesy by Joe, proposed to relieve Capt. Fisher of his. They both misunderstood what Hall and Nelson meant, and offered to shake hands with them. In an instant the barrels of four glittering revolvers informed them that death was their doom if they refused to be prisoners. Resistance was useless and they surrendered. All now mounted quickly and we left the pike. As we started, both officers burst out laughing. I asked them what they were laughing at. They said they had laughed so much about their people being gobbled up by me that they were now enjoying the joke being turned on themselves. They were then informed that I knew that they had despatches for Pleasanton, and that they could relieve me of performing a disagreeable duty by handing them over. Maj. Stirling promptly complied. I then went to a farmer's house near by, got a light, and read them. They contained just such information as Gen. Lee wanted, and were the "open sesame" to Hooker's army. I wrote a note to Stuart to go with the despatches, which were sent with the prisoners under charge of Norman Smith. He got to Stuart's headquarters about daybreak. The skies were red that night in every direction with the light of the fires of the Union army. We slept soundly within a mile of Birney's corps at Gum Spring, and in the morning began operations on the pike. We soon got as many fish in our nets as we could haul out, and then returned into the Confederate lines. Stuart was delighted to see me ; he had also learned from the captured despatches that a cavalry reconnoissance would be sent to Warrenton the next day. Notice of it was sent to Gen. Hampton, who met and repulsed it.

. . . On the afternoon when Pleasanton followed the Confederate cavalry through Upperville to the mountain, I was with my command on

Dulony's farm, about a mile from the pike, as he passed. I determined again to strike at his rear. . . . We slept in a drenching rain on the top of the mountain, and started early in the morning. As we were going through Dr. Ewell's farm, I stopped to talk with him ; but the men went on. Presently, I saw them halt near a church in the woods ; and one of them beckoned to me. I galloped up, and saw a body of about thirty cavalry drawn up not a hundred yards in front of us. I instantly ordered a charge ; and, just as we got upon them, they ran away, while a heavy fire was poured into us by a company of infantry concealed in the church. A negro had carried the news of our being on the mountain to Gen. Meade, who had prepared this ambuscade for me. Three of my men — Charlie Hall, Mountjoy, and Ballard — were wounded ; the latter losing a leg. The lieutenant commanding the Federal cavalry was killed. I was not ten steps from the infantry when they fired the volley. We fell back to the mountain ; and, no doubt, Gen. Meade thought that I was done for — at least for that day. After taking care of my wounded, I started again for the Little River Pike, which we reached by flanking Gen. Meade. Pretty soon we caught a train of twenty wagons, and proceeded to unhitch the mules. I did not have more than one man to a wagon. The guard to the train rallied, and recaptured some of the animals, and two of my men ; but we got away with most of them. That night they were delivered to Stuart's quartermaster. This raid is a fine illustration of the great results that may be achieved by a partisan force co-operating with the movements of an army. My principal aim in these operations was to get information for Stuart, and, by harassing the communications of the Federal army, to neutralize with my small command Stahel's three brigades of cavalry in Fairfax.

It happened that on June 22 — the very day we captured the wagon train — Gen. Stahel, in obedience to Hooker's orders, had gone from Fairfax with three cavalry brigades and a battery of artillery, on a reconnoissance to the Rappahannock. On June 23, just as one of his brigades had crossed over the river, and the other two were in the act of crossing, he received an order from Gen. Hooker to return immediately, and to dispose his force so as to catch the party inside his lines that had captured his wagon train. We had got to Stuart's headquarters with Hooker's mules before Stahel got the order. He did not come there to search for them. . . .

John S. Mosby, *Mosby's War Reminiscences and Stuart's Cavalry Campaigns* (New York, [1888]), 162–172 *passim*.

U

CHAPTER XVII — WAR–TIME GOVERNMENT

96. At the White House (1861)

BY WILLIAM HOWARD RUSSELL

Russell was first an English barrister; later, during the Crimean War and during the first part of the Civil War in America, special correspondent of the London *Times*. The *Times* was the great conservative organ of England, and its correspondent was received, both north and south, as a kind of unofficial British envoy; hence his published criticisms, especially on the rout at Bull Run, drew upon him the disfavor of the administration. This extract is from his diary. — Bibliography of government during the war: J. F. Rhodes *History of the United States*, III–IV, *passim;* Channing and Hart, *Guide*, §§ 208, 212, 213.

[March 27, 1861.] SOON afterwards there entered, with a shambling, loose, irregular, almost unsteady gait, a tall, lank, lean man, considerably over six feet in height, with stooping shoulders, long pendulous arms, terminating in hands of extraordinary dimensions, which, however, were far exceeded in proportion by his feet. He was dressed in an ill-fitting, wrinkled suit of black, which put one in mind of an undertaker's uniform at a funeral ; round his neck a rope of black silk was knotted in a large bulb, with flying ends projecting beyond the collar of his coat ; his turned-down shirt-collar disclosed a sinewy muscular yellow neck, and above that, nestling in a great black mass of hair, bristling and compact like a ruff of mourning pins, rose the strange quaint face and head, covered with its thatch of wild republican hair, of President Lincoln. The impression produced by the size of his extremities, and by his flapping and wide projecting ears, may be removed by the appearance of kindliness, sagacity, and the awkward bonhomie of his face ; the mouth is absolutely prodigious ; the lips, straggling and extending almost from one line of black beard to the other, are only kept in order by two deep furrows from the nostril to the chin ; the nose itself — a prominent organ — stands out from the face, with an inquiring, anxious air, as though it were sniffing for some good thing in the wind ; the eyes dark, full, and deeply set, are penetrating, but full of an expression which almost amounts to tenderness ; and above them projects the shaggy brow, running into the small hard frontal space, the development of which can scarcely be estimated accurately, owing to the irregular flocks of thick hair carelessly brushed across it.   One would say that, although the mouth was made to enjoy a joke, it could also utter the severest sentence which the head could dictate, but that Mr. Lincoln would be ever more willing to temper justice with mercy, and to enjoy what he considers the amenities of life, than to take a harsh view of men's nature and of the world, and to estimate things in an ascetic or puritan spirit.   A person who met Mr. Lincoln in the street would not take him to be what — according to the usages of European society — is called a " gentleman ; " and, indeed, since I came to the United States, I have heard more disparaging allusions made by Americans to him on that account than I could have expected among simple republicans, where all should be equals ; but, at the same time, it would not be possible for the most indifferent observer to pass him in the street without notice. . . .

[March 28.]   In the evening I repaired to the White House. . . .

. . . Whilst we were waiting, Mr. Seward took me round, and introduced me to the Ministers, and to their wives and daughters, among the latter, Miss Chase, who is very attractive, agreeable, and sprightly.   Her father, the Finance Minister, struck me as one of the most intelligent and distinguished persons in the whole assemblage ; tall, of a good presence, with a well-formed head, fine forehead, and a face indicating energy and power . . . he is one who would not pass quite unnoticed in a European crowd of the same description. . . .

Mr. Cameron, the Secretary for War, a slight man, above the middle height, with grey hair, deep-set keen grey eyes, and a thin mouth, gave me the idea of a person of ability and adroitness.   His colleague, the Secretary of the Navy, a small man, with a great long grey beard and spectacles, did not look like one of much originality or ability ; but people who know Mr. Welles declare that he is possessed of administrative power, although they admit that he does not know the stem from the stern of a ship, and are in doubt whether he ever saw the sea in his life.   Mr. Smith, the Minister of the Interior, is a bright-eyed, smart (I use the word in the English sense) gentleman, with the reputation of being one of the most conservative members of the cabinet. Mr. Blair, the Postmaster-General, is a person of much greater influence than his position would indicate.   He has the reputation of being one of the most determined republicans in the Ministry; but he held peculiar notions with reference to the black and the white races, which, if carried out, would not by any means conduce to the comfort or happiness of free negroes in the United States. . . .

In the conversation which occurred before dinner, I was amused to observe the manner in which Mr. Lincoln used the anecdotes for which he is famous. Where men bred in courts, accustomed to the world, or versed in diplomacy, would use some subterfuge, or would make a polite speech, or give a shrug of the shoulders as the means of getting out of an embarrassing position, Mr. Lincoln raises a laugh by some bold west-country anecdote, and moves off in the cloud of merriment produced by his joke. . . .

. . . The first "state dinner," as it is called, of the President was not remarkable for ostentation. . . . The conversation was suited to the state dinner of a cabinet at which women and strangers were present, . . . and except where there was an attentive silence caused by one of the President's stories, there was a Babel of small talk round the table. . . .

[October 9.] Calling on the General [McClellan] the other night at his usual time of return, I was told by the orderly, who was closing the door, "The General's gone to bed tired, and can see no one. He sent the same message to the President, who came inquiring after him ten minutes ago."

This poor President! He is to be pitied; surrounded by such scenes, and trying with all his might to understand strategy, naval warfare, big guns, the movements of troops, military maps, reconnaissances, occupations, interior and exterior lines, and all the technical details of the art of slaying. He runs from one house to another, armed with plans, papers, reports, recommendations, sometimes good humoured, never angry, occasionally dejected, and always a little fussy. The other night, as I was sitting in the parlour at head-quarters, with an English friend who had come to see his old acquaintance the General, walked in a tall man with a navvy's cap, and an ill-made shooting suit, from the pockets of which protruded paper and bundles. "Well," said he to Brigadier Van Vliet, who rose to receive him, "is George in?"

"Yes, sir. He's come back, but is lying down, very much fatigued. I'll send up, sir, and inform him you wish to see him."

"Oh, no; I can wait. I think I'll take supper with him. Well, and what are you now, — I forget your name — are you a major, or a colonel, or a general?" "Whatever you like to make me, sir."

Seeing that General M'Clellan would be occupied, I walked out with my friend, who asked me when I got into the street why I stood up when that tall fellow came into the room. " Because it was the President." " The President of what ? " " Of the United States." " Oh ! come, now you're humbugging me. Let me have another look at him." He came back more incredulous than ever, but when I assured him I was quite serious, he exclaimed, " I give up the United States after this."

But for all that, there have been many more courtly presidents who, in a similar crisis, would have displayed less capacity, honesty, and plain dealing than Abraham Lincoln.

William Howard Russell, *My Diary North and South* (London, 1863), I, 54–65 *passim* ; II, 371–373.

97. The Secretary and the Master (1861)

BY SECRETARY WILLIAM HENRY SEWARD AND PRESIDENT ABRAHAM LINCOLN

For Seward, see No. 22 above. — For Lincoln, see No. 44 above. — Bibliography of foreign relations : J. F. Rhodes, *History of the United States*, III–IV, *passim ;* Frederic Bancroft, *Life of Seward*, II *passim*.

A. SEWARD'S MEMORANDUM

SOME Thoughts for the President's Consideration, April 1, 1861.

First. We are at the end of a month's administration, and yet without a policy either domestic or foreign.

Second. This, however, is not culpable, and it has even been unavoidable. The presence of the Senate, with the need to meet applications for patronage, have prevented attention to other and more grave matters.

Third. But further delay to adopt and prosecute our policies for both domestic and foreign affairs would not only bring scandal on the administration, but danger upon the country.

Fourth. To do this we must dismiss the applicants for office. Bu how ? I suggest that we make the local appointments forthwith, leaving foreign or general ones for ulterior and occasional action.

Fifth. The policy at home. I am aware that my views are singular, and perhaps not sufficiently explained. My system is built upon this idea as a ruling one, namely, that we must

CHANGE THE QUESTION BEFORE THE PUBLIC FROM ONE UPON SLAVERY, OR ABOUT SLAVERY, for a question upon UNION OR DISUNION :

In other words, from what would be regarded as a party question, to one of patriotism or union.

The occupation or evacuation of Fort Sumter, although not in fact a slavery or a party question, is so regarded. Witness the temper manifested by the Republicans in the free States, and even by the Union men in the South.

I would therefore terminate it as a safe means for changing the issue. I deem it fortunate that the last administration created the necessity.

For the rest, I would simultaneously defend and reinforce all the ports in the gulf, and have the navy recalled from foreign stations to be prepared for a blockade. Put the island of Key West under martial law.

This will raise distinctly the question of union or disunion. I would maintain every fort and possession in the South.

FOR FOREIGN NATIONS.

I would demand explanations from Spain and France, categorically, at once.

I would seek explanations from Great Britain and Russia, and send agents into Canada, Mexico, and Central America to rouse a vigorous continental spirit of independence on this continent against European intervention.

And, if satisfactory explanations are not received from Spain and France, Would convene Congress and declare war against them.

But whatever policy we adopt, there must be an energetic prosecution of it.

For this purpose it must be somebody's business to pursue and direct it incessantly.

Either the President must do it himself, and be all the while active in it, or Devolve it on some member of his cabinet. Once adopted, debates on it must end, and all agree and abide.

It is not in my especial province ;

But I neither seek to evade nor assume responsibility.

B. LINCOLN'S REPLY

EXECUTIVE MANSION, April 1, 1861.

HON. W. H. SEWARD.

MY dear Sir : Since parting with you I have been considering your paper dated this day, and entitled "Some Thoughts for the

President's Consideration." The first proposition in it is, "*First,* We are at the end of a month's administration, and yet without a policy either domestic or foreign."

At the beginning of that month, in the inaugural, I said : "The power confided to me will be used to hold, occupy, and possess the property and places belonging to the government, and to collect the duties and imposts." This had your distinct approval at the time ; and, taken in connection with the order I immediately gave General Scott, directing him to employ every means in his power to strengthen and hold the forts, comprises the exact domestic policy you now urge, with the single exception that it does not propose to abandon Fort Sumter.

Again, I do not perceive how the reinforcement of Fort Sumter would be done on a slavery or a party issue, while that of Fort Pickens would be on a more national and patriotic one.

The news received yesterday in regard to St. Domingo certainly brings a new item within the range of our foreign policy ; but up to that time we have been preparing circulars and instructions to ministers and the like, all in perfect harmony, without even a suggestion that we had no foreign policy.

Upon your closing propositions — that "whatever policy we adopt, there must be an energetic prosecution of it.

"For this purpose it must be somebody's business to pursue and direct it incessantly.

"Either the President must do it himself, and be all the while active in it, or

"Devolve it on some member of his cabinet. Once adopted, debates on it must end, and all agree and abide " — I remark that if this must be done, I must do it. When a general line of policy is adopted, I apprehend there is no danger of its being changed without good reason, or continuing to be a subject of unnecessary debate ; still, upon points arising in its progress I wish, and suppose I am entitled to have, the advice of all the cabinet.

Your obedient servant,   A. LINCOLN.

Abraham Lincoln, *Complete Works* (edited by John G. Nicolay and John Hay, New York, 1894), II, 29-30.

98.　A Friend in Need (1861)

BY JOHN BRIGHT, M.P.

Bright was a Quaker and one of the leaders of the Liberal party in the British Parliament, and from the first placed himself unreservedly on the Union side, voicing the sympathy of the great nonconformist body.　This extract is from a speech delivered at a public dinner during the Trent excitement. — Bibliography as in No. 97 above.

THE question is a very different and a far more grave question.　It is a question of slavery, — (Cheers,) — and for thirty years it has constantly been coming to the surface, disturbing social life, and overthrowing almost all political harmony in the working of the United States.　(Cheers.)　In the North there is no secession ; there is no collision.　These disturbances and this insurrection are found wholly in the South and in the Slave States ; and therefore I think that the man who says otherwise, who contends that it is the tariff, or anything whatsoever else than slavery, is either himself deceived or endeavors to deceive others.　(Cheers.)　The object of the South is this, to escape from the majority who wish to limit the area of slavery.　(Hear ! Hear !)　They wish to found a Slave State freed from the influence and the opinions of freedom.　The Free States in the North now stand before the world the advocates and defenders of freedom and civilization.　The Slave States offer themselves for the recognition of a Christian nation, based upon the foundation, the unchangeable foundation in their eyes, of slavery and barbarism.

. . . I say that slavery has sought to break up the most free government in the world, and to found a new state, in the nineteenth century, whose corner-stone is the perpetual bondage of millions of men. . . .

. . . It has been said, " How much better it would be " — not for the United States, but — " for us, that these States should be divided." . . .

There cannot be a meaner motive than this I am speaking of, in forming a judgment on this question, — that it is " better for us " — for whom? the people of England, or the government of England ? — that the United States should be severed, and that that continent should be as the continent of Europe is, in many states, and subject to all the contentions and disasters which have accompanied the history of the states of Europe.　(Applause.)　I should say that, if a man had a great heart within him, he would rather look forward to the day when, from that point of land which is habitable nearest to the Pole, to the shores of the great Gulf, the whole of that vast continent might become one great confederation of States, — without a great army, and without a great navy, — not mixing itself up with the entanglements of European politics, — without a custom-house inside, through the whole length and breadth of its territory, — and with freedom everywhere, equality everywhere, law everywhere, peace everywhere, — such a confederation would afford at least some hope that man is not forsaken of Heaven, and that the future of our race might be better than the past. . . .

. . . what is this people, about which so many men in England at this moment are writing, and speaking, and thinking, with harshness, I think with injustice, if not with great bitterness? Two centuries ago, multitudes of the people of this country found a refuge on the North American continent, escaping from the tyranny of the Stuarts, and from the bigotry of Laud. Many noble spirits from our country made great experiments in favor of human freedom on that continent. Bancroft, the great historian of his own country, has said, in his own graphic and emphatic language, "The history of the colonization of America is the history of the crimes of Europe." . . .

At this very moment . . . there are millions in the United States who personally, or whose immediate parents, have at one time been citizens of this country, and perhaps known to some of the oldest of those whom I have now the honor of addressing. They found a home in the Far West; they subdued the wilderness; they met with plenty there, which was not afforded them in their native country; and they became a great people. There may be persons in England who are jealous of those States. There may be men who dislike democracy, and who hate a republic; there may be even those whose sympathies warm towards the slave oligarchy of the South. But of this I am certain, that only misrepresentation the most gross or calumny the most wicked can sever the tie which unites the great mass of the people of this country with their friends and brethren beyond the Atlantic. (Loud cheers.)

Now, whether the Union will be restored or not, or the South achieve an unhonored independence or not, I know not, and I predict not. But this I think I know, — that in a few years, a very few years, the twenty millions of freemen in the North will be thirty millions, or even fifty millions, — a population equal to or exceeding that of this kingdom. (Hear! Hear!) When that time comes, I pray that it may not be said amongst them, that, in the darkest hour of their country's trials England, the land of their fathers, looked on with icy coldness and saw unmoved the perils and calamities of their children. (Cheers.) As for me, I have but this to say : I am one in this audience, and but one in the citizenship of this country ; but if all other tongues are silent, mine shall speak for that policy which gives hope to the bondsmen of the South, and which tends to generous thoughts, and generous words, and generous deeds, between the two great nations who speak the English language, and from their origin are alike entitled to the English name.

John Bright, *Speeches on the American Question* (edited by Frank Moore, Boston, 1865), 26–67 *passim*.

———◆———

99. The Trent Affair (1861)

BY SECRETARY WILLIAM HENRY SEWARD

The letter to the British minister at Washington, Lord Lyons, from which this extract is taken — on the Trent affair — was Seward's most important and most studied state paper; it expresses the matured judgment of the administration, which was, not to bring on war with England. — For Seward, see No. 22 above. — Bibliography as in No. 97 above.

ONLY the fifth question remains, namely : Did Captain Wilkes exercise the right of capturing the contraband in conformity with the law of nations? . . .

. . . the question here concerns the mode of procedure in regard, not to the vessel that was carrying the contraband, nor yet to contraband things which worked the forfeiture of the vessel, but to contraband persons. . . .

. . . But only courts of admiralty have jurisdiction in maritime cases, and these courts have formulas to try only claims to contraband chattels, but none to try claims concerning contraband persons. . . .

It was replied all this was true ; but you can reach in those courts a decision which will have the moral weight of a judicial one by a circuitous proceeding. Convey the suspected men, together with the suspected vessel, into port, and try there the question whether the vessel is contraband. You can prove it to be so by proving the suspected men to be contraband, and the court must then determine the vessel to be contraband. If the men are not contraband the vessel will escape condemnation. Still, there is no judgment for or against the captured persons. But it was assumed that there would result from the determination of the court concerning the vessel a legal certainty concerning the character of the men. . . .

In the present case, Captain Wilkes, after capturing the contraband persons and making prize of the Trent in what seems to be a perfectly lawful manner, instead of sending her into port, released her from the capture, and permitted her to proceed with her whole cargo upon her voyage. He thus effectually prevented the judicial examination which might otherwise have occurred.

If, now, the capture of the contraband persons and the capture of the contraband vessel are to be regarded, not as two separate or distinct transactions under the law of nations, but as one transaction, one capture only, then it follows that the capture in this case was left unfinished, or was abandoned. . . .

I have not been unaware that, in examining this question, I have fallen into an argument for what seems to be the British side of it against my own country. But I am relieved from all embarrassment on that subject. I had hardly fallen into that line of argument when I discovered that I was really defending and maintaining, not an exclusively British interest, but an old, honored, and cherished American cause, not upon British authorities, but upon principles that constitute a large portion of the distinctive policy by which the United States have developed the resources of a continent, and thus becoming a considerable maritime power, have won the respect and confidence of many nations. These principles were laid down for us in 1804, by James Madison, when Secretary of State in the administration of Thomas Jefferson, in instructions given to James Monroe, our Minister to England. Although the case before him concerned a description of persons different from those who are incidentally the subjects of the present discussion, the ground he assumed then was the same I now occupy, and the arguments by which he sustained himself upon it, have been an inspiration to me in preparing this reply.

"Whenever," he says, "property found in a neutral vessel is supposed to be liable on any ground to capture and condemnation, the rule in all cases is, that the question shall not be decided by the captor, but be carried before a legal tribunal, where a regular trial may be had, and where the captor himself is liable to damages for an abuse of his power. Can it be reasonable, then, or just, that a belligerent commander who is thus restricted, and thus responsible in a case of mere property of trivial amount, should be permitted, without recurring to any tribunal whatever, to examine the crew of a neutral vessel, to decide the important question of their respective allegiances, and to carry that decision into execution by forcing every individual he may choose into a service abhorrent to his feelings, cutting him off from his most tender connexions, exposing his mind and his person to the most humiliating discipline, and his life itself to the greatest danger. Reason, justice and humanity unite in protesting against so extravagant a proceeding."

If I decide this case in favor of my own government, I must disavow its most cherished principles, and reverse and forever abandon its essential policy. The country cannot afford the sacrifice. If I maintain those principles, and adhere to that policy, I must surrender the case itself. It will be seen, therefore, that this government could not deny the justice of the claim presented to us in this respect upon its merits. We are asked to do to the British nation just what we have always insisted all nations ought to do to us.

The claim of the British government is not made in a discourteous manner. This government, since its first organization, has never used more guarded language in a similar case.

In coming to my conclusion I have not forgotten that, if the safety of this Union required the detention of the captured persons, it would be the right and duty of this government to detain them. But the effectual check and waning proportions of the existing insurrection, as well as the comparative unimportance of the captured persons themselves, when dispassionately weighed, happily forbid me from resorting to that defence. . . .

Nor have I been tempted at all by suggestions that cases might be found in history where Great Britain refused to yield to other nations, and even to ourselves, claims like that which is now before us. . . . It would tell little for our own claims to the character of a just and magnanimous people if we should so far consent to be guided by the law of retaliation as to lift up buried injuries from their graves to oppose against what national consistency and the national conscience compel us to regard as a claim intrinsically right.

Putting behind me all suggestions of this kind, I prefer to express my satisfaction that, by the adjustment of the present case upon principles confessedly American, and yet, as I trust, mutually satisfactory to both of the nations concerned, a question is finally and rightly settled between them, which, heretofore exhausting not only all forms of peaceful d[i]scussion, but also the arbitrament of war itself, for more than half a century alienated the two countries from each other, and perplexed with fears and apprehensions all other nations.

The four persons in question are now held in military custody at Fort Warren, in the State of Massachusetts. They will be cheerfully liberated. Your lordship will please indicate a time and place for receiving them.

Senate Executive Documents, 37 Cong., 2 sess. (Washington, 1862), IV, No. 8, pp. 8–13 *passim*.

---

100. Interview with Napoleon Third (1863)

BY COMMISSIONER JOHN SLIDELL

Slidell, senator from Louisiana at the time of secession, was an able man who had had diplomatic experience in Mexico. Davis appointed him commissioner to France. Prudence forbade Napoleon's recognition of the Confederacy, but Slidell received the emperor's private sympathy and secret influence in negotiating for a loan. — Bibliography as in No. 97 above.

ON Wednesday I received from the Duke de Bassano, First Chamberlain, a note informing me that the emperor would receive me at the Tuileries on the following day at ten o'clock. The emperor received me with great cordiality. He said that he had read the memorandum presented to him by the Count de Persigny . . . that he was more fully convinced than ever of the propriety of the general recognition by the European powers of the Confederate States, but that the commerce of France and the success of the Mexican expedition would be jeopardized by a rupture with the United States ; that no other power than England possessed a sufficient navy to give him efficient aid in war on the ocean, an event which, indeed, could not be anticipated, if England would co-operate with him in recognition.

I replied that I was well satisfied that recognition by France and other Continental powers, or even by France alone, would not lead to a war with the United States, as they already found ample occupation for all their energies at home ; that he could count on the co-operation of Spain, Austria, Prussia, Belgium, Holland, Sweden, and Denmark. He remarked that none of those powers possessed a navy of any consequence. I suggested that Spain had a very respectable navy and was daily increasing it. I adverted to the instructions in your despatch No. 16, of the 9th of May, and that I was authorized to give the adhesion of my government to the tripartite treaty for the guarantee of Cuba to Spain ; and I thought it was probable that such an adhesion might induce Spain, if assured in advance of the concurrence of France, to take the initiative of our recognition. Would the emperor be willing to give such an assurance? He said he would. I asked, will the emperor authorize me to say so to the Spanish Ambassador, Mr. Isturitz, to whom I had already communicated the substance of my instructions. He replied that he was willing that I should do so. . . .

. . . He, however, after a little reflection, added, " I think that I can do something better ; make a direct proposition to England for joint recognition. This will effectually prevent Lord Palmerston from misrepresenting my position and wishes on the American question." He said, " I shall bring the question before the cabinet meeting to-day. . . ."

I then said it may, perhaps, be an indiscretion to ask whether your majesty prefers to see the Whigs or Tories in power in England, and he said, " I rather prefer the Whigs." I remarked that Lord Malmesbury would under a conservative administration probably be the Secretary for Foreign Affairs, and that I had always understood that intimate relations existed between the emperor and him. He said, " That is true ; personally we are excellent friends, but personal relations have very little influence in great affairs where party interests are involved." He playfully remarked, " The Tories are very good friends of mine when in a minority, but their tone changes very much when they get into power."

He then spoke of the different spirit in which the news of the fall of Puebla had been received North and South ; that the Northern papers showed their disappointment and hostility, while Richmond had been illuminated on the occasion. This is reported by the newspapers. I, of course, did not express any doubt of the fact, although I considered it somewhat apocryphal. I said that there could be no doubt of the bitterness of the Northern people at the success of his arms in Mexico, while all our sympathies were with France, and urged the importance of securing the lasting gratitude and attachment of a people already so well disposed ; that there could be no doubt that our Confederacy was to be the strongest power of the American continent, and that our alliance was worth cultivating. He said that he was quite convinced of the fact, and spoke with great admiration of the bravery of our troops, the skill of our generals, and the devotion of our people. He expressed his regret at the death of Stonewall Jackson, whom he considered as one of the most remarkable men of the age.

I expressed my thanks to him for his sanction of the contracts made for the building of four ships-of-war at Bordeaux and Nantes. I then informed him that we were prepared to build several iron-clad ships-of-war, and that it only required his verbal assurance that they would be allowed to proceed to sea under the Confederate flag to enter into contracts for that purpose. He said that we might build the ships, *but it would be necessary that their destination should be concealed.* I replied that the permission to build, equip, and proceed to sea would be no violation of neutrality, and invoked the precedent of a ship built for the Chilian government under the circumstances mentioned in my despatch No. 32, of April 20. *The emperor remarked that there was a distinction to be drawn between that case and what I desired to do. Chili was a government recognized by France.*

The conversation then closed. The audience was shorter than the two previous occasions of my seeing the emperor. It lasted half an hour, but I did not think it discreet again to go over the ground covered by my note, and the points discussed in the former interviews, although they were occasionally brought into the conversation. . . .

John Bigelow, *France and the Confederate Navy* (London, 1888), 135–138 *passim.*

---

101. Speeches on Liberty (1864)

BY PRESIDENT ABRAHAM LINCOLN

In spite of the great burden of responsibility placed upon him, no president was more approachable than Lincoln. His direct intercourse with the people was one of his methods of gauging public opinion; and these brief impromptu speeches are among his most noble utterances. — For Lincoln, see No. 44 above. — Bibliography: Channing and Hart, *Guide,* §§ 208, 213.

MARCH 18, 1864. — REMARKS ON CLOSING A SANITARY FAIR IN WASHINGTON.

Ladies and Gentlemen: I appear to say but a word. This extraordinary war in which we are engaged falls heavily upon all classes of people, but the most heavily upon the soldier. For it has been said, all that a man hath will he give for his life; and while all contribute of their substance, the soldier puts his life at stake, and often yields it up in his country's cause. The highest merit, then, is due to the soldier.

In this extraordinary war, extraordinary developments have manifested themselves, such as have not been seen in former wars; and amongst these manifestations nothing has been more remarkable than these fairs for the relief of suffering soldiers and their families. And the chief agents in these fairs are the women of America.

I am not accustomed to the use of language of eulogy ; I have never studied the art of paying compliments to women ; but I must say, that if all that has been said by orators and poets since the creation of the world in praise of women were applied to the women of America, it would not do them justice for their conduct during this war. I will close by saying, God bless the women of America. . . .

March 21, 1864. — REPLY TO A COMMITTEE FROM THE WORKINGMEN'S ASSOCIATION OF NEW YORK.

Gentlemen of the Committee : The honorary membership in your association, as generously tendered, is gratefully accepted.

You comprehend, as your address shows, that the existing rebellion means more, and tends to more, than the perpetuation of African slavery — that it is, in fact, a war upon the rights of all working people. . . .

. . . None are so deeply interested to resist the present rebellion as the working people. Let them beware of prejudice, working division and hostility among themselves. The most notable feature of a disturbance in your city last summer was the hanging of some working people by other working people. It should never be so. The strongest bond of human sympathy, outside of the family relation, should be one uniting all working people, of all nations, and tongues, and kindreds. Nor should this lead to a war upon property, or the owners of property. Property is the fruit of labor ; property is desirable ; is a positive good in the world. That some should be rich shows that others may become rich, and hence is just encouragement to industry and enterprise. Let not him who is houseless pull down the house of another, but let him work diligently and build one for himself, thus by example assuring that his own shall be safe from violence when built. . . .

August 18, 1864. — ADDRESS TO THE 164TH OHIO REGIMENT.

Soldiers : You are about to return to your homes and your friends, after having, as I learn, performed in camp a comparatively short term of duty in this great contest. I am greatly obliged to you, and to all who have come forward at the call of their country. I wish it might be more generally and universally understood what the country is now engaged in. We have, as all will agree, a free government, where every man has a right to be equal with every other man. In this great struggle, this form of government and every form of human right is endangered if our enemies succeed. There is more involved in this contest than is realized by every one. There is involved in this struggle the question whether your children and my children shall enjoy the privileges we have enjoyed. I say this in order to impress upon you, if you are not already so impressed, that no small matter should divert us from our great purpose.

There may be some inequalities in the practical application of our system. It is fair that each man shall pay taxes in exact proportion to the value of his property ; but if we should wait, before collecting a tax, to adjust the taxes upon each man in exact proportion with every other man, we should never collect any tax at all. There may be mistakes made sometimes ; things may be done wrong, while the officers of the government do all they can to prevent mistakes. But I beg of you, as citizens of this great republic, not to let your minds be carried off from the great work we have before us. This struggle is too large for you to be diverted from it by any small matter. When you return to your homes, rise up to the height of a generation of men worthy of a free government, and we will carry out the great work we have commenced. I return to you my sincere thanks, soldiers, for the honor you have done me this afternoon. . . .

August 22, 1864. — ADDRESS TO THE 166TH OHIO REGIMENT.

Soldiers : I suppose you are going home to see your families and friends. For the services you have done in this great struggle in which we are all engaged, I present you sincere thanks for myself and the country.

I almost always feel inclined, when I happen to say anything to soldiers, to impress upon them, in a few brief remarks, the importance of success in this contest. It is not merely for to-day, but for all time to come, that we should perpetuate for our children's children that great and free government which we have enjoyed all our lives. I beg you to remember this, not merely for my sake, but for yours. I happen, temporarily, to occupy this White House. I am a living witness that any one of your children may look to come here as my father's child has. It is in order that each one of you may have, through this free government which we have enjoyed, an open field and a fair chance for your industry, enterprise, and intelligence ; that you may all have equal privileges in the race of life, with all its desirable human aspirations. It is for this the struggle should be maintained, that we may not lose our birthright — not only for one, but for two or three years. The nation is worth fighting for, to secure such an inestimable jewel.

Abraham Lincoln, *Complete Works* (edited by John G. Nicolay and John Hay, New York, 1894), II, 500–567 *passim.*

PART VI

PROGRESS OF THE WAR

CHAPTER XVIII — YEAR OF PREPARATION

102. The War of Liberty (1861)

BY WENDELL PHILLIPS

In selecting the materials for this important Part, two principles have been kept in view: to give some first-hand accounts of the great battles on land or river or sea, and also to give extracts from many of the principal commanders on both sides. The details of nearly all the seventeen hundred engagements must be omitted, and also a great mass of materials by many participants in the war. — Bibliography of the Civil War is to be found in J. R. Bartlett, *Literature of the Rebellion;* Robert Clarke & Co., *Catalogue of Books relating to America;* footnotes to John C. Ropes, *Story of the Civil War*, and J. F. Rhodes, *History of the United States;* Channing and Hart, *Guide*, §§ 208–210. The great source for all military histories is the *Official Records*, published in more than one hundred large volumes by the United States government.

Phillips was the great orator of abolitionism. A man of the highest social position in Boston, he gave to the doctrine his adhesion and the service of his magnetic oratory at a time when abolitionism was under the ban of society. He became one of the strongest supporters of Garrison's extreme views. This extract is from an address entitled "Under the Flag," delivered in Boston on April 21, 1861, as the regular Sunday discourse before the Twenty-Eighth Congregational society. — For Phillips, see G. L. Austin, *Life and Times of Wendell Phillips.* — Bibliography as in 101 above. — For Garrison's views on the war, see No. 126 below.

MANY times this winter, here and elsewhere, I have counselled peace, — urged, as well as I knew how, the expediency of acknowledging a Southern Confederacy, and the peaceful separation of these thirty-four States. One of the journals announces to you that I come here this morning to retract those opinions. No, not one of them! I need them all, — every word I have spoken this winter, — every act of twenty-five years of my life, to make the welcome I give this war hearty and hot. Civil war is a momentous evil. It needs the soundest, most solemn justification. I rejoice before God to-day for every word that I have spoken counselling peace; but I rejoice also with an especially profound gratitude, that now, the first time in my antislavery life, I speak under the stars and stripes, and welcome the tread of Massachusetts men marshalled for war. No matter what the past has been or said; to-day the slave asks God for a sight of this banner, and counts it the pledge of his redemption. Hitherto it may have meant what you thought, or what I did; to-day it represents sovereignty and justice. The only mistake that I have made, was in supposing Massachusetts wholly choked with cotton-dust and cankered with gold. The South thought her patience and generous willingness for peace were cowardice; to-day shows the mistake. She has been sleeping on her arms since '83, and the first cannon-shot brings her to her feet with the war-cry of the Revolution on her lips. Any man who loves either liberty or manhood must rejoice at such an hour.

. . . I do not acknowledge the motto, in its full significance, "Our country, right or wrong." If you let it trespass on the domain of morals, it is knavish. But there is a full, broad sphere for loyalty; and no war-cry ever stirred a generous people that had not in it much of truth and right. . . .

Plain words, therefore, now, before the nation goes mad with excitement, is every man's duty. Every public meeting in Athens was opened with a curse on any one who should not speak what he really thought. "I have never defiled my conscience from fear or favor to my superiors," was part of the oath every Egyptian soul was supposed to utter in the Judgment-Hall of Osiris, before admission to heaven. Let us show to-day a Christian spirit as sincere and fearless. No mobs in this hour of victory, to silence those whom events have not converted. We are strong enough to tolerate dissent. That flag which floats over press or mansion at the bidding of a mob, disgraces both victor and victim.

All winter long, I have acted with that party which cried for peace. The antislavery enterprise to which I belong started with peace written on its banner. We imagined that the age of bullets was over; that the age of ideas had come; that thirty millions of people were able to take a great question, and decide it by the conflict of opinions; that, without letting the ship of state founder, we could lift four millions of men into Liberty and Justice. We thought that if your statesmen would throw away personal ambition and party watchwords, and devote themselves to the great issue, this might be accomplished. To a certain extent it has been. The North has answered to the call. Year after year, event by event, has indicated the rising education of the people, — the readiness for a higher moral life, the calm, self-poised confidence in our own convictions that patiently waits — like master for a pupil — for a neighbor's conversion. The North has responded to the call of that peaceful, moral, intellectual agitation which the antislavery idea has initiated. Our mistake, if any, has been that we counted too much on the intelligence of the masses, on the honesty and wisdom of statesmen as a class. Perhaps we did not give weight enough to the fact we saw, that this nation is made up of different ages; not homogeneous, but a mixed mass of different centuries. The North *thinks,* — can appreciate argument, — is the nineteenth century, — hardly any struggle left in it but that between the working class and the money-kings. The South *dreams,* — it is the thirteenth and fourteenth century, — baron and serf, — noble and slave. Jack Cade and Wat Tyler loom over its horizon, and the serf, rising, calls for another Thierry to record his struggle. There the fagot still burns which the Doctors of the Sorbonne called, ages ago, " the best light to guide the erring." There men are tortured for opinions, the only punishment the Jesuits were willing their pupils should look on. This is, perhaps, too flattering a picture of the South. Better call her, as Sumner does, " the Barbarous States." Our struggle, therefore, is between barbarism and civilization. Such can only be settled by arms. The government has waited until its best friends almost suspected its courage or its integrity; but the cannon shot against Fort Sumter has opened the only door out of this hour. There were but two. One was compromise; the other was battle. The integrity of the North closed the first; the generous forbearance of nineteen States closed the other. The South opened this with cannon-shot, and Lincoln shows himself at the door. The war, then, is not aggressive, but in self-defence, and Washington has become the Thermopylæ of Liberty and Justice. Rather than surrender that Capital, cover every square foot of it with a living body; crowd it with a million of men, and empty every bank vault at the North to pay the cost. Teach the world once for all, that North America belongs to the Stars and Stripes, and under them no man shall wear a chain. In the whole of this conflict, I have looked only at Liberty, — only at the slave. Perry entered the battle of the Lakes with " DON'T GIVE UP THE SHIP ! " floating from the masthead of the Lawrence. When with his fighting flag he left her crippled, heading north, and, mounting the deck of the Niagara, turned her bows due west, he did all for one and the same purpose, — to rake the decks of the foe. Steer north or west, acknowledge secession or cannonade it, I care not which; but "Proclaim liberty throughout all the land unto all the inhabitants thereof." . . .

The noise and dust of the conflict may hide the real question at issue. Europe may think, some of us may, that we are fighting for forms and parchments, for sovereignty and a flag. But really the war is one of opinions: it is Civilization against Barbarism: it is Freedom against Slavery. The cannon-shot against Fort Sumter was the yell of pirates against the DECLARATION OF INDEPENDENCE; the war-cry of the North is the echo of that sublime pledge. The South, defying Christianity, clutches its victim. The North offers its wealth and blood in glad atonement for the selfishness of seventy years. The result is as sure as the throne of God. I believe in the possibility of justice, in the certainty of union. Years hence, when the smoke of this conflict clears away, the world will see under our banner all tongues, all creeds, all races, — one brotherhood, — and on the banks of the Potomac, the Genius of Liberty, robed in light, four and thirty stars for her diadem, broken chains under feet, and an olive-branch in her right hand.

Wendell Phillips, *Speeches, Lectures, and Letters* (Boston, 1863), 396–414 *passim.*

---

103. Battle of Bull Run (1861)

BY WILLIAM HOWARD RUSSELL

The account from which this extract is taken was sent by Russell to the London *Times.* It created much comment, and secured for its writer the title of "Bull Run Russell." — For Russell, see No. 96 above. — Bibliography: J. G. Nicolay, *Outbreak of Rebellion, passim;* J. C. Ropes, *Story of the Civil War,* I, xi-xiv; Channing and Hart, *Guide,* § 210.

[July 22, 1861.] I SIT down to give an account — not of the action yesterday, but of what I saw with my own eyes, hitherto not often deceived, and of what I heard with my own ears, which in this country are not so much to be trusted. Let me, however, express an opinion as to the affair of yesterday. In the first place, the repulse of the Federalists, decided as it was, might have had no serious effects whatever beyond the mere failure — which politically was of greater consequence than it was in a military sense — but for the disgraceful conduct of the troops. The retreat on their lines at Centreville seems to have ended in a cowardly route — a miserable, causeless panic.

Such scandalous behaviour on the part of soldiers I should have considered impossible, as with some experience of camps and armies I have
never even in alarms among camp followers seen the like of it. . . .

The North will, no doubt, recover the shock. Hitherto she has only
said, "Go and fight for the Union." The South has exclaimed, "Let us
fight for our rights." The North must put its best men into the battle,
or she will inevitably fail before the energy, the personal hatred, and the
superior fighting powers of her antagonist. In my letters, as in my conversation, I have endeavoured to show that the task which the Unionists
have set themselves is one of no ordinary difficulty, but in the state of
arrogance and supercilious confidence, either real or affected to conceal
a sense of weakness, one might as well have preached to the Pyramid of
Cheops. Indeed, one may form some notion of the condition of the
public mind by observing that journals conducted avowedly by men of
disgraceful personal character — the be-whipped and be-kicked and unrecognized pariahs of society in New York — are, nevertheless, in the
very midst of repulse and defeat, permitted to indulge in ridiculous
rhodomontade towards the nations of Europe, and to move our laughter by impotently malignant attacks on "our rotten old monarchy,"
while the stones of their bran new republic are tumbling about their
ears. It will be amusing to observe the change of tone, for we can afford
to observe and to be amused at the same time. . . .

. . . At last Centreville appeared in sight — a few houses on our front,
beyond which rose a bald hill, the slopes covered with bivouac huts,
commissariat carts, and horses, and the top crested with spectators of
the fight. . . .

. . . The scene was so peaceful a man might well doubt the evidence
of one sense that a great contest was being played out below in bloodshed. . . . But the cannon spoke out loudly from the green bushes,
and the plains below were mottled, so to speak, by puffs of smoke and
by white rings from bursting shells and capricious howitzers. . . . With
the glass I could detect now and then the flash of arms through the dust
clouds in the open, but no one could tell to which side the troops who
were moving belonged, and I could only judge from the smoke whether
the guns were fired towards or away from the hill. . . . In the midst
of our little reconnaissance Mr. Vizetelly, who has been living and, indeed, marching with one of the regiments as artist of the *Illustrated
London News*, came up and told us the action had been commenced in
splendid style by the Federalists, who had advanced steadily, driving the

Confederates before them — a part of the plan, as I firmly believe, to bring them under the range of their guns.   He believed the advantages on the Federalist side were decided, though won with hard fighting.
. . . As I turned down into the narrow road, or lane . . . there was a forward movement among the large four-wheeled tilt waggons . . . when suddenly there arose a tumult in front of me at a small bridge across the road, and then I perceived the drivers of a set of waggons with the horses turned towards me, who were endeavouring to force their way against the stream of vehicles setting in the other direction.   By the side of the new set of waggons there were a number of commissariat men and soldiers, whom at first sight I took to be the baggage guard. They looked excited and alarmed, and were running by the side of the horses — in front the dust quite obscured the view.   At the bridge the currents met in wild disorder.   " Turn back !   Retreat ! " shouted the men from the front, " We 're whipped, we 're whipped ! "   They cursed and tugged at the horses' heads, and struggled with frenzy to get past.
. . . I got my horse up into the field out of the road, and went on rapidly towards the front.   Soon I met soldiers who were coming through the corn, mostly without arms ; and presently I saw firelocks, cooking tins, knapsacks, and greatcoats on the ground, and observed that the confusion and speed of the baggage-carts became greater, and that many of them were crowded with men, or were followed by others, who clung to them.   The ambulances were crowded with soldiers, but it did not look as if there were many wounded.   Negro servants on led horses dashed frantically past ; men in uniform, whom it were a disgrace to the profession of arms to call " soldiers," swarmed by on mules, chargers, and even draught horses, which had been cut out of carts or waggons, and went on with harness clinging to their heels, as frightened as their riders. Men literally screamed with rage and fright when their way was blocked up.   On I rode, asking all " What is all this about ? " and now and then, but rarely, receiving the answer, " We 're whipped ; " or, " We 're repulsed."   Faces black and dusty, tongues out in the heat, eyes staring — it was a most wonderful sight.   On they came like him —

> " — who having once turned round goes on,
>   And turns no more his head,
> For he knoweth that a fearful fiend
>   Doth close behind him tread."

But where was the fiend ?   I looked in vain.   There was, indeed, some cannonading in front of me and in their rear, but still the firing was com-

paratively distant, and the runaways were far out of range. As I advanced the number of carts diminished, but the mounted men increased,
and the column of fugitives became denser. . . . I had ridden, I suppose, about three or three and a-half miles from the hill, though it is
not possible to be sure of the distance; when . . . I came out on an
open piece of ground, beyond and circling which was forest. Two field
pieces were unlimbered and guarding the road; the panting and jaded
horses in the rear looked as though they had been hard worked, and the
gunners and drivers looked worn and dejected. Dropping shots sounded
close in front through the woods; but the guns on the left no longer
maintained their fire. I was just about to ask one of the men for a
light, when a sputtering fire on my right attracted my attention, and out
of the forest or along the road rushed a number of men. The gunners
seized the trail of the nearest piece to wheel it round upon them; others
made for the tumbrils and horses as if to fly, when a shout was raised,
" Don't fire; they're our own men;" and in a few minutes on came
pell-mell a whole regiment in disorder. I rode across one and stopped
him. " We're pursued by cavalry," he gasped; " They've cut us all to
pieces." As he spoke a shell burst over the column; another dropped
on the road, and out streamed another column of men, keeping together
with their arms, and closing up the stragglers of the first regiment. I
turned, and to my surprise saw the artillerymen had gone off, leaving
one gun standing by itself. They had retreated with their horses. . . .
it was now well established that the retreat had really commenced, though
I saw but few wounded men, and the regiments which were falling back
had not suffered much loss. No one seemed to know anything for certain. Even the cavalry charge was a rumour. Several officers said they
had carried guns and lines, but then they drifted into the nonsense
which one reads and hears everywhere about " masked batteries." One
or two talked more sensibly about the strong positions of the enemy, the
fatigue of their men, the want of a reserve, severe losses, and the bad
conduct of certain regiments. Not one spoke as if he thought of retiring beyond Centreville. The clouds of dust rising above the woods
marked the retreat of the whole army, and the crowds of fugitives continued to steal away along the road. . . . There was no choice for me
but to resign any further researches. . . . On approaching Centreville
. . . I turned up on the hill half a mile beyond. . . . I swept the
field once more. The clouds of dust were denser and nearer. That
was all. There was no firing — no musketry. I turned my horse's head,

and rode away through the village, and after I got out upon the road the same confusion seemed to prevail. Suddenly the guns on the hill opened, and at the same time came the thuds of artillery from the wood on the right rear. The stampede then became general. What occurred at the hill I cannot say, but all the road from Centreville for miles presented such a sight as can only be witnessed in the track of the runaways of an utterly demoralized army. Drivers flogged, lashed, spurred, and beat their horses, or leaped down and abandoned their teams, and ran by the side of the road; mounted men, servants, and men in uniform, vehicles of all sorts, commissariat waggons thronged the narrow ways. At every shot a convulsion as it were seized upon the morbid mass of bones, sinew, wood, and iron, and thrilled through it, giving new energy and action to its desperate efforts to get free from itself. Again the cry of "Cavalry" arose. . . . In silence I passed over the Long-bridge. Some few hours later it quivered under the steps of a rabble of unarmed men . . . the Federalists, utterly routed, had fallen back upon Arlington to defend the capital, leaving nearly five batteries of artillery, 8,000 muskets, immense quantity of stores and baggage, and their wounded and prisoners in the hands of the enemy!

The Times (London), August 6, 1861.

---

104. "Manassas" (1861)

BY MRS. CATHARINE ANN (WARE) WARFIELD

Before the Civil War Mrs. Warfield was well known as a novelist and poet. Her home was in Kentucky; her sympathies were all with the Confederacy, and in behalf of the southern cause she wrote several passionate lyrics. "Manassas" was the name given by the Confederates to the battle of Bull Run. — Bibliography as in No. 103 above.

THEY have met at last, as storm-clouds
    Meet in heaven,
And the Northmen, back and bleeding
    Have been driven;
And their thunder has been stilled,
And their leaders crushed or killed,
And their ranks with terror thrilled,
    Rent and riven.

Like the leaves of Vallambrosa
They are lying,
In the midnight and the moonlight,
Dead or dying ;
Like those leaves before the gale,
Fled their legions — wild and pale —
While the host that made them quail
Stood defying !

When in the morning sunlight
Flags were flaunted,
And "Vengeance on the Rebels"
Proudly vaunted,
They little dreamed that night
Would close upon their flight,
And the victor of the fight
Stand undaunted.

But peace to those who perished
In our passes,
Light be the earth above them,
Green the grasses.
Long shall Northmen rue the day,
When in battle's wild affray,
They met the South's array
At Manassas.

The Southern Poems of the War (compiled by Emily V. Mason, Baltimore, 1867), 52–53.

———◆———

105. Northern Preparations (1861)

BY LOUIS PHILIPPE D'ORLEANS, COMTE DE PARIS (1874)

(TRANSLATED BY LOUIS FITZGERALD TASISTRO, 1875)

As grandson of Louis Philippe, the Comte de Paris was the head of the royal house of Orleans, and later legitimist claimant to the throne of France. He and his brother became members of McClellan's staff in September, 1861, and remained with the Union army until after the battles before Richmond in 1862. His excellent history of the war was never completed. — Bibliography as in No. 103 above.

CONGRESS on the 22d of July [1861] had correctly expressed the sentiments which animated the entire North at the news of

McDowell's defeat.   The loyal States understood at last the magnitude of the undertaking they had before them, and determined to neglect nothing that could compass its success.   Everybody set to work ; patriotic donations flowed in ; subscription funds were opened for the benefit of the soldiers ; women manifested as much zeal to induce men to enlist as in the South ; the largest iron mills in the United States were turned into cannon foundries or into outfitting establishments ; finally, enlistments became more and more numerous.   The three months' volunteers raised on the first call of April 15th were discharged, but a great many of them re-enlisted.   Those who had responded to the second call of May 4th, instead of the forty battalions asked for, already formed 208 battalions on the 21st of July.   In order to complete the effective force of 250,000 men authorized by Congress, it was only necessary to encourage this movement and to receive into the service of the Union all the new battalions thus created. . . .   As soon as they were received into the Federal service by the mustering-officer, who had charge of the registry, they were forwarded to the armies of the West or to the army of the Potomac, which were rather vast camps of instruction than armies in the field ; and as soon as they were able to defile without too much confusion they were formed into brigades of one or two battalions somewhat less inexperienced than themselves, whose example could be of use to them.

The interior organization of the armies thus formed was modelled precisely upon that of the old regular army . . . and this old army ceased to have a separate existence except in the annual Army Register. . . .

The first thing required was the appointment of a certain number of generals to assume the commands indispensable to such a large assemblage of troops. . . . the President . . . had the merit of listening to the opinions expressed by the comrades of every old officer, and his first list of generals, composed almost entirely of West Pointers, furnished him, together with a few chiefs who were to play a distinguished part in the war, a considerable number of educated and industrious men, who contributed powerfully to the organization of the volunteers.   Selections were unquestionably made which were dictated either by political influence or personal favor ; and among the first major-generals appointed by Mr. Lincoln we find two — Messrs. Banks and Butler — who are the two types of the class then styled political generals. . . .   But, on the other hand, the names of Grant, Sherman, Meade, Kearney, Hooker, Slocum, and Thomas, which were among the first promotions, show that

Mr. Lincoln knew from the outset how to select men worthy of his entire
confidence. . . .

All the administrative branches of the service were reinforced, both in
the war department and in the armies in the field, by large promotions
of officers appointed by the President, like the generals of volunteers, to
serve during the war.   But, notwithstanding their number, the *personnel*
of all these corps, like that of the staffs, was always found insufficient for
the task imposed upon it by the necessity of providing for the support
and management of an army of 500,000 men, which at the end of the
war was to number nearly 1,000,000 ; most of these officers, besides,
were utterly unaccustomed to the duties confided to them. . . .   It
required months of assiduous labor to introduce order and method in this
vast administrative machinery.   There was constantly occasion to regret
the absence of a general staff, such as is to be found in European armies,
serving as a direct medium between the chief and all the subordinate
agents placed under his command, and enabling him to enforce the execution of his wishes at all times.

When General McClellan commanded an army of 150,000 men, he had
only about him, besides four topographical engineers especially detailed
to study the ground, concerning which no map gave any precise information, eight aides-de-camp to carry his orders, to ascertain the position of
the several army corps, to accompany important reconnoissances, to convey directions to a general on the day of battle, and to receive despatches
during the night at general head-quarters and during the day, the generals, civil functionaries, bearers of flags of truce from the enemy, and,
finally, to question the inhabitants or prisoners of importance from whom
information might be obtained.

An exception should be made in favor of the medical branch of the
service ; for, if officers were scarce, physicians before the war were
numerous. . . .   It may be said that there was no branch of the service
in the whole army, unless it be that of the chaplains, which understood
and performed its duties so well as the regimental surgeons — all physicians by profession.

The composition of the *personnel* of an army, notwithstanding its importance, is not, however, either the first element of military organizations
or the most difficult to create : the most important is discipline, that
moral force without which no army can exist.   When it is established by
tradition the new-comers submit to it without difficulty.   But the Federal
government had not only to introduce it among a vast multitude of men,

all equally strangers to its severe requirements, but it did not possess any really effective means to enforce respect for it.   In the first place, if the government had the right to deprive officers of their rank, it had not the power to replace them.   It could only punish regimental officers by dismissing them, and had no rewards to offer them.   The States, fearing lest the Federal government should possess too much influence, had, in refusing the right of appointment and promotion, deprived it of the best guarantee of good service. . . .

The establishment of examining commissions operated largely in favor of discipline, and raised the dignity of the epaulette in the estimation of the soldiers by purging the *personnel* of the list of officers. . . . the examining commissions were . . . instructed to subject all the officers of the various contingents to a rigid examination before they were finally accepted by the President.   These examinations only took place several months after those contingents had been formed into divisions, so that the generals who had them under their respective commands were able to furnish the commissioners with suggestions in regard to the officers about to be examined, which more or less controlled their decisions.

The examiners always favored those who were known to be disposed to learn their profession, but those convicted of downright ignorance had no mercy shown to them. . . .

It was thus that discipline and respect for authority began to take root in the army, and their salutary influence was soon felt, although the observer, judging only from appearances, might not yet have been able to realize the fact.   Indeed, what may be called the hierarchical sentiment has never existed in the United States, where the uncertain rounds of the social ladder offer to no one a pedestal so high but that a man may descend from it without ruin, where the citizen who has deserved well of his country in a high position does not think it derogatory to his dignity to serve that country in a more modest capacity. . . .   In the volunteer army . . . no prestige could attach to the mere *epaulette*, for the soldier was the more able to criticise the ignorance of his immediate chiefs because he almost always belonged to the same county or village and had long known them personally.   The absence of that moral authority which is based upon length of service and superior experience was still more unfortunate among the non-commissioned officers, to whom it was even more indispensable in order to enforce obedience from the soldier.

But, on the other hand, the intelligence and education which lifted

most of the privates to a level with their superiors inspired them with a
natural respect for those among their chiefs in whom they recognized
the necessary qualities for command, and induced them to accept, without a murmur, the obligations and restraints of military life when they
were made to understand the necessity.   Leaving the entire monopoly
of insubordination to a few regiments, mostly composed of European
adventurers, they exhibited none of that turbulence which is frequently
associated with the name of volunteers.   A few words of caution were
sufficient to remind them that, having once taken the oath, there were no
longer *amateurs* in the ranks of the army. . . .

The *personnel* of staffs and administrative departments being once
organized and that of the contingents purified, and the first principles
of discipline established among the officers, as well as among the soldiers, the great task of drilling the army had yet hardly begun. . . .   In
order that it may acquire suppleness and agility the recruits must go
through a series of exercises and evolutions equally irksome to the
teachers and the taught — first singly, then by platoons, by battalions
next, and finally by brigades.   This task was the more difficult in the
American army because instruction was as necessary for the officers as
for the men, and because the latter, having no example to encourage
them, did not understand the utility of so long an apprenticeship.
Their intelligence, however, which rendered them submissive to the voice
of chiefs really worthy to command them, soon made them undertake it
with ardor.   Full of confidence in themselves, they made up their minds,
not that it was useless to learn, but that it would be very easy for them
to learn anything they wished, the trade of war as well as any other ;
having enlisted voluntarily, they were determined to do everything in
their power to become good soldiers capable of victory.

They were, therefore, of as much value as their chiefs, whose examples
exercised an all-powerful influence over the collective spirit, if we may
use such an expression, which animates a body of troops.   A rapid change
took place in those regiments in which the superior officers went assidu-
ously to work and began by learning themselves what they desired to
teach their inferiors. . . .

The special services found great resource in the aptitude of the American to pass from one trade to another.   This is a great and valuable
quality which the practice of true liberty engenders by protecting the
individual against excesses in the pursuit of specialties which confine the
faculties of man within a narrow prison. . . .

In order to organize the engineer service it was also found necessary to appeal to the ardor of volunteers who had no military instruction. The officers of that arm scattered among the various corps were not sufficiently numerous to direct in person all the works required by the military operations, nor to instruct the soldiers employed in them. But there were found, on the one hand, useful auxiliaries among civil engineers, a large and educated class, composed of practical men accustomed to struggle with the difficulties of the virgin soil of America ; while, on the other hand, a rapid course of special instruction imparted to a few regiments sufficed to qualify them for the most important works of engineering art, while the rougher work was entrusted indiscriminately to the various regiments of volunteers, among whom some skilful artisans were always sure to be found. The construction of these works was never entirely new to them. Even the most populous States, which still possessed vast forests, all furnished a considerable contingent of woodmen or lumbermen and pioneers, inured from their infancy to the use of the axe, the pick, and the spade, and one regiment a thousand strong might be seen felling more than eighty acres (*quarantes hectares*) of tall forests in a single day.

Comte de Paris, *History of the Civil War in America* (edited by Henry Coppée, Philadelphia, 1875), I, 262–277 *passim*.

---

106. Supplies for the Confederacy (1861)

BY EX-PRESIDENT JEFFERSON DAVIS (1881)

The work from which this extract is taken was prepared under Davis's dictation, a method which makes it liable to inaccuracy of detail. It is, however, a kind of official defence of the South by the man who knew most about the beginnings and progress of the Confederacy. — For Davis, see No. 62 above. — Bibliography : Channing and Hart, *Guide*, §§ 209, 210.

TO furnish one hundred and fifty thousand men, on both sides of the Mississippi, in May, 1861, there were no infantry accoutrements, no cavalry arms or equipments, no artillery, and, above all, no ammunition ; nothing save arms, and these almost wholly the old pattern smooth-bore muskets, altered to percussion from flint locks.

Within the limits of the Confederate States the arsenals had been used only as depots, and no one of them, except that at Fayetteville, North Carolina, had a single machine above the grade of a foot-lathe. Except at Harper's Ferry Armory, all the work of preparation of material had been carried on at the North; not an arm, not a gun, not a gun-carriage, and, except during the Mexican War, scarcely a round of ammunition, had for fifty years been prepared in the Confederate States. There were consequently no workmen, or very few, skilled in these arts. Powder, save perhaps for blasting, had not been made at the South. No saltpeter was in store at any Southern point; it was stored wholly at the North. There were no worked mines of lead except in Virginia, and the situation of those made them a precarious dependence. The only cannon-foundry existing was at Richmond. Copper, so necessary for field-artillery and for percussion-caps, was just being obtained in East Tennessee. There was no rolling-mill for bar-iron south of Richmond, and but few blast-furnaces, and these, with trifling exceptions, were in the border States of Virginia and Tennessee.

The first efforts made to obtain powder were by orders sent to the North, which had been early done both by the Confederate Government and by some of the States. These were being rapidly filled when the attack was made on Fort Sumter. The shipments then ceased. . . .

For the supply of arms an agent was sent to Europe, who made contracts to the extent of nearly half a million dollars. Some small-arms had been obtained from the North, and also important machinery. The machinery at Harper's Ferry Armory had been saved from the flames by the heroic conduct of the operatives, headed by Mr. Armistead M. Ball, the master armorer. Of the machinery so saved, that for making rifle-muskets was transported to Richmond, and that for rifles with sword-bayonets to Fayetteville, North Carolina. In addition to the injuries suffered by the machinery, the lack of skilled workmen caused much embarrassment. . . .

In field-artillery the manufacture was confined almost entirely to the Tredegar Works in Richmond. . . . The State of Virginia possessed a number of old four-pounder iron guns which were reamed out to get a good bore, and rifled with three grooves, after the manner of Parrott. The army at Harper's Ferry and that at Manassas were supplied with old batteries of six-pounder guns and twelve-pounder howitzers. A few Parrott guns, purchased by the State of Virginia, were with General Magruder at Big Bethel.

For the ammunition and equipment required for the infantry and artillery, a good laboratory and workshop had been established at Richmond. The arsenals were making preparations for furnishing ammunition and knapsacks; but generally, what little was done in this regard was for local purposes. Such was the general condition of ordnance and ordnance stores in May, 1861.

The progress of development, however, was steady. A refinery of saltpeter was established near Nashville during the summer, which received the niter from its vicinity, and from the caves in East and Middle Tennessee. Some inferior powder was made at two small mills in South Carolina. North Carolina established a mill near Raleigh; and a stamping-mill was put up near New Orleans, and powder made there before the fall of the city. Small quantities were also received through the blockade. . . .

. . . It was . . . necessary that we should establish a Government powder-mill. . . .

These Government powder-mills were located at Augusta, Georgia, and satisfactory progress was made in the construction during the year. All the machinery, including the very heavy rollers, was made in the Confederate States. Contracts were made abroad for the delivery of niter through the blockade; and, for obtaining it immediately, we resorted to caves, tobacco-houses, cellars, etc. The amount delivered from Tennessee was the largest item in the year's supply, but the whole was quite inadequate to existing and prospective needs.

The consumption of lead was mainly met by the Virginia lead-mines at Wytheville, the yield from which was from sixty to eighty thousand pounds per month. Lead was also collected by agents in considerable quantities throughout the country, and the battle-field of Manassas was closely gleaned, from which much lead was collected. . . .

By the close of 1861, eight arsenals and four depots had been supplied with materials and machinery, so as to be efficient in producing the various munitions and equipments, the want of which had caused early embarrassment. Thus a good deal had been done to produce the needed material of war, and to refute the croakers who found in our poverty application for the maxim, " *Ex nihilo nihil fit.*" . . .

. . . To provide the iron needed for cannon and projectiles, it had been necessary to stimulate by contracts the mining and smelting of its ores.

. . . A niter and mining bureau was organized. . . .

Niter was to be obtained from caves and other like sources, and by the formation of niter-beds, some of which had previously been begun at Richmond. . . . The whole country was laid off into districts, each of

Y

which was under the charge of an officer, who obtained details of work-men from the army, and made his monthly reports. Thus the niter production, in the course of a year, was brought up to something like half of the total consumption. . . . The supervision of the production of iron, lead, copper, and all the minerals which needed development, as well as the manufacture of sulphuric and nitric acids (the latter required for the supply of the fulminate of mercury for percussion-caps), without which the firearms of our day would have been useless, was added to the niter bureau. Such was the progress that, in a short time, the bureau was aiding or managing some twenty to thirty furnaces with an annual yield of fifty thousand tons or more of pig-iron. The lead- and copper-smelting works erected were sufficient for all wants, and the smelting of zinc of good quality had been achieved. The chemical works were placed at Charlotte, North Carolina, to serve as a reserve when the supply from abroad might be cut off.

In equipping the armies first sent into the field, the supply of acces-sories was embarrassingly scant. There were arms, such as they were, for over one hundred thousand men, but no accoutrements nor equip-ments, and a meager supply of ammunition. In time the knapsacks were supplanted by haversacks, which the women could make. But soldiers' shoes and cartridge-boxes must be had; leather was also needed for artillery-harness and for cavalry-saddles; and, as the amount of leather which the country could furnish was quite insufficient for all these purposes, it was perforce apportioned among them. Soldiers' shoes were the prime necessity. Therefore, a scale was established, by which first shoes and then cartridge-boxes had the preference; after these, artillery-harness, and then saddles and bridles. To economize leather, the waist and cartridge-box belts were made of prepared cotton cloth stitched in three or four thicknesses. Bridle-reins were likewise so made, and then cartridge-boxes were thus covered, except the flap. Saddle-skirts, too, were made of heavy cotton cloth strongly stitched. To get leather, each department procured its quota of hides, made con-tracts with the tanners, obtained hands for them by exemptions from the army, got transportation over the railroads for the hides and for sup-plies. To the varied functions of this bureau was finally added that of assisting the tanners to procure the necessary supplies for the tanneries. A fishery, even, was established on Cape Fear River to get oil for me-chanical purposes, and at the same time food for the workmen. . . . One of the most difficult wants to supply in this branch of the service was the horseshoe for cavalry and artillery. The want of iron and of skilled labor was strongly felt. Every wayside blacksmith-shop accessible, especially those in and near the theatre of operations, was employed. These, again, had to be supplied with material, and the employees exempted from service.

It early became manifest that great reliance must be placed on the introduction of articles of prime necessity through the blockaded ports. A vessel, capable of stowing six hundred and fifty bales of cotton, was purchased by the agent in England, and kept running between Bermuda and Wilmington. Some fifteen to eighteen successive trips were made before she was captured. Another was added, which was equally successful. These vessels were long, low, rather narrow, and built for speed. They were mostly of pale sky-color, and, with their lights out and with fuel that made little smoke, they ran to and from Wilmington with considerable regularity. Several others were added, and devoted to bringing in ordnance, and finally general supplies. Depots of stores were likewise made at Nassau and Havana. Another organization was also necessary, that the vessels coming in through the blockade might have their return cargoes promptly on their arrival. These resources were also supplemented by contracts for supplies brought through Texas from Mexico. . . .

The chief armories were at Richmond and Fayetteville, North Carolina. . . . A great part of the work of the armories consisted in the repair of arms. In this manner the gleanings of the battle-fields were utilized. Nearly ten thousand stands were saved from the field of Manassas, and from those about Richmond in 1862 about twenty-five thousand excellent arms. All the stock of inferior arms disappeared from the armories during the first two years of the war, and were replaced by a better class of arms, rifled and percussioned. Placing the good arms lost previous to July, 1863, at one hundred thousand, there must have been received from various sources four hundred thousand stands of infantry arms in the first two years of the war.

Jefferson Davis, *The Rise and Fall of the Confederate Government* (New York, D. Appleton & Co., 1881), I, 472–480 *passim*.

CHAPTER XIX — YEAR OF DISCOURAGE-
MENT

107. Capture of Fort Donelson (1862)

FROM THE CHICAGO TRIBUNE

The great newspapers of the North were noted for their enterprise in securing quick and usually accurate news from the front, and their correspondents were exposed to all the trials and hardships of combatants. This account is deficient in not stating that General Smith personally led the charge on the Union left. — For the *Chicago Tribune*, see No. 77 above. — Bibliography: M. F. Force, *From Fort Henry to Corinth, passim ;* J. C. Ropes, *Story of the Civil War*, II, vii–xii; Channing and Hart, *Guide*, § 210.

[February 17, 1862.] AFTER the capture of Fort Henry, General Grant as soon as possible moved across the twelve mile strip of land between the rivers and invested the place by throwing McClernand's division upon the right, at the creek — extending his pickets down to the river beyond. General Wallace occupied the centre, while General Smith closed up all communication with the outside world on the North. Our forces occupied a range of hills almost one mile distant from the enemy's outer works. . . .

The army made no movement on Friday [February 14] of consequence, but waited any demonstration the rebels might make. They were elated with the repulse of the gunboats, and undoubtedly concluded that, they would either repulse the army, or if not that they would cut their way through and escape to Clarksville.

Prepared to do either, as circumstances might decide, at six o'clock on Saturday morning they appeared in solid column upon the road, which seems partly parallel to the creek, at McClernand's right. It was a few minutes past six when our pickets exchanged shots with their skirmishers.

Immediately the whole division was astir, waiting for what might turn up. As the rebels neared our forces they deployed and formed in line of battle, making the most furious attack upon the right ; also sending their Mississippi sharp shooters, as one of the Captains, now a pris·oner, informed me, to the left to throw the 11th and 20th regiments into confusion.

It was about seven o'clock when the firing began on the right, and in a few minutes it was running like a train of powder on a floor, along the entire line. The rebels advanced with determination — not in a regular line, but in the guerilla mode — availing themselves of the trees and the undulations of the ground. Their design was to cut the division at the centre, turn the regiments on the right composing Oglesby's Brigade up against the creek and capture them. But their movements to that end were foiled. The regiments at the center being pressed, after standing a hot fire, begun gradually to fall back, which rendered it necessary for Oglesby to do the same as he separated, from the division, and the entire right wing of the division accordingly swung back, slowly at first. . . .

And now occurred one of those wonders common in warfare. The enemy pressing hard upon our forces, Gen. McClernand sent Major Brayman for reinforcements. He rode rapidly to the rear and came upon Col. Cruft's brigade, who moved forward, crossed the road, and came up in rear of the 30th and 31st. These regiments were lying down and firing over the crest of a ridge. As Col. Cruft came in rear of them they rose to their feet, not knowing whether the force in their rear was friend or foe. The 25th Ky. supposing them to be rebels, poured in a volley, which did terrible execution. It is not possible to ascertain how many fell under the fire, but it was sufficient to throw the entire division into disorder, and at once there was almost a panic. . . .

The enemy improved the opportunity, and advanced upon Dresser's and Schwartz's batteries, capturing five guns, taking possession of General McClernand's headquarters, and driving our forces nearly a mile and a half. They had opened the gap ; and not only that, but had in the joust driven us, captured five guns, and had reason to feel that the day was theirs.

But now they committed a fatal mistake. Instead of adhering to the original plan, to escape, they resolved to follow up their advantage by pursuit, cut us up and capture the entire army.

The fight had lasted nearly four hours, and McClernand's division was exhausted ; besides they were out of ammunition.

At this juncture General Wallace's division was thrown in front. They took up a position on a ridge, with Captain Taylor's battery in the center at the road, commanding it down the ridge to the bottom of a ravine. McClernand's division was making up its scattered ranks, ready to support Wallace. It was now just noon — nearly one o'clock. The rebels formed upon the ridge which General McClernand had occupied through the night. They were flushed with success and descended the ridge with the expectation of routing the Yankees. As they came in range, Taylor opened upon them with shell, grape and canister. They quailed before it, advanced at a slow pace, came to a halt, and as the infantry opened, began to fall back. Wallace improved the moment, moved on, drove them before him, regained the lost ground, recovered McClernand's tent and occupied the old ground. . . .

The rebels might have escaped when Wallace was driving them back, but by some fatuity neglected the opportunity and were again boxed up. This made two distinct fights, but the day was not thus to close. There was to be a second display of coolness, daring and determined bravery of Union troops, fighting under the Stars and Stripes, resulting in a signal victory.

The Iowa and Indiana boys composing Lauman's brigade of Smith's division, were ready to do their part in crushing out rebellion, and General Grant decided that they should have an opportunity to show their valor. Directly west of Fort Donelson, and beyond the breastworks there was a second ridge of land running parallel to that on which the breastworks were erected. The distance across from ridge to ridge, as near as I could judge by a somewhat minute survey, is about forty rods. On this outer ridge were ten rifle pits, made of logs, with a shallow ditch behind and the excavated earth thrown up in front. The western slope of the ridge was quite steep. The distance to the base was thirty rods as I judged, opening upon a meadow and cornfield. The slope had been forest, but the rebels had used their axes and cut down the trees, forming an abbatis not impassible because the forest was not dead, but a serious obstruction to the advance of an army. It was desirable that the rebels should be driven out of their pits, for they in part commanded Fort Donelson, lying about sixty rods farther east. . . .

Col. Lauman gave the 2d Iowa the honor of leading the charge. They moved across the meadow through a little belt of woods, came to the base of the hill, and met the leaden rain. But they paused not a moment. Then they encountered the fallen trees, but instead of being disheartened, they seemed to feel new life and energy. Without firing a shot, without flinching a moment or faltering as their ranks were thinned, they rushed up the hill, regardless of the fire in front or on their flank, jumped upon the rifle pits and drove the rebels down the eastern slope. They escaped into their inner line of defenses. Col. Lauman did not deem it prudent to follow, but halted his men and poured a deadly fire upon the foe, in force, with four cannon behind the works. ·

Then for ten minutes the fire was exceedingly severe. I visited the spot on Sunday afternoon and found the ground thick with bullets fired by the rebels. The trees were scarred but bore evidence on their limbs that the aim of the rebels had been much too high. Col. Lauman called his men back to their rifle pits, and there they lay down upon their arms, holding the position through the night, ready with the first flash of dawn to make a breach into the line beyond. . . .

Col. Lauman was apprised during the night that the rebels were about to surrender, by a negro who escaped to his lines. Soon after daylight an officer, Major Calsbry, appeared, bearing a white flag and a note from General Buckner to General Grant, proposing a cessation of hostilities and the appointment of commissioners. . . .

The victory was won, and Fort Donelson was ours, with its seventeen heavy size guns, its forty-eight field pieces, its fifteen thousand soldiers, its twenty thousand stand of arms, its tents and ammunition — all were unconditionally ours.

Wild were the cheers, loud were the salutes from the fleet and from Taylor's batteries when the Stars and Stripes, the glorious old flag, was flung to the breeze upon the ramparts of Fort Donelson.

I cannot give you the sights or the incidents. You must imagine them. Neither have I time to tell of the appearance of the rebels in their snuff-colored, shabby clothes — their bedquilts, pieces of carpeting, coverlids, sacking — but there they were, gloomy, downcast, humbled, apprehensive for the future ; and yet I think that many of them were not sorry that there was to be no more fighting. I made myself at home among them, talked with them freely, heard their indignant utterances against Floyd, who had sneaked away with his Virginia regiments, the 36th, 50th and 51st, and a host of stragglers — officers many of them — who did not hesitate to desert their men in the hour of adversity. They went away at midnight after an angry altercation, as I was informed by a secession officer, between Pillow, Floyd and Buckner. I am also informed that about five thousand rebels escaped, the boats being loaded to the guards. Forest's Louisiana cavalry escaped on their horses along the creek. But the great bulk of the army is ours. Fifteen thousand prisoners! What shall we do with them? We have indeed drawn an elephant. . . .

The following correspondence passed between Gen. Grant, commanding the Federal forces, and Gen. S. B. Buckner, commanding the Confederates:

HEADQUARTERS FORT DONELSON, February 16, 1862.

Sir: In consideration of all the circumstances governing the present situation of affairs at this station, I propose to the commanding officer of the Federal forces, the appointment of Commissioners to agree upon terms of capitulation of the forces and post under my command, and in that view suggest an armistice until 2 o'clock to-day.

I am, sir, very respectfully,
Your obedient servant,
S. B. BUCKNER, Brig. Gen. C.S.A.

To Brig. Gen. U. S. GRANT, Com'g U. S. forces near Fort Donelson. . . .

HEADQUARTERS ARMY IN THE FIELD, NEAR DONELSON, Feb. 16, 1862.

To Gen. S. B. Buckner, Confederate Army . . .

No terms except unconditional and immediate surrender can be accepted. I propose to move immediately upon your works.

I am, sir, very respectfully,
Your obd't serv't,
U. S. GRANT, Brig. Gen. Commanding.

HEADQUARTERS, DOVER, Tenn., Feb. 16, 1862.

To Brig. Gen. U. S. Grant, U. S. A.:

SIR: The distribution of the forces under my command, incident to an unexpected change of commanders and the overwhelming force under your command, compel me, notwithstanding the brilliant success of the Confederate arms yesterday, to accept the ungenerous and unchivalrous terms which you propose. I am, dear sir,

Your very obedient servant,
S. B. BUCKNER,
Brig. Gen. C. S. A.

Chicago Weekly Tribune, February 20, 1862.

108. "The Cumberland" (1862)

BY HENRY WADSWORTH LONGFELLOW

Longfellow lacked the aggressive temperament that made Whittier and Lowell prominent in reform causes, but he loved his country with a deep wholesomeness that often found voice in his poems. The event here described occurred in the first day's attack of the Confederate ironclad Merrimac upon the Union vessels in Hampton Roads. — For Longfellow, see Henry Matson, *References for Literary Workers*, 324-326. — Bibliography: J. R. Soley, *The Blockade and the Cruisers*, ch. iii; J. F. Rhodes, *History of the United States*, III, 613, note; Channing and Hart, *Guide*, § 210.

AT anchor in Hampton Roads we lay,
  On board of the Cumberland, sloop-of-war;
And at times from the fortress across the bay
    The alarum of drums swept past,
    Or a bugle blast
  From the camp on the shore.

Then far away to the south uprose
  A little feather of snow-white smoke,
And we know that the iron ship of our foes
    Was steadily steering its course
    To try the force
  Of our ribs of oak.

Down upon us heavily runs,
  Silent and sullen, the floating fort;
Then comes a puff of smoke from her guns,
    And leaps the terrible death,
    With fiery breath,
  From each open port

We are not idle, but send her straight
  Defiance back in a full broadside!
As hail rebounds from a roof of slate,
    Rebounds our heavier hail
    From each iron scale
  Of the monster's hide.

"Strike your flag!" the rebel cries,
  In his arrogant old plantation strain.
"Never!" our gallant Morris replies;

"It is better to sink than to yield !"
And the whole air pealed
With the cheers of our men.

Then, like a kraken huge and black,
She crushed our ribs in her iron grasp !
Down went the Cumberland all a wrack,
With a sudden shudder of death,
And the cannon's breath
For her dying gasp.

Next morn, as the sun rose over the bay,
Still floated our flag at the mainmast head.
Lord, how beautiful was Thy day !
Every waft of the air
Was a whisper of prayer,
Or a dirge for the dead.

Ho ! brave hearts that went down in the seas !
Ye are at peace in the troubled stream ;
Ho ! brave land ! with hearts like these,
Thy flag, that is rent in twain,
Shall be one again,
And without a seam !

Henry Wadsworth Longfellow, *Poetical Works* (Boston, 1867), 330.

---

109. The Monitor and the Merrimac (1862)

BY MEDICAL-DIRECTOR CHARLES MARTIN (1886)

Martin was a surgeon in the navy, and rose to the rank of medical director. This extract is from a paper of personal reminiscences read before the New York Commandery of the Loyal Legion in 1886. — Bibliography as in No. 108 above.

COMPANIONS : I will tell you what I saw at Newport News when the *Merrimac* destroyed the *Congress* and the *Cumberland,* and fought with the *Monitor.* It was a drama in three acts, and twelve hours will elapse between the second and third acts.

"Let us begin at the beginning" — 1861. The North Atlantic squadron is at Hampton Roads, except the frigate *Congress* and the razee *Cumberland;* they are anchored at Newport News, blockading the James River and Norfolk. The *Merrimac,* the Rebel ram, is in the dry dock of the Norfolk navy-yard. . . .

The *Monitor* is building in New York City. . . . It is determined to keep the *Merrimac* in the dry dock, wait the arrival of the *Monitor,* send her out to meet her, and in the action it is positive that an opportunity will offer to pierce and sink her. The ram is a terror, and both sides say, " When the *Merrimac* comes out ! " The last of February, 1862, the *Monitor* is ready for sea ; she will sail for Hampton Roads in charge of a steamer. There is a rumor that she has broken her steering gear before reaching Sandy Hook. She will be towed to Washington for repairs. The Rebel spies report her a failure — steering defective, turret revolves with difficulty, and when the smoke of her guns in action is added to the defects of ventilation, it will be impossible for human beings to live aboard of her. No *Monitor* to fight, the Southern press and people grumble ; they pitch into the *Merrimac.* Why does she lie idle ? Send her out to destroy the *Congress* and the *Cumberland,* that have so long bullied Norfolk, then sweep away the fleet at Hampton Roads, starve out Fortress Monroe, go north to Baltimore and New York and Boston, and destroy and plunder ; and the voice of the people, not always an inspiration, prevails, and the ram is floated and manned and armed, and March 8th is bright and sunny when she steams down the Elizabeth River to carry out the first part of her programme. And all Norfolk and Portsmouth ride and run to the bank of the James, to have a picnic, and assist at a naval battle and victory. The cry of " Wolf ! " has so often been heard aboard the ships that the *Merrimac* has lost much of her terrors. They argue : " If she is a success, why don't she come out and destroy us ? " And when seen this morning at the mouth of the river : " It is only a trial trip or a demonstration." But she creeps along the opposite shore, and both ships beat to quarters and get ready for action. The boats of the *Cumberland* are lowered, made fast to each other in line, anchored between the ship and the shore, about an eighth of a mile distant.

Here are two large sailing frigates, on a calm day, at slack water, anchored in a narrow channel, impossible to get under weigh and manœuvre, and must lie and hammer, and be hammered, so long as they hold together, or until they sink at their anchors. To help them is a tug, the *Zouave,* once used in the basin at Albany to tow canal boats under the grain elevator. The *Congress* is the senior ship ; the tug makes fast to her.   The *Congress* slips her cable and tries to get under weigh. The tug does her best and breaks her engine.   The *Congress* goes aground in line with the shore.   The *Zouave* floats down the river, firing her pop-guns at the *Merrimac* as she drifts by her.   The captain of the *Congress* was detached on the 7th.   He is waiting a chance to go North.   He serves as a volunteer in the action, refusing to resume command and deprive the first lieutenant of a chance for glory.   The captain of the *Cumberland* has been absent since the 3d.   He is president of a court-martial at this moment in session on board the *Roanoke* at Hampton Roads, so the command of both the ships devolves on the first lieutenants. On board the *Cumberland* all hands are allowed to remain on deck, watching the slow approach of the *Merrimac*, and she comes on so slowly, the pilot declares she has missed the channel ; she draws too much water to use her ram.   She continues to advance, and two gun-boats, the *Yorktown* and the *Teazer*, accompany her.   Again they beat to quarters, and every one goes to his station.   There is a platform on the roof of the *Merrimac*.   Her captain is standing on it.   When she is near enough, he hails, " Do you surrender ? "   " *Never!* " is the reply.   The order to fire is given ; the shot of the starboard battery rattles on the iron roof of the *Merrimac*.   She answers with a shell ; it sweeps the forward pivot gun, it kills and wounds ten of the gun's crew.   A second slaughters the marines at the after pivot gun.   The *Yorktown* and the *Teazer* keep up a constant fire.   She bears down on the *Cumberland*.   She rams her just aft the starboard bow.   The ram goes into the sides of the ship as a knife goes into a cheese.   The *Merrimac* tries to back out ; the tide is making ; it catches against her great length at a right angle with the *Cumberland ;* it slews her around ; the weakened, lengthened ram breaks off ; she leaves it in the *Cumberland*.   The battle rages, broadside answers broadside, and the sanded deck is red and slippery with the blood of the wounded and dying; they are dragged amidships out of the way of the guns ; there is no one and no time to take them below.   Delirium seizes the crew ; they strip to their trousers, tie their handkerchiefs round their heads, kick off their shoes, fight and yell like demons, load and fire at will, keep it up for the rest of the forty-two minutes the ship is sinking, and fire a last gun as the water rushes into her ports. . . .

The *Merrimac* turns to the *Congress*.   She is aground, but she fires her guns till the red-hot shot from the enemy sets her on fire, and the flames drive the men away from the battery.   She has forty years of seasoning; she burns like a torch. Her commanding officer is killed, and her deck strewn with killed and wounded. The wind is off shore; they drag the wounded under the windward bulwark, where all hands take refuge from the flames. The sharpshooters on shore drive away a tug from the enemy. The crew and wounded of the *Congress* are safely landed. She burns the rest of the afternoon and evening, discharging her loaded guns over the camp. At midnight the fire has reached her magazines — the *Congress* disappears.

When it is signalled to the fleet at Hampton Roads that the *Merrimac* has come out, the *Minnesota* leaves her anchorage and hastens to join the battle. Her pilot puts her aground off the Elizabeth River, and she lies there helpless. The *Merrimac* has turned back for Norfolk. She has suffered from the shot of the *Congress* and the *Cumberland*, or she would stop and destroy the *Minnesota;* instead, with the *Yorktown* and *Teazer*, she goes back into the river. Sunday morning, March 9th, the *Merrimac* is coming out to finish her work. She will destroy the *Minnesota*. As she nears her, the *Monitor* appears from behind the helpless ship; she has slipped in during the night, and so quietly, her presence is unknown in the camp. And David goes out to meet Goliath, and every man who can walk to the beach sits down there, spectators of the first iron-clad battle in the world. The day is calm, the smoke hangs thick on the water, the low vessels are hidden by the smoke. They are so sure of their invulnerability, they fight at arms' length. They fight so near the shore, the flash of their guns is seen, and the noise is heard of the heavy shot pounding the armor. They haul out for breath, and again disappear in the smoke. The *Merrimac* stops firing, the smoke lifts, she is running down the *Monitor*, but she has left her ram in the *Cumberland*. The *Monitor* slips away, turns, and renews the action. One P.M. — they have fought since 8:30 A.M.: The crews of both ships are suffocating under the armor. The frames supporting the iron roof of the *Merrimac* are sprung and shattered. The turret of the *Monitor* is dented with shot, and is revolved with difficulty. The captain of the *Merrimac* is wounded in the leg; the captain of the *Monitor* is blinded with powder. It is a drawn game. The *Merrimac*, leaking badly, goes back to Norfolk; the *Monitor* returns to Hampton Roads.

Personal Recollections of the War of the Rebellion, Second Series (edited by A. Noel Blakeman. New York, etc., 1897), 1–6 *passim.*

110. Pittsburg Landing (1862)

BY BRIGADIER-GENERAL BENJAMIN MAYBERRY PRENTISS

Prentiss was a volunteer officer, and at the battle of Pittsburg Landing, or Shiloh, he commanded one of the divisions of Grant's army. This extract is from his official report. It is now very generally recognized that the valiant and stubborn defence by the divisions of Prentiss and W. H. L. Wallace prevented the Confederate army from attaining a victory on the first day, and made possible the Union victory on the second day of the battle. — Bibliography as in No. 107 above.

AT 3 o'clock on the morning of Sunday, April 6, Col. David Moore, Twenty-first Missouri, with five companies of his infantry regiment, proceeded to the front, and at break of day the advance pickets were driven in, whereupon Colonel Moore pushed forward and engaged the enemy's advance, commanded by General Hardee. At this stage a messenger was sent to my headquarters, calling for the balance of the Twenty-first Missouri, which was promptly sent forward. This information received, I at once ordered the entire force into line, and the remaining regiments of the First Brigade, commanded by Col. Everett Peabody, consisting of the Twenty-fifth Missouri, Sixteenth Wisconsin, and Twelfth Michigan Infantry, were advanced well to the front. I forthwith at this juncture communicated the fact of the attack in force to Major-General Smith and Brig. Gen. S. A. Hurlbut.

Shortly before 6 o'clock, Col. David Moore having been severely wounded, his regiment commenced falling back, reaching our front line at about 6 o'clock, the enemy being close upon his rear. Hereupon the entire force, excepting only the Sixteenth Iowa, which had been sent to the field the day previous without ammunition, and the cavalry, which was held in readiness to the rear, was advanced to the extreme front, and thrown out alternately to the right and left.

Shortly after 6 o'clock the entire line was under fire, receiving the assault made by the entire force of the enemy, advancing in three columns simultaneously upon our left, center, and right. This position was held until the enemy had passed our right flank, this movement being effected by reason of the falling back of some regiment to our right not belonging to the division.

Perceiving the enemy was flanking me, I ordered the division to retire in line of battle to the color line of our encampment, at the same time communicating to Generals Smith and Hurlbut the fact of the falling back, and asking for re-enforcements.

Being again assailed, in position described, by an overwhelming force, and not being able longer to hold the ground against the enemy, I ordered the division to fall back to the line occupied by General Hurlbut, and at 9.05 a.m. reformed to the right of General Hurlbut, and to the left of Brig. Gen. W. H. L. Wallace, who I found in command of the division assigned to Major-General Smith. At this point the Twenty-third Missouri Infantry, commanded by Colonel Tindall, which had just disembarked from a transport, and had been ordered to report to me as a part of the Sixth Division, joined me. This regiment I immediately assigned to position on the left. My battery (Fifth Ohio) was posted to the right on the road.

At about 10 o'clock my line was again assailed, and finding my command greatly reduced by reason of casualties and because of the falling back of many of the men to the river, they being panic-stricken — a majority of them having now for the first time been exposed to fire — I communicated with General W. H. L. Wallace, who sent to my assistance the Eighth Iowa Infantry, commanded by Col. J. L. Geddes.

After having once driven the enemy back from this position Maj. Gen. U. S. Grant appeared upon the field. I exhibited to him the disposition of my entire force, which disposition received his commendation, and I received my final orders, which were to maintain that position at all hazards. This position I did maintain until 4 o'clock p.m., when General Hurlbut, being overpowered, was forced to retire. I was then compelled to change front with the Twenty-third Missouri, Twenty-first Missouri, Eighteenth Wisconsin, Eighteenth Missouri, and part of the Twelfth Michigan, occupying a portion of the ground vacated by General Hurlbut. I was in constant communication with Generals Hurlbut and Wallace during the day, and both of them were aware of the importance of holding our position until night. When the gallant Hurlbut was forced to retire General Wallace and myself consulted, and agreed to hold our positions at all hazards, believing that we could thus save the army from destruction; we having been now informed for the first time that all others had fallen back to the vicinity of the river. A few minutes after General W. H. L. Wallace received the wound of which he shortly afterwards died. Upon the fall of General Wallace, his division, excepting the Eighth Iowa, Colonel Geddes, acting with me, and the Fourteenth Iowa, Colonel Shaw; Twelfth Iowa, Colonel Woods, and Fifty-eighth Illinois, Colonel Lynch, retired from the field.

Perceiving that I was about to be surrounded, and having dispatched my aide, Lieut. Edwin Moore, for re-enforcements, I determined to assail the enemy, which had passed between me and the river, charging upon him with my entire force. I found him advancing in mass, completely encircling my command, and nothing was left but to harass him and retard his progress so long as might be possible. This I did until 5.30 p.m., when, finding that further resistance must result in the slaughter of every man in the command, I had to yield the fight. The enemy succeeded in capturing myself and 2,200 rank and file, many of them being wounded.

The War of the Rebellion: Official Records of the Union and Confederate Armies, First Series (Washington, 1884), X, pt. i, 278–279.

---

111. Passing the Forts at New Orleans (1862)

BY CAPTAIN THEODORUS BAILEY

Bailey was a naval officer of long experience, having been appointed a midshipman in 1818. He was Farragut's second in command in the great naval conflict below New Orleans during the Civil War, and in the little gunboat Cayuga led the line of battle, Farragut's column being behind Bailey's. This extract is from Bailey's official report to the secretary of the navy. — Bibliography: A. T. Mahan, *The Gulf and Inland Waters,* ch. iii; J. F. Rhodes, *History of the United States,* III, 629, note; Channing and Hart, *Guide,* § 210.

THAT brave, resolute, and indefatigable officer, Commander D.D. Porter, was at work with his mortar fleet, throwing shells at and into Fort Jackson, while General Butler, with a division of his army, in transports, was waiting a favorable moment to land. After the mortar fleet had been playing upon the forts for six days and nights, (without perceptibly diminishing their fire,) and one or two changes of programme, Flag-Officer Farragut formed the ships into two columns, "line ahead;" the column of the red, under my orders, being formed on the right, and consisting of the Cayuga, Lieutenant Commanding Harrison, bearing my flag, and leading the Pensacola, Captain Morris; the Mississippi, Commander M. Smith; Oneida, Commander S. P. Lee; Varuna, Commander C. S. Boggs; Katahdin, Lieutenant Commanding Preble; Kineo, Lieutenant Commanding Ransom; and the Wissahickon, Lieutenant Commanding A. N. Smith. The column of the blue was formed on the left, heading up the river, and consisted of the flag-ship Hartford, Commander R. Wainwright, and bearing the flag of the commander-in-chief, Farragut;

the Brooklyn, Captain T. T. Craven ; the Richmond, Commander Alden ; the Sciota, bearing the divisional flag of Fleet-Captain H. H. Bell ; followed by the Iroquois, Itasca, Winona, and Kennebec.

At 2 a.m. on the morning of the 24th [April] the signal " to advance " was thrown out from the flag-ship. The Cayuga immediately weighed anchor and led on the column. We were discovered at the boom, and, a little beyond, both forts opened their fire. When close up with St. Philip we opened with grape and canister, still steering on. After passing this line of fire, we encountered the " Montgomery flotilla," consisting of eighteen gunboats, including the ram Manassas and iron battery Louisiana, of twenty guns.

This was a moment of anxiety, as no supporting ship was in sight. By skilful steering, however, we avoided their attempts to butt and board, and had succeeded in forcing the surrender of three, when the Varuna, Captain Boggs, and Oneida, Captain Lee, were discovered near at hand. The gallant exploits of these ships will be made known by their commanders. At early dawn discovered a rebel camp on the right bank of the river. Ordering Lieutenant Commanding N. B. Harrison to anchor close alongside, I hailed and ordered the colonel to pile up his arms on the river bank and come on board. This proved to be the Chalmette regiment, commanded by Colonel Szymanski. The regimental flag, tents, and camp equipage were captured.

On the morning of the 25th, still leading, and considerably ahead of the line, the Chalmette batteries, situated three miles below the city, opened a cross fire on the Cayuga. To this we responded with our two guns. At the end of twenty minutes the flag-ship ranged up ahead and silenced the enemy's guns.

From this point no other obstacles were encountered, except burning steamers, cotton ships, fire rafts, and the like. Immediately after anchoring in front of the city I was ordered on shore by the flag-officer to demand the surrender of the city, and that the flag should be hoisted on the post office, custom-house, and mint. . . .

. . . On the 28th General Butler landed above Fort St. Philip, under the guns of the Mississippi and Kineo. This landing of the army above, together with the passage of the fleet, appears to have put the finishing touch to the demoralization of their garrisons, (300 having mutinied in Fort Jackson.) Both forts surrendered to Commander Porter, who was near at hand with the vessels of his flotilla.

As I left the river General Butler had garrisoned Forts Jackson and

z

St. Philip, and his transports, with troops, were on their way to occupy New Orleans.

I cannot too strongly express my admiration of the cool and able management of all the vessels of my line by their respective captains. After we had passed the forts it was a contest between iron hearts in wooden vessels and iron-clads with iron beaks, and the "iron hearts" won.

House Executive Documents, 37 Cong., 3 sess. (Washington, 1862), III, No. 1, pp. 289–290 *passim*.

---

112. Peninsular Campaign (1862)

BY MAJOR-GENERAL GEORGE BRINTON McCLELLAN

McClellan became commander of the Army of the Potomac after the battle of Bull Run. His powers of organization were great, and he slowly brought the chaotic mass of men around Washington into an orderly, well-trained, and well-disciplined army. But his ability in the field was not equal to his opportunity ; for his over-caution, tardiness, and proneness to magnify the enemy's force handicapped him in an advance against Lee, and there was a mutual lack of confidence between him and the administration. These extracts, except the letter to Stanton, which is here inserted in its chronological order, are taken from private letters and telegrams to his wife. — For McClellan, see G. S. Hillard, *Life and Campaigns of G. B. McClellan*. — Bibliography : A. S. Webb, *The Peninsula, passim ;* J. C. Ropes, *Story of the Civil War*, II, vii–xii ; Channing and Hart, *Guide*, § 210.

JUNE 15, 10.15 P.M., *Camp Lincoln.* . . . The chances now are that I will make the first advance on Tuesday or Wednesday. By that time I think the ground will be fit for the movements of artillery and that all our bridges will be completed. I think the rebels will make a desperate fight, but I feel sure that we will gain our point. Look on the maps I sent you a day or two ago, and find "Old Tavern," on the road from New bridge to Richmond ; it is in that vicinity that the next battle will be fought. I think that they see it in that light, and that they are fully prepared to make a desperate resistance. I shall make the first battle mainly an artillery combat. As soon as I gain possession of the "Old Tavern" I will push them in upon Richmond and behind their works ; then I will bring up my heavy guns, shell the city, and carry it by assault. I speak very confidently, but if you could see the faces of the troops as I ride among them you would share my confidence. They will do anything I tell them to do. . . .

June 22, [*Trent's House*]. . . . By an arrival from Washington to-day

I learn that Stanton and Chase have fallen out; that McDowell has deserted his friend C. and taken to S.! Alas! poor country that should have such rulers. I tremble for my country when I think of these things; but still can trust that God in His infinite wisdom will not punish us as we deserve, but will in His own good time bring order out of chaos and restore peace to this unhappy country. His will be done, whatever it may be! I am as anxious as any human being can be to finish this war. Yet when I see such insane folly behind me I feel that the final salvation of the country demands the utmost prudence on my part, and that I must not run the slightest risk of disaster, for if anything happened to this army our cause would be lost. I got up some heavy guns to-day, and hope to give secesh a preliminary pounding to-morrow and to make one good step next day. The rascals are very strong, and outnumber me very considerably; they are well entrenched also, and have all the advantages of position, so I must be prudent; but I will yet succeed, notwithstanding all they do and leave undone in Washington to prevent it. I would not have on my conscience what those men have for all the world. . . .

. . . *McClellan's Headquarters, June* 27.— Have had a terrible fight against vastly superior numbers. Have generally held our own, and we may thank God that the Army of the Potomac has not lost its honor. It is impossible as yet to tell what the result is. . . .

. . . *McClellan's Headquarters, June* 28. . . . They have outnumbered us everywhere, but we have not lost our honor. This army has acted magnificently. I thank my friends in Washington for our repulse. . . .

HEADQUARTERS, ARMY OF THE POTOMAC,
SAVAGE'S STATION, June 28, 1862, 12.20 A.M.

Hon. E. M. Stanton, Secretary of War:

I now know the full history of the day. On this side of the river (the right bank) we repulsed several strong attacks. On the left bank our men did all that men could do, all that soldiers could accomplish, but they were overwhelmed by vastly superior numbers, even after I brought my last reserves into action. The loss on both sides is terrible. I believe it will prove to be the most desperate battle of the war. The sad remnants of my men behave as men. Those battalions who fought most bravely and suffered most are still in the best order. My regulars were superb, and I count upon what are left to turn another battle in company with their gallant comrades of the volunteers. Had I twenty thousand (20,000), or even ten thousand (10,000), fresh troops to use to-morrow, I could take Richmond ; but I have not a man in reserve, and shall be glad to cover my retreat and save the material and *personnel* of the army.

If we have lost the day we have yet preserved our honor, and no one need blush for the Army of the Potomac. I have lost this battle because my force was too small.

I again repeat that I am not responsible for this, and I say it with the earnestness of a general who feels in his heart the loss of every brave man who has been needlessly sacrificed to-day. I still hope to retrieve our fortunes ; but to do this the government must view the matter in the same earnest light that I do. You must send me very large reinforcements, and send them at once. I shall draw back to this side of the Chickahominy, and think I can withdraw all our material. Please understand that in this battle we have lost nothing but men, and those the best we have.

In addition to what I have already said, I only wish to say to the President that I think he is wrong in regarding me as ungenerous when I said that my force was too weak. I merely intimated a truth which to-day has been too plainly proved. If, at this instant, I could dispose of ten thousand (10,000) fresh men, I could gain the victory to-morrow.

I know that a few thousand more men would have changed this battle from a defeat to a victory. As it is, the government must not and cannot hold me responsible for the result.

I feel too earnestly to-night. I have seen too many dead and wounded comrades to feel otherwise than that the government has not sustained this army. If you do not do so now the game is lost.

If I save this army now, I tell you plainly that I owe no thanks to you or to any other persons in Washington.

You have done your best to sacrifice this army.

G. B. McClellan.

July 2, . . . Berkley, James river.— . . . I have only energy enough left to scrawl you a few lines to say that I have the whole army here, with all its material and guns. . . .

. . . 11 P.M. — I will now take a few moments from the rest which I really need, and write at least a few words. . . . We have had a terrible time. On Wednesday the serious work commenced. I commenced driving the enemy on our left, and, by hard fighting, gained my point. Before that affair was over I received news that Jackson was probably about to attack my right. I galloped back to camp, took a fresh horse, and went over to Porter's camp, where I remained all night making the best arrangements I could, and returned about daybreak to look out for the left. On Thursday afternoon Jackson began his attack on McCall, who was supported by Porter. Jackson being repulsed, I went over there in the afternoon and remained until two or three A.M. I was satisfied that Jackson would have force enough next morning to turn Porter's right, so I removed all the wagons, heavy guns, etc., during the night, and caused Porter to fall back to a point nearer the force on the other side of the Chickahominy. This was most handsomely effected, all our material being saved. The next day Porter was attacked in his new position by the whole force of Jackson, Longstreet, Ewell, Hill, and Whiting. I sent what supports I could, but was at the same time attacked on my own front, and could only spare seven brigades. With these we held our own at all points after most desperate fighting. . . . I was forced that night to withdraw Porter's force to my side of the Chickahominy, and therefrom to make a very dangerous and difficult movement to reach the James river. . . .

July 4. . . . I am ready for an attack now; give me twenty-four hours even, and I will defy all secession. The movement has been a magnificent one; I have saved all our material, have fought every day for a week, and marched every night. You can't tell how nervous I became; everything seemed like the opening of artillery, and I had no rest, no peace, except when in front with my men. The duties of my position are such as often to make it necessary for me to remain in the rear. It is an awful thing. . . .

July 8. . . . I have written a strong, frank letter to the President, which I send by your father. If he acts upon it the country will be saved. . . . I understood the state of affairs long ago, and . . . had my advice been followed we should not have been in our present difficulties. . . . I have done the best I could. . . .

July 13. . . . There never was such an army; but there have been plenty of better generals. When I spoke about being repulsed I meant our failure to take Richmond. In no battle were we repulsed. We always at least held our own on the field, if we did not beat them. . . . I still hope to get to Richmond this summer, unless the government commits some extraordinarily idiotic act; but I have no faith in the administration, and shall cut loose from public life the very moment my country can dispense with my services. . . .

July 17. . . . You ask me when I expect to reach Richmond and whether I shall act on the offensive this summer.   I am at the mercy of the government.   After the first 9,000 or 10,000 men sent to me they have withheld all further reinforcements.   Burnside is halted at Fortress Monroe.   With his own troops and those of Hunter he can bring me some 20,000 troops ; but I have no idea of the intentions of the government.   If I am reinforced to that extent I will try it again with the least possible delay.   I am not at all in favor of baking on the banks of this river, but am anxious to bring matters to an issue. . . .

July 18. . . . I am inclined now to think that the President will make Halleck commander of the army, and that the first pretext will be seized to supersede me in command of this army.   Their game seems to be to withhold reinforcements, and then to relieve me for not advancing, well knowing that I have not the means to do so. . . .

Berkley, Aug. 14. . . . Porter's corps starts this evening, Franklin in the morning, the remaining three to-morrow and next day.   Headquarters will remain here until nearly the last.   We are going, not to Richmond, but to Fort Monroe, I am ashamed to say ! . . . It is a terrible blow to me, but I have done all that could be done to prevent it, without success, so I must submit as best I can and carry it out. . . .

George B. McClellan, *McClellan's Own Story* (New York, 1887), 404–468 *passim.*

---

113. Second Battle of Bull Run (1862)

BY MAJOR-GENERAL THOMAS JONATHAN JACKSON

"Stonewall" Jackson was the most remarkable character on the Confederate side of the Civil War.   He lived, prayed, disciplined, and fought with all the rigidity and strenuousness born of his Presbyterian creed and Scotch-Irish ancestors.   He was a born fighter, self-dependent to the extreme of not even informing his principal lieutenants of his plans; and so rapid were his movements that his troops came to be called "Jackson's Foot Cavalry."   Of the southern generals he has been ranked as next to Lee, under whom he commanded; and his death after Chancellorsville was a great blow to the Confederate cause.   This extract is from his official report. — For Jackson, see Carl Hovey, *Stonewall Jackson*, 129–131. — Bibliography: Military Historical Society of Massachusetts, *Papers* (ed. 1895), II, xi-xxi ; Channing and Hart, *Guide*, § 210.

PURSUING the instructions of the commanding general, I left Jeffersonton on the morning of the 25th [August] to throw my command between Washington City and the army of General Pope and to break up his railroad communication with the Federal capital. . . .

On the next day (26th) the march was continued, diverging to the right at Salem, crossing the Bull Run Mountain through Thoroughfare Gap, and passing Gainesville, reached Bristoe Station, on the Orange and Alexandria Railroad, after sunset. . . . My command was now in rear of General Pope's army, separating it from the Federal capital and its base of supply. . . .

Learning that the enemy had collected at Manassas Junction, a station about 7 miles distant, stores of great value, I deemed it important that no time should be lost in securing them. . . . The duty was cheerfully undertaken by all who were assigned to it and most promptly and successfully executed. . . .

The next morning the divisions under command of Generals Hill and Taliaferro moved to Manassas Junction, the division of General Ewell remaining at Bristoe Station. . . .

. . . Orders were given to supply the troops with rations and other articles which they could properly make subservient to their use from the captured property. It was vast in quantity and of great value, comprising 50,000 pounds of bacon, 1,000 barrels of corned beef, 2,000 barrels of salt pork, 2,000 barrels of flour, quartermaster's, ordnance, and sutler's stores deposited in buildings and filling two trains of cars. Having appropriated all that we could use, and unwilling that the residue should again fall into the hands of the enemy, who took possession of the place next day, orders were given to destroy all that remained after supplying the immediate wants of the army. This was done during the night. General Taliaferro moved his division that night across to the Warrenton and Alexandria turnpike, pursuing the road to Sudley's Mill, and crossing the turnpike in the vicinity of Groveton, halted near the battle-field of July 21, 1861. Ewell's and Hill's divisions joined Jackson's on the 28th.

My command had hardly concentrated north of the turnpike before the enemy's advance reached the vicinity of Groveton from the direction of Warrenton. General Stuart kept me advised of the general movements of the enemy, while Colonel Rosser, of the cavalry, with his command, and Col. Bradley T. Johnson, commanding Campbell's brigade, remained in front of the Federals and operated against their advance. Dispositions were promptly made to attack the enemy, based upon the idea that he would continue to press forward upon the turnpike toward Alexandria ; but as he did not appear to advance in force, and there was reason to believe that his main body was leaving the road and inclining toward Manassas Junction, my command was advanced through the woods, leaving Groveton on the left, until it reached a commanding position near Brawner's house. By this time it was sunset; but as his column appeared to be moving by, with its flank exposed, I determined to attack at once, which was vigorously done by the divisions of Talia-ferro and Ewell. The batteries of Wooding, Poague, and Carpenter were placed in position in front of Starke's brigade and above the village of Groveton, and, firing over the heads of our skirmishers, poured a heavy fire of shot and shell upon the enemy. This was responded to by a very heavy fire from the enemy, forcing our batteries to select another position. By this time Taliaferro's command, with Lawton's and Trim-ble's brigades on his left, was advanced from the woods to the open field, and was now moving in gallant style until it reached an orchard on the right of our line and was less than 100 yards from a large force of the enemy. The conflict here was fierce and sanguinary. Although largely re-enforced, the Federals did not attempt to advance, but maintained their ground with obstinate determination.

Both lines stood exposed to the discharges of musketry and artillery until about 9 o'clock, when the enemy slowly fell back, yielding the field to our troops. . . .

Although the enemy moved off under cover of the night and left us in quiet possession of the field, he did not long permit us to remain inac-tive or in doubt as to his intention to renew the conflict.

The next morning (29th) I found that he had abandoned the ground occupied as the battle-field the evening before and had moved farther to the east and to my left, placing himself between my command and the Federal capital. . . .

In the morning, about 10 o'clock, the Federal artillery opened with spirit and animation upon our right, which was soon replied to by the batteries of Poague, Carpenter, Dement, Brockenbrough, and Latimer, under Major (L. M.) Shumaker. This lasted for some time, when the enemy moved around more to our left to another point of attack. His next effort was directed against our left. This was vigorously repulsed by the batteries of Braxton, Crenshaw, and Pegram.

About 2 p. m. the Federal infantry in large force advanced to the attack of our left, occupied by the division of General Hill. It pressed forward, in defiance of our fatal and destructive fire, with great deter-mination, a portion of it crossing a deep cut in the railroad track and penetrating in heavy force an interval of nearly 175 yards, which sepa-

rated the right of Gregg's from the left of Thomas' brigade.   For a short
time Gregg's brigade, on the extreme left, was isolated from the main
body of the command ; but the Fourteenth South Carolina Regiment,
then in reserve, with the Forty-ninth Georgia, left of Colonel Thomas,
attacked the exultant enemy with vigor, and drove them back across the
railroad track with great slaughter.   General McGowan reports that the
opposing forces at one time delivered their volleys into each other at
the distance of 10 paces.   Assault after assault was made on the left, exhibiting on the part of the enemy great pertinacity and determination,
but every advance was most successfully and gallantly driven back.

General Hill reports that six separate and distinct assaults were thus
met and repulsed by his division, assisted by Hays' brigade, Colonel
Forno commanding.

By this time the brigade of General Gregg, which from its position on
the extreme left was most exposed to the enemy's attack, had nearly expended its ammunition. . . .   It was now retired to the rear to take
some repose after seven hours of severe service, and General Early's
brigade, of Ewell's division, with the Eighth Louisiana Regiment, took
its place.   On reaching his position General Early found that the enemy
had obtained possession of the railroad and a piece of wood in front,
there being at this point a deep cut, which furnished a strong defense.
Moving through a field he advanced upon the enemy, drove them from
the wood and railroad cut with great slaughter, and followed in pursuit
some 200 yards. . . .   As it was not desirable to bring on a general
engagement that evening General Early was recalled to the railroad,
where Thomas, Pender, and Archer had firmly maintained their positions
during the day.   Early kept his position there until the following morning. . . .

On the following day (30th) my command occupied the ground and
the divisions the same relative position to each other and to the field
which they held the day before, forming the left wing of the army, General Longstreet's command forming the right wing. . . . the Federal
infantry, about 4 o'clock in the evening, moved from under cover of the
wood and advanced in several lines, first engaging the right, but soon
extending its attack to the center and left.   In a few moments our entire
line was engaged in a fierce and sanguinary struggle with the enemy.
As one line was repulsed another took its place and pressed forward as
if determined by force of numbers and fury of assault to drive us from
our positions.   So impetuous and well sustained were these onsets as to

induce me to send to the commanding general for re-enforcements, but the timely and gallant advance of General Longstreet on the right re-lieved my troops from the pressure of overwhelming numbers and gave to those brave men the chances of a more equal conflict. As Longstreet pressed upon the right the Federal advance was checked, and soon a general advance of my whole line was ordered. Eagerly and fiercely did each brigade press forward, exhibiting in parts of the field scenes of close encounter and murderous strife not witnessed often in the turmoil of battle. The Federals gave way before our troops, fell back in disor-der, and fled precipitately, leaving their dead and wounded on the field. During their retreat the artillery opened with destructive power upon the fugitive masses. The infantry followed until darkness put an end to the pursuit.

The War of the Rebellion: Official Records of the Union and Confederate Armies, First Series (Washington, 1885), XII, pt. ii, 642–647 *passim*.

———◆———

114. Antietam (1862)

BY GEORGE WASHBURN SMALLEY

Smalley was educated for the law, but became one of the *New York Tribune's* many war correspondents. His enterprise in getting to the press his account of the battle of Antietam, or Sharpsburg, and the vividness of the description itself, secured him high rank as a war correspondent. He became a member of the editorial staff of the *Tribune*, and after the war went to England as European correspondent of the paper, where he remained about thirty years.— Bibliography: F. W. Palfrey, *Antietam and Fredericksburg, passim ;* J. C. Ropes, *Story of the Civil War*, II, vii–xii ; Chan-ning and Hart, *Guide*, § 210.

BATTLE-FIELD OF SHARPSBURG, ⎫
Wednesday Evening, Sept 17, 1862. ⎭

FIERCE and desperate battle between 200,000 men has raged since daylight, yet night closes on an uncertain field. . . .

The position on either side was peculiar. When Richardson advanced on Monday he found the enemy deployed and displayed in force on a crescent-shaped ridge, the outline of which followed more or less exactly the course of Antietam Creek. . . .

. . . What from our front looked like only a narrow summit fringed with woods was a broad table-land of forest and ravine ; cover for troops everywhere. nowhere easy access for an enemy. The smoothly sloping surface in front and the sweeping crescent of slowly mingling lines was only a delusion. It was all a Rebel stronghold beyond.

Under the base of these hills runs the deep stream called Antietam Creek, fordable only at distant points. . . .

The plan was generally as follows : Hooker was to cross on the right, establish himself on the enemy's left if possible, flanking his position, and to open the fight. Sumner, Franklin, and Mansfield were to send their forces also to the right, co-operating with and sustaining Hooker's attack while advancing also nearer the center. The heavy work in the center was left mostly to the batteries, Porter massing his infantry supports in the hollows. On the left Burnside was to carry the bridge already referred to, advancing then by a road which enters the pike at Sharpsburg, turning at once the Rebel left flank and destroying his line of retreat. Porter and Sykes were held in reserve. . . .

Hooker moved on Tuesday afternoon at four, crossing the creek at a ford above the bridge and well to the right, without opposition. . . .

Gen. Hooker formed his lines with precision and without hesitation. Ricketts's Division went into the woods on the left in force. Meade, with the Pennsylvania Reserves, formed in the center. Doubleday was sent out on the right. . . .

The battle began with the dawn. Morning found both armies just as they had slept, almost close enough to look into each other's eyes. The left of Meade's reserves and the right of Ricketts's line became engaged at nearly the same moment, one with artillery, the other with infantry. A battery was almost immediately pushed forward beyond the central woods, over a plowed field, near the top of the slope where the corn-field began. On this open field, in the corn beyond, and in the woods which stretched forward into the broad fields, like a promontory into the ocean, were the hardest and deadliest struggles of the day. . . .

The half hour passed, the Rebels began to give way a little, only a little, but at the first indication of a receding fire, Forward, was the word, and on went the line with a cheer and a rush. . . .

Meade and his Pennsylvanians followed hard and fast — followed till they came within easy range of the woods, among which they saw their beaten enemy disappearing — followed still, with another cheer, and flung themselves against the cover.

But out of those gloomy woods came suddenly and heavily terrible volleys — volleys which smote, and bent, and broke in a moment that eager front, and hurled them swiftly back for half the distance they had won. . . .

In ten minutes the fortune of the day seemed to have changed — it was the Rebels now who were advancing, pouring out of the woods in endless lines, sweeping through the corn-field from which their comrades had just fled. Hooker sent in his nearest brigade to meet them, but it could not do the work. He called for another. There was nothing close enough, unless he took it from his right. His right might be in danger if it was weakened, but his center was already threatened with annihilation. Not hesitating one moment, he sent to Doubleday : "Give me your best brigade instantly."

The best brigade came down the hill to the right on the run, went through the timber in front through a storm of shot and bursting shell and crashing limbs, over the open field beyond, and straight into the corn-field, passing as they went the fragments of three brigades shattered by the Rebel fire, and streaming to the rear. They passed by Hooker, whose eyes lighted as he saw these veteran troops led by a soldier whom he knew he could trust. " I think they will hold it," he said. . . .

. . . They began to go down the hill and into the corn, they did not stop to think that their ammunition was nearly gone, they were there to win that field and they won it. The Rebel line for the second time fled through the corn and into the woods. . . .

. . . With his left . . . able to take care of itself, with his right impregnable with two brigades of Mansfield still fresh and coming rapidly up, and with his center a second time victorious, Gen. Hooker determined to advance. Orders were sent to Crawford and Gordon — the two Mansfield brigades — to move directly forward at once, the batteries in the center were ordered on, the whole line was called on, and the General himself went forward.

. . . He rode out in front of his furthest troops on a hill to examine the ground for a battery. At the top he dismounted and went forward on foot, completed his reconnoissance, returned and remounted. . . . Remounting on this hill he had not ridden five steps when he was struck in the foot by a ball. . . .

Sumner arrived just as Hooker was leaving, and assumed command. Crawford and Gordon had gone into the woods, and were holding them stoutly against heavy odds. . . .

Sedgwick's division was in advance, moving forward to support Crawford and Gordon. . . .

To extend his own front as far as possible, he ordered the 34th New-York to move by the left flank. The maneuver was attempted under a fire of the greatest intensity, and the regiment broke. At the same moment the enemy, perceiving their advantage, came round on that flank. Crawford was obliged to give on the right, and his troops pouring in confusion through the ranks of Sedgwick's advance brigade, threw it into disorder and back on the second and third lines. The enemy advanced, their fire increasing. . . .

. . . The test was too severe for volunteer troops under such a fire. Sumner himself attempted to arrest the disorder, but to little purpose. . . . It was impossible to hold the position. Gen. Sumner withdrew the division to the rear, and once more the corn-field was abandoned to the enemy. . . .

At this crisis Franklin came up with fresh troops and formed on the left. Slocum, commanding one division of the corps, was sent forward along the slopes lying under the first ranges of Rebel hills, while Smith, commanding the other division, was ordered to retake the corn-fields and woods which all day had been so hotly contested. It was done in the handsomest style. His Maine and Vermont regiments and the rest went forward on the run, and, cheering as they went, swept like an avalanche through the corn-fields, fell upon the woods, cleared them in ten minutes, and held them. They were not again retaken. . . .

Up to 3 o'clock Burnside had made little progress. His attack on the bridge had been successful, but the delay had been so great that to the observer it appeared as if McClellan's plans must have been seriously disarranged. It is impossible not to suppose that the attacks on right and left were meant in a measure to correspond, for otherwise the enemy had only to repel Hooker on the one hand, then transfer his troops, and hurl them against Burnside. . . .

Finally, at 4 o'clock, McClellan sent simultaneous orders to Burnside and Franklin ; to the former to advance and carry the batteries in his front at all hazards and any cost ; to the latter to carry the woods next in front of him to the right, which the Rebels still held. The order to Franklin, however, was practically countermanded, in consequence of a message from Gen. Sumner that if Franklin went on and was repulsed, his own corps was not yet sufficiently reorganized to be depended on as a reserve. . . .

. . . Burnside hesitated for hours in front of the bridge which should have been carried at once by a *coup de main*. Meantime Hooker had been fighting for four hours with various fortune, but final success. Sumner had come up too late to join in the decisive attack which his earlier arrival would probably have converted into a complete success; and Franklin reached the scene only when Sumner had been repulsed. . . .

. . . It was at this point of time that McClellan sent him [Burnside] the order above given.

Burnside obeyed it most gallantly. Getting his troops well in hand, and sending a portion of his artillery to the front, he advanced them with rapidity and the most determined vigor, straight up the hill in front, on top of which the Rebels had maintained their most dangerous battery. . . .

. . . His guns opening first from this new position in front, soon entirely controlled and silenced the enemy's artillery. The infantry came on at once, moving rapidly and steadily up long dark lines, and broad, dark masses, being plainly visible without a glass as they moved over the green hill-side.

The next moment the road in which the Rebel battery was planted was canopied with clouds of dust swiftly descending into the valley. Underneath was a tumult of wagons, guns, horses, and men flying at speed down the road. Blue flashes of smoke burst now and then among them, a horse or a man or half dozen went down, and then the whirlwind swept on.

The hill was carried, but could it be held? . . .

In another moment a Rebel battle-line appears on the brow of the ridge above them, moves swiftly down in the most perfect order, and though met by incessant discharges of musketry, of which we plainly see the flashes, does not fire a gun. . . .

There is a halt, the Rebel left gives way and scatters over the field, the rest stand fast and fire. More infantry comes up, Burnside is outnumbered; flanked, compelled to yield the hill he took so bravely. His position is no longer one of attack; he defends himself with unfaltering firmness, but he sends to McClellan for help. McClellan's glass for the last half hour has seldom been turned away from the left. . . .

. . . Looking down into the valley where 15,000 troops are lying, he turns a half-questioning look on Fitz John Porter, who stands by his side, gravely scanning the field. They are Porter's troops below, are fresh and only impatient to share in this fight. But Porter slowly shakes his head, and one may believe that the same thought is passing through the minds of both generals: "They are the only reserves of the army; they cannot be spared." . . .

Burnside's messenger rides up. His message is, "I want troops and guns. If you do not send them I cannot hold my position for half an hour." McClellan's only answer for the moment is a glance at the western sky. Then he turns and speaks very slowly : " Tell Gen. Burnside that this is the battle of the war. He must hold his ground till dark at any cost. I will send him Miller's battery. . . ." . . .

The sun is already down ; not half-an-hour of daylight is left. . . . None suspected how near was the peril of defeat, of sudden attack on exhausted forces — how vital to the safety of the army and the nation were those fifteen thousand waiting troops of Fitz John Porter in the hollow. But the Rebels halted instead of pushing on, their vindictive cannonade died away as the light faded. Before it was quite dark the battle was over. Only a solitary gun of Burnside's thundered against the enemy, and presently this also ceased, and the field was still.

New York Daily Tribune, September 20, 1862.

---

115. Fredericksburg (1862)

BY MAJOR-GENERAL AMBROSE EVERETT BURNSIDE

Burnside had gained an early substantial success for the Union army on the coast of North Carolina, and, on McClellan's removal after the battle of Antietam, he was put in command of the Army of the Potomac. He assumed the responsibility reluctantly, failed at Fredericksburg, and was relieved of the command. This extract is from his official report. — For Burnside, see B. P. Poore, *Life and Public Services of Ambrose E. Burnside.* — Bibliography as in No. 114 above.

IN my interview with General Halleck I represented to him that soon after commencing the movement in the direction of Fredericksburg my telegraphic communication with Washington would be broken, and that I relied upon him to see that such parts of my plan as required action in Washington would be carried out. He told me that everything required by me would receive his attention, and that he would at once order, by telegraph, the pontoon trains spoken of in my plan, and would, upon his return to Washington, see that they were promptly forwarded. . . .

On my arrival at Falmouth, on the 19th [November], I dispatched to General Halleck's chief of staff the report . . . which . . . states the fact of the non-arrival of the pontoon train. These pontoon trains and supplies, which were expected to meet us on our arrival at Falmouth, could have been readily moved overland in time for our purposes in perfect safety. . . .

. . . Colonel Spaulding . . . arrived at Belle Plain with his pontoons on the 24th, and by the night of the 25th he was encamped near general headquarters.

By this time the enemy had concentrated a large force on the opposite side of the river, so that it became necessary to make arrangements to cross in the face of a vigilant and formidable foe. These arrangements were not completed until about December 10. . . .

. . . Before issuing final orders, I concluded that the enemy would be more surprised by a crossing at or near Fredericksburg, where we were making no preparations. . . . It was decided to throw four or five pontoon bridges across the river—two . . . opposite the upper part of the town, one . . . at the lower part of the town, one about a mile below, and, if there were pontoons sufficient, two at the latter point.

Final orders were now given to the commanders of the three grand divisions to concentrate their troops near the places for the proposed bridges. . . .

The right grand division (General Sumner's) was directed to concentrate near the upper and middle bridges ; the left grand division (General Franklin's) near the bridges, below the town ; the center grand division (General Hooker) near to and in rear of General Sumner. . . . The enemy held possession of the city of Fredericksburg and the crest or ridge running from a point on the river, just above Falmouth, to the Massaponax, some 4 miles below. This ridge was in rear of the city, forming an angle with the Rappahannock. Between the ridge and the river there is a plain, narrow at the point, where Fredericksburg stands, but widening out as it approaches the Massaponax. . . .

During the night of the 10th the bridge material was taken to the proper points on the river, and soon after 3 o'clock on the morning of the 11th the working parties commenced throwing the bridges, protected by infantry, placed under cover of the banks, and by artillery, on the bluffs above. One of the lower bridges, for General Franklin's command, was completed by 10.30 a. m. without serious trouble, and afterward a second bridge was constructed at the same point. The upper bridge . . . and the middle bridge . . . were about two-thirds built at 6 a. m., when the enemy opened upon the working parties with musketry with such severity as to cause them to leave the work. Our artillery was unable to silence this fire, the fog being so dense as to make accurate firing impossible. Frequent attempts were made to continue the work, but to no purpose.

About noon the fog cleared away, and we were able, with our artillery, to check the fire of the enemy. . . . I decided to resume the work on the bridges, and gave directions . . . to send men over in pontoons to the other shore as rapidly as possible, to drive the enemy from his position on the opposite bank. This work was most gallantly performed by Colonel Hall's brigade — the Seventh Michigan and Nineteenth and Twentieth Massachusetts — at the upper bridges, and by the Eighty-ninth New York at the middle bridge, and the enemy were soon driven from their position. The throwing of the bridges was resumed, and they were soon afterward finished.

No more difficult feat has been performed during the war than the throwing of these bridges in the face of the enemy by these brave men. . . .

It was now near night-fall. One brigade of Franklin's division crossed over to the south side ; drove the enemy's pickets from the houses near the bridge head, and Howard's division, together with a brigade from the Ninth Corps, both of General Sumner's command, crossed over on the upper and middle bridges, and, after some sharp skirmishing, occupied the town before daylight on the morning of the 12th.

During this day, the 12th, Sumner's and Franklin's commands crossed over and took position on the south bank, and General Hooker's grand division was held in readiness to support either the right or left, or to press the enemy in case the other command succeeded in moving him. . . .

The old Richmond road . . . runs from the town in a line nearly parallel with the river, to a point near the Massaponax, where it turns to the south, and passes near the right of the crest, or ridge, which runs in rear of the town, and was then occupied by the enemy in force. In order to pass down this road it was necessary to occupy the extreme right of this crest, which was designated on the map then in use by the army as " Hamilton's." . . .

It was my intention, in case this point had been gained, to push Generals Sumner and Hooker against the left of the crest, and prevent at least the removal of the artillery of the enemy, in case they attempted a retreat. . . .

. . . General Franklin was directed to seize, if possible, the heights near Captain Hamilton's, and to send at once a column of attack for that purpose, composed of a division at least, in the lead, well supported, and to keep his whole command in readiness to move down the old Richmond road. The object of this order is clear. It was necessary to seize this height in order to enable the remainder of his forces to move down the old Richmond road, with a view of getting in rear of the enemy's line on the crest. He was ordered to seize these heights, if possible, and to do it at once. I sent him a copy of the order to General Sumner, in which . . . I directed General Sumner's column not to move until he received orders from me, while he (General Franklin) was ordered to move at once. The movements were not intended to be simultaneous; in fact, I did not intend to move General Sumner until I learned that Franklin was about to gain the heights near Hamilton's, which I then supposed he was entirely able to do. . . .

. . . one of the smallest divisions of the command (General Meade's) led the attack. . . .

From General Meade's report it seems that he had great difficulty in getting his command into position to assault the hill. The time occupied for that purpose was from 9 a. m. till 1.15 p. m. . . . but, once in position, his division moved forward with the utmost gallantry. He broke the enemy's line; captured many prisoners and colors; crossed the road that ran in the rear of the crest, and established himself at the desired point on the crest; and, had he been able to hold it, our forces would have had free passage to the rear of the enemy's line along the crest. The supports which the order contemplated were not with him, and he found himself across the enemy's line, with both flanks unprotected. He dispatched staff officers to Generals Gibbon and Birney, urging them to advance to his right and left, in support of his flanks; but before the arrival of these divisions he was forced to withdraw from his advanced position, with his lines broken. These two divisions met his division as it was retreating, and by their gallant fighting aided materially in its safe withdrawal. An unsuccessful effort was made to reform the division, after which it was marched to the rear and held in reserve. . . .

No further attempt was made to carry this point on the crest. . . .

General Sumner's corps was held in position until after 11 o'clock, in the hope that Franklin would make such an impression upon the enemy as would enable him (Sumner) to carry the enemy's line near the Telegraph and Plank roads. Feeling the importance of haste, I now directed General Sumner to commence his attack. . . .

The enemy was strongly posted along the crest in his front, covered by rifle-pits and batteries, which gave him a commanding sweep of the ground over which our troops had to pass. I supposed when I ordered General Sumner to attack that General Franklin's attack on the left would have been made before General Sumner's men would be engaged, and would have caused the enemy to weaken his forces in front of Sumner, and I therefore hoped to break through their lines at this point. It subsequently appeared that this attack had not been made at the time General Sumner moved, and, when it was finally made, proved to be in such small force as to have had no permanent effect upon the enemy's line.

. . . Never did men fight more persistently than this brave grand division of General Sumner. The officers and men seemed to be inspired with the lofty courage and determined spirit of their noble commander, but the position was too strong for them. . . .

At 1.30 p. m. I ordered General Hooker to support General Sumner with his command. Soon after receiving this order, he (General Hooker) sent an aide-de-camp to me with the statement that he did not think the attack would be successful. I directed him to make the assault. Some time afterward General Hooker came to me in person with the same statement. I reiterated my order, which he then proceeded to obey. The afternoon was now well advanced. General Franklin before this had been positively ordered to attack with his whole force, and I hoped before sundown to have broken through the enemy's line. This order was not carried out.

At 4 p. m. General Humphreys was directed to attack, General Sykes' division moving in support of Humphreys' right. All these men fought with determined courage, but without success. . . .

Our forces had been repulsed at all points, and it was necessary to look upon the day's work as a failure. . . .

From the night of the 13th until the night of the 15th, our men held their positions. Something was done in the way of intrenching, and some angry skirmishing and annoying artillery firing was indulged in in the mean time. . . .

On the night of the 15th, I decided to remove the army to the north side of the river, and the work was accomplished without loss of mén or *matériel.* . . .

The War of the Rebellion: Official Records of the Union and Confederate Armies, First Series (Washington, 1888), XXI, 84–95 *passim.*

116. Experience of a Blockade-Runner (1862)

BY CAPTAIN JOHN WILKINSON (1877)

Wilkinson was an officer in the navy when his state, Virginia, seceded. He resigned and offered his services to the Confederacy. He was captured by Farragut at
New Orleans, and on being exchanged performed various services for the Confederacy
afloat and ashore : he engaged in blockade-running, had charge of various naval
affairs at Wilmington, and commanded a cruiser. This piece is inserted as evidence
of the importance and general efficiency of the blockading service. — Bibliography :
J. R. Soley, *The Blockade and the Cruisers, passim ;* Channing and Hart, *Guide,*
§§ 209, 210.

THE natural advantages of Wilmington for blockade-running were
very great, chiefly owing to the fact, that there are two separate
and distinct approaches to Cape Fear River, i.e., either by "New
Inlet" to the north of Smith's Island, or by the "western bar" to the
south of it. This island is ten or eleven miles in length ; but the Frying
Pan Shoals extend ten or twelve miles further south, making the distance
by sea between the two bars thirty miles or more, although the direct
distance between them is only six or seven miles. From Smithville, a
little village nearly equi-distant from either bar, both blockading fleets
could be distinctly seen, and the outward bound blockade-runners could
take their choice through which of them to run the gauntlet. The inward bound blockade-runners, too, were guided by circumstances of
wind and weather ; selecting that bar over which they would cross, after
they had passed the Gulf Stream ; and shaping their course accordingly. The approaches to both bars were clear of danger, with the
single exception of the "Lump" . . . and so regular are the soundings that the shore can be coasted for miles within a stone's throw of
the breakers.

These facts explain why the United States fleet were unable wholly to
stop blockade-running. It was, indeed, impossible to do so ; the result
to the very close of the war proves this assertion ; for in spite of the
vigilance of the fleet, many blockade-runners were afloat when Fort
Fisher was captured. In truth the passage through the fleet was little
dreaded ; for although the blockade-runner might receive a shot or two,
she was rarely disabled ; and in proportion to the increase of the fleet,
the greater would be the danger (we knew,) of their firing into each
other. As the boys before the deluge used to say, they would be very
apt "to miss the cow and kill the calf." The chief danger was upon

the open sea ; many of the light cruisers having great speed. As soon as one of them discovered a blockade-runner during daylight she would attract other cruisers in the vicinity by sending up a dense column of smoke, visible for many miles in clear weather. A " cordon " of fast steamers stationed ten or fifteen miles apart *inside the Gulf Stream,* and in the course from Nassau and Bermuda to Wilmington and Charleston, would have been more effectual in stopping blockade-running than the whole United States Navy concentrated off those ports ; and it was unaccountable to us why such a plan did not occur to good Mr. Welles ; but it was not our place to suggest it. I have no doubt, however, that the fraternity to which I then belonged would have unanimously voted thanks and a service of plate to the Hon. Secretary of the United States Navy for this oversight. I say *inside the Gulf Stream,* because every experienced captain of a blockade-runner made a point to cross "the stream " early enough in the afternoon, if possible, to establish the ship's position by chronometer so as to escape the influence of that current upon his dead reckoning. The lead always gave indication of our distance from the land, but not, of course, of our position ; and the numerous salt works along the coast, where evaporation was produced by fire, and which were at work night and day were visible long before the low coast could be seen. Occasionally the whole inward voyage would be made under adverse conditions. Cloudy, thick weather and heavy gales would prevail so as to prevent any solar or lunar observations, and reduce the dead reckoning to mere guess work. In these cases the nautical knowledge and judgment of the captain would be taxed to the utmost. The current of the Gulf Stream varies in velocity and (within certain limits) in direction ; and the stream, itself almost as well defined as a river within its banks under ordinary circumstances, is impelled by a strong gale toward the direction in which the wind is blowing, overflowing its banks as it were. The counter current, too, inside of the Gulf Stream is much influenced by the prevailing winds. Upon one occasion, while in command of the R. E. Lee, we had experienced very heavy and thick weather ; and had crossed the Stream and struck soundings about midday. The weather then clearing so that we could obtain an altitude near meridian we found ourselves at least forty miles north of our supposed position and near the shoals which extend in a southerly direction off Cape Lookout. It would be more perilous to run out to sea than to continue on our course, for we had passed through the off shore line of blockaders, and the sky had become perfectly clear.   I determined to personate a transport bound to Beaufort, which was in the possession of the United States forces, and the coaling station of the fleet blockading Wilmington.   The risk of detection was not very great, for many of the captured blockade-runners were used as transports and dispatch vessels.   Shaping our course for Beaufort, and slowing down, as we were in no haste to get there, we passed several vessels, showing United States colors to them all. Just as we were crossing through the ripple of shallow water off the " tail " of the shoals, we dipped our colors to a sloop of war which passed three or four miles to the south of us.   The courtesy was promptly responded to ; but I have no doubt her captain thought me a lubberly and careless seaman to shave the shoals so closely.   We stopped the engines when no vessel was in sight ; and I was relieved from a heavy burden of anxiety as the sun sank below the horizon ; and the course was shaped at full speed for Masonboro' Inlet. . . .

. . . A blockade-runner did not often pass through the fleet without receiving one or more shots, but these were always preceded by the flash of a calcium light, or by a blue light ; and immediately followed by two rockets thrown in the direction of the blockade-runner.   The signals were probably concerted each day for the ensuing night, as they appeared to be constantly changed ; but the rockets were invariably sent up.   I ordered a lot of rockets from New York.   Whenever all hands were called to run through the fleet, an officer was stationed alongside of me on the bridge with the rockets.   One or two minutes after our immediate pursuer had sent up his rockets, I would direct ours to be discharged at a right angle to our course.   The whole fleet would be misled, for even if the vessel which had discovered us were not deceived, the rest of the fleet would be baffled. . . .

The staid old town of Wilmington was turned " topsy turvy " during the war.   Here resorted the speculators from all parts of the South, to attend the weekly auctions of imported cargoes ; and the town was infested with rogues and desperadoes, who made a livelihood by robbery and murder. . . .   The agents and employès of the different blockade-running companies, lived in magnificent style, paying a king's ransom (in Confederate money) for their household expenses, and nearly monopolizing the supplies in the country market. . . .

J[ohn] Wilkinson, *The Narrative of a Blockade-Runner* (New York, 1877), 130–199 *passim*.

CHAPTER XX — YEAR OF ADVANCE

117. Chancellorsville (1863)

BY GENERAL ROBERT EDWARD LEE

Lee's genius was not recognized until the battles before Richmond in 1862. From that time on he was the greatest general on the southern side, and in 1865 public opinion forced Davis to make him generalissimo of the Confederate forces. This extract is from his official report. — For Lee, see No. 47 above. — Bibliography: Abner Doubleday, *Chancellorsville and Gettysburg, passim ;* J. F. Rhodes, *History of the United States,* IV, 264, note ; Channing and Hart, *Guide,* § 210.

. . . AFTER the battle of Fredericksburg, the army remained encamped on the south side of the Rappahannock until the latter part of April. The Federal Army occupied the north side of the river opposite Fredericksburg, extending to the Potomac. . . .

At 5.30 a. m. on April 28, the enemy crossed the Rappahannock in boats near Fredericksburg . . . in . . . considerable force . . . and was massed out of view under the high banks of the river. . . .

No demonstration was made opposite any other part of our lines at Fredericksburg, and the strength of the force that had crossed and its apparent indisposition to attack indicated that the principal effort of the enemy would be made in some other quarter. This impression was confirmed by intelligence received from General Stuart that a large body of infantry and artillery was passing up the river. . . . The routes they were pursuing after crossing the Rapidan converge near Chancellorsville, whence several roads lead to the rear of our position at Fredericksburg.

On the night of the 29th, General Anderson was directed to proceed toward Chancellorsville. . . .

The enemy in our front near Fredericksburg continued inactive, and it was now apparent that the main attack would be made upon our flank and rear. It was, therefore, determined to leave sufficient troops to hold our lines, and with the main body of the army to give battle to the approaching column. Early's division, of Jackson's corps, and Barksdale's brigade, of McLaws' division, with part of the Reserve Artillery, under General (W. N.) Pendleton, were intrusted with the defense of

359

our position at Fredericksburg, and, at midnight on the 30th, General McLaws marched with the rest of his command toward Chancellorsville. General Jackson followed at dawn next morning with the remaining divisions of his corps. He reached the position occupied by General Anderson at 8 a. m., and immediately began preparations to advance.

At 11 a. m. the troops moved forward upon the Plank and old Turnpike roads. . . . The enemy was soon encountered on both roads, and heavy skirmishing with infantry and artillery ensued, our troops pressing steadily forward. . . . General Wright . . . turned the enemy's right. His whole line thereupon retreated rapidly, vigorously pursued by our troops until they arrived within about 1 mile of Chancellorsville. Here the enemy had assumed a position of great natural strength, surrounded on all sides by a dense forest filled with a tangled undergrowth, in the midst of which breastworks of logs had been constructed, with trees felled in front, so as to form an almost impenetrable abatis. . . .

It was evident that a direct attack upon the enemy would be attended with great difficulty and loss, in view of the strength of his position and his superiority of numbers. It was, therefore, resolved to endeavor to turn his right flank and gain his rear, leaving a force in front to hold him in check and conceal the movement. The execution of this plan was intrusted to Lieutenant-General Jackson with his three divisions. The commands of Generals McLaws and Anderson . . . remained in front of the enemy.

Early on the morning of the 2d, General Jackson marched by the Furnace and Brock roads, his movement being effectually covered by Fitzhugh Lee's cavalry, under General Stuart in person. . . .

After a long and fatiguing march, General Jackson's leading division, under General Rodes, reached the old turnpike, about 3 miles in rear of Chancellorsville, at 4 p. m. As the different divisions arrived, they were formed at right angles to the road — Rodes in front . . . Colston, in the second, and A. P. Hill's in the third, line.

At 6 p. m. the advance was ordered. The enemy were taken by surprise, and fled after a brief resistance. General Rodes' men pushed forward with great vigor and enthusiasm, followed closely by the second and third lines. Position after position was carried, the guns captured, and every effort of the enemy to rally defeated by the impetuous rush of our troops. . . . It was now dark, and General Jackson ordered the third line, under General Hill, to advance to the front, and relieve the troops of Rodes and Colston, who were completely blended and in such disorder, from their rapid advance through intricate woods and over broken ground, that it was necessary to reform them. As Hill's men moved forward, General Jackson, with his staff and escort, returning from the extreme front, met his skirmishers advancing, and in the obscurity of the night were mistaken for the enemy and fired upon. . . . General Jackson himself received a severe injury, and was borne from the field. The command devolved upon Major-General Hill. . . . General Hill was soon afterward disabled, and Major-General Stuart . . . was sent for to take command. . . .

. . . The darkness of the night and the difficulty of moving through the woods and undergrowth rendered it advisable to defer further operations until morning, and the troops rested on their arms in line of battle. . . .

Early on the morning of the 3d, General Stuart renewed the attack upon the enemy. . . . Anderson, in the meantime, pressed gallantly forward directly upon Chancellorsville. . . . As the troops advancing upon the enemy's front and right converged upon his central position, Anderson effected a junction with Jackson's corps, and the whole line pressed irresistibly on. The enemy was driven from all his fortified positions, with heavy loss in killed, wounded, and prisoners, and retreated toward the Rappahannock. By 10 a. m. we were in full possession of the field.

The troops, having become somewhat scattered by the difficulties of the ground and the ardor of the contest, were immediately reformed preparatory to renewing the attack. . . . Our preparations were just completed when further operations were arrested by intelligence received from Fredericksburg. . . .

Before dawn on the morning of the 3d, General Barksdale reported to General Early that the enemy had occupied Fredericksburg in large force and laid down a bridge at the town. . . .

. . . The success of the enemy enabled him . . . to come upon our rear at Chancellorsville by the Plank road . . . his progress being gallantly disputed by the brigade of General Wilcox. . . . General Wilcox fell back slowly until he reached Salem Church, on the Plank road, about 5 miles from Fredericksburg.

Information of the state of affairs in our rear having reached Chancellorsville, as already stated, General McLaws, with his three brigades and one of General Anderson's, was ordered to re-enforce General Wilcox. He arrived at Salem Church early in the afternoon, where he found

General Wilcox in line of battle, with a large force of the enemy — consisting, as was reported, of one army corps and part of another, under Major-General Sedgwick — in his front. . . . The enemy's . . . infantry advanced in three strong lines. . . . The assault was met with the utmost firmness, and after a fierce struggle the first line was repulsed with great slaughter. The second then came forward, but immediately broke under the close and deadly fire which it encountered, and the whole mass fled in confusion to the rear. . . .

The next morning General Early advanced along the Telegraph road, and recaptured Marye's and the adjacent hills without difficulty, thus gaining the rear of the enemy's left. . . .

In the meantime the enemy had so strengthened his position near Chancellorsville that it was deemed inexpedient to assail it with less than our whole force, which could not be concentrated until we were relieved from the danger that menaced our rear. It was accordingly resolved still further to re-enforce the troops in front of General Sedgwick, in order, if possible, to drive him across the Rappahannock.

Accordingly, on the 4th, General Anderson was directed to proceed with his remaining three brigades to join General McLaws. . . . Anderson reached Salem Church about noon, and was directed to gain the left flank of the enemy and effect a junction with Early. McLaws' troops were disposed as on the previous day, with orders to hold the enemy in front, and to push forward his right brigades as soon as the advance of Anderson and Early should be perceived, so as to connect with them and complete the continuity of our line. . . . The attack did not begin until 6 p. m., when Anderson and Early moved forward and drove General Sedgwick's troops rapidly before them across the Plank road in the direction of the Rappahannock. . . .

The next morning it was found that General Sedgwick had made good his escape and removed his bridges. Fredericksburg was also evacuated, and our rear no longer threatened ; but as General Sedgwick had it in his power to recross, it was deemed best to leave General Early, with his division and Barksdale's brigade, to hold our lines as before, McLaws and Anderson being directed to return to Chancellorsville. They reached their destination during the afternoon, in the midst of a violent storm, which continued throughout the night and most of the following day.

Preparations were made to assail the enemy's works at daylight on the 6th, but, on advancing our skirmishers, it was found that under cover of the storm and darkness of the night he had retreated over the river. . . .

The movement by which the enemy's position was turned and the fortune of the day decided was conducted by the lamented Lieutenant-General Jackson, who, as has already been stated, was severely wounded near the close of the engagement on Saturday evening. I do not propose here to speak of the character of this illustrious man, since removed from the scene of his eminent usefulness by the hand of an inscrutable but all-wise Providence. I nevertheless desire to pay the tribute of my admiration to the matchless energy and skill that marked this last act of his life, forming, as it did, a worthy conclusion of that long series of splendid achievements which won for him the lasting love and gratitude of his country.

The War of the Rebellion: Official Records of the Union and Confederate Armies, First Series (Washington, 1889), XXV, pt. i, 795–803 *passim*.

---

118. Gunboat Warfare (1863)

BY ADMIRAL DAVID DIXON PORTER (1885)

Porter, a son of Commodore David Porter, was of the fourth generation of naval commanders in the service of the United States. He assisted his foster-brother, Farragut, in the attack on New Orleans; and, after taking part in the various operations before Vicksburg and in the unsuccessful Red River expedition, he commanded the vast naval forces at the attack on Fort Fisher. This piece is inserted to show the difficulties of the gunboat service in the western rivers. — For Porter, see J. R. Soley, *Admiral Porter.* — Bibliography: F. V. Greene, *The Mississippi, passim;* A. T. Mahan, *The Gulf and Inland Waters, passim;* J. F. Rhodes, *History of the United States*, IV, 319, note; Channing and Hart, *Guide*, § 210.

ONE of the liveliest reminiscences I have of the siege is what is called the Yazoo Pass expedition — one of three attempts we made to get behind Vicksburg with a fleet of ironclads and a detachment of the army — in which I have to say that we failed most egregiously.

At one period of the siege the rains had swollen the Mississippi River so much that it had backed its waters up into its tributaries, which had risen seventeen feet, and, overflowing, had inundated the country for many miles.

Great forests had become channels admitting the passage of large steamers between the trees, and now and then wide lanes were met with where a frigate might have passed.

The ironclads drew only seven feet of water and had no masts or yards to encumber them, and but little about their decks that could be swept away by the bushes or lower branches of the trees. I had thoughts of trying the experiment of getting the vessels back of Vicksburg in that way. . . .

I determined to go myself, and, to make it a success, I omitted nothing that might possibly be wanted on such an expedition. I selected the ironclads Louisville, Lieutenant-Commanding Owen; Cincinnati, Lieutenant-Commanding Bache; Carondelet, Lieutenant-Commanding Murphy; Mound City, Lieutenant-Commanding Wilson; Pittsburgh, Lieutenant-Commanding Hoel, and four tugs; also two light mortar-boats built for the occasion, to carry each a thirteen-inch mortar and shells enough to bombard a city. . . .

At the same time General Sherman prepared his contingent to accompany the expedition. . . .

It was a curious sight to see a line of ironclads and mortar-boats, tugs and transports, pushing their way through the long, wide lane in the woods without touching on either side, though sometimes a rude tree would throw Briarean arms around the smoke-stack of the tin-clad Forest Rose, or the transport Molly Miller, and knock their bonnets sideways. . . .

We ran on, in line of battle, eight or ten miles through the open way in the trees, carrying fifteen feet of water by the lead-line. Let the nautical reader imagine an old quartermaster in the "chains" of an ironclad steaming through the woods and singing out, "Quarter less three!" Truth is stranger than fiction.

At last we came to a point where the forest was close and composed of very large trees — old monarchs of the woods which had spread their arms for centuries over those silent solitudes : Titans, like those in the old fables, that dominate over all around them. . . .

We had to knock down six or eight of these large trees before we could reach the point where Sherman was disembarking part of his troops. When I came up he was on a piece of high ground, on an old white horse some of his "boys" had captured.

"Halloo, old fellow," he sang out, "what do you call this? This must be traverse sailing. You think it's all very fine just now, don't you ; but, before you fellows get through, you wont have a smoke-stack or a boat among you. . . .

"steam on about twenty yards to the west, and you will find a hole through a kind of levee wide enough, I think, for your widest vessel.

That is Cypress Bayou; it leads into the Sunflower about seventy-five miles distant, and a devil of a time you'll have of it. Look out those fellows don't catch you. I'll be after you." . . .

I pushed on, my fleet following, and soon found myself inside the bayou. It was exactly forty-six feet wide. My vessel was forty-two feet wide, and that was the average width of the others. This place seemed to have been a bayou with high levees bordering, reaching, indeed, above the vessel's guns.

. . . This bayou had not been used for many years for the purposes of navigation. It had almost closed up, and the middle of it was filled with little willows which promised to be great impediments to us, but, as there was nine feet of water in the ditch, I pushed on. . . .

I was in the leading vessel, and necessarily had to clear the way for the others. The bayou was full of logs that had been there for years. They had grown soggy and heavy, and sometimes one end, being heavier than the other, would sink to the bottom, while the other end would remain pointing upward, presenting the appearance of *chevaux-de-frise*, over which we could no more pass than we could fly. We had to have working parties in the road with tackles and hook-ropes to haul these logs out on the banks before we could pass on. . . .

Then, again, we would get jammed between two large, overhanging trees. We could not ram them down as we did in the woods, with plenty of "sea room" around us. We had to chop away the sides of the trees with axes. . . .

An hour after entering the very narrow part of the ditch, where we really had not a foot to spare, we had parted with everything like a boat, and cut them away as useless appendages. . . .

That day, by sunset, we had made eight miles, which was a large day's work, considering all the impediments, but when night came — which it did early in the deep wood — we had to tie up to the bank, set watches, and wait until daylight. . . .

At daylight next morning we moved ahead, and all that day toiled as men never toiled before. . . . Evening found us fourteen miles ahead, but where was Sherman? There was only one road, so he couldn't have taken the wrong one. . . .

It were vain to tell all the hardships of the third day. The plot seemed to thicken as we advanced, and old logs, small Red River rafts, and rotten trees overhanging the banks, seemed to accumulate. . . .

We had steamed, or rather bumped, seventy-five miles, and had only six hundred yards to go before getting into the Rolling Fork, where all would be plain sailing; but I waited for all the vessels to come up to repair damages, and start together.

I noticed right at the head of the pass a large green patch extending all the way across. It looked like the green scum on ponds.

" What is that? " I asked of one of the truthful contrabands.

" It's nuffin but willers, sah," he replied. . . .

I thought I would try it while the vessels were " coming into port." I sent the tug on ahead with the mortar-boat, and followed on after.

The tug went into it about thirty yards, began to go slower and slower, and finally stuck so fast that she could move neither ahead nor astern. I hailed her and told them that I would come along and push them through. We started with a full head of steam, and did not even reach the tug. The little withes caught in the rough iron ends of the over-hang and held us as if in a vise. I tried to back out, but 'twas no use. We could not move an inch, no matter how much steam we put on. Ah, I thought, this is only a temporary delay.

We got large hooks out and led the hook-ropes aft, and tried to break off the lithe twigs, but it was no use ; we could not move. We got saws, knives, cutlasses, and chisels over the side, with the men handling them sitting on planks, and cut them off, steamed ahead, and only moved three feet. Other withes sprang up from under the water and took a fresher grip on us, so we were worse off than ever. . . .

Just then a rebel steamer was reported coming up the Rolling Fork and landing about four miles below. . . .

There was nothing easier than for two thousand men to charge on us from the bank and carry us by boarding. Only the enemy didn't know the fix we were in. They didn't know how it was that we could fire those thirteen-inch shell, that would burst now and then at the root of a great tree and throw it into the air. They didn't know that we had only four smooth-bore howitzers free to work, that our heavy guns were useless, below the bank. So much for their not being properly posted. But I was quite satisfied that they would know all this before Sherman came up.

We drove the artillery away about four o'clock in the afternoon. Then I sent a hawser to the tug, and another to the ironclad astern of me, while the latter made fast to another ironclad. Then we all backed together and, after an hour's hard pull, we slipped off the willows into soft water. *Laus Deo!*

Then went forth the orders to unship the rudders and let the vessels drift down stern foremost, and away we all went together with a four-knot current taking us — bumping badly — down at the rate of two miles an hour — which was twice as fast as we came up. . . .

Sharp-shooters made their appearance in the morning. About sixty of them surrounded us. First it was like an occasional drop of rain. Then it was *pat, pat* against the iron hull all the time. . . .

Suddenly the Louisville, Captain Owen, brought up all standing. There were eight large trees cut down ahead of us — four from either bank, and they seemed to be so interlaced that it was apparently impossible to remove them.

I sent out two hundred riflemen, and found that they were quite equal to the enemy. They drove them to a safe distance with the aid of the mortar fire. . . .

Under fire from the sharp-shooters we removed the eight trees in three hours, and started to push on, when we found those devils had sunk two large trees across the bayou under water, and *pinned* them down.

Another hour was spent in getting them up, and under renewed sharp-shooting. . . .

We had no sooner got rid of these obstructions than we saw a large column of gray-uniformed soldiers swooping down on us from the woods.

We opened mortar fire on them. They didn't mind it. On they came. They were no doubt determined to overwhelm us by numbers, and close us in. Their artillery was coming on with them. Now would come the tug of war. We were jammed up against the bank, and the stream was so narrow where we were we could not increase our distance from it. Their sharp-shooters had now taken up positions behind trees about one hundred yards from us, and our men were firing rapidly at them as they opened on us. . . .

The sharp-shooters were becoming very troublesome about this time, when suddenly I saw the advancing column begin to fall into confusion ; then they jumped behind trees, or fell into groups, and kept up a rapid fire of musketry. It looked as if they were fighting among themselves. But no ! they were retreating before some one. They had run foul of Sherman's army, which was steadily driving them back. . . .

The game was up, and we bumped on homeward. . . .

I am quite satisfied that no one who went on that party desired to try it again. It was the hardest cruise that any Jack Tar ever made, and we all determined to cultivate the army more than we had done, in case we should go on a horse-marine excursion.

Admiral [David D.] Porter, *Incidents and Anecdotes of the Civil War* (New York, D. Appleton & Co., 1885), 137–172 *passim*.

———◆———

119. Taking of Vicksburg (1863)

BY " CLINT "

The *Mobile Advertiser*, controlled by John Forsyth, was very zealous for the southern cause both before and during the Civil War, and was rather more enterprising than other prominent papers in the South, in having its own correspondents at the front. Correspondents for southern papers were often soldiers, but in this case the man was sent by the paper to the front at Jackson. The account from which this extract is taken is a fair example of the news furnished from unofficial sources to the southern reader. — Bibliography as in No. 118 above.

[May 23.] THE enemy having moved from Jackson directly to the Big Black and after the disasters of Saturday [May 16], or more particularly that of Sunday, threw his columns across the river and commenced extending his lines around Vicksburg. Our forces evacuated Snyder's Bluff, destroying the works. This opened up the Yazoo to the enemy, who immediately availed himself of the advantage, and entering the river ascended it to Yazoo City and took possession, our forces destroying the navy yard and the two embryo gunboats in course of construction there, and which would have been finished in some six or eight months. This enables Grant to supply his army without the necessity of using his wagon road from Milliken's Bend to Carthage, or of the gunboats running the gauntlet of the Vicksburg batteries, as the transports can go up the Yazoo and safely land whatever is needed. Vicksburg being nearly or completely invested, you will see that it is with much difficulty that any information can be obtained from that point. . . .

Procrastination is the thief of time, says the poet, and I might add that he who dallies is damned. The golden moment for taking Vicksburg has passed, and future events rapidly culminating will soon settle the question of its future destiny — either of its being the strongest stronghold of the Confederacy or a Federal garrison. If Grant, after compelling Pemberton to abandon the indecisive field of Baker's Creek and then forcing him to hurriedly throw the Big Black in his rear — I say if he had followed up his advantage by advancing his fresh troops, he might have gone pell mell into Vicksburg with a large portion of Pemberton's discomfited soldiers.

The point at which he made his attack on Tuesday was the most vulnerable, and on Sunday night *it is my opinion* that Grant could have carried it like a " flash," but he dallied until Tuesday.   Meanwhile Pemberton eat no " idle bread."   It was dig, work, work ; and by the time General Grant was ready to " go and see Gen. Pemberton," his house had been set in order, and he was prepared to " receive company," and Grant received one of the most bloody entertainments of modern history.   Right gallantly did Grant's men rush to the charge — they had been flushed with an ephemeral success, the booty of Jackson and an abundant supply of whiskey, and forward they dashed with an energy worthy of a better cause.   But all in vain — they were numbered with the dead — and with all of their freshly committed crimes suddenly ushered into the presence of God.   The robbers of Jackson have met with speedy bloody deaths, but no Christian burial — their bodies are the food of beasts and birds of prey.   I have not learned whether Grant wanted to bury his dead or not.   If he had Pemberton would not have permitted it, for it would require stouter hearts than there are in Grant's army to march or charge over the Golgotha in front of the Vicksburg batteries. . . .

[June 10.] . . . The enemy having become tired of directly carrying the place by assault, has set himself down before its fortifications, awaiting reinforcements, and has gone to digging up the big hills of Vicksburg.   It is a gigantic undertaking, but I imagine he will ultimately succeed in his approaches to our works, but will be again foiled and driven back with heavy slaughter. — By day and by night the enemy is constantly shelling, and strange to say, does but very little damage. This will be the story for several days yet. . . .

[July 2.] . . . All eyes are now turned towards Vicksburg, but when Johnston will move and strike his blow, is known only to himself.   It is the opinion of many that he is fighting Grant daily by giving him a "terrible letting alone," and after all it may be the safest and surest way of whipping Grant.   With the Navigation of the Mississippi closed, his supplies cut off, and harassed and menaced at every point, he will have but one alternative, that of raising the siege and giving Johnston battle on his own ground. . . .

Grant has fortified himself well in his rear against attack, and if Pemberton is well supplied with provisions, the longer a battle is de ferred may *possibly* be for the better. At night Grant works his men on his entrenchments, and perfects them as much as possible for offensive and defensive purposes. If Johnston cuts his supplies off, his only chance of escape will be by the way of Grand Gulf, and down the Mississippi river to New Orleans, a retrograde movement that must be attended with immense loss and almost entire destruction of his army, but then we must have Grant cut off and whipped first, before all this disaster can occur. . . .

[July 8.] What judgment the people will pass upon the unfortunate result of affairs in this department and the loss of Vicksburg, I feel confident will be correct, and although the blow has been heavy and is a great disaster, instead of " crying over spilt milk," we should be but the more strongly nerved and determined to win back, not only that which has been lost, but to gain all for which we have been so long bloodily contending. Let us throw aside all bickerings, forget everything save the precious boon for which we are contending, and rally to the defense of our country, our liberties and our homes. All the fault-finding and croaking that may be done will not cap a gun or let slip one of the bull dogs of war. Let the brave man remain determined — the irresolute take courage, and the timid take heart, and all rally together and strike for their " altars and their fires."

Vicksburg is lost to us, and that stronghold has passed into the possession of the enemy. The hour of misfortune has come, and let us rise above the storm-cloud and battle more resolutely than ever. Gen. Johnston could not by possibility, with the means at his command, have relieved Vicksburg. All that skill, energy and zeal could do, has been done, although his efforts have not resulted as we fondly anticipated. He had to create an army and all its appliances before he could move with any reasonable hope of success, and to have moved at an earlier day without adequate preparation for the emergency of the conflict, would have been but to expose his army to the blows of the enemy, with the certainty of its defeat ; for to have attacked Grant would have resulted in the sacrifice of the only army which remains for the protection of the interior, while this sacrifice could not have saved Vicksburg.

Grant occupied a country with double our numbers, over which an army could not have been marched in line of battle if there were no foe to meet and dispute its advance. . . . This position was obtained, fortified and defended in every possible way, *before* Johnston had an army with which he could commence offensive operations.

The root of the disaster is twofold.   First, Grant's flank movement by way of Port Gibson, which should have been checked at all hazards. This might have been done with competent and prompt action.   It was not done, neither was it attempted.   Grant was suffered, with but a feeble resistance by inadequate numbers, to move where he pleased, and secure all he desired.   The second cause of disaster was, that Vicksburg had been supplied with but *one month's* scant rations to stand the siege with !   This was the preparation of a year !   All accounts, however, previous to the unfortunate capitulation, went to insure the belief that the garrison was amply supplied with provisions for a long time, and believing these assertions to be true, I so telegraphed and wrote.

The garrison was *starved out*, and our glorious boys staggered from utter exhaustion when they left the trenches !   What in Heaven's name has the commissariat been doing?   I am reminded that last winter the garrison at one time were reduced to but four days' rations, and the " Southern Crisis " was so severe with its lash that an alarm prevailed, but which soon subsided when it was made known that provisions were being sent forward.   That there has been a crying incompetency in the antecedent management of affairs is apparent to all.   With the credit of the Government at command, an ample supply of provisions in the land, when speculators were brushed out of the way, I am at a loss to account for the shortness of supplies within the fortifications.   Would to God the sugar and molasses crop had been sunk in the Mississippi river before ever it had been moved by way of Vicksburg.

That Gen. Pemberton is disloyal to our cause no sensible man believes, and none will so assert who know anything about him or the affairs of the country.   He has certainly done the best he knew how — if he lacked capacity it was his misfortune and not his fault.   The appointing power must take the responsibility before the country with respect to Vicksburg and the Trans-Mississippi Department.   Our ablest men believe that we have magnified the importance of Vicksburg far beyond its intrinsic importance to the Confederacy in any military point of view.

The army of Vicksburg is not lost to us, and in a few days these brave men will again be in our ranks ; and the question of resisting Lee on the part of the enemy and of our strengthening Bragg must be settled.   Those who calmly survey the field — whose nerves do not sway like the aspen — are to-day as hopeful, firm and confident of our glorious ultimate success and independence as at any time during the struggle.

Mobile Advertiser and Register, May 26, June 4, 16, July 7, 11, 1863.

120. Pickett's Charge at Gettysburg (1863)

BY LIEUTENANT-GENERAL JAMES LONGSTREET (1895)

Longstreet was Lee's best and hardest-fighting lieutenant. He never held an independent command; but after Gettysburg he was sent west to assist Bragg, and rejoined Lee in time for the Wilderness campaign. After the war he accepted reconstruction, and held offices under Republican presidents. The battle of Gettysburg and the capture of Vicksburg were the climax of the war, and the charge here described was the decisive feature of the battle. — Bibliography: Abner Doubleday, *Chancellorsville and Gettysburg, passim;* J. F. Rhodes, *History of the United States,* IV, 298, note; Channing and Hart, *Guide,* § 210.

GENERAL LEE has reported of arrangements for the day, —

"The general plan was unchanged. Longstreet, reinforced by Pickett's three brigades, which arrived near the battle-field during the afternoon of the 2d [July], was ordered to attack the next morning, and General Ewell was ordered to attack the enemy's right at the same time. . . ."

This is disingenuous. He did not give or send me orders for the morning of the third day, nor did he reinforce me by Pickett's brigades for morning attack. As his head-quarters were about four miles from the command, I did not ride over, but sent, to report the work of the second day. In the absence of orders, I had scouting parties out during the night in search of a way by which we might strike the enemy's left, and push it down towards his centre. I found a way that gave some promise of results, and was about to move the command, when he rode over after sunrise and gave his orders. His plan was to assault the enemy's left centre by a column to be composed of McLaws's and Hood's divisions reinforced by Pickett's brigades. I thought that it would not do; that the point had been fully tested the day before, by more men, when all were fresh; that the enemy was there looking for us, as we heard him during the night putting up his defences; that the divisions of McLaws and Hood were holding a mile along the right of my line against twenty thousand men, who would follow their withdrawal, strike the flank of the assaulting column, crush it, and get on our rear towards the Potomac River; that thirty thousand men was the minimum of force necessary for the work; that even such force would need close co-operation on other parts of the line; that the column as he proposed to organize it would have only about thirteen thousand men (the divisions having lost a third of their numbers the day before); that the column would have to march a mile under concentrating battery

fire, and a thousand yards under long-range musketry ; that the conditions were different from those in the days of Napoleon, when field
batteries had a range of six hundred yards and musketry about sixty
yards.

He said the distance was not more than fourteen hundred yards.
General Meade's estimate was a mile or a mile and a half (Captain
Long, the guide of the field of Gettysburg in 1888, stated that it was a
trifle over a mile). He then concluded that the divisions of McLaws
and Hood could remain on the defensive line ; that he would reinforce
by divisions of the Third Corps and Pickett's brigades, and stated the
point to which the march should be directed. I asked the strength of
the column. He stated fifteen thousand. Opinion was then expressed
that the fifteen thousand men who could make successful assault over
that field had never been arrayed for battle ; but he was impatient of
listening, and tired of talking, and nothing was left but to proceed.
General Alexander was ordered to arrange the batteries of the front
of the First and Third Corps, those of the Second were supposed to be
in position ; Colonel Walton was ordered to see that the batteries of the
First were supplied with ammunition, and to prepare to give the signal-guns for the opening combat. The infantry of the Third Corps
to be assigned were Heth's and Pettigrew's divisions and Wilcox's
brigade. . . .

The director of artillery was asked to select a position on his line
from which he could note the effect of his practice, and to advise
General Pickett when the enemy's fire was so disturbed as to call for the
assault. General Pickett's was the division of direction, and he was
ordered to have a staff-officer or courier with the artillery director to
bear notice of the moment to advance.

The little affair between the skirmish lines quieted in a short time,
and also the noise on our extreme left. The quiet filing of one or two
of our batteries into position emphasized the profound silence that prevailed during our wait for final orders. Strong battle was in the air, and
the veterans of both sides swelled their breasts to gather nerve and
strength to meet it. Division commanders were asked to go to the
crest of the ridge and take a careful view of the field, and to have their
officers there to tell their men of it, and to prepare them for the sight
that was to burst upon them as they mounted the crest. . . .

The signal-guns broke the silence, the blaze of the second gun mingling in the smoke of the first, and salvoes rolled to the left and repeated

themselves, the enemy's fine metal spreading its fire to the converging lines, ploughing the trembling ground, plunging through the line of batteries, and clouding the heavy air. The two or three hundred guns seemed proud of their undivided honors and organized confusion. The Confederates had the benefit of converging fire into the enemy's massed position, but the superior metal of the enemy neutralized the advantage of position. The brave and steady work progressed. . . .

General Pickett rode to confer with Alexander, then to the ground upon which I was resting, where he was soon handed a slip of paper. After reading it he handed it to me. It read:

"If you are coming at all, come at once, or I cannot give you proper support, but the enemy's fire has not slackened at all. At least eighteen guns are still firing from the cemetery itself. ALEXANDER."

Pickett said, "General, shall I advance?"

The effort to speak the order failed, and I could only indicate it by an affirmative bow. He accepted the duty with seeming confidence of success, leaped on his horse, and rode gayly to his command. I mounted and spurred for Alexander's post. He reported that the batteries he had reserved for the charge with the infantry had been spirited away by General Lee's chief of artillery; that the ammunition of the batteries of position was so reduced that he could not use them in proper support of the infantry. He was ordered to stop the march at once and fill up his ammunition-chests. But, alas! there was no more ammunition to be had.

The order was imperative. The Confederate commander had fixed his heart upon the work. Just then a number of the enemy's batteries hitched up and hauled off, which gave a glimpse of unexpected hope. Encouraging messages were sent for the columns to hurry on, — and they were then on elastic springing step. The officers saluted as they passed, their stern smiles expressing confidence. General Pickett, a graceful horseman, sat lightly in the saddle, his brown locks flowing quite over his shoulders. Pettigrew's division spread their steps and quickly rectified the alignment, and the grand march moved bravely on. As soon as the leading columns opened the way, the supports sprang to their alignments. General Trimble mounted, adjusting his seat and reins with an air and grace as if setting out on a pleasant afternoon ride. When aligned to their places solid march was made down the slope and past our batteries of position.

Confederate batteries put their fire over the heads of the men as they moved down the slope, and continued to draw the fire of the enemy until the smoke lifted and drifted to the rear, when every gun was turned upon the infantry columns. The batteries that had been drawn off were replaced by others that were fresh. Soldiers and officers began to fall, some to rise no more, others to find their way to the hospital tents. Single files were cut here and there, then the gaps increased, and an occasional shot tore wider openings, but, closing the gaps as quickly as made, the march moved on. . . .

Colonel Latrobe was sent to General Trimble to have his men fill the line of the broken brigades, and bravely they repaired the damage. The enemy moved out against the supporting brigade in Pickett's rear. Colonel Sorrel was sent to have that move guarded, and Pickett was drawn back to that contention. McLaws was ordered to press his left forward, but the direct line of infantry and cross-fire of artillery was telling fearfully on the front. Colonel Fremantle ran up to offer congratulations on the apparent success, but the big gaps in the ranks grew until the lines were reduced to half their length. I called his attention to the broken, struggling ranks. Trimble mended the battle of the left in handsome style, but on the right the massing of the enemy grew stronger and stronger. Brigadier Garnett was killed, Kemper and Trimble were desperately wounded; Generals Hancock and Gibbon were wounded. General Lane succeeded Trimble, and with Pettigrew held the battle of the left in steady ranks.

Pickett's lines being nearer, the impact was heaviest upon them. Most of the field officers were killed or wounded. Colonel Whittle, of Armistead's brigade, who had been shot through the right leg at Williamsburg and lost his left arm at Malvern Hill, was shot through the right arm, then brought down by a shot through his left leg.

General Armistead, of the second line, spread his steps to supply the places of fallen comrades. His colors cut down, with a volley against the bristling line of bayonets, he put his cap on his sword to guide the storm. The enemy's massing, enveloping numbers held the struggle until the noble Armistead fell beside the wheels of the enemy's battery. Pettigrew was wounded, but held his command.

General Pickett, finding the battle broken, while the enemy was still reinforcing, called the troops off. There was no indication of panic. The broken files marched back in steady step. The effort was nobly made, and failed from blows that could not be fended. . . .

Looking confidently for advance of the enemy through our open field, I rode to the line of batteries, resolved to hold it until the last gun was lost. As I rode, the shells screaming over my head and ploughing the ground under my horse, an involuntary appeal went up that one of them might take me from scenes of such awful responsibility; but the storm to be met left no time to think of one's self. The battery officers were prepared to meet the crisis, — no move had been made for leaving the field. . . . Our men passed the batteries in quiet walk, and would rally, I knew, when they reached the ridge from which they started.

General Lee was soon with us, and with staff-officers and others assisted in encouraging the men and getting them together.

James Longstreet, *From Manassas to Appomattox* (Philadelphia, 1896), 385–395 *passim*.

---

121. The Draft Riot (1863)

BY ANNA ELIZABETH DICKINSON (1868)

Miss Dickinson became prominent during the Civil War as an orator who spoke often in the different states in favor of Republican candidates and on war issues. After the war she continued to lecture, usually on subjects of political or of social importance. Her account of the great draft riot in New York City appeared in a novel in 1868; the substantial features were generally accepted at that time, but some details have never been proved. The riot was not fully suppressed until the fifth day, after troops had arrived from the front. — Bibliography: J. F. Rhodes, *History of the United States*, IV, 328, note.

ON the morning of Monday, the thirteenth of July, began this outbreak, unparalleled in atrocities by anything in American history, and equalled only by the horrors of the worst days of the French Revolution. Gangs of men and boys, composed of railroad *employées*, workers in machine-shops, and a vast crowd of those who lived by preying upon others, thieves, pimps, professional ruffians, — the scum of the city, — jail-birds, or those who were running with swift feet to enter the prison-doors, began to gather on the corners, and in streets and alleys where they lived; from thence issuing forth they visited the great establishments on the line of their advance, commanding their instant close and the companionship of the workmen, — many of them peaceful and orderly men, — on pain of the destruction of one and a murderous assault upon the other, did not their orders meet with instant compliance.

A body of these, five or six hundred strong, gathered about one of the enrolling-offices in the upper part of the city, where the draft was quietly proceeding, and opened the assault upon it by a shower of clubs, bricks, and paving-stones torn from the streets, following it up by a furious rush into the office. Lists, records, books, the drafting-wheel, every article of furniture or work in the room was rent in pieces, and strewn about the floor or flung into the street; while the law officers, the newspaper reporters, — who are expected to be everywhere, — and the few peaceable spectators, were compelled to make a hasty retreat through an opportune rear exit, accelerated by the curses and blows of the assailants.

. . . And then, finding every portable article destroyed, — their thirst for ruin growing by the little drink it had had, — and believing, or rather hoping, that the officers had taken refuge in the upper rooms, set fire to the house, and stood watching the slow and steady lift of the flames, filling the air with demoniac shrieks and yells, while they waited for the prey to escape from some door or window, from the merciless fire to their merciless hands. One of these, who was on the other side of the street, courageously stepped forward, and, telling them that they had utterly demolished all they came to seek, informed them that helpless women and little children were in the house, and besought them to extinguish the flames and leave the ruined premises; to disperse, or at least to seek some other scene.

By his dress recognizing in him a government official, so far from hearing or heeding his humane appeal, they set upon him with sticks and clubs, and beat him till his eyes were blind with blood, and he — bruised and mangled — succeeded in escaping to the handful of police who stood helpless before this howling crew, now increased to thousands. With difficulty and pain the inoffensive tenants escaped from the rapidly spreading fire, which, having devoured the house originally lighted, swept across the neighboring buildings till the whole block stood a mass of burning flames. . . .

The work thus begun, continued, — gathering in force and fury as the day wore on. Police-stations, enrolling-offices, rooms or buildings used in any way by government authority, or obnoxious as representing the dignity of law, were gutted, destroyed, then left to the mercy of the flames. Newspaper offices, whose issues had been a fire in the rear of the nation's armies by extenuating and defending treason, and through violent and incendiary appeals stirring up " lewd fellows of the baser sort " to this very carnival of ruin and blood, were cheered as the

crowd went by.   Those that had been faithful to loyalty and law were
hooted, stoned, and even stormed by the army of miscreants who
were only driven off by the gallant and determined charge of the police,
and in one place by the equally gallant, and certainly unique defence,
which came from turning the boiling water from the engines upon the
howling wretches, who, unprepared for any such warm reception as this,
beat a precipitate and general retreat.   Before night fell it was no longer
one vast crowd collected in a single section, but great numbers of
gatherings, scattered over the whole length and breadth of the city, —
some of them engaged in actual work of demolition and ruin ; others
with clubs and weapons in their hands, prowling round apparently with
no definite atrocity to perpetrate, but ready for any iniquity that might
offer, — and, by way of pastime, chasing every stray police officer, or
solitary soldier, or inoffensive negro, who crossed the line of their vision ;
these three objects — the badge of a defender of the law, — the uniform
of the Union army, — the skin of a helpless and outraged race — acted
upon these madmen as water acts upon a rabid dog.

Late in the afternoon a crowd which could have numbered not less
than ten thousand, the majority of whom were ragged, frowzy, drunken
women, gathered about the Orphan Asylum for Colored Children, — a
large and beautiful building, and one of the most admirable and noble
charities of the city.   When it became evident, from the menacing
cries and groans of the multitude, that danger, if not destruction, was
meditated to the harmless and inoffensive inmates, a flag of truce appeared, and an appeal was made in their behalf, by the principal, to
every sentiment of humanity which these beings might possess, — a vain
appeal !   Whatever human feeling had ever, if ever, filled these souls
was utterly drowned and washed away in the tide of rapine and blood in
which they had been steeping themselves.   The few officers who stood
guard over the doors, and manfully faced these demoniac legions, were
beaten down and flung to one side, helpless and stunned, whilst the vast
crowd rushed in.   All the articles upon which they could seize — beds,
bedding, carpets, furniture, — the very garments of the fleeing inmates,
some of these torn from their persons as they sped by — were carried
into the streets, and hurried off by the women and children who stood
ready to receive the goods which their husbands, sons, and fathers flung
to their care.   The little ones, many of them, assailed and beaten ;
all, — orphans and care-takers, — exposed to every indignity and every
danger, driven on to the street, — the building was fired. . . .

. . . The house was fired in a thousand places, and in less than two hours the walls crashed in, — a mass of smoking, blackened ruins; whilst the children wandered through the streets, a prey to beings who were wild beasts in everything save the superior ingenuity of man to agonize and torture his victims.

Frightful as the day had been, the night was yet more hideous; since to the horrors which were seen was added the greater horror of deeds which might be committed in the darkness; or, if they were seen, it was by the lurid glare of burning buildings, — the red flames of which — flung upon the stained and brutal faces, the torn and tattered garments, of men and women who danced and howled around the scene of ruin they had caused — made the whole aspect of affairs seem more like a gathering of fiends rejoicing in Pandemonium than aught with which creatures of flesh and blood had to do. . . .

The next morning's sun rose on a city which was ruled by a reign of terror. Had the police possessed the heads of Hydra and the arms of Briareus, and had these heads all seen, these arms all fought, they would have been powerless against the multitude of opposers. Outbreaks were made, crowds gathered, houses burned, streets barricaded, fights enacted, in a score of places at once. Where the officers appeared they were irretrievably beaten and overcome; their stand, were it ever so short, but inflaming the passions of the mob to fresh deeds of violence. Stores were closed; the business portion of the city deserted; the large works and factories emptied of men, who had been sent home by their employers, or were swept into the ranks of the marauding bands. The city cars, omnibuses, hacks, were unable to run, and remained under shelter. Every telegraph wire was cut, the posts torn up, the operators driven from their offices. The mayor, seeing that civil power was helpless to stem this tide, desired to call the military to his aid, and place the city under martial law, but was opposed by the Governor, — a governor, who, but a few days before, had pronounced the war a failure; and not only predicted, but encouraged this mob rule, which was now crushing everything beneath its heavy and ensanguined feet. This man, through almost two days of these awful scenes, remained at a quiet sea-side retreat but a few miles from the city. Coming to it on the afternoon of the second day, — instead of ordering cannon planted in the streets, giving these creatures opportunity to retire to their homes, and, in the event of refusal, blowing them there by powder and ball, — he first went to the point where was collected the chiefest mob, and proceeded to address them. Before him stood incendiaries, thieves, and murderers, who even then were sacking dwelling-houses, and butchering powerless and inoffensive beings. These wretches he apostrophized as " My friends," repeating the title again and again in the course of his harangue, assuring them that he was there as a proof of his friendship, — which he had demonstrated by "sending his adjutant-general to Washington, to have the draft stopped ;" begging them to "wait for his return ;" "to separate now as good citizens ;" with the promise that they "might assemble again whenever they wished to do so ;" meanwhile, he would "take care of their rights." This model speech was incessantly interrupted by tremendous cheering and frantic demonstrations of delight, — one great fellow almost crushing the Governor in his enthusiastic embrace. . . .

His allies in newspaper offices attempted to throw the blame upon the loyal press and portion of the community. This was but a repetition of the cry, raised by traitors in arms, that the government, struggling for life in their deadly hold, was responsible for the war : " If thou wouldst but consent to be murdered peaceably, there could be no strife."

These editors outraged common sense, truth, and decency, by speaking of the riots as an " uprising of the people to defend their liberties," — " an opposition on the part of the workingmen to an unjust and oppressive law, enacted in favor of the men of wealth and standing." As though the *people* of the great metropolis were incendiaries, robbers, and assassins ; as though the poor were to demonstrate their indignation against the rich by hunting and stoning defenceless women and children ; torturing and murdering men whose only offence was the color God gave them, or men wearing the self-same uniform as that which they declared was to be thrust upon them at the behest of the rich and the great.

It was absurd and futile to characterize this new Reign of Terror as anything but an effort on the part of Northern rebels to help Southern ones, at the most critical moment of the war, — with the State militia and available troops absent in a neighboring Commonwealth, — and the loyal people unprepared. These editors and their coadjutors, men of brains and ability, were of that most poisonous growth, — traitors to the Government and the flag of their country, — renegade Americans. Let it, however, be written plainly and graven deeply, that the tribes of savages — the hordes of ruffians — found ready to do their loathsome bidding, were not of native growth, nor American born. . . .

By far the most infamous part of these cruelties was that which wreaked every species of torture and lingering death upon the colored people of the city, — men, women, and children, old and young, strong and feeble alike.   Hundreds of these fell victims to the prejudice fostered by public opinion, incorporated in our statute-books, sanctioned by our laws, which here and thus found legitimate outgrowth and action. The horrors which blanched the face of Christendom were but the bloody harvest of fields sown by society, by cultured men and women, by speech, and book, and press, by professions and politics, nay, by the pulpit itself, and the men who there make God's truth a lie, — garbling or denying the inspired declaration that " He has made of one blood all people to dwell upon the face of the earth ;" and that he, the All-Just and Merciful One, " is no respecter of persons."

Anna E. Dickinson, *What Answer ?* (Boston, 1868), 243–257 *passim.*

————◆————

122. Chickamauga (1863)

BY WILLIAM FRANKLIN GORE SHANKS

Shanks became a war correspondent of the *New York Herald* at the beginning of the Civil War, and at the close a member of the *Herald's* editorial staff.   Since then he has held various prominent positions as a journalist.   The *Herald* was established as an independent paper by James Gordon Bennett ; but until the firing on Sumter it supported southern interests, and after that event, though it upheld the war for the Union, it continued to denounce the anti-slavery cause. — Bibliography : H. M. Cist, *Army of the Cumberland, passim ;* J. F. Rhodes, *History of the United States,* IV, 407, note ; Channing and Hart, *Guide,* § 210.

[September 21.] . . . ROSECRANS' army had been concentrated on West Chickamauga creek, about ten or twelve miles northwest of Lafayette, Ga. . . .

. . . Bragg . . . moved to the right, nearly parallel with the creek, with the intention of getting upon our right flank and rear, or forcing Rosecrans to move with him to such point upon the stream as was naturally less calculated to offer a good defensive position against a strong attack on the left, in which plan Bragg persisted to the last.   That it was his plan and purpose to throw himself between Rosecrans and Chattanooga, with the aim of preventing a junction with Burnside, now no longer remains doubtful. . . .

. . . on the night of the 18th the line was changed to accommodate itself with that of Bragg, Gen. Thomas' corps moving all night for that purpose, and becoming the left of the army. . . .

. . . the enemy pushed up vigorously on the left, and simultaneously the three divisions of Brannan, Baird and Johnston were hotly engaged against a force fully equal, pressing forward most persistently. . . . Twice repulsed in their daring attack upon the left, with their dead strewing the field, the enemy had the boldness to make a third charge, this time pushing forward a heavy force on the entire front of Thomas and Crittenden, the line from Brannan to Van Cleve going in with vigor. For nearly an hour this engagement lasted, with success alternating between our banner and theirs. The musketry firing was very heavy, and in the densely timbered plain in which the fight occurred the sounds and echoes were demoniac, mingled as they were with the cries of the infuriated combatants. It is vain that one attempts to give the various incidents of this magnificent engagement of an hour and a half. . . .

. . . the enemy in front of Thomas' four divisions (Brannan, Baird, Johnston and Reynolds) became less persistent in their efforts, and upon a charge being ordered by Thomas, they, the elite of Lee, broke. . . . For the fourth time they were driven over ground that they had thrice contested, at frightful cost ; but their fourth repulse appeared to me to cost them more than all the rest. They fell at every step, mercilessly shot down, as they fled like sheep. The glory and renown of Longstreet had departed. Thomas pursued him for nearly a mile, driving him from every position which he assumed west of the creek, and forcing him beyond it in such great disorder that he was unable to recover from it during the day. The charge of that corps should go down to posterity in language that would insure the immortality of the story. . . .

. . . the fruits of Thomas' victory over Longstreet were lost. It was in this wise. When Thomas' corps made the charge upon Longstreet, which drove him such a distance in disastrous rout, Crittenden's corps failed to push the rebel centre, but remained in his original position. Crittenden thus allowed a great gap to be made between him and Thomas, and permitted the latter's right flank to be much exposed. At the same time the enemy was allowed time to gather fresh strength in front of McCook and Crittenden . . . until he had penetrated our centre. . . . But, as if unaware of the damage he had done us — unaware that Palmer was cut off, Van Cleve destroyed for the time, and Davis much pressed and wearied — the enemy had partially withdrawn, and the centre was re-established without any great effort, but somewhat in the rear of the former line.   Having in the meantime learned of this new disaster on his right, and fearful of further exposure of his right flank, General Thomas reluctantly gave the order to fall back to the old position, which the men did in the most excellent order. . . .

On the morning of the 20th (Sunday) General Rosecrans . . . found the line stretched in the following order, from right to left . . . Davis' right, then Sheridan, with one brigade in reserve ; Wood, two brigades of Brannan, with the other and all of Van Cleve in reserve ; Reynolds, Palmer, Baird, Johnston and Negley on the extreme left, the latter three divisions furnishing their own reserves. . . .

Along Thomas' front there had been built during the night a rude breastwork for the protection of the men. . . . Generals Crittenden and McCook had not taken the same wise precautions, or the day might, perhaps, have gone otherwise.

. . . Longstreet still held the right, D. H. Hill had the centre and Polk the left of the rebel line, now well established west of the Chickamauga creek.

The fog on the morning of the 20th lifted slowly . . . when the battle opened with a furious assault on Thomas' left.

. . . the storm, in all its fury, burst along the plain, enveloping the lines of Negley, Johnston, Baird and Palmer — no farther — and to this part it was confined for nearly two hours.   I despair of giving any correct idea of this engagement. . . .   For two hours that line never wavered. Can you not guess the result on the other side ? . . .

At this time it was noon, and Thomas had not budged an inch from his position. . . .

Lying under Reynolds' works at this hour, my attention was called to evident movements in the thick woods in his front and on his right.   The dust revealed that the enemy was there, and soon it was known all along the line that he was pushing forward to attack the right and centre.   The fight on the left continued with great fury : but Brannan had arrived in time to save that flank.   The danger was now in the front and right. The enemy . . . advanced with great rapidity, and in a moment Reynolds, Brannan, Palmer, Wood and Sheridan were hotly engaged.   But the fight was of short duration.   The right and centre — I will not attempt to explain how — gave way in ten minutes after the fight began, and fled rapidly across the fields towards the mountains.   Davis, struck in flank, was cut off with Sheridan, while Palmer and Wood, making desperate efforts to repel the overwhelming assault of the rebels, made with an impetus which of itself should have insured success, were forced back in the opposite direction. Van Cleve, struck while *en route* to aid the left, made no resistance deserving of the name, but was seen flying in mad retreat across an open field, where Rosecrans' headquarters were. I can remember seeing in the distance the vain endeavors of Rosecrans and his staff to rally them. The rebels pushed on after the flying columns, increasing the wild panic which possessed them, and all the personal exertions of the chief and his staff were in vain. The rout of Sheridan, Davis, Van Cleve, and the most of Wood and Palmer, was now complete. General Rosecrans, cut off with Sheridan, Davis and Van Cleve, was forced, with McCook and Crittenden, far to the right, and in three hours after, borne along by the current, and cut off from Thomas, all three were pushed by the flying columns into Rossville and Chattanooga. . . .

Thomas still remained on the field, with remnants of his glorious old corps ; and the man who had the day before, in equal contest, defeated the boastful chivalry of Longstreet, now bent all his energies, with an unequal force, to cover the retreat and save the flying army from absolute destruction.

. . . But this abandonment of the field by the centre and right enabled the enemy to do with Thomas' right what he had signally failed, at frightful cost, to do with his left, and soon the rebels were pushing forward upon Wood and Palmer, doubling them up and pushing them back upon Brannan and Reynolds. . . .

. . . The raid had begun at twelve o'clock ; the stand of Thomas was made in half an hour, and the repulse and check of the enemy had been effected in a desperate engagement along the whole of this little line of not over fifteen minutes' duration.

Imagine this line — a thread without supports — the whole force to the front line — a force not over 20,000 — and no one who saw it and who writes of it will put it at so much — and you have in your mind's eye the heroic corps which saved the whole army. And imagine the black lines of a powerful enemy marching upon it flank and front, and all the time pressing it closely in front and flank. . . .

General Thomas, near the centre of the army, was engaged, about one o'clock . . . watching a heavy cloud of dust in his rear, in such a direction that it might be General Granger with reinforcements, or it might be the enemy. . . .

. . . In a few minutes . . . emerged . . . the red, white and blue crescent-shaped battle flag of Gordon Granger. . . . At a quarter-past one, Steadman first, and Gordon Granger afterwards, had wrung the hand of the statue Thomas, who had gone all through the terrible scenes of the last two days' battle to be melted and moved at this hour. . . .

. . . Steadman in position, and the others notified as to his purpose, Thomas, with all the assurance of power and strength, assumed the offensive, and, while the enemy were actually moving on his flanks, intending to envelop him, positively made an attack and, in a fight of ten minutes of desperate encounter, knocked the centre out of their line and dislodged them from the position which they had held. . . .

Driven from his pressing position in the centre, the enemy did not fail to continue his manœuvres on our flanks, and at times succeeded in pushing them in, giving the line more and more the appearance of a horseshoe. But a general lull had followed the fight I have last mentioned, and that lull lasted until about sunset. Thomas was not disposed to attack, and the enemy were contented to manœuvre upon the flanks, perfectly confident, as he seemed, of surrounding our little force.

. . . the rebels, as if eager to consummate the victory ere the day should die out, pushed up for a last and overwhelming attack. It was five o'clock when the last combat of the battle began, and the sun refused to look upon its end. . . .

Our men were short of ammunition, and had orders to make what they had serve the best effect. Yet, despite this precaution, all along our line a most furious fire was kept up. I do not say that ammunition was wasted; for we had reason subsequently to know that the fire had been marked by most deadly effect, and that the last repulse of the battle was one of the most bloody to the rebels. There were but two charges, but each so admirably sustained by the rebels that only the desperate defence of our men could have repulsed them. . . .

. . . The aim of the enemy, persistently pursued from the beginning, was to get possession of Chattanooga. In that he was foiled, foiled for the present and the future; for it is now impossible to gain it. . . .

During the night of Sunday Gen. Thomas fell back from his position on the field to Rossville, where he held a strong position in the gap of Missionary Ridge, in which the town is situated. The enemy reconnoitered this position the next day, but failed to attack. During the same day the corps fell back to Chattanooga. . . .

New York Herald, September 27, 1863.

123. "Battle above the Clouds" (1863)

BY MAJOR-GENERAL GEORGE HENRY THOMAS

Thomas, like most of the other successful generals in the Civil War, was educated at West Point. He was a Virginian; but he remained loyal, and through the confidence inspired in his reliability gradually became one of the great generals of the western armies. His claim to fame rests equally upon his sturdy defence at Chickamauga (see No. 122 above) and his skilful attack at Nashville (see No. 138 below). His official report of the battles of Lookout Mountain and Missionary Ridge, from which this extract is taken, embraced only the operations of his own army; but his forces were the dominant factor in the victory. — For Thomas, see T. B. Van Horne, *Life of Major-General George H. Thomas.* — Bibliography as in No. 122 above.

A S soon as communications with Bridgeport had been made secure, and the question of supplying the army at this point rendered certain, preparations were at once commenced for driving the enemy from his position in our immediate front on Lookout Mountain and Missionary Ridge. . . .

. . . Major-General Sherman, commanding Army of the Tennessee, having been ordered with the Fifteenth Corps to this point to participate in the operations against the enemy, reached Bridgeport with two divisions on the 15th [November]. He came to the front himself, and having examined the ground, expressed himself confident of his ability to execute his share of the work. The plan of operations was then written out substantially as follows : Sherman, with the Fifteenth Corps, strengthened with one division from my command, was to effect a crossing of the Tennessee River just below the mouth of the South Chickamauga, on Saturday, November 21, at daylight. . . . After crossing his force, he was to carry the heights of Missionary Ridge from their northern extremity to about the railroad tunnel before the enemy could concentrate a force against him. I was to co-operate with Sherman by concentrating my troops in Chattanooga Valley, on my left flank. . . . I was then to effect a junction with Sherman, making my advance from the left well toward the north end of Mission Ridge, and moving as near simultaneously with Sherman as possible. . . .

. . . In consequence of the bad condition of the roads General Sherman's troops were occupied all of Sunday in getting into position. In the meantime, the river having risen, both pontoon bridges were broken by rafts sent down the river by the enemy, cutting off Osterhaus' division from the balance of Sherman's troops. It was thought this would delay us another day, but during the night of the 22d, two deserters reported Bragg had fallen back, and that there was only a strong picket line in our front. Early on the morning of the 23d, I received a note from Major-General Grant, directing me to ascertain by a demonstration the truth or falsity of this report.

Orders were accordingly given to General Granger, commanding the Fourth Corps, to form his troops and to advance directly in front of Fort Wood, and thus develop the strength of the enemy. General Palmer, commanding the Fourteenth Corps, was directed to support General Granger's right, with Baird's division refused and *en échelon*. . . . The two divisions of Granger's corps (Sheridan's and Wood's) were formed in front of Fort Wood; Sheridan on the right, Wood on the left, with his left extending nearly to Citico Creek. The formation being completed about 2 p. m. the troops were advanced steadily and with rapidity directly to the front, driving before them first the rebel pickets, then their reserves, and falling upon their grand guards stationed in their first line of rifle-pits, captured something over 200 men, and secured themselves in their new positions before the enemy had sufficiently recovered from his surprise to attempt to send re-enforcements from his main camp. Orders were then given to General Granger to make his position secure by constructing temporary breastworks and throwing out strong pickets to his front. . . . The troops remained in that position for the night. The Tennessee River having risen considerably from the effect of the previous heavy rain-storm, it was found difficult to rebuild the pontoon bridge at Brown's Ferry. Therefore it was determined that General Hooker should take Osterhaus' division, which was still in Lookout Valley, and Geary's division, Whitaker's and Grose's brigades, of the First Division, Fourth Corps, under Brigadier-General Cruft, and make a strong demonstration on the western slope of Lookout Mountain, for the purpose of attracting the enemy's attention in that direction and thus withdrawing him from Sherman while crossing the river at the mouth of the South Chickamauga.

General Hooker was instructed that in making this demonstration, if he discovered the position and strength of the enemy would justify him in attempting to carry the point of the mountain, to do so. By 4 a. m. on the morning of the 24th, General Hooker reported his troops in position and ready to advance.

. . . Hooker's movements were facilitated by the heavy mist which overhung the mountain, enabling Geary to get into position without attracting attention.

Finding himself vigorously pushed by a strong column on his left and rear, the enemy began to fall back with rapidity, but his resistance was obstinate, and the entire point of the mountain was not gained until about 2 p. m., when General Hooker reported by telegraph that he had carried the mountain as far as the road from Chattanooga Valley to the white house. Soon after, his main column coming up, his line was extended to the foot of the mountain, near the mouth of Chattanooga Creek. . . .

With the aid of the steamer Dunbar, which had been put in condition and sent up the river at daylight of the 24th, General Sherman by 11 a. m. had crossed three divisions of the Fifteenth Corps, and was ready to advance. . . .

. . . Instructions were sent to General Hooker to be ready to advance on the morning of the 25th from his position on the point of Lookout Mountain to the Summertown road, and endeavor to intercept the enemy's retreat, if he had not already withdrawn, which he was to ascertain by pushing a reconnaissance to the top of Lookout Mountain.

The reconnaissance was made as directed, and having asertained that the enemy had evacuated during the night, General Hooker was then directed to move on the Rossville road with the troops under his command . . . carry the pass at Rossville, and operate upon the enemy's left and rear. Palmer's and Granger's troops were held in readiness to advance directly on the rifle-pits in their front as soon as Hooker could get into position at Rossville. . . . About noon, General Sherman becoming heavily engaged by the enemy, they having massed a strong force in his front, orders were given for General Baird to march his division within supporting distance of General Sherman. Moving his command promptly in the direction indicated, he was placed in position to the left of Wood's division of Granger's corps.

. . . The whole line then advanced against the breastworks, and soon became warmly engaged with the enemy's skirmishers; these, giving way, retired upon their reserves, posted within their works. Our troops advancing steadily in a continuous line, the enemy, seized with panic abandoned the works at the foot of the hill and retreated precipitately to the crest, where they were closely followed by our troops, who, apparently inspired by the impulse of victory, carried the hill simultaneously at six different points, and so closely upon the heels of the enemy that many of them were taken prisoners in the trenches. W captured all their cannon and ammunition before they could be removed or destroyed.

After halting for a few moments to reorganize the troops, who had become somewhat scattered in the assault of the hill, General Sheridan pushed forward in pursuit, and drove those in his front who escaped capture across Chickamauga Creek. Generals Wood and Baird, being obstinately resisted by re-enforcements from the enemy's extreme right, continued fighting until darkness set in, slowly but steadily driving the enemy before them. In moving upon Rossville, General Hooker encountered Stewart's division and other troops. Finding his left flank threatened, Stewart attempted to escape by retreating toward Graysville, but some of his force, finding their retreat threatened from that quarter, retired in disorder toward their right, along the crest of the ridge, when they were met by another portion of General Hooker's command, and were driven by these troops in the face of Johnson's division of Palmer's corps, by whom they were nearly all made prisoners.

. . . On the 26th, the enemy were pursued by Hooker's and Palmer's commands. . . . The pursuit was continued on the 27th. . . .

The War of the Rebellion: Official Records of the Union and Confederate Armies, First Series (Washington, 1890), XXXI, pt. ii, 92–97 *passim*.

CHAPTER XXI — EMANCIPATION

124. "Contraband of War" (1861)

BY MAJOR-GENERAL BENJAMIN FRANKLIN BUTLER

Butler, a former Breckinridge Democrat, was one of the earliest appointed major-generals of the volunteer forces. The appointment was for political reasons; and although he remained in active command throughout the war, he never gained a reputation as a good general. In 1861 he was in command at Fortress Monroe, and his somewhat humorous definition of negroes as "contraband of war" was the first official intimation that the slaves of Confederates would be held free. This extract is from his report to General Scott, May 24, 1861. — Bibliography: Channing and Hart, *Guide*, § 214.

ON Thursday night, three negroes, field hands, belonging to Col. Charles Mallory, now in command of the secession forces in this district, delivered themselves up to my picket guard, and, as I learned from the report of the officer of the guard in the morning, had been detained by him. I immediately gave personal attention to the matter, and found satisfactory evidence that these men were about to be taken to Carolina for the purpose of aiding the secession forces there; that two of them left wives and children (one a free woman) here; that the other had left his master from fear that he would be called upon to take part in the rebel armies. Satisfied of these facts from cautious examination of each of the negroes apart from the others, I determined for the present, and until better advised, as these men were very serviceable, and I had great need of labor in my quartermaster's department, to avail myself of their services, and that I would send a receipt to Colonel Mallory that I had so taken them, as I would for any other property of a private citizen which the exigencies of the service seemed to require to be taken by me, and especially property that was designed, adapted, and about to be used against the United States.

As this is but an individual instance in a course of policy which may be required to be pursued with regard to this species of property, I have detailed to the Lieutenant-General this case, and ask his direction. I am credibly informed that the negroes in this neighborhood are now being employed in the erection of batteries and other works by the rebels, which it would be nearly or quite impossible to construct without their labor. Shall they be allowed the use of this property against the United States, and we not be allowed its use in aid of the United States ? . . .

Major Cary demanded to know with regard to the negroes what course I intended to pursue. I answered him substantially as I have written above, when he desired to know if I did not feel myself bound by my constitutional obligations to deliver up fugitives under the fugitive-slave act. To this I replied that the fugitive-slave act did not affect a foreign country, which Virginia claimed to be, and that she must reckon it one of the infelicities of her position that in so far at least she was taken at her word ; that in Maryland, a loyal State, fugitives from service had been returned, and that even now, although so much pressed by my necessities for the use of these men of Colonel Mallory's, yet if their master would come to the fort and take the oath of allegiance to the Constitution of the United States I would deliver the men up to him and endeavor to hire their services of him if he desired to part with them. To this Major Cary responded that Colonel Mallory was absent.

The War of the Rebellion: Official Records of the Union and Confederate Armies, First Series (Washington, 1880), II, 649–650 *passim*.

———◆———

125. " At Port Royal " (1861)

BY JOHN GREENLEAF WHITTIER

Whittier was an early recruit to the cause of immediate emancipation, and much of his early fame rested upon his abolition lyrics. This poem commemorates the capture of Port Royal by the Union forces under General T. W. Sherman and Commodore Du Pont, who thus secured control over the country where the famous Sea Island cotton was grown and where the slave population greatly exceeded the white. The whites all fled and the slaves of the neighborhood became practically free, and later negro troops were raised here. — For Whittier, see Providence Public Library, *Monthly Reference Lists*, III, 3 ; *Contemporaries*, III, No. 178. — Bibliography as in No. 124 above.

THE tent-lights glimmer on the land,
   The ship-lights on the sea ;
The night-wind smooths with drifting sand
   Our track on lone Tybee.

At last our grating keels outslide,
　Our good boats forward swing;
And while we ride the land-locked tide,
　Our negroes row and sing.

For dear the bondman holds his gifts
　Of music and of song:
The gold that kindly Nature sifts
　Among his sands of wrong;

The power to make his toiling days
　And poor home-comforts please;
The quaint relief of mirth that plays
　With sorrow's minor keys.

Another glow than sunset's fire
　Has filled the West with light,
Where field and garner, barn and byre
　Are blazing through the night.

The land is wild with fear and hate,
　The rout runs mad and fast;
From hand to hand, from gate to gate,
　The flaming brand is passed.

The lurid glow falls strong across
　Dark faces broad with smiles:
Not theirs the terror, hate, and loss
　That fire yon blazing piles.

With oar-strokes timing to their song,
　They weave in simple lays
The pathos of remembered wrong,
　The hope of better days, —

The triumph-note that Miriam sung,
　The joy of uncaged birds:
Softening with Afric's mellow tongue
　Their broken Saxon words.

"At Port Royal"

SONG OF THE NEGRO BOATMEN

O, praise an' tanks! De Lord he come
  To set de people free;
An' massa tink it day ob doom,
  An' we ob jubilee.
De Lord dat heap de Red Sea waves
  He jus' as 'trong as den;
He say de word: we las' night slaves;
  To-day, de Lord's freemen.
      De yam will grow, de cotton blow,
        We'll hab de rice an' corn;
      O nebber you fear, if nebber you hear
        De driver blow his horn!

Ole massa on he trabbels gone;
  He leaf de land behind:
De Lord's breff blow him furder on,
  Like corn-shuck in de wind.
We own de hoe, we own de plough,
  We own de hands dat hold;
We sell de pig, we sell de cow,
  But nebber chile be sold.
      De yam will grow, de cotton blow,
        We'll hab de rice an' corn:
      O nebber you fear, if nebber you hear
        De driver blow his horn!

We pray de Lord: he gib us signs
  Dat some day we be free;
De Norf-wind tell it to de pines,
  De wild-duck to de sea;
We tink it when de church-bell ring,
  We dream it in de dream;
De rice-bird mean it when he sing,
  De eagle when he scream.
      De yam will grow, de cotton blow,
        We'll hab de rice an' corn:
      O nebber you fear, if nebber you hear
        De driver blow his horn!

We know de promise nebber fail,
  An' nebber lie de word ;
So, like de 'postles in de jail,
  We waited for de Lord :
An' now he open ebery door,
  An' trow away de key ;
He tink we lub him so before,
  We lub him better free.
      De yam will grow, de cotton blow,
        He'll gib de rice an' corn :
      O nebber you fear, if nebber you hear
        De driver blow his horn !

So sing our dusky gondoliers ;
  And with a secret pain,
And smiles that seem akin to tears,
  We hear the wild refrain.

We dare not share the negro's trust,
  Nor yet his hope deny ;
We only know that God is just,
  And every wrong shall die.

Rude seems the song ; each swarthy face,
  Flame-lighted, ruder still :
We start to think that hapless race
  Must shape our good or ill ;

That laws of changeless justice bind
  Oppressor with oppressed ;
And, close as sin and suffering joined,
  We march to Fate abreast.

Sing on, poor hearts ! your chant shall be
  Our sign of blight or bloom, —
The Vala-song of Liberty,
  Or death-rune of our doom !

John Greenleaf Whittier, *In War Time and other Poems* (Boston, 1864)
  51-57.

126. " Thank God for War " (1862)

BY WILLIAM LLOYD GARRISON

Garrison was one of the first abolitionists, and the leader of the cause in New England. His views were extreme and impracticable; but, though he refused to be governed himself by the political situation of the emancipation question, he did not fail to understand that point of view, as is seen in his address delivered at the annual meeting of the Massachusetts Anti-Slavery Society, from which this extract is taken. — For Garrison, see F. J. Garrison and W. P. Garrison, *William Lloyd Garrison; Contemporaries*, III, No. 174. — Bibliography as in No. 124 above.

WHAT have we to rejoice over? Why, I say, the war! " What! this fratricidal war? What! this civil war? What! this treasonable dismemberment of the Union?" Yes, thank God for it all! — for it indicates the waning power of slavery, and the irresistible growth of freedom, and that the day of Northern submission is past. It is better that we should be so virtuous that the vicious cannot live with us, than to be so vile that they can endure and relish our company. No matter what may be said of the Government — how it timidly holds back — how it lacks courage, energy and faith — how it refuses to strike the blow which alone will settle the rebellion. No matter what may be said of President Lincoln or Gen. McClellan, by way of criticism — and a great deal can be justly said to their condemnation — one cheering fact overrides all these considerations, making them as dust in the balance, and that is, that our free North is utterly unendurable to the slaveholding South ; that we have at last so far advanced in our love of liberty and sympathy for the oppressed, as a people, that it is not possible any longer for the " traffickers in slaves and souls of men " to walk in union with us. I call that a very cheering fact. Yes, the Union is divided ; but better division, than that we should be under the lash of Southern overseers ! Better civil war, if it must come, than for us to crouch in the dust, and allow ourselves to be driven to the wall by a miserable and merciless slave oligarchy ! This war has come because of the increasing love of liberty here at the North ; and although, as a people, we do not yet come up to the high standard of duty in striking directly at the slave system for its extirpation as the root and source of all our woe — nevertheless, the sentiment of the North is deepening daily in the right direction. I hold that it is not wise for us to be too microscopic in endeavoring to find disagreeable and annoying things, still less to assume that everything is waxing worse and worse, and that there is little or no hope. No ; broaden your views ; take a more philosophical grasp of the great question ; and see that, criticise and condemn as you may and should, in certain directions, the fountains of the great deep are broken up — see that this is fundamentally a struggle between all the elements of freedom on the one hand, and all the elements of despotism on the other, with whatever of alloy in the mixture.

I repeat, the war furnishes ground for high encouragement. "Why," some may exclaim, "we thought you were a peace man!" Yes, verily, I am, and none the less so because of these declarations. Would the cause of peace be the gainer by the substitution of the power of the rebel traitors over the nation for the supremacy of the democratic idea? Would the cause of peace be promoted by the North basely yielding up all her rights, and allowing her free institutions to be overthrown? Certainly not. Then, as a peace man, I rejoice that the issue is at last made up, and that the struggle is going on, because I see in it the sign of ultimate redemption. Besides, whether we would have it so or not, it comes inevitably, because of our great national transgression, which is slavery. . . .

I do not know that some margin of allowance may not be made even for the Administration. I would rather be over magnanimous than wanting in justice. Supposing Mr. Lincoln could answer to-night, and we should say to him — "Sir, with the power in your hands, slavery being the cause of the rebellion beyond all controversy, why don't you put the trump of jubilee to your lips, and proclaim universal freedom?" possibly he might answer — "Gentlemen, I understand this matter quite as well as you do. I do not know that I differ in opinion from you ; but will you insure me the support of a united North if I do as you bid me? Are all parties and all sects at the North so convinced and so united on this point, that they will stand by the Government? If so, give me the evidence of it, and I will strike the blow. But, gentlemen, looking over the entire North, and seeing in all your towns and cities papers representing a considerable, if not a formidable portion of the people, menacing and bullying the Government in case it dare to liberate the slaves, even as a matter of self-preservation, I do not feel that the hour has yet come that will render it safe for the Government to take that step." I am willing to believe that something of this feeling weighs in the mind of the President and the Cabinet, and that there is some ground for hesitancy, as a mere matter of political expediency. My reply, however, to the President would be — "Sir, the power is in your hands as President of the United States, and Commander-in-chief of the army and navy. Do *your* duty; give to the slaves their liberty by proclamation, as far as that can give it; and if the North shall betray you, and prefer the success of the rebellion to the preservation of the Union, let the dread responsibility be hers, but stand with God and Freedom on your side, come what may!" But men high in office are not apt to be led by such lofty moral considerations; and, therefore, we should not judge the present incumbents too harshly. Doubtless, they want to be assured of the Northern heart, feeling, coöperation, approval. Can these be safely relied upon when the decisive blow shall be struck? That is the question; and it is a very serious question. . . .

. . . Nevertheless, I think the Administration is unnecessarily timid, and not undeserving of rebuke. I think that this bellowing, bullying, treasonable party at the North has, after all, but very little left, either in point of numbers or power: the fangs of the viper are drawn, though the venomous feeling remains. Still, it has its effect, and produces a damaging, if not paralyzing impression at Washington. . . .

I have great faith in the future. We shall not go back to "the beggarly elements" of old. The "covenant with death" is annulled; the "agreement with hell" no longer stands. Under the new order of things, new relations exist, and the Government is invested with extraordinary powers. . . .

Liberator (Boston), February 7, 1862.

———◆———

127. Slavery and the Union (1862)

BY HORACE GREELEY AND PRESIDENT ABRAHAM LINCOLN

Greeley was liable to an excess of fervor that made his views impracticable. During the Civil War he often lost patience with the administration and berated it through the editorial columns of the *New York Tribune*, as shown in the first of these extracts. The importance of the letter is that it was an attempt to force Lincoln's hand in the issuance of a proclamation of emancipation.— For Greeley, see No. 28 above. — For Lincoln, see No. 44 above. — Bibliography as in No. 124 above.

A. GREELEY TO LINCOLN

[NEW YORK, August 19, 1862.]

. . . I DO not intrude to tell you — for you must know already — that a great proportion of those who triumphed in your election, and of all who desire the unqualified suppression of the Rebellion now desolating our country, are sorely disappointed and deeply pained by the policy you seem to be pursuing with regard to the slaves of Rebels. . . .

VIII. On the face of this wide earth, Mr. President, there is not one disinterested, determined, intelligent champion of the Union cause who does not feel that all attempts to put down the Rebellion and at the same time uphold its inciting cause are preposterous and futile — that the Rebellion, if crushed out to-morrow, would be renewed within a year if Slavery were left in full vigor — that Army officers who remain to this day devoted to Slavery can at best be but half-way loyal to the Union — and that every hour of deference to Slavery is an hour of added and deepened peril to the Union.   I appeal to the testimony of your Embassadors in Europe.   It is freely at your service, not at mine.   Ask them to tell you candidly whether the seeming subserviency of your policy to the slaveholding, slavery-upholding interest, is not the perplexity, the despair, of statesmen of all parties, and be admonished by the general answer !

IX. I close as I began with the statement that what an immense majority of the Loyal Millions of your countrymen require of you is a frank, declared, unqualified, ungrudging execution of the laws of the land, more especially of the Confiscation Act.   That Act gives freedom to the slaves of Rebels coming within our lines, or whom those lines may at any time inclose — we ask you to render it due obedience by publicly requiring all your subordinates to recognize and obey it.   The Rebels are everywhere using the late anti-negro riots in the North, as they have long used your officers' treatment of negroes in the South, to convince the slaves that they have nothing to hope from a Union success — that we mean in that case to sell them into a bitterer bondage to defray the cost of the war. Let them impress this as a truth on the great mass of their ignorant and credulous bondmen, and the Union will never be restored — never.   We cannot conquer Ten Millions of People united in solid phalanx against us, powerfully aided by Northern sympathizers and European allies.   We must have scouts, guides, spies, cooks, teamsters, diggers and choppers from the Blacks of the South, whether we allow them to fight for us or not, or we shall be baffled and repelled.   As one of the millions who would gladly have avoided this struggle at any sacrifice but that of Principle and Honor, but who now feel that the triumph of the Union is indispensable not only to the existence of our country but to the well-being of mankind, I entreat you to render a hearty and unequivocal obedience to the law of the land.

B. LINCOLN TO GREELEY

EXECUTIVE MANSION, WASHINGTON, August 22, 1862.

. . . I HAVE just read yours of the 19th, addressed to myself through the New York "Tribune." If there be in it any statements or assumptions of fact which I may know to be erroneous, I do not, now and here, controvert them. If there be in it any inferences which I may believe to be falsely drawn, I do not, now and here, argue against them. If there be perceptible in it an impatient and dictatorial tone, I waive it in deference to an old friend whose heart I have always supposed to be right.

As to the policy I "seem to be pursuing," as you say, I have not meant to leave any one in doubt.

I would save the Union. I would save it the shortest way under the Constitution. The sooner the national authority can be restored, the nearer the Union will be "the Union as it was." If there be those who would not save the Union unless they could at the same time save slavery, I do not agree with them. If there be those who would not save the Union unless they could at the same time destroy slavery, I do not agree with them. My paramount object in this struggle is to save the Union, and is not either to save or to destroy slavery. If I could save the Union without freeing any slave, I would do it; and if I could save it by freeing all the slaves, I would do it; and if I could save it by freeing some and leaving others alone, I would also do that. What I do about slavery and the colored race, I do because I believe it helps to save the Union; and what I forbear, I forbear because I do not believe it would help to save the Union. I shall do less whenever I shall believe what I am doing hurts the cause, and I shall do more whenever I shall believe doing more will help the cause. I shall try to correct errors when shown to be errors, and I shall adopt new views so fast as they shall appear to be true views.

I have here stated my purpose according to my view of official duty; and I intend no modification of my oft-expressed personal wish that all men everywhere could be free.

New York Daily Tribune, August 20, 1862.
Abraham Lincoln, *Complete Works* (edited by John G. Nicolay and John Hay, New York, 1894), II, 227–228.

128. Debate in the Cabinet (1862)

BY SECRETARY SALMON PORTLAND CHASE

Chase entered public life as an anti-slavery man, and remained consistently such throughout his career. As a member of Lincoln's cabinet, his sympathies were with the demands of the radicals for emancipation, and he was their spokesman within the president's council. His best claim to fame, however, lies in the constructive statesmanship shown in his financial measures, especially in his organization of the national banking system. This extract is from his diary. — For Chase, see Hart, *Salmon Portland Chase;* Channing and Hart, *Guide,* § 25. — Bibliography as in No. 124 above.

[September 22, 1862.] TO department about nine. State Department messenger came with notice to heads of departments to meet at twelve. Received sundry callers. Went to the White House. All the members of the Cabinet were in attendance. There was some general talk, and the President mentioned that Artemus Ward had sent him his book. Proposed to read a chapter which he thought very funny. Read it, and seemed to enjoy it very much ; the heads also (except Stanton). The chapter was " High-Handed Outrage at Utica."

The President then took a graver tone, and said : " Gentlemen, I have, as you are aware, thought a great deal about the relation of this war to slavery, and you all remember that, several weeks ago, I read to you an order I had prepared upon the subject, which, on account of objections made by some of you, was not issued. Ever since then my mind has been much occupied with this subject, and I have thought all along that the time for acting on it might probably come. I think the time has come now. I wish it was a better time. I wish that we were in a better condition. The action of the army against the rebels has not been quite what I should have best liked. But they have been driven out of Maryland, and Pennsylvania is no longer in danger of invasion. When the rebel army was at Frederick I determined, as soon as it should be driven out of Maryland, to issue a proclamation of emancipation, such as I thought most likely to be useful. I said nothing to any one, but I made a promise to myself and (hesitating a little) to my Maker. The rebel army is now driven out, and I am going to fulfill that promise. I have got you together to hear what I have written down. I do not wish your advice about the main matter, for that I have determined for myself. This I say without intending any thing but respect for any one of you. But I already know the views of each on this question. They have been heretofore expressed, and I have considered them as thoroughly and carefully as I can. What I have written is that which my reflections have determined me to say. If there is any thing in the expressions I use or in any minor matter which any one of you thinks had best be changed, I shall be glad to receive your suggestions. One other observation I will make. I know very well that many others might, in this matter as in others, do better than I can; and if I was satisfied that the public confidence was more fully possessed by any one of them than by me, and knew of any constitutional way in which he could be put in my place, he should have it. I would gladly yield it to him. But though I believe that I have not so much of the confidence of the people as I had some time since, I do not know that, all things considered, any other person has more; and, however this may be, there is no way in which I can have any other man put where I am. I am here. I must do the best I can, and bear the responsibility of taking the course which I feel I ought to take."

The President then proceeded to read his Emancipation Proclamation, making remarks on the several parts as he went on, and showing that he had fully considered the subject in all the lights under which it had been presented to him.

After he had closed, Governor Seward said: "The general question having been decided, nothing can be said further about that. Would it not, however, make the proclamation more clear and decided to leave out all reference to the act being sustained during the incumbency of the present President; and not merely say that the Government 'recognizes,' but that it will maintain the freedom it proclaims?"

I followed, saying: "What you have said, Mr. President, fully satisfies me that you have given to every proposition which has been made a kind and candid consideration. And you have now expressed the conclusion to which you have arrived clearly and distinctly. This it was your right, and, under your oath of office, your duty to do. The proclamation does not, indeed, mark out the course I would myself prefer; but I am ready to take it just as it is written and to stand by it with all my heart. I think, however, the suggestions of Governor Seward very judicious, and shall be glad to have them adopted."

The President then asked us severally our opinions as to the modifications proposed, saying that he did not care much about the phrases he had used. Every one favored the modification, and it was adopted. Governor Seward then proposed that in the passage relating to coloniza-

2 D

tion some language should be introduced to show that the colonization proposed was to be only with the consent of the colonists, and the consent of the States in which the colonies might be attempted. This, too, was agreed to ; and no other modification was proposed. Mr. Blair then said that the question having been decided, he would make no objection to issuing the proclamation ; but he would ask to have his paper, presented some days since, against the policy, filed with the proclamation. The President consented to this readily. And then Mr. Blair went on to say that he was afraid of the influence of the proclamation on the border States and on the army, and stated, at some length, the grounds of his apprehensions. He disclaimed most expressly, however, all objections to emancipation *per se*, saying he had always been personally in favor of it — always ready for immediate emancipation in the midst of slave States, rather than submit to the perpetuation of the system.

J. W. Schuckers, *Life and Public Services of Salmon Portland Chase* (New York, D. Appleton & Co., 1874), 453–455.

129. A Peace Democrat's View of Emancipation (1863)

BY REPRESENTATIVE CLEMENT LAIRD VALLANDIGHAM

Vallandigham was a representative from Ohio, and the most prominent and outspoken of the copperheads, or opponents of the war. The speech from which this extract is taken was delivered in the House of Representatives on January 14, 1863. In the succeeding spring Vallandigham attacked the administration so violently in his speeches in Ohio that he was arrested, tried, and convicted by court-martial, and was banished by Lincoln across the Confederate lines. But he found in the South little sympathy for his reunion ideas, and so made his way to Canada, whence he was suffered to return unmolested the following year. — Bibliography : Channing and Hart, *Guide*, §§ 213, 214.

NOW, sir, on the 14th of April [1861], I believed that coercion would bring on war, and war disunion. More than that, I believed, what you all in your hearts believe to-day, that the South could never be conquered — never. And not that only, but I was satisfied — and you of the abolition party have now proved it to the world — that the secret but real purpose of the war was to abolish slavery in the States. In any event, I did not doubt that whatever might be the momentary impulses of those in power, and whatever pledges they might make in the midst of the fury for the Constitution, the Union, and the flag, yet the natural and inexorable logic of revolutions would, sooner or later, drive them into that policy, and with it to its final but inevitable result, the change of our present democratical form of government into an imperial despotism. . . .

And now, sir, I recur to the state of the Union to-day. . . .

Money and credit . . . you have had in prodigal profusion. . . . The fabled hosts of Xerxes have been outnumbered. And yet victory strangely follows the standards of the foe. From Great Bethel to Vicksburg, the battle has not been to the strong. . . . you have utterly, signally, disastrously — I will not say ignominiously — failed to subdue ten millions of "rebels," whom you had taught the people of the North and West not only to hate but to despise. Rebels, did I say? Yes, your fathers were rebels, or your grandfathers. He who now before me on canvas looks down so sadly upon us, the false, degenerate, and imbecile guardians of the great Republic which he founded, was a rebel. And yet we, cradled ourselves in rebellion, and who have fostered and fraternized with every insurrection in the nineteenth century everywhere throughout the globe, would now, forsooth, make the word "rebel" a reproach. Rebels certainly they are ; but all the persistent and stupendous efforts of the most gigantic warfare of modern times have, through your incompetency and folly, availed nothing to crush them out, cut off though they have been by your blockade from all the world, and dependent only upon their own courage and resources. And yet they were to be utterly conquered and subdued in six weeks, or three months ! Sir, my judgment was made up and expressed from the first. I learned it from Chatham : " My lords, you cannot conquer America." And you have not conquered the South. You never will. It is not in the nature of things possible ; much less under your auspices. But money you have expended without limit, and blood poured out like water. Defeat, debt, taxation, sepulchres, these are your trophies. In vain the people gave you treasure and the soldier yielded up his life. " Fight, tax, emancipate, let these," said the gentleman from Maine, (Mr. PIKE,) at the last session, " be the trinity of our salvation." Sir, they have become the trinity of your deep damnation. The war for the Union is, in your hands, a most bloody and costly failure. The President confessed it on the 22d of September, solemnly, officially, and under the broad seal of the United States. And he has now repeated the confession. The priests and rabbis of abolition taught him that God would not prosper such a cause. War for the

Union was abandoned; war for the negro openly begun, and with stronger battalions than before. With what success? Let the dead at Fredericksburg and Vicksburg answer. . . .

And now, sir, I come to the great and controlling question within which the whole issue of union or disunion is bound up : is there " an irrepressible conflict " between the slaveholding and non-slaveholding States? . . . If so, then there is an end of all union and forever. You cannot abolish slavery by the sword ; still less by proclamations, though the President were to " proclaim " every month. Of what possible avail was his proclamation of September? Did the South submit? Was she even alarmed? And yet he has now fulmined another "bull against the comet " — *brutum fulmen* — and, threatening servile insurrection with all its horrors, has yet coolly appealed to the judgment of mankind, and invoked the blessing of the God of peace and love ! But declaring it a military necessity, an essential measure of war to subdue the rebels, yet, with admirable wisdom, he expressly exempts from its operation the only States and parts of States in the South where he has the military power to execute it.

Neither, sir, can you abolish slavery by argument. As well attempt to abolish marriage or the relation of paternity. The South is resolved to maintain it at every hazard and by every sacrifice ; and if " this Union cannot endure part slave and part free," then it is already and finally dissolved. Talk not to me of " West Virginia." Tell me not of Missouri, trampled under the feet of your soldiers. As well talk to me of Ireland. Sir, the destiny of those States must abide the issue of the war. But Kentucky you may find tougher. And Maryland —

> " E'en in her ashes live their wonted fires."

Nor will Delaware be found wanting in the day of trial.

But I deny the doctrine. It is full of disunion and civil war. It is disunion itself. Whoever first taught it ought to be dealt with as not only hostile to the Union, but an enemy of the human race. Sir, the fundamental idea of the Constitution is the perfect and eternal compatibility of a union of States " part slave and part free ; " else the Constitution never would have been framed, nor the Union founded ; and sevent years of successful experiment have approved the wisdom of the plan In my deliberate judgment, a confederacy made up of slaveholding and non-slaveholding States is, in the nature of things, the strongest of a popular governments. African slavery has been, and is, eminently com servative. It makes the absolute political equality of the white race everywhere practicable. It dispenses with the English order of nobility, and leaves every white man, North and South, owning slaves or owning none, the equal of every other white man. It has reconciled universal suffrage throughout the free States with the stability of government. I speak not now of its material benefits to the North and West, which are many and more obvious. But the South, too, has profited many ways by a union with the non-slaveholding States. Enterprise, industry, self-reliance, perseverance, and the other hardy virtues of a people living in a higher latitude and without hereditary servants, she has learned or received from the North. Sir, it is easy, I know, to denounce all this, and to revile him who utters it. Be it so. The English is, of all languages, the most copious in words of bitterness and reproach. "Pour on : I will endure." . . .

. . . Whoever hates negro slavery more than he loves the Union, must demand separation at last. I think that you can never abolish slavery by fighting. Certainly you never can till you have first destroyed the South, and then, in the language, first of Mr. Douglas and afterwards of Mr. Seward, converted this Government into an imperial despotism. And, sir, whenever I am forced to a choice between the loss to my own country and race, of personal and political liberty with all its blessings, and the involuntary domestic servitude of the negro, I shall not hesitate one moment to choose the latter alternative. The sole question to-day is between the Union with slavery, or final disunion, and, I think, anarchy and despotism. I am for the Union. It was good enough for my fathers. It is good enough for us and our children after us.

Appendix to the Congressional Globe, 37 Cong., 3 sess. (John C. Rives, Washington, 1863), 53–59 *passim,* January 14, 1863.

———◆———

130. "The Black Regiment" (1863)

BY GEORGE HENRY BOKER

Boker was an author and poet, and a man of prominent social position in Philadelphia. He was one of the founders of the Union League of Philadelphia, and a moving spirit in the aid furnished to the Union cause by that notable organization, while his pen was active in writing patriotic lyrics and vigorous prose in behalf of his country. The action here described took place at Port Hudson, May 27, 1863. — Bibliography as in No. 124 above.

DARK as the clouds of even,
        Ranked in the western heaven,
Waiting the breath that lifts
All the dread mass, and drifts
Tempest and falling brand
Over a ruined land ; —
So still and orderly,
Arm to arm, knee to knee,
Waiting the great event,
Stands the black regiment.

Down the long dusky line
Teeth gleam and eyeballs shine ;
And the bright bayonet,
Bristling and firmly set,
Flashed with a purpose grand,
Long ere the sharp command
Of the fierce rolling drum
Told them their time had come,
Told them what work was sent
For the black regiment.

" Now," the flag-sergeant cried,
" Though death and hell betide,
Let the whole nation see
If we are fit to be
Free in this land ; or bound
Down, like the whining hound, —
Bound with red stripes of pain
In our old chains again ! "
O, what a shout there went
From the black regiment !

" Charge ! "   Trump and drum awoke,
Onward the bondmen broke ;
Bayonet and sabre-stroke
Vainly opposed their rush.
Through the wild battle's crush,
With but one thought aflush,
Driving their lords like chaff,
In the guns' mouths they laugh ;

Or at the slippery brands
Leaping with open hands,
Down they tear man and horse,
Down in their awful course ;
Trampling with bloody heel
Over the crashing steel,
All their eyes forward bent,
Rushed the black regiment.

" Freedom ! ' their battle-cry, —
" Freedom ! or leave to die ! "
Ah ! and they meant the word,
Not as with us 'tis heard,
Not a mere party shout :
They gave their spirits out ;
Trusted the end to God,
And on the gory sod
Rolled in triumphant blood.
Glad to strike one free blow,
Whether for weal or woe ;
Glad to breathe one free breath,
Though on the lips of death.
Praying — alas ! in vain ! —
That they might fall again,
So they could once more see
That burst to liberty !
This was what " freedom " lent
To the black regiment.

Hundreds on hundreds fell ;
But they are resting well ;
Scourges and shackles strong
Never shall do them wrong.
O, to the living few,
Soldiers, be just and true !
Hail them as comrades tried ;
Fight with them side by side ;
Never, in field or tent,
Scorn the black regiment !

George H. Boker, *Poems of the War* (Boston, 1864), 99–103.

131. Contrabands (1864)

BY CHARLES CARLETON COFFIN (1866)

Coffin, as a war correspondent of the *Boston Journal*, witnessed many battles in both the eastern and the western campaigns. He wrote under the name of "Carleton," and after the war gathered his records into a series of books written under the same name. Many of these are for juvenile readers, for whom he has also written other books dealing with interesting periods of American history. — Bibliography as in No. 124 above.

DURING the march the next day towards the North Anna, I halted at a farm-house. The owner had fled to Richmond in advance of the army, leaving his overseer, a stout, burly, red-faced, tobacco-chewing man. There were a score of old buildings on the premises. It had been a notable plantation, yielding luxuriant harvests of wheat, but the proprietor had turned his attention to the culture of tobacco and the breeding of negroes. He sold annually a crop of human beings for the southern market. The day before our arrival, hearing that the Yankees were coming, he hurried forty or fifty souls to Richmond. He intended to take all, — forty or fifty more, — but the negroes fled to the woods. The overseer did his best to collect them, but in vain. The proprietor raved, and stormed, and became violent in his language and behavior, threatening terrible punishment on all the runaways, but the appearance of a body of Union cavalry put an end to maledictions. He had a gang of men and women chained together, and hurried them toward Richmond.

The runaways came out from their hiding-places when they saw the Yankees, and advanced fearlessly with open countenances. The first pleasure of the negroes was to smile from ear to ear, the second to give everybody a drink of water or a piece of hoe-cake, the third to pack up their bundles and be in readiness to join the army.

"Are you not afraid of us?"

"Afraid ! Why, boss, I's been praying for yer to come ; and now yer is here, thank de Lord."

"Are you not afraid that we shall sell you?"

"No, boss, I is n't. The overseer said you would sell us off to Cuba, to work in the sugar-mill, but we did n't believe him."

Among the servants was a bright mulatto girl, who was dancing, singing, and manifesting her joy in violent demonstration.

"What makes you so happy?" I asked.

" Because you Yankees have come.   I can go home now."

" Is not this your home ? "

" No.   I come from Williamsport in Maryland."

" When did you come from there ? "

" Last year.   Master sold me.   I spect my brother is 'long with the army.   He ran away last year.   Master was afraid that I should run away, and he sold me."

The negroes came from all the surrounding plantations.   Old men with venerable beards, horny hands, crippled with hard work and harder usage ; aged women, toothless, almost blind, steadying their steps with sticks ; little negro boys, driving a team of skeleton steers, — mere bones and tendons covered with hide, — or wall-eyed horses, spavined, foundered, and lame, attached to rickety carts and wagons, piled with beds, tables, chairs, pots and kettles, hens, turkeys, ducks, women with infants in their arms, and a sable cloud of children trotting by their side.

" Where are you going ? " I said to a short, thick-set, gray-bearded old man, shuffling along the road ; his toes bulging from his old boots, and a tattered straw hat on his head, — his gray wool protruding from the crown.

" I do'no, boss, where I 's going, but I reckon I 'll go where the army goes."

" And leave your old home, your old master, and the place where you have lived all your days ? "

" Yes, boss ; master, he 's gone.   He went to Richmond.   Reckon he went mighty sudden, boss, when he heard you was coming.   Thought I 'd like to go along with you."

His face streamed with perspiration.   He had been sorely afflicted with the rheumatism, and it was with difficulty that he kept up with the column ; but it was not a hard matter to read the emotions of his heart. He was marching towards freedom.   Suddenly a light had shined upon him.   Hope had quickened in his soul.   He had a vague idea of what was before him.   He had broken loose from all which he had been accustomed to call his own, — his cabin, a mud-chinked structure, with the ground for a floor, his garden patch, — to go out, in his old age, wholly unprovided for, yet trusting in God that there would be food and raiment on the other side of Jordan.

It was a Jordan to them.   It was the Sabbath-day, — bright, clear, calm, and delightful.   There was a crowd of several hundred colored people at a deserted farm-house.

"Will it disturb you if we have a little singing? You see we feel so happy to-day that we would like to praise the Lord."

It was the request of a middle-aged woman.

"Not in the least. I should like to hear you."

In a few moments a crowd had assembled in one of the rooms. A stout young man, black, bright-eyed, thick-wooled, took the centre of the room. The women and girls, dressed in their best clothes, which they had put on to make their exodus from bondage in the best possible manner, stood in circles round him. The young man began to dance. He jumped up, clapped his hands, slapped his thighs, whirled round, stamped upon the floor.

"Sisters, let us bless the Lord. Sisters, join in the chorus," he said, and led off with a kind of recitative, improvised as the excitement gave him utterance. From my note-book I select a few lines : —

RECITATIVE.

"We are going to the other side of Jordan."

CHORUS.

"So glad! so glad!
Bless the Lord for freedom,
So glad! so glad!
We are going on our way,
So glad! so glad!
To the other side of Jordan,
So glad! so glad!
Sisters, won't you follow?
So glad! so glad!
Brothers, won't you follow?"

And so it went on for a half-hour, without cessation, all dancing, clapping their hands, tossing their heads. It was the ecstasy of action. It was a joy not to be uttered, but demonstrated. The old house partook of their rejoicing. It rang with their jubilant shouts, and shook in all its joints. . . .

It was late at night before the dancers ceased, and then they stopped, not because of a surfeit of joy, but because the time had come for silence in the camp. It was their first Sabbath of freedom, and like the great king of Israel, upon the recovery of the ark of God, they danced before the Lord with all their might.

We had a hard, dusty ride from the encampment at Mongohick to the

Pamunkey . . . and halted beneath the oaks, magnolias, and button-woods of an old Virginia mansion. . . .

When the war commenced, the owner of this magnificent estate enlisted in the army and was made a Colonel of cavalry. He furnished supplies and kept open house for his comrades in arms; but he fell in a cavalry engagement on the Rappahannock, in October, 1863, leaving a wife and three young children. The advance of the army, its sudden appearance on the Pamunkey, left Mrs. —— no time to remove her personal estate, or to send her negroes to Richmond for safe keeping. Fitz-Hugh Lee disputed Sheridan's advance. The fighting began on this estate. Charges by squadrons and regiments were made through the corn-fields. Horses, cattle, hogs, sheep, were seized by the cavalrymen. The garden, filled with young vegetables, was spoiled. In an hour there was complete desolation. The hundred negroes — cook, steward, chambermaid, house and field hands, old and young — all left their work and followed the army. Mrs. —— was left to do her own work. The parlors of the stately mansion were taken by the surgeons for a hospital. The change which Mrs. —— experienced was from affluence to abject poverty, from power to sudden helplessness.

Passing by one of the negro cabins on the estate, I saw a middle-aged colored woman packing a bundle.

"Are you going to move?" I asked.

"Yes, sir; I am going to follow the army."

"What for? Where will you go?"

"I want to go to Washington, to find my husband. He ran away awhile ago, and is at work in Washington."

"Do you think it right, auntie, to leave your mistress, who has taken care of you so long?"

She had been busy with her bundle, but stopped now and stood erect before me, her hands on her hips. Her black eyes flashed.

"Taken care of me! What did she ever do for me? Have n't I been her cook for more than thirty years? Have n't I cooked every meal she ever ate in that house? What has she done for me in return? She has sold my children down South, one after another. She has whipped me when I cried for them. She has treated me like a hog, sir! Yes, sir, like a hog!"

Charles Carleton Coffin, *Four Years of Fighting* (Boston, 1866), 343–349 *passim.*

CHAPTER XXII — YEAR OF VICTORY

132. In the Wilderness (1864)

BY CHARLES ANDERSON DANA (1897)

Before the Civil War Dana was managing editor of the *New York Tribune;* but, resigning because his views on the conduct of the war did not agree with Greeley's, in 1863 he became assistant secretary of war, with headquarters in the field. He acted as the personal representative of Lincoln and Stanton at the front, and was often with the armies under the command of Grant. In 1868 he began to publish the *Sun,* and made it famous as an organ of personal opinion. — Bibliography: A. A. Humphreys, *Virginia Campaign of '64 and '65, passim;* J. F. Rhodes, *History of the United States,* IV, 448, note; Channing and Hart, *Guide,* § 210.

. . . IT was Grant, the lieutenant general of the armies of the United States, who was really directing the movements. The central idea of the campaign had not developed to the army when I reached headquarters, but it was soon clear to everybody. Grant's great operation was the endeavor to interpose the Federal army between Lee's army and Richmond, so as to cut Lee off from his base of supplies. He meant to get considerably in advance of Lee — between him and Richmond — thus compelling Lee to leave his intrenchments and hasten southward. If in the collision thus forced Grant found that he could not smash Lee, he meant to make another move to get behind his army. That was to be the strategy of the campaign of 1864. That was what Lee thwarted, though he had a narrow escape more than once.

The first encounter with Lee had taken place in the Wilderness on May 5th and 6th. The Confederates and many Northern writers love to call the Wilderness a drawn battle. It was not so; in every essential light it was a Union victory. Grant had not intended to fight a battle in those dense, brushy jungles, but Lee precipitated it just as he had precipitated the battle of Chancellorsville one year before, and not six miles to the eastward of this very ground. In doing so he hoped to neutralize the superior numbers of Grant as he had Hooker's, and so to mystify and handle the Union leader as to compel a retreat across the Rapidan. But he failed. Some of the fighting in the brush was a draw, but the Union army did not yield a rood of ground; it held the roads southward, inflicted great losses on its enemy, and then, instead of re-crossing the river, resumed its march toward Richmond as soon as Lee's attacks had ceased.   Lee had palpably failed in his objects.   His old-time tactics had made no impression on Grant.   He never offered gen-eral battle in the open afterward.

The previous history of the Army of the Potomac had been to advance and fight a battle, then either to retreat or to lie still, and finally to go into winter quarters.   Grant did not intend to proceed in that way.   As soon as he had fought a battle and had not routed Lee, he meant to move nearer to Richmond and fight another battle.   But the men in the army had become so accustomed to the old methods of campaign-ing that few, if any, of them believed that the new commander in chief would be able to do differently from his predecessors.   I remember dis-tinctly the sensation in the ranks when the rumor first went around that our position was south of Lee's.   It was the morning of May 8th. The night before the army had made a forced march on Spottsylvania Courthouse.   There was no indication the next morning that Lee had moved in any direction.   As the army began to realize that we were really moving south, and at that moment were probably much nearer Richmond than was our enemy, the spirits of men and officers rose to the highest pitch of animation.   On every hand I heard the cry, " On to Richmond ! "

But there were to be a great many more obstacles to our reaching Rich-mond than General Grant himself, I presume, realized on May 8, 1864. We met one that very morning ; for when our advance reached Spott-sylvania Courthouse it found Lee's troops there, ready to dispute the right of way with us, and two days later Grant was obliged to fight the battle of Spottsylvania before we could make another move south.

. . . The battle had begun on the morning of May 10th, and had con-tinued all day.   On the 11th the armies had rested, but at half past four on the morning of the 12th fighting had been begun by an attack by Hancock on a rebel salient.   Hancock attacked with his accustomed impetuosity, storming and capturing the enemy's fortified line, with some four thousand prisoners and twenty cannon.   The captures in-cluded nearly all of Major-General Edward Johnson's division, together with Johnson himself and General George H. Steuart. . . .

It was quite early in the morning when Hancock's prisoners were brought in.   The battle raged without cessation throughout the day, Wright and Hancock bearing the brunt of it.   Burnside made several attacks, in which his troops generally bore themselves like good soldiers. The results of the battle of Spottsylvania were that we had crowded the enemy out of some of his most important positions, had weakened him by losses of between nine thousand and ten thousand men killed, wounded, and captured, besides many battle flags and much artillery, and that our troops rested victorious upon the ground they had fought for.

After the battle was over and firing had nearly ceased, Rawlins and I went out to ride over the field. We went first to the salient which Hancock had attacked in the morning. The two armies had struggled for hours for this point, and the loss had been so terrific that the place has always been known since as the " Bloody Angle." The ground around the salient had been trampled and cut in the struggle until it was almost impassable for one on horseback, so Rawlins and I dismounted and climbed up the bank over the outer line of the rude breastworks. Within we saw a fence over which earth evidently had been banked, but which now was bare and half down. It was here the fighting had been fiercest. We picked our way to this fence, and stopped to look over the scene. The night was coming on, and, after the horrible din of the day, the silence was intense ; nothing broke it but distant and occasional firing or the low groans of the wounded. I remember that as I stood there I was almost startled to hear a bird twittering in a tree. All around us the underbrush and trees, which were just beginning to be green, had been riddled and burnt. The ground was thick with dead and wounded men, among whom the relief corps was at work. The earth, which was soft from the heavy rains we had been having before and during the battle, had been trampled by the fighting of the thousands of men until it was soft, like thin hasty pudding. . . .

The first news which passed through the ranks the morning after the battle of Spottsylvania was that Lee had abandoned his position during the night. Though our army was greatly fatigued from the enormous efforts of the day before, the news of Lee's departure inspired the men with fresh energy, and everybody was eager to be in pursuit. Our skirmishers soon found the enemy along the whole line, however, and the conclusion was that their retrograde movement had been made to correct their position after the loss of the key points taken from them the day before, and that they were still with us in a new line as strong as the old one. Of course, we could not determine this point without a battle, and nothing was done that day to provoke one. It was necessary to rest the men.

In changing his lines Lee had left more uncovered the roads leading southward along his right wing, and Grant ordered Meade to throw the corps of Warren, which held the right, and the corps of Wright, which held the center of Meade's army, to the left of Burnside, leaving Hancock upon our right. If not interrupted, Grant thought by this ma-neuvre to turn Lee's flank and compel him to move southward.

The movement of the two corps to our left was executed during the night of May 13th and 14th, but for three days it had rained steadily, and the roads were so bad that Wright and Warren did not get up to surprise the enemy at daylight as ordered. . . .

The two armies were then lying in a semicircle, the Federal left well around toward the south. We were concentrated to the last degree, and, so far as we could tell, Lee's forces were equally compact. On the 15th, 16th, and 17th, we lay in about the same position. This inactivity was caused by the weather. A pouring rain had begun on the 11th, and it continued until the morning of the 16th; the mud was so deep that any offensive operation, however successful, could not be followed up. . . .

While waiting for the rain to stop, we had time to consider the field returns of losses as they were handed in. The army had left winter quarters at Culpeper Courthouse on May 4th, and on May 16th the total of killed, wounded, and missing in both the Army of the Potomac and the Ninth Corps amounted to a little over thirty-three thousand men. The missing alone amounted to forty-nine hundred, but some of these were, in fact, killed or wounded. When Grant looked over the returns, he expressed great regret at the loss of so many men. Meade, who was with him, remarked, as I remember, " Well, General, we can't do these little tricks without losses."

By the afternoon of May 17th the weather was splendid, and the roads were rapidly becoming dry, even where the mud was worst. Grant determined to engage Lee, and orders for a decisive movement of the army were issued, to be executed during the night. . . . Hancock and Wright . . . attacked at daylight . . . but . . . both corps having artfully but unsuccessfully sought for a weak point where they might break through, Grant, at nine o'clock, ordered the attack to cease. The attempt was a failure. Lee was not to be ousted ; and Grant, convinced of it, issued orders . . . to slip away from Lee and march on toward Richmond again.

Charles A. Dana, *Recollections of the Civil War* (New York, D. Appleton & Co., 1898), 192-201 *passim*.

133. End of the Alabama (1864)

BY CAPTAIN RAPHAEL SEMMES

Semmes left the United States navy to become the most famous of the Confederate naval officers. As commander of the cruiser Alabama, an English-built vessel, he caused great loss to the merchant marine of the United States, and for two years evaded capture by the numerous war vessels sent out against him. The Alabama never entered the ports of the Confederacy during her career, depending entirely upon captures and neutral ports for supplies and recruits. This report was addressed to Samuel Barron, who was the general European naval agent of the Confederacy. — Bibliography as in No. 116 above.

SOUTHAMPTON, *June 21, 1864.*

. . . I HAVE the honor to inform you, in accordance with my intention as previously announced to you, I steamed out of the harbor of Cherbourg between 9 and 10 o'clock on the morning of June 19 for the purpose of engaging the enemy's steamer *Kearsarge,* which had been lying off and on the port for several days previously. After clearing the harbor we descried the enemy, with his head offshore, at a distance of about 9 miles. We were three-quarters of an hour in coming up with him. I had previously pivoted my guns to starboard, and made all my preparations for engaging the enemy on that side. When within about a mile and a quarter of the enemy he suddenly wheeled, and bringing his head inshore presented his starboard battery to me. By this time we were distant about 1 mile from each other, when I opened on him with solid shot, to which he replied in a few minutes, and the engagement became active on both sides. The enemy now pressed his ship under a full head of steam, and to prevent our passing each other too speedily, and to keep our respective broadsides bearing, it became necessary to fight in a circle, the two ships steaming around a common center and preserving a distance from each other of from a quarter to half a mile. When we got within good shell range, we opened upon him with shell. Some ten or fifteen minutes after the commencement of the action our spanker gaff was shot away and our ensign came down by the run. This was immediately replaced by another at the mizzenmast-head. The firing now became very hot, and the enemy's shot and shell soon began to tell upon our hull, knocking down, killing, and disabling a number of men in different parts of the ship. Perceiving that our shell, though apparently exploding against the enemy's sides, were doing but little damage, I returned to solid shot firing, and from this time onward alternated with shot and shell. After the lapse of about one hour and ten minutes our ship was ascertained to be in a sinking condition, the enemy's shell having exploded in our sides and between decks, opening large apertures, through which the water rushed with great rapidity. For some few minutes I had hopes of being able to reach the French coast, for which purpose I gave the ship all steam and set such of the fore-and-aft sails as were available. The ship filled so rapidly, however, that before we had made much progress the fires were extinguished in the furnaces, and we were evidently on the point of sinking. I now hauled down my colors to prevent the further destruction of life, and dispatched a boat to inform the enemy of our condition. Although we were now but 400 yards from each other, the enemy fired upon me five times after my colors had been struck, dangerously wounding several of my men. It is charitable to suppose that a ship of war of a Christian nation could not have done this intentionally. We now turned all our exertions toward the wounded and such of the boys as were unable to swim. These were dispatched in my quarter boats, the only boats remaining to me, the waist boats having been torn to pieces.

Some twenty minutes after my furnace fires had been extinguished, and the ship being on the point of settling, every man, in obedience to a previous order which had been given to the crew, jumped overboard and endeavored to save himself. There was no appearance of any boat coming to me from the enemy until after the ship went down. Fortunately, however, the steam yacht *Deerhound*, owned by a gentleman of Lancashire, England (Mr. John Lancaster), who was himself on board, steamed up in the midst of my drowning men and rescued a number of both officers and men from the water. I was fortunate enough myself thus to escape to the shelter of the neutral flag, together with about forty others, all told. About this time the *Kearsarge* sent one and then, tardily, another boat.

Accompanying you will find lists of the killed and wounded, and of those who were picked up by the *Deerhound*. The remainder there is reason to hope were picked up by the enemy and by a couple of French pilot boats, which were also fortunately near the scene of action. At the end of the engagement it was discovered by those of our officers who went alongside the enemy's ship with the wounded that her midship section on both sides was thoroughly iron-coated, this having been done with chains constructed for the purpose, placed perpendicularly from the rail to the water's edge, the whole covered over by a thin

2 E

outer planking, which gave no indication of the armor beneath. This planking had been ripped off in every direction by our shot and shell, the chain broken and indented in many places, and forced partly into the ship's side. She was most effectually guarded, however, in this section from penetration. The enemy was much damaged in other parts, but to what extent it is now impossible to tell. It is believed he was badly crippled.

My officers and men behaved steadily and gallantly, and though they have lost their ship they have not lost honor. Where all behaved so well it would be invidious to particularize ; but I can not deny myself the pleasure of saying that Mr. Kell, my first lieutenant, deserves great credit for the fine condition in which the ship went into action, with regard to her battery, magazine, and shell rooms ; also that he rendered me great assistance by his coolness and judgment as the fight proceeded.

The enemy was heavier than myself, both in ship, battery, and crew ; but I did not know until the action was over that she was also ironclad. Our total loss in killed and wounded is 30, to wit, 9 killed and 21 wounded.

Official Records of the Union and Confederate Navies in the War of the Rebellion, First Series (Washington, 1896), III, 649–651.

---

134. In Mobile Bay (1864)

BY REAR-ADMIRAL DAVID GLASGOW FARRAGUT

Farragut was a southerner, but remained loyal to the nation and to the navy, in which he had served from the time when as a boy of twelve he fought in the Essex under his foster-father, Commodore Porter. He was the most prominent naval officer in the Civil War ; and for his daring exploits in passing the forts on the Mississippi and in Mobile Bay, and defeating the enemy's fleet at the same time, he is ranked as one of the world's great naval commanders. This extract is from his official report. — For Farragut, see James Barnes, *David G. Farragut*, 129–132. — Bibliography: A. T. Mahan, *The Gulf and Inland Waters*, ch. viii; Channing and Hart, *Guide*, § 210.

AS mentioned in my previous despatch, the vessels outside the bar, which were designed to participate in the engagement, were all under way by forty minutes past five in the morning [August 5] . . . two abreast, and lashed together. . . . The ironclads . . . were already inside the bar, and had been ordered to take up their positions on the starboard side of the wooden ships, or between them and Fort Morgan, for the double purpose of keeping down the fire from the water battery and the parapet guns of the fort, as well as to attack the ram Tennessee as soon as the fort was passed.

It was only at the urgent request of the captains and commanding officers that I yielded to the Brooklyn being the leading ship of the line, as she had four chase guns and an ingenious arrangement for picking up torpedoes, and because, in their judgment, the flag-ship ought not to be too much exposed. This I believe to be an error ; for, apart from the fact that exposure is one of the penalties of rank in the navy, it will always be the aim of the enemy to destroy the flag-ship, and, as will appear in the sequel, such attempt was very persistently made, but Providence did not permit it to be successful.

The attacking fleet steamed steadily up the main ship-channel, the Tecumseh firing the first shot at forty-seven minutes past six o'clock. At six minutes past seven the fort opened upon us, and was replied to by a gun from the Brooklyn, and immediately after the action became general.

It was soon apparent that there was some difficulty ahead. The Brooklyn, for some cause which I did not then clearly understand . . . arrested the advance of the whole fleet, while, at the same time, the guns of the fort were playing with great effect upon that vessel and the Hartford. A moment after I saw the Tecumseh, struck by a torpedo, disappear almost instantaneously beneath the waves, carrying with her her gallant commander and nearly all her crew. I determined at once, as I had originally intended, to take the lead ; and after ordering the Metacomet to send a boat to save, if possible, any of the perishing crew, I dashed ahead with the Hartford, and the ships followed on, their officers believing that they were going to a noble death with their commander-in-chief.

I steamed through between the buoys, where the torpedoes were supposed to have been sunk. These buoys had been previously examined by my flag-lieutenant, J. Crittenden Watson, in several nightly reconnoissances. Though he had not been able to discover the sunken torpedoes, yet we had been assured by refugees, deserters, and others, of their existence, but believing that, from their having been some time in the water they were probably innocuous, I determined to take the chance of their explosion.

From the moment I turned to the northwestward, to clear the middle ground, we were enabled to keep such a broadside fire upon the batteries of Fort Morgan that their guns did us comparatively little injury.

Just after we passed the fort, which was about ten minutes before eight o'clock, the ram Tennessee dashed out at this ship, as had been expected, and in anticipation of which I had ordered the monitors on our starboard side. I took no further notice of her than to return her fire.

The rebel gunboats Morgan, Gaines, and Selma were ahead, and the latter particularly annoyed us with a raking fire, which our guns could not return. At two minutes after eight o'clock I ordered the Metacomet to cast off and go in pursuit of the Selma. Captain Jouett was after her in a moment, and in an hour's time he had her as a prize. . . . The Morgan and Gaines succeeded in escaping under the protection of the guns of Fort Morgan, which would have been prevented had the other gunboats been as prompt in their movements as the Metacomet; the want of pilots, however, I believe, was the principal difficulty. The Gaines was so injured by our fire that she had to be run ashore, where she was subsequently destroyed, but the Morgan escaped to Mobile during the night, though she was chased and fired upon by our cruisers.

Having passed the forts and dispersed the enemy's gunboats, I had ordered most of the vessels to anchor, when I perceived the ram Tennessee standing up for this ship. This was at forty-five minutes past eight. I was not long in comprehending his intentions to be the destruction of the flag-ship. The monitors, and such of the wooden vessels as I thought best adapted for the purpose, were immediately ordered to attack the ram, not only with their guns, but bows on at full speed, and then began one of the fiercest naval combats on record.

The Monongahela, Commander Strong, was the first vessel that struck her, and in doing so carried away his own iron prow, together with the cutwater, without apparently doing her adversary much injury. The Lackawanna, Captain Marchand, was the next vessel to strike her, which she did at full speed; but though her stem was cut and crushed to the plank ends for the distance of three feet above the water's edge to five feet below, the only perceptible effect on the ram was to give her a heavy list.

The Hartford was the third vessel which struck her, but, as the Tennessee quickly shifted her helm, the blow was a glancing one, and as she rasped along our side, we poured our whole port broadside of nine-inch solid shot within ten feet of her casement.

The monitors worked slowly, but delivered their fire as opportunity offered. The Chickasaw succeeded in getting under her stern, and a fifteen-inch shot from the Manhattan broke through her iron plating and heavy wooden backing, though the missile itself did not enter the vessel.

Immediately after the collision with the flag-ship, I directed Captain Drayton to bear down for the ram again. He was doing so at full speed when, unfortunately, the Lackawanna run into the Hartford just forward of the mizzen-mast, cutting her down to within two feet of the water's edge. We soon got clear again, however, and were fast approaching our adversary, when she struck her colors and run up the white flag.

She was at this time sore beset ; the Chickasaw was pounding away at her stern, the Ossipee was approaching her at full speed, and the Monongahela, Lackawanna, and this ship were bearing down upon her, determined upon her destruction. Her smoke-stack had been shot away, her steering chains were gone, compelling a resort to her relieving tackles, and several of her port shutters were jammed. Indeed, from the time the Hartford struck her, until her surrender, she never fired a gun. As the Ossipee, Commander LeRoy, was about to strike her, she hoisted the white flag, and that vessel immediately stopped her engine, though not in time to avoid a glancing blow.

During this contest with the rebel gunboats and the ram Tennessee, and which terminated by her surrender at ten o'clock, we lost many more men than from the fire of the batteries of Fort Morgan.

Admiral Buchanan was wounded in the leg ; two or three of his men were killed, and five or six wounded. Commander Johnston, formerly of the United States navy, was in command of the Tennessee, and came on board the flag-ship, to surrender his sword, and that of Admiral Buchanan. The surgeon, Doctor Conrad, came with him, stated the condition of the admiral, and wished to know what was to be done with him. . . .

As I had an elevated position in the main rigging near the top, I was able to overlook not only the deck of the Hartford, but the other vessels of the fleet. I witnessed the terrible effects of the enemy's shot, and the good conduct of the men at their guns, and although no doubt their hearts sickened, as mine did, when their shipmates were struck down beside them, yet there was not a moment's hesitation to lay their comrades aside, and spring again to their deadly work.

House Executive Documents, 38 Cong., 2 sess. (Washington, 1864), VI, No. 1, pp. 400–403 *passim*.

135. Sheridan's Ride (1864)

BY GENERAL PHILIP HENRY SHERIDAN (1888)

Sheridan was a West Point graduate, and served continuously in the army until his death. His service at Perryville and Murfreesboro made him one of the most prominent of the young officers in the western armies, and his intrepid attack on Missionary Ridge led Grant to appoint him commander of the cavalry of the Army of the Potomac. Here his skilful boldness brought him almost constant success, and at the end of the war he ranked in popular estimation as next to Grant and Sherman. — For Sheridan, see H. E. Davies, *General Sheridan.* — Bibliography: G. E. Pond, *The Shenandoah Valley in 1864, passim ;* Channing and Hart, *Guide,* § 210.

TOWARD 6 o'clock the morning of the 19th [October], the officer on picket duty at Winchester came to my room, I being yet in bed, and reported artillery firing from the direction of Cedar Creek. . . . I asked him if it sounded like a battle, and as he . . . said that it did not, I . . . inferred that the cannonading was caused by Grover's division banging away at the enemy simply to find out what he was up to. However, I went down-stairs and requested that breakfast be hurried up, and at the same time ordered the horses to be saddled and in readiness, for I concluded to go to the front before any further examinations were made in regard to the defensive line.

We mounted our horses between half-past 8 and 9. . . . On reaching the edge of the town I halted a moment, and there heard quite distinctly the sound of artillery firing in an unceasing roar. . . . Moving on, I put my head down toward the pommel of my saddle and listened intently, trying to locate and interpret the sound, continuing in this position till we had crossed Mill Creek, about half a mile from Winchester. The result of my efforts in the interval was the conviction that the travel of the sound was increasing too rapidly to be accounted for by my own rate of motion, and that therefore my army must be falling back.

At Mill Creek my escort fell in behind, and we were going ahead at a regular pace, when, just as we made the crest of the rise beyond the stream, there burst upon our view the appalling spectacle of a panic stricken army — hundreds of slightly wounded men, throngs of other unhurt but utterly demoralized, and baggage-wagons by the score, all pressing to the rear in hopeless confusion, telling only too plainly that a disaster had occurred at the front. On accosting some of the fugitives they assured me that the army was broken up, in full retreat, and that all was lost; all this with a manner true to that peculiar indifference that takes possession of panic-stricken men. I was greatly disturbed by the sight, but at once sent word to Colonel Edwards, commanding the brigade in Winchester, to stretch his troops across the valley, near Mill Creek, and stop all fugitives, directing also that the transportation be passed through and parked on the north side of the town. . . .

For a short distance I traveled on the road, but soon found it so blocked with wagons and wounded men that my progress was impeded, and I was forced to take to the adjoining fields to make haste. When most of the wagons and wounded were past I returned to the road, which was thickly lined with unhurt men, who, having got far enough to the rear to be out of danger, had halted, without any organization, and begun cooking coffee, but when they saw me they abandoned their coffee, threw up their hats, shouldered their muskets, and as I passed along turned to follow with enthusiasm and cheers. To acknowledge this exhibition of feeling I took off my hat, and with Forsyth and O'Keefe rode some distance in advance of my escort, while every mounted officer who saw me galloped out on either side of the pike to tell the men at a distance that I had come back. In this way the news was spread to the stragglers off the road, when they, too, turned their faces to the front and marched toward the enemy, changing in a moment from the depths of depression to the extreme of enthusiasm. . . . I said nothing except to remark, as I rode among those on the road : "If I had been with you this morning this disaster would not have happened. We must face the other way ; we will go back and recover our camp."

. . . At Newtown I was obliged to make a circuit to the left, to get round the village. I could not pass through it, the streets were so crowded, but meeting on this détour Major McKinley, of Crook's staff, he spread the news of my return through the motley throng there.

When nearing the Valley pike, just south of Newtown I saw about three-fourths of a mile west of the pike a body of troops, which proved to be Ricketts's and Wheaton's divisions of the Sixth Corps, and then learned that the Nineteenth Corps had halted a little to the right and rear of these ; but I did not stop, desiring to get to the extreme front. Continuing on parallel with the pike, about midway between Newtown and Middletown I crossed to the west of it, and a little later came up in rear of Getty's division of the Sixth Corps. When I arrived, this division and the cavalry were the only troops in the presence of and resisting the enemy ; they were apparently acting as a rear guard at a point about three miles north of the line we held at Cedar Creek when the battle began. General Torbert was the first officer to meet me, saying as he rode up, " My God ! I am glad you've come." Getty's division, when I found it, was about a mile north of Middletown, posted on the reverse slope of some slightly rising ground, holding a barricade made with fence-rails, and skirmishing slightly with the enemy's pickets. Jumping my horse over the line of rails, I rode to the crest of the elevation, and there taking off my hat, the men rose up from behind their barricade with cheers of recognition. . . . I then turned back to the rear of Getty's division, and as I came behind it, a line of regimental flags rose up out of the ground, as it seemed, to welcome me. They were mostly the colors of Crook's troops, who had been stampeded and scattered in the surprise of the morning. The color-bearers, having withstood the panic, had formed behind the troops of Getty. The line with the colors was largely composed of officers, among whom I recognized Colonel R. B. Hayes, since president of the United States, one of the brigade com-manders. . . . In a few minutes some of my staff joined me, and the first directions I gave were to have the Nineteenth Corps and the two divisions of Wright's corps brought to the front, so they could be formed on Getty's division, prolonged to the right ; for I had already decided to attack the enemy from that line as soon as I could get matters in shape to take the offensive. . . .

All this had consumed a great deal of time, and I concluded to visit again the point to the east of the Valley pike, from where I had first observed the enemy, to see what he was doing. Arrived there, I could plainly see him getting ready for attack, and Major Forsyth now sug-gested that it would be well to ride along the line of battle before the enemy assailed us, for although the troops had learned of my return, but few of them had seen me. Following his suggestion I started in behind the men, but when a few paces had been taken I crossed to the front and, hat in hand, passed along the entire length of the infantry line. . . .

Between half-past 3 and 4 o'clock, I was ready to assail, and . . . the men pushed steadily forward with enthusiasm and confidence . . . Gen-eral McMillan . . . doing his work so well that the enemy's flanking troops were cut off from their main body and left to shift for themselves. Custer, who was just then moving in from the west side of Middle Marsh Brook, followed McMillan's timely blow with a charge of cavalry, but before starting out on it, and while his men were forming, riding at full speed himself, to throw his arms around my neck. By the time he had disengaged himself from this embrace, the troops broken by McMillan had gained some little distance to their rear, but Custer's troopers sweeping across the Middletown meadows and down toward Cedar Creek, took many of them prisoners before they could reach the stream — so I forgave his delay.

My whole line as far as the eye could see was now driving everything before it, from behind trees, stone walls, and all such sheltering obstacles, so I rode toward the left to ascertain how matters were getting on there. . . . When I reached the Valley pike Crook had reorganized his men, and as I desired that they should take part in the fight, for they were the very same troops that had turned Early's flank at the Opequon and at Fisher's Hill, I ordered them to be pushed forward; and the alacrity and celerity with which they moved on Middletown demonstrated that their ill-fortune of the morning had not sprung from lack of valor.

Meanwhile Lowell's brigade of cavalry, which . . . had been holding on, dismounted, just north of Middletown ever since the time I arrived from Winchester, fell to the rear for the purpose of getting their led horses. A momentary panic was created in the nearest brigade of infantry by this withdrawal of Lowell, but as soon as his men were mounted they charged the enemy clear up to the stone walls in the edge of Middletown; at sight of this the infantry brigade renewed its attack, and the enemy's right gave way. The accomplished Lowell received his death-wound in this courageous charge.

All our troops were now moving on the retreating Confederates, and as I rode to the front Colonel Gibbs, who succeeded Lowell, made ready for another mounted charge, but I checked him from pressing the enemy's right, in the hope that the swinging attack from my right would throw most of the Confederates to the east of the Valley pike, and hence off their line of retreat through Strasburg to Fisher's Hill. The eagerness of the men soon frustrated this anticipation, however, the left insisting on keeping pace with the centre and right, and all pushing ahead till we regained our old camps at Cedar Creek. Beyond Cedar Creek, at Strasburg, the pike makes a sharp turn to the west toward Fisher's Hill, and here Merritt uniting with Custer, they together fell on the flank of the retreating columns, taking many prisoners, wagons, and guns, among the prisoners being Major-General Ramseur, who, mortally wounded, died the next day.

P. H. Sheridan, *Personal Memoirs* (New York, 1888), II, 68–92 *passim.*

136. "Sheridan's Ride" (1864)

BY THOMAS BUCHANAN READ

Read was both a poet and an artist; but he is remembered chiefly for his poems, of which the one here given is the most famous, but by no means the best. It was written under the influence of the event, and rendered with much dramatic effect at various loyal and political gatherings. — Bibliography as in No. 135 above.

UP from the South at break of day,
　Bringing to Winchester fresh dismay,
The affrighted air with a shudder bore,
Like a herald in haste, to the chieftain's door,
The terrible grumble, and rumble, and roar,
Telling the battle was on once more,
And Sheridan twenty miles away.

And wider still those billows of war,
Thundered along the horizon's bar;
And louder yet into Winchester rolled
The roar of that red sea uncontrolled,
Making the blood of the listener cold,
As he thought of the stake in that fiery fray,
And Sheridan twenty miles away.

But there is a road from Winchester town,
A good broad highway leading down;
And there, through the flush of the morning light,
A steed as black as the steeds of night,
Was seen to pass, as with eagle flight,
As if he knew the terrible need;
He stretched away with his utmost speed;
Hills rose and fell; but his heart was gay,
With Sheridan fifteen miles away.

Still sprung from those swift hoofs, thundering South,
The dust, like smoke from the cannon's mouth;
Or the trail of a comet, sweeping faster and faster,
Foreboding to traitors the doom of disaster.
The heart of the steed, and the heart of the master
Were beating like prisoners assaulting their walls,

Impatient to be where the battle-field calls ;
Every nerve of the charger was strained to full play,
With Sheridan only ten miles away.

Under his spurning feet the road
Like an arrowy Alpine river flowed,
And the landscape sped away behind
Like an ocean flying before the wind,
And the steed, like a bark fed with furnace ire,
Swept on, with his wild eye full of fire.
But lo ! he is nearing his heart's desire ;
He is snuffing the smoke of the roaring fray,
With Sheridan only five miles away.

The first that the general saw were the groups
Of stragglers, and then the retreating troops,
What was done? what to do? a glance told him both,
Then striking his spurs, with a terrible oath,
He dashed down the line, 'mid a storm of huzzas,
And the wave of retreat checked its course there, because
The sight of the master compelled it to pause.
With foam and with dust, the black charger was gray ;
By the flash of his eye, and the red nostril's play,
He seemed to the whole great army to say,
" I have brought you Sheridan all the way
From Winchester, down to save the day ! "

Hurrah ! hurrah for Sheridan !
Hurrah ! hurrah for horse and man !
And when their statues are placed on high,
Under the dome of the Union sky,
The American soldiers' Temple of Fame ;
There with the glorious general's name,
Be it said, in letters both bold and bright,
    " Here is the steed that saved the day,
By carrying Sheridan into the fight,
    From Winchester, twenty miles away ! "

Thomas Buchanan Read, *Poetical Works* (Philadelphia, 1867), III, 265–267.

137. March to the Sea (1864)

BY GENERAL WILLIAM TECUMSEH SHERMAN (1875)

Sherman was a brother of John Sherman (see No. 52 above), and a West Point graduate. He served throughout the Civil War, remaining with the western armies after the first battle of Bull Run. Grant considered him his best lieutenant, and as he rose in command he carried Sherman with him. When Grant became commander of all the Federal armies, Sherman succeeded him in command of the Division of the Mississippi, and carried out most successfully the part assigned to him in Grant's grand tactics. The march to the sea, however, was Sherman's own conception. It was a startling innovation in practical warfare. — For Sherman, see M. F. Force, *General Sherman.* — Bibliography : J. D. Cox, *The March to the Sea, Franklin and Nashville, passim;* Channing and Hart, *Guide,* § 210.

ON the 12th of November the railroad and telegraph communications with the rear were broken, and the army stood detached from all friends, dependent on its own resources and supplies. . . .

The strength of the army, as officially reported . . . shows an aggregate of fifty-five thousand three hundred and twenty-nine infantry, five thousand and sixty-three cavalry, and eighteen hundred and twelve artillery — in all, sixty-two thousand two hundred and four officers and men. . . .

The most extraordinary efforts had been made to purge this army of non-combatants and of sick men . . . so that all on this exhibit may be assumed to have been able-bodied, experienced soldiers, well armed, well equipped and provided, as far as human foresight could, with all the essentials of life, strength, and vigorous action. . . .

The two general orders made for this march appear to me, even at this late day, so clear, emphatic, and well-digested, that no account of that historic event is perfect without them . . . and, though they called for great sacrifice and labor on the part of the officers and men, I insist that these orders were obeyed as well as any similar orders ever were, by an army operating wholly in an enemy's country, and dispersed, as we necessarily were, during the subsequent period of nearly six months.

(Special Field Orders, No. 119.) . . .

The general commanding deems it proper at this time to inform the officers and men of the Fourteenth, Fifteenth, Seventeenth, and Twentieth Corps, that he has organized them into an army for a special purpose, well known to the War Department and to General Grant. It is sufficient for you to know that it involves a departure from our present base, and a long and difficult march to a new one. All the chances of war have been considered and provided for, as far as human sagacity can. . . . Of all things, the most important is, that the men, during marches and in camp, keep their places and do not scatter about as stragglers or foragers, to be picked up by a hostile people in detail. It is also of the utmost importance that our wagons should not be loaded with any thing but provisions and ammunition. . . . With these few simple cautions, he hopes to lead you to achievements equal in importance to those of the past. . . .

(Special Field Orders, No. 120.) . . .

1. For the purpose of military operations, this army is divided into two wings viz.: The right wing, Major-General O. O. Howard commanding, composed of the Fifteenth and Seventeenth Corps; the left wing, Major-General H. W. Slocum commanding, composed of the Fourteenth and Twentieth Corps.

2. The habitual order of march will be, wherever practicable, by four roads, as nearly parallel as possible, and converging at points hereafter to be indicated in orders. The cavalry, Brigadier-General Kilpatrick commanding, will receive special orders from the commander-in-chief.

3. There will be no general train of supplies, but each corps will have its ammunition-train and provision-train. . . . The separate columns will start habitually at 7 A.M., and make about fifteen miles per day, unless otherwise fixed in orders.

4. The army will forage liberally on the country during the march. To this end, each brigade commander will organize a good and sufficient foraging party, under the command of one or more discreet officers, who will gather, near the route traveled, corn or forage of any kind, meat of any kind, vegetables, corn-meal, or whatever is needed by the command, aiming at all times to keep in the wagons at least ten days' provisions for his command, and three days' forage. Soldiers must not enter the dwellings of the inhabitants, or commit any trespass; but, during a halt or camp, they may be permitted to gather turnips, potatoes, and other vegetables, and to drive in stock in sight of their camp. To regular foraging-parties must be intrusted the gathering of provisions and forage, at any distance from the road traveled.

5. To corps commanders alone is intrusted the power to destroy mills, houses, cotton-gins, etc.; and for them this general principle is laid down: In districts and neighborhoods where the army is unmolested, no destruction of such property should be permitted; but should guerrillas or bushwhackers molest our march, or should the inhabitants burn bridges, obstruct roads, or otherwise manifest local hostility, then army commanders should order and enforce a devastation more or less relentless, according to the measure of such hostility.

6. As for horses, mules, wagons, etc., belonging to the inhabitants, the cavalry and artillery may appropriate freely and without limit; discriminating, however, between the rich, who are usually hostile, and the poor and industrious, usually neutral or friendly. Foraging-parties may also take mules or horses, to replace the jaded animals of their trains, or to serve as pack-mules for the regiments or brigades. . . .

7. Negroes who are able-bodied and can be of service to the several columns may be taken along; but each army commander will bear in mind that the question of supplies is a very important one, and that his first duty is to see to those who bear arms. . . .

The wagon-trains were divided equally between the four corps, so that each had about eight hundred wagons, and these usually on the march occupied five miles or more of road. . . .

The march from Atlanta began on the morning of November 15th, the right wing and cavalry following the railroad southeast toward Jonesboro', and General Slocum with the Twentieth Corps leading off to the east by Decatur and Stone Mountain, toward Madison. These were divergent lines, designed to threaten both Macon and Augusta at the same time, so as to prevent a concentration at our intended destination, or "objective," Milledgeville, the capital of Georgia, distant southeast about one hundred miles. . . .

About 7 A.M. of November 16th we rode out of Atlanta by the Decatur road, filled by the marching troops and wagons of the Fourteenth Corps; and reaching the hill, just outside of the old rebel works, we naturally paused to look back upon the scenes of our past battles. We stood upon the very ground whereon was fought the bloody battle of July 22d, and could see the copse of wood where McPherson fell. Behind us lay Atlanta, smouldering and in ruins, the black smoke rising high in air, and hanging like a pall over the ruined city. Away off in the distance, on the McDonough road, was the rear of Howard's column, the gun-barrels glistening in the sun, the white-topped wagons stretching away to the south; and right before us the Fourteenth Corps, marching steadily and rapidly, with a cheery look and swinging pace, that made light of the thousand miles that lay between us and Richmond. Some band, by accident, struck up the anthem of "John Brown's soul goes marching on;" the men caught up the strain, and never before or since have I heard the chorus of "Glory, glory, hallelujah!" done with more spirit, or in better harmony of time and place. . . .

The first night out we camped by the road-side near Lithonia. . . . the whole horizon was lurid with the bonfires of rail-ties, and groups of men all night were carrying the heated rails to the nearest trees, and bending them around the trunks. Colonel Poe had provided tools for ripping up the rails and twisting them when hot; but the best and easiest way is the one I have described, of heating the middle of the iron-rails on bonfires made of the cross-ties, and then winding them around a telegraph-pole or the trunk of some convenient sapling. I attached much importance to this destruction of the railroad, gave it my own personal attention, and made reiterated orders to others on the subject. . . .

. . . We found abundance of corn, molasses, meal, bacon, and sweet-potatoes. We also took a good many cows and oxen, and a large number of mules. In all these the country was quite rich, never before having been visited by a hostile army; the recent crop had been excellent, had been just gathered and laid by for the winter. As a rule, we destroyed none, but kept our wagons full, and fed our teams bountifully.

The skill and success of the men in collecting forage was one of the features of this march. Each brigade commander had authority to detail a company of foragers, usually about fifty men, with one or two commissioned officers selected for their boldness and enterprise. This party would be dispatched before daylight with a knowledge of the intended day's march and camp; would proceed on foot five or six miles from the route traveled by their brigade, and then visit every plantation and farm within range. They would usually procure a wagon or family carriage, load it with bacon, corn-meal, turkeys, chickens, ducks, and every thing that could be used as food or forage, and would then regain the main road, usually in advance of their train. When this came up, they would deliver to the brigade commissary the supplies thus gathered by the way. Often would I pass these foraging-parties at the road-side, waiting for their wagons to come up, and was amused at their strange collections — mules, horses, even cattle, packed with old saddles and loaded with hams, bacon, bags of corn-meal, and poultry of every character and description. Although this foraging was attended with great danger and hard work, there seemed to be a charm about it that attracted the soldiers, and it was a privilege to be detailed on such a party. Daily they returned mounted on all sorts of beasts, which were at once taken from them and appropriated to the general use; but the next day they would start out again on foot, only to repeat the experience of the day before. No doubt, many acts of pillage, robbery, and violence, were committed by these parties of foragers, usually called "bummers;" for I have since heard of jewelry taken from women, and the plunder of articles that never reached the commissary; but these acts were exceptional and incidental. . . . no army could have carried along sufficient food and forage for a march of three hundred miles; so that foraging in some shape was necessary. . . . By it our men were well supplied with all the essentials of life and health, while the wagons retained enough in case of unexpected delay, and our animals were well fed. Indeed, when we reached Savannah, the trains were pronounced by experts to be the finest in flesh and appearance ever seen with any army. . . .

. . . November 23d, we rode into Milledgeville, the capital of the State, whither the Twentieth Corps had preceded us; and during that

day the left wing was all united, in and around Milledgeville. . . .
The first stage of the journey was, therefore, complete, and absolutely
successful. . . .

. . . I was in Milledgeville with the left wing, and was in full communication with the right wing at Gordon. The people of Milledgeville
remained at home, except the Governor (Brown), the State officers, and
Legislature, who had ignominiously fled, in the utmost disorder and
confusion. . . .

Meantime orders were made for the total destruction of the arsenal
and its contents, and of such public buildings as could be easily converted to hostile uses. . . . Meantime the right wing continued its
movement along the railroad toward Savannah, tearing up the track
and destroying its iron. . . . Kilpatrick's cavalry was brought into
Milledgeville, and crossed the Oconee by the bridge near the town;
and on the 23d I made the general orders for the next stage of the
march as far as Millen. . . .

General William T. Sherman, *Memoirs* (New York, D. Appleton & Co., 1875),
II, 171–190 *passim*.

---

138. Last Campaign in the West (1864)

BY GENERAL JOHN BELL HOOD

Hood resigned from the Union army, where he held the rank of lieutenant, and
entered the Confederate service, rising rapidly to the command of a brigade under
Lee. He was sent west, and commanded a corps in the Atlanta campaign in 1864,
until Davis removed Johnston and gave Hood command of the army. When Sherman started for the sea, Hood, with more bravery than skill, took the offensive
against Thomas and penetrated as far as Nashville, but was finally defeated as described in this extract, which is taken from his official report. — Bibliography as in
No. 137 above.

. . . WHEN our army arrived at Florence [October 31] it
had entirely recovered from the depression that fre-
quent retreats had created. The enemy having for the first time divided
his forces, I had to determine which of the two parts to direct my operations against. To follow the forces about to move through Georgia under
Sherman would be to again abandon the regained territory to the forces
under Thomas, with little hope of being able to reach the enemy in time
to defeat his movement, and also to cause desertion and greatly impair
the morale or fighting spirit of the army by what would be considered a

compulsory retreat. I thought the alternative clear that I should move upon Thomas. If I succeeded in beating him the effect of Sherman's movement would not be great, and I should gain in men sufficiently to compensate for the damages he might inflict. If beaten I should leave the army in better condition than it would be if I attempted a retrograde movement against Sherman. . . .

The want of a good map of the country, and the deep mud through which the army marched, prevented our overtaking the enemy before he reached Columbia, but on the evening of the 27th of November our army was placed in position in front of his works at that place. During the night, however, he evacuated the town. . . .

. . . We pursued the enemy rapidly and compelled him to burn a number of his wagons. He made a feint as if to give battle on the hills about four miles south of Franklin, but as soon as our forces began to deploy for the attack and to flank him on his left he retired slowly to Franklin.

I learned from dispatches captured at Spring Hill, from Thomas to Schofield, that the latter was instructed to hold that place till the position at Franklin could be made secure, indicating the intention of Thomas to hold Franklin and his strong works at Murfreesborough. Thus I knew that it was all important to attack Schofield before he could make himself strong, and if he should escape at Franklin he would gain his works about Nashville. The nature of the position was such as to render it inexpedient to attempt any further flank movement, and I therefore determined to attack him in front, and without delay.

On the 30th of November Stewart's corps was placed in position on the right, Cheatham's on the left, and the cavalry on either flank, the main body of the cavalry on the right, under Forrest. Johnson's division, of Lee's corps, also became engaged on the left during the engagement. The line advanced at 4 p. m., with orders to drive the enemy into or across the Big Harpeth River, while General Forrest, if successful, was to cross the river and attack and destroy his trains and broken columns. The troops moved forward most gallantly to the attack. We carried the enemy's first line of hastily constructed works handsomely. We then advanced against his interior line, and succeeded in carrying it also in some places. Here the engagement was of the fiercest possible character. Our men possessed themselves of the exterior of the works, while the enemy held the interior. Many of our men were killed entirely inside the works. The brave men captured were taken inside his

2 F

works in the edge of the town. The struggle lasted till near midnight, when the enemy abandoned his works and crossed the river, leaving his dead and wounded in our possession. Never did troops fight more gallantly. The works of the enemy were so hastily constructed that while he had a slight abatis in front of a part of his line there was none on his extreme right. During the day I was restrained from using my artillery on account of the women and children remaining in the town. At night it was massed ready to continue the action in the morning, but the enemy retired.

We captured about 1,000 prisoners and several stand of colors. Our loss in killed, wounded, and prisoners was 4,500. . . .

The number of dead left by the enemy on the field indicated that his loss was equal or near our own.

The next morning at daylight, the wounded being cared for and the dead buried, we moved forward toward Nashville, Forrest with his cavalry pursuing the enemy vigorously.

On the 2d of December the army took position in front of Nashville, about two miles from the city. Lieutenant-General Lee's corps constituted our center, resting upon the Franklin pike, with Cheatham's corps upon the right and Stewart's on the left, and the cavalry on either flank, extending to the river. I was causing strong detached works to be built to cover our flanks, intending to make them inclosed works, so as to defeat any attempt of the enemy should he undertake offensive movements against our flank and rear. The enemy still held Murfreesborough with about 6,000 men, strongly fortified; he also held small forces at Chattanooga and Knoxville. It was apparent that he would soon have to take the offensive to relieve his garrisons at those points or cause them to be evacuated, in which case I hoped to capture the forces at Murfreesborough, and should then be able to open communication with Georgia and Virginia. Should he attack me in position I felt that I could defeat him, and thus gain possession of Nashville with abundant supplies for the army. This would give me possession of Tennessee . . . Having possession of the State, we should have gained largely in recruits, and could at an early day have moved forward to the Ohio, which would have frustrated the plans of the enemy, as developed in his campaign toward the Atlantic coast.

I had sent Major-General Forrest, with the greatest part of his cavalry and Bate's division of infantry, to Murfreesborough, to ascertain if it was possible to take the place. After a careful examination and reconnais sance in force, in which, I am sorry to say, the infantry behaved badly, it was determined that nothing could be accomplished by assault. Bate's division was then withdrawn, leaving Forrest with Jackson's and Buford's divisions of cavalry in observation. Mercer's and Palmer's brigades of infantry were sent to replace Bate's division. Shortly afterward Buford's division was withdrawn and ordered to the right of the army, on the Cumberland River.

Nothing of importance occurred until the morning of the 15th of December when the enemy, having received heavy re-enforcements, attacked simultaneously both our flanks. On our right he was handsomely repulsed, with heavy loss, but on our left, toward evening, he carried some partially completed redoubts of those before mentioned.

During the night of the 15th our whole line was shortened and strengthened ; our left was also thrown back ; dispositions were made to meet any renewed attack. The corps of Major-General Cheatham was transferred from our right to our left, leaving Lieutenant-General Lee on our right, who had been previously in the center, and placing Lieutenant-General Stewart's corps in the center, which had been previously the left.

Early on the 16th of December the enemy made a general attack on our lines, accompanied by a heavy fire of artillery. All his assaults were repulsed with heavy loss till 3.30 p. m., when a portion of our line to the left of the center, occupied by Bate's division, suddenly gave way. Up to this time no battle ever progressed more favorably ; the troops in excellent spirits, waving their colors and bidding defiance to the enemy. The position gained by the enemy being such as to enfilade our line caused in a few moments our entire line to give way and our troops to retreat rapidly down the pike in the direction of Franklin, most of them, I regret to say, in great confusion, all efforts to reform them being fruitless. Our loss in artillery was heavy — 54 guns. Thinking it impossible for the enemy to break our line, the horses were sent to the rear for safety, and the giving way of the line was so sudden that it was not possible to bring forward the horses to move the guns which had been placed in position. Our loss in killed and wounded was small. At Brentwood, some four miles from our line of battle, the troops were somewhat collected, and Lieutenant-General Lee took command of the rear guard, encamping for the night in the vicinity. On leaving the field I sent a staff officer to inform General Forrest of our defeat, and to direct him to rejoin the army with as little delay as possible to protect its rear, but owing to the swollen condition of the creeks, caused by the heavy rain then falling, he was unable to join us until we reached Columbia, with the exception of a portion of his command, which reached us while the enemy was moving from Franklin to Spring Hill.

On the 17th we continued the retreat toward Columbia, encamping for the night at Spring Hill. During this day's march the enemy's cavalry pressed with great boldness and activity, charging our infantry repeatedly with the saber, and at times penetrating our lines. The country being open was favorable to their operations. I regret to say that also on this day Lieutenant-General Lee, commanding the covering force, was severely wounded in the foot. We continued our retreat across Duck River to Columbia, the corps alternating as rear guards to the army. Lieutenant-General Lee and the corps commanded by him deserve great credit.

. . . on the 21st the army resumed its march for Pulaski. . . . From Pulaski I moved by the most direct road to the Bainbridge crossing on the Tennessee River, which was reached on the 25th, where the army crossed without interruption, completing the crossing on the 27th, including our rear guard, which the enemy followed with all his cavalry and three corps of infantry to Pulaski, and with cavalry between Pulaski and the Tennessee River. After crossing the river the army moved by easy marches to Tupelo, Miss. . . . Here, finding so much dissatisfaction throughout the country as in my judgment to greatly impair, if not destroy, my usefulness and counteract my exertions, and with no desire but to serve my country, I asked to be relieved, with the hope that another might be assigned to the command who might do more than I could hope to accomplish. Accordingly, I was so relieved on the 23d of January by authority of the President. . . .

. . . It is my firm conviction that, notwithstanding that disaster, I left the army in better spirits and with more confidence in itself than it had at the opening of the campaign. The official records will show that my losses, including prisoners, during the entire campaign do not exceed 10,000 men. Were I again placed in such circumstances I should make the same marches and fight the same battles, trusting that the same unforseen and unavoidable accident would not again occur to change into disaster a victory which had been already won.

The War of the Rebellion: Official Records of the Union and Confederate Armies, First Series (Washington, 1892–1894), XXXIX, pt. i, 803; XLV, pt. i, 652–656 *passim.*

139. Surrender of Lee (1865)

BY GENERAL ULYSSES SIMPSON GRANT (1885)

The capture of Vicksburg (see No. 119 above) settled the question of Grant's ability; and when, after the campaign at Chattanooga (see No. 123 above), Lincoln appointed him commander of all the Union armies, the selection met with public approval; for Grant was considered the man most able to cope with the great antagonist, Lee, especially if he had power to move the other Federal armies in unison with the plan of his attack. — For Grant, see No. 12 above. — Bibliography: A. A. Humphreys, *Virginia Campaign of '64 and '65, passim;* Channing and Hart, *Guide,* § 210.

ON the 8th [April, 1865] I had followed the Army of the Potomac in rear of Lee. . . . During the night I received Lee's answer to my letter of the 8th, inviting an interview between the lines on the following morning. But it was for a different purpose from that of surrendering his army, and I answered him as follows . . .

[April 9.] Your note of yesterday is received. As I have no authority to treat on the subject of peace, the meeting proposed for ten A.M. to-day could lead to no good. I will state, however, General, that I am equally anxious for peace with yourself, and the whole North entertains the same feeling. The terms upon which peace can be had are well understood. By the South laying down their arms they will hasten that most desirable event, save thousands of human lives, and hundreds of millions of property not yet destroyed. Sincerely hoping that all our difficulties may be settled without the loss of another life, I subscribe myself, etc. . .

Lee . . . sent . . . this message . . . to me.

[April 9.] . . . I received your note of this morning on the picket-line whither I had come to meet you and ascertain definitely what terms were embraced in your proposal of yesterday with reference to the surrender of this army. I now request an interview in accordance with the offer contained in your letter of yesterday for that purpose. . . .

. . . I found him at the house of a Mr. McLean, at Appomattox Court House, with Colonel Marshall, one of his staff officers, awaiting my arrival. . . .

. . . We greeted each other, and after shaking hands took our seats. I had my staff with me, a good portion of whom were in the room during the whole of the interview.

What General Lee's feelings were I do not know. As he was a man of much dignity, with an impassible face, it was impossible to say whether he felt inwardly glad that the end had finally come, or felt sad over the result, and was too manly to show it. Whatever his feelings, they were entirely concealed from my observation ; but my own feelings, which had been quite jubilant on the receipt of his letter, were sad and depressed. I felt like anything rather than rejoicing at the downfall of a foe who had fought so long and valiantly, and had suffered so much for a cause, though that cause was, I believe, one of the worst for which a people ever fought, and one for which there was the least excuse. I do not question, however, the sincerity of the great mass of those who were opposed to us.

General Lee was dressed in a full uniform which was entirely new, and was wearing a sword of considerable value, very likely the sword which had been presented by the State of Virginia ; at all events, it was an entirely different sword from the one that would ordinarily be worn in the field. In my rough traveling suit, the uniform of a private with the straps of a lieutenant-general, I must have contrasted very strangely with a man so handsomely dressed, six feet high and of faultless form. But this was not a matter that I thought of until afterwards.

We soon fell into a conversation about old army times. He remarked that he remembered me very well in the old army ; and I told him that as a matter of course I remembered him perfectly, but from the difference in our rank and years (there being about sixteen years' difference in our ages), I had thought it very likely that I had not attracted his attention sufficiently to be remembered by him after such a long interval. Our conversation grew so pleasant that I almost forgot the object of our meeting. After the conversation had run on in this style for some time, General Lee called my attention to the object of our meeting, and said that he had asked for this interview for the purpose of getting from me the terms I proposed to give his army. I said that I meant merely that his army should lay down their arms, not to take them up again during the continuance of the war unless duly and properly exchanged. He said that he had so understood my letter.

Then we gradually fell off again into conversation about matters foreign to the subject which had brought us together. This continued for some little time, when General Lee again interrupted the course of the conversation by suggesting that the terms I proposed to give his army ought to be written out. I called to General Parker, secretary on my staff, for writing materials, and commenced writing out the following terms . . .

[April 9.] . . . In accordance with the substance of my letter to you of the 8th inst., I propose to receive the surrender of the Army of N. Va. on the following terms, to wit: Rolls of all the officers and men to be made in duplicate. One copy to be given to an officer designated by me, the other to be retained by such officer or officers as you may designate. The officers to give their individual paroles not to take up arms against the Government of the United States until properly exchanged, and each company or regimental commander sign a like parole for the men of their commands. The arms, artillery and public property to be parked and stacked, and turned over to the officer appointed by me to receive them. This will not embrace the side-arms of the officers, nor their private horses or baggage. This done, each officer and man will be allowed to return to their homes, not to be disturbed by United States authority so long as they observe their paroles and the laws in force where they may reside. . . .

When I put my pen to the paper I did not know the first word that I should make use of in writing the terms. I only knew what was in my mind, and I wished to express it clearly, so that there could be no mistaking it. As I wrote on, the thought occurred to me that the officers had their own private horses and effects, which were important to them, but of no value to us; also that it would be an unnecessary humiliation to call upon them to deliver their side arms.

No conversation, not one word, passed between General Lee and myself, either about private property, side arms, or kindred subjects. He appeared to have no objections to the terms first proposed; or if he had a point to make against them he wished to wait until they were in writing to make it. When he read over that part of the terms about side arms, horses and private property of the officers, he remarked, with some feeling, I thought, that this would have a happy effect upon his army.

Then, after a little further conversation, General Lee remarked to me again that their army was organized a little differently from the army of the United States (still maintaining by implication that we were two countries); that in their army the cavalrymen and artillerists owned their own horses; and he asked if he was to understand that the men who so owned their horses were to be permitted to retain them. I told him that as the terms were written they would not; that only the officers were permitted to take their private property. He then, after reading over the terms a second time, remarked that that was clear.

I then said to him that I thought this would be about the last battle of the war — I sincerely hoped so; and I said further I took it that most of the men in the ranks were small farmers. The whole country had been so raided by the two armies that it was doubtful whether they would be able to put in a crop to carry themselves and their families through the next winter without the aid of the horses they were then riding. The United States did not want them and I would, therefore, instruct the officers I left behind to receive the paroles of his troops to let every man of the Confederate army who claimed to own a horse or mule take the animal to his home. Lee remarked again that this would have a happy effect.

He then sat down and wrote out the following letter :

[April 9.] . . . I received your letter of this date containing the terms of the surrender of the Army of Northern Virginia as proposed by you. As they are substantially the same as those expressed in your letter of the 8th inst., they are accepted. I will proceed to designate the proper officers to carry the stipulations into effect. . . .

General Lee, after all was completed and before taking his leave, remarked that his army was in a very bad condition for want of food, and that they were without forage ; that his men had been living for some days on parched corn exclusively, and that he would have to ask me for rations and forage. I told him "certainly," and asked for how many men he wanted rations. His answer was "about twenty-five thousand :" and I authorized him to send his own commissary and quartermaster to Appomattox Station, two or three miles away, where he could have, out of the trains we had stopped, all the provisions wanted. As for forage, we had ourselves depended almost entirely upon the country for that. . . .

When news of the surrender first reached our lines our men commenced firing a salute of a hundred guns in honor of the victory. I at once sent word, however, to have it stopped. The Confederates were now our prisoners, and we did not want to exult over their downfall.

U. S. Grant, *Personal Memoirs* (New York, 1886), II, 483-496 *passim*.

———◆———

140. "Robbutleeh Layeth down his Arms" (1865)

BY RICHARD GRANT WHITE

This almost rollicking satire sufficiently represents the elation of the North at the end of the war. The characters will be recognized : Sherman, Lee, Grant, Thomas ("Safety"), and Jefferson Davis ; as also the places, — Atlanta, Nashville. — For White, see No. 74 above. — Bibliography as in No. 139 above.

AND it came to pass that after these things the captain of the Bhum Urs marched westward through the breadth of the land of Dicksee even unto the sea-shore. And the Phiretahs spoke very fierce words against him, and prophesied evil against him, and filled the land with their roarings after their fashion.

2. But the Shear-man heeded not the fierceness of their words or their prophesying or their roarings, and marched onward. And the Phiretahs called upon Robbutleeh to send help unto them, but Ulysses held him fast so that he could not. And the Phiretahs fled from before the Bhum Urs, and the Shear-man cut his way onward through the land.

3. Moreover, about this time, the Phiretah captain whom the Shear-man had driven out of Hadal-antah, gathered together a great army and marched against a mighty captain in the armies of Unculpsalm, who was named of his soldiers Saiphtee.

4. (Now this captain came out of Pharjinnee, and was one of the Ephephvees. Yet was he faithful to the land of Unculpsalm.)

5. And Saiphtee marched backward, and drew the Phiretahs after him and away from the army of the Bhum Urs. And when he had drawn them far westward into the land, he went into a little city there; and the Phiretahs sat down before it, and boasted that they would take him captive and put his army to the sword.

6. Then he gathered his army together, and marched out of the city, and fell upon the Phiretahs while their boastings and their cursings were in their mouths: And he discomfited them with great slaughter, and they fled from before him, and he pursued after them many days, and slew them as they fled; and their boasting was turned into wailing and gnashing of teeth, so that the city where Saiphtee fell upon them is called Gnashfill unto this day.

7. And after these things Ulysses saw that his time was come, and that the occasion wherefor he had waited and watched and toiled for many days had been given unto him.

8. And he marched upon Robbutleeh while his army was yet in the forts and the strong places that he had made. And Ulysses had the victory, and drove Robbutleeh out of his forts and his strong places.

9. And it was the Sabbath day. And Jeph the Repudiator sat in the synagogue which was in the chief city of the Phiretahs; and the chief men of the Phiretahs, Ephephvees, were about him, and as he sat, there came a messenger to him from Robbutleeh, saying,

10. Thy servant is discomfited, but not yet destroyed. Nevertheless he can no longer hold the city. Save thyself, thou and thy household and thy counsellors, and flee, for Ulysses is upon thee.

11. And Jeph went straightway out of the synagogue to his house, and began to gather his gold and his silver and his stuff. And the thing was noised abroad in the city, and there was great commotion. And the Phiretahs fled from that city and from the villages round about, leaving only their women and children. And Jeph fled southward before them, uttering boastings, and making proclamations.

12. And as Jeph was fleeing out of the city, a company of Niggahs, which had joined themselves unto the armies of Unculpsalm entered it from the other side ; and as they entered they lifted up their voices with one accord and sang, saying,

13. Tell unto me, Niggahs, and declare unto me, oh ye of woolly locks and dark countenance, have you seen the lord, have you seen the master?

14. Whose beard is upon his face and above his mouth upon his face?

15. Have you seen him pass this way since the dawning, looking like one who goeth hastily into a far country?

VER. 13-23. This passage, as all oriental scholars will see, is much older in style than the rest of the book, and has traces of the period of the most ancient Hebrew and Chaldee writers. Although it is a song and is rhythmical, a comparison will show that it belongs rather to the period of the author of the song of Deborah, or even of Lamech, than to that of the more cultivated writers of the time of David and Solomon. It was probably an ancient song preserved by tradition among that strange and recordless people, the Niggahs. Yet there has been discovered a coincidence of thought between this song and the following stanza : —

> " Say, darkies, have you seen de massa,
>   Wid de muffstash on he face,
> Go 'long de road some time dis mornin',
>   Like he gwine for leabe de place ?
> He see de smoke way up de ribber
>   Whar de Lincum gun-boats lay;
> He took he hat and leff berry sudden,
>   And I 'spose he's runned away.
>   De massa run, ha! ha!
>   De darky stay, ho! ho!
>   It mus' be now de kingdum comin',
>   An' de yar of Jubilo."

It cannot be denied that the coincidence noticed does exist to a certain degree. This can only be accounted for upon the plausible and ingenious hypothesis of Dr. Trite, that either the former was written before the latter or the latter before the former. — RICHARD GRANT WHITE.

16. He saw the smoke, the smoke rose up before him on the river, and he said,

17. O my soul, these are the ships of Father Abraham.

18. Then he covered his head ; he put on the covering of his head ; he covered his head speedily ; his head-covering he put on with haste. He departed, he went swiftly ; he departed covering his head with haste.

19. It seemeth unto me that he hath fled, and my soul saith within herself, he hath skedaddled.

20. Behold the master fleeth, the lord passeth away.

21. But the servant remaineth, the Niggah abideth forever.

22. For he is the everlasting Niggah.

23. Lo, now the kingdom cometh, and the year of Jubilee is at hand ; and the Niggah shall rule in the land, and the master shall be cast down under his feet.

24. And the news of the fall of the city was spread abroad over the land upon the lightnings of the heavens. And there were great rejoicings, and feastings, so that that night all the city of Gotham was drunken with wine. Likewise was it in many other cities of the Iangkies. And the Kopur-hedds were abased, and the Oueecneas vanished away, so that not one of them was found thereafter, and the sect of Smalphri among the Dimmichrats was swallowed up in the victory of the Eunyunmen.

25. And Robbutleeh essayed to flee westward with his army among the mountains. But Ulysses pursued after him and overtook him, and fell upon him with great slaughter.

26. And his army saw that their cause was lost, and many of them fell behind, and wandered into the wilderness, or went homeward, for there was no power to keep them. But many were faithful unto the end.

27. And it came to pass that Ulysses with his army got before Robbutleeh with his army, and cut him off and hemmed him in on every side. And he could have fallen upon Robbutleeh and the remnant of his army and put every man to the sword and cut them off from the face of the earth.

28. But he had compassion upon them and respect unto them ; for Ulysses was not a man of blood. And he sent a messenger unto Robbutleeh, saying :

29. Behold now the end has come, and thou and thine army are in

the hands of thy servant. Lay down thine arms now, and let there be peace between thee and me ; and our Father Abraham shall pardon thee, and receive thee again as one of the children of Unculpsalm, and treat thee with honor, thee and thine officers, and all that are with thee.

30. But at first Robbutleeh would not ; for he was stout-hearted and stiff-necked. But afterward he considered the matter, and for the sake of them that were with him he consented.

31. And he and his captains and his officers and his soldiers laid down their arms, and gave themselves up captive.

32. And there was an apple-tree where Robbutleeh gave himself up. That it might be fulfilled as it was written, We will hang Jeph the Re-pudiator upon a bitter apple-tree. And that tree grew and multiplied so that it filled the whole land of Unculpsalm.

33. But Ulysses sent them every man to his own home, saying, See only, that ye obey the laws of the land of Unculpsalm, and have respect unto the proclamations of our Father Abraham. And he gave them horses to ride upon ; for the way was long and the road that they had travelled was hard. And he said keep the horses, that ye may till your fields and gather in your harvests.

34. Now, when the other Phiretah captains saw that Robbutleeh had laid down his arms, they laid down their arms, all save one upon the farthest border on the south-west as thou goest into the land of Mecsicho.

35. And it was in the spring time, in the fourth month, on the ninth day of the month, that Robbutleeh laid down his arms ; and before the sowing of the latter wheat was accomplished the other captains had done likewise. And about the time of the barley harvest, there was peace in the land of Unculpsalm; so that the men who fought gathered in the latter wheat harvest. For when the war was over each man returned unto his own home.

[Richard Grant White], *The New Gospel of Peace according to St. Benjamin* (New York, 1866), Book IV, 267–274.

PART VII

RECONSTRUCTION

CHAPTER XXIII — CONDITIONS IN THE SOUTH

141. Among the Freedmen (1864)

BY MRS. ELIZABETH HYDE BOTUME (1892)

In 1864 Mrs. Botume was appointed by the New England Freedmen's Aid Society a teacher to the freed people at Beaufort, South Carolina. This was in the famous Port Royal region, which was occupied by the Federal troops in 1861 and became a headquarters for negroes during the war; great efforts were here made to alleviate the mental, moral, and physical condition of the freedmen. Mrs. Botume remained in charge of her school, and what she called her "parish," for several years. — Bibliography as in No. 124 above.

"THE poor ye have always with you." This was impressed upon me all the time. It was necessary to inspect my district, now crowded with new-comers, to find out the condition and needs of these people.

I went first to the negro quarters at the "Battery Plantation," a mile and a half away. A large number of Georgia refugees who had followed Sherman's army were quartered here. Around the old plantation house was a small army of black children, who swarmed like bees around a hive. There were six rooms in the house, occupied by thirty-one persons, big and little. In one room was a man whom I had seen before. He was very light, with straight red hair and a sandy complexion, and I mistook him for an Irishman. He had been to me at one time grieving deeply for the loss of his wife, but he had now consoled himself with a buxom girl as black as ink. His sister, a splendidly developed creature, was with them. He had also four sons. Two were as light as himself, and two were very black. These seven persons occupied this one room. A rough box bedstead, with a layer of moss and a few old rags in it, a hom-iny pot, two or three earthen plates, and a broken-backed chair, com-prised all the furniture of the room.   I had previously given one of the women a needle and some thread, and she now sat on the edge of the rough bedstead trying to sew the dress she ought, in decency, to have had on.

In the old kitchen, not far from the house, more refugees had been placed.   Two women were very ill, lying on the floor with only moss and corn-husks under them.   It was a most pitiful sight.   One of these women begged for a blanket, but the other asked for better food.

" I cannot eat only dry hominy, ma'am," she said.   " I lived in massa's house, and used to have white bread and coffee, and I want something sweet in my mouth."

She had belonged to kind and careful owners in Georgia, and suffered severely from all these changes. . . .

Both of these women died.   Feeling they could not live, to my sur-prise and consternation, they willed me their children.   In one family there were five children, and in the other but one boy.   The old feeling, born of slavery, that the white race had a right of possession over the blacks, still clung to them.   They not only gave me their children, but tried to exact from me a promise to keep them and take good care of them.   When I hesitated, they implored me most piteously not to desert them. . . .

The plantation people lived in "the nigger houses."   Most of these people had been carried "up country" by their old owners, but had now got back, delighted to see again the familiar places and the cabins where they were born.   They seemed to me, as I talked with them, a superior class ; more tidy and self-respecting than most of the new-comers, — owing, doubtless, to the care and good management of their former owners.

On the next plantation was a curious collection of the original people and new-comers.   All might be called refugees, for they had recently returned "from the main," where they had been carried — not fled to.

In one cabin I found a man in a most wretched condition.   Years before he had fallen from a building and broken his back. . . .   He was only able to use his hands, and he looked like a human ball rolling over the floor.

I had his cabin cleaned and whitewashed, and fresh, clean clothes put on the poor fellow.   He tried in vain to find words to express his gratitude. In all my interviews with him I never heard a word of complaint, although his sufferings must have been extreme.

"Bless the Lord, missis!" he said, "'tain't no use to fret about it, for it can't be helpt; an' I ain't all the time so racket about wid pain as I used to bin. Sometimes at night I'se so painful I can't shet my eye, an' den I look out de doah, up at the stars, an' t'ink dem de eyes of de Lord looking straight down at me one. An' I 'member what de white folks tell me, 'De Lord is my Shepherd, I shall not want;' for in course I is His little sheep, an' I is so glad! It 'pears like the pain don't hurt me no more. I done forget it altogedder." . . .

In my district there were over five hundred contrabands, men, women, and children. All expressed a desire to have their children learn something, if they themselves knew nothing. But all, from the oldest to the youngest, were eager to "come fur larn too."

I found but one person, a young soldier, who disdained to attempt anything, saying, almost with insolence, that he had a right to learn when young, like other boys; this was denied him then, and he was not allowed to touch a book, and now it was too late. This man had indomitable will, with boldness, unceasing activity, and great physical strength. He was a power with his race. I wished to gain his influence for the school, as well as his own good, but could never do it.

One contraband said to me, "Liberty is as good for us as for the birds of the air. Slavery is not so bad, but liberty is so good."

He spoke with great affection of his master, who he said had gone to live in Delaware. . . .

Seeing so much destitution around us made our own lives, meagre as they were, seem luxurious by comparison. But we were not posing as "saints without bodies," and it was sometimes a desperate struggle to keep ourselves comfortable. At first there was nothing by which to note time; no clocks nor bells nor steam-whistles. There were two watches belonging to our "mess." When one was at the schoolhouse there was nothing to guide the cook at home.

The dial of the contrabands was: "When the first fowl crow" — "At crack o' day" — "W'en de sun stan' straight ober head" — "At frog peep" — "When fust star shine" — "At flood tide," or "ebb tide," or "young flood" — "On las' moon," or "new moon." Now they add to this list "quarterly meeting."

But these data did not help our cook to work, nor us to regular meals. . . .

In some places the first people who were freed were treated with injudicious consideration. They were told they were by right the owners of the land upon which they had worked so long, etc.

Whatever sentiment there was in this, we had to remember we were dealing with people just born into a new life, who had to learn the meanings of their new conditions. Like children, they were to be given what they could assimilate.

For instance, I was advised not to ask the old house servants to work for me ; for they were in fact the masters and mistresses of the place, — of the situation they were for a time, if they only knew it, but of nothing else. Said my adviser, " I have no more right to ask Cornelia, the old laundress, to wash for me, than she has to ask me to do her washing."

I replied that laundry work had not been my business : I came to teach the freed people to help themselves.

Whatever they could do better than I, in so far they were my superiors. In consideration of their " previous condition," I gave them my time and instruction, whilst I should pay regular wages for their labor. But I should expect good work, and no make-believe.

Elizabeth Hyde Botume, *First Days amongst the Contrabands* (Boston, Lee & Shepard, 1893), 82–129 *passim.*

---

142. "The South as it is" (1865–1866)

BY EDWIN LAWRENCE GODKIN

From his establishment of the *Nation* in 1865, until his retirement from active life in 1899, Godkin exercised a potent influence on American journalism.   He was an uncompromising critic of all political measures and tendencies which he deemed of dubious worth.   Soon after the Civil War closed he spent nine months journeying through the South, and during this time he wrote a letter for each issue of the *Nation*, minutely delineating the social, economic, and political conditions in the subjugated region.   This extract is from these letters. — There is no available bibliography upon this or the remaining numbers in this chapter.

LYNCHBURG, Va., July 31, 1865. . . .

THE rough little city is built on several round-topped hills that descend abruptly to the banks of the James, which is here an insignificant stream at the bottom of a rocky valley hardly wider than the river's bed.   The streets, which run towards the water, are almost precipitous, and all the streets, whether steep or not, are dirty and ill-paved. At present they are unlighted at night, and, though guarded by soldiers, are considered unsafe after nightfall. The warehouses, manufactories, and private residences are, for the most part, mean in appearance, and the stranger is surprised to learn that, before the war, in proportion to the number of inhabitants, Lynchburg was, with the single exception of New Bedford, Massachusetts, the richest city in the United States. But if there is little which, to the casual eye, is indicative of wealth, there are many signs that the reputation of the place as a famous tobacco mart was well deserved. . . .

The opinion seems to prevail among the people that the renown of their city as the tobacco metropolis has passed away with slavery, and that, for a long time at least, it will not return. They say that free labor cannot be profitably applied to the culture of tobacco on a large scale. This opinion may or not be of weight. The men who hold it express great contempt for free negro labor in general. " Free nigger labor may do on a trucking farm, or something like that, but it won't raise tobacco. You can't place any dependence on it. We may be able to do something with white labor by-and-bye."

These gentlemen firmly believe that the negro not only will be, but that in most parts of the South he to-day is, a pauper. Yet I find no man who does not admit that in his own particular neighborhood the negroes are doing tolerably well — are performing whatever agricultural labor is done. From the most trustworthy sources I learn that, in the vicinity of Lynchburg, of Danville, of Wytheville — in counties embracing a great part of southern and southwestern Virginia — the colored population may be truly described as orderly, industrious, and self-supporting. And this seems to be plainly shown by the reports, drawn up by Government officials, of the issue to citizens of what are known as " Destitute Rations." . . .

This distribution has been going on ever since the end of May, but very recently the general commanding in this district has deemed it proper to stop all issues of rations to citizens, except in well authenticated instances of actual pauperism.

. . . Whatever may have been the case immediately after the occupation of this part of Virginia by the Federal troops, for some time past it has been plainly discernible that the very large majority of those claiming to be destitute might easily support life without taxing the charity of the Government. . . .

. . . An order made in May last, by General Gregg, which allows farmers, in order that they may be the better able to provide for the laborers upon their plantations, to buy supplies from the military stores, paying for them in cash, or giving bonds to pay for them in cash or in kind when the crops shall have been harvested, has not, I think, been rescinded by General Curtis, but is still in force.   In the earlier part of the season many planters availed themselves of the permission thus granted, which was doubtless of advantage to them and to the negroes. In reference to the remarkable fact that so very few negroes of all the great number inhabiting the region round about Lynchburg have sought food from the Government, it is fair to say that the military authorities, when the matter was wholly in their hands, and in those of the agency of the Freedmen's Bureau recently established, have not permitted the planters to set adrift all or any of the negroes from their homes.   It is considered that the crops, which in part were planted before the slaves became free, and which have all been worked by them throughout the year, are justly chargeable with the support of the laborers and those dependent upon them.   Some planters have shown a disposition to turn loose all such negroes as were neither able-bodied themselves nor had near relations able to work, and whose labor could be taken as payment for the board and lodging of all.   One gentleman, somewhat advanced in years and averse to the trouble of managing free negroes, wished to let his farm stand idle, and to send away at once about sixty people, who might, very likely, have become a burden on the community at large.   He was very angry when informed that no such discharge could be permitted, and that for the present, at least, the negroes must stay where they were. But the large majority of farmers have kept with them those of their former slaves who would stay, and the large majority of these latter willingly remain in their old homes and work for wages.   The amount of pay given them varies a good deal.   When wages are paid in money, five dollars per month seems to be the usual rate.   But it is believed that on many plantations nothing more is given than the food and clothes of the laborer and his family. . . .   Some plantations are "worked on shares."   In one case which has fallen under my observation, the employer agrees to feed and clothe the laborers, to allow each family a patch of ground for a garden, and at the end of the year to divide among them one-seventh of the total produce of the farm.   The crops planted are corn, oats, wheat, potatoes, and sorghum.   The wheat has been already divided. . . .

ATLANTA, Ga., December 31, 1865. . . .

. . . The inducements to Northern men to come here and engage in agriculture, lumbering, and similar branches of business which, being carried on mainly by the services of the freedmen and for a foreign market, are not subject to the drawbacks above-mentioned, seem to be very great. There is apparent a willingness, often an anxiety even, to secure Northern men as lessees of plantations, and large tracts of land, well improved and productive, are everywhere offered for sale at low prices, sometimes at prices that may be called ruinously low. "These freedmen will work a heap better for a Yankee than they will for one of us," it is frequently said. Other causes of this sacrifice of lands and rents are to be found in the belief that the free labor of the negroes cannot be made profitable, and in the fact that many men who have much land have no money with which to cultivate it. But although much land may still be bought cheap, there are some signs that these causes will not continue to operate so extensively as heretofore. Often I hear it predicted that cotton is going to command a very high price for some years to come ; that therefore its culture may be profitable, though the laborers should work a smaller number of acres than in old times ; and occasionally some local newspaper announces that the gloomy prospects of the planters are brightening, that the negroes who, after all, showed so commendable a spirit of devotion, faithfulness, and obedience during the war, are beginning, in certain districts, to make contracts and profess a willingness to receive a share of the crop as wages.

But, however the case may be as regards the business relations of Northern men in the South, I should consider it advisable for the new-comer, if he desires agreeable social intercourse with his neighbors, in almost any part of the South that I have yet seen, to restrain the free expression of any social or political opinions distinctively Northern. Frequently this hostility is avowed, frequently men make a merit of disclaiming it, but no one denies its existence. . . .

MACON, Ga., January 12, 1866. . . .

The negroes, I was told, are very generally entering into contracts with the planters, and it is thought that almost all will have found employers before the 1st of February. All negroes who at that time shall be unemployed and not willing to make contracts, it is the intention of the Commissioner to arrest and treat as vagrants. The demand for labor is greater than the supply, and the Commissioner has frequent calls made upon him for able-bodied men to go to other States and to other parts of Georgia. . . .

MONTGOMERY, Ala., January 24, 1866. . . .

Cotton-planting was of course discussed — two of the men around the fire asserting that without slavery there can be no cotton : on a well-regulated plantation, in old times, of course the niggers was made to work a heap harder than any man ought to work ; well, a heap closer, anyhow ; as for workin' harder, a nigger won't be drove to work more'n so much, like a mule in that respect.   Now a free nigger a'n't goin' to work from before daylight, from the time he can see a cotton-stalk, till nine o'clock at night, and a white man can't stand it, and of course it stands to reason that cotton-raisin's gone up. . . .

This provoked a Georgian to say that on a plantation where nobody worked before nor after daylight he could raise more bales of cotton than on a plantation where the other plan was followed.   And as to white men not being able to work in the field, that was all a mistake.   They could work ; he'd seen white men working cotton in Texas, and was mighty nigh being run out of his own town for saying so, and for telling 'em that the doom of slavery was written by them Germans.   It would n't be long before you'd see white men raisin' cotton in every State in the Confederacy.

Not our white men a'n't goin' to work, said the former speaker. . . .

[Edwin Lawrence Godkin], *The South as it is*, in *The Nation*, August 17, 1865, January 25 and February 1-8, 1866 (New York), I, 209-210; II, 110-173 *passim.*

——————◆——————

143. An Impartial View (1865)

BY MAJOR-GENERAL CARL SCHURZ

Schurz was obliged to flee from Germany because of his participation in the uprising of 1848.   He came to the United States and was prominent as a speaker in the Republican party in the campaign of 1856, possessing much influence, especially over the German voters.   He became an officer in the Union army during the Civil War, and rose to the rank of major-general.   At the close of the war President Johnson sent him to the South as a special commissioner to investigate the political and social conditions there.   This extract is from his report.   Since the war he has been senator and secretary of the interior, and very earnest in behalf of civil-service reform.

. . . THERE is, at present, no danger of another insurrection against the authority of the United States on a large scale, and the people are willing to reconstruct their State governments, and to send their senators and representatives to Congress.

But as to the moral value of these results, we must not indulge in any delusions. There are two principal points to which I beg to call your attention. In the first place, the rapid return to power and influence of so many of those who but recently were engaged in a bitter war against the Union, has had one effect which was certainly not originally contemplated by the government. Treason does, under existing circumstances, not appear odious in the south. The people are not impressed with any sense of its criminality. And, secondly, there is, as yet, among the southern people an *utter absence of national feeling.* . . .

The principal cause of that want of national spirit which has existed in the south so long, and at last gave birth to the rebellion, was, that the southern people cherished, cultivated, idolized their peculiar interests and institutions in preference to those which they had in common with the rest of the American people. Hence the importance of the negro question as an integral part of the question of union in general, and the question of reconstruction in particular. . . .

That the result of the free labor experiment made under circumstances so extremely unfavorable should at once be a perfect success, no reasonable person would expect. Nevertheless, a large majority of the southern men with whom I came into contact announced their opinions with so positive an assurance as to produce the impression that their minds were fully made up. In at least nineteen cases of twenty the reply I received to my inquiry about their views on the new system was uniformly this : " You cannot make the negro work without physical compulsion." . . .

A belief, conviction, or prejudice, or whatever you may call it, so widely spread and apparently so deeply rooted as this . . . is certainly calculated to have a very serious influence upon the conduct of the people entertaining it. It naturally produced a desire to preserve slavery in its original form as much and as long as possible — and you may, perhaps, remember the admission made by one of the provisional governors, over two months after the close of the war, that the people of his State still indulged in a lingering hope slavery might yet be preserved — or to introduce into the new system that element of physical compulsion which would make the negro work. . . . Here and there planters succeeded for a limited period to keep their former slaves in ignorance, or at least doubt, about their new rights ; but the main agency employed for that purpose was force and intimidation. In many instances negroes who walked away from the plantations, or were found upon the roads, were shot or otherwise severely punished, which was calculated to produce the impression among those remaining with their masters that an attempt to escape from slavery would result in certain destruction.   A large proportion of the many acts of violence committed is undoubtedly attributable to this motive. . . .

. . . Aside from the assumption that the negro will not work without physical compulsion, there appears to be another popular notion prevalent in the south, which stands as no less serious an obstacle in the way of a successful solution of the problem.   It is that the negro exists for the special object of raising cotton, rice and sugar *for the whites*, and that it is illegitimate for him to indulge, like other people, in the pursuit of his own happiness in his own way.   Although it is admitted that he has ceased to be the property of a master, it is not admitted that he has a right to become his own master. . . .   An ingrained feeling like this is apt to bring forth that sort of class legislation which produces laws to govern one class with no other view than to benefit another.   This tendency can be distinctly traced in the various schemes for regulating labor which here and there see the light. . . .

. . . As to what is commonly termed " reconstruction," it is not only the political machinery of the States and their constitutional relations to the general government, but the whole organism of southern society that must be reconstructed, or rather constructed anew, so as to bring it in harmony with the rest of American society.   The difficulties of this task are not to be considered overcome when the people of the south take the oath of allegiance and elect governors and legislatures and members of Congress, and militia captains. . . .

The true nature of the difficulties of the situation is this : The general government of the republic has, by proclaiming the emancipation of the slaves, commenced a great social revolution in the south, but has, as yet, not completed it.   Only the negative part of it is accomplished.   The slaves are emancipated in point of form, but free labor has not yet been put in the place of slavery in point of fact. . . .

In my despatches from the south I repeatedly expressed the opinion that the people were not yet in a frame of mind to legislate calmly and understandingly upon the subject of free negro labor. . . .   When the rebellion was put down they found themselves not only conquered in a political and military sense, but economically ruined.   The planters, who represented the wealth of the southern country, are partly laboring under the severest embarrassments, partly reduced to absolute poverty.   Many

who are stripped of all available means, and have nothing but their land,
cross their arms in gloomy despondency, incapable of rising to a manly
resolution.   Others, who still possess means, are at a loss how to use
them, as their old way of doing things is, by the abolition of slavery,
rendered impracticable, at least where the military arm of the government has enforced emancipation.   Others are still trying to go on in
the old way, and that old way is in fact the only one they understand,
and in which they have any confidence.   Only a minority is trying to
adopt the new order of things.   A large number of the plantations,
probably a considerable majority of the more valuable estates, is under
heavy mortgages, and the owners know that, unless they retrieve their
fortunes in a comparatively short space of time, their property will pass
out of their hands.   Almost all are, to some extent, embarrassed.   The
nervous anxiety which such a state of things produces extends also to
those classes of society which, although not composed of planters, were
always in close business connexion with the planting interest, and there
was hardly a branch of commerce or industry in the south which was
not directly or indirectly so connected.   Besides, the southern soldiers,
when returning from the war, did not, like the northern soldiers, find a
prosperous community which merely waited for their arrival to give them
remunerative employment.   They found, many of them, their homesteads
destroyed, their farms devastated, their families in distress ; and those
that were less unfortunate found, at all events, an impoverished and
exhausted community which had but little to offer them.   Thus a great
many have been thrown upon the world to shift as best they can.   They
must do something honest or dishonest, and must do it soon, to make a
living, and their prospects are, at present, not very bright.   Thus that
nervous anxiety to hastily repair broken fortunes, and to prevent still
greater ruin and distress, embraces nearly all classes, and imprints upon
all the movements of the social body a morbid character.

In which direction will these people be most apt to turn their eyes?
Leaving the prejudice of race out of the question, from early youth they
have been acquainted with but one system of labor, and with that one
system they have been in the habit of identifying all their interests.
They know of no way to help themselves but the one they are accustomed to.   Another system of labor is presented to them, which, however, owing to circumstances which they do not appreciate, appears at
first in an unpromising light.   To try it they consider an experiment
which they cannot afford to make while their wants are urgent.   They

have not reasoned calmly enough to convince themselves that the trial must be made. It is, indeed, not wonderful that, under such circumstances, they should study, not how to introduce and develop free labor, but how to avoid its introduction, and how to return as much and as quickly as possible to something like the old order of things. Nor is it wonderful that such studies should find an expression in their attempts at legislation. But the circumstance that this tendency is natural does not render it less dangerous and objectionable. The practical question presents itself: Is the immediate restoration of the late rebel States to absolute self-control so necessary that it must be done even at the risk of endangering one of the great results of the war, and of bringing on in those States insurrection or anarchy, or would it not be better to postpone that restoration until such dangers are passed? If, as long as the change from slavery to free labor is known to the southern people only by its destructive results, these people must be expected to throw obstacles in its way, would it not seem necessary that the movement of social " reconstruction " be kept in the right channel by the hand of the power which originated the change, until that change can have disclosed some of its beneficial effects?

. . . One reason why the southern people are so slow in accommodating themselves to the new order of things is, that they confidently expect soon to be permitted to regulate matters according to their own notions. Every concession made to them by the government has been taken as an encouragement to persevere in this hope, and, unfortunately for them, this hope is nourished by influences from other parts of the country. Hence their anxiety to have their State governments restored *at once*, to have the troops withdrawn, and the Freedmen's Bureau abolished, although a good many discerning men know well that, in view of the lawless spirit still prevailing, it would be far better for them to have the general order of society firmly maintained by the federal power until things have arrived at a final settlement. . . . If, therefore, the national government firmly and unequivocally announces its policy not to give up the control of the free-labor reform until it is finally accomplished, the progress of that reform will undoubtedly be far more rapid and far less difficult than it will be if the attitude of the government is such as to permit contrary hopes to be indulged in.

Senate Executive Documents, 39 Cong., 1 sess. (Washington, 1866), I, No. 2, pp. 13–40 *passim*.

144. A Soldier's Observations (1865)

BY LIEUTENANT-GENERAL ULYSSES SIMPSON GRANT

This extract is from a report made to the president by General Grant, after a tour of inspection through a portion of the South. — For Grant, see No. 12 above.

WITH your approval, and also that of the honorable Secretary of War, I left Washington city on the 27th of last month [November] for the purpose of making a tour of inspection through some of the southern States, or States lately in rebellion, and to see what changes were necessary to be made in the disposition of the military forces of the country; how these forces could be reduced and expenses curtailed, &c.; and to learn, as far as possible, the feelings and intentions of the citizens of those States towards the general government.

The State of Virginia being so accessible to Washington city, and information from this quarter, therefore, being readily obtained, I hastened through the State without conversing or meeting with any of its citizens. In Raleigh, North Carolina, I spent one day; in Charleston, South Carolina, two days; Savannah and Augusta, Georgia, each one day. Both in travelling and whilst stopping I saw much and conversed freely with the citizens of those States as well as with officers of the army who have been stationed among them. The following are the conclusions come to by me.

I am satisfied that the mass of thinking men of the south accept the present situation of affairs in good faith. The questions which have heretofore divided the sentiment of the people of the two sections — slavery and State rights, or the right of a State to secede from the Union — they regard as having been settled forever by the highest tribunal — arms — that man can resort to. I was pleased to learn from the leading men whom I met that they not only accepted the decision arrived at as final, but, now that the smoke of battle has cleared away and time has been given for reflection, that this decision has been a fortunate one for the whole country, they receiving like benefits from it with those who opposed them in the field and in council.

Four years of war, during which law was executed only at the point of the bayonet throughout the States in rebellion, have left the people possibly in a condition not to yield that ready obedience to civil authority the American people have generally been in the habit of yielding. This would render the presence of small garrisons throughout those

States necessary until such time as labor returns to its proper channel, and civil authority is fully established. I did not meet any one, either those holding places under the government or citizens of the southern States, who think it practicable to withdraw the military from the south at present. The white and the black mutually require the protection of the general government.

There is such universal acquiescence in the authority of the general government throughout the portions of country visited by me, that the mere presence of a military force, without regard to numbers, is sufficient to maintain order. The good of the country, and economy, require that the force kept in the interior, where there are many freedmen, (elsewhere in the southern States than at forts upon the seacoast no force is necessary,) should all be white troops. The reasons for this are obvious without mentioning many of them. The presence of black troops, lately slaves, demoralizes labor, both by their advice and by furnishing in their camps a resort for the freedmen for long distances around. White troops generally excite no opposition, and therefore a small number of them can maintain order in a given district. Colored troops must be kept in bodies sufficient to defend themselves. It is not the thinking men who would use violence towards any class of troops sent among them by the general government, but the ignorant in some places might; and the late slave seems to be imbued with the idea that the property of his late master should, by right, belong to him, or at least should have no protection from the colored soldier. There is danger of collisions being brought on by such causes.

My observations lead me to the conclusion that the citizens of the southern States are anxious to return to self-government, within the Union, as soon as possible; that whilst reconstructing they want and require protection from the government; that they are in earnest in wishing to do what they think is required by the government, not humiliating to them as citizens, and that if such a course were pointed out they would pursue it in good faith. It is to be regretted that there cannot be a greater commingling, at this time, between the citizens of the two sections, and particularly of those intrusted with the law-making power.

Senate Executive Documents, 39 Cong., 1 sess. (Washington, 1866), I, No. 2, pp. 106–107.

CHAPTER XXIV — PRINCIPLES OF RECON-STRUCTION

145. The First Theory (1863)

BY PRESIDENT ABRAHAM LINCOLN

This proclamation was sent to Congress with the president's annual message, which contained comments upon it. — For Lincoln, see No. 44 above. — Bibliography : W. A. Dunning, *Essays on the Civil War and Reconstruction*, footnotes *passim ;* Lalor, *Cyclopædia*, III, 556.

WHEREAS, in and by the Constitution of the United States, it is provided that the President " shall have power to grant reprieves and pardons for offenses against the United States, except in cases of impeachment ; " and

Whereas a rebellion now exists whereby the loyal State governments of several States have for a long time been subverted, and many persons have committed, and are now guilty of, treason against the United States ; and

Whereas, with reference to said rebellion and treason, laws have been enacted by Congress, declaring forfeitures and confiscation of property and liberation of slaves, all upon terms and conditions therein stated, and also declaring that the President was thereby authorized at any time thereafter, by proclamation, to extend to persons who may have participated in the existing rebellion, in any State or part thereof, pardon and amnesty, with such exceptions and at such times and on such conditions as he may deem expedient for the public welfare ; and

Whereas the congressional declaration for limited and conditional pardon accords with well-established judicial exposition of the pardoning power ; and

Whereas, with reference to said rebellion, the President of the United States has issued several proclamations, with provisions in regard to the liberation of slaves ; and

Whereas it is now desired by some persons heretofore engaged in said rebellion to resume their allegiance to the United States, and to reinaugurate loyal State governments within and for their respective States; therefore

I, Abraham Lincoln, President of the United States, do proclaim, declare, and make known to all persons who have, directly or by implication, participated in the existing rebellion, except as hereinafter excepted, that a full pardon is hereby granted to them and each of them, with restoration of all rights of property, except as to slaves, and in property cases where rights of third parties shall have intervened, and upon the condition that every such person shall take and subscribe an oath, and thenceforward keep and maintain said oath inviolate; and which oath shall be registered for permanent preservation, and shall be of the tenor and effect following, to wit:

I, ————, do solemnly swear, in presence of almighty God, that I will henceforth faithfully support, protect, and defend the Constitution of the United States, and the union of the States thereunder; and that I will, in like manner, abide by and faithfully support all acts of Congress passed during the existing rebellion with reference to slaves, so long and so far as not repealed, modified, or held void by Congress, or by decision of the Supreme Court; and that I will, in like manner, abide by and faithfully support all proclamations of the President made during the existing rebellion having reference to slaves, so long and so far as not modified or declared void by decision of the Supreme Court. So help me God.

The persons exempted from the benefits of the foregoing provisions are all who are, or shall have been, civil or diplomatic officers or agents of the so-called Confederate Government; all who have left judicial stations under the United States to aid the rebellion; all who are or shall have been military or naval officers of said so-called Confederate Government above the rank of colonel in the army or of lieutenant in the navy; all who left seats in the United States Congress to aid the rebellion; all who resigned commissions in the army or navy of the United States and afterward aided the rebellion; and all who have engaged in any way in treating colored persons, or white persons in charge of such, otherwise than lawfully as prisoners of war, and which persons may have been found in the United States service as soldiers, seamen, or in any other capacity.

And I do further proclaim, declare, and make known that whenever, in any of the States of Arkansas, Texas, Louisiana, Mississippi, Tennessee, Alabama, Georgia, Florida, South Carolina, and North Carolina, a number of persons, not less than one tenth in number of the votes cast in such State at the presidential election of the year of our Lord one thousand eight hundred and sixty, each having taken the oath aforesaid and not having since violated it, and being a qualified voter by the election law of the State existing immediately before the so-called act of secession, and excluding all others, shall reëstablish a State government which shall be republican, and in no wise contravening said oath, such shall be recognized as the true government of the State, and the State shall receive thereunder the benefits of the constitutional provision which declares that " the United States shall guaranty to every State in this Union a republican form of government, and shall protect each of them against invasion ; and, on application of the legislature, or the executive (when the legislature cannot be convened), against domestic violence."

And I do further proclaim, declare, and make known, that any provision which may be adopted by such State government in relation to the freed people of such State, which shall recognize and declare their permanent freedom, provide for their education, and which may yet be consistent as a temporary arrangement with their present condition as a laboring, landless, and homeless class, will not be objected to by the national executive.

And it is suggested as not improper that, in constructing a loyal State government in any State, the name of the State, the boundary, the subdivisions, the constitution, and the general code of laws, as before the rebellion, be maintained, subject only to the modifications made necessary by the conditions hereinbefore stated, and such others, if any, not contravening said conditions, and which may be deemed expedient by those framing the new State government.

To avoid misunderstanding, it may be proper to say that this proclamation, so far as it relates to State governments, has no reference to States wherein loyal State governments have all the while been maintained.

And, for the same reason, it may be proper to further say, that whether members sent to Congress from any State shall be admitted to seats, constitutionally rests exclusively with the respective houses, and not to any extent with the executive. And still further, that this proclamation is intended to present the people of the States wherein the national authority has been suspended, and loyal State governments have been subverted, a mode in and by which the national authority and loyal State governments may be reëstablished within said States, or in any of them ; and while the mode presented is the best the executive can suggest, with his present impressions, it must not be understood that no other possible mode would be acceptable.

[L. S.]

    Given under my hand at the city of Washington, the eighth day of December, in the year of our Lord one thousand eight hundred and sixty-three, and of the independence of the United States of America the eighty-eighth.   ABRAHAM LINCOLN.

Abraham Lincoln, *Complete Works* (edited by John G. Nicolay and John Hay, New York, 1894), II, 442–444.

---

146. The State-Suicide Theory (1863)

BY SENATOR CHARLES SUMNER

    Sumner's official career was confined to the United States Senate, where he held a seat from 1851 until his death in 1874. From first to last he faithfully championed the cause of negro freedom and rights. For many years he was chairman of the Committee on Foreign Affairs, a position for which he was peculiarly fitted by his training and ability; but this duty and all others were subordinate to his self-imposed stewardship in behalf of an enslaved race. The theory set forth in this extract was first advanced by him in a speech in the Senate in 1862. — For Sumner, see E. L. Pierce, *Memoir and Letters of Charles Sumner*. — Bibliography as in No. 145 above.

IT is argued that the Acts of Secession are all inoperative and void, and that therefore the States continue precisely as before, with their local constitutions, laws, and institutions in the hands of traitors, but totally unchanged, and ready to be quickened into life by returning loyalty. Such, I believe, is a candid statement of the pretension for State Rights against Congressional governments, which, it is argued, cannot be substituted for the State governments. . . .

    It is true, beyond question, that the Acts of Secession are all inoperative and void against the Constitution of the United States. Though matured in successive conventions, sanctioned in various forms, and maintained ever since by bloody war, these acts — no matter by what name they may be called — are all equally impotent to withdraw an acre of territory or a single inhabitant from the rightful jurisdiction of the United States. But while thus impotent against the United States, it does not follow that they were equally impotent in the work of self-destruction. Clearly, the Rebels, by utmost efforts, could not impair the National jurisdiction ; but it remains to be seen if their enmity did not act back with fatal rebound upon those very State Rights in behalf of which they commenced their treason. . . .

    . . . On this important question I discard all theory, whether it be of State suicide or State forfeiture or State abdication, on the one side, or of State rights, immortal and unimpeachable, on the other side. . . .

It is enough, that, for the time being, and *in the absence of a loyal government,* they can take no part and perform no function in the Union, *so that they cannot be recognized by the National Government.* The reason is plain. There are in these States no local functionaries bound by constitutional oaths, so that, in fact, there are no constitutional functionaries ; and since the State government is necessarily composed of such functionaries, there can be no State government. . . . Therefore to all pretensions in behalf of State governments in the Rebel States I oppose the simple FACT, that for the time being no such governments exist. The broad spaces once occupied by those governments are now abandoned and vacated. . . .

. . . It is enough that the Rebel States be declared *vacated,* as *in fact* they are, by all local government which we are bound to recognize, so that the way is open to the exercise of a rightful jurisdiction.

And here the question occurs, How shall this rightful jurisdiction be established in the vacated States? Some there are, so impassioned for State rights, and so anxious for forms even at the expense of substance, that they insist upon the instant restoration of the old State governments in all their parts, through the agency of loyal citizens, who meanwhile must be protected in this work of restoration. But, assuming that all this is practicable, as it clearly is not, it attributes to the loyal citizens of a Rebel State, however few in numbers, — it may be an insignificant minority, — a power clearly inconsistent with the received principle of popular government, that the majority must rule. . . .

. . . The new governments can all be organized by Congress, which is the natural guardian of people without any immediate government, and within the jurisdiction of the Constitution of the United States. Indeed, with the State governments already *vacated* by rebellion, the Constitution becomes, for the time, the supreme and only law, binding alike on President and Congress, so that neither can establish any law or institution incompatible with it. And the whole Rebel region, deprived of all local government, lapses under the exclusive jurisdiction of Congress, precisely as any other territory ; or, in other words, the lifting of the local governments leaves the whole vast region without any other government than Congress, unless the President should undertake to govern it by military power. . . .

If we look at the origin of this power in Congress, we shall find that it comes from three distinct fountains, any one of which is ample to supply it. . . .

First. From the necessity of the case, *ex necessitate rei*, Congress must have jurisdiction over every portion of the United States *where there is no other government;* and since in the present case there is no other government, the whole region falls within the jurisdiction of Congress. This jurisdiction . . . can be questioned only in the name of the local government; but since this government has disappeared in the Rebel States, the jurisdiction of Congress is uninterrupted there.   The whole broad Rebel region is *tabula rasa*, or "a clean slate," where Congress, under the Constitution of the United States, may write the laws. . . .

Secondly. This jurisdiction may also be derived from the *Rights of War*, which surely are not less abundant for Congress than for the President. . . . It is Congress that conquers; and the same authority that conquers must govern. . . .

Thirdly. But there is another source for this jurisdiction which is common alike to Congress and the President.   It will be found in the constitutional provision, that "the United States shall guarantee to every State in this Union a republican form of government, and shall protect each of them against invasion." . . . If there be any ambiguity, it is only as to what constitutes a republican form of government.   But for the present this question does not arise.   It is enough that a wicked rebellion has undertaken to detach certain States from the Union, and to take them beyond the protection and sovereignty of the United States, with the menace of seeking foreign alliance and support, even at the cost of every distinctive institution. . . .

. . . When a State fails to maintain a republican government *with officers sworn according to the requirements of the Constitution*, it ceases to be a constitutional State.   The very case contemplated by the Constitution has arrived, and the National Government is invested with plenary powers, whether of peace or war. . . .

But there are yet other words of the Constitution which cannot be forgotten : " New States may be admitted by the Congress into this Union." Assuming that the Rebel States are no longer *de facto* States of this Union, but that the territory occupied by them is within the jurisdiction of Congress, then these words become completely applicable.   It will be for Congress, in such way as it shall think best, to regulate the return of these States to the Union, whether in time or manner.   No special form is prescribed.   But the vital act must proceed from Congress. . . .

Charles Sumner, *Our Domestic Relations, or How to Treat the Rebel States*, in *Atlantic Monthly*, October, 1863 (Boston), XII, 518–526 *passim*.

147. Adoption of the Thirteenth Amendment (1865)

FROM THE NEW YORK TRIBUNE

The Senate passed the amendment, by a vote of thirty-eight to six, on April 8, 1864. In the House of Representatives the vote on June 15 was ninety-three to sixty-five, not the necessary two-thirds. The measure was made a prominent feature of the political campaign in 1864, and when it was reconsidered in 1865 it passed. The account given below is taken from the telegraphic reports to the *New York Tribune.* — Bibliography : Channing and Hart, *Guide*, § 214.

WASHINGTON, Tuesday, Jan. 21, 1865.

THE hour has come ! The proposed Amendment to the Constitution immediately abolishing and forever prohibiting Slavery comes up for final decision. An anxious throng of witnesses pours into the galleries ; there is an air of confidence rising almost to exultation on the Union side, while a sullen gloom settles over the pro-Slavery benches.

Archibald McAllister, Dem., of the XVIIIth Pennsylvania District, reads a beautiful paper, in which he justifies his change of vote, and casts his ballot against the corner-stone of the Rebellion. Alexander H. Coffroth, Dem., of Pennsylvania, XVIth District, follows in an unanswerable and manly argument, to show the power to amend and the policy to amend. Applause on the Republican side greeted these new accessions to Freedom.

12 : 45. — William H. Miller of Pennsylvania, XIVth District, (who was beaten at the last election by Geo. F. Miller, Union,) espouses pro-Slavery Democracy, and insists on keeping his party foot on the niggers.

The galleries are getting crowded, the floor of the House filling up.

Anson Herrick, Dem., IXth District of New-York, next gives frank and statesmanlike reasons why he has changed his views, and shall change his vote.

In the midst of the speaking, and that buzzing which always characterizes a critical vote upon a great question, it is whispered that three Rebel Peace Commissioners, Stevens, Hunter and Campbell, are on their way here — that they were at City Point last night. A few believe, but most people say " gold gamblers' news."

1 : 30 *p. m.* — The crowd increases. Senators, Heads of Bureaus, prominent civilians and distinguished strangers, fill the spaces outside of the circle.

The interest becomes intense. The disruption of the Democratic party now going on is watched with satisfaction and joy upon the

2 H

Republican side of the House ; anxiety and gloom cover the obstinate body-guard of Slavery, whose contracting lines break with the breaking up of their party.

James S. Brown, Democrat, of Wisconsin, spitefully indicates his intention to vote against freedom.   Aaron Harding of Kentucky, a " Border State Unionist," bless the mark ! makes a melancholy effort to poke fun at young Democratic converts, and rams the struggling nigger back under the protection of the sacred Constitution.

Martin Kalbfleisch, Democrat, of Brooklyn reads a long pro-Slavery composition which excites little attention and no interest.

3 *p. m.* — The hour for voting has arrived, and the fact is announced by the Speaker.   Mr. Kalbfleisch is only at the 22d page of his composition, and begs to be endured through six pages more.   This request is granted, with much reluctance.

The galleries are wonderfully crowded, and women are invading the reporters' seats.   The Supreme Court and the Senate appear to have been transferred bodily to the floor of the House.

3 : 20 *p. m.* — A motion to lay the motion to reconsider on the table assumes the character of a test vote.   The most earnest attention is given to the calling of the roll.   Division lists appear on all sides, and members, reporters, and spectators devote themselves to keeping tally.

Of course the attempt to table the amendment will fail ; but there are not votes enough to pass the bill.   Absentees drop in ; one "aye," one " no."   The roll is called over by the Reading Clerk, but the count has already been declared in whispers through the House — 57 ayes, 111 noes. It is not tabled.

3 : 30 *p. m.* — Question is taken now on the motion to reconsider the vote of last session by which the proposed amendment was lost for want of two-thirds.   The House vote to reconsider, Ayes 112, Nays 57.

Now commence efforts to stave off the final vote.   Robert Mallory (Dem.) of Ky., with a menace as to what course he should decide to pursue, appeals to Mr. Ashley to let the vote go over till to-morrow. Other Democrats clamor for this delay.

Mr. Ashley refuses and stands firm, this being the accepted time and the day of salvation.

The final vote begins.   Down the roll we go to James E. English (Dem.) of Conn., who votes " aye."   A burst of applause greets this unexpected result, and the interest becomes thrilling.   The Speaker's hammer falls heavily, and restores silence.

Clerk — " John Ganson." " Aye." Applause again, repressed again by the Speaker. Angry calls among the Democrats and great irritation of feeling.

Clerk — " Wells A. Hutchins." " Aye." A stir of astonishment in the reporters' gallery.

" William Radford." " Aye." A movement of satisfaction all over the House.

" John B. Steele." " Aye." Wonder and pleasure are manifested.

" Dwight Townsend." " No." " Ah, if Harry Stebbins had been well enough to stay *that* vote had not been given," said a Senator.

Clerk — " Schuyler Colfax." " Aye."

The voting is done. Swift pencils run up the division lists. " One hundred and nineteen to fifty-six ! " Hurrah ! *Seven more than two-thirds !*

The Clerk whispers the result to the Speaker. The Speaker announces to the House what the audience quickly interpreted to be THE MIGHTY FACT THAT THE XXXVIIITH AMERICAN CONGRESS HAD ABOLISHED AMERICAN SLAVERY.

The tumult of joy that broke out was vast, thundering, and uncontrollable. Representatives and Auditors on the floor, soldiers and spectators in the gallery, Senators and Supreme Court Judges, women and pages, gave way to the excitement of the most august and important event in American Legislation and American History since the Declaration of Independence.

God Bless the XXXVIIIth Congress !

The work done in securing the passage of this bill has been immense. It has taken the labor of an entire month, night and day, to secure the majority which to-day so delighted the friends of freedom and of humanity, and so astounded the allies of Slavery.

To two Republicans in particular does the nation owe a debt of gratitude — to James M. Ashley of Toledo, Ohio, and Augustus Frank of Warsaw, New-York. They held the laboring oars.

The Democrats were sure of defeating the measure by a large majority up to this noon ; indeed, they felt sure of it up to the final voting. The Republicans were not sure of success till last night.

Three batteries of regular artillery have just saluted the grand result with a hundred guns, in the heart of the city.

New York Daily Tribune, February 1, 1865.

148. The President's Policy (1866)

BY PRESIDENT ANDREW JOHNSON

Johnson became president upon the death of Lincoln. He was a resident of Tennessee, and a Democrat before the Civil War; but he became a pronounced Unionist, and by his unequivocal opposition to secession placed himself in the ranks of the Republican or Union party. Lincoln made him military governor of Tennessee, and because of his record as a War Democrat the Republican convention named him for vice-president. He made no recantation of his Democratic principles, and by reason of his belief in states' rights soon found himself opposed to the reconstruction measures of the Republican Congress, a strife in which the president failed to preserve a dignity worthy of his high position. This extract is from his famous "Washington's Birthday" speech. — For Johnson, see Frank Moore, *Speeches of Andrew Johnson, with a Biographical Introduction.* — Bibliography as in No. 145 above.

. . . THE resolutions, as I understand them, are complimentary of the policy which has been adopted and pursued by the Administration since it came into power. I am free to say to you on this occasion that it is extremely gratifying to me to know that so large a portion of our fellow-citizens endorse the policy which has been adopted and which is intended to be carried out.

This policy has been one which was intended to restore the glorious Union — to bring those great States, now the subject of controversy, to their original relations to the Government of the United States. . . .

I assume nothing here to-day but the citizen — one of you — who has been pleading for his country and the preservation of the Constitution. These two parties have been arrayed against each other, and I stand before you as I did in the Senate of the United States in 1860. I denounced there those who wanted to disrupt the Government. . . . I remarked, though, that there were two parties. One would destroy the Government to preserve slavery. The other would break up the Government to destroy slavery. The objects to be accomplished were different, it is true, so far as slavery was concerned ; but they agreed in one thing — the destruction of the Government, precisely what I was always opposed to ; and whether the disunionists came from the South or from the North, I stand now where I did then, vindicating the Union of these States and the Constitution of our country. The rebellion manifested itself in the South. I stood by the Government. I said I was for the Union with slavery. I said I was for the Union without slavery. In either alternative I was for the Government and the Constitution. The Government has stretched forth its strong arm, and with its physical power it has put down treason in the field. . . . Now, what had we said to those people? We said: " No compromise; we can settle this question with the South in eight and forty hours."

I have said it again and again, and I repeat it now, " Disband your armies, acknowledge the supremacy of the Constitution of the United States, give obedience to the law, and the whole question is settled."

What has been done since? Their armies have been disbanded. They come now to meet us in a spirit of magnanimity and say, " We were mistaken; we made the effort to carry out the doctrine of secession and dissolve this Union, and having traced this thing to its logical and physical results, we now acknowledge the flag of our country, and promise obedience to the Constitution, and the supremacy of the law."

I say, then, when you comply with the Constitution, when you yield to the law, when you acknowledge allegiance to the Government, I say let the door of the Union be opened and the relation be restored to those that had erred and had strayed from the fold of our fathers.

Who has suffered more than I have? I ask the question. I shall not recount the wrongs and the sufferings inflicted upon me. It is not the course to deal with a whole people in a spirit of revenge. I know there has been a great deal said about the exercise of the pardon power, as regards the Executive; and there is no one who has labored harder than I to have the principals, the intelligent and conscious offenders, brought to justice and have the principle vindicated that " treason is a crime." . . .

. . . But as for the great mass who have been forced into the rebellion — misled in other instances — let there be clemency and kindness, and a trust and a confidence in them. . . . The rebellion is put down by the strong arm of the Government, in the field. But . . . we are now almost inaugurated into another rebellion . . . there is an attempt now to concentrate all power in the hands of a few at the Federal head, and thereby bring about a consolidation of the Republic which is equally objectionable with its dissolution. . . . By a resolution reported by a committee upon whom and in whom the legislative power of the Government has been lodged, that great principle in the Constitution which authorizes and empowers the legislative department, the Senate and House of Representatives, to be the judges of elections, returns, and qualifications of its own members, has been virtually taken away from the two respective branches of the National Legislature, and conferred upon a committee, who must report before the body can act on the question of the admission of members to their seats. By this rule they assume a State is out of the Union, and to have its practical relations restored by that rule, before the House can judge of the qualifications of its own members. What position is that? You have been struggling for four years to put down a rebellion. You contended at the beginning of that struggle that a State had not a right to go out. You said it had neither the right nor the power, and it has been settled that the States had neither the right nor the power to go out of the Union. And when you determine by the executive, by the military, and by the public judgment, that these States cannot have any right to go out, this committee turns around and assumes that they are out, and that they shall not come in.

I am free to say to you as your Executive that I am not prepared to take any such position. . . . I am opposed to the Davises, the Toombses, the Slidells, and the long list of such. But when I perceive on the other hand men . . . still opposed to the Union, I am free to say to you that I am still with the people. I am still for the preservation of these States — for the preservation of this Union, and in favor of this great Government accomplishing its destiny. . . .

The gentleman calls for three names. I am talking to my friends and fellow-citizens here. Suppose I should name to you those whom I look upon as being opposed to the fundamental principles of this Government, and as now laboring to destroy them. I say Thaddeus Stevens, of Pennsylvania ; I say Charles Sumner, of Massachusetts ; I say Wendell Phillips, of Massachusetts. . . .

. . . I know, my countrymen, that it has been insinuated — nay, said directly, in high places — that if such a usurpation of power had been exercised two hundred years ago, in particular reigns, it would have cost an individual his head. What usurpation has Andrew Johnson been guilty of? My only usurpation has been committed by standing between the people and the encroachments of power. . . .

They may talk about beheading, but when I am beheaded I want the American people to be the witness. . . . Are they not satisfied with one martyr? Does not the blood of Lincoln appease the vengeance and wrath of the opponents of this Government? Is their thirst still unslaked? Do they want more blood? Have they not honor and courage enough to effect the removal of the Presidential obstacle otherwise than through the hands of the assassin? . . . But . . . if my blood is to be shed because I vindicate the Union and the preservation of this Government in its original purity and character, let it be so ; but when it is done, let an altar of the Union be erected, and then, if necessary, lay me upon it, and the blood that now warms and animates my frame shall be poured out in a last libation as a tribute to the Union, and let the opponents of this Government remember that when it is poured out, the blood of the martyr will be the seed of the church.   The Union will grow.   It will continue to increase in strength and power, though it may be cemented and cleansed with blood. . . .

Have you heard them at any time quote my predecessor, who fell a martyr to his cause, as coming in controversy with anything I advocated? An inscrutable Providence saw proper to remove him to, I trust, a better world than this, and I came into power.   Where is there one principle in reference to this restoration that I have departed from?   Then the war is not simply upon me, but it is upon my predecessor. . . .

Daily National Intelligencer (Washington), February 23, 1866.

---

149. The Congressional Theory (1866)

BY THE JOINT COMMITTEE ON RECONSTRUCTION

When the Thirty-Ninth Congress met in December, 1865, a joint committee on reconstruction, of fifteen members, was appointed in accordance with a resolution offered in the House by Thaddeus Stevens, the mainspring of the reconstruction measures (see No. 152 below).   The committee was directed to " inquire into the condition of the States which formed the so-called Confederate States of America, and report whether they or any of them are entitled to be represented in either house of Congress, with leave to report by bill or otherwise."   From this committee came resolutions which in a modified form were ultimately embodied in the fourteenth amendment; and on June 18, 1866, a majority of the committee made the report from which this extract is taken.   It was accompanied by a large amount of testimony to prove the persistence of disloyal sentiments in the South. — Bibliography as in No. 145 above.

. . . IT is the opinion of your committee —

I.   That the States lately in rebellion were, at the close of the war, disorganized communities, without civil government, and without constitutions or other forms, by virtue of which political relations could legally exist between them and the federal government.

II.   That Congress cannot be expected to recognize as valid the election of representatives from disorganized communities, which, from the very nature of the case, were unable to present their claim to representation under those established and recognized rules, the observance of which has been hitherto required.

III. That Congress would not be justified in admitting such communities to a participation in the government of the country without first providing such constitutional or other guarantees as will tend to secure the civil rights of all citizens of the republic; a just equality of representation; protection against claims founded in rebellion and crime; a temporary restoration of the right of suffrage to those who have not actively participated in the efforts to destroy the Union and overthrow the government, and the exclusion from positions of public trust of, at least, a portion of those whose crimes have proved them to be enemies to the Union, and unworthy of public confidence.

Your committee will, perhaps, hardly be deemed excusable for extending this report further; but inasmuch as immediate and unconditional representation of the States lately in rebellion is demanded as a matter of right, and delay and even hesitation is denounced as grossly oppressive and unjust, as well as unwise and impolitic, it may not be amiss again to call attention to a few undisputed and notorious facts, and the principles of public law applicable thereto, in order that the propriety of that claim may be fully considered and well understood. . . .

To ascertain whether any of the so-called Confederate States "are entitled to be represented in either house of Congress," the essential inquiry is, whether there is, in any one of them, a constituency qualified to be represented in Congress. . . .

We now propose to re-state, as briefly as possible, the general facts and principles applicable to all the States recently in rebellion :

First. The seats of the senators and representatives from the so-called Confederate States became vacant in the year 1861, during the second session of the thirty-sixth Congress, by the voluntary withdrawal of their incumbents, with the sanction and by direction of the legislatures or conventions of their respective States. This was done as a hostile act against the Constitution and government of the United States, with a declared intent to overthrow the same by forming a southern confederation. This act of declared hostility was speedily followed by an organization of the same States into a confederacy, which levied and waged war, by sea and land, against the United States. . . . From the time these confederated States thus withdrew their representation in Congress and levied war against the United States, the great mass of their people became and were insurgents, rebels, traitors, and all of them assumed and occupied the political, legal, and practical relation of enemies of the United States. This position is established by acts of Congress and judicial decisions, and is recognized repeatedly by the President in public proclamations, documents, and speeches.

Second. The States thus confederated prosecuted their war against the United States to final arbitrament, and did not cease until all their armies were captured, their military power destroyed, their civil officers, State and confederate, taken prisoners or put to flight, every vestige of State and confederate government obliterated, their territory overrun and occupied by the federal armies, and their people reduced to the condition of enemies conquered in war, entitled only by public law to such rights, privileges, and conditions as might be vouchsafed by the conqueror. This position is also established by judicial decisions, and is recognized by the President in public proclamations, documents, and speeches.

Third. . . . they have no right to complain of temporary exclusion from Congress ; but, on the contrary, having voluntarily renounced the right to representation, and disqualified themselves by crime from participating in the government, the burden now rests upon them, before claiming to be reinstated in their former condition, to show that they are qualified to resume federal relations. In order to do this, they must prove that they have established, with the consent of the people, republican forms of government in harmony with the Constitution and laws of the United States, that all hostile purposes have ceased, and should give adequate guarantees against future treason and rebellion — guarantees which shall prove satisfactory to the government against which they rebelled, and by whose arms they were subdued.

Fourth. Having, by this treasonable withdrawal from Congress, and by flagrant rebellion and war, forfeited all civil and political rights and privileges under the federal Constitution, they can only be restored thereto by the permission and authority of that constitutional power against which they rebelled and by which they were subdued.

Fifth. These rebellious enemies were conquered by the people of the United States, acting through all the co-ordinate branches of the government, and not by the executive department alone. The powers of conqueror are not so vested in the President that he can fix and regulate the terms of settlement and confer congressional representation on conquered rebels and traitors. Nor can he, in any way, qualify enemies of the government to exercise its law-making power. The authority to restore rebels to political power in the federal government can be exercised only with the concurrence of all the departments in which political power is vested; and hence the several proclamations of the President to the people of the Confederate States cannot be considered as extending beyond the purposes declared, and can only be regarded as provisional permission by the commander-in-chief of the army to do certain acts, the effect and validity whereof is to be determined by the constitutional government, and not solely by the executive power.

Sixth. The question before Congress is, then, whether conquered enemies have the right, and shall be permitted at their own pleasure and on their own terms, to participate in making laws for their conquerors. . . .

Seventh. The history of mankind exhibits no example of such madness and folly. The instinct of self-preservation protests against it. The surrender by Grant to Lee, and by Sherman to Johnston, would have been disasters of less magnitude, for new armies could have been raised, new battles fought, and the government saved. The anti-coercive policy, which, under pretext of avoiding bloodshed, allowed the rebellion to take form and gather force, would be surpassed in infamy by the matchless wickedness that would now surrender the halls of Congress to those so recently in rebellion until proper precautions shall have been taken to secure the national faith and the national safety.

Eighth. As has been shown in this report, and in the evidence submitted, no proof has been afforded to Congress of a constituency in any one of the so-called Confederate States, unless we except the State of Tennessee, qualified to elect senators and representatives in Congress. No State constitution, or amendment to a State constitution, has had the sanction of the people. All the so-called legislation of State conventions and legislatures has been had under military dictation. If the President may, at his will, and under his own authority, whether as military commander or chief executive, qualify persons to appoint senators and elect representatives, and empower others to appoint and elect them, he thereby practically controls the organization of the legislative department. The constitutional form of government is thereby practically destroyed, and its powers absorbed in the Executive. And while your committee do not for a moment impute to the President any such design, but cheerfully concede to him the most patriotic motives, they cannot but look with alarm upon a precedent so fraught with danger to the republic. . . .

Tenth. The conclusion of your committee therefore is, that the so-called Confederate States are not, at present, entitled to representation in the Congress of the United States ; that, before allowing such representation, adequate security for future peace and safety should be required ; that this can only be found in such changes of the organic law as shall determine the civil rights and privileges of all citizens in all parts of the republic, shall place representation on an equitable basis, shall fix a stigma upon treason, and protect the loyal people against future claims for the expenses incurred in support of rebellion and for manumitted slaves, together with an express grant of power in Congress to enforce these provisions. . . .

> W. P. FESSENDEN.
> JAMES W. GRIMES.
> IRA HARRIS.
> J. M. HOWARD.
> GEORGE H. WILLIAMS.
> THADDEUS STEVENS.
> JUSTIN S. MORRILL.
> JNO. A. BINGHAM.
> ROSCOE CONKLING.
> GEORGE S. BOUTWELL.

House Reports, 39 Cong., 1 sess. (Washington, 1866), II, No. 30, xviii–xxi *passim*.

———◆———

150. Arraignment of Reconstruction (1868)

BY SAMUEL JONES TILDEN

Throughout the Civil War, Tilden, though nominally a War Democrat, objected to the extra-constitutional measures developed during the war, and from this attitude was led naturally to an opposition to the congressional theory and practice of reconstruction. When the speech from which this extract is taken was delivered, he was the recognized head of the Democratic party in New York, a position which he retained until his party selected him as its presidential candidate in 1876. — For Tilden, see John Bigelow, *Life of Samuel J. Tilden.* — Bibliography as in No. 145 above.

THE Republican party recoiled for a while on the fatal brink of the policy on which it at last embarked. It had not the courage to conciliate by magnanimity, and to found its alliances and its hopes of success upon the better qualities of human nature. It totally abandoned all relations to the white race of the ten States. It resolved to make the black race the governing power in those States, and by means of them to bring into Congress twenty senators and fifty representatives,— practically appointed by itself in Washington. . . .

The effect of a gain to the Republican party of twenty senators and fifty representatives is to strengthen its hold on the Federal Government against the people of the North.　Nor is there the slightest doubt that the paramount object and motive of the Republican party is by these means to secure itself against a reaction of opinion adverse to it in our great populous Northern commonwealths.　The effect of its system and its own real purpose is to establish a domination over us of the Northern States.

When the Republican party resolved to establish negro supremacy in the ten States in order to gain to itself the representation of those States in Congress, it had to begin by governing the people of those States by the sword.　The four millions and a half of whites composed the electoral bodies.　If they were to be put under the supremacy of the three millions of negroes, and twenty senators and fifty representatives were to be obtained through these three millions of negroes, it was necessary to obliterate every vestige of local authority, whether it had existed before the rebellion, or been instituted since by Mr. Lincoln or by the people.　A bayonet had to be set to supervise and control every local organization.　The military dictatorship had to be extended to the remotest ramifications of human society.　That was the first necessity.

The next was the creation of new electoral bodies for those ten States, in which, by exclusions, by disfranchisements and proscriptions, by control over registration, by applying test-oaths operating retrospectively and prospectively, by intimidation, and by every form of influence, three millions of negroes are made to predominate over four and a half millions of whites.　These three millions of negroes . . . have been organized in compact masses to form the ruling power in these ten States.　They have been disassociated from their natural relations to the intelligence, humanity, virtue, and piety of the white race, set up in complete antagonism to the whole white race, for the purpose of being put over the white race, and of being fitted to act with unity and become completely impervious to the influence of superior intellect and superior moral and social power in the communities of which they form a part.

Of course such a process has repelled, with inconsiderable exceptions, the entire white race in the ten States.　It has repelled the moderate portion who had reluctantly yielded to secession.　It has repelled those who had remained Unionists. The first fruit of the Republican policy is the complete separation of the two races, and to some extent their antagonism. . . .

If those three millions of negroes elect twenty senators and fifty representatives, they will have ten times as much power in the Senate of the United States as the four millions of whites in the State of New York. . . . These three millions of blacks will have twice the representation in the Senate which will be possessed by the five great commonwealths, — New York, Pennsylvania, Ohio, Indiana, and Illinois, — embracing thirteen and a half millions of our people.

Let me not be told that this enormous wrong is nothing more than an original defect of the Constitution. I answer that it derives most of its evil and its danger from the usurpations of the Republican party. . . .

Changes are dared and attempted by it with a success which, I trust, is but temporary, — changes which revolutionize the whole nature of our government.

1. . . . The Constitution left the States with exclusive power over the suffrage, and the States have always defined and protected the suffrage from change by their fundamental laws. Congress now usurps control over the whole subject in the ten States, and creates negro constituencies, and vests them with nearly a third of the whole representation in the Senate, and nearly a quarter of the whole representation in the House. The leaders of the Republican party also claim the power by Congressional act to regulate the suffrage in the loyal States, and, without the consent of the people of those States, to alter their constitutions, and involve them in a political partnership with inferior races.

2. Congress, by the methods and means I have traced, usurps control over the representation in the two branches of the national legislature, and packs those bodies with delegates, admitting or rejecting for party ends, and at length attempting to create a permanent majority by deputies from negro constituencies formed for that purpose. . . .

4. Congress is systematically breaking down all the divisions of power between the co-ordinate departments of the Federal Government which the Constitution established, and which have always been considered as essential to the very existence of constitutional representative government. . . .

. . . Congress has stripped the President of his constitutional powers over his subordinates in the executive function, and even over his own confidential advisers, and vested these powers in the Senate. It is now exercising the power of removing from office the President elected by the people and appointing another in his place, under the form of a trial, but without the pretence of actual crime, or anything more than a mere difference of opinion.

It has menaced the Judiciary : at one time proposing to create by law an incapacity in the Supreme Court to act by a majority in any case where it should disagree with Congress ; at another time proposing to divest that tribunal of jurisdiction, exercised by it from the foundation of the government, to decide between an ordinary law and the Constitution, which is the fundamental and supreme law. There is reason to believe also that a plan has been matured to overthrow the Court by the creation of new judges, to make a majority more subservient to Congress than the judges appointed by Mr. Lincoln are found to be.

These changes are organic. They would revolutionize the very nature of the government. They would alter every important part of its structure on which its authors relied to secure good laws and good administration, and to preserve civil liberty. They would convert it into an elective despotism. The change could not by possibility stop at that stage.

I avow the conviction, founded on all history and on the concurring judgment of all our great statesmen and patriots, that such a system, if continued, would pass into imperialism. I feel not less certain that the destruction of all local self-government in a country so extensive as ours, and embracing such elements of diversity in habits, manners, opinions, and interests, and the exercise by a single, centralized authority of all the powers of society over so vast a region and over such populations, would entail upon us an indefinite series of civil commotions, and repeat here the worst crimes and worst calamities of history.

Samuel J. Tilden, *Writings and Speeches* (edited by John Bigelow, New York, 1885), I, 399–407 *passim*.

CHAPTER XXV — PROCESS OF RECONSTRUCTION

151. Legislation on the Freedmen (1865–1866)

BY SOUTHERN LEGISLATURES

These laws respecting the freedmen, commonly called the " vagrant " laws, were passed by the legislatures of southern states reconstructed under Johnson's proclamation of May 29, 1865. The legislatures were controled by those recently in arms against the Union; and this legislation was one of the main causes of the passage of the fourteenth amendment. — Bibliography as in No. 145 above.

A. MISSISSIPPI: "THE VAGRANT ACT," NOVEMBER 24, 1865

SEC. 2 provides that all freedmen, free negroes, and mulattoes in this State, over the age of eighteen years, found on the second Monday in January, 1866, or thereafter, with no lawful employment or business, or found unlawfully assembling themselves together, either in the day or night time . . . shall be deemed vagrants, and on conviction thereof shall be fined in the sum of not exceeding . . . fifty dollars . . . and imprisoned, at the discretion of the court . . . not exceeding ten days. . . .

SEC. 5 provides that . . . in case any freedman, free negro or mulatto, shall fail for five days after the imposition of any fine or forfeiture upon him or her, for violation of any of the provisions of this act to pay the same, that it shall be, and is hereby made, the duty of the sheriff of the proper county to hire out said freedman, free negro or mulatto, to any person who will, for the shortest period of service, pay said fine or forfeiture and all costs : *Provided*, A preference shall be given to the employer, if there be one, in which case the employer shall be entitled to deduct and retain the amount so paid from the wages of such freedman, free negro or mulatto, then due or to become due ; and in case such freedman, free negro or mulatto cannot be hired out, he or she may be dealt with as a pauper.

SEC. 6 provides that . . . it is hereby made the duty of the boards of county police of each county in this State, to levy a poll or capitation tax on each and every freedman, free negro or mulatto, between the ages of eighteen and sixty years, not to exceed the sum of one dollar annually to each person so taxed, which tax when collected shall be paid into the county treasurer's hands, and constitute a fund to be called the freedmen's pauper fund, which shall be applied by the commissioners of the poor for the maintenance of the poor of the freedmen, free negroes and mulattoes. . . .

SEC. 7 provides that if any freedman, free negro or mulatto shall fail or refuse to pay any tax levied according to the provisions of the sixth section of this act, it shall be *prima facie* evidence of vagrancy. . . .

B. FLORIDA: "AN ACT IN RELATION TO CONTRACTS OF PERSONS OF COLOR," JANUARY 12, 1866

SEC. 1 Provides that all contracts with persons of color shall be made in writing and fully explained to them before two credible witnesses . . . with the affidavit of one or both witnesses, setting forth that the terms and effect of such contract were fully explained to the colored person, and that he, she, or they had voluntarily entered into and signed the contract and no contract shall be of any validity against any person of color unless so executed and filed : *Provided*, That contracts for service or labor may be made for less time than thirty days by parol.

SEC. 2 Provides, that whereas it is essential to the welfare and prosperity of the entire population of the State that the agricultural interest be sustained and placed upon a permanent basis, it is provided that when any person of color shall enter into a contract as aforesaid, to serve as a laborer for a year, or any other specified term, on any farm or plantation in this State, if he shall refuse or neglect to perform the stipulations of his contract by wilful disobedience of orders, wanton impudence or disrespect to his employer, or his authorized agent, failure or refusal to perform the work assigned to him, idleness, or abandonment of the premises or the employment of the party with whom the contract was made, he or she shall be liable, upon the complaint of his employer or his agent, made under oath before any justice of the peace of the county, to be arrested and tried before the criminal court of the county, and upon conviction shall be subject to all the pains and penalties prescribed for the punishment of vagrancy : *Provided*, That it shall be optional with the employer to require that such laborer be remanded to his service, instead of being subjected to the punishment aforesaid : *Provided, further*, That if it shall on such trial appear that the complaint made is not well founded, the court shall dismiss such complaint, and give judgment in favor of such laborer against the employer, for such sum as may appear to be due under the contract, and for such damages as may be assessed by the jury.

C.   FLORIDA : " AN ACT PRESCRIBING ADDITIONAL PENALTIES FOR THE COMMISSION OF OFFENSES AGAINST THE STATE," JANUARY 15, 1866

SEC. 12 provides that it shall not be lawful for any negro, mulatto, or other person of color, to own, use, or keep in his possession or under his control any bowie-knife, dirk, sword, fire-arms, or ammunition of any kind, unless he first obtain a license to do so from the judge of probate of the county in which he may be a resident for the time being ; and the said judge of probate is hereby authorized to issue license, upon the recommendation of two respectable citizens of the county, certifying to the peaceful and orderly character of the applicant ; and any negro, mulatto, or other person of color, so offending, shall be deemed to be guilty of a misdemeanor, and upon conviction shall forfeit to the use of the informer all such fire-arms and ammunition, and in addition thereto, shall be sentenced to stand in the pillory for one hour, or be whipped, not exceeding thirty-nine stripes, or both, at the discretion of the jury.

SEC. 14 provides that if any negro, mulatto, or other person of color, shall intrude himself into any religious or other public assembly of white persons, or into any railroad car or other public vehicle set apart for the exclusive accommodation of white people, he shall be deemed to be guilty of a misdemeanor, and upon conviction shall be sentenced to stand in the pillory for one hour, or be whipped, not exceeding thirty-nine stripes, or both, at the discretion of the jury ; nor shall it be lawful for any white person to intrude himself into any religious or other public assembly of colored persons, or into any railroad car or other public vehicle, set apart for the exclusive accommodation of persons of color, under the same penalties.

Edward McPherson, *A Political Manual for 1866* (Washington, 1866), 30–40 *passim*.

152. The Fourteenth Amendment (1866)

BY REPRESENTATIVE THADDEUS STEVENS

From the beginning of the Civil War Stevens was the leader of the radical Republicans in the House. He was intolerant of compromises; as chairman of the Committee on Ways and Means, prompt and unsparing in enabling the government to meet its financial obligations; urgent for confiscation; and defiant to "rebels, traitors, and copperheads." His theory of reconstruction was that the southern states had forfeited all their rights, and under his leadership this theory became the foundation of the congressional action on this question ; but his extreme views often had to be modified before they were acceptable to the majority. He was chairman of the House reconstruction committee, and reported the fourteenth amendment. After the House had passed the amendment the Senate modified it, — leniency of which Stevens disapproved. — For Stevens, see S. W. McCall, *Thaddeus Stevens*. — Bibliography as in No. 145 above.

THIS proposition is not all that the committee desired. It falls far short of my wishes, but it fulfills my hopes. I believe it is all that can be obtained in the present state of public opinion. Not only Congress but the several States are to be consulted. Upon a careful survey of the whole ground, we did not believe that nineteen of the loyal States could be induced to ratify any proposition more stringent than this. I say nineteen, for I utterly repudiate and scorn the idea that any State not acting in the Union is to be counted on the question of ratification. It is absurd to suppose that any more than three fourths of the States that propose the amendment are required to make it valid ; that States not here are to be counted as present. Believing, then, that this is the best proposition that can be made effectual, I accept it. . . .

The first section prohibits the States from abridging the privileges and immunities of citizens of the United States, or unlawfully depriving them of life, liberty, or property, or of denying to any person within their jurisdiction the " equal " protection of the laws.

I can hardly believe that any person can be found who will not admit that every one of these provisions is just. They are all asserted, in some form or other, in our DECLARATION or organic law. But the Constitution limits only the action of Congress, and is not a limitation on the States. This amendment supplies that defect, and allows Congress to correct the unjust legislation of the States, so far that the law which operates upon one man shall operate *equally* upon all. Whatever law punishes a white man for a crime shall punish the black man precisely in the same way and to the same degree. Whatever law protects the white man shall afford " equal " protection to the black man. Whatever means of redress is afforded to one shall be afforded to all. Whatever law allows the white man to testify in court shall allow the man of color to do the same. These are great advantages over their present codes. Now different degrees of punishment are inflicted, not on account of the magnitude of the crime, but according to the color of the skin. Now color disqualifies a man from testifying in courts, or being tried in the same way as white men. I need not enumerate these partial and oppressive laws. Unless the Constitution should restrain them those States will all, I fear, keep up this discrimination, and crush to death the hated freedmen. Some answer, " Your civil rights bill secures the same things." That is partly true, but a law is repealable by a majority. And I need hardly say that the first time that the South with their copperhead allies obtain the command of Congress it will be repealed. The veto of the President and their votes on the bill are conclusive evidence of that. And yet I am amazed and alarmed at the impatience of certain well-meaning Republicans at the exclusion of the rebel States until the Constitution shall be so amended as to restrain their despotic desires. This amendment once adopted cannot be annulled without two thirds of Congress. That they will hardly get. And yet certain of our distinguished friends propose to admit State after State before this becomes a part of the Constitution. What madness ! Is their judgment misled by their kindness ; or are they unconsciously drifting into the haven of power at the other end of the avenue ? I do not suspect it, but others will.

The second section I consider the most important in the article. It fixes the basis of representation in Congress. If any State shall exclude any of her adult male citizens from the elective franchise, or abridge that right, she shall forfeit her right to representation in the same proportion. The effect of this provision will be either to compel the States to grant universal suffrage or so to shear them of their power as to keep them forever in a hopeless minority in the national Government, both legislative and executive. If they do not enfranchise the freedmen, it would give to the rebel States but thirty-seven Representatives. Thus shorn of their power, they would soon become restive. Southern pride would not long brook a hopeless minority. True it will take two, three, possibly five years before they conquer their prejudices sufficiently to allow their late slaves to become their equals at the polls. That short delay would not be injurious. In the mean time the freedmen would become more

enlightened, and more fit to discharge the high duties of their new condition.   In that time, too, the loyal Congress could mature their laws
and so amend the Constitution as to secure the rights of every human
being, and render disunion impossible.   Heaven forbid that the southern
States, or *any one of them*, should be represented on this floor until such
muniments of freedom are built high and firm.   Against our will they
have been absent for four bloody years ; against our will they must not
come back until we are ready to receive them.   Do not tell me that
there are loyal representatives waiting for admission — until their States
are loyal they can have no standing here.   They would merely *mis*represent their constituents.

   I admit that this article is not as good as the one we sent to death in
the Senate.   In my judgment, we shall not approach the measure of
justice until we have given every adult freedman a homestead on the land
where he was born and toiled and suffered.   Forty acres of land and a
hut would be more valuable to him than the immediate right to vote.
Unless we give them this we shall receive the censure of mankind and
the curse of Heaven.   That article referred to provided that if *one* of the
injured race was excluded the State should forfeit the right to have any
of them represented.   That would have hastened their full enfranchisement.   This section allows the States to discriminate among the same
class, and receive proportionate credit in representation.   This I dislike.
But it is a short step forward.   The large stride which we in vain proposed is dead ; the murderers must answer to the suffering race.   I
would not have been the perpetrator.   A load of misery must sit heavy
on their souls.

   The third section may encounter more difference of opinion here.
Among the people I believe it will be the most popular of all the provisions ; it prohibits rebels from voting for members of Congress and
electors of President until 1870.   My only objection to it is that it is too
lenient.   I know that there is a morbid sensibility, sometimes called
mercy, which affects a few of all classes, from the priest to the clown,
which has more sympathy for the murderer on the gallows than for his
victim.   I hope I have a heart as capable of feeling for human woe as
others.   I have long since wished that capital punishment were abolished.
But I never dreamed that all punishment could be dispensed with in
human society.   Anarchy, *treason*, and violence would reign triumphant.
Here is the mildest of all punishments ever inflicted on traitors.   I might
not consent to the extreme severity denounced upon them by a pro-

visional governor of Tennessee — I mean the late lamented Andrew Johnson of blessed memory — but I would have increased the severity of this section. I would be glad to see it extended to 1876, and to include all State and municipal as well as national elections. In my judgment we do not sufficiently protect the loyal men of the rebel States from the vindictive persecutions of their victorious rebel neighbors. Still I will move no amendment, nor vote for any, lest the whole fabric should tumble to pieces.

I need say nothing of the fourth section, for none dare object to it who is not himself a rebel. To the friend of justice, the friend of the Union, of the perpetuity of liberty, and the final triumph of the rights of man and their extension to every human being, let me say, sacrifice as we have done your peculiar views, and instead of vainly insisting upon the instantaneous operation of all that is right accept what is possible, and " all these things shall be added unto you."

Congressional Globe, 39 Cong., 1 sess. (F. and J. Rives, Washington, 1866), 2459–2460 *passim*, May 8, 1866.

———◆———

153. Military Government (1867–1868)

BY MILITARY GOVERNORS

These extracts are from digests of orders of the military governors appointed under the reconstruction act of 1867. — Bibliography as in No. 145 above.

First Military District — Virginia. . . .

MAY 28 [1867] — Where civil authorities fail to give adequate protection to all persons in their rights of person and property, it was announced that military commissioners would be appointed ; trials by the civil courts preferred in all cases where there is satisfactory reason to believe that justice will be done. . . .

June 26 — It was decided that, as the laws of Congress declared there was no legal government in Virginia, the Alexandria constitution does not disfranchise any persons. . . .

April 4 [1868] — The office of Governor of Virginia having become vacant by the expiration of Governor Pierpoint's term, and he being ineligible for the next term, Henry H. Wells was appointed. . . .

Second Military District — North and South Carolina. . . .

April 27 [1867] — Local election in Newbern suspended ; and officers appointed, and required to take the oath of March 23, 1867. . . .

May 30 . . .   In public conveyances, on railroads, highways, streets, or navigable waters, no discrimination because of color or caste shall be made, and the common rights of all citizens therein shall be recognized and respected ; a violation of this regulation to be deemed a misdemeanor, and to render the offender liable to arrest and trial by a military tribunal, besides such damages as may be recovered in the civil courts. The remedy by distress for rent is abolished, where lands are leased or let out for hire or rent.   No license for the sale of intoxicating liquors in quantities less than one gallon, or to be drank on the premises, shall be granted to any person other than an inn-keeper. . . .

August 1 — The session of the Legislature of North Carolina, elected in 1866, indefinitely postponed. . . .

September 5 — The act of the Legislature of North Carolina, of March 7, 1867, " for the relief of executors, administrators, &c.," annulled as in violation of the Constitution of the United States, and in violation of the acts of Congress passed prohibiting all acts in aid of the late rebellion.   Courts directed to dismiss judgments, orders, and decrees, under said legislation. . . .

September 13 — General Canby ordered that all citizens assessed for taxes, and who shall have paid taxes for the current year, and who are qualified and have been or may be duly registered as voters, are declared qualified to serve as jurors.   Any requirement of a property qualification for jurors is hereby abrogated.   The collection of certain illegal and oppressive taxes, imposed in parts of North and South Carolina, was suspended.

October 16 — An election ordered in South Carolina, November 19 and 20, for or against a " convention," and for delegates to constitute the Convention.   Violence, or threats of violence, or of discharge from employment, or other oppressive agencies against the free exercise of the right of suffrage, prohibited. . . .

October 19 . . .   The election of municipal officers in Charleston forbidden. . . .

December 3 — A system of taxation established, for the support of the provisional government of South Carolina for the year from October 1, 1867, to September 30, 1868.   Appropriations ordered for the various offices and expenses of the State.

December 28 — The election declared to have resulted in favor of a convention; and the delegates notified to meet in Charleston, January 14, 1868. . . .

1868, January 14 — Conventions of both States met, and adjourned March 17.

February 6 — Ordinance of South Carolina Convention for the collection of taxes, promulgated, and the assessors ordered to collect the taxes therein levied. State Treasurer authorized to pay the expenses of the Convention. . . .

May 2 — Constitution announced ratified by a majority of the votes actually cast by the qualified electors of South Carolina. . . .

Third Military District — Georgia, Alabama, and Florida. . . .

April 12 [1867] — General Wager Swayne issued this order at Montgomery, Alabama:

General Orders, No. 3.

I. Complaints of hardship in the needless apprenticing of minors, particularly in pursuance of the preference given to the "former owner" in the law, have been almost incessant. It is enjoined upon probate judges, upon application, to revise the action taken in such cases, and as a rule to revoke indentures made within the past two years of minors who were capable of self-support. . . .

III. The use of "chain-gangs" as a mode of legal punishment being found to involve serious abuses, will be henceforth discontinued, except in connection with the penitentiary. . . .

August 2 — No civil court will entertain any action against officers or soldiers, or others, for acts performed in accordance with the orders of the military authorities. All such suits now pending to be dismissed.

August 12 — Ordered, that all advertisements or other official publications under State or municipal authority shall be made in such newspapers only as have not opposed and do not oppose reconstruction under acts of Congress, nor attempt to obstruct the civil officers appointed by the military authorities. . . .

January 13 [1868] — This order was issued : " Charles J. Jenkins, Provisional Governor, and Jno. Jones, provisional treasurer, of the State of Georgia, having declined to respect the instructions of and failed to co-operate with the major general commanding the third military district, are hereby removed from office." Brevet Brigadier General Thomas H.

Ruger appointed Governor, and Brevet Captain Charles F. Rockwell to be treasurer of Georgia. . . .

February 28 — All civil courts and officers whose duty it is to provide for the relief of paupers, shall extend relief to all persons entitled to relief, as such, without any discrimination as to race or color. . . .

March 18 — In all the jails and other prisons, colored prisoners are to receive the same food, in quality and quantity, as white prisoners, and the sheriffs shall get the same fees for victualling all classes of prisoners.

March 26 — Freedmen being threatened with discharge, "for the purpose of controlling their votes, or of restraining them from voting," bureau officers were directed by the superintendent of registration, E. Hulbert, to report all cases of interference with their political rights. . . .

Fourth Military District — Mississippi and Arkansas. . . .

July 29 [1867] — An order issued notifying all State and municipal officers that any attempt to render nugatory the action of Congress designed to promote the better government of the rebel States, by speeches or demonstrations at public meetings in opposition thereto, will be deemed sufficient cause for their summary removal. The same prohibition in regard to speeches will be applied to all officers holding appointments from these headquarters, and to officers of the army in this district. . . .

September 6 — Where a person, indicted for a criminal offence, can prove by two credible witnesses that he was a loyal man during the rebellion, believes that he cannot by reason of that fact get a fair and impartial trial by jury, the court will not proceed to try the case, but the papers shall be transmitted to these headquarters. As freed people bear their share of taxation, no denial to them of the benefit of those laws will be tolerated, and a refusal or neglect to provide properly for colored paupers will be treated as a dereliction of official duty. . . .

December 5 — It was ordered that, in consequence of stolen goods being sold or delivered after dark, traders and all other parties are forbid purchasing or delivering country supplies after sunset till market hour in the morning, and making such sale or delivery a military offence. . . .

Fifth Military District — Louisiana and Texas. . . .

April 8 [1867] — An election in the parish of Livingston, Louisiana, annulled. . . .

April 27 — General Griffin, reciting that persons disqualified by law are drawn to serve as jurors in the civil courts of Texas, directed that hereafter no person shall be eligible to serve as a juryman until he shall have taken the test-oath of July 2, 1862. . . .

May 2 . . . New Orleans. . . . The mayor, Edward Heath, ordered to adjust the police force so that at least one-half shall be composed of ex-Union soldiers. . . .

May 25 — Collection of taxes in Texas levied during the rebellion prohibited. . . .

July 30 — J. W. Throckmorton, Governor of Texas, removed as an impediment to reconstruction, and E. M. Pease appointed. . . .

Aug. 8 — Judge Edward Dougherty, 12th district of Texas, removed for denying the supremacy of the laws of Congress, and Edward Basse appointed.

Edward McPherson, *A Hand Book of Politics for 1868* (Washington, 1868), 316–323 *passim*.

---

154. Issue in the Impeachment of the President (1868)

BY MANAGER BENJAMIN FRANKLIN BUTLER AND WILLIAM MAXWELL EVARTS

The impeachment of the president was the climax of the strife between him and Congress growing out of the reconstruction measures (see No. 148 above), although the alleged ground of impeachment was but indirectly connected with these measures. Evarts, then recognized as one of the first lawyers in the country, was Johnson's leading defender. Butler was one of the managers of the impeachment for the House ; his political affiliations were at that time with the radical Republicans. — For Butler, see No. 124 above. — Bibliography as in No. 145 above.

THE CHIEF JUSTICE. Senators, the Chief Justice . . . will . . . direct the Secretary to read the offer to prove, and will then submit the question directly to the Senate. . . .

The chief clerk read the offer, as follows :

We offer to prove that at the meetings of the cabinet at which Mr. Stanton was present, held while the tenure-of-civil-office bill was before the President for approval, the advice of the cabinet in regard to the same was asked by the President and given by the cabinet, and thereupon the question whether Mr. Stanton and the other Secretaries who had received their appointment from Mr. Lincoln were within the restrictions upon the President's power of removal from office created by said act was considered, and the opinion expressed that the Secretaries appointed by Mr. Lincoln were not within such restrictions. . . .

The yeas and nays were ordered, and being taken resulted — yeas 22, nays 26. . . .

So the evidence proposed to be offered was decided to be inadmissible.

Mr. EVARTS, (to the witness.)   Mr. Welles, at any of the cabinet meetings held between the time of the passage of the civil-tenure act and the removal of Mr. Stanton, did the subject of the public service as affected by the operation of that act come up for the consideration of the cabinet? . . .

The WITNESS. I answer yes.

  By Mr. EVARTS:

Q. Was it considered repeatedly?

A. It was on two occasions, if not more.

Q. During those considerations and discussions was the question of the importance of having some determination judicial in its character of the constitutionality of this law considered?

Mr. Manager BUTLER. Stay a moment; we object. . . .

The CHIEF JUSTICE. If the question be objected to it will be reduced to writing. . . .

The offer was handed to the desk and read, as follows:

We offer to prove that at the cabinet meetings between the passage of the tenure-of-civil-office bill and the order of the 21st of February, 1868, for the removal of Mr. Stanton, upon occasions when the condition of the public service as affected by the operation of that bill came up for the consideration and advice of the cabinet, it was considered by the President and cabinet that a proper regard to the public service made it desirable that upon some proper case a judicial determination on the constitutionality of the law should be obtained.

Mr. Manager BUTLER. Mr. President and Senators, we, of the managers, object, and we should like to have this question determined in the minds of the senators upon this principle. We understand here that the determination of the Senate is, that cabinet discussions, of whatever nature, shall not be put in as a shield to the President. That I understand, for one, to be the broad principle upon which this class of questions stand and upon which the Senate has voted; and, therefore, these attempts to get around it, to get in by detail and at retail — if I may use that expression — evidence which in its wholesale character cannot be admitted, are simply tiring out and wearing out the patience of the Senate. I should like to have it settled, once for all, if it can be, whether the cabinet consultations upon any subject are to be a shield. Upon this particular offer, however, I will leave the matter with the Senate after a single suggestion.

It is offered to show that the cabinet consulted upon the desirability of getting up a case to test the constitutionality of the law. It is either material or immaterial. It might possibly be material in one view if they mean to say that they consulted upon getting up this case in the mode and manner that it is brought here, and only in that event could it be material. Does the question mean to ask if they consulted and agreed together to bring up this case in the form in which it has been done? If they agreed upon any other proceeding it is wholly immaterial; but if they agreed upon this case, then we are in this condition of things, that they propose to justify the President's act by the advice of his subordinates, and substitute their opinion upon the legality of his action in this case for yours.

Senators, you passed this tenure-of-office act. That might have been done by inadvertence. The President then presented it to you for your revision, and you passed it again notwithstanding his constitutional argument upon it. The President then removed Mr. Stanton, and presented its unconstitutionality again, and presented also the question whether Mr. Stanton was within it, and you, after solemn deliberation and argument, again decided that Mr. Stanton was within its provisions so as to be protected by it, and that the law was constitutional. Then he removed Mr. Stanton on the 21st of February, and presented the same question to you again; and again, after solemn argument, you decided that Mr. Stanton was within its provisions and that the law was constitutional. Now they offer to show the discussions of the cabinet upon its constitutionality to overrule the quadruple opinion solemnly expressed by the Senate upon these very questions — four times upon the constitutionality of the law, and twice upon its constitutionality and upon the fact that Mr. Stanton was within it. Is that testimony to be put in here? The proposition whether it was desirable to have this constitutional question raised is the one presented. If it was any other constitutional question in any other case, then it is wholly immaterial. If it is this case, then you are trying that question, and they propose to substitute the judgment of the cabinet for the judgment of the Senate.

Mr. EVARTS. . . . Now, senators, the proposition can be very briefly submitted to you.

By decisive determinations upon certain questions of evidence arising in this cause, you have decided that, at least, what in point of time is so near to this action of the President as may fairly import to show that in his action he was governed by a desire to raise a question for judicial determination, shall be admitted.   About that there can be no question that the record will confirm my statement.   Now, my present inquiry is to show that within this period, thus extensively and comprehensively named for the present, in his official duty and in his consultations concerning his official duty with the heads of departments, it became apparent that the operation of this law raised embarrassments in the public service, and rendered it important as a practical matter that there should be a determination concerning the constitutionality of the law, and that it was desirable that upon a proper case such a determination should be had.   I submit the matter to the Senate with these observations. . . .

The question being taken by yeas and nays, resulted — yeas 19, nays 30. . . .

So the Senate ruled the offer to be inadmissible.

Trial of Andrew Johnson . . . before the Senate . . . on Impeachment by the House of Representatives for High Crimes and Misdemeanors (Washington, 1868), I, 696–700 *passim*.

———◆———

155. The Fifteenth Amendment (1869)

BY SENATOR HENRY WILSON

Although Wilson entered the Senate, in 1855, with the reputation of a skilful politician who had made use of the Know-Nothing movement in order to float himself into office, his early and earnest attachment to the anti-slavery cause, and his great faith in the success of the Republican party, soon secured for him recognition as a worthy colleague of Sumner. His loyalty to freedom and the negro race continued during the reconstruction period, at the end of which he was elected vice-president. This extract is from a speech in the Senate. — Bibliography as in No. 145 above.

SIR, it is now past six o'clock in the morning — a continuous session of more than eighteen hours.   For more than seventeen hours the ear of the Senate has been wearied and pained with anti-republican, inhuman, and unchristian utterances, with the oft-repeated warnings, prophecies, and predictions, with petty technicalities, and carping criticisms.   The majority in this Chamber, in the House, and in the country, too, have been arraigned, assailed, and denounced, their ideas, principles, and policies misrepresented, and their motives questioned.   Sir, will our assailants never forget anything nor learn anything? Will they never see themselves as others see them?   Year after year they have continuously and vehemently, as grand historic questions touching the interests of the country and the rights of our countrymen have arisen to be grappled with and solved, blurted into our unwilling ears these same warnings, prophecies, and predictions, their unreasoning prejudices and passionate declamations. Time and events, which test all things, have brought discomfiture to their cause and made their illogical and ambitious rhetoric seem to be but weak and impotent drivel.

In spite of the discomfitures of the past, the champions of slavery and of the ideas, principles, and policies pertaining to it are again doing battle for their perishing cause. Again, sir, we are arraigned, again misrepresented, again denounced. Why are we again thus misrepresented, arraigned, and denounced? We, the friends of human rights, simply propose to submit to our countrymen an amendment of the Constitution of our country to secure the priceless boon of suffrage to citizens of the United States to whom the right to vote and be voted for is denied by the constitutions and laws of some of the States. This effort to remove the disabilities of the emancipated victims of the perished slave systems, to clothe them with power to maintain the dignity of manhood and the honor and rights of citizenship, spring from our love of freedom, our sense of justice, our reverence for human nature, and our recognition of the fatherhood of God and the brotherhood of man. This effort, sanctified by patriotism, liberty, justice, and humanity, is stigmatized in this Chamber as a mere partisan movement. Who make it a partisan movement? The men who are actuated by an imperative sense of duty, or the men who instinctively seize the occasion to arouse the unreasoning passions of race and caste and the prejudices of ignorance and hate? . . .

 . . . Because frivolity and fashion put their ban upon the black man, be his character ever so pure or his intelligence ever so great, statesmen in this Christian land of republican institutions must deny to him civil and political rights and privileges. Because social life has put and continues to put its brand of exclusion upon the black man, it is therefore the duty of statesmanship to maintain by class legislation the abhorrent doctrine of caste in this Christian Republic. This is the argument, the logic, the position of Senators. . . .

Honorable Senators have grown weary in reminding us that it would be a breach of our plighted faith to submit to the State Legislatures this amendment to the Constitution to secure to American citizens the right to vote and to be voted for. They tell us we were pledged by our national convention of 1868 ; that we were committed to the doctrine that the right to regulate the suffrage properly belonged to the loyal States.

So the earlier Republican national conventions proclaimed that slavery in the States was a local institution, for which the people of each State only were responsible. But that declaration did not stand in the way of the proclamation of emancipation, did not stand in the way of the thirteenth article of the amendments of the Constitution, did not stand in the way of that series of aggressive measures by which slavery was extirpated in the States. Slavery struck at the life of the nation, and the Republican party throttled its mortal foe. The Republican party in the national convention of 1868 pronounced the guarantee by Congress of equal suffrage of all loyal men at the South as demanded by every consideration of public safety, gratitude, and of justice, and determined that it should be maintained. That declaration unreservedly committed the Republican party to the safety and justice of equal suffrage. The declaration that the suffrage in the loyal States properly belonged to the people of those States meant this, no more, no less : that under the Constitution it belonged to the people of each of the loyal States to regulate suffrage therein. . . .

Senators accuse us of being actuated by partisanship, by the love of power, and the hope of retaining power ; yet they never tire of reminding us that the people have in several States pronounced against equal suffrage and will do so again. I took occasion early in the debate to express the opinion that in the series of measures for the extirpation of slavery and the elevation and enfranchisement of the black race the Republican party had lost at least a quarter of a million of voters. In every great battle of the last eight years the timid, the weak faltered, fell back or slunk away into the ranks of the enemy. Yes, sir ; while we have been struggling often against fearful odds, timid men, weak men, and bad men, too, following the examples of timid men, weak men, and bad men, in all the great struggles for the rights of human nature, have broken from our advancing ranks and fallen back to the rear or gone over to the enemy, thus giving to the foe the strength they had pledged to us. But we have gone on prospering, and we shall go on prospering in spite of treacheries on the right hand and on the left. The timid may chide us, the weak reproach us, and the bad malign us, but we shall strive on, for in struggling to secure and protect the rights of others we assure our own.

Appendix to the Congressional Globe, 40 Cong., 3 sess. (Rives and Bailey, Washington, 1869), 153–154 *passim*, February 8, 1869.

156. The Ku-Klux Klan (1871)

BY THE FEDERAL GRAND JURY

The opposition in the southern states to the fourteenth amendment took the form of secret societies, the members of which were sworn to intimidate the negroes from exerting their new-born rights, and also to put down both the " carpet-baggers " and their southern supporters, the " scalawags." The most prominent of these societies, the Ku-Klux Klan, was especially active in South Carolina, where the worst results of carpet-bag government had been shown (see No. 157 below), and where in October, 1871, the president, under the authority granted to him by an act to enforce the fourteenth amendment, had suspended the privilege of the writ of *habeas corpus* in nine counties. The presentment of the grand jury here given was made at the Circuit Court held at Columbia after the privilege of the writ had been suspended. Many arrests were made by military authorities, and the jury found 785 true bills. — Bibliography as in No. 145 above.

To the Judges of the United States Circuit Court:

IN closing the labors of the present term, the grand jury beg leave to submit the following presentment : During the whole session we have been engaged in investigations of the most grave and extraordinary character — investigations of the crimes committed by the organization known as the Ku-Klux Klan. The evidence elicited has been voluminous, gathered from the victims themselves and their families, as well as those who belong to the Klan and participated in its crimes. The jury has been shocked beyond measure at the developments which have been made in their presence of the number and character of the atrocities committed, producing a state of terror and a sense of utter insecurity among a large portion of the people, especially the colored population. The evidence produced before us has established the following facts :

1. That there has existed since 1868, in many counties of the State, an organization known as the " Ku-Klux Klan," or " Invisible Empire of the South," which embraces in its membership a large proportion of the white population of every profession and class.

2. That this Klan [is] bound together by an oath, administered to its members at the time of their initiation into the order, of which the following is a copy :

OBLIGATION.

I, (name,) before the immaculate Judge of Heaven and Earth, and upon the Holy Evangelists of Almighty God, do, of my own free will and accord, subscribe to the following sacredly binding obligation :

" 1. We are on the side of justice, humanity, and constitutional liberty, as bequeathed to us in its purity by our forefathers.

" 2. We oppose and reject the principles of the radical party.

" 3. We pledge mutual aid to each other in sickness, distress, and pecuniary embarrassment.

" 4. Female friends, widows, and their households, shall ever be special objects of our regard and protection.

" Any member divulging, or causing to be divulged, any of the foregoing obligations, shall meet the fearful penalty and traitor's doom, which is Death ! Death ! Death ! "

That in addition to this oath the Klan has a constitution and by-laws, which provides, among other things, that each member shall furnish himself with a pistol, a Ku-Klux gown, and a signal instrument.   That the operations of the Klan were executed in the night, and were invariably directed against members of the republican party by warnings to leave the country, by whippings, and by murder.

3. That in large portions of the counties of York, Union, and Spartanburgh, to which our attention has been more particularly called in our investigations during part of the time for the last eighteen months, the civil law has been set at defiance, and ceased to afford any protection to the citizens.

4. That the Klan, in carrying out the purposes for which it was organized and armed, inflicted summary vengeance on the colored citizens of these counties, by breaking into their houses at the dead of night, dragging them from their beds, torturing them in the most inhuman manner, and in many instances murdering them ; and this, mainly, on account of their political affiliations.   Occasionally additional reasons operated, but in no instance was the political feature wanting.

5. That for this condition of things, for all these violations of law and order, and the sacred rights of citizens, many of the leading men of those counties were responsible.   It was proven that large numbers of the most prominent citizens were members of the order.   Many of this class attended meetings of the Grand Klan.   At a meeting of the Grand Klan, held in Spartanburgh County, at which there were representatives from the various dens of Spartanburgh, York, Union, and Chester Counties, in this State, besides a number from North Carolina, a resolution was adopted that no raids should be undertaken, or any one whipped or injured by members of the Klan, without orders from the Grand Klan.   The penalty for violating this resolution was one hundred

lashes on the bare back for the first offense, and for the second, death. This testimony establishes the nature of the discipline enforced in the order, and also the fact that many of the men who were openly and publicly speaking against the Klan, and pretending to deplore the work of this murderous conspiracy, were influential members of the order, and directing its operations even in detail.

The jury has been appalled as much at the number of outrages as at their character, it appearing that eleven murders and over six hundred whippings have been committed in York County alone. Our investigation in regard to the other counties named has been less full; but it is believed, from the testimony, that an equal or greater number has been committed in Union, and that the number is not greatly less in Spartanburgh and Laurens.

We are of the opinion that the most vigorous prosecution of the parties implicated in these crimes is imperatively demanded; that without this there is great danger that these outrages will be continued, and that there will be no security to our fellow-citizens of African descent.

We would say further, that unless the strong arm of the Government is interposed to punish these crimes committed upon this class of citizens, there is every reason to believe that an organized and determined attempt at retaliation will be made, which can only result in a state of anarchy and bloodshed too horrible to contemplate.

House Reports, 42 Cong., 2 sess. (Washington, 1872), II, pt. i, No. 22, pt. i, pp. 48–49.

———————◆———————

157. Carpet-Bag Government (1873)

BY JAMES SHEPHERD PIKE

Before the Civil War Pike was a prominent member of the editorial staff of the *New York Tribune*, and its Washington correspondent. During the war he was minister to the Netherlands. In 1872 he supported the Liberal Republican movement in its opposition to further coercive measures in the southern states, and in 1873 he visited South Carolina in order to write up the evils of carpet-bag government. — Bibliography as in No. 145 above.

. . . WE will enter the House of Representatives. Here sit one hundred and twenty-four members. Of these, twenty-three are white men, representing the remains of the old civilization. . . .

Deducting the twenty-three members referred to, who comprise the entire strength of the opposition, we find one hundred and one remain-

ing.   Of this one hundred and one, ninety-four are colored, and seven
are their white allies.   Thus the blacks outnumber the whole body of
whites in the House more than three to one. . . .   As things stand, the
body is almost literally a Black Parliament, and it is the only one on the
face of the earth which is the representative of a white constituency and
the professed exponent of an advanced type of modern civilization.
But the reader will find almost any portraiture inadequate to give a vivid
idea of the body, and enable him to comprehend the complete meta-
morphosis of the South Carolina Legislature, without observing its details.
The Speaker is black, the Clerk is black, the door-keepers are black, the
little pages are black, the chairman of the Ways and Means is black, and
the chaplain is coal-black.   At some of the desks sit colored men whose
types it would be hard to find outside of Congo ; whose costume, visages,
attitudes, and expression, only befit the forecastle of a buccaneer.   It
must be remembered, also, that these men, with not more than half a
dozen exceptions, have been themselves slaves, and that their ancestors
were slaves for generations. . . .

The corruption of the State government of South Carolina is a topic
that has grown threadbare in the handling.   The last administration
stole right hand and left with a recklessness and audacity without parallel.
The robbers under it embraced all grades of people.   The thieves had
to combine to aid one another.   It took a combination of the principal
authorities to get at the Treasury, and they had to share the plunder
alike.   All the smaller fry had their proportions, the legislators and
lobbymen included.   The principal men of the Scott administration are
living in Columbia, and nobody undertakes to call them to account.
They do not attempt even to conceal their plunder.   If everybody was
not implicated in the robberies of the Treasury, some way would be
found to bring them to light.   All that people know is, that the State
bonded debt has been increased from five to fifteen millions, and that,
besides this, there are all sorts of current obligations to pay afloat, issued
by State officers who had authority to bind the Treasury.   They are all
tinctured with fraud, and some of them are such scandalous swindles that
the courts have been able temporarily to stop their payment.

The whole of the late administration, which terminated its existence
in November, 1872, was a morass of rottenness, and the present administration was born of the corruptions of that ; but for the exhaustion of the
State, there is no good reason to believe it would steal less than its predecessor.   There seems to be no hope, therefore, that the villainies of

the past will be speedily uncovered.   The present Governor was Speaker
of the last House, and he is credited with having issued during his term
in office over $400,000 of pay " certificates " which are still unredeemed
and for which there is no appropriation, but which must be saddled on
the tax-payers sooner or later. . . .

   . . . Then it has been found that some of the most unscrupulous
white and black robbers who have, as members or lobbyists, long plied
their nefarious trade at the capital, still disfigure and disgrace the present
Assembly.   So tainted is the atmosphere with corruption, so universally
implicated is everybody about the government, of such a character are
the ornaments of society at the capital, that there is no such thing as an
influential local opinion to be brought against the scamps.   They plunder,
and glory in it.   They steal, and defy you to prove it.   The legalization
of fraudulent scrip is regarded simply as a smart operation.   The
purchase of a senatorship is considered only a profitable trade.   Those
who make the most out of the operation are the best fellows.   " How
did you get your money ? " was asked of a prominent legislator and
lobbyist.   " I stole it," was the prompt reply. . . .   As has been already
said, it is believed that the lank impoverishment of the Treasury and
the total abasement and destruction of the State credit alone prevent the
continuance of robbery on the old scale.   As it is, taxation is not in the
least diminished, and nearly two millions per annum are raised for State
expenses where $400,000 formerly sufficed.   This affords succulent
pasturage for a large crowd.   For it must be remembered that not a
dollar of it goes for interest on the State debt.   The barter and sale of
the offices in which the finances of the State are manipulated, which are
divided among the numerous small counties under a system offering
unusual facilities for the business, go on with as much activity as ever.
The new Governor has the reputation of spending $30,000 or $40,000 a
year on a salary of $3,500, but his financial operations are taken as a mat-
ter of course, and only referred to with a slight shrug of the shoulders.

   . . . The narration I have given sufficiently shows how things have
gone and are going in this State, but its effect would be much heightened
if there were time and room for details.   Here is one : The total amount
of the stationery bill of the House for the twenty years preceding 1861
averaged $400 per annum.   Last year it was $16,000. . . .   The influence of a free press is well understood in South Carolina.   It was understood and dreaded under the old *régime*, and was muzzled accordingly.
Nearly all the newspapers in the State are now subsidized. . . .   The

whole amount of the printing bills of the State last year, it is computed (for every thing here has to be in part guess-work), aggregated the immense sum of $600,000. . . .

The black men who led the colored forces the other day against a railroad charter, because their votes had not been purchased, were models of hardihood in legislative immorality.   They were not so wily nor so expert, perhaps, as the one white man who was their ally in debate, but who dodged the vote from fear of his constituency ; but they exhibited on that, as they have on other occasions, an entire want of moral tone, and a brazen effrontery in pursuing their venal purposes that could not be surpassed by the most accomplished " striker " of Tweed's old gang. I have before alluded to the fact that on this occasion the blacks voted alone, not one white man going with them in opposing the measure they had conspired to defeat in order to extort money from the corporators.

This mass of black representatives, however ignorant in other respects, were here seen to be well schooled in the arts of corruption.   They knew precisely what they were about and just what they wanted, and they knew the same when they voted for Patterson for Senator.

This is the kind of moral education the ignorant blacks of the State are getting by being made legislators.   The first lessons were, to be sure, given by whites from abroad.   But the success of the carpet-baggers has stimulated the growth of knavish native demagogues, who bid fair to surpass their instructors.   The imitative powers of the blacks and their destitution of *morale* put them already in the front ranks of the men who are robbing and disgracing the State, and cheating the gallows of its due.

James S. Pike, *The Prostrate State : South Carolina under Negro Government* (New York, D. Appleton & Co., 1874), 12–50 *passim.*

PART VIII

THE NEW UNITED STATES

CHAPTER XXVI — POLITICAL AFFAIRS

158. The Tidal Wave (1874)

BY REPRESENTATIVE HILARY ABNER HERBERT (1890)

Herbert enlisted in the Confederate army from Alabama, and after the war practised law in that state. He entered Congress in 1877 and served until 1893, when he became secretary of the navy in Cleveland's cabinet, a position for which he had been eminently fitted by long service on the Committee on Naval Affairs. He is a representative statesman of the new South. The return to power of the Democrats in 1874 was general throughout the South, a condition which has continued to exist and has given rise to the term "solid South." This extract is from a symposium on reconstruction called "Why the Solid South?" written by prominent southern statesmen in 1890, when the bill for regulating national elections, known as the Force Bill, was before Congress. The book was intended to show "the consequences which once followed an interference in the domestic affairs of certain states." — Bibliography: Brookings and Ringwalt, *Briefs for Debate*, No. ii; and as in No. 145 above.

THE year 1874, which was to mark another era in the history of Alabama, had now come. The government "born of the bayonet" had been in existence six years. A general election was to be held in November, and both parties began early to prepare for the conflict. The Republicans who represented the state in Congress had made their contributions at an early date. They had secured, in the Act of March 28th, 1874, authority for the President to issue army rations and clothing to the destitute along the Alabama, Tombigbee and Warrior Rivers, all in Alabama; and, to carry out this and a similar Act relating to the Mississippi, four hundred thousand dollars were appropriated by the Sundry Civil Act, approved June 23d, 1874.

It may be as well here to give the history of this adventure, which was based on the pretense of a disastrous overflow. There had really been no unusual overflows anywhere in the state. The money sent to Alabama was distributed as an electioneering fund; some of it at points like Opelika, which had not been under water since the days of Noah's flood. This open prostitution of public funds, became a most effective weapon in the hands of the Democrats. To crown the misadventure, the Republican Governor, Lewis, probably to stamp with the seal of his condemnation the folly of the superserviceable politicians, who had secured this hapless appropriation, in his message to the Legislature, just after the election, took occasion to say, pointedly, that the state had during the year been " free from floods."

The Republicans renominated Governor Lewis and the Democrats selected as their candidate George S. Houston. And now began the great struggle which was to redeem Alabama from Republican rule.

The state was bankrupt — its credit gone.

Governor Lewis had reported to the Legislature, November 17th, 1873, that he was "unable to sell for money any of the state bonds."

The debt, which had been at the beginning of Republican administration in the state $8,356,083.51, was now, as appears by the official report, September 30th, 1874, including straight and endorsed railroad bonds, $25,503,593.30.

City and county indebtedness had in many cases increased in like proportion, with no betterments to show for expenditures.

The administration of public affairs in the state for many years preceding the Civil War had been notably simple and economical. Taxes had been low, honestly collected and faithfully applied.

To a people trained in such a school of government the extravagance and corruption now everywhere apparent, coupled with the higher rates of taxation and bankrupt condition of the treasury, were appalling.

More intolerable still were the turmoil and strife between whites and blacks, created and kept alive by those who, as the Republican Governor Smith had said, " would like to have a few colored men killed every week to furnish a semblance of truth to Spencer's libels upon the people of the state generally," as well as to make them more "certain of the vote of the negroes." Not only was immigration repelled by these causes, but good citizens were driven out of the state. It is absolutely safe to say that Alabama during the six years of Republican rule gained practically nothing by immigration, and at the same time lost more inhabitants by emigration than by that terrible war, which destroyed fully one-fifth of her people able to bear arms. Thousands more were now resolved to leave the state if, after another and supreme effort, they should fail to rid themselves of a domination that was blighting all hope of the future. Few things are more difficult than to overcome political prejudices as bitter as those which had formerly divided the white people of Alabama, but six years of Republican misrule had been, in most cases, sufficient for the purpose. In 1874 the people seemed to forget that they had ever been Whigs and Democrats, Secessionists and Union men ; and when this came about the days of the black man's party in Alabama were numbered. Although the whites had lost over twenty thousand men in the war who would now have been voting, they had in the state, by the census of 1870, a majority of 7,651 of those within the voting age. In 1880 this majority, as the census showed, was 23,038, and by the coming of age of boys too young to have been in the war, the white voters certainly outnumbered the blacks in 1874 by over ten thousand.

The Republicans had forced the color line upon an unwilling people. The first resolution of the Democratic platform of July, 1874, was that " the radical and dominant faction of the Republican party in this state persistently and by false and fraudulent representations have inflamed the passions and prejudices of the negroes, as a race, against the white people, and have thereby made it necessary for white people to unite and act together in self-defense and for the preservation of white civilization."

That the people of the state accepted this issue in this manner is the rock of offense against which partisan clamor in distant states has so often since that day lashed itself into fury.

The campaign of 1874 was not unattended by the usual efforts to inflame the public mind of the North and to intimidate Democratic voters at home by the display of Federal power, both civil and military. Troops were, of course, loudly called for. . . .

There were, during the year 1874, conflicts between whites and blacks, in which both parties received injuries and losses. These were incited, Democrats claimed, by Republican leaders to invoke the aid of Federal authorities, civil and military, in the pending election. . . . The Republican press, however, claimed that the acts which were to bring United States troops into the state to superintend the elections always resulted from the folly of the Democrats, who did not desire the presence of troops, and that the troubles were never instigated by the Republicans, who were anxious to have the troops. The political training of the colored man had been such that it was perfectly natural for him to look upon United States soldiers, when he saw them come into the state, as sent to see that he voted the Republican ticket. . . .

. . . The presence of troops . . . while it encouraged the negroes, served greatly to intensify the zeal of Democrats. Thousands of whites were inspired during that campaign with the feeling that their future homes depended upon the result of the election. The aliens among the Republican leaders also felt that their future habitations depended on the election, for they had no business in Alabama, except office-holding.

The Democrats were successful. They carried by over ten thousand majority all the state offices and they elected large majorities in both branches of the Legislature.

The clutch of the carpet-bagger was broken; most of them left the State; and there was at once peace between whites and blacks. A new Constitution was adopted. Superfluous offices were abolished. Salaries were cut down and fixed by the Constitution, some of them, perhaps, at too low a figure; and it is believed that, in many respects, the limitations upon the power of the Legislature were made too stringent. It was the necessary reaction, the swing of the pendulum from corruption and extravagance to the severest simplicity and economy in government. The consequences have been most happy. . . .

The facts of history are that the people of Alabama, prostrated by an unsuccessful war, and divided by the bitter memories of the past, were very loth to oppose what seemed to be the behests of the strongest government man had ever seen. They were utterly unable to unite and agree on any policy whatever. For six long years they suffered degradation, poverty and detraction, before they made up their minds to come together to assert, as they finally did, their supremacy in numbers, wealth, education and moral power. They have now in successful operation a government that, for the protection it affords to the lives, liberties and property of all its people, white and black, may safely challenge comparison with that of any state in the Union. Education and the liberalizing influences of the age . . . will gradually . . . solve every problem that can arise within her borders if she herself is left to deal with them. . . .

Hilary A. Herbert and others, *Why the Solid South? or Reconstruction and its Results* (Baltimore, R. H. Woodward Co., 1890), 61–69 *passim*.

———◆———

159. Electoral Crisis of 1877

BY MAJOR-GENERAL WINFIELD SCOTT HANCOCK

Hancock was the most prominent of the Federal officers during the Civil War who exercised no independent command. He was a Democrat by birth and breeding, and was opposed to the congressional policy of reconstruction. His name was before the Democratic national convention in 1868, and in 1880 he was the candidate of that party for president.   During the excitement over the contested election of 1876–77, when he was in command of the Division of the Atlantic, the false report was circulated that he had been selected to lead an armed force to Washington to compel the inauguration of Tilden, and that to prevent this the government had ordered him to the Pacific coast, but that he had refused to go. During the prevalence of that rumor the letter from which this extract is taken was written to General Sherman, then commanding the army; it shows the perplexities of the situation and the attitude of a prominent Union general. — For Hancock, see [Almira R. Hancock], *Reminiscences of Winfield Scott Hancock.* — Bibliography: W. E. Foster, *Presidential Administrations,* 51.

WHEN I heard the rumor that I was ordered to the Pacific coast, I thought it probably true, considering the past discussion on the subject. . . .   I was not exactly prepared to go to the Pacific, however, and I therefore felt relieved when I received your note informing me that there was no truth in the rumors. Then I did not wish to appear to be escaping from responsibilities and possible danger which may cluster around military commanders in the East, especially in the critical period fast approaching.

" All's well that ends well." The whole matter of the Presidency seems to me to be simple and to admit of a peaceful solution. The machinery for such a contingency as threatens to present itself has been all carefully prepared. It only requires lubricating, owing to disuse. The army should have nothing to do with the selection or inauguration of Presidents. The people elect the Presidents. Congress declares, in a joint session, who he is. We of the Army have only to obey his mandates, and are protected in so doing only so far as they may be lawful. Our commissions express that.

I like Jefferson's way of inauguration ; it suits our system. . . . He inaugurated himself simply by taking the oath of office. There is no other legal inauguration in our system. . . . Our system does not provide that one President should inaugurate another. There might be danger in that, and it was studiously left out of the Charter. But you are placed in an exceptionally important position in connection with coming events. The Capitol is in my jurisdiction, also, but I am a subordinate, and not on the spot, and if I were, so also would my superior in authority, for there is the station of the General-in-Chief. On the principle that a regularly elected President's term of office expires with the 3d of March (of which I have not the slightest doubt, and which the laws bearing on the subject uniformly recognize), and in consideration of the possibility that the lawfully elected President may not appear until

the 5th of March, a great deal of responsibility may necessarily fall upon
you. You hold over. You will have power and prestige to support you.
The Secretary of War, too, probably holds over; but, if no President
appears, he may not be able to exercise functions in the name of a
President, for his proper acts are of a known superior, a lawful President. You act on your own responsibility, and by virtue of a Commission only restricted by the law. The Secretary of War is only the
mouth-piece of a President. You are not. If neither candidate has a
Constitutional majority of the Electoral College, or the Senate and House
on the occasion of the count do not unite in declaring some person legally
elected by the people, there is a lawful machinery already provided to
meet that contingency, and to decide the question peacefully. It has
not been recently used, no occasion presenting itself; but our forefathers provided it. It has been exercised, and has been recognized
and submitted to as lawful on every hand. That machinery would
probably elect Mr. Tilden President and Mr. Wheeler Vice-President.
That would be right enough, for the law provides that in failure to elect
duly by the people, the House shall immediately elect the President, and
the Senate the Vice-President. Some tribunal must decide whether the
people have duly elected a President.

I presume, of course, that it is in the joint affirmative action of the
Senate and House; why are they present to witness the count, if not to
see that it is fair and just? If a failure to agree arises between the two
bodies, there can be no lawful affirmative decision that the people have
elected a President, and the House must then proceed to act, not the
Senate. The Senate elects Vice-Presidents, not Presidents. Doubtless,
in case of a failure by the House to elect a President by the 4th of
March, the President of the Senate (if there be one) would be the
legitimate person to exercise Presidential authority for the time being,
or until the appearance of a lawful President, or for the time laid down
in the Constitution. Such a course would be a peaceful and, I have a
firm belief, a lawful one.

I have no doubt Governor Hayes would make an excellent President.
I have met him, and know of him. For a brief period he served under
my command ; but as the matter stands I can't see any likelihood of his
being duly declared elected by the people, unless the Senate and House
come to be in accord as to that fact, and the House would of course, not
otherwise elect him.

What the people want is a peaceful determination of this matter, as fair a determination as possible, and a lawful one.   No other determination could stand the test.

The country, if not plunged into revolution, would become poorer day by day, business would languish, and our bonds would come home to find a depreciated market. . . .

As I have been writing thus freely to you, I may still further unbosom myself by stating that I have not thought it lawful or wise to use Federal troops in such matters as have transpired east of the Mississippi, within the last few months, save as far as they may be brought into action under the Constitution, which contemplates meeting armed resistance and invasion of a State, more powerful than the State authorities can subdue by the ordinary processes, and then only when requested by the Legislature, or, if that body could not be convened in season, by the Governor; and if the President of the United States intervenes in the matter it is a state of war, not peace.   The Army is laboring under disadvantages, and has been used unlawfully at times, in the judgment of the people (in mine certainly), and we have lost a great deal of the kindly feeling which the community at large once felt for us.   It is time to stop and unload. Officers in command of troops often find it difficult to act wisely and safely, when superiors in authority have different views of the laws from them, and when legislation has sanctioned action seemingly in conflict with the fundamental law, and they generally defer to the known judgment of their superiors.   Yet the superior officers of the Army are so regarded in such great crises, and are held to such responsibility, especially those at or near the head of it, that it is necessary on such momentous occasions to determine for themselves what is lawful and what is not lawful under our system, if the military authorities should be invoked, as might possibly be the case in such exceptional times when there existed such divergent views as to the correct result.   The Army will suffer from its past action if it has acted wrongfully.   Our regular Army has little hold upon the affections of the people of to-day, and its superior officers should certainly, as far as lies in their power, legally, and with righteous intent, aim to defend the right, which to us is *the law*, and the institution which they represent.   It is a well-meaning institution, and it would be well if it should have an opportunity to be recognized as a bulwark in support of the right of the people and of the law.

[Mrs. Almira Russell Hancock], *Reminiscences of Winfield Scott Hancock* (New York, 1887), 152–157 *passim*.

160. Appeal to the Voters (1880)

BY SENATOR JAMES GILLESPIE BLAINE

Blaine was a prominent figure in national politics from 1861 to 1892: his name was before the Republican national convention five times as a candidate for the presidential nomination, and in 1884 he was the nominee, but was defeated at the election. He was noted as a parliamentarian and as a political orator of great power. He possessed a personal magnetism that won for him an enthusiastic following, while at the same time he incurred an enmity such as has developed against few public characters of such prominence. In 1880 he was deprived of the nomination for president by the attempt to nominate Grant. The campaign that followed, during which this speech was delivered, was a bitter one, and on the Republican side there were many invocations to the spirit that had prevailed during the Civil War. — For Blaine, see Gail Hamilton (Mary Abigail Dodge), *Biography of James G. Blaine.* — Bibliography: Brookings and Ringwalt, *Briefs for Debate*, No. vi; Edward Stanwood, *History of the Presidency*, ch. xxvi.

I BELIEVE . . . that the Republican party in 1876 presented the solitary exception of a political organization strong enough and deeply-grounded enough in the affections and confidence of the people to survive the financial disaster and win a signal victory in the face of the business depression then existing. . . . And when the trust reposed in the Republican party has been so amply justified; when everything they predicted and promised in regard to the finances of the country has been more than justified; when prosperity is general, industry revived, and every man willing to work is able to get work at good wages, and when capital has found remunerative employment in conjunction with labor, it seems to me what the boys would call the height of impudence for the Democratic party to ask to be allowed to take control at such a time.

Well, says some very sensible man, pray tell me why this prosperity may not continue, and what check can possibly come of it if Hancock be chosen President rather than Garfield? . . .

. . . If you elect General Hancock you inevitably, within the space of a twelvemonth — I am not sure that it would not be within the space of ninety days — hand over to the Democratic party, led by Southern men, the control of the Supreme Court of the United States absolutely. Five of those Judges are to-day beyond seventy, or in that neighborhood. They may accept retirement at full pay. If they are reluctant to do so, a Democratic President backed by a Democratic Senate and House would swamp that Court by superior numbers; and by way of advice to the North let me say that a bill is pending on the calendar of the Senate to make that Court consist of twenty members.

"Well," says my inquiring friend, "what of that? Suppose the Court itself does become Democratic; if you have honest Judges it makes no difference about their politics." No, but when you come to that great class of political cases in which are points relative to upholding the reconstruction of the Southern States, the upholding of the Constitutional Amendments, in which are garnered up and preserved the fruits of the war — upon all these questions such Judges would be as inevitably and as radically wrong as the men who fought in the ranks of the rebel army. I beg you to remember that the Democrats after 1834 bent all their energies to building up a Supreme Court that would uphold the State Rights theory, and the first fruits of it was the Dred Scott decision of 1857, in which slavery was made national. Do not believe for one moment that you may intrust the Supreme Court to such men, though they are honest men. I may say their honesty is the trouble. They believe in these doctrines, and it is this which makes them so powerful for mischief.

I will tell you another thing that will happen if Hancock is elected. We shall have a thorough overhauling of the whole revenue and financial system of the United States. . . . I ask you to look back at the prosperity of the last twenty years and then say if you are willing to put the whole of it to the hazard of an experiment of trying a new theory with new men? I could detain you until morning in recording instances of how the prosperity of the American people has been so enormously developed by reason of a protective tariff, but it is useless at this late date to ask the value of protection.

Another thing that will happen if Hancock is elected — and I only speak of those things publicly vouched as the policy of the party — will arise from a vindication of the theory of States Rights, the underlying principle and guiding inspiration of the Democratic party. If he comes into power, in accordance with bills that have been perpetually renewed in Congress for the last eight years, the old State bank system will be renewed, and the "shin-plaster" currency will be revived. If, outside of the humanitarian achievement of the Republican party there was but this one thing — the abolition of State banks — upon which the party could pride itself, that should be sufficient to entitle it to the country's gratitude. In abolishing this system the Republican party abolished bad money. There has not been a bad bill in circulation since the National Bank system was established.

See how it will clog trade and paralyze industry, all for the sake of an experiment to vindicate State rights. I must call your attention to one or two other things in the history of the past ten years. One is, that the Republican party has been held up to the scorn and indignation of the country by the Democratic party on account of its harsh and cruel treatment of the South, as they say. Well, ten years have gone by, and we have reached the year of the decennial enumeration . . . this Southern census will disclose, and will intentionally disclose—it is not for me to say who the intender is, who plotted the plan — the fact that there are one and a half to two millions in the South who are not there — names of men in the grave and babes which are not yet born.

Now take four and a half millions of negroes in the South who don't have anything more to do with the Government of the United States than they do with the Government of Great Britain ; endowed with American citizenship and yet as capable of exercising the right of franchise as if they were in the moon. Take four and a half millions of these men, and what do we see ? . . . In Mississippi there are 225,000 colored men to 100,000 white men — that is nine to four. In Mississippi to-day four soldiers of the Confederate army will exercise as much power in electing Hancock, by throwing their votes for him, as nine Union soldiers in New-York or New-Jersey will exercise by voting for Garfield. I don't know whether you relish that or not ; I don't. And now on the top of the four and a half millions of actual men of flesh and blood deprived entirely of their power as a political element in the Government, we have a million [and] a half of imaginary men to overcome : there are seven millions which are counted on the other side before we start in the race. I say that this sort of thing must be stopped.

. . . We shall not fight over this to-morrow, or next day or next year, but I repeat in another form what I have said, that you cannot continue the Government of the United States when the party in power bases itself on the joint operation of fraud and violence.

Now, gentlemen . . . if you comprehend these issues as coming to your own doors and firesides, that you throw your Supreme Court and your tariff and your financial system and your currency all into the scale of a new experiment to be wrought out by incompetent and dangerous men, I have no doubt of the result. If you believe, as believe every reflecting man must, that the safe thing for this people to do is to stand still while we stand well ; that the wise thing for this people to do is to stand by that which has proved itself so stable and so true ; if you believe in the policy of the Republican party, which has brought the country through a great revolution of blood and through another great revolution of distress and finance; if you believe that party is to be trusted again, it is for New-Jersey as much as that of any State in the Union, upon this great industrial and financial system, to do her duty. . . .

New York Tribune, September 24, 1880.

———◆———

161. Change of Party (1884)

BY EBENEZER HANNAFORD

Hannaford served in the ranks of the 6th Ohio Regiment for three years during the Civil War, and saw service in most of the campaigns of the Army of the Cumberland; later he was adjutant in the 197th Ohio Regiment. The campaign of 1884 was noted not only for the first Democratic victory since 1856, but also for a wide severance of previous political affiliation. This is a letter from Hannaford to the *Nation.* — Bibliography: Edward Stanwood, *History of the Presidency*, ch. xxvii.

. . . *HARPER'S WEEKLY* is no doubt right in saying that the ultimate effects of Cleveland's election cannot yet be foreseen — so multitudinous and diverse are the interests through which these effects will ramify. But it seems to me impossible not to feel that its effects on the future of the Republican party depend in no minor degree on the course of the Republican leaders and the Republican press during the next six, or at most twelve, months. Among the many "lessons of the election" is not this an obvious one, that the American people are ready to smooth out and iron down "the bloody shirt," do it up with care and camphor, and put it away in the back closet of party politics? Not that the nation's heart for one moment throbs less true to the Union or the cause of universal freedom than it did twelve, sixteen, or twenty years ago, but simply that the plain, practical men who make up (as may they long continue to make up) the great mass of our voters, have come to regard the settlement of the war issues as safe beyond the possibility of undoing; and, further, to require of political parties that their aspirations and endeavors "fall in" with the soul of Capt. John Brown, and keep marching on.

That this, at any rate, is the attitude of mind in which most Independent Republicans find themselves, the morning after victory, is, I think, very certain. They are satisfied that in no shape whatever is the principle of secession any more an issue in American politics than the "peculiar institution" is a factor in American industry or a problem in American sociology. With all their heart they believe in progress — a movement straightforward, that is, and not round and round in a circle, like the wheelings of a hunted ostrich, or the wanderings of some lost wretch in a snowstorm. They have their convictions, and the " courage of them " too. Nobody crusades more vigorously than they. But it is against the living hordes of despoiling infidels that they demand to be led, not against those elder evaporated infidels, the mummies of the Pharaohs.

In forecasting the future of the Republican party no one can with reason shut his eyes to two things. One is that for the party to forfeit permanently the confidence of its " Independent " element would be a fatal blow to its every prospect of recovered ascendancy. The other is that the influential and steadily increasing class of voters in question can never be rallied around the ghost of a dead past. They will, as heretofore, fight in the front rank, but they will insist on being placed face to face with existing verities, real issues, living questions. The party that leaves them the most free, and gives them the best opportunity for working out what they believe to be their own and the country's salvation, is the party they will support, the party which their decisive vote will place or maintain in power.

Will that party be the Republican? Will its doctors of the law and Talmud-wise scribes be able to discern the signs of the times ? Is it capable of " rising on stepping-stones of its dead self to higher things " ? I, for one, shall await the unfolding of its plans and policy in the new sphere of " the opposition " with solicitous interest.

Meanwhile, what shall we say to the Mumbo-Jumbos of journalism in New York, in Chicago, in Cincinnati, who are still loudly mouthing " the Solid South " and " the Rebel yell," as though these outworn catch phrases embodied the profoundest and the saintliest of human wisdom, instead of being, in their *present* application, little better than mere gibberish? This much at least: " Such veteran Nimrods in the field of politics as you are, ought to show more skill. You should better know the habits of your game. They are too old birds, these Independents, to be caught with chaff from a thrice-beaten sheaf, or frightened by a scarecrow rigged out in their own discarded feathers."

The Nation, November 20, 1884 (New York), XXXIX, 435.

CHAPTER XXVII — COMMERCE

162. The American Railway System (1865)

BY SIR SAMUEL MORTON PETO, BART., M.P.

Peto became very prominent in England as a constructor of railways both at home and abroad. He visited the United States in 1865, and incorporated his observations in the book from which this extract is taken. English capitalists held much of the stock of American railroads. — Bibliography: Brookings and Ringwalt, *Briefs for Debate*, Nos. xlvii, lii; Library of Leland Stanford Junior University, *Catalogue of the Hopkins Railway Library*.

THE system . . . on which railroads have been permitted to be constructed in America has been one of great simplicity. . . . In America . . . every one in the country has felt, from the first . . . that the construction of a railroad through his property, or to the city, town, or village he inhabited, was a source of prosperity and wealth, not only to the district in which he resided, but to himself personally. . . .

As a rule, nothing has been easier than to obtain from the legislative authority of a State in America a concession, or as it is there styled, a "charter," to lay down a road. The land in many cases, especially where it belonged to the public, has been freely given for the line ; in other cases, where landed proprietors were affected, comparatively small compensations have sufficed to satisfy their claims. The citizens residing in the towns and populous places of the different districts, have hailed the approach of a railroad as a blessing. Under certain regulations, lines have been permitted to be laid down in the main streets and thoroughfares of the cities, so that the trains may traverse them at prescribed speeds, and so that goods may be put upon trucks at the very doors of the warehouses and shops. . . .

The influence of railroads on the value of real estates along their lines, and in the cities in which they terminate, is so well understood in America, as to have afforded important financial facilities to their construction. It is not the public who are invited in America to take railway shares ; they are subscribed for in a wholly different manner. In order to promote the construction of a line, not only does the State which it traverses frequently afford it facilities with respect to land, but pecuniary facilities are often given by the cities and towns giving securities for certain amounts on their Municipal Bonds. The cities in which it is to have its termini also agree to subscribe for portions of its share capital, and so do the inhabitants of the towns and villages through which it is to pass. This is a very important feature of the American railway system, inasmuch as it gives the inhabitants of each district which a railway traverses, a direct local and individual interest in the promotion and well-working of the line. Every one, in fact, is interested in contributing traffic to his own railway.

Not only the whole cost of maintaining the roads, but a very considerable proportion of the cost of their construction, has, in the case of the majority of the lines in America, been thrown *upon revenue*. I am afraid that the consequence of this has been injurious to public confidence in the American railways as commercial securities. Where lines are imperfectly constructed in the first instance — where they have to bear all the effects of climate and of wear and tear, whilst in indifferent condition, it is quite obvious that the cost of reparations, even in the very early stages of their working, must be a serious burden. And where all this is thrown, at once, on revenue, adequate dividends cannot be expected. . . .

Most of the American lines were originally made in short lengths, as lines of communication between different towns in the same State ; and without regard to any general system of communication for the nation. It follows, that even in the cases of lines which are now united and brought under a single management, much diversity of construction, and a great want of unity of system is observable. One of the great deficiencies of the American railroad system is, in fact, the absence of a general policy of management. Scarcely any attempts are made to render the working of lines convenient to travellers, by working the trains of one company in conjunction with another ; and this gives rise to complaints on the part of the public, which may, some day or other, be made to afford a ground of excuse for governmental interference. Nothing can be more desirable for the success of American railroad enterprises than well-considered general arrangements for the working and interchange of traffic.

Remarkable as has been the rapidity with which the American railroads have been constructed, and great as is the total mileage already made, the railroad accommodation of the United States is not to be regarded as by any means meeting the requirements of the country.

The rapid growth of the system has only been co-equal with the rapid growth of the population : the extent of mileage is attributable to the vast extent of territory settled, and the great distances between the seats of population.

In many parts of the States, indeed, the existing railways are quite insufficient. In the South, the system is very imperfectly developed. Whilst slaves existed, there was a determined hostility in the Southern States to the expansion of any general railway system, arising from the apprehension that it would be used for the escape of slaves. . . .

From West to East, also, the present railways are quite insufficient for the growing traffic. The lines of communication from the West by canal, &c., which existed previously to railways, have not been affected by their construction. The produce of the Western States has, in fact, increased faster than the means of transport, and additional facilities for the conveyance of goods are urgently required. It is of the utmost importance to the development of the West that no time should be lost in making this additional provision.

Sir S. Morton Peto, *Resources and Prospects of America* (New York, 1866), 255–265 *passim*.

———◆———

163. Completion of the Pacific Railroad (1869)

BY HENRY VARNUM POOR

Poor established *Poor's Manual of Railroads*, and was for many years an authority on railroad interests. — Bibliography: Library of Leland Stanford Junior University, *Catalogue of the Hopkins Railway Library*, 73–86.

THE present year witnesses the completion of the most important enterprise of the kind ever executed in any country — a line of railroad from the Missouri River across the Continent, and with connecting lines, from the Atlantic to Pacific Ocean, a distance of 3,250 miles. This great undertaking was commenced in the latter part of 1863, but no considerable amount of work was made till 1865, in which year only about 100 miles were constructed; in 1866, about 300 miles were opened ; in 1867, about the same number ; in 1868, about 800 miles ; and in the present year, about 300 : the whole distance from the Missouri to Sacramento being 1,800 miles. . . . Toward the construction of these roads the Government has, or will, issue its 6 per cent. *currency* bonds, to the amount of about $63,616,000, viz. : upon 300 miles at the rate of $48,000 per mile; upon 976 miles at the rate of $32,000 per mile; and upon 1,124 miles at the rate of $16,000 per mile. The annual interest upon the above sum will equal $3,816,960. These bonds are a second mortgage upon the respective lines, the several Companies being authorized to issue their own bonds to an amount equal to the Government subsidy, and to make them a first mortgage upon their roads.

The influence of these works . . . upon the commerce and welfare of the country, must be immense. A vast commerce, yet in its infancy, already exists between the two shores of the Continent. With the advantage and stimulus of the railroad this commerce must soon assume colossal proportions. Fronting the Pacific slope are hundreds of millions of people in Eastern Asia, who are rapidly taking part in the commerce of the world, and who will have the most intimate relations with our own Continent, which produces the gold and silver which at present forms one of the chief staples of commerce with them. It is hardly possible to estimate the magnitude of the commerce which will eventually exist between the Pacific coast and China and Japan. It is a commerce in which the world is to engage, and in which the Pacific Railroad is to be one of the most important instruments.

This road, too, will open up to settlement vast tracts of hitherto inaccessible territory, either fertile in soil, or rich in the more valuable minerals which are likely amply to compensate for the want of agricultural wealth. The main line will serve as the trunk from which lateral roads, constructed by private enterprise, will branch off in every direction. Already several important branches are in progress — one to Denver, Colorado; one to Salt Lake City; and one to connect it with the Columbia River. These branches will open up wide sections and add largely to the traffic of the trunk line.

The construction of this, and of similar works, by the aid of the Federal Government, has excited great interest, and although at present public opinion seems to be against any further grants of money, there can be no doubt that Government has been largely the gainer by the aid it has extended to the Pacific Railroad and its branches. The public taxes equal, at the present time, ten dollars per head of our population. These works have been instrumental in adding more than 500,000 to our population, whose contributions to the National treasury have far exceeded the interest on the bonds issued to them. They have certainly been instrumental in securing the construction of an equal extent of line which, but for them, would not have been built. Assuming the tonnage of these roads to equal 2,000 tons to the mile of road, the aggregate will be 9,800,000 tons, having a value of $490,000,000. The gain to the Federal Government from the creation of such an immense tonnage and value far exceeds the sums it has paid in aid of their construction, while the gain will, in a very short time, more than equal the principal sum of the bonds issued. Equally beneficent results will follow the construction of similar works. The people of the United States cannot afford to have extensive portions of their wide domain remain without means of access. In cases where such means have not been supplied by navigable water-courses they must be by a railway, or vast territories must remain, what they now are, deserts. The argument in favor of Government aid is as conclusive as it is simple. . . .

There can be no doubt, if the railroads of the United States could have been secured in no other way, it would have been the soundest policy for Government to have assumed their construction, even without the expectation of realizing a dollar of direct income from them. The actual cost of these works have been about $1,200,000,000. The interest on this sum is $72,000,000. They have created a commerce worth $10,000,000,000 annually. Such a commerce has enabled the people to pay $400,000,000 into the public treasury with far greater ease than they could have paid $100,000,000 without them. No line of ordinary importance was ever constructed that did not, from the wealth it created, speedily repay its cost, although it may never have returned a dollar to its share or bondholders. If this be true of local and unimportant works, how much more so must it be of great lines, which will open vast sections of our public domain, now a desert, but abounding in all the elements of wealth.

While, therefore, there are but few cases which would justify the Government in extending aid to railroads, there are some in which its interposition becomes an imperative duty. In addition to the Central line now constructed, nothing could be more promotive of the general welfare than the opening, by its aid, both the Northern and Southern routes. Upon each of these are immense extents of territory, full of natural wealth, but which, without a railroad, are utterly beyond the reach of settlement or commerce. Aid extended to both lines, instead of weakening the public credit, would greatly strengthen it. . . .

Henry V. Poor, *Manual of the Railroads of the United States*, 1869–1870 (New York, 1869), xlvi–xlviii *passim*.

164. "A Condition, not a Theory" (1887)

BY PRESIDENT GROVER CLEVELAND

President Cleveland's annual message to Congress in December, 1887, from which this extract is taken, was devoted entirely to the question of surplus revenue, its causes and remedy. This unique presentation of the need of tariff reform as an issue of such paramount importance that, in a message devoted to the "state of the Union," no other subject was worthy of a place beside it, made tariff reform the issue in the presidential contest of the ensuing year. This was Cleveland's most famous message. — For Cleveland, see J. L. Whittle, *Grover Cleveland.* — Bibliography: Brookings and Ringwalt, *Briefs for Debate,* Nos. xxxvii–xliv; Bowker and Iles, *Reader's Guide in Economic, Social, and Political Science,* 54–64. — For other discussions of the tariff question, see *Contemporaries,* III, Nos. 78, 130; below, No. 166.

OUR scheme of taxation, by means of which this needless surplus is taken from the people and put into the public treasury, consists of a tariff or duty levied upon importations from abroad, and internal-revenue taxes levied upon the consumption of tobacco and spirituous and malt liquors. It must be conceded that none of the things subjected to internal-revenue taxation are, strictly speaking, necessaries; there appears to be no just complaint of this taxation by the consumers of these articles, and there seems to be nothing so well able to bear the burden without hardship to any portion of the people.

But our present tariff laws, the vicious, inequitable, and illogical source of unnecessary taxation, ought to be at once revised and amended. These laws, as their primary and plain effect, raise the price to consumers of all articles imported and subject to duty by precisely the sum paid for such duties. Thus the amount of the duty measures the tax paid by those who purchase for use these imported articles. Many of these things, however, are raised or manufactured in our own country, and the duties now levied upon foreign goods and products are called protection to these home manufactures, because they render it possible for those of our people who are manufacturers to make these taxed articles and sell them for a price equal to that demanded for the imported goods that have paid customs duty. So it happens that while comparatively a few use the imported articles, millions of our people, who never use and never saw any of the foreign products, purchase and use things of the same kind made in this country, and pay therefor nearly or quite the same enhanced price which the duty adds to the imported articles. Those who buy imports pay the duty charged thereon into the public treasury, but the great majority of our citizens, who buy domestic articles of the same class, pay a sum at least approximately equal to this duty to the home manufacturer. . . .

It is not proposed to entirely relieve the country of this taxation. It must be extensively continued as the source of the Government's income ; and in a readjustment of our tariff the interests of American labor engaged in manufacture should be carefully considered, as well as the preservation of our manufacturers. It may be called protection, or by any other name, but relief from the hardships and dangers of our present tariff laws should be devised with especial precaution against imperiling the existence of our manufacturing interests. But this existence should not mean a condition which, without regard to the public welfare or a national exigency, must always insure the realization of immense profits instead of moderately profitable returns. As the volume and diversity of our national activities increase, new recruits are added to those who desire a continuation of the advantages which they conceive the present system of tariff taxation directly affords them. So stubbornly have all efforts to reform the present condition been resisted by those of our fellow-citizens thus engaged, that they can hardly complain of the suspicion, entertained to a certain extent, that there exists an organized combination all along the line to maintain their advantage.

We are in the midst of centennial celebrations, and with becoming pride we rejoice in American skill and ingenuity, in American energy and enterprise, and in the wonderful natural advantages and resources developed by a century's national growth. Yet when an attempt is made to justify a scheme which permits a tax to be laid upon every consumer in the land for the benefit of our manufacturers, quite beyond a reasonable demand for governmental regard, it suits the purposes of advocacy to call our manufactures infant industries still needing the highest and greatest degree of favor and fostering care that can be wrung from Federal legislation. . . .

But the reduction of taxation demanded should be so measured as not to necessitate or justify either the loss of employment by the workingman nor the lessening of his wages ; and the profits still remaining to the manufacturer, after a necessary readjustment, should furnish no excuse for the sacrifice of the interests of his employés either in their opportunity to work or in the diminution of their compensation. . . .

Under our present laws more than four thousand articles are subject to duty. Many of these do not in any way compete with our own manufactures, and many are hardly worth attention as subjects of revenue. A considerable reduction can be made in the aggregate, by adding them to the free list. The taxation of luxuries presents no features of hardship ; but the necessaries of life used and consumed by all the people, the duty upon which adds to the cost of living in every home, should be greatly cheapened.

The radical reduction of the duties imposed upon raw material used in manufactures, or its free importation, is of course an important factor in any effort to reduce the price of these necessaries ; it would not only relieve them from the increased cost caused by the tariff on such material, but the manufactured products being thus cheapened, that part of the tariff now laid upon such product, as a compensation to our manufacturers for the present price of raw material, could be accordingly modified. Such reduction, or free importation, would serve beside to largely reduce the revenue. It is not apparent how such a change can have any injurious effect upon our manufacturers. On the contrary, it would appear to give them a better chance in foreign markets with the manufacturers of other countries, who cheapen their wares by free material. Thus our people might have the opportunity of extending their sales beyond the limits of home consumption — saving them from the depression, interruption in business, and loss caused by a glutted domestic market, and affording their employés more certain and steady labor, with its resulting quiet and contentment. . . .

Our progress toward a wise conclusion will not be improved by dwelling upon the theories of protection and free trade. This savors too much of bandying epithets. It is a *condition* which confronts us — not a theory. Relief from this condition may involve a slight reduction of the advantages which we award our home productions, but the entire withdrawal of such advantages should not be contemplated. The question of free trade is absolutely irrelevant ; and the persistent claim made in certain quarters, that all the efforts to relieve the people from unjust and unnecessary taxation are schemes of so-called free-traders, is mischievous and far removed from any consideration for the public good.

The simple and plain duty which we owe the people is to reduce taxation to the necessary expenses of an economical operation of the Government, and to restore to the business of the country the money which we hold in the Treasury through the perversion of governmental powers. . . .

Senate Journal, 50 Cong., 1 sess. (Washington, 1887), 11–16 *passim*.

165. The Interstate Commerce Commission (1887–1891)

BY ALDACE FREEMAN WALKER (1891)

Walker is a prominent lawyer and financier. When the Interstate Commerce Commission was organized in 1887, President Cleveland appointed him a member of the body. He served two years, and then held important positions in railroad-traffic associations until 1894, when he became a receiver of the Santa Fé railroad system, and, later, chairman of the board of directors of the reorganized company. — Bibliography: Brookings and Ringwalt, *Briefs for Debate*, Nos. xlvii, lii; Bowker and Iles, *Reader's Guide in Economic, Social, and Political Science*, 47–51; Library of Leland Stanford Junior University, *Catalogue of the Hopkins Railway Library*, 150–152.

THIS universal reliance upon competition as the safeguard of the public has had two noticeable results : first, it has tended to entrench railroad managers in the belief that the public was protected sufficiently thereby, and that carriers by rail, like carriers by sea, were entitled to fix rates at will, subject only to the control of competitive conditions. . . .

In the second place, in its practical working, competition bred discrimination. The evils of unjust discrimination in railway methods cannot be too vividly portrayed. As time went on they became more and more pronounced, until they were too great to be endured. Legislative investigations were demanded. . . .

The remedy proposed was the forbidding of unjust discrimination under pains and penalties. That was the essence of the Interstate Commerce law. In other words, the result was prohibited while the cause was left in full operation. It was thought that free and unrestricted competition must be maintained as an essential principle of the American railway system. . . .

. . . Of course discriminations in railway rates are necessary; for example, the rate upon silk and upon sand should not be the same, and the question is often a doubtful one whether a particular discrimination is or is not unjust. The determination of this question, arising in innumerable forms, is the matter which has chiefly occupied the attention of the Commission since the passage of the law. . . .

. . . When the law first went into operation it was felt that a new era had arrived. The statute demanded the undeviating and inflexible maintenance of the published tariff rates. . . . This was just what conservative and influential railway managers desired. It was not only just, but it protected their revenues. The new rule was cheerfully accepted and imperative orders were issued for its obedience. But toward the close of 1887 it began to be perceived that there were difficulties, which became much more serious in 1888. On even rates the traffic naturally flowed to the direct lines, which could give the best service and make the best time. Roads less direct or of less capacity, roads with higher grades or less advantageous terminals and roads otherwise at a disadvantage, found that business was leaving them. It was discovered that the law in this its most essential feature, as well as in other respects, was practically a direct interference by the government in favor of the strong roads and against the weak. Dissatisfaction arose among officials of roads whose earnings were reduced and which were often near the edge of insolvency. It had been customary for them to obtain business by rebates and other like devices, and they knew no other method. It presently became to some of them a case of desperation. There was nothing in the law specifically forbidding the payment of " commissions," and it was found that the routing of business might be secured to a given line by a slight expenditure of that nature to a shipper's friend. Other kindred devices were suggested, some new, some old ; the payment of rent, clerk hire, dock charges, elevator fees, drayage, the allowance of exaggerated claims, free transportation within some single State — a hundred ingenious forms of evading the plain requirements of the law — were said to be in use. The demoralization was not by any means confined to the minor roads ; shippers were ready to give information to other lines concerning concessions which were offered them, and to state the sum required to control their patronage. A freight agent thus appealed to at first perhaps might let the business go, but when the matter became more serious and he saw one large shipper after another seeking a less desirable route, he was very apt to throw up his hands and fall in with the procession.

Meanwhile nothing was done in the way of the enforcement of the law. It was found that the sixth or administrative section had been so framed as to require the exact maintenance of the tariffs of each carrier, but that this important provision had been omitted respecting " joint tariffs," in which two or more carriers participate ; rates upon interstate traffic are usually joint. . . .

Toward the end of the second year came a reaching out for a remedy. In the closing days of the Fiftieth Congress amendments to the law were adopted by which shippers as well as carriers were made subject to its penalties, and the punishment of imprisonment was added to the fine in cases of unjust discrimination ; joint tariffs were also distinctly brought within the jurisdiction of the Commission and the courts.

These amendments became effective March 2, 1889, and their influence was immediately felt. . . . The third year therefore exhibited an almost entire cessation of the use of illegitimate methods for securing business, and until near its close little complaint was heard. The fourth year, 1890, witnessed a renewed relaxation of the spirit of obedience. The conditions that had prevailed in 1888 again became pressing, and evasions secretly inaugurated were not efficiently dealt with ; for a considerable time no prosecutions were commenced ; customers began to renew their appeals for favors, or as they term it, for relief; and it was presently a common statement among shippers and traffic agents that the law was after all a dead letter, and that its penalties need not be feared. A short corn crop added its pressure by threatening a deficiency in the usual tonnage ; and at the end of last year, although irregularities were more carefully concealed, they were generally believed to exist to a considerable extent. . . .

Aldace F. Walker, *The Operation of the Interstate Commerce Law*, in *Forum*, July, 1891 (New York), XI, 524–533 *passim*.

---

166. The Tariff and Reciprocity (1890)

BY PRESIDENT BENJAMIN HARRISON

Harrison was elected president on a platform advocating protection to home industries;. and, two months before he sent to Congress the annual message from which this extract is taken, he had approved of the " McKinley Act," a tariff measure which greatly increased protection, while it reduced the revenue from import duties. This law contained a section providing for a limited reciprocity in the manner described in the text, a measure that had been strongly advocated by James G. Blaine (see No. 160 above), the secretary of state. Immediately after its passage the McKinley law was subjected to much severe criticism both at home and abroad. — For Harrison, see Lew Wallace, *Life of General Benjamin Harrison*. — Bibliography : Bowker and Iles, *Reader's Guide in Economic, Social, and Political Science*, 65; and as in No. 164 above.

THE misinformation as to the terms of the act which has been so widely disseminated at home and abroad will be corrected by experience, and the evil auguries as to its results confounded by the market reports, the savings-banks, international trade balances, and the general prosperity of our people. Already we begin to hear from abroad and from our custom-houses that the prohibitory effect upon importations imputed to the act is not justified. . . . And so far from being an act to limit exports, I confidently believe that under it we shall secure a larger and more profitable participation in foreign trade than we have ever enjoyed, and that we shall recover a proportionate participation in the ocean carrying trade of the world. . . .

There is no disposition among any of our people to promote prohibitory or retaliatory legislation. Our policies are adopted not to the hurt of others, but to secure for ourselves those advantages that fairly grow out of our favored position as a nation. Our form of government, with its incident of universal suffrage, makes it imperative that we shall save our working people from the agitations and distresses which scant work and wages that have no margin for comfort always beget. But after all this is done it will be found that our markets are open to friendly commercial exchanges of enormous value to the other great powers.

From the time of my induction into office the duty of using every power and influence given by law to the Executive Department for the development of larger markets for our products, especially our farm products, has been kept constantly in mind, and no effort has been or will be spared to promote that end. We are under no disadvantage in any foreign market, except that we pay our workmen and workwomen better wages than are paid elsewhere — better abstractly, better relatively to the cost of the necessaries of life. I do not doubt that a very largely increased foreign trade is accessible to us without bartering for it either our home market for such products of the farm and shop as our own people can supply or the wages of our working people.

In many of the products of wood and iron, and in meats and breadstuffs, we have advantages that only need better facilities of intercourse and transportation to secure for them large foreign markets. The reciprocity clause of the tariff act wisely and effectively opens the way to secure a large reciprocal trade in exchange for the free admission to our ports of certain products. The right of independent nations to make special reciprocal trade concessions is well established, and does not impair either the comity due to other powers or what is known as the "favored-nation clause," so generally found in commercial treaties. What is given to one for an adequate agreed consideration can not be claimed by another freely. The state of the revenues was such that we could dispense with any import duties upon coffee, tea, hides, and the lower grades of sugar and molasses. That the large advantage resulting to the countries producing and exporting these articles by placing them on the free list entitled us to expect a fair return in the way of customs concessions upon articles exported by us to them was so obvious that to have gratuitously abandoned this opportunity to enlarge our trade would have been an unpardonable error.

There were but two methods of maintaining control of this question open to Congress : to place all of these articles upon the dutiable list, subject to such treaty agreements as could be secured, or to place them all presently upon the free list, but subject to the reimposition of specified duties if the countries from which we received them should refuse to give to us suitable reciprocal benefits. This latter method, I think, possesses great advantages. It expresses in advance the consent of Congress to reciprocity arrangements affecting these products, which must otherwise have been delayed and unascertained until each treaty was ratified by the Senate and the necessary legislation enacted by Congress. Experience has shown that some treaties looking to reciprocal trade have failed to secure a two-thirds vote in the Senate for ratification, and others having passed that stage have for years awaited the concurrence of the House and Senate in such modifications of our revenue laws as were necessary to give effect to their provisions. We now have the concurrence of both Houses in advance in a distinct and definite offer of free entry to our ports of specific articles. The Executive is not required to deal in conjecture as to what Congress will accept. Indeed, this reciprocity provision is more than an offer. Our part of the bargain is complete ; delivery has been made ; and when the countries from which we receive sugar, coffee, tea, and hides have placed on their free lists such of our products as shall be agreed upon, as an equivalent for our concession, a proclamation of that fact completes the transaction ; and in the mean time our own people have free sugar, tea, coffee, and hides.

The indications thus far given are very hopeful of early and favorable action by the countries from which we receive our large imports of coffee and sugar, and it is confidently believed that if steam communication with these countries can be promptly improved and enlarged the next year will show a most gratifying increase in our exports of breadstuffs and provisions, as well as of some important lines of manufactured goods.

Senate Journal, 51 Cong., 2 sess. (Washington, 1890), 8 *passim*.

167. The Clearing-House System (1890–1893)

BY COMPTROLLERS EDWARD SAMUEL LACEY AND JAMES H. ECKELS

Lacey was comptroller of the currency during the major portion of Harrison's administration, and Eckels held the position during Cleveland's second administration. The comptroller has charge of all matters relating to national banks; his annual report includes also the condition of state and savings-banks, and is, in consequence, a *résumé* of the banking interests of the nation during the year. The issuance of clearing-house certificates during the financial stringency of 1893, contemporary with the agitation for the repeal of the Sherman Law, was denounced by the advocates of free silver. This extract is from the official reports. — Bibliography: Brookings and Ringwalt, *Briefs for Debate*, No. xxxvi; Bowker and Iles, *Reader's Guide in Economic, Social, and Political Science*, 35–44; Horace White, *Money and Banking*, 469–477.

A. LACEY'S REPORT, 1891

THE effect of a general monetary stringency is felt first and most seriously by banks located in the larger of the reserve cities. Whenever financial affairs are in a normal condition the surplus funds of the local banks find their way to the vaults of their correspondent banks located in the great centers of business activity. This is undoubtedly due in part to the fact that these deposits may be made available for lawful money reserve and that a small rate of interest is, as a rule, paid upon bank balances by associations in the larger cities, and to the further fact that the maintenance of a good balance with their city correspondents strengthens the claim of the interior banks upon the former for rediscounts when the temporary condition of redundancy passes away and the increased demand for money is greater than the interior banks from their resources can conveniently supply.

Thus it results that the wants of a continent in case of general depression are at last brought through various channels of business activity, by way of withdrawals or loans, to the bankers of the great metropolitan cities for relief, and they are presented in such a form, in many cases, as to preclude the possibility of refusal, if general bankruptcy is to be avoided.

During the period of the stringency [1890] . . . the cities of New York, Philadelphia, and Boston were subjected to the most pressing demands, and after very careful consideration it was decided by the associated banks that the exigency made necessary a resort to the issuing of clearing-house loan certificates, for the purpose of settling clearing-house balances. This expedient had been successfully resorted to during the panics of 1873 and 1884.

At a meeting of the New York Clearing-House Association, on the 11th day of November, 1890, the following resolution was unanimously adopted :

Resolved, That a committee of five be appointed by the chair, of which the chairman shall be one, to receive from banks members of the association bills receivable and other securities, to be approved by said committee, who shall be authorized to issue therefor, to such depositing banks, loan certificates bearing interest at 6 per cent per annum, and in addition thereto a commission of one-quarter of 1 cent for every thirty days such certificates shall remain unpaid, and such loan certificates shall not be in excess of 75 per cent of the market value of the securities of bills receivable so deposited, and such certificates shall be received and paid in settlement of balances at the clearing house. . . .

These certificates were, by unanimous agreement upon the part of the clearing-house banks, accepted in lieu of money in the settlement of clearing-house balances.

In order to provide for the retirement of these securities in case the collaterals pledged were found insufficient, the several boards of directors of the associated banks were requested to, and did, pass a resolution in the following form :

Resolved, That any loss resulting from the issue of loan certificates shall be borne by the banks comprising the Clearing-House Association pro rata of capital and surplus, and this resolution shall be ratified by the boards of the respective banks, members of the association, and a certified copy of such consent delivered to the chairman of the loan committee.

B. ECKELS'S REPORT, 1893

THE unprecedented condition of the money market from June to September called for extraordinary remedies, not only to avert general disaster to the banks but to prevent commercial ruin. This remedy was the issuing of clearing-house loan certificates, which were brought into use as in 1873, 1884, 1890–'91, by the associated banks of New York, Boston, Philadelphia, Baltimore, and other cities where needed. The service rendered by them was invaluable, and to their timely issuance by the associated banks of the cities named is due the fact that the year's record of suspensions and failures is not greatly augmented.

. . . The subject . . . constitutes a very important part of the year's banking history, and for the additional reason that here and there are to be found those who entertain an entirely erroneous idea of the purpose for which these certificates were issued and what was accomplished by their issuance. Briefly stated, they were temporary loans made by the banks associated together as a clearing-house association, to the members of such association, and were available to such banks only for the purpose of settling balances due from and to each other, these balances under normal conditions of business being always settled in coin or currency. . . .

At a time when vast sums of coin and currency were being withdrawn from the banks, to be hoarded, these loan certificates, by performing the functions of the currency or coin customarily required for settling daily balances at the clearing house, released so much currency or coin to the legitimate and current demands of business and unquestionably placed it within the power of the banks in the cities named to extend to outside banks the aid needed on the one hand and liberally granted on the other. In no instance were these certificates designed to nor did they circulate as money. They were but due-bills and their sole function consisted in discharging the single obligation at the clearing house. An attempt on the part of a bank in any of the associations issuing these certificates to use them otherwise would have incurred a fine and other penalties provided in the rules governing such associations. Their issuance at so early a date in the financial derangement of the country was most opportune in not only preventing an acute panic, but in tending to restore public confidence, such action demonstrating that by mutual agreement of all, the weak banks of the association would be, so far as depositors and other creditors were concerned, as strong as the strongest. . . .

The following figures, showing the movement and amount of the issue of loan certificates in 1893 in the cities named, will indicate the measure of relief afforded by them:

	Date of issue of first certificate.	Date of largest amount outstanding.	Largest amount outstanding.	Date of surrender of last certificate.	Amount outstanding Oct. 31.
New York......	June 21	Aug. 29 to Sept. 6	$38,280,000	Nov. 1	....
Philadelphia....	June 16	Aug. 15.........	10,965,000	......	$3,835,000
Boston.........	June 27	Aug. 23 to Sept. 1	11,445,000	Oct. 20	....
Baltimore......	...do...	Aug. 24 to Sept. 9	1,475,000	......	845,000
Pittsburg.......	Aug. 11	Sept. 15.........	987,000	......	332,000
Total........	....	....	$63,152,000		

House Executive Documents, 52 Cong., 1 sess. (Washington, 1892), XXIV, No. 3, pt. 1, pp. 12–13 *passim*; 53 Cong., 2 sess. (Washington, 1895), XXIII, pt. i, No. 3, pt. 1, pp. 15–16 *passim*.

CHAPTER XXVIII — FINANCES AND CURRENCY

168. Demonetization of Silver (1872)

BY MEMBERS OF THE HOUSE OF REPRESENTATIVES

The Mint Law, or Coinage Act, of 1873, as the bill discussed in this extract was called, was prepared in the treasury department and passed the Senate during the Forty-First Congress. At that time the bill did not provide for the coinage of the silver dollar. In the House of Representatives the bill was considered during the next Congress, when a clause was added providing for the coinage of a subsidiary silver dollar. The discussion of this clause and the passage of the bill in the House are shown in this extract. The bill then went to the Senate, where the coinage of the subsidiary silver dollar was cut out and a substitute added providing for the coinage of the " trade " dollar. In this form the act became a law. Later it was contended that the bill passed the House by fraud because the purpose to demonetize silver was not stated. — Bibliography : Brookings and Ringwalt, *Briefs for Debate*, Nos. xxxiv, xxxv; Bowker and Iles, *Reader's Guide in Economic, Social, and Political Science*, 38–40 ; Providence Public Library, *Monthly Bulletin*, II, 233–241. — For a detailed history of the bill, see Edward McPherson, *Hand Book of Politics for 1890*, 157–169.

[April 9. Mr. HOOPER.] SECTION fourteen declares what the gold coins shall be, and their respective weights, and makes them a legal tender in all payments at their nominal value, when not below the standard weight and limit of tolerance prescribed, and at a valuation proportioned to their actual weight when below the standard weight and tolerance. Thus far the section is a reënactment of existing laws. In addition, it declares the gold dollar of twenty-five and eight tenths grains of standard gold to be the unit of value, gold practically having been in this country for many years the standard or measure of value, as it is legally in Great Britain and most of the European countries. The silver dollar, which by law is now the legally declared unit of value, does not bear a correct relative proportion to the gold dollar. . . .

. . . The committee, after careful consideration, concluded that twenty-five and eight tenths grains of standard gold constituting the gold dollar should be declared the money unit or metallic representative of the dollar of account. . . .

Section sixteen reënacts the provisions of existing laws defining the silver coins and their weights respectively, except in relation to the silver dollar, which is reduced in weight from four hundred and twelve and a half to three hundred and eighty-four grains ; thus making it a subsidiary coin in harmony with the silver coins of less denomination, to secure its concurrent circulation with them. The silver dollar of four hundred and twelve and a half grains, by reason of its bullion or intrinsic value being greater than its nominal value, long since ceased to be a coin of circulation, and is melted by manufacturers of silverware. . . .

Section eighteen provides that no coins other than those prescribed in this act shall hereafter be issued. The effect of it is to discontinue the coinage of the one and two cent bronze coins. . . .

[Mr. STOUGHTON.] The gold coins provided for . . . are declared to be a legal tender for all sums at their denominational value. Aside from the three-dollar gold piece, which is a deviation from our metrical ratio, and therefore objectionable, the only change in the present law is in more clearly specifying the gold dollar as the unit of value. This was probably the intention, and perhaps the effect of the act of March 3, 1849, but it ought not to be left to inference or implication. The value of silver depends, in a great measure, upon the fluctuations of the market, and the supply and demand. Gold is practically the standard of value among all civilized nations, and the time has come in this country when the gold dollar should be distinctly declared to be the coin representative of the money unit. . . .

The silver coins provided for are the dollar, 384 grains troy, the half dollar, quarter dollar, and dime of the value and weight of one half, one quarter, and one tenth of the dollar respectively ; and they are made a legal tender for all sums not exceeding five dollars at any one payment. . . .

[Mr. POTTER.] . . . this bill provides for the making of changes in the legal-tender coin of the country, and for substituting as legal-tender coin of only one metal instead as heretofore of two. I think myself this would be a wise provision, and that legal-tender coins, except subsidiary coin, should be of gold alone ; but why should we legislate on this now when we are not using either of those metals as a circulating medium? . . .

[May 27.] Mr. HOOPER. . . . I desire to call up the bill (H. R. No. 1427) revising and amending the laws relative to mints, assay offices, and coinage of the United States. I do so for the purpose of offering an amendment to the bill in the nature of a substitute, one which has been very carefully prepared and which I have submitted to the different gentlemen in this House who have taken a special interest in the bill. . . .

The SPEAKER. Does the gentleman from Massachusetts (Mr. HOOPER) move that the reading of the bill be dispensed with?

Mr. HOOPER. . . . I will so frame my motion to suspend the rules that it will dispense with the reading of the bill. . . .

The question was put on suspending the rules and passing the bill without reading ; and (two thirds not voting in favor thereof) the rules were not suspended. . . .

Mr. HOOPER. . . . I now move that the rules be suspended, and the substitute for the bill in relation to mints and coinage passed ; and I ask that the substitute be read.

The Clerk began to read the substitute. . . .

The question being taken on the motion of Mr. HOOPER, of Massachusetts, to suspend the rules and pass the bill, it was agreed to ; there being — ayes 110, noes 13.

Congressional Globe, 42 Cong., 2 sess. (Rives and Bailey, Washington, 1872), 2305–3883 *passim*, April 9 and May 27, 1872.

———————◆———————

169. Resumption of Specie Payments (1879)
BY SECRETARY JOHN SHERMAN (1895)

The law providing for the resumption of specie payments was passed in 1875. Sherman was secretary of the treasury when the law was finally carried into effect. — For Sherman, see No. 52 above. — Bibliography : Bowker and Iles, *Reader's Guide in Economic, Social, and Political Science*, 35–38 ; Horace White, *Money and Banking*, 469–477.

ON the 1st of January, 1879, when the resumption act went into effect, the aggregate amount of gold coin and bullion in the treasury exceeded $140,000,000. United States notes, when presented, were redeemed with gold coin, but instead of the notes being presented for redemption, gold coin in exchange for them was deposited, thus increasing the gold in the treasury.

The resumption of specie payments was generally accepted as a fortunate event by the great body of the people of the United States, but there was a great diversity of opinion as to what was meant by resumption. The commercial and banking classes generally treated resumption as if it involved the payment and cancellation of United States notes and all forms of government money except coin and bank notes. Another class was opposed to resumption, and favored a large issue of paper money without any promise or expectation of redemption in coin. The body of the people, I believe, agreed with me in opinion that resumption meant, not the cancellation and withdrawal of greenbacks, but the bringing them up to par and maintaining them as the equivalent of coin by the payment of them in coin on demand by the holder. This was my definition of resumption. I do not believe that any commercial nation can conduct modern operations of business upon the basis of coin alone. Prior to our Civil War the United States undertook to collect its taxes in specie and to pay specie for its obligations; this was the bullion theory. This narrow view of money compelled the states to supply paper currency, and this led to a great diversity of money, depending upon the credit, the habits and the wants of the people of the different states. The United States notes, commonly called greenbacks, were the creature of necessity, but proved a great blessing, and only needed one attribute to make them the best substitute for coin money that has ever been devised. That quality was supplied by their redemption in coin, when demanded by the holder.

The feeling in the treasury department on the day of resumption is thus described by J. K. Upton, assistant secretary, in an article written at the close of 1892 :

"The year, however, closed with no unpleasant excitement, but with unpleasant forebodings. The 1st day of January was Sunday and no business was transacted. On Monday anxiety reigned in the office of the secretary. Hour after hour passed; no news came from New York. Inquiry by wire showed all was quiet. At the close of business came this message: '$135,000 of notes presented for coin — $400,000 of gold for notes.' That was all. Resumption was accomplished with no disturbance. By five o'clock the news was all over the land, and the New York bankers were sipping their tea in absolute safety.

"Thirteen years have since passed, and the redemption fund still remains intact in the sub-treasury vaults. The prediction of the secretary has become history. When gold could with certainty be obtained for notes, nobody wanted it. The experiment of maintaining a limited amount of United States notes in circulation, based upon a reasonable reserve in the treasury pledged for that purpose, and supported also by the credit of the government, has proved generally satisfactory, and the exclusive use of these notes for circulation may become, in time, the fixed financial policy of the government."

The immediate effect of resumption of specie payments was to advance the public credit, which made it possible to rapidly fund all the bonds of the United States then redeemable into bonds bearing four per cent. interest. . . .

. . . Letters written about this date will show my view better than anything I can say now. . . .

WASHINGTON, D. C., January 8, 1879.

R. C. STONE, ESQ., Secretary Bullion Club, New York. . . .

I regret that my official duties will not permit me, in person, to respond to the toast you send me, and I cannot do so, by letter, in words more expressive than the toast itself, 'To Resumption — may it be forever.'

Irredeemable money is always the result of war, pestilence, or some great misfortune. A nation would not, except in dire necessity, issue its promises to pay money when it is unable to redeem those promises. I know that when the legal tenders were first issued, in February, 1862, we were under a dire necessity. The doubt that prevented several influential Senators, like Fessenden and Collamer, from voting for the legal tender clause, was that they were not convinced that our necessities were so extreme as to demand the issue of irredeemable paper money. Most of those who voted for it justified their vote upon the ground that the very existence of the country depended upon its ability to coin into money its promises to pay. That was the position taken by me. We were assured by Secretary Chase that nearly one hundred millions of unpaid requisitions were lying upon his table, for money due to soldiers in the presence of the enemy, and for food and clothing to maintain them at the front. We then provided for the issue of legal tender United States notes, as an extreme remedy in the nation's peril. It has always seemed strange that so large and respectable a body of our fellow-citizens should regard the continuance of irredeemable money as the permanent policy of a nation so strong and rich as ours, able to pay every dollar of its debts on demand, after the causes of its issue had disappeared. To resume is to recover from illness, to escape danger, to stand sound and healthy in the financial world, with our currency based upon the intrinsic value of solid coin.

Therefore I say, may resumption be perpetual. To wish otherwise is to hope for war, danger and national peril, calamities to which our nation, like others, may be subject, but against which the earnest aspiration of every patriot will be uttered.

John Sherman, *Recollections of Forty Years in the House, Senate, and Cabinet* (Chicago, etc., 1895), II, 701–704 *passim*. [By permission of the Saalfield Publishing Co., Akron, O.]

———◆———

170. The Sherman Act (1890)

BY PROFESSOR FRANK WILLIAM TAUSSIG

Taussig is professor of political economy at Harvard University, and an authority upon subjects connected with the financial and economic development of the United States. — Bibliography as in No. 168 above.

FIRST of all, it must be noted that the present act makes no important change from the provisions of the Bland act of 1878, except in the amount of silver currency to be issued. It is true there is a change in form ; instead of silver dollars and silver certificates we are to have treasury notes, redeemable at the government's option in gold or in silver coin, which notes are made legal tender for debts.   But under the act of 1878 the silver dollars were a legal tender, and the silver certificates were practically so.   Both, moreover, were practically redeemable either in gold or in silver ; directly of course in silver, and indirectly, but none the less effectually, in gold.   This indirect redemption arose because the government was always willing to accept the certificates and dollars freely in payment of all public dues ; while, on the other hand, it was always willing and able to pay each one of its creditors gold, if he wanted it.   The effect of the double willingness was to keep the silver currency always equal in value to gold, and the new legislation does no more than to simplify matters by making the treasury notes redeemable in gold or silver coin directly.   It is safe to say — even without the express declaration, wedged into the act, that it is " the established policy of the United States to maintain the two metals on a parity on the present legal ratio " — that every administration, in the future as in the past, will wish to keep the notes equal to gold, and will redeem them in gold whenever that metal is demanded.   The only important change, therefore, from the act of 1878, is as to amount.   In both measures the annual increment of new silver currency is determined in a cumbrous way, depending on the price of silver bullion.   The outcome under the old act was an annual issue of about thirty millions of dollars ; under the new one it will be between fifty and sixty millions — for several years probably nearer sixty millions than fifty. . . .

    . . . Twenty millions a year, perhaps thirty millions, will find use in the increase of retail transactions arising from the general growth of the community.   There is an inevitable elasticity about this item.   In any one year, more or less may be absorbed.   Present indications point to the use, for the first year or two, of rather more than twenty millions.   Then there is the gap left by retired bank notes, where again the count must be uncertain . . . but, on the whole, some temporary aid in finding a lodgment for the new notes in the retail currency will doubtless be found in this direction.   Between general growth and retired bank notes, so large a part of the new notes will probably find their way into general circulation for retail transactions that the government will be able to hoard any unused excess without great financial embarrassment.   Barring unexpected revulsions in foreign and domestic trade, we may therefore expect that the new silver currency will be issued at the start as

smoothly and with as little immediate effect as that of the past.   Those
who expect any prompt effect on prices, on bank operations, or on government finances, are likely to be disappointed.

Next, as to the more ultimate effects, assuming that there will be no
fresh legislation by Congress on the bank-note, silver, or greenback
issues.   We shall reach after a year or two the stage when more notes
will be put out than can find a place in the old way.   It is almost certain
that sixty millions of new notes of the smaller denominations cannot be
got into circulation every year.   Of course it is possible that the government then will simply hoard the excess, as it did at an earlier period
already referred to — the years 1885 and 1886.   A continued surplus of
income over expenditure might enable it, if it chose, to maintain such a
policy for a long time — to buy the silver, and simply to hoard so many
of the notes as did not readily find their way into circulation or came
back into its hands.   But this escape from the difficulties of the situation is not likely to be resorted to, except as a makeshift to tide over a
temporary emergency, or one expected to be temporary.   In the end,
the treasury will doubtless have to pay out the notes, whether they find
a ready circulation or not.   Then, at last, it may be said, we shall have a
forced issue of new currency, and surely a period of inflation, with all its
intoxicating and demoralizing effects.

No doubt the inflation must come, but the how and when are not so
clear.   The reader's attention must again be called to the importance
of banking operations, and to the consequences which flow from the fact
that all large payments are made by checks resting on bank deposits.
No issue of government notes, large or small, can greatly affect prices,
unless it affects the volume of bank deposits and that of the payments
made through them.   It would be wearisome, and indeed — since the
precise turn which events may take is quite uncertain — hardly profitable, to speculate on the various possibilities of a future several years
distant ; but it may illustrate what I have said of the part which bank
operations must play in any process of inflation, if I indicate the working
of the silver notes under two simple and very possible sets of conditions.
First, the notes may be issued at one of the ordinary periods of depression and business inactivity.   At such times the banks have plenty of
cash in their vaults ; they find it difficult to induce business men to increase their credits and deposits ; the industrial current is sluggish and
is not easily moved by a fresh inflow.   The notes which the government
would pay out to bullion-sellers, or to other creditors, would accumulate

in bank vaults, and thence more and more of them would flow back into the treasury. A larger and larger proportion of the government's revenue would be received in these treasury notes. Meanwhile, gold would be paid out to such as called for it, and, the bank reserves being already over-full, the gold would tend to flow out in foreign payments; the more so because at such times securities, which form ordinarily a considerable part of our resources for foreign payments, would be difficult to sell abroad. By a process of this sort, the treasury might be drained of its gold, and even brought to a suspension of gold payments, while yet the note issues which had brought this about had had no effect on prices. Eventually, no doubt, the continuance of these issues would lead to a movement toward inflation; but only when, in the time of activity which usually follows in due course the time of depression, the banks, and still more the business community, were in a humor to respond.

F. W. Taussig, *The Working of the New Silver Act*, in *Forum*, October, 1890 (New York), X, 165–171 *passim*.

------

171. Defence of Silver (1896)

BY WILLIAM JENNINGS BRYAN

Bryan entered Congress from Nebraska in 1891, and soon became noted for his advocacy of a bimetallic standard. His speech before the Democratic national convention in 1896, from which this extract is taken, was instrumental in securing for him the nomination for president by that convention. Both during that year and in 1900, when he was again candidate for the presidency, his name was considered as inseparably connected with the free-silver policy. — For Bryan, see W. J. Bryan, *The First Battle.* — Bibliography as in No. 168 above.

. . . WHEN you (turning to the gold delegates) come before us and tell us that we are about to disturb your business interests, we reply that you have disturbed our business interests by your course.

We say to you that you have made the definition of a business man too limited in its application. The man who is employed for wages is as much a business man as his employer; the attorney in a country town is as much a business man as the corporation counsel in a great metropolis; the merchant at the cross-roads store is as much a business man as the merchant of New York; the farmer who goes forth in the morning and toils all day — who begins in the spring and toils all summer — and who by the application of brain and muscle to the natural resources of the country creates wealth, is as much a business man as the man who goes upon the board of trade and bets upon the price of grain; the miners who go down a thousand feet into the earth, or climb two thousand feet upon the cliffs, and bring forth from their hiding places the precious metals to be poured into the channels of trade are as much business men as the few financial magnates who, in a back room, corner the money of the world. We come to speak for this broader class of business men.

. . . We do not come as aggressors. Our war is not a war of conquest; we are fighting in the defense of our homes, our families, and posterity. We have petitioned, and our petitions have been scorned; we have entreated, and our entreaties have been disregarded; we have begged, and they have mocked when our calamity came. We beg no longer; we entreat no more; we petition no more. We defy them. . . .

Let me call your attention to two or three important things. The gentleman from New York says that he will propose an amendment to the platform providing that the proposed change in our monetary system shall not affect contracts already made. Let me remind you that there is no intention of affecting those contracts which according to present laws are made payable in gold; but if he means to say that we cannot change our monetary system without protecting those who have loaned money before the change was made, I desire to ask him where, in law or in morals, he can find justification for not protecting the debtors when the act of 1873 was passed, if he now insists that we must protect the creditors. . . .

And now, my friends, let me come to the paramount issue. If they ask us why it is that we say more on the money question than we say upon the tariff question, I reply that, if protection has slain its thousands, the gold standard has slain its tens of thousands. If they ask us why we do not embody in our platform all the things that we believe in, we reply that when we have restored the money of the Constitution all other necessary reforms will be possible; but that until this is done there is no other reform that can be accomplished. . . .

Mr. Carlisle said in 1878 that this was a struggle between " the idle holders of idle capital " and " the struggling masses, who produce the wealth and pay the taxes of the country; " and, my friends, the question we are to decide is: Upon which side will the Democratic party fight; upon the side of " the idle holders of idle capital " or upon the side of " the struggling masses? " That is the question which the party must answer first, and then it must be answered by each individual hereafter.

The sympathies of the Democratic party, as shown by the platform, are on the side of the struggling masses who have ever been the foundation of the Democratic party.   There are two ideas of government.   There are those who believe that, if you will only legislate to make the well-to-do prosperous, their prosperity will leak through on those below.   The Democratic idea, however, has been that if you legislate to make the masses prosperous, their prosperity will find its way up through every class which rests upon them.

You come to us and tell us that the great cities are in favor of the gold standard ; we reply that the great cities rest upon our broad and fertile prairies.   Burn down your cities and leave our farms, and your cities will spring up again as if by magic ; but destroy our farms and the grass will grow in the streets of every city in the country.

My friends, we declare that this nation is able to legislate for its own people on every question, without waiting for the aid or consent of any other nation on earth ; and upon that issue we expect to carry every State in the Union.   I shall not slander the inhabitants of the fair State of Massachusetts nor the inhabitants of the State of New York by saying that, when they are confronted with the proposition, they will declare that this nation is not able to attend to its own business.   It is the issue of 1776 over again.   Our ancestors, when but three millions in number, had the courage to declare their political independence of every other nation ; shall we, their descendants, when we have grown to seventy millions, declare that we are less independent than our forefathers ? No, my friends, that will never be the verdict of our people.   Therefore, we care not upon what lines the battle is fought.   If they say bimetallism is good, but that we cannot have it until other nations help us, we reply that, instead of having a gold standard because England has, we will restore bimetallism, and then let England have bimetallism because the United States has it.   If they dare to come out in the open field and defend the gold standard as a good thing, we will fight them to the uttermost.   Having behind us the producing masses of this nation and the world, supported by the commercial interests, the laboring interests, and the toilers everywhere, we will answer their demand for a gold standard by saying to them : You shall not press down upon the brow of labor this crown of thorns, you shall not crucify mankind upon a cross of gold.

William J. Bryan, *The First Battle: A Story of the Campaign of 1896* (Chicago, [1896]), 200–206 *passim*.

172. The Gold-Standard Act (1900)

BY SECRETARY LYMAN JUDSON GAGE

Gage was a prominent banker in Chicago who in 1897 became secretary of the treasury in McKinley's cabinet. The chief issue in the presidential contest of 1896 was that of the monetary standard. The Republicans, advocating a single gold standard unless bimetallism should be adopted by international agreement, were successful, and the gold-standard law of 1900 was the outcome of their success. Secretary Gage took an active interest in the matter and was one of the chief promoters of the bill. The article from which this extract is taken is in the nature of a reply to an article written by Professor J. L. Laughlin, in the *Journal of Political Economy*, June, 1900. — Bibliography as in No. 168 above.

I AM satisfied that the new law establishes the gold standard beyond assault, unless it is deliberately violated. . . .

It is quite true that the legal tender quality has not been taken away from the silver and paper money of the United States. It would have been a remarkable and disquieting thing to do and it would have been quite as likely to weaken as to strengthen our monetary system. It makes no difference to anybody to-day whether he is paid in gold or silver, so long as the two metals circulate at par with each other and are received on deposit by the banks without discrimination. What difference would it make to me if I held some bonds and Mr. Bryan should direct his Secretary of the Treasury to sort out some of his limited stock of silver dollars for the purpose of redeeming the bonds? Would I not immediately deposit the silver in my bank and draw checks against it, just as I would if the Secretary had exercised the more rational policy of paying me with a Sub-Treasury check?

I believe that silver will never drop below par in gold? The crux of the proposition is that adequate measures have been taken by the new law to prevent such a contingency. . . .

The question is largely an academic one whether any provision is made for maintaining the parity of gold and silver beyond the provisions of previous laws, for the simple reason that methods were already in operation which maintained this parity under severe strain from the first coinage of the Bland dollars in 1878 down to the repeal of the silver purchase law in 1893 and have maintained such parity ever since. Prof. Laughlin understands the practical operation of these methods of redemption through the receipt of silver for public dues. This method will unquestionably prove adequate, upon the single condition that our mints are not opened to the free coinage of silver and no further considerable purchase or coinage of silver takes place. The facts of the situation and the experience of other countries with a considerable amount of silver coins plainly show that the suspension of free coinage and the receipt of the silver coins without discrimination for public dues are in themselves sufficient to maintain parity.

But I think Prof. Laughlin is mistaken in his criticism that no means whatever have been provided for maintaining the parity between gold and silver. He admits that the first section of the Act declares that " All forms of money issued or coined by the United States shall be maintained at a parity of value with this standard, and it shall be the duty of the Secretary of the Treasury to maintain such parity." He criticises this provision upon the ground that it gives absolutely nothing with which to maintain parity. . . .

It is to be regretted that the provision on this subject is not put in plainer language. I understand that it was urged upon the Conference Committee that this clause should read, " it shall be the duty of the Secretary of the Treasury to use all appropriate means to maintain such parity." This would have conveyed sweeping and complete authority to buy gold, sell bonds, or take any other steps in execution of a solemn duty imposed by Congress. But there is another provision of the bill which Prof. Laughlin seems to have disregarded. This is in section 2, providing for the gold reserve, where it is prescribed that when bonds are sold for the maintenance of the reserve the Secretary of the Treasury, after exchanging the gold for notes and depositing the latter in the general fund of the Treasury, " may, in his discretion, use said notes in exchange for gold, or to purchase or redeem any bonds of the United States, or for any other lawful purpose the public interest may require, except that they shall not be used to meet deficiencies in the current revenues." The declaration that notes may be used " for any lawful purpose," certainly includes the maintenance of parity between gold and silver, since it is distinctly made a legal obligation of the Secretary by the first section. If the Secretary of the Treasury, therefore, finds a considerable fund of redeemed notes in the general fund of the Treasury, and fears that silver will fall below parity with gold, he is able under this provision to pay for silver in United States notes which are redeemable in gold on demand. It seems to me this affords an important and almost perfect means of maintaining the parity of gold and silver. It amounts in substance to the ability of the holder of silver dollars to obtain gold notes for them, if the Secretary of the

Treasury, under the mandate laid upon him by law, finds it necessary to offer such notes in order to maintain the parity of silver.

But suppose that there were no notes in the general fund of the Treasury which could be used for this purpose? — if, in other words, there was no demand for gold by the presentation of United States notes, which had resulted in an accumulation of the latter — it is pretty plain that there would be no demand for the exchange of silver for gold. The entire body of the law on this subject is calculated for a period of distrust and demand for gold. If such a demand occurs it must fall upon the gold resources of the Government by the presentation of notes. The notes then become available for exchange for silver. If the criticism is made that this puts the notes afloat again in excessive quantities, it may be answered that the quantity of silver in circulation has been diminished, that a gold note has taken its place, and that if this note comes back for redemption in gold the Treasury is fully equipped by law for obtaining additional gold by the sale of bonds and holding the note until financial conditions have changed. . . .

Objection is made to the new law that it does not make the bonds of the United States redeemable in gold. That is true in a narrow sense. The new law, as finally enacted, does not change the contract between the Government and the holder of the bond, which was an agreement to pay coin. . . . I think that upon many grounds the conference committee acted wisely in refusing to make this change. It establishes a dangerous precedent to enact a retroactive law. . . . For those who prefer a gold bond Congress provided the means of obtaining it by offering the new two per cent bonds upon terms of conversion approaching the market value of the old bonds. . . . Nobody doubts that these bonds will be as good as gold, and it is wholly immaterial whether some Secretary of the Treasury pursues the infantile policy of paying silver dollars upon these bonds instead of checks, when as I have shown all money of the United States is convertible into gold. These are the distinct provisions of the new law and they cannot fail to maintain the gold standard except by the deliberate violation of the duty imposed by the law upon the Secretary of the Treasury.

Lyman J. Gage, *The Gold Standard Law*, in *Sound Currency*, July, 1900 (New York), VII, 113–115 *passim*.

CHAPTER XXIX — FOREIGN RELATIONS

173. Northeastern Fishery Question (1854–1887)

BY CHARLES BURKE ELLIOTT (1887)

Elliott is well known as a jurist, and as a lecturer on international law. Under the treaty of peace in 1783 the United States continued to exercise all the privileges of fishing off the Newfoundland coast which the states had possessed as colonies. The War of 1812 abrogated the right; and since 1818, except during periods covered by temporary treaties, the privileges have been such as were granted by a treaty ratified in that year, and the main controversies over the fisheries have been as to the interpretation of this treaty. After the period covered by this extract a treaty was framed, but it was rejected by the Senate in 1888; hence the international status is still based on the treaty of 1818. — Bibliography: C. B. Elliott, *The United States and the Northeastern Fisheries*, 135–144.

LORD ELDON [Elgin], Governor-General of Canada, evidently believing that the fishery controversy had now reached a point when it could with truth be called "a tender case," came to Washington in 1854 for the purpose of securing to Canadian fishermen that most desirable object — a Reciprocity Treaty. . . .

This treaty was signed by Secretary Marcy on the part of the United States and by Lord Eldon [Elgin] acting as Minister Plenipotentiary on the part of Great Britain.

By the First Article, "It is agreed by the high contracting parties, that, in addition to the liberty secured to the United States fishermen by the above mentioned Convention of October 20, 1818, of taking, curing, and drying fish on certain coasts of the British North American colonies therein defined, the inhabitants of the United States shall have, in common with the subjects of Her Britannic Majesty, the liberty to take fish of every kind, except shell fish, on the sea coasts and shores, and in the bays, harbors and creeks of Canada, New Brunswick, Nova Scotia, Prince Edward Island, and of the several islands thereunto adjacent, without being restricted to any distance from the shore ; with permission to land upon the coasts and shores of those colonies and the islands thereof, and also upon the Magdalen Islands, for the purpose of drying their nets and curing their fish ; *provided*, that, in so doing, they do not interfere with the rights of private property, or with British fishermen in the peaceable use of any part of the said coast in their occupancy for the same purpose."

By this treaty the American fishermen gained fishing rights analogous to those enjoyed under the treaty of 1783, while the Canadians obtained a market for their natural products free of duty.

Now commenced a period of unexampled prosperity for the Canadian fishery interests. The trade quadrupled and American fishermen were now received on the former inhospitable coasts with open arms. . . .

But the American fishermen were not satisfied with thus contributing so materially towards building up the business of their competitors at the expense of their own interests.

It soon became evident that the loss of revenue from the remission of duty on Canadian importations far exceeded the value of the fishing rights conceded to American fishermen. The Canadian fishermen by reason of their proximity to the fishing ground and the cheapness of labor and material for building boats were enabled to compete with the Americans to such an extent as to render their business unprofitable. The result was that in March, 1865, the treaty was terminated in pursuance of notice given by the United States one year before. . . .

On the 8th of January, 1870, the Governor-General of Canada issued an order "that henceforth all foreign fishermen shall be prevented from fishing in the waters of Canada." This was such a gross and palpable violation of the treaty [of 1818] then in force that, on May 31st, 1870, the Secretary of State called the attention of the British Minister to the illegal order and requested its modification. The negotiations thus commenced resulted in the fishery articles of the treaty of 1871, known as the treaty of Washington. By Article XVIII of this treaty, Article I of the Reciprocity Treaty of 1854 was revived with the stipulation that it should exist for a term of ten years and for two years after notice of its termination by either party. . . . By Article XXI it was agreed that for the term of years stated, " Fish oil and fish of all kinds (except fish of the inland lakes and of the rivers falling into them, and except fish preserved in oil,) being the produce of the fisheries of the United States or of the Dominion of Canada, or of Prince Edward's Island, shall be admitted into each country, respectively, free of duty."

During the negotiations that led to the Treaty of Washington, the United States offered one million of dollars for the inshore fisheries in perpetuity, not because they were of that value but in order to avoid future inconvenience and annoyance.

The British Government asserting that the privileges accorded to the citizens of the United States were of greater value than those accorded to the citizens of Great Britain, it was provided by Article XXII of the Treaty of Washington that a commission should be appointed to determine the value of these additional privileges, — "having regard to the privileges accorded by the United States to the subjects of Her Britannic Majesty." . . .

The award was not made until the 23rd of November, 1887 [1877], when, by a vote of two to one, the Commissioners decided that the United States was to pay five million five hundred thousand dollars for the use of the fishing privileges for twelve years. The decision produced profound astonishment in the United States. . . .

The customs receipts for the four full years from 1873 to 1877 showed that the United States had remitted duties on fish amounting to three hundred fifty thousand dollars a year, and that adding this to the award it was equivalent to almost ten million dollars for the use of the inshore fisheries for twelve years, while they were not worth more than twenty-five thousand dollars a year. Notwithstanding these facts the Committee recommended the payment of the award if Great Britain was willing to accept it.

On a motion to approve the report of the Committee, Senator Edmunds offered an amendment declaring that "Article XVIII and XXI of the Treaty between the United States and Great Britain concluded on the 8th of May, 1871, ought to be terminated at the earliest period consistent with the provisions of Article XXXIII of the same treaty." This was adopted and the money necessary to pay the award was appropriated. . . .

In pursuance of instructions from Congress the President gave the required notice of the desire of the United States to terminate the Fishery Articles of the Treaty of Washington, which consequently came to an end the 1st of July, 1885. . . .

During the season of 1886 the Canadian authorities pursued a course little adapted to lead to the end they so much desired, — a new reciprocity treaty. Notwithstanding the fact that the Government of the United States emphatically denied the applicability of local customs regulations to the case of the fishermen pursuing their occupation under the protection of the treaty of 1818, the Canadians persisted in enforcing their construction of the treaty with reckless and uncalled for severity ; even to the extent of refusing to sell articles of food to the captain of an American fishing vessel who had exhausted his supply by rendering assistance to the starving crew of a wrecked Canadian boat. Many American vessels were seized, warned, or molested in such manner as to break up their voyages and entail heavy loss upon the owners.

These seizures and the constant complaints of the fishermen led to an elaborate correspondence between the two governments. In order to justify their acts, the Canadian authorities resort to a very strict and literal interpretation of the language of the convention of 1818, and assume the power to enact legislation for the purpose of construing a contract entered into by the Imperial Government, " an assumption of jurisdiction entirely unwarranted and which is wholly denied by the United States." They also deny to the fishing vessels any commercial privileges, thus assuming the right to decide upon the efficacy of permits to " touch and trade," issued by properly qualified officials of the United States, on the ground that to allow fishing vessels to enter the harbors under such permits would in effect operate as a repeal of the restrictive clauses of the treaty.

The United States Government claims that the Treaty of 1818 related solely to the fishing rights of American vessels on the British North American coasts, and that it in no way affects their commercial rights ; that a vessel may be a fisher and yet be entitled to all the privileges of a trader, and that the language of the treaty should be liberally construed. . . .

The United States also claims for its fishermen the right to enter Canadian harbors for the purpose of selling and purchasing goods, procuring bait to be used in deep sea fishing, landing and trans-shipping fish, and, generally that each party should allow to the fishing vessels of the other such commercial privileges as are permitted her own shipping in the ports of the others. . . .

Admitting that the words " for no other purpose whatever " in the fishery clause of 1818, rebut the idea that commercial privileges were to be granted to the United States, as at that time Great Britain had closed all her colonial ports to foreign vessels by law, it is claimed that she opened them in the same way by the proclamation of 1830, and that they stand open until closed by law. " Since the proclamation (of 1830) the fishing vessels of Canada have enjoyed in the ports of the United States every privilege of commerce flowing from those proclamations.

Not only did Canada know this, but a perverse disposition has induced her, while continuing in their unrestricted use and enjoyment, to endeavor to deprive our fishermen of their similar rights in Canada."

In May, 1886, Congress gave to the President power to suspend commercial relations with Canada, in addition to the power possessed since 1823, of discriminating against foreign vessels in the ports of the United States. During the Second Session of the Forty-ninth Congress the indignation of the country found expression in two bills looking towards retaliation. The one introduced in the House of Representatives prohibited all commercial intercourse with Canada, by land or water.

The Senate would not agree to so radical a measure and proposed a bill intended to apply to that portion of our commerce with Canada carried on in Canadian vessels. This bill was the occasion of a debate in the Senate in which some of the Senators, notably Senator Ingalls, took advantage of the opportunity to refer to Great Britain in terms far from complimentary.

For several weeks the fishery question was the all-absorbing topic, and threats of war were freely made. The power thus vested in the President has not been exercised and negotiations have been continued looking to a settlement of the question by other means. . . .

The Canadian authorities have taken a position and seem inclined to defend to the end what they consider their rights. Their cruisers are guarding the fishery grounds, and collisions with the fishermen are liable to take place at any time. The United States has also sent a war vessel to the coast with instructions to watch over American interests.

What was practically the Senate bill passed both houses and received the President's approval on the 3rd of March, 1887.

The enforcement of the provisions of this so-called retaliatory law was left entirely in the discretion of the President, but as the administration was pledged to the British Government to attempt to solve the questions by means of another Joint Commission, the President has not seen fit to infuse life into it. The British statesmen continued to urge the plan of a Commission until success again crowned their efforts and a new Fishery Commission is announced to meet in Washington in the near future. It is to be hoped that its labors, should they receive the sanction of the Senate will prove less prejudicial to the interests of the United States, than those of its predecessor.

Charles B. Elliott, *The United States and the Northeastern Fisheries* (Minneapolis, 1887), 74-100 *passim.*

174. Purchase of Alaska (1867)

BY SENATOR CHARLES SUMNER

Sumner was at this time chairman of the Senate Committee on Foreign Relations. He presented the treaty to the Senate, and in executive session made a very elaborate speech, giving in detail a description of the character and value of Alaska. Later he wrote out his speech for publication; this extract is taken from the oration in that form. — For Sumner, see No. 146 above. — Bibliography: H. H. Bancroft, *History of the Pacific States*, XXVIII, xxiii–xxxviii.

1. *ADVANTAGES to the Pacific Coast.* — Foremost in order, if not in importance, I put the desires of our fellow-citizens on the Pacific coast, and the special advantages they will derive from this enlargement of boundary. They were the first to ask for it, and will be the first to profit by it. . . .

These well-known desires were founded, of course, on supposed advantages; and here experience and neighborhood were prompters. Since 1854 the people of California have received their ice from the fresh-water lakes in the island of Kadiak, not far westward from Mount St. Elias. Later still, their fishermen have searched the waters about the Aleutians and the Shumagins, commencing a promising fishery. Others have proposed to substitute themselves for the Hudson's Bay Company in their franchise on the coast. But all are looking to the Orient, as in the time of Columbus, although like him they sail to the west. To them China and Japan, those ancient realms of fabulous wealth, are the Indies. . . .

The absence of harbors belonging to the United States on the Pacific limits the outlets of the country. On that whole extent, from Panama to Puget Sound, the only harbor of any considerable value is San Francisco. Further north the harbors are abundant, and they are all nearer to the great marts of Japan and China. But San Francisco itself will be nearer by the way of the Aleutians than by Honolulu. . . .

The advantages to the Pacific coast have two aspects, — one domestic, and the other foreign. Not only does the treaty extend the coasting trade of California, Oregon, and Washington Territory northward, but it also extends the base of commerce with China and Japan.

To unite the East of Asia with the West of America is the aspiration of commerce now as when the English navigator recorded his voyage. Of course, whatever helps this result is an advantage. The Pacific Railroad is such an advantage; for, though running westward, it will be, when completed, a new highway to the East. This treaty is another advantage ; for nothing can be clearer than that the western coast must exercise an attraction which will be felt in China and Japan just in proportion as it is occupied by a commercial people communicating readily with the Atlantic and with Europe. This cannot be without consequences not less important politically than commercially. Owing so much to the Union, the people there will be bound to it anew, and the national unity will receive another confirmation. Thus the whole country will be a gainer. So are we knit together that the advantages to the Pacific coast will contribute to the general welfare.

2. *Extension of Dominion.* — The extension of dominion is another consideration calculated to captivate the public mind. . . .

The passion for acquisition, so strong in the individual, is not less strong in the community. A nation seeks an outlying territory, as an individual seeks an outlying farm. . . . It is common to the human family. There are few anywhere who could hear of a considerable accession of territory, obtained peacefully and honestly, without a pride of country, even if at certain moments the judgment hesitated. With increased size on the map there is increased consciousness of strength, and the heart of the citizen throbs anew as he traces the extending line.

3. *Extension of Republican Institutions.* — More than the extension of dominion is the extension of republican institutions, which is a traditional aspiration. . . .

John Adams, in the preface to his Defence of the American Constitutions . . . thus for a moment lifts the curtain : " Thirteen governments," he says plainly, " thus founded on the natural authority of the people alone, without a pretence of miracle or mystery, and *which are destined to spread over the northern part of that whole quarter of the globe,* are a great point gained in favor of the rights of mankind." . . .

By the text of our Constitution, the United States are bound to guaranty "a republican form of government" to every State in the Union ; but this obligation, which is applicable only at home, is an unquestionable indication of the national aspiration everywhere. The Republic is something more than a local policy ; it is a general principle, not to be forgotten at any time, especially when the opportunity is presented of bringing an immense region within its influence. . . .

The present treaty is a visible step in the occupation of the whole North American continent. As such it will be recognized by the world and accepted by the American people. But the treaty involves some-

thing more. We dismiss one other monarch from the continent. One
by one they have retired, — first France, then Spain, then France again,
and now Russia, — all giving way to the absorbing Unity declared in
the national motto, *E pluribus unum.*

4. *Anticipation of Great Britain.* — Another motive to this acquisition may be found in the desire to anticipate imagined schemes or
necessities of Great Britain. With regard to all these I confess doubt ;
and yet, if we credit report, it would seem as if there were already a
British movement in this direction. . . .

5. *Amity of Russia.* — There is still another consideration concerning this treaty not to be disregarded. It attests and assures the amity
of Russia. Even if you doubt the value of these possessions, the treaty
is a sign of friendship. It is a new expression of that *entente cordiale*
between the two powers which is a phenomenon of history. Though
unlike in institutions, they are not unlike in recent experience. Sharers
of common glory in a great act of Emancipation, they also share together
the opposition or antipathy of other nations. Perhaps this experience
has not been without effect in bringing them together. At all events,
no coldness or unkindness has interfered at any time with their good
relations.

. . . The Rebellion, which tempted so many other powers into its
embrace, could not draw Russia from her habitual good-will. Her
solicitude for the Union was early declared. She made no unjustifiable
concession of *ocean belligerence,* with all its immunities and powers, to
Rebels in arms against the Union. She furnished no hospitality to Rebel
cruisers, nor was any Rebel agent ever received, entertained, or encouraged at St. Petersburg, — while, on the other hand, there was an understanding that the United States should be at liberty to carry prizes into
Russian ports. So natural and easy were the relations between the two
Governments, that such complaints as incidentally arose on either side
were amicably adjusted by verbal explanations without written controversy. . . .

In relations such as I have described, the cession of territory seems
a natural transaction, entirely in harmony with the past. It remains to
hope that it may be a new link in an amity which, without effort, has
overcome differences of institutions and intervening space on the
globe. . . .

At all events, now that the treaty has been signed by plenipotentiaries
on each side duly empowered, it is difficult to see how we can refuse to

complete the purchase without putting to hazard the friendly relations which happily subsist between the United States and Russia. The overtures originally proceeded from us. After a delay of years, and other intervening propositions, the bargain was at length concluded. It is with nations as with individuals. A bargain once made must be kept. Even if still open to consideration, it must not be lightly abandoned. I am satisfied that the dishonoring of this treaty, after what has passed, would be a serious responsibility for our country. As an international question, it would be tried by the public opinion of the world ; and there are many who, not appreciating the requirement of our Constitution by which a treaty must have " the advice and consent of the Senate," would regard its rejection as bad faith. There would be jeers at us, and jeers at Russia also : at us for levity in making overtures, and at Russia for levity in yielding to them. . . .

Charles Sumner, *Works* (Boston, 1875), XI, 216–232 *passim*.

---

175. The Geneva Award (1872)

BY THE ARBITRATORS

In 1871 a treaty was signed submitting to arbitration the claims of the United States against Great Britain arising out of depredations committed during the Civil War on the commerce and merchant vessels of the United States by the Alabama and other cruisers fitted out in Great Britain. There were five arbitrators, three of them foreign, one appointed by Great Britain, and one by the United States. The British arbitrator, Sir Alexander Cockburn, refused to sign the award. — Bibliography : J. B. Moore, *History and Digest of International Arbitrations*, I, lxxxiii–xcviii.

THE United States of America and Her Britannic Majesty having agreed by Article I of the treaty concluded and signed at Washington the 8th of May, 1871, to refer all the claims " generically known as the Alabama claims " to a tribunal of arbitration . . .

And the five arbitrators . . . having assembled at Geneva . . . on the 15th of December, 1871 . . .

The agents named by each of the high contracting parties . . . then delivered to each of the arbitrators the printed case prepared by each of the two parties, accompanied by the documents, the official correspondence, and other evidence on which each relied, in conformity with the terms of the third article of the said treaty. . . .

The tribunal, in accordance with the vote of adjournment passed at their second session, held on the 16th of December, 1871, re-assembled at Geneva on the 15th of June, 1872 ; and the agent of each of the parties duly delivered to each of the arbitrators, and to the agent of the other party, the printed argument referred to in Article V of the said treaty.

The tribunal having since fully taken into their consideration the treaty, and also the cases, counter-cases, documents, evidence, and arguments, and likewise all other communications made to them by the two parties during the progress of their sittings, and having impartially and carefully examined the same,

Has arrived at the decision embodied in the present award :

Whereas, having regard to the VIth and VIIth articles of the said treaty, the arbitrators are bound under the terms of the said VIth article, " in deciding the matters submitted to them, to be governed by the three rules therein specified and by such principles of international law, not inconsistent therewith, as the arbitrators shall determine to have been applicable to the case ; "

[" RULES. — A neutral Government is bound —

"First, to use due diligence to prevent the fitting out, arming, or equipping, within its jurisdiction, of any vessel which it has reasonable ground to believe is intended to cruise or to carry on war against a Power with which it is at peace ; and also to use like diligence to prevent the departure from its jurisdiction of any vessel intended to cruise or carry on war as above, such vessel having been specially adapted, in whole or in part, within such jurisdiction, to warlike use.

"Secondly, not to permit or suffer either belligerent to make use of its ports or waters as the base of naval operations against the other, or for the purpose of the renewal or augmentation of military supplies or arms, or the recruitment of men.

"Thirdly, to exercise due diligence in its own ports and waters, and, as to all persons within its jurisdiction, to prevent any violation of the foregoing obligations and duties."]

And whereas the " due diligence " referred to in the first and third of the said rules ought to be exercised by neutral governments in exact proportion to the risks to which either of the belligerents may be exposed, from a failure to fulfil the obligations of neutrality on their part ;

And whereas the circumstances out of which the facts constituting the subject-matter of the present controversy arose were of a nature to call for the exercise on the part of Her Britannic Majesty's government of all possible solicitude for the observance of the rights and the duties involved in the proclamation of neutrality issued by Her Majesty on the 13th day of May, 1861 ;

And whereas the effects of a violation of neutrality committed by means of the construction, equipment, and armament of a vessel are not done away with by any commission which the government of the belligerent power, benefited by the violation of neutrality, may afterwards have granted to that vessel ; and the ultimate step, by which the offense is completed, cannot be admissible as a ground for the absolution of the offender, nor can the consummation of his fraud become the means of establishing his innocence ;

And whereas the privilege of exterritoriality accorded to vessels of war has been admitted into the law of nations, not as an absolute right, but solely as a proceeding founded on the principle of courtesy and mutual deference between different nations, and therefore can never be appealed to for the protection of acts done in violation of neutrality ;

And whereas the absence of a previous notice cannot be regarded as a failure in any consideration required by the law of nations, in those cases in which a vessel carries with it its own condemnation ;

And whereas, in order to impart to any supplies of coal a character inconsistent with the second rule, prohibiting the use of neutral ports or waters, as a base of naval operations for a belligerent, it is necessary that the said supplies should be connected with special circumstances of time, of persons, or of place, which may combine to give them such character ;

And whereas, with respect to the vessel called the Alabama, it clearly results from all the facts relative to the construction of the ship at first designated by the number " 290 " in the port of Liverpool, and its equipment and armament in the vicinity of Terceira through the agency of the vessels called the " Agrippina " and the " Bahama," dispatched from Great Britain to that end, that the British government failed to use due diligence in the performance of its neutral obligations ; and especially that it omitted, notwithstanding the warnings and official representations made by the diplomatic agents of the United States during the construction of the said number " 290," to take in due time any effective measures of prevention, and that those orders which it did give at last, for the detention of the vessel, were issued so late that their execution was not practicable ;

And whereas, after the escape of that vessel, the measures taken for its pursuit and arrest were so imperfect as to lead to no result, and therefore cannot be considered sufficient to release Great Britain from the responsibility already incurred ;

And whereas, in despite of the violations of the neutrality of Great Britain committed by the " 290," this same vessel, later known as the confederate cruiser Alabama, was on several occasions freely admitted into the ports of colonies of Great Britain, instead of being proceeded against as it ought to have been in any and every port within British jurisdiction in which it might have been found ;

And whereas the government of Her Britannic Majesty cannot justify itself for a failure in due diligence on the plea of insufficiency of the legal means of action which it possessed :

Four of the arbitrators, for the reasons above assigned, and the fifth for reasons separately assigned by him,

Are of opinion —

That Great Britain has in this case failed, by omission, to fulfill the duties prescribed in the first and the third of the rules established by the VIth article of the treaty of Washington.

And whereas, with respect to the vessel called the " Florida," it results from all the facts relative to the construction of the " Oreto " in the port of Liverpool, and to its issue therefrom, which facts failed to induce the authorities in Great Britain to resort to measures adequate to prevent the violation of the neutrality of that nation, notwithstanding the warnings and repeated representations of the agents of the United States, that Her Majesty's government has failed to use due diligence to fulfil the duties of neutrality ;

And whereas it likewise results from all the facts relative to the stay of the " Oreto " at Nassau, to her issue from that port, to her enlistment of men, to her supplies, and to her armament, with the co-operation of the British vessel " Prince Alfred," at Green Cay, that there was negligence on the part of the British colonial authorities ;

And whereas, notwithstanding the violation of the neutrality of Great Britain committed by the Oreto, this same vessel, later known as the confederate cruiser Florida, was nevertheless on several occasions freely admitted into the ports of British colonies ;

And whereas the judicial acquittal of the Oreto at Nassau cannot relieve Great Britain from the responsibility incurred by her under the principles of international law ; nor can the fact of the entry of the

Florida into the confederate port of Mobile, and of its stay there during four months, extinguish the responsibility previously to that time incurred by Great Britain :

For these reasons,

The tribunal, by a majority of four voices to one, is of opinion —

That Great Britain has in this case failed, by omission, to fulfil the duties prescribed in the first, in the second, and in the third of the rules established by Article VI of the treaty of Washington.

And whereas, with respect to the vessel called the "Shenandoah," it results from all the facts relative to the departure from London of the merchant-vessel the "Sea King," and to the transformation of that ship into a confederate cruiser under the name of the Shenandoah, near the island of Madeira, that the government of Her Britannic Majesty is not chargeable with any failure, down to that date, in the use of due diligence to fulfil the duties of neutrality ;

But whereas it results from all the facts connected with the stay of the Shenandoah at Melbourne, and especially with the augmentation which the British government itself admits to have been clandestinely effected of her force, by the enlistment of men within that port, that there was negligence on the part of the authorities at that place :

For these reasons,

The tribunal is unanimously of opinion —

That Great Britain has not failed, by any act or omission, "to fulfil any of the duties prescribed by the three rules of Article VI in the treaty of Washington, or by the principles of international law not inconsistent therewith," in respect to the vessel called the Shenandoah during the period of time anterior to her entry into the port of Melbourne ;

And, by a majority of three to two voices, the tribunal decides that Great Britain has failed, by omission, to fulfil the duties prescribed by the second and third of the rules aforesaid, in the case of this same vessel, from and after her entry into Hobson's Bay, and is therefore responsible for all acts committed by that vessel after her departure from Melbourne, on the 18th day of February, 1865.

And so far as relates to the vessels called —

The Tuscaloosa, (tender to the Alabama,)

The Clarence,

The Tacony, and

The Archer, (tenders to the Florida,)

The tribunal is unanimously of opinion —

That such tenders or auxiliary vessels, being properly regarded as accessories, must necessarily follow the lot of their principals, and be submitted to the same decision which applies to them respectively.

And so far as relates to the vessel called " Retribution,"

The tribunal, by a majority of three to two voices, is of opinion —

That Great Britain has not failed by any act or omission to fulfil any of the duties prescribed by the three rules of Article VI in the treaty of Washington, or by the principles of international law not inconsistent therewith.

And so far as relates to the vessels called —

The Georgia,

The Sumter,

The Nashville,

The Tallahasse, and

The Chickamauga, respectively,

The tribunal is unanimously of opinion —

That Great Britain has not failed, by any act or omission, to fulfil any of the duties prescribed by the three rules of Article VI in the treaty of Washington, or by the principles of international law not inconsistent therewith.

And so far as relates to the vessels called —

The Sallie,

The Jefferson Davis,

The Music,

The Boston, and

The V. H. Joy, respectively,

The tribunal is unanimously of opinion —

That they ought to be excluded from consideration for want of evidence.

And whereas, so far as relates to the particulars of the indemnity claimed by the United States, the costs of pursuit of the confederate cruisers are not, in the judgment of the tribunal, properly distinguishable from the general expenses of the war carried on by the United States :

The tribunal is, therefore, of opinion, by a majority of three to two voices —

That there is no ground for awarding to the United States any sum by way of indemnity under this head.

And whereas prospective earnings cannot properly be made the subject of compensation, inasmuch as they depend in their nature upon future and uncertain contingencies :

The tribunal is unanimously of opinion —

That there is no ground for awarding to the United States any sum by way of indemnity under this head.

And whereas, in order to arrive at an equitable compensation for the damages which have been sustained, it is necessary to set aside all double claims for the same losses, and all claims for " gross freights," so far as they exceed " net freights ; "

And whereas it is just and reasonable to allow interest at a reasonable rate ;

And whereas, in accordance with the spirit and letter of the treaty of Washington, it is preferable to adopt the form of adjudication of a sum in gross, rather than to refer the subject of compensation for further discussion and deliberation to a board of assessors, as provided by Article X of the said treaty :

The tribunal, making use of the authority conferred upon it by Article VII of the said treaty, by a majority of four voices to one, awards to the United States a sum of $15,500,000 in gold, as the indemnity to be paid by Great Britain to the United States, for the satisfaction of all the claims referred to the consideration of the tribunal, conformably to the provisions contained in Article VII of the aforesaid treaty.

And, in accordance with the terms of Article XI of the said treaty, the tribunal declares that " all the claims referred to in the treaty as submitted to the tribunal are hereby fully, perfectly, and finally settled."

Furthermore it declares, that " each and every one of the said claims, whether the same may or may not have been presented to the notice of, or made, preferred, or laid before the tribunal, shall henceforth be considered and treated as finally settled, barred, and inadmissible." . . .

Made and concluded at the Hôtel de Ville of Geneva, in Switzerland, the 14th day of the month of September, in the year of our Lord one thousand eight hundred and seventy-two.

CHARLES FRANCIS ADAMS.
FREDERICK SCLOPIS.
STÄMPFLI.
VICOMTE D'ITAJUBÁ.

House Executive Documents, 42 Cong., 3 sess. (Washington, 1873), I, pt. ii, No. 1, pt. 1, p. 14; I, pt. v, No. 1, pt. 1, pp. 49–54 *passim.*

176. Proposed Intervention in Cuba (1875)

BY SECRETARY HAMILTON FISH

Fish was United States senator for one term before the Civil War; he was secretary of state during both of Grant's administrations, playing an important part in negotiating the Treaty of Washington and in discussing with Spain the questions arising from the insurrection then in progress in Cuba. Diplomatic negotiations with Spain concerning Cuba began soon after the United States had acknowledged the independence of the South and Central American States; and these questions were repeatedly revived until they finally culminated, in 1898, in war between the two nations. This extract is from an official letter to Caleb Cushing, minister to Spain. — Bibliography: A. P. C. Griffin, *List of Books relating to Cuba* (Senate Document, 55 Cong., 2 sess., No. 161). — For other articles on American interests in Cuba, see *Contemporaries*, III, No. 149; below, ch. xxx and No. 189.

A T the time of your departure for Madrid, apart from the general question of the unsatisfactory condition of affairs in Cuba and the failure to suppress the revolution, several prominent questions remained unadjusted, the settlement of which was deemed necessary before any satisfactory relations with Spain could be established or maintained. Upon all of these you were instructed.

The most prominent among them were the questions arising from the embargo and confiscation of estates of American citizens in Cuba; those relating to the trial of American citizens in that island, in violation of treaty obligations, and the claims arising out of the capture of the Virginius, including the trial and punishment of General Burriel.

After the expiration of more than eighteen months, it seems advisable to examine what progress has been made and to consider our present relations with Spain. . . .

. . . the promises made and repeated, the assurances given from time to time that something should be done, the admission of the justice of the demands of this country, at least to the extent of expressing regret for these wrongs and promising redress, followed as they have been by absolutely no performance and no practical steps whatever towards performance, need no extended comment.

In the cases of embargo and confiscation, not only have wrongs been long since done, but continuing and repeated wrongs are daily inflicted. . . .

Turning to the questions which arose from the capture of the Virginius, and the executions which followed, no extended reference is required.

The particulars of the delivery of the vessel to this Government, and the payment to both Great Britain and the United States of considerable sums as compensation for the acts of the authorities in ordering the execution of fifty-three of the passengers and crew under circumstances of peculiar brutality, have passed into history.

So far as a payment of money can atone for the execution of these unprotected prisoners, that has been accomplished.

The higher and more imperative duty which the government of Spain assumed by the protocol of November 29, 1873, namely, to bring to justice General Burriel and the other principal offenders in this tragedy, has been evaded and entirely neglected. . . .

Having touched on these particular questions which have lately been prominent as disturbing causes with Spain, it is necessary to also refer to the general condition of affairs in Cuba as affecting our relations with the mother country.

In my No. 2, of February 6, 1874, (the first instruction addressed to you on general matters pertaining to your mission,) I referred at length to the views entertained by the President and to the position of this Government.

It was then more than five years since an organized insurrection had broken out which the government of Spain had been entirely unable to suppress. . . .

Almost two years have passed since those instructions were issued . . . and it would appear that the situation has in no respect improved.

The horrors of war have in no perceptible measure abated ; the inconveniences and injuries which we then suffered have remained, and others have been added ; the ravages of war have touched new parts of the island, and well-nigh ruined its financial and agricultural system and its relations to the commerce of the world.   No effective steps have been taken to establish reforms or remedy abuses, and the effort to suppress the insurrection, by force alone, has been a complete failure. . . .

The United States purchases more largely than any other people of the productions of the island of Cuba, and therefore, more than any other for this reason, and still more by reason of its immediate neighborhood, is interested in the arrest of a system of wanton destruction which disgraces the age and affects every commercial people on the face of the globe.

Under these circumstances, and in view of the fact that Spain has rejected all suggestions of reform or offers of mediation made by this

Government, and has refused all measures looking to a reconciliation, except on terms which make reconciliation an impossibility, the difficulty of the situation becomes increased.

When, however, in addition to these general causes of difficulty, we find the Spanish government neglectful also of the obligations of treaties and solemn compacts, and unwilling to afford any redress for long-continued and well-founded wrongs suffered by our citizens, it becomes a serious question how long such a condition of things can or should be allowed to exist, and compels us to inquire whether the point has not been reached where longer endurance ceases to be possible.

During all this time, and under these aggravated circumstances, this Government has not failed to perform her obligations to Spain as scrupulously as toward other nations. . . .

It will be apparent that such a state of things cannot continue. It is absolutely necessary to the maintenance of our relations with Spain, even on their present footing, that our just demands for the return to citizens of the United States of their estates in Cuba, unincumbered, and for securing to them a trial for offenses according to treaty provisions and all other rights guaranteed by treaty and by public law, should be complied with. . . .

Moreover, apart from these particular questions, in the opinion of the President, the time has arrived when the interests of this country, the preservation of its commerce, and the instincts of humanity alike demand that some speedy and satisfactory ending be made of the strife that is devastating Cuba. . . .

The contest and disorder in Cuba affect the United States directly and injuriously by the presence in this country of partisans of the revolt who have fled hither (in consequence of the proximity of territory) as to a political asylum, and who, by their plottings, are disturbers of the public peace.

The United States has exerted itself to the utmost, for seven years, to repress unlawful acts on the part of these self-exiled subjects of Spain, relying on the promise of Spain to pacify the island. Seven years of strain on the powers of this Government to fulfill all that the most exacting demands of one government can make, under any doctrine or claim of international obligation, upon another, have not witnessed the much hoped for pacification. The United States feels itself entitled to be relieved of this strain.

The severe measures, injurious to the United States and often in conflict with public law, which the colonial officers have taken to subdue the insurrection; the indifference, and ofttimes the offensive assaults upon the just susceptibilities of the people of the United States and their Government, which have characterized that portion of the peninsular population of Havana which has sustained and upheld, if it has not controlled, successive governors-general, and which have led to the disregard of orders and decrees which the more enlarged wisdom and the more friendly councils of the home government had enacted; the cruelty and inhumanity which have characterized the contest, both on the part of the colonial government and of the revolt, for seven years, and the destruction of valuable properties and industries by arson and pillage, which Spain appears unable, however desirous, to prevent and stop, in an island three thousand miles distant from her shores, but lying within sight of our coast, with which trade and constant intercourse are unavoidable, are causes of annoyance and of injury to the United States, which a people cannot be expected to tolerate without the assured prospect of their termination.

The United States has more than once been solicited by the insurgents to extend to them its aid, but has for years hitherto resisted such solicitation, and has endeavored by the tender of its good offices, in the way of mediation, advice, and remonstrance, to bring to an end a great evil, which has pressed sorely upon the interests both of the Government and of the people of the United States, as also upon the commercial interests of other nations. . . .

The President hopes that Spain may spontaneously adopt measures looking to a reconciliation, and to the speedy restoration of peace, and the organization of a stable and satisfactory system of government in the island of Cuba.

In the absence of any prospect of a termination of the war, or of any change in the manner in which it has been conducted on either side, he feels that the time is at hand when it may be the duty of other governments to intervene, solely with the view of bringing to an end a disastrous and destructive conflict, and of restoring peace in the island of Cuba. No government is more deeply interested in the order and peaceful administration of this island than is that of the United States, and none has suffered as has the United States from the condition which has obtained there during the past six or seven years. He will, therefore, feel it his duty at an early day to submit the subject in this light, and accompanied by an expression of the views above presented, for the consideration of Congress. . . .

It is believed to be a just and friendly act to frankly communicate this conclusion to the Spanish government.

You will, therefore, take an early occasion thus to inform that government.

House Executive Documents, 44 Cong., 1 sess. (Washington, 1876), XII, No. 90, pp. 3–11 *passim*.

---

177. Relations to Latin-America (1881)

BY SECRETARY JAMES GILLESPIE BLAINE

Blaine was secretary of state in Garfield's cabinet, and for a few months in Arthur's also. His foreign policy was much criticised, especially for its tendency to dictate to the South American nations. His policy of intervention in the Chileno-Peruvian War was reversed by his successor in office. This extract is from an official letter to H. J. Kilpatrick, minister to Chili. — For Blaine, see No. 160 above. — Bibliography as in No. 179 below.

. . . THE unfortunate condition of the relations between Chili and Peru makes the mission upon the duties of which you are now entering one of grave responsibility and great delicacy. Difficult as would be any intervention of the United States under ordinary circumstances, our position is further embarrassed by the failure of the conference at Arica, undertaken at our suggestion. It is evident from the protocols of that conference that Chili was prepared to dictate and not to discuss terms of peace, and that the arbitration of the United States upon any questions of difference with the allied powers of Peru and Bolivia was not acceptable and would not be accepted by the Chilian Government. Since that time the war has closed in the complete success of Chili, and in what can scarcely be considered less than the conquest of Peru and Bolivia.

This government cannot therefore anticipate that the offer of friendly intervention in the settlement of the very serious questions now pending would be agreeable to the Government of Chili. It would scarcely comport with self-respect that such an offer should be refused, and it would be of no benefit to Peru and Bolivia that it should be offered and declined. But I am sure the Chilian Government will appreciate the natural and deep interest which the United States feels in the termination of a condition so calamitous in its consequences to the best interests of all the South American republics. It should also know that if at any time the interposition of the good offices of this government can contribute to the restoration of friendly relations between the belligerent powers, they will, upon proper intimation, be promptly offered.

While, therefore, no instructions are given you to tender officially any advice to the Government of Chili which is unsought, you will, on such opportunity as may occur, govern your conduct and representations by the considerations to which I shall now call your attention.

Without entering upon any discussion as to the causes of the late war between Chili on the one side and Peru and Bolivia on the other, this government recognizes the right which the successful conduct of that war has conferred upon Chili ; and, in doing so, I will not undertake to estimate the extent to which the Chilian Government has the right to carry its calculations of the indemnities to which it is entitled, nor the security for the future, which its interests may seem to require. But if the Chilian Government, as its representatives have declared, seeks only a guarantee of future peace, it would seem natural that Peru and Bolivia should be allowed to offer such indemnity and guarantee before the annexation of territory, which is the right of conquest, is insisted upon. If these powers fail to offer what is a reasonably sufficient indemnity and guarantee, then it becomes a fair subject of consideration whether such territory may not be exacted as the necessary price of peace.

But at the conclusion of a war avowedly not of conquest, but for the solution of differences which diplomacy had failed to settle, to make the acquisition of territory a *sine qua non* of peace is calculated to cast suspicions on the professions with which war was originally declared. . . . At this day, when the right of the people to govern themselves, the fundamental basis of republican institutions, is so widely recognized, there is nothing more difficult or more dangerous than the forced transfer of territory, carrying with it an indignant and hostile population ; and nothing but a necessity proven before the world can justify it. It is not a case in which the power desiring the territory can be accepted as a safe or impartial judge.

While the United States Government does not pretend to express an opinion whether or not such an annexation of territory is a necessary consequence of this war, it believes that it would be more honorable to the Chilian Government, more conducive to the security of a permanent peace, and more in consonance with those principles which are professed by all the republics of America, that such territorial changes should be avoided as far as possible ; that they should never be the result of mere force, but, if necessary, should be decided and tempered by full and equal discussion between all the powers whose people and whose national interests are involved.

At the present moment, the completeness of the victory of Chili seems to render such a diplomatic discussion impossible. The result of the conflict has been not only the defeat of the allied armies, but the dissolution of all responsible government in Peru. . . .

An effort, and apparently a very earnest and honest one, has been made to create a provisional government, which shall gradually restore order and the reign of law. But it is obvious that for such a government to succeed in obtaining the confidence either of its own people or foreign powers, it must be allowed a freedom and force of action which cannot be exercised while Chili holds absolute possession and governs by military authority. This government, therefore, has been glad to learn from its minister in Chili, whom you succeed, that the Chilian authorities have decided to give their support to the efforts of Señor Calderon to establish on a steady footing a provisional government in Peru.

You will, as far as you can do so with propriety and without officious intrusion, approve and encourage this disposition on the part of the Chilian Government, and this Department will be exceedingly gratified if your influence as the representative of the United States shall be instrumental in inducing the Government of Chili to give its aid and support to the restoration of regular, constitutional government in Peru, and to postpone the final settlement of all questions of territorial annexation to the diplomatic negotiations which can then be resumed with the certainty of a just, friendly, and satisfactory conclusion.

In any representation which you may make, you will say that the hope of the United States is that the negotiations for peace shall be conducted, and the final settlement between the two countries determined, without either side invoking the aid or intervention of any European power.

The Government of the United States seeks only to perform the part of a friend to all the parties in this unhappy conflict between South American republics, and it will regret to be compelled to consider how far that feeling might be affected, and a more active interposition forced upon it, by any attempted complication of this question with European politics.

House Executive Documents, 47 Cong., 1 sess. (Washington, 1882), I, No. 1, pt. 1, pp. 131–133 *passim*.

178. Bering Sea Arbitration (1893)

BY PRESIDENT BARON ALPHONSE DE COURCEL, JAMES LORD HANNEN, AND SENATOR JOHN TYLER MORGAN

In 1892 Great Britain and the United States submitted to arbitration the question as to the jurisdictional rights of the United States in the waters of Bering Sea, especially her right to regulate or prohibit pelagic sealing. The treaty further provided that, in case the award was against the claims of the United States, the arbitrators should decide upon a set of concurrent regulations for the protection and preservation of the fur seals resorting to Bering Sea; and the two nations agreed to coöperate in securing the adhesion of other powers to such regulations. The award was against the claims of the United States; regulations were drawn up and included in it, but they proved ineffectual. This extract is taken from the speeches of the arbitrators at the time of the presentation of the award. — Bibliography as in No. 175 above.

[Baron Courcel.] GENTLEMEN : Now we have come to the end of our task. We have done our best to accomplish it, without concealing from ourselves the difficulties which complicated it, nor the heavy responsibilities which it has imposed upon us. Selected from various nationalities, we have not considered ourselves the representatives of any one in particular, nor of any government or any human power, but, solely guided by our conscience and our reason, we have wished only to act as one of those councils of wise men, whose duties were so carefully defined by the old capitularies of France.

To assist us, we have had at our disposition a library of documents, compiled with extreme care, and in order that we might not lose our way among so many sources of information, men holding a high rank among the most learned jurists and eloquent orators of which the Old or New Worlds could boast have been willing so liberally to bestow upon us their advice.

During weeks and months our labors have been prolonged, and it constantly appeared that some new matter had risen before us and that some new problem pressed upon our attention.

To-day . . . we are assembled to inform you of the result of our labors, hoping with all our hearts that they may be profitable to man, and conformable to the designs of Him who rules his destiny. . . .

We have felt obliged to maintain intact the fundamental principles of that august law of nations, which extends itself like the vault of heaven above all countries, and which borrows the laws of nature herself to protect the peoples of the earth, one against another, by inculcating in them the dictates of mutual good will.

In the regulations which we were charged to draw up we have had to decide between conflicting rights and interests which it was difficult to reconcile.   The Governments of the United States of America and Great Britain have promised to accept and execute our decisions.   Our desire is that this voluntary engagement may not cause regret to either of them, though we have required of both sacrifices which they may, perhaps, regard as serious.   This part of our work inaugurates great innovation.

Hitherto, the nations were agreed to leave out of special legislation the vast domain of the seas, as in times of old, according to the poets, the earth itself was common to all men, who gathered its fruits at their will, without limitation or control.   You know that even to-day, dreamers believe it possible to bring back humanity to that golden age.   The sea, however, like the earth, has become small for men, who, like the hero, Alexander, and no less ardent for labor than he was for glory, feel confined in a world too narrow.   Our work is a first attempt at a sharing of the products of the ocean, which has hitherto been undivided, and at applying a rule to things which escaped every other law but that of the first occupant.   If this attempt succeeds, it will doubtless be followed by numerous imitations, until the entire planet, until the waters as well as the continents will have become the subject of a careful partition.   Then, perhaps, the conception of property may change amongst men. . . .

[Lord Hannen.] . . .   Mr. de Courcel, I have to discharge a duty which gives me peculiar satisfaction.   I have to express to you our high appreciation of the manner in which you have presided over our deliberations.   The public has had the opportunity of witnessing the sagacity, the learning, and the courtesy with which you have guided the proceedings during the arguments.   Your colleagues only can know how greatly those qualities have assisted us in our private conferences.   Let me add, that our intimate relations with you have taught us to regard you with the warmest esteem and affection.   Permit me to say that you have won in each of us an attached friend.

I must not conclude without an allusion to the remarkable occasion which has brought us together.   We trust that the result will prove that we have taken part in a great historical transaction fruitful in good for the world.   Two great nations, in submitting their differences to arbitration, have set an example which I doubt not will be followed from time to time by others, so that the scourge of war will be more and more repressed. Few can be so sanguine as to expect that all international quarrels will be speedily settled by arbitration, instead of by the dread arbitrament of

war ; but each occasion on which the peaceful method is adopted will
hasten the time when it will be the rule and not the exception.

One of our poets has said that every prayer for universal peace avails
to expedite its coming.

We have done more than join in such a supplication ; we may hope
that we have been the humble instruments through whom an answer has
been granted to that prayer which I doubt not ascends from the hearts
of these two kindred nations, that peace may forever prevail between
them. . . .

[Senator Morgan.] The arbitrators on the part of the United States
most sincerely unite in the very happy expressions that have fallen from
Lord Hannen, of grateful appreciation of the splendid hospitality of the
French Government and people. . . .

If we should take a narrow view of the results of this arbitration, the
United States would have a regret that the important judicial questions
we have been considering were not stated in a broader form in the treaty
between these great Powers. The opportunity was offered when the
treaty was in process of formation to have presented in a more equitable
light the rights of the nations to whose islands and coasts the fur-seals
habitually resort for places of abode and shelter in the summer season ;
to control and protect them under the legal rules and intendments that
apply universally to the animals that are classed as domestic, or domesti-
cated animals, because of their usefulness to men.

My colleague and I concurred in the view that the treaty presented
this subject for consideration in its broadest aspect. Our honorable colleagues, however, did not so construe the scope of the duty prescribed to
the Tribunal by the treaty. They considered that these questions of the
right of property and protection in respect to the fur-seals were to be
decided upon the existing state of the law, and, finding no existing precedent in the international law, they did not feel warranted in creating one.

As the rights claimed by the United States could only be supported by
international law, in their estimation, and inasmuch as that law is silent
on the subject, they felt that under the treaty they could find no legal
foundation for the rights claimed that extended beyond the limits of the
territorial jurisdiction of the United States.

This ruling made it necessary to resort to the power conferred upon
the Tribunal to establish, by the authority of both Governments, regulations for the preservation and protection of the fur-seals, to which the
treaty relates. In this new and untried field of experiment, much embar-

rassment was found in conflicting interests of an important character, and yet more difficulty in the uncertainty as to the facts upon which regulations could be based that would be at once just to those interests, and would afford to the fur-seals proper preservation and protection.

The United States will fully understand and appreciate those difficulties, and will accept the final award as the best possible result, under existing conditions. A very large measure of protection is secured by the regulations adopted by the Tribunal to the Alaskan herd of fur-seals ; and the virtual repression of the use of firearms in pelagic sealing is an earnest and wise guaranty that those common interests may be pursued without putting in serious peril the peace of the two countries.

Senate Executive Documents, 53 Cong., 2 sess. (Washington, 1895), VII, pt. i, No. 177, pt. 1, pp. 71–73 *passim.*

---

179. The Olney Doctrine (1895)

BY SECRETARY RICHARD OLNEY

Olney was a prominent corporation lawyer in New England. He became attorney-general in Cleveland's cabinet in 1893, and later was made secretary of state. In 1895, when the administration took an active interest in the boundary dispute between Venezuela and British Guiana, he sent to Bayard, the United States ambassador to Great Britain, the letter of instruction from which this extract is taken. The interpretation given to the Monroe Doctrine in Olney's letter was generally considered to enlarge the scope of that policy, and hence has been popularly called the Olney Doctrine. In 1896, acting in behalf of Venezuela, he negotiated a treaty with Great Britain which submitted the boundary question to arbitration. — Bibliography : D. C. Gilman, *James Monroe,* 269–280 ; Providence Public Library, *Monthly Bulletin,* II, 12–21 ; Channing and Hart, *Guide,* § 178. — For other expositions of American foreign policy, see *Contemporaries,* III, Nos. 84, 106, 147, 148 ; below, Nos. 192, 196.

IT is not proposed, and for present purposes is not necessary, to enter into any detailed account of the controversy between Great Britain and Venezuela respecting the western frontier of the colony of British Guiana. The dispute is of ancient date and began at least as early as . . . 1814. . . . The claims of both parties, it must be conceded, are of a somewhat indefinite nature. . . .

. . . Great Britain . . . apparently remained indifferent as to the exact area of the colony until 1840, when she commissioned an engineer, Sir Robert Schomburgk, to examine and lay down its boundaries. . . .

. . . the exploitation of the Schomburgk line in 1840 was at once followed by the protest of Venezuela and by proceedings on the part of

Great Britain which could fairly be interpreted only as a disavowal of that line. . . . Notwithstanding this, however, every change in the British claim since that time has moved the frontier of British Guiana farther and farther to the westward of the line thus proposed. . . .

The important features of the existing situation . . . may be briefly stated.

1. The title to territory of indefinite but confessedly very large extent is in dispute between Great Britain on the ône hand and the South American Republic of Venezuela on the other.

2. The disparity in the strength of the claimants is such that Venezuela can hope to establish her claim only through peaceful methods — through an agreement with her adversary either upon the subject itself or upon an arbitration. . . .

5. Great Britain, however, has always and continuously refused to arbitrate, except upon the condition of a renunciation of a large part of the Venezuelan claim and of a concession to herself of a large share of the territory in controversy.

6. By the frequent interposition of its good offices at the instance of Venezuela, by constantly urging and promoting the restoration of diplomatic relations between the two countries, by pressing for arbitration of the disputed boundary, by offering to act as arbitrator, by expressing its grave concern whenever new alleged instances of British aggression upon Venezuelan territory have been brought to its notice, the Government of the United States has made it clear to Great Britain and to the world that the controversy is one in which both its honor and its interests are involved and the continuance of which it can not regard with indifference.

. . . those charged with the interests of the United States are now forced to determine exactly what those interests are and what course of action they require. It compels them to decide to what extent, if any, the United States may and should intervene in a controversy between and primarily concerning only Great Britain and Venezuela and to decide how far it is bound to see that the integrity of Venezuelan territory is not impaired by the pretensions of its powerful antagonist. Are any such right and duty devolved upon the United States? If . . . any such right and duty exist, their due exercise and discharge will not permit of any action that shall not be efficient and that, if the power of the United States is adequate, shall not result in the accomplishment of the end in view. . . .

That there are circumstances under which a nation may justly inter-pose in a controversy to which two or more other nations are the direct and immediate parties is an admitted canon of international law. . . . We are concerned at this time, however, not so much with the general rule as with a form of it which is peculiarly and distinctively American. Washington, in the solemn admonitions of the Farewell Address, ex-plicitly warned his countrymen against entanglements with the politics or the controversies of European powers. . . .

. . . The Monroe administration . . . did not hesitate to accept and apply the logic of the Farewell Address by declaring in effect that American non-intervention in European affairs necessarily implied and meant European non-intervention in American affairs. . . .

. . . It was realized that it was futile to lay down such a rule unless its observance could be enforced. It was manifest that the United States was the only power in this hemisphere capable of enforcing it. It was therefore courageously declared not merely that Europe ought not to interfere in American affairs, but that any European power doing so would be regarded as antagonizing the interests and inviting the oppo-sition of the United States.

. . . The precise scope and limitations of this rule cannot be too clearly apprehended. It does not establish any general protectorate by the United States over other American states. It does not relieve any American state from its obligations as fixed by international law nor prevent any European power directly interested from enforcing such obligations or from inflicting merited punishment for the breach of them. It does not contemplate any interference in the internal affairs of any American state or in the relations between it and other American states. It does not justify any attempt on our part to change the established form of government of any American state. . . . The rule in question has but a single purpose and object. It is that no European power or combination of European powers shall forcibly deprive an American state of the right and power of self-government and of shaping for itself its own political fortunes and destinies.

That the rule thus defined has been the accepted public law of this country ever since its promulgation cannot fairly be denied. . . .

. . . every administration since President Monroe's has had occasion, and sometimes more occasions than one, to examine and consider the Monroe doctrine and has in each instance given it emphatic endorse-ment. . . .

. . . It rests . . . upon facts and principles that are both intelligible and incontrovertible. That distance and three thousand miles of intervening ocean make any permanent political union between an European and an American state unnatural and inexpedient will hardly be denied. But physical and geographical considerations are the least of the objections to such a union. . . .

. . . whether moral or material interests be considered, it can not but be universally conceded that those of Europe are irreconcilably diverse from those of America, and that any European control of the latter is necessarily both incongruous and injurious. If, however . . . the forcible intrusion of European powers into American politics is to be deprecated — if, as it is to be deprecated, it should be resisted and prevented — such resistance and prevention must come from the United States . . . since only the United States has the strength adequate to the exigency.

Is it true, then, that the safety and welfare of the United States are so concerned with the maintenance of the independence of every American state as against any European power as to justify and require the interposition of the United States whenever that independence is endangered? The question can be candidly answered in but one way. The states of America, South as well as North, by geographical proximity, by natural sympathy, by similarity of governmental constitutions, are friends and allies, commercially and politically, of the United States. To allow the subjugation of any of them by an European power is, of course, to completely reverse that situation and signifies the loss of all the advantages incident to their natural relations to us. But that is not all. The people of the United States have a vital interest in the cause of popular self-government. . . . But . . . they are content with such assertion and defense of the right of popular self-government as their own security and welfare demand. It is in that view more than in any other that they believe it not to be tolerated that the political control of an American state shall be forcibly assumed by an European power.

. . . To-day the United States is practically sovereign on this continent, and its fiat is law upon the subjects to which it confines its interposition. Why? . . . It is because, in addition to all other grounds, its infinite resources combined with its isolated position render it master of the situation and practically invulnerable as against any or all other powers.

All the advantages of this superiority are at once imperiled if the principle be admitted that European powers may convert American states into colonies or provinces of their own. . . . The disastrous consequences to the United States of such a condition of things are obvious. The loss of prestige, of authority, and of weight in the councils of the family of nations, would be among the least of them. Our only real rivals in peace as well as enemies in war would be found located at our very doors. Thus far in our history we have been spared the burdens and evils of immense standing armies. . . . But, with the powers of Europe permanently encamped on American soil, the ideal conditions we have thus far enjoyed can not be expected to continue. We too must be armed to the teeth." . . .

How a greater calamity than this could overtake us it is difficult to see. . . . The people of the United States have learned in the school of experience to what extent the relations of states to each other depend not upon sentiment nor principle, but upon selfish interest. . . . They have yet in mind that France seized upon the apparent opportunity of our civil war to set up a monarchy in the adjoining state of Mexico. They realize that had France and Great Britain held important South American possessions to work from and to benefit, the temptation to destroy the predominance of the Great Republic in this hemisphere by furthering its dismemberment might have been irresistible. From that grave peril they have been saved in the past and may be saved again in the future through the operation of the sure but silent force of the doctrine proclaimed by President Monroe. . . .

. . . The application of the doctrine to the boundary dispute between Great Britain and Venezuela remains to be made and presents no real difficulty. Though the dispute relates to a boundary line, yet, as it is between states, it necessarily imports political control to be lost by one party and gained by the other. . . .

. . . Great Britain cannot be deemed a South American state within the purview of the Monroe doctrine, nor, if she is appropriating Venezuelan territory, is it material that she does so by advancing the frontier of an old colony instead of by the planting of a new colony. . . . It is not admitted, however, and therefore cannot be assumed, that Great Britain is in fact usurping dominion over Venezuelan territory. While Venezuela charges such usurpation, Great Britain denies it, and the United States, until the merits are authoritatively ascertained, can take sides with neither. But while this is so . . . it is certainly within its right to demand that the truth shall be ascertained. . . .

. . . It being clear, therefore, that the United States may legitimately insist upon the merits of the boundary question being determined, it is equally clear that there is but one feasible mode of determining them, viz., peaceful arbitration. . . .

You are instructed, therefore, to present the foregoing views to Lord Salisbury. . . .   They call for a definite decision upon the point whether Great Britain will consent or will decline to submit the Venezuelan boundary question in its entirety to impartial arbitration.   It is the earnest hope of the President that the conclusion will be on the side of arbitration. . . .   If he is to be disappointed in that hope . . . it is his wish to be made acquainted with the fact at such early date as will enable him to lay the whole subject before Congress in his next annual message.

House Documents, 54 Cong., 1 sess. (Washington, 1896), I, No. 1, pt. 1, pp. 545–562 *passim*.

PART IX

AMERICAN PROBLEMS

CHAPTER XXX — THE SPANISH WAR

180. Reasons for War (1898)

ANONYMOUS

Bibliography of all the numbers in this chapter: *Independent, Nation, Outlook, Public Opinion, Review of Reviews*, and kindred publications for 1898 and 1899.

. . . WE have had a Cuban question for more than ninety years. At times it has disappeared from our politics, but it has always reappeared. Once we thought it wise to prevent the island from winning its independence from Spain, and thereby, perhaps, we entered into moral bonds to make sure that Spain governed it decently. Whether we definitely contracted such an obligation or not, the Cuban question has never ceased to annoy us. The controversies about it make a long series of chapters in one continuous story of diplomatic trouble. Many of our ablest statesmen have had to deal with it as secretaries of state and as ministers to Spain, and not one of them has been able to settle it. One President after another has taken it up, and every one has transmitted it to his successor. It has at various times been a "plank" in the platforms of all our political parties, — as it was in both the party platforms of 1896, — and it has been the subject of messages of nearly all our Presidents, as it was of President Cleveland's message in December, 1896, in which he distinctly expressed the opinion that the United States might feel forced to recognize "higher obligations" than neutrality to Spain. In spite of periods of apparent quiet, the old trouble has always reappeared in an acute form, and it has never been settled ; nor has there recently been any strong reason for hope that it could be settled merely by diplomatic negotiation with Spain. Our diplomats have long had an experience with Spanish character and methods such as the public can better understand since war has been in progress. The pathetic inefficiency and the continual indirection of the Spanish character are now apparent to the world; they were long ago apparent to those who have had our diplomatic duties to do.

Thus the negotiations dragged on. We were put to trouble and expense to prevent filibustering, and filibustering continued in spite of us. More than once heretofore has there been danger of international conflict, as for instance when American sailors on the Virginius were executed in Cuba in 1873. Propositions have been made to buy the island, and plans have been formed to annex it. All the while there have been American interests in Cuba. Our citizens have owned property and made investments there, and done much to develop its fertility. They have paid tribute, unlawful as well as lawful, both to insurgents and to Spanish officials. They have lost property, for much of which no indemnity has been paid. All the while we have had a trade with the island, important during periods of quiet, irritating during periods of unrest.

The Cuban trouble is, therefore, not a new trouble even in an acute form. It had been moving toward a crisis for a long time. Still, while our government suffered these diplomatic vexations, and our citizens these losses, and our merchants these annoyances, the mass of the American people gave little serious thought to it. The newspapers kept us reminded of an opera-bouffe war that was going on, and now and then there came information of delicate and troublesome diplomatic duties for our minister to Spain. If Cuba were within a hundred miles of the coast of one of our populous states and near one of our great ports, periods of acute interest in its condition would doubtless have come earlier and oftener, and we should long ago have had to deal with a crisis by warlike measures. Or if the insurgents had commanded respect instead of mere pity, we should have paid heed to their struggle sooner; for it is almost an American maxim that a people cannot govern itself till it can win its own independence.

When it began to be known that Weyler's method of extermination was producing want in the island, and when appeals were made to American charity, we became more interested. . . .

The American public was in this mood when the battleship Maine was blown up in the harbor of Havana. The masses think in events, and not in syllogisms, and this was an event. This event provoked suspicions in the public mind. The thought of the whole nation was instantly directed to Cuba. The fate of the sailors on the Virginius, twenty-five years ago, was recalled. The public curiosity about everything Cuban and Spanish became intense. The Weyler method of warfare became more generally known. The story of our long diplomatic trouble with Spain was recalled. . . .

There is no need to discuss minor and accidental causes that hastened the rush of events ; but such causes were not lacking either in number or in influence. . . . But all these together could not have driven us to war if we had not been willing to be driven, — if the conviction had not become firm in the minds of the people that Spanish rule in Cuba was a blot on civilization that had now begun to bring reproach to us ; and when the President, who favored peace, declared it " intolerable," the people were ready to accept his judgment.

. . . We rushed into war almost before we knew it, not because we desired war, but because we desired something to be done with the old problem that should be direct and definite and final. Let us end it once for all. . . .

Not only is there in the United States an unmistakable popular approval of war as the only effective means of restoring civilization in Cuba, but the judgment of the English people promptly approved it, — giving evidence of an instinctive race and institutional sympathy. If Anglo-Saxon institutions and methods stand for anything, the institutions and methods of Spanish rule in Cuba are an abomination and a reproach. And English sympathy is not more significant as an evidence of the necessity of the war and as a good omen for the future of free institutions than the equally instinctive sympathy with Spain that has been expressed by some of the decadent influences on the Continent ; indeed, the real meaning of American civilization and ideals will henceforth be somewhat more clearly understood in several quarters of the world.

American character will be still better understood when the whole world clearly perceives that the purpose of the war is only to remove from our very doors this cruel and inefficient piece of mediævalism which is one of the two great scandals of the closing years of the century ; for it is not a war of conquest. . . .

The War with Spain, and After, in *Atlantic Monthly*, June, 1898 (Boston, etc.), LXXXI, 722–725 *passim*.

181. Outbreak of War (1898)

FROM THE INTERNATIONAL YEAR BOOK

For earlier articles on the relations of the United States to Cuba, see *Contemporaries*, III, No. 149 ; above, No. 176.

BOTH Congress and the people had sunk the question of the *Maine* in the larger one of Cuban independence.   Destitution among the *reconcentrados* was constantly growing worse, thousands dying slowly from starvation.   American supplies were distributed to the sufferers through Miss Clara Barton, President of the Red Cross Society, and General Fitzhugh Lee, our Consul at Havana. . . .

On March 31 Captain-General Blanco issued a decree putting an end to reconcentration in the provinces of Pinar del Rio, Havana, Matanzas, and Santa Clara, and on April 9 the Spanish Cabinet decided to grant an armistice to the insurgents, while both the Pope and the great Powers of Europe were using their influence to avert a Spanish-American war.   Nevertheless the replies at this time of the Madrid government to President McKinley's demands concerning the pacification of Cuba, notwithstanding the Spanish offer to arbitrate the *Maine* trouble, led the authorities at Washington to believe that pacification could not be attained without the armed intervention of the United States.   The President's message to Congress, which was daily expected, was withheld . . . until April 11. . . .   Both Congress and the people had grown impatient waiting for the message, and when it finally came excitement was at such a height that many condemned it for its conservatism. It was, however, a wise and ably conceived document.   The President stated the entire issue, rightly considering the *Maine* disaster a subordinate matter, and passed in review Spanish mismanagement and outrage in Cuba, and the repeated promises and the repeated failures of the Spanish government to effect suitable reforms. . . .

The conclusion of the long message and the really important part was as follows :

" The only hope of relief and repose from a condition which can no longer be endured is the enforced pacification of Cuba.   In the name of humanity, in the name of civilization, in behalf of endangered American interests, which give us the right and the duty to speak and act, the war in Cuba must stop.

" In view of these facts and of these considerations, I ask the Congress to authorize and empower the President to take measures to secure a full and final termination of hostilities between the government of Spain and the people of Cuba, and to secure in the island the establishment of a stable government capable of maintaining order and observing its international obligations, insuring peace and tranquility and the security of its citizens, as well as our own, and to use the military and naval forces of the United States as may be necessary for these purposes.

"And in the interest of humanity and to aid in preserving the lives of the starving people of the island, I recommend that the distribution of food and supplies be continued, and that an appropriation be made out of the public treasury to supplement the charity of our citizens.

"The issue is now with the Congress. It is a solemn responsibility. I have exhausted every effort to relieve the intolerable condition of affairs which is at our doors. Prepared to execute every obligation imposed upon me by the Constitution and the law, I await your action.". . .

. . . The resolutions . . . were accepted by both Houses in the small hours of the morning of April 19, — by the Senate, by a vote of 42 to 35, and by the House by a vote of 310 to 6, — and were signed by the President on the following day. . . . The following is the text of the act . . .

" . . . be it resolved :

"First — That the people of the island of Cuba are, and of right ought to be, free and independent.

"Second — That it is the duty of the United States to demand, and the government of the United States does hereby demand, that the government of Spain at once relinquish its authority and government in the island of Cuba and withdraw its land and naval forces from Cuba and Cuban waters.

"Third — That the President of the United States be, and he hereby is, directed and empowered to use the entire land and naval forces of the United States, and to call into active service the militia of the several States to such an extent as may be necessary to carry these resolutions into effect.

"Fourth — That the United States hereby disclaims any disposition or intention to exercise sovereignty, jurisdiction, or control over said island, except for the pacification thereof, and asserts its determination when that is accomplished to leave the government and control of the island to its people."

On the 20th of April the President signed his ultimatum to the Spanish government, a copy of which was handed to Minister Polo, who immediately demanded his passports and started for Canada, leaving the interests of the Spanish legation in charge of M. Cambon, the French Minister. Before receiving the ultimatum the Spanish Cabinet delivered to Minister Woodford his passports and informed him that diplomatic relations with the United States were at an end. On the 25th a bill was passed by Congress declaring that a state of war existed between the United States and Spain, and had so existed since and including April 21.

In the meantime war preparations were being pushed forward by both governments. The Queen-Regent signed a decree asking for a national subscription to the navy, our own navy was increased by the purchase of many more ships of various kinds, and by the middle of the month the troops throughout the country were preparing to move towards the Gulf. On the 17th two companies of the Twenty-fifth Infantry reached Key West and two days later a general movement of regular troops began. The principal rendezvous was Chickamauga, but New Orleans, Mobile, and Tampa were also places of mobilization. The President issued a call for 125,000 volunteers on April 23, which though meeting with immediate response received not a little adverse criticism, the dissatisfaction arising from the fact that in some States the infantry and artillery requisitions were not consistently apportioned, and from the fact that the Department of War proposed to use its privilege, if it chose, of destroying the integrity of State organizations when the troops were beyond State boundaries. A few days later orders were issued for recruiting the regular army up to its war strength, 61,000. On the 21st the fleet under acting Rear-Admiral Sampson at Key West was ordered to proceed to Havana and then institute a general blockade of the western end of Cuba. Commodore Schley with the "flying squadron" was detained at Hampton Roads in order to meet any attack which might be made on the coast cities by the Spanish Cape Verde fleet, reports from which for a number of weeks subsequent were contradictory and alarming.

During the rest of the month many prizes were taken in western Cuban waters. It was not the purpose of Admiral Sampson to bombard Havana or expose his fleet to the enemy's fire from coast fortifications before he was assured of the destination of the Spanish Cape Verde and Cadiz fleets ; but at the same time he determined to prevent the erection of any new fortifications. This brought about the first action of the war, the bombardment of the works . . . at Matanzas, April 27. . . .

The International Year Book, 1898 (edited by Frank Moore Colby, New York [1899]), 727–729 *passim*.

182. Battle of Manila Bay (1898)

BY COMMODORE GEORGE DEWEY

Dewey's overwhelming victory at Manila Bay within a fortnight of the declaration of war made him the chief character of the Spanish War; and the dignity and skill with which he maintained his position before Manila under trying circumstances confirmed his reputation gained in battle. As a reward for these services the rank of admiral was revived for him. This extract is from his first telegram and official report. — For Dewey, see John Barrett, *Admiral George Dewey.*

HONGKONG, *May 7, 1898.* (Manila, May 1.)

SECRETARY OF THE NAVY, *Washington :*

THE squadron arrived at Manila at daybreak this morning. Immediately engaged enemy and destroyed the following Spanish vessels : *Reina Christina, Castillia, Don Antonio de Biloa, Don Juan de Austria, Isla de Luzon, Isla de Cuba, General Lezo, Marquis del Duaro, El Curreo, Velasco,* one transport, *Isla de Mandano,* water battery at Cavite. I shall destroy Cavite arsenal dispensatory. The squadron is uninjured. Few men were slightly wounded. I request the Department will send immediately from San Francisco fast steamer with ammunition. The only means of telegraphing is to the American consul at Hongkong.

DEWEY. . . .

U. S. NAVAL FORCE ON ASIATIC STATION,

Flagship Olympia, Cavite, Philippine Islands, May 4, 1898.

SIR : I have the honor to submit the following report of the operations of the squadron under my command :

The squadron left Mirs Bay on April 27, immediately on the arrival of Mr. O. F. Williams, United States consul at Manila, who brought important information and who accompanies the squadron.

Arrived off Bolinao on the morning of April 30 and, finding no vessels there, proceeded down the coast and arrived off the entrance to Manila Bay on the same afternoon. . . .

The *Boston* and *Concord* were sent to reconnoiter Port Subic, I having been informed that the enemy intended to take position there. A thorough search of the port was made by the *Boston* and *Concord,* but the Spanish fleet was not found, although, from a letter afterwards found in the arsenal . . . it appears that it had been their intention to go there.

Entered the Boca Grande, or south channel, at 11.30 p.m., steaming in column at distance at 8 knots. After half the squadron had passed, a battery on the south side of the channel opened fire, none of the shots taking effect. The *Boston* and *McCulloch* returned the fire.

The squadron proceeded across the bay at slow speed, and arrived off Manila at daybreak, and was fired upon at 5.15 a.m. by three batteries at Manila and two at Cavite and by the Spanish fleet anchored in an approximately east and west line across the mouth of Bakor Bay, with their left in shoal water in Canacao Bay.

The squadron then proceeded to the attack, the flagship *Olympia*, under my personal direction, leading, followed at distance by the *Baltimore, Raleigh, Petrel, Concord,* and *Boston,* in the order named, which formation was maintained throughout the action. The squadron opened fire at 5.41 a. m. While advancing to the attack, two mines were exploded ahead of the flagship, too far to be effective.

The squadron maintained a continuous and precise fire at ranges varying from 5,000 to 2,000 yards, countermarching in a line approximately parallel to that of the Spanish fleet. The enemy's fire was vigorous, but generally ineffective.

Early in the engagement two launches put out toward the *Olympia* with the apparent intention of using torpedoes. One was sunk and the other disabled by our fire and beached before an opportunity occurred to fire torpedoes. At 7 a.m. the Spanish flagship *Reina Christina* made a desperate attempt to leave the line and come out to engage at short range, but was received with such galling fire, the entire battery of the *Olympia* being concentrated upon her, that she was barely able to return to the shelter of the point. The fires started in her by our shell at this time were not extinguished until she sank.

At 7.35 a.m., it having been erroneously reported to me that only 15 rounds per gun remained for the 5-inch rapid-fire battery, I ceased firing and withdrew the squadron for consultation and a redistribution of ammunition, if necessary.

The three batteries at Manila had kept up a continuous fire from the beginning of the engagement, which fire was not returned by this squadron. The first of these batteries was situated on the south mole head at the entrance to the Pasig River, the second on the south bastion of the walled city of Manila, and the third at Malate, about one-half mile farther south. At this point I sent a message to the Governor-General to the effect that if the batteries did not cease firing the city would be shelled. This had the effect of silencing them.

At 11.16 a.m., finding that the report of scarcity of ammunition was incorrect, I returned with the squadron to the attack. By this time the flagship and almost the entire Spanish fleet were in flames, and at 12.30 p.m. the squadron ceased firing, the batteries being silenced and the ships sunk, burnt, and deserted.

At 12.40 p.m. the squadron returned and anchored off Manila, the *Petrel* being left behind to complete the destruction of the smaller gunboats, which were behind the point of Cavite. This duty was performed by Commander E. P. Wood in the most expeditious and complete manner possible.

The Spanish lost the following vessels :

Sunk — *Reina Christina, Castilla, Don Antonio de Ulloa.*

Burnt — *Don Juan de Austria, Isla de Luzon, Isla de Cuba, General Lezo, Marques del Duero, El Correo, Velasco,* and *Isla de Mindanao* (transport).

Captured — *Rapido* and *Hercules* (tugs) and several small launches.

I am unable to obtain complete accounts of the enemy's killed and wounded, but believe their loss to be very heavy. The *Reina Christina* alone had 150 killed, including the captain, and 90 wounded.

I am happy to report that the damage done to the squadron under my command was inconsiderable. There were none killed, and only 7 men in the squadron very slightly wounded. As will be seen by the reports of the commanding officers which are herewith inclosed, several of the vessels were struck and even penetrated, but the damage was of the slightest, and the squadron is in as good condition now as before the battle. . . .

On May 2, the day following the engagement, the squadron again went to Cavite, where it remains. . . .

On the 3d the military forces evacuated the Cavite Arsenal, which was taken possession of by a landing party. On the same day the *Raleigh* and *Baltimore* secured the surrender of the batteries on Corregidor Island, paroling the garrison and destroying the guns.

On the morning of May 4 the transport *Manila,* which had been aground in Bakor Bay, was towed off and made a prize.

House Documents, 55 Cong., 3 sess. (Washington, 1898), XII, No. 3, pp. 68–72 *passim.*

183. The Navy in the Spanish War (1898)

BY CAPTAIN ALFRED THAYER MAHAN

Mahan is a retired naval officer.   His works on naval history have gained for him the reputation of being a preëminent authority on the subject.   During the Spanish War he was a member of the Naval War Board.

. . . UNLESS, and until, the United States fleet available for service in the Caribbean Sea was strong enough to control permanently the waters which separated the Spanish islands from our territory nearest to them, the admitted vast superiority of this country in potential resources for land warfare was completely neutralized.   If the Spanish Navy preponderated over ours, it would be evidently impossible for transports carring troops and supplies to traverse the seas safely ; and, unless they could so do, operations of war in the enemy's colonies could neither be begun nor continued.   If, again, the two fleets were so equally balanced as to make the question of ultimate preponderance doubtful, it was clearly foolish to land in the islands men whom we might be compelled, by an unlucky sea-fight, to abandon there.

This last condition was that which obtained, as war became imminent. The force of the Spanish Navy — on paper, as the expression goes — was so nearly equal to our own that it was well within the limits of possibility that an unlucky incident — the loss, for example, of a battleship — might make the Spaniard decisively superior in nominal, or even in actual, available force. . . .   It was clearly recognized that war cannot be made without running risks ; but it was also held, unwaveringly, that no merely possible success justified risk, unless it gave a fair promise of diminishing the enemy's naval force, and so of deciding the control of the sea, upon which the issue of the war depended.   This single idea, and concentration of purpose upon it, underlay and dictated every step of the Navy Department from first to last. . . .

It was this consideration that brought the *Oregon* from the Pacific to the Atlantic, — a movement initiated before hostilities opened, though not concluded until after they began.   The wisdom of the step was justified not merely, nor chiefly, by the fine part played by that ship on July 3, but by the touch of certainty her presence imparted to the grip of our fleet upon Cervera's squadron during the preceding month, and the consequent power to move the army without fear by sea to Santiago. Few realize the doubts, uncertainties, and difficulties of the sustained watchfulness which attends such operations as the "bottling" of the Spanish fleet by Admiral Sampson; for "bottling" a hostile fleet does not resemble the chance and careless shoving of a cork into a half-used bottle, — it is rather like the wiring down of champagne by bonds that cannot be broken and through which nothing can ooze. This it is which constitutes the claim of the American Commander-in-Chief upon the gratitude of his countrymen; for to his skill and tenacity in conducting that operation is primarily due the early ending of the war, the opportunity to remove our stricken soldiery from a sickly climate, the ending of suspense, and the saving of many lives. "The moment Admiral Cervera's fleet was destroyed," truly said the London "Times" (August 16), "the war was practically at an end, unless Spain had elected to fight on to save the point of honor;" for she could have saved nothing else by continued war.

To such successful operation, however, there is needed not only ships individually powerful, but numbers of such ships; and that the numbers of Sampson's fleet were maintained — not drawn off to other, though important, operations — even under such sore temptation as the dash of Cámara's fleet from Cadiz towards the Philippines, was due to the Department's ability to hold fast the primary conception of concentration upon a single purpose, even though running thereby such a risk as was feared from Cámara's armored ships reaching Dewey's unarmored cruisers before they were reinforced. The chances of the race to Manila, between Cámara, when he started from Cadiz, and the two monitors from San Francisco, were deliberately taken, in order to ensure the retention of Cervera's squadron in Santiago, or its destruction in case of attempted escape. . . .

. . . But Cuba and Puerto Rico, points for attack, were not, unluckily, the only two considerations forced upon the attention of the United States. We have a very long coast-line, and it was notorious that the defences were not so far advanced, judged by modern standards, as to inspire perfect confidence, either in professional men or in the inhabitants. . . .

Under these combined influences the United States Government found itself confronted from the beginning with two objects of military solicitude, widely divergent one from the other, both in geographical position and in method of action; namely, the attack upon Cuba and the protection of its own shores. As the defences did not inspire confidence, the navy had to supplement their weakness, although it is essentially an offensive, and not a defensive, organization. Upon this the enemy counted

much at the first. . . .   Our total force for the order of battle, prior to
the arrival of the *Oregon*, was nominally only equal to that of the enemy,
and, when divided between the two objects named, the halves were not
decisively superior to the single squadron under Cervera, — which also
might be reinforced by some of the armored ships then in Spain.   The
situation, therefore, was one that is not infrequent, but always embarrassing, — a double purpose and a single force, which, although divisible,
ought not to be divided. . . .

. . . The Flying Squadron was kept in Hampton Roads to calm the
fears of the seaboard, and to check any enterprise there of Cervera, if
intended or attempted.   The other division of the armored fleet, however, was placed before Havana, where its presence not only strengthened adequately the blockading force proper, but assured also the safety
of our naval base at Key West, both objects being attainable by the
same squadron, on account of their nearness to each other. . . .

. . . Cervera's destination was believed — as it turned out, rightly
believed — to be the West Indies.   His precise point of arrival was a
matter of inference only, as in fact was his general purpose.   A natural
surmise was that he would go first to Puerto Rico. . . .   Whatever the
particular course of reasoning, it was decided that a squadron under
Admiral Sampson's command should proceed to the Windward Passage
for the purpose of observation, with a view to going further eastward if
it should appear advisable.   Accordingly, on the 4th of May, five days
after Cervera left the Cape de Verde, the Admiral sailed for the appointed
position. . . .

. . . He then decided to go on to San Juan, the chief seaport of
Puerto Rico, upon the chance of finding the Spanish squadron there . . .
and on the early morning of the 12th arrived off San Juan.   An attack
upon the forts followed at once, lasting from 5.30 to 7.45 A.M. ; but,
as it was evident that the Spanish division was not there, the Admiral
decided not to continue the attack, although satisfied that he could
force a surrender. . . .

. . . The squadron started back immediately to the westward.   During
the night of this same day . . . towards midnight, reliable information
was received at the Navy Department that Cervera's squadron had arrived
off Martinique, — four armored cruisers and three torpedo destroyers. . . .

The departure of Admiral Cervera from Martinique for Curaçao was
almost simultaneous with that of Admiral Sampson from San Juan for
Key West. . . .   When he began thus to retrace his steps, he was still

ignorant of Cervera's arrival. . . . But on the morning of the 15th — Sunday — at 3.30, his despatch-boat returned to him with the official intelligence, not only of the enemy's being off Martinique, but of his arrival at Curaçao, which occurred shortly after daylight of the 14th. The same telegram informed him that the Flying Squadron was on its way to Key West, and directed him to regain that point himself with all possible rapidity. . . .

The Flying Squadron had sailed at 4 P.M. of the 13th. . . . It is to be inferred from the departure of these vessels that the alarm about our own coast, felt while the whereabouts of the hostile division was unknown, vanished when it made its appearance. . . .

The Department could calculate certainly that, by the time its message reached Sampson, his division would be so far advanced as to ensure interposing between Havana and the Spaniards, if the latter came by the Windward Passage — from the eastward. It was safe, therefore, or at least involved less risk of missing the enemy, to send the Flying Squadron to Cienfuegos, either heading him off there, or with a chance of meeting him in the Yucatan Channel, if he tried to reach Havana by going west of Cuba. But . . . Cienfuegos was thought the more likely destination. . . .

On the 19th of May the Department received probable, but not certain, information that the enemy's division had entered Santiago. . . .

Although the information received of Cervera's entering Santiago was not reliable enough to justify detaching Sampson's ships from before Havana, it was probable to a degree that made it imperative to watch the port in force at once. . . .

The intention of Commodore Schley to return to Key West precipitated the movement of Admiral Sampson, with his two fastest ships, to Santiago ; but the step would certainly have been taken as soon as the doubt whether all the Spanish division had entered was removed. . . .

. . . Fortunately, on second thoughts, the Commodore decided to remain ; but before that was known to the Department, Sampson had been directed, on May 29th, to proceed with the *New York* and the *Oregon*, the latter of which had only joined him on the 28th. . . .

Admiral Sampson with his two ships arrived off Santiago on the 1st of June at 6 A.M., and established at once the close watch of the port which lasted until the sally and destruction of Cervera's squadron. . . .

Alfred T. Mahan, *Lessons of the War with Spain* (Boston, 1899), 30–180 *passim.*

184. Capture of Santiago (1898)

BY JOHN BLACK ATKINS

Atkins was war correspondent for the *Manchester Guardian*, an English newspaper, and in that capacity accompanied General Shafter's army in the campaign against Santiago.

ABOUT five o'clock on the evening of Sunday, July 10, began what is known as the second bombardment. The firing was desultory, and almost entirely on the American side. But even there it was very slight: the guns in one battery, for example, were being fired only once in nine minutes. . . .

When I awoke the next morning the first thing I saw was a new regiment of volunteers just come to the front, with the sunlight aslant on their faces. They all expected to receive their baptism of fire that day; their friends rallied them on the expectation, and they on their side replied facetiously. After the first sunlight came a dulness over the whole sky, so that the day was like night sick — to reverse Shakspere's phrase. A mist still lay over part of Santiago; everything was still, and dead, and wet, and silent; the leaves of the palms seemed as though they must fall for very heaviness. Perhaps the valley was never more strangely rich and beautiful. A shell came up from the American fleet, fired blindly at a range of over 8,000 yards, and plunged with a shrill cry into the mist; we could not see it burst. The American artillery was now a little stronger than on July 1. To the sixteen guns with which the fighting had begun eight mortars had been added and were now in position. But I heard an officer say that the ammunition for them could be fired away in half an hour with only four mortars in use. The siege guns which came with the first expedition had never been taken off the ships. General Randolph, who had lately arrived with General Miles, brought with him six batteries, and some of these guns were at the front and some were on their way there, but apparently none had yet been put in position. The artillery was of course delayed by the badness of the roads. When I left the front for the last time some of General Randolph's guns were still stuck in a mud pool. The engineers appeared to do little. Where were they? Were they all building permanent forts in the United States? Of the brooks that one crossed on the ordinary route between General Shafter's headquarters and the front not one was bridged over; one would think that with so much timber handy they could have been bridged at about the rate of one an hour. As it was, waggons sometimes overturned in them, and soldiers who had to wade through them were made unnecessarily wet.

The American intention was to surround the city as nearly as possible by extending the right of the line till it reached beyond the end of the harbour. Most of the infantry firing was in that direction, and for this reason General Lawton's division was strengthened by the transference to it of a brigade from General Kent's division. As on the previous evening, the firing was slight; the most active guns of all were those of the Rough Riders. Perhaps there never were volunteers who went about their business with greater zest than these, or who learned more in so short a time. Not content with the amount of ordinary artillery, they carried about with them quick-firing guns as a kind of personal equipment. Someone had presented this Colt to the regiment, someone else that Gatling, others had bought among them the dynamite gun. Sometimes there was a noise exactly like rapping on a door — that was one of the Colts at work; sometimes there was a noise like the grinding of coffee — that was one of the Gatlings. One of these nights I spent in the Rough Riders' camp. The men in the trenches were like men out for a holiday; their chief characteristic was a habit of cheering on every possible occasion; they used to cheer when they went into the trenches, and cheer when they came out; they used to cheer when there was food, but also when there was no food. The camp used to laugh for hours over some quite silly joke, which seemed at the time to be mightily amusing and witty, and afterwards it would turn out that it was only that the silliness had been opportune. It was vastly amusing, for example, to hear a certain officer, whose name had incessantly to be repeated, spoken of as General Mango, or another officer spoken of as Lieutenant-Colonel Cocoanut. These light-hearted people did as much firing as they were allowed to do with the quick-firing instruments which one had come to look upon almost as their playthings. The dynamite gun was not fired very often, because it used to become jammed, but everybody loved it as a great big expensive toy. The firing string was not very long — not longer than that of an ordinary field-piece — but, as the operator used to explain, if the gun blew up you were no better off fifty yards away than five. When the gun was fired there was very little noise — only the sound of a rocket; but when the shell exploded there was a tremendous detonation. It was said that everything near the explosion was devastated. In one case a Spanish gun and a tree were seen to be hurled bodily into the air. It was my singular misfortune, however, to find no traces of the devastation done by this terrible instrument.

Colonel Roosevelt, the lieutenant-colonel of the Rough Riders, since elected Governor of New York, was a man who impressed one. He is the typical strong man, with the virtues and defects of the strong man ; creating opposition and making enemies, but in the end beating down in his own direct, honest, didactic way the opposition which he himself has created, and turning, often, into friends the enemies whom he himself has made. So that in every adventure he almost inevitably — to use the expressive American phrase — 'gets there.' The impulse of which he is capable was illustrated by his sudden resignation of his Assistant Secretaryship to the Navy to command this whimsical, gallant regiment. The Rough Riders were the devotees of his person.

All the morning of July 11 the bombardment was a half-hearted affair. Neither side left its trenches. At noon General Toral, who had succeeded General Linares, sent out a flag of truce saying that he would meet General Miles personally in conference the next day. With the flag the firing ceased, and, as all the world knows, never began again. . . .

John Black Atkins, *The War in Cuba* (London, 1899), 176–182 *passim.*

---

185. Ultimatum in the Negotiation of Peace (1898)

BY ENVOY WILLIAM RUFUS DAY

Day was assistant secretary of state from the beginning of McKinley's administration, and when Sherman resigned the state portfolio at the outbreak of the Spanish War, Day was appointed his successor. Later in the year he resigned, and became head of the commission to negotiate peace with Spain. This extract is from his official letter to the head of the Spanish commission.

Paris. November 22, 1898.

. . . HAVING received and read your letter of today, touching the final proposition presented by the American Commissioners at yesterday's conference, I hasten to answer your enquiries *seriatim*, first stating your question, and then giving my reply.

" First. Is the proposition you make based on the Spanish colonies being transferred free of all burdens, all, absolutely all outstanding obligations and debts, of whatsoever kind and whatever may have been their origin and purpose, remaining thereby chargeable exclusively to Spain?"

In reply to this question, it is proper to call attention to the fact that the American Commissioners, in their paper of yesterday, expressed the hope that they might receive within a certain time "a definite and final acceptance" of their proposal as to the Philippines, and also "of the demands as to Cuba, Porto Rico and other Spanish Islands in the West Indies, and Guam, in the form in which those demands have been provisionally agreed to."

The form in which they have thus been agreed to is found in the proposal presented by the American Commissioners on the 17th of October and annexed to the protocol of the 6th conference, and is as follows :

"ARTICLE 1. Spain hereby relinquishes all claim of sovereignty over and title to Cuba.

"ARTICLE 2. Spain hereby cedes to the United States the Island of Porto Rico and other islands now under Spanish sovereignty in the West Indies, and also the Island of Guam in the Ladrones."

These articles contain no provision for the assumption of debt by the United States.

In this relation, I desire to recall the statements in which the American Commissioners have in our conferences repeatedly declared that they would not accept any articles that required the United States to assume the so-called colonial debts of Spain.

To these statements I have nothing to add.

But, in respect of the Philippines, the American Commissioners, while including the cession of the archipelago in the article in which Spain "cedes to the United States the Island of Porto Rico and other islands now under Spanish sovereignty in the West Indies, and also the Island of Guam in the Ladrones," or in an article expressed in similar words, will agree that their Government shall pay to Spain the sum of twenty million dollars ($20,000,000).

"Second. Is the offer made by the United States to Spain to establish for a certain number of years similar conditions in the ports of the archipelago for vessels and merchandise of both nations, an offer which is preceded by the assertion that the policy of the United States is to maintain an open door to the world's commerce, to be taken in the sense that the vessels and goods of other nations are to enjoy or can enjoy the same privilege (*situación*) which for a certain time is granted those of Spain, while the United States do not change such policy?"

The declaration that the policy of the United States in the Philippines will be that of an open door to the world's commerce necessarily implies that the offer to place Spanish vessels and merchandise on the same footing as American is not intended to be exclusive. But, the offer to give Spain that privilege for a term of years, is intended to secure it to her for a certain period by special treaty stipulation, whatever might be at any time the general policy of the United States.

"Third. The Secretary of State having stated in his note of July 30 last that the cession by Spain of the Island of Porto Rico and the other islands now under Spanish sovereignty in the West Indies, as well as one of the Ladrones, was to be as compensation for the losses and expenses of the United States during the war, and of the damages suffered by their citizens during the last insurrection in Cuba, what claims does the proposition refer to on requiring that there shall be inserted in the treaty a provision for the mutual relinquishment of all claims, individual and national, that have arisen from the beginning of the last insurrection in Cuba to the conclusion of the treaty of peace?"

While the idea doubtless was conveyed in the note of the Secretary of State of the United States of the 30th of July last that the cession of " Porto Rico and other islands now under the sovereignty of Spain in the West Indies, and also the cession of an island in the Ladrones, to be selected by the United States," was required on grounds of indemnity, and that "on similar grounds the United States is entitled to occupy and will hold the city, bay, and harbor of Manila, pending the conclusion of a treaty of peace which shall determine the control, disposition and government of the Philippines," no definition has as yet been given of the extent or precise effect of the cessions in that regard. The American Commissioners therefore propose, in connection with the cessions of territory, "the mutual relinquishment of all claims for indemnity, national and individual, of every kind, of the United States against Spain and of Spain against the United States, that may have arisen since the beginning of the late insurrection in Cuba and prior to the conclusion of a treaty of peace."

Senate Documents, 55 Cong., 3 sess. (Washington, 1899), VIII, No. 62, pt. 2, pp. 217–219.

CHAPTER XXXI — QUESTIONS OF COLO-NIZATION

186. American Experience of Colonization (1898)

BY PROFESSOR ABBOTT LAWRENCE LOWELL

Lowell is professor of the science of government at Harvard University, and an authority on questions relating to the organization and government of colonies. — Bibliography: A. P. C. Griffin, *List of Books relating to the Theory of Colonization*, 11-22.

IT is commonly said that the recent annexations mark a departure from our traditional policy, in that they present the first attempt the nation has made to acquire colonies. The former half of this state-ment is substantially correct; for, with the exception of Alaska, the lands we have annexed have bordered upon those we already possessed. Moreover, they have been, for the most part, uninhabited or very thinly peopled. The other half of the statement — that we have entered for the first time in the path of colonization — cannot be accepted without careful examination. . . . Properly speaking, a colony is a territory, not forming, for political purposes, an integral part of the mother country, but dependent upon her, and peopled in part, at least, by her emigrants. If this is true, there has never been a time, since the adoption of the first ordinance for the government of the Northwest Territory in 1784, when the United States has not had colonies. Nor is there anything artificial or strained about this definition. The very essence of a colony lies in the fact that it is a new land, to which citizens can go and carry with them the protection of the parent state; and this has been emi-nently the case in the territories of the United States. They have been administered, it is true, with a view to their becoming at the earliest possible moment members of the Union, with full equality of rights; but this is not inconsistent with their being colonies in the strictest sense, so long as they remained territories at all. Until admitted as states, their position has not differed in any essential particular from that of the North American colonies of England before the outbreak of the Revolution. . . .

The existence of vast regions in North America uninhabited by civilized man enabled our fathers to plant an ever extending series of new
communities to which the people of the older settlements could emigrate
without becoming foreigners, and the process has added enormously to
the prosperity of the nation. . . .

Nor has the process of planting new communities in the West been
less successful from a political than from an economic point of view.
With the exception of the troubles in Kansas during the contest over
slavery, a quarrel imported from the older states, and the disturbances
in Utah, where polygamy was a rock of offense, the United States has
had scarcely any friction with the territories. The course of their government has run smoothly ; and if the conditions have been peculiarly
favorable and such as can never occur again, this fact has not been the
sole cause of success. That the expansion to the Mississippi and the
plains beyond has been a source of strength, that it has promoted
the welfare of the nation to an incalculable degree, no man will feel
inclined to deny. To realize this, one has only to recall what the position of our country would have been to-day if the ocean or a foreign
power had encompassed the boundaries of the original thirteen states ;
if the Alleghanies had been our western frontier. Since the Revolutionary War the inhabitants of the United States have increased twentyfold ;
and of the present population one half live in communities that have at
some time been organized as territories, — in other words, that have
been founded by the process of colonization. It may safely be asserted,
therefore, that the United States has been one of the greatest and most
successful colonizing powers the world has ever known.

. . . The conditions that made possible the expansion of our people
westward at a furious and constantly accelerated pace are surely, and
not very slowly, coming to an end. . . . We have no reason to expect,
therefore, that the Western movement will continue much longer at the
present rate. The United States as a whole is capable, no doubt, of
supporting a far larger population than it contains to-day, but the filling
up of country already settled is a much slower process than that of pushing into vacant territories, and hence the rate of expansion must inevitably be checked. . . . The expansion into new regions, within the old
limits of the United States, must cease, because there will be no new
fertile regions there ; and we shall be confined to filling up what we
have already occupied.

If we look, then, at the past and the future, the question is, not whether we shall enter upon a career of colonization or not, but whether we shall shift into other channels the colonization which has lasted as long as our national existence, or whether we shall abandon it; whether we shall expand in other directions, or cease to expand into new territory at all. Although the acquisition of the Spanish colonies was an accident, in the sense that the war was not waged with any deliberate intention of expansion, yet the question was sure to present itself in some form before long; and there can be little doubt how it would have been answered. . . .

. . . That a tendency so firmly rooted should die out as the country fills up, that the custom of pushing into any favorable opening should not operate beyond the present limits of the United States, seems incredible. . . .

It seems altogether probable, therefore, that if the war with Spain had not broken out, the question of expansion would have arisen in some concrete form before many decades had passed, and that it would ultimately have been answered in the affirmative. The war has forced the issue, prematurely, perhaps, and rightly or wrongly, for good or for evil, the die is cast. Hence it behooves us to consider the causes of our past success in expansion or colonization, and see how far they are applicable to our new possessions. Of these causes two are preëminent: the territories have been treated as infant states, subject to tutelage only until they came of age; and they have been managed unselfishly. . . .

. . . The application of the principle that their people had equal political rights with those of the older parts of the country has been justified by the fact that the population of states and territories has been substantially homogeneous. . . . Now, these conditions are not true in our new possessions. No one of them has a population homogeneous with our own, or the experience of a long training in self-government. . . . They must be trained for it, as our forefathers were trained, beginning with local government under a strong judicial system, and the process will necessarily be slow. . . .

One element of our success in the management of the territories — their treatment as infant states, with institutions like our own and prospective equality of rights — cannot therefore be applied to our new possessions; and this very fact ought to make us the more earnest in using every other means at our disposal.

The second great cause of our success has been that we have treated the territories unselfishly. . . . This principle of unselfish management

2 Q

can be applied perfectly to our new possessions, and to any others we may ever acquire. The revolt of North America taught England the lesson that colonies cannot be a permanent source of wealth and strength unless they are managed with a single eye to their own welfare ; and the subsequent experience of European nations has confirmed the principle, for it is one that is universally true. We must treat fairly not only each of our possessions as a whole, but also every race that inhabits it. . . .

Moreover, it is not enough that Congress legislate unselfishly. The men sent to conduct the administration must have in view solely the welfare of the colonies committed to their charge, and this cannot be the case if they are appointed for political motives. . . . If our colonies are to thrive and add to our own prosperity, we must select only thoroughly trained administrators, fit them for their work by long experience, and retain them in office irrespective of party. To do this, it is necessary to create a permanent and highly paid colonial administrative service, which shall offer an honorable and attractive career for young men of ability. . . .

A. Lawrence Lowell, *The Colonial Expansion of the United States*, in *Atlantic Monthly*, February, 1899 (Boston, etc.), LXXXIII, 145-154 *passim*.

---

187. In the Philippines (1898)

BY FREDERIC H. SAWYER

Sawyer was, in 1885, acting British consul for the Philippines ; he resided for fourteen years in Luzon, and travelled extensively throughout the archipelago. This extract is from a paper apparently sent to the United States naval *attaché* in London. — Bibliography : A. P. C. Griffin, *List of Books relating to the Theory of Colonization*, 11-22, 100-108.

THE most important race in the archipelago is the Tagal or Tagaloc, inhabiting Manila and the central provinces of Luzon, and as my long experience of them is extremely favorable, I am loth to see them described as they have been — as ferocious savages, intent on bloodshed.

The Tagal, as I knew him, possesses a good deal of self-respect, and is of a quiet and calm demeanor. On great provocation he is liable to give way to a sudden burst of fury, in which condition he is very dangerous. But in general he shows great docility, and bears no malice if justly punished. He is fairly industrious, and sometimes is very hard working. Anyone who has seen him poling barges against the current of the Pasig will admit this. He is a sportsman, and will readily put his money on his favorite horse or gamecock. He is also prone to other forms of gambling. He rarely gives way to intemperance. . . .

The Tagal makes a good soldier ; he can march long distances barefooted, and find food in the forests where European soldiers would starve.

In action his officer has more trouble to hold him in than to urge him on. . . .

The Tagals are good agriculturists. Their sugar plantations are worked on the " métayage " system, a sort of cooperative arrangement which gives good results. All the cultivation is done by natives of the islands, no Chinamen being employed on the land, except a few market gardeners near Manila.

I think that the Tagals and other natives might be easily governed. Latterly they have shown themselves rebellious against the Spanish Government and especially against the priests, but the causes are not far to seek.

In former times, when communication with Spain was by sailing vessel round the Cape, the number of Spaniards in the islands was small.

Each province was under an alcalde — mayor — who was both governor and judge ; a province with a hundred thousand inhabitants had perhaps not more than five resident Spanish officials besides the priests. All the wealthy parishes had Spanish monks as parish priests. The poor ones had native clergy. The government was carried on according to the old " Leyes de Indias." By these wise laws the native was afforded great protection against extortion.

He was in some sense a perpetual minor, and could not be sued for more than $5. . . .

These laws also conferred upon the native the perpetual usufruct of all the land that he cleared and cultivated, and he could not be removed from it. In consequence, most of the cultivated land in Luzon is to this day the property of the natives.

The native also had the right to cut timber in the forests to build or repair his house or ship, and could cut bamboos for his roofs and fences. . . .

The taxes were light, the principal one being a poll tax called the " tributo." The customs duties were light and machinery for the sugar plantations came in free of duty. A friendly feeling then existed between the Spaniard and the native ; the maintenance of such an economical administration was not burdensome to the latter.

With the opening of the Suez Canal, and the subsequent establishment of a Spanish line of steamers, all this changed. Hordes of hungry Spaniards arrived by every steamer, for whom places must be found. A bureaucratic administration was gradually substituted for the old paternal régime.

New departments were organized and the old ones greatly extended. Officials fresh from Spain were poured into every province. . . .

A policy was now announced and acted upon to assimilate all the institutions of the archipelago to those of the peninsula — a policy almost too imbecile for belief, but credible now we have seen to what depths of inaptitude a Spanish cabinet can descend. . . .

. . . every year some new and oppressive tax was imposed. The customs duties were several times raised and articles formerly exempt were made to pay. An export tax on sugar and hemp, a tax on all trades and professions, on horses and carriages, a port tax, stamp tax, a vexatious tax on all animals slaughtered, taxes on the hand looms used by the women in their spare time, taxes on sugar, rice, and oil mills, on ships, boats, and lighters ; all these and many more were imposed. All these duties and taxes, collected by a horde of rapacious and unscrupulous employees, might well disgust the native with the Government. All classes felt the oppression. The rich were blackmailed under threats of being reported as disaffected, while the poor suffered from illegal exactions.

Serious agrarian troubles arose between the monastic orders and the tenants on their vast estates. Toward the end of General Weyler's government a perilous state of unrest prevailed. But the arrival of Gen. Don Emilio Despujols, Conde de Caspe, to take over the government soon produced a better feeling. He meted out justice alike to priest and tenant, to Spaniard and native, and sent back to Spain several notorious offenders who were a disgrace to the Spanish name. The natives, seeing justice done them for the first time, became most fervent admirers of the Conde de Caspe, whom they looked upon as a savior. He became the idol of the people. This state of things was unfortunately of short duration, for the priests seeing that he was not their champion obtained his recall by cable. It is said that they paid $100,000 in Madrid to obtain this. His departure was a wonderful sight ; never had there been seen such demonstrations of affection to a governor-general.   Innumerable multitudes of natives crowded the shores to see him embark, and every steamer belonging to the port accompanied him far out to sea.

With the sudden departure of the Conde de Caspe there settled down on the native mind the gloomy conviction that force alone could plead their cause and that their only hope was to rise in arms.

Who can wonder at it?   With that horde of hungry taxgatherers ever vexing them, with all justice denied them, with exile from their homes to some distant island ever hanging over them, what else could they do?   Their fight almost unarmed against the Spaniards was heroic and merits the admiration of all brave men.   With few exceptions, their humanity has been equal to their valor.

Altogether, I consider the Tagals to be a brave, kindly, intelligent, and interesting people, worthy of a better government than they have had.   At the same time they are not advanced enough to take the administration of the archipelago, nor even of Luzon, entirely into their own hands.

If an honest administration could be conferred upon them, I am convinced that in a very few years they would attain such a degree of prosperity as no other colony has hitherto achieved, and thus fully justify their release from the curse of Spanish domination.

Senate Documents, 55 Cong., 3 sess. (Washington, 1899), VIII, No. 62, pt. 2, pp. 552–555 *passim.*

---

188. The Porto Ricans (1899)

BY COMMISSIONER HENRY KING CARROLL

Carroll, author-journalist, was for many years religious and political editor of the *Independent.* In 1898, after the Spanish war had been suspended by the protocol, President McKinley sent him to Porto Rico as a special commissioner to study the conditions of the island. This extract is from his report. — Bibliography as in No. 187 above.

THE system of public schools was antiquated, and few improvements seem to have been made. In practice it was decidedly. inferior and insufficient. Most attention was given, naturally, to urban schools, and these were inadequate in almost every respect. Less attention was given to schools in the rural districts, where the difficulties were greatest. Something was done for the boys, but little for the girls. Indeed, the first rural school for girls is said to have been established no longer ago than 1880. . . . The school population of the island, as reported by Secretary Carbonell, on the 1st of November, 1898, was 125,695. Of these 27,938 had attended school and 93,757 had not. . . .

The last census does not give returns for literacy and illiteracy except in certain districts. There are no later figures than those of the census of 1860, when the population was 583,181. Of this number 51,250 were literate and 531,931 illiterate. Over 90 per cent were unable to read. The estimates of present conditions vary; some say that 15, others 18 or 20 per cent, of the population are literates. . . .

. . . Porto Rico had a cheap and fairly effective telegraph and postal system, both under Government direction, but its roads, with few exceptions, were bad, and its railroads incomplete and not altogether satisfactory. There exists on paper a plan for a railroad system all the way around the island, but the gaps are much longer than the lines. . . .

The demand for good roads was more general than any other presented to the commissioner. A memorial from Arroyo stated that "without roads the riches of the island can not be developed." Another, from the municipal council of Utuado, said : "Real roads do not exist from the interior to the coast ; only tracks, dangerous even to travelers, are available, preventing the development of the country and sapping its life every day." . . .

The policy which has governed in Porto Rico hitherto seems to have been to put all its energy into the production of sugar, coffee, tobacco, and cattle, and import most of its food supply. Its crops, under a system of cultivation not the most advantageous, have been so large that it could pay its heavy bills for foreign goods, meet enormous interest charges on its working capital, and have generally a profit left. . . .

Those who depend upon daily wages for support constitute the great majority of the people. The sources of employment are not numerous. The raising, harvesting, and grinding of cane require many more hands than the care and cure of coffee or tobacco ; but even on sugar estates the work is not continuous. Some are kept the year round ; others only during the busiest season. The daily wages of the common field laborer range generally from 35 to 50 cents, native money. . . .

The field laborer is usually illiterate and is bringing up his children as he himself was raised, entirely without schooling. This is due in part to the lack of school accommodations in rural districts, partly to the want of suitable clothing, and in some measure to the failure of parents to appreciate the importance of education. . . .

It is evident that the condition of the laboring classes can not be greatly improved unless agriculture becomes prosperous and minor industries are developed. This means practically a revolution in the methods of raising and marketing crops, and it can not be accomplished without the influx of new capital. How this shall be attracted is one of the problems for those interested in the regeneration of Porto Rico. It is manifest that the great object to be gained is the raising of the working classes to a higher level of intelligence, of efficiency as laborers, of power and influence as citizens, and of comfort and enjoyment as social creatures. Give them remunerative work, and all the rest is possible. They will then . . . want better houses, better furniture, better food and clothing, and this in turn will give increased employment to masons and carpenters and to producers of foodstuffs and the various fabrics. The great wheel would turn all the lesser wheels. Laborers are good consumers when their labor is sufficiently paid, and there can be no real prosperity in which they do not share. . . .

All classes of natives of the island welcomed the American Army, American occupation, and American methods, and accepted without hesitation the Stars and Stripes in place of the red and yellow bars. They had not been disloyal to the old flag ; but it had come to represent to them, particularly during the present century, in which a class feeling developed between the insular and the peninsular Spaniard, partiality and oppression. . . . Porto Ricans generally complained that the former Government discriminated in favor of the Spaniard, who, in the distribution of the offices, was preferred to the native, and who, aided by the powerful influence of the authorities, prospered in business as banker, merchant, manufacturer, or agriculturist. They also insist that the internal improvement of the island was neglected ; that agriculture bore more than its share of the burden of taxation ; that the assessments were very inequitable and unequal ; that education was not fostered, and that in general the welfare of the people was not the first concern of their rulers. . . .

The question of capacity for self-government lies at the threshold of the whole subject. It may be said, without fear of contradiction, that Porto Ricans have had little opportunity to show their capacity, and such experience as they may have gained in the government of cities and in minor official positions was under a system not the most suitable for developing efficient, independent, impartial, and honest public servants. They, themselves, see this clearly and admit it. They condemn unsparingly the old methods, and say that they want to begin the era of their new relations with better institutions, under sounder and juster principles, and with improved methods. . . .

If the desire to assume the burdens of local self-government may be taken as indicating some degree of capacity for self-government, the people of Porto Rico certainly have the desire. They may be poor, but they are proud and sensitive, and would be bitterly disappointed if they found that they had been delivered from an oppressive yoke to be put under a tutelage which proclaimed their inferiority. Apart from such qualifications as general education and experience constitute, the commissioner has no hesitation in affirming that the people have good claims to be considered capable of self-government. . . .

The unswerving loyalty of Porto Rico to the Crown of Spain, as demonstrated by the truth of history, is no small claim to the confidence and trust of the United States. The people were obedient under circumstances which provoked revolt after revolt in other Spanish colonies. The habit of obedience is strong among them.

Their respect for law is another notable characteristic. They are not turbulent or violent. Riots are almost unknown in the island ; so is organized resistance to law ; brigandage flourished only for a brief period after the war and its object was revenge rather than rapine.

They are not a criminal people. The more violent crimes are by no means common. Burglary is almost unknown. There are many cases of homicide, but the number in proportion to population is not as large as in the United States. Thievery is the most common crime, and petty cases make up a large part of this list of offences. The people as a whole are a moral, law-abiding class, mild in disposition, easy to govern, and possess the possibilities of developing a high type of citizenship. . . .

They are industrious, and are not disposed to shirk the burdens which fall, often with crushing force, upon the laboring class. Their idleness is usually an enforced idleness. No doubt the ambition of many needs to be stimulated, for their lot has been so hopeless of an improvement that the desire for more conveniences and comforts may have been well-nigh lost. They seem to have few customs or prejudices which would prevent them from becoming good American citizens.

The question remains whether, in view of the high rate of illiteracy which exists among them, and of their lack of training in the responsibilities of citizenship, it would be safe to intrust them with the power of self-government. The commissioner has no hesitation in answering this question in the affirmative. . . .

Henry K. Carroll, *Report on the Island of Porto Rico* (Washington, 1899), 32-58 *passim*.

---

189. Government in Cuba (1899)

BY GOVERNOR-GENERAL LEONARD WOOD

Wood was an assistant surgeon in the United States army before the Spanish War. He recruited the " Rough Riders " and commanded them during the Santiago campaign, being promoted to the rank of brigadier-general, and later to that of major-general, of volunteers. After the capture of the city he was made the military governor, and administered affairs so satisfactorily that in 1899 he was appointed governor-general of Cuba, and in 1901 brigadier-general in the regular army. — Bibliography as in No. 187 above.

WHEN the American authorities took charge of the Province of Santiago de Cuba they found the civil affairs of the province in a condition of complete chaos. The treasuries of all the different municipalities were empty ; the offices were vacant ; public records, such as had not been burnt or destroyed, were bundled up in abandoned buildings. The courts had ceased to exist. In fact, there was only a semblance of any form of civil government. In many of the towns a few members of the old " Guardia Civil " still continued to maintain an appearance of order, but, practically speaking, there had been a complete destruction of civil government, and it rested with the newcomers to do what they could toward re-establishing a proper form of government which would give the people necessary protection, and guarantee such a condition of order as would once more tend to re-establish business and invite the confidence of outside capital. . . .

The idea with which this work has been done is first to re-establish the municipalities upon the simplest and most economical basis consistent with a fair degree of efficiency. Of course it was impossible to change altogether the old system. We have had to begin, even in the little towns, by appointing a mayor, a secretary and one or two municipal police officers, simply because this was the system to which the people for many generations had been accustomed ; but in making these appointments every effort has been made to select the best men and an adequate service for the salary paid has been insisted upon. Under the old system men went to their offices at 9 a. m., left at 11 a. m. and came back for an hour in the afternoon. There were a great many clerks, many of whom were totally unnecessary. In each little town one found a great many officials doing very little, no school houses, no sanitary regulations — in fact nothing indicative of a high degree of civilization. It was a pedantic humbug from top to bottom. In place of this condition, we, so far as possible with the limited time and means at our command, have re-established these little towns, giving them the officers absolutely necessary to maintain an efficient administration of the public business. We insisted upon a thorough sanitary supervision of the towns, a thorough cleaning up of the streets, private houses, yards, courts, etc., the re-establishing of the schools in the best buildings obtainable ; a prompt monthly payment of the teachers' salaries ; the forbidding of public school teachers having private pupils in the public schools — a condition which existed formerly and led to great abuses. Every effort has been made toward the re-establishment of the courts upon the most economical basis consistent with prompt transaction of the public business. The entire judicial machinery of the province has been put in operation upon an economical basis. At the head of this judicial system stands the Supreme Court of the province, which is supreme only for the time being, as upon the establishment of the Supreme Court for the island it will continue simply as the Audiencia or Superior Court of the province, from which an appeal can be taken to Havana. The greatest evil of the present system is in the method of criminal procedure. Persons accused are often months in prison before trial. . . . I have done what I could to remedy this condition by making offenses not capital bailable, and by establishing the writ of habeas corpus. The police is also to apply a large portion of the public revenue to the reconstruction of roads, bridges, etc., and to encourage, throughout the province, in all the larger towns, such sanitary reformation as the means at hand would permit. . . .

To the people was given a " Bill of Rights," which guaranteed to them the freedom of the press, the right to assemble peaceably, the right to seek redress for grievances, the right of habeas corpus, and the right to present bail for all offenses not capital. Every effort was made to impress upon them the fact that the civil law must in all free countries be absolutely supreme, and that all classes of people must recognize the authority of the officers of the law, whether represented by the ordinary policeman or by the judges of the Supreme Court. . . . In fact every effort was made to impress upon them the fact that people can do as they wish so long as they do not violate the law. On the other hand they were told, in unmistakable terms, that any and all infractions of the civil law would be punished severely, and that individuals resisting arrest would be taken even at the cost of their lives. Of course all this was under military government. Every effort was made, however, to remove the military as far as practicable from the situation. The intention was to re-establish rather than to replace the civil government. Men were appointed to office solely for their fitness for the position, and their selection was never made arbitrarily, but always upon the recommendation of the best citizens. I do not mean the best men in the social sense, or in any other sense than those best qualified by experience and ability to judge of the fitness of the various applicants for office. . . . I do not believe that just at present the people are in a condition to be taken further into the administration of civil affairs than indicated above. Before proceeding further it will be necessary to complete the organization of the schools ; get the courts into thorough running order and, what is very important, to get all the municipalities established upon an efficient basis, making them thoroughly self-supporting ; to do all that can be done to get the people back to their plantations and at work ; to reopen the roads and make them passable, thus enabling people to get their produce to the seacoast and to the markets ; to establish enough rural police to keep things quiet and orderly in the interior. After these conditions have been well established and found to be in good working order then we can begin to consider seriously the remaining details of civil government. Just at present it is well to stop, for a short time at least, where we are.

. . . It must be remembered that a large portion of the population is illiterate and they have never had any extensive participation in the affairs of government, not even in municipal affairs, and, until they thoroughly understand the handling of small affairs, they certainly are not fitted to undertake larger ones. In other words, let us begin from the bottom and build on a secure foundation rather than start at the top to remodel the whole fabric of civil government. . . .

Brigadier-General Leonard Wood, *The Establishment of the Civil Government in the Province of Santiago*, in *Independent*, June 15, 1899 (New York). LI, 1601–1604 *passim*.

190. Duty to Dependencies (1900)

BY PRESIDENT WILLIAM McKINLEY

McKinley began his legislative career in 1877, when he entered the House of Representatives as a Republican. He made a specialty of tariff legislation, became a prominent advocate of the protective system, and in 1890, as chairman of the Committee on Ways and Means, drafted the extreme protective-tariff law that bore his name. He was elected president in 1896 as a supporter of this system and of a single monetary standard; but his administration became prominent in other directions by reason of the problems imposed upon it by the Spanish War. This extract is from his instructions to the Philippine commission, transmitted through the secretary of war. — For McKinley, see Murat Halstead, *Life and Distinguished Services of Hon. Wm. McKinley.* — Bibliography as in No. 186 above.

IN the Message transmitted to the Congress on the 5th of December 1899, I said, speaking of the Philippine Islands : "As long as the insurrection continues the military arm must necessarily be supreme. But there is no reason why steps should not be taken from time to time to inaugurate governments essentially popular in their form as fast as territory is held and controlled by our troops. To this end I am considering the advisability of the return of the commission, or such of the members thereof as can be secured, to aid the existing authorities and facilitate this work throughout the islands."

To give effect to the intention thus expressed, I have appointed . . . commissioners to the Philippine Islands, to continue and perfect the work of organizing and establishing civil government already commenced by the military authorities, subject in all respects to any laws which the Congress may hereafter enact. . . .

. . . Without hampering them by too specific instructions, they should in general be enjoined, after making themselves familiar with the conditions and needs of the country, to devote their attention in the first instance to the establishment of municipal governments, in which the natives of the islands, both in the cities and in the rural communities, shall be afforded the opportunity to manage their own local affairs to the fullest extent of which they are capable and subject to the least degree of supervision and control which a careful study of their capacities and observation of the workings of native control show to be consistent with the maintenance of law, order, and loyalty.

The next subject in order of importance should be the organization of government in the larger administrative divisions corresponding to counties, departments, or provinces, in which the common interests of many or several municipalities falling within the same tribal lines, or the same natural geographical limits, may best be subserved by a common administration. Whenever the commission is of the opinion that the condition of affairs in the islands is such that the central administration may safely be transferred from military to civil control they will report that conclusion to you, with their recommendations as to the form of central government to be established for the purpose of taking over the control.

Beginning with the 1st day of September, 1900, the authority to exercise, subject to my approval, through the Secretary of War, that part of the power of government in the Philippine Islands which is of a legislative nature is to be transferred from the military governor of the islands to this commission. . . .

The commission will also have power . . . to appoint to office such officers under the judicial, educational, and civil-service systems and in the municipal and departmental governments as shall be provided for. . . .

The many different degrees of civilization and varieties of custom and capacity among the people of the different islands preclude very definite instruction as to the part which the people shall take in the selection of their own officers ; but these general rules are to be observed : That in all cases the municipal officers, who administer the local affairs of the people, are to be selected by the people, and that wherever officers of more extended jurisdiction are to be selected in any way natives of the islands are to be preferred, and if they can be found competent and willing to perform the duties, they are to receive the offices in preference to any others.

It will be necessary to fill some offices for the present with Americans which after a time may well be filled by natives of the islands. As soon as practicable a system for ascertaining the merit and fitness of candidates for civil office should be put in force. An indispensable qualification for all offices and positions of trust and authority in the islands must be absolute and unconditional loyalty to the United States, and absolute and unhampered authority and power to remove and punish any officer deviating from that standard must at all times be retained in the hands of the central authority of the islands.

In all the forms of government and administrative provisions which they are authorized to prescribe the commission should bear in mind that the government which they are establishing is designed not for our satisfaction, or for the expression of our theoretical views, but for the happiness, peace, and prosperity of the people of the Philippine Islands, and the measures adopted should be made to conform to their customs, their habits, and even their prejudices, to the fullest extent consistent with the accomplishment of the indispensable requisites of just and effective government.

At the same time the commission should bear in mind, and the people of the islands should be made plainly to understand, that there are certain great principles of government which have been made the basis of our governmental system which we deem essential to the rule of law and the maintenance of individual freedom, and of which they have, unfortunately, been denied the experience possessed by us ; that there are also certain practical rules of government which we have found to be essential to the preservation of these great principles of liberty and law, and that these principles and these rules of government must be established and maintained in their islands for the sake of their liberty and happiness, however much they may conflict with the customs or laws of procedure with which they are familiar.

It is evident that the most enlightened thought of the Philippine Islands fully appreciates the importance of these principles and rules, and they will inevitably within a short time command universal assent. Upon every division and branch of the government of the Philippines, therefore, must be imposed these inviolable rules :

That no person shall be deprived of life, liberty, or property without due process of law ; that private property shall not be taken for public use without just compensation ; that in all criminal prosecutions the accused shall enjoy the right to a speedy and public trial, to be informed of the nature and cause of the accusation, to be confronted with the witnesses against him, to have compulsory process for obtaining witnesses in his favor, and to have the assistance of counsel for his defense ; that excessive bail shall not be required, nor excessive fines imposed, nor cruel and unusual punishment inflicted ; that no person shall be put twice in jeopardy for the same offense, or be compelled in any criminal case to be a witness against himself ; that the right to be secure against unreasonable searches and seizures shall not be violated ; that neither slavery nor involuntary servitude shall exist except as a punishment for crime ; that no bill of attainder or ex-post-facto law shall be passed ; that no law shall be passed abridging the freedom of speech or of the press, or the rights of the people to peaceably assemble and petition the

Government for a redress of grievances ; that no law shall be made respecting an establishment of religion, or prohibiting the free exercise thereof, and that the free exercise and enjoyment of religious profession and worship without discrimination or preference shall forever be allowed. . . .

It will be the duty of the commission to promote and extend, and, as they find occasion, to improve the system of education already inaugurated by the military authorities. In doing this they should regard as of first importance the extension of a system of primary education which shall be free to all, and which shall tend to fit the people for the duties of citizenship and for the ordinary avocations of a civilized community. This instruction should be given in the first instance in every part of the islands in the language of the people. . . .

It may be well that the main changes which should be made in the system of taxation and in the body of the laws under which the people are governed, except such changes as have already been made by the military government, should be relegated to the civil government which is to be established under the auspices of the Commission. It will, however, be the duty of the Commission to inquire diligently as to whether there are any further changes which ought not to be delayed, and if so, they are authorized to make such changes, subject to your approval. In doing so they are to bear in mind that taxes which tend to penalize or repress industry and enterprise are to be avoided ; that provisions for taxation should be simple, so that they may be understood by the people ; that they should affect the fewest practicable subjects of taxation which will serve for the general distribution of the burden.

The main body of the laws which regulate the rights and obligations of the people should be maintained with as little interference as possible. Changes made should be mainly in procedure, and in the criminal laws to secure speedy and impartial trials, and at the same time effective administration and respect for individual rights. . . .

Upon all officers and employees of the United States, both civil and military, should be impressed a sense of the duty to observe not merely the material but the personal and social rights of the people of the islands, and to treat them with the same courtesy and respect for their personal dignity which the people of the United States are accustomed to require from each other.

Senate Journal, 56 Cong., 2 sess. (Washington, 1901), 11–12 *passim.*

191. Right of Self-Government (1900)

BY SENATOR GEORGE FRISBIE HOAR

Hoar is one of the oldest and most prominent members of the United States Senate. He is a Republican, but has not agreed with his party as to the acquisition or the retention of the Philippine Islands. This extract is from a speech in the Senate. — Bibliography as in No. 186 above.

. . . WE are told if we oppose the policy of our imperialistic and expanding friends we are bound to suggest some policy of our own as a substitute for theirs. We are asked what we would do in this difficult emergency. It is a question not difficult to answer. I for one am ready to answer it.

1. I would declare now that we will not take these islands to govern them against their will.

2. I would reject a cession of sovereignty which implies that sovereignty may be bought and sold and delivered without the consent of the people. Spain had no rightful sovereignty over the Philippine Islands. She could not rightfully sell it to us. We could not rightfully buy it from her.

3. I would require all foreign governments to keep out of these islands.

4. I would offer to the people of the Philippines our help in maintaining order until they have a reasonable opportunity to establish a government of their own.

5. I would aid them by advice, if they desire it, to set up a free and independent government.

6. I would invite all the great powers of Europe to unite in an agreement that that independence shall not be interfered with by us, by themselves, or by any one of them with the consent of the others. As to this I am not so sure. I should like quite as well to tell them it is not to be done whether they consent or not.

7. I would declare that the United States will enforce the same doctrine as applicable to the Philippines that we declared as to Mexico and Haiti and the South American Republics. It is true that the Monroe Doctrine, a doctrine based largely on our regard for our own interests, is not applicable either in terms or in principle to a distant Asiatic territory. But undoubtedly, having driven out Spain, we are bound, and have the right, to secure to the people we have liberated an opportunity, undisturbed and in peace, to establish a new government for themselves.

8. I would then, in a not distant future, leave them to work out their own salvation, as every nation on earth, from the beginning of time, has wrought out its own salvation. . . . To attempt to confer the gift of freedom from without, or to impose freedom from without on any people, is to disregard all the lessons of history. It is to attempt

> " A gift of that which is not to be given
> By all the blended powers of earth and heaven."

9. I would strike out of your legislation the oath of allegiance to us and substitute an oath of allegiance to their own country. . . .

Mr. President, there lies at the bottom of what is called imperialism a doctrine which, if adopted, is to revolutionize the world in favor of despotism. It directly conflicts with and contradicts the doctrine on which our own revolution was founded, and with which, so far, our example has revolutionized the world. It is the doctrine that when, in the judgment of any one nation or any combination of nations, the institutions which a people set up and maintain for themselves are disapproved they have a right to overthrow that government and to enter upon and possess it themselves. . . .

Our imperialistic friends seem to have forgotten the use of the vocabulary of liberty. They talk about giving good government. "We shall give them such a government as we think they are fitted for." "We shall give them a better government than they had before." Why, Mr. President, that one phrase conveys to a free man and a free people the most stinging of insults. In that little phrase, as in a seed, is contained the germ of all despotism and of all tyranny. Government is not a gift. Free government is not to be given by all the blended powers of earth and heaven. It is a birthright. It belongs, as our fathers said and as their children said, as Jefferson said and as President McKinley said, to human nature itself. There can be no good government but self-government. . . .

I have failed to discover in the speech, public or private, of the advocates of this war, or in the press which supports it and them, a single expression anywhere of a desire to do justice to the people of the Philippine Islands, or of a desire to make known to the people of the United States the truth of the case. . . .

The catchwords, the cries, the pithy and pregnant phrases of which all their speech is full, all mean dominion. They mean perpetual dominion. When a man tells you that the American flag must not be hauled down where it has once floated, or demands of a shouting audience, "Who will haul it down?" if he mean anything, he means that that people shall be under our dominion forever. The man who says, "We will not treat with them till they submit; we will not deal with men in arms against the flag," says, in substance, the same thing. One thing there has been, at least, given to them as Americans not to say. There is not one of these gentlemen who will rise in his place and affirm that if he were a Filipino he would not do exactly as the Filipinos are doing; that he would not despise them if they were to do otherwise. So much, at least, they owe of respect to the dead and buried history — the dead and buried history, so far as they can slay and bury it — of their country.

Why, the tariff schemes which are proposed are schemes in our interest and not in theirs. If you propose to bring tobacco from Porto Rico or from the Philippine Islands on the ground that it is for the interest of the people whom you are undertaking to govern, for their best interests to raise it and sell it to you, every imperialist in Connecticut will be up in arms. The nerve in the pocket is still sensitive, though the nerve in the heart may be numb. You will not let their sugar come here to compete with the cane sugar of Louisiana or the beet sugar of California or the Northwest, and in determining that question you mean to think not of their interest but of yours. The good government you are to give them is a government under which their great productive and industrial interests, when peace comes, are to be totally and absolutely disregarded by their government. You are not only proposing to do that, but you expect to put another strain on the Constitution to accomplish it.

Why, Mr. President, the atmosphere of both legislative chambers, even now, is filled with measures proposing to govern and tax these people for our interest, and not for theirs. Your men who are not alarmed at the danger to constitutional liberty are up in arms when there is danger to tobacco. . . .

Is there any man so bold as to utter in seriousness the assertion that where the American flag has once been raised it shall never be hauled down? I have heard it said that to haul down or to propose to haul down this national emblem where it has once floated is poltroonery. Will any man say it was poltroonery when Paul Jones landed on the northeast coast of England that he took his flag away with him when he departed? Was Scott a poltroon, or was Polk a poltroon? Was Taylor a poltroon? Was the United States a nation of poltroons when they retired from the City of Mexico or from Vera Cruz without leaving the flag behind them? . . .

Mr. President, this talk that the American flag is never to be removed where it has once floated is the silliest and wildest rhetorical flourish ever uttered in the ears of an excited populace. No baby ever said anything to another baby more foolish.

Now, what are the facts as to the Philippine Islands and the American flag? We have occupied a single city, part of one of four hundred islands, and with a population of 120,000 or thereabouts out of 10,000,000. The Spanish forces were invested and hemmed in by the people of those islands, who had risen to assert their own freedom when we got there. Now, what kind of Americanism, what kind of patriotism, what kind of love of liberty is it to say that we are to turn our guns on that patriot people and wrest from them the freedom that was almost within their grasp and hold these islands for our own purposes in subjection and by right of conquest because the American flag ought not to be hauled down where it has once floated, or, for the baser and viler motive still, that we can make a few dollars a year out of their trade?

Congressional Record, 56 Cong., 1 sess. (Washington, 1900), XXXIII, 4303–4305 *passim*, April 17, 1900.

CHAPTER XXXII — FOREIGN PROBLEMS

192. Our Foreign Policy (1899)

BY RICHARD OLNEY

For Olney, see No. 179 above. — Bibliography: A. P. C. Griffin, *List of Books relating to the Theory of Colonization*, 112–114.

THOUGH historians will probably assign the abandonment of the isolation policy of the United States to the time when this country and Spain went to war over Cuba, and though the abandonment may have been precipitated by that contest, the change was inevitable, had been long preparing, and could not have been long delayed. . . . when our troubles with Spain came to a head, it had, it is believed, already dawned upon the American mind that the international policy suitable to our infancy and our weakness was unworthy of our maturity and our strength ; that the traditional rules regulating our relations to Europe, almost a necessity of the conditions prevailing a century ago, were inapplicable to the changed conditions of the present day ; and that both duty and interest required us to take our true position in the European family and to both reap all the advantages and assume all the burdens incident to that position. . . .

. . . That relinquishment — the substitution of international fellowship — the change from passive and perfunctory membership of the society of civilized states to real and active membership — is to be ascribed . . . above all to that instinct and impulse in the line of national growth and expansion whose absence would be a sure symptom of our national deterioration. For it is true of states as of individuals — they never stand still, and if not going forward, are surely retrogressing. This evolution of the United States as one of the great Powers among the nations has, however, been accompanied by another departure radical in character and far-reaching in consequences. The United States has come out of its shell and ceased to be a hermit among the nations, naturally and properly. What was not necessary and is certainly of the most doubtful expediency is that it should at the same time become a colonizing Power on an immense scale. . . .

. . . The United States now asserting itself not only as one of the great Powers of the world but as a Power with very large Asiatic dependencies — what consequent changes in respect of its foreign relations must reasonably be anticipated?

It goes without saying that the United States cannot play the part in the world's affairs it has just assumed without equipping itself for the part with all the instrumentalities necessary to make its will felt either through pacific intercourse and negotiation or through force. . . . But the equipment required for our new international rôle need not be discussed at any length. We must have it — the need will be forced upon us by facts the logic of which will be irresistible — and however slow to move or indisposed to face the facts, the national government must sooner or later provide it. It is more important as well as interesting to inquire how the new phase of our foreign relations will affect the principles regulating our policy and conduct towards foreign states.

In dealing with that topic, it should be kept in mind that membership of the society of civilized states does not mean that each member has the same rights and duties as respects every subject-matter. On the contrary . . . while the United States as regards Europe in general may . . . be regarded as an insular Power, its remoteness and separation from Europe by a great expanse of ocean make its interest in the internal affairs of European states almost altogether speculative and sentimental. Abstention from interference in any such affairs . . . should be and must be the rule of the United States for the future as it has been in the past.

Again, as between itself and the states of Europe, the primacy of the United States as respects the affairs of the American continents is a principle of its foreign policy which will no doubt hold good and be as firmly asserted in the future as in the past. . . .

It is to be remembered, however, that no rule of policy is so inflexible as not to bend to the force of extraordinary and anomalous conditions. . . . It is hardly necessary to add that the status of the United States as an Asiatic Power must have some tendency to qualify the attitude which, as a strictly American Power, the United States has hitherto successfully maintained towards the states of Europe. They are Asiatic Powers as well as ourselves — we shall be brought in contact with them as never before — competition and irritation are inevitable and contro-

versies not improbable — and when and how far a conflict in the East may
spread and what domestic as well as foreign interests and policies may be
involved, is altogether beyond the reach of human sagacity to foretell.

Subject to these exceptions . . . our new departure in foreign affairs
will require no change in the cardinal rules already alluded to. . . . It
can not be doubted, however, that our new departure not merely unties
our hands but fairly binds us to use them in a manner we have thus far
not been accustomed to. We can not assert ourselves as a Power whose
interests and sympathies are as wide as civilization without assuming
obligations corresponding to the claim. . . . The first duty of every
nation, as already observed, is to itself — is the promotion and conserva-
tion of its own interests. . . . But, just weight being given to that
principle, and its abilities and resources and opportunities permitting,
there is no reason why the United States should not act for the relief of
suffering humanity and for the advancement of civilization wherever and
whenever such action would be timely and effective. Should there, for
example, be a recurrence of the Turkish massacres of Armenian Christians,
not to stop them alone or in concert with others, could we do so without
imperiling our own substantial interests, would be unworthy of us and
inconsistent with our claims and aspirations as a great Power. We
certainly could no longer shelter ourselves behind the time-honored
excuse that we are an American Power exclusively, without concern with
the affairs of the world at large.

On similar grounds, the position we have assumed in the world and
mean to maintain justifies us in undertaking to influence and enables us
to greatly influence the industrial development of the American people.
The "home market" fallacy disappears with the proved inadequacy of
the home market. Nothing will satisfy us in the future but free access
to foreign markets — especially to those markets in the East now for the
first time beginning to fully open themselves to the Western nations. . . .
In the markets of the Orient especially, American citizens have always
been at a decided disadvantage as compared with those of the great
European Powers. The latter impress themselves upon the native
imagination by their display of warlike resources and their willingness
to use them in aid not merely of the legal rights of their citizens but in
many cases of their desires and ambitions as well. . . . Obstacles of
this sort to the extension of American trade can not but be greatly
lessened in the future under the operation of the new foreign policy of
the United States and its inevitable accompaniments. . . . Our diplo-

matic representatives, no matter how certain of the greatness of their country, have hitherto labored under the difficulty that nations to whom they were accredited, especially the Oriental nations, were not appreciative of the fact. That difficulty is unlikely to embarrass them in the future. They will, like the nation itself, cease to be isolated and of small consideration, and will speak and act with something of the same persuasiveness and authority as the representatives of European Powers.

Along with the Monroe doctrine and non-interference in the internal concerns of European states . . . has gone another which our changed international attitude will undoubtedly tend to modify. It has heretofore been considered that anything like an alliance between the United States and an European Power, for any purpose or any time, was something not to be thought of. . . . Yet there may be "alliances" which are not "entangling" but wholly advantageous. . . . Nevertheless, up to this time the theory and practice of the United States have been against all alliances peremptorily, and, were the Philippines not on our hands, might perhaps have been persisted in for a longer or shorter period. Whether they could have been or not is a contingency not worth discussing. We start our career as a world Power with the Philippine handicap firmly fastened to us, and that situation being accepted, how about "alliances"? The true, the ideal position for us, would be complete freedom of action, perfect liberty to pick allies from time to time as special occasions might warrant and an enlightened view of our own interests might dictate. Without the Philippines, we might closely approach that position. With them, not merely is our need of friendship imperative, but it is a need which only one of the great Powers can satisfy or is disposed to satisfy. Except for Great Britain's countenance, we should almost certainly never have got the Philippines — except for her continued support, our hold upon them would be likely to prove precarious, perhaps altogether unstable. It follows that we now find ourselves actually caught in an entangling alliance, forced there not by any treaty, or compact of any sort, formal or informal, but by the stress of the inexorable facts of the situation. It is an alliance that entangles because we might be and should be friends with all the world and because our necessary intimacy with and dependence upon one of them is certain to excite the suspicion and ill-will of other nations. Still, however much better off we might have been, regrets, the irrevocable having happened, are often worse than useless, and it is much more profitable to note such compensatory advantages as the actual situation offers. In that view, it is consoling to reflect that, if we must single out an ally from among the nations at the cost of alienating all others, and consequently have thrown ourselves into the arms of England, our choice is probably unexceptionable. . . .

In undertaking any forecast of the future of our foreign relations, it is . . . not rash to affirm . . . that a consequence of the new international position of the United States must be to give to foreign affairs a measure of popular interest and importance far beyond what they have hitherto enjoyed. Domestic affairs will cease to be regarded as alone deserving the serious attention of Americans generally. . . . Such a change will import . . . if not for us, for coming generations, a larger knowledge of the earth and its diverse peoples ; a familiarity with problems world-wide in their bearings ; the abatement of racial prejudices ; in short . . . enlarged mental and moral vision. . . .

Richard Olney, *Growth of our Foreign Policy*, in *Atlantic Monthly*, March, 1900 (Boston, etc.), LXXXV, 290–301 *passim*.

---

193. The Open Door (1899)

BY SECRETARY JOHN HAY

Hay began his public career as Lincoln's private secretary. Later he held several minor diplomatic appointments and became prominent as a writer. McKinley appointed him ambassador to Great Britain in 1897, and secretary of state in 1898. In this last position his name has become inseparably associated with the policy of the United States in respect to the far-eastern question. This extract is from a letter addressed to Charlemagne Tower, the United States ambassador at St. Petersburg. Similar letters were sent to the legations at London, Paris, Berlin, Rome, and Tokyo, and favorable replies were received from all the foreign governments thus addressed. — Bibliography : A. P. C. Griffin, *List of Books relating to the Theory of Colonization*, 115–131.

Washington, September 6, 1899.

. . . IN 1898, when His Imperial Majesty had, through his diplomatic representative at this capital, notified this Government that Russia had leased from His Imperial Chinese Majesty the ports of Port Arthur, Ta-lien-wan, and the adjacent territory in the Liao-tung Peninsula in north-eastern China for a period of twenty-five years, your predecessor received categorical assurances from the Imperial Minister for Foreign Affairs that American interests in that part of the Chinese Empire would in no way be affected thereby, neither was it the desire of Russia to interfere with the trade of other nations, and that our citizens would continue to enjoy within said leased territory all the rights and privileges guaranteed them under existing treaties with China.   Assurances of a similar purport were conveyed to me by the Emperor's Ambassador at this capital; while fresh proof of this is afforded by the Imperial Ukase of $\frac{\text{July } 30}{\text{August } 11}$ last, creating the free port of Dalny, near Ta-lien-wan, and establishing free trade for the adjacent territory.

However gratifying and reassuring such assurances may be in regard to the territory actually occupied and administered, it can not but be admitted that a further, clearer, and more formal definition of the conditions which are henceforth to hold within the so-called Russian "sphere of interest" in China as regards the commercial rights therein of our citizens is much desired by the business world of the United States, inasmuch as such a declaration would relieve it from the apprehensions which have exercised a disturbing influence during the last four years on its operations in China.

The present moment seems particularly opportune for ascertaining whether His Imperial Russian Majesty would not be disposed to give permanent form to the assurances heretofore given to this Government on this subject.

The Ukase of the Emperor of August 11 of this year, declaring the port of Ta-lien-wan open to the merchant ships of all nations during the remainder of the lease under which it is held by Russia, removes the slightest uncertainty as to the liberal and conciliatory commercial policy His Majesty proposes carrying out in northeastern China, and would seem to insure us the sympathetic and, it is hoped, favorable consideration of the propositions hereinafter specified.

The principles which this Government is particularly desirous of seeing formally declared by His Imperial Majesty and by all the great Powers interested in China, and which will be eminently beneficial to the commercial interests of the whole world, are:

First. The recognition that no Power will in any way interfere with any treaty port or any vested interest within any leased territory or within any so-called "sphere of interest" it may have in China.

Second. That the Chinese treaty tariff of the time being shall apply to all merchandise landed or shipped to all such ports as are within said "sphere of interest" (unless they be "free ports"), no matter to what nationality it may belong, and that duties so leviable shall be collected by the Chinese Government.

Third. That it will levy no higher harbor dues on vessels of another nationality frequenting any port in such "sphere" than shall be levied on vessels of its own nationality, and no higher railroad charges over lines built, controlled, or operated within its "sphere" on merchandise belonging to citizens or subjects of other nationalities transported through such "sphere" than shall be levied on similar merchandise belonging to its own nationals transported over equal distances.

The declaration of such principles by His Imperial Majesty would not only be of great benefit to foreign commerce in China, but would powerfully tend to remove dangerous sources of irritation and possible conflict between the various Powers ; it would reestablish confidence and security ; and would give great additional weight to the concerted representations which the treaty Powers may hereafter make to His Imperial Chinese Majesty in the interest of reform in Chinese administration so essential to the consolidation and integrity of that Empire, and which, it is believed, is a fundamental principal of the policy of His Majesty in Asia.

Germany has declared the port of Kiao-chao, which she holds in Shangtung under a lease from China, a free port and has aided in the establishment there of a branch of the Imperial Chinese Maritime Customs.   The Imperial German Minister for Foreign Affairs has also given assurances that American trade would not in any way be discriminated against or interfered with, as there is no intention to close the leased territory to foreign commerce within the area which Germany claims. These facts lead this Government to believe that the Imperial German Government will lend its cooperation and give its acceptance to the proposition above outlined, and which our Ambassador at Berlin is now instructed to submit to it.

That such a declaration will be favorably considered by Great Britain and Japan, the two other Powers most interested in the subject, there can be no doubt ; the formal and oft-repeated declarations of the British and Japanese Governments in favor of the maintenance throughout China of freedom of trade for the whole world insure us, it is believed, the ready assent of these Powers to the declaration desired.

The acceptance by His Imperial Majesty of these principles must therefore inevitably lead to their recognition by all the other Powers interested, and you are instructed to submit them to the Emperor's Minister for Foreign Affairs and urge their immediate consideration.

Department of State, *Correspondence concerning American Commercial Rights in China* (Washington, 1900), 15-17.

194. Besieged in Pekin (1900)

BY MRS. KATHARINE MULLIKIN LOWRY

Mrs. Lowry resided for five years in China, where her husband was formerly connected with the United States embassy at Pekin.   When the Boxer insurrection
began, she was living at the Methodist Episcopal mission settlement in Pekin.   The
"Sir Claude" in the text was the British minister, Sir Claude MacDonald. — Bibliography as in No. 193 above.

WEDNESDAY, June 13 [1900] : About 6.30 P.M. there is excitement and loud voices at the Ha-ta gate, and from the Woman's
Foreign Missionary Society's upper windows soldiers can be seen on the
wall looking into the street.   Later, smoke and flame announce that our
street chapel is being burned.   All night long fires spring up in different
parts of the city.   (All the different mission compounds and Catholic
churches were first looted and then burned, except the Pei-Tang, which
was guarded). . . .

THURSDAY, June 14 : To-day some of our number went to the Legation carrying the records, mission history, deeds, etc. . . .

FRIDAY, June 15 : Last night for two hours awful sounds of raging
heathen filled the air, and seemed to surge against the wall in the
southern city, opposite our place.   Some estimated there were 50,000
voices.   " Kill the foreign devil !   Kill, kill, kill !" they yelled till it
seemed hell was let loose. . . .

WEDNESDAY, June 20 : About nine A.M. . . . great excitement was
caused by the word that Baron von Ketteler, the German Minister, had
been shot on his way to the Tsungli Yamen, and his interpreter wounded.
. . . Captain Hall thought as it would be impossible to hold the compound against soldiers, our only chance would be to abandon it immediately, while it is still possible for women and children to walk on the
street.   He therefore sends word to the Legation that he wishes to be
relieved, and sets the time for leaving the compound at eleven A.M.,
with no baggage except what we can carry in our hands. . . . At
eleven o'clock the melancholy file takes up its march, the seventy
foreigners at the front, two and two, the gentlemen, with their guns,
walking by the side of the ladies and children, while behind follow over
500 Chinese refugees who have been with us all these twelve mournful
days, the twenty marines with Captain Myers bringing up the rear — 656
persons in all.   Sad, indeed, did we feel to thus march away from our
homes, leaving them with all their contents to certain destruction. . . .

The nationalities represented here (British Legation) are American, Austrian, Belgian, Boer, British, Chinese, Danish, Dutch, French, Finn, German, Italian, Japanese, Norwegian, Portuguese, Russian, Spanish, Swedish. . . . They are divided into men, 245 ; women, 149 ; children, 79 ; total, 473 ; not including the marines, of whom there were 409. . . . The Chinese here number about 700 to 800 Protestants and 2,000 Catholics. . . .

THURSDAY, June 21 : To-day Sir Claude requests that Mr. Gamewell take full charge of fortifying this place, and that committees be appointed with full authority to control our defenses. This is done. Mr. Tewkesbury is made head of the general committees. Other committees are appointed for fire, food, fuel, Chinese labor, foreign labor, sanitation, and water, and in a remarkably short time this motley crowd of many nationalities is thoroughly organized for the best good of all. Mr. Gamewell suggests the use of sand-bags in the defense, and the making of them begins, the church being headquarters for this work. Large fires are seen raging in many parts of the city. . . .

SATURDAY, June 23 : To-day has been one of great excitement. Five big fires rage close about us, and bucket lines are formed several times. Some of the fires are started by the Chinese ; some by our people, to burn out places which are dangerous to us, because the Chinese may burn them or can fire from them. After burning the Russian Bank the Chinese start a fire in the Han Lin College, with a wind blowing from the north, which makes it very dangerous for us. Hardly is the fire under way, however, when the wind providentially changes and we are saved from that danger, though much hard work is required in passing water. Sentiment and fear of antagonizing the Chinese caused our people to refrain from firing this Han Lin College, the very foundation of Chinese literature and culture. The intense hatred of the Chinese for us is shown by the fact that they themselves set fire to this relic of the ages. . . . It is said the destruction of this Han Lin Library is only paralleled by the burning of the Alexandrian Library.

SUNDAY, June 24 : To-day the Chinese do their first shelling. . . .

WEDNESDAY, June 27 : The usual nerve strain is endured all day from the bullets and shells. We shall forget how it feels to be without their sound. The nights are dreadful with the sound of shattering tiles and falling bricks, and there is so much echo in the courts that at night it is hard to locate where an attack is being made, and harder still to sleep at all. At eleven P.M. an alarm is rung at the bell tower for all to assemble there with their firearms. This is the second or third general alarm we have had, and they frighten us almost worse than the attacks. . . .

FRIDAY, June 29. . . . To-day many gentlemen are busy constructing bomb-proof houses, to which we may retreat if necessary. . . .

FRIDAY, July 6. . . . Another unsuccessful sortie is made from the Fu after the big gun to the northeast which does so much damage, the Japanese commander being killed and a Japanese and an Austrian wounded. . . .

TUESDAY, July 17 : Last night, about six P.M., the . . . messenger . . . brought a letter and a telegram in cipher. The latter when translated read, "Washington, Conger, send tidings, bearer." Mr. Conger is puzzled, as the code can be none other than that of the State Department, yet it is incomplete, as there is no date nor signature. . . .

WEDNESDAY, July 18 : Major Conger asks in his reply . . . to have his cablegram completed, as he does not know from whom it comes. They send back the whole thing. The first message proves to be included in a cablegram from Chinese Minister Wu to his Government, which accounts for the lack of date and signature. Complete message from Wu is as follows : " United States gladly assist China, but they are thinking of Major Conger. Inclosed is message inquiring for his health. Please deliver and forward reply." Major Conger sent in cipher cable the following : " Surrounded and fired upon by Chinese for a month. If not relieved soon, massacre will follow." This the Tsungli Yamen promises to send. . . .

FRIDAY, July 27. . . . To-day there was sent in with the compliments of the Tsungli Yamen 1,000 catties of flour, and over a hundred each of watermelons, cucumbers, egg plants, and squashes.

SATURDAY, July 28. . . . It is estimated that from July 10th to 25th 2,800 cannon-balls or shells came into these premises, between sixty and seventy striking Sir Claude's house alone. There have been as many as 400 in one day. . . .

TUESDAY, August 14 : Last night was certainly the most frightful we have had. Although they had fired all day yesterday, the Chinese began with renewed vigor about eight P.M., at the very moment that a terrific thunderstorm with lightning and torrents of rain set in. Shells, bullets, and fire-crackers vied with the noise of the elements, while our big guns, the Colt's automatic, the Nordenfeldt, the Austrian and Italian guns, and " Betsey " added to the noise ; for our men were wild, and felt like doing their best, for it was now certain that the foreign troops could not be far distant. In fact, the boom of the distant cannon could easily be heard, and no one felt like sleeping, had it been possible in the din. Our American gunner, Mitchell, is wounded. All the morning we have heard the thundering of the foreign troops, and while it seems too good to be true, our hearts rejoice that deliverance is near. The Chinese exhausted themselves last night, and have doubtless spent the day in fleeing. Between three and four o'clock this afternoon the British Sikhs came through the water-gate, and the rest of the foreign troops came pouring in from various directions. We are released and saved after eight horrible weeks.

Mrs. E. K. Lowry, *A Woman's Diary of the Siege of Pekin*, in *McClure's Magazine*, November, 1900 (New York), XVI, 66-76 *passim*.

---

195. The Nicaragua Canal (1900)

BY THE ISTHMIAN CANAL COMMISSION

The question of connecting the Atlantic and Pacific oceans by canal is a very old one; interest in it became strong in the United States after the acquisition of California and the discovery of gold there. Within the last six years three commissions have been appointed to examine and report on the feasibility and advisability of having a canal through Nicaragua; and the last one, from whose preliminary report this extract is taken, was authorized to inspect all the possible routes, including that through the Isthmus of Panama, where for years a French company has been spasmodically active in constructing a canal. — Bibliography: United States Superintendent of Documents, *Bibliography of United States Public Documents relating to Interoceanic Communication;* Ira D. Travis, *History of the Clayton-Bulwer Treaty* (Michigan Political Science Association, *Publications*, III, No. 8), 309-312.

THE use that would be made of an isthmian canal by the United States and other nations, and the effects of that use upon the development of our resources and the extension of our domestic and foreign trade have been carefully investigated, and the commercial advantages derivable from the Nicaragua and Panama routes have been compared in order that every factor having a bearing upon the location of the canal might be considered. . . .

The statistics of entrances and clearances show that the net register tonnage of the American and foreign shipping that would have passed through a canal had it existed during the year 1898–99 was 4,582,128 tons, in addition to a part of the commerce between Europe and the

Orient. The opening of the American Isthmian Canal will accentuate
the present tendency of traffic to follow round-the-world lines, and not
less than one-fourth of the present traffic of Europe with Eastern
countries may be expected to use this route. One-fourth of the vessel
tonnage employed in the European-Oriental commerce during the
calendar year 1898 amounted to 1,154,328 tons net, and this added to
4,582,128 gives a total of 5,736,456, the number of tons of shipping that
would have used a canal had it been in existence in 1898–99. . . .

The increase during the decade preceding 1899 in the tonnage of
the vessels that would have used the canal was 22.55 per cent. Upon
the safe assumption that this rate of increase per decade will continue . . . the basis of estimate . . . would make the figures for 1909,
7,030,027 tons, and for 1914, 7,782,240 tons net register.

. . . The unmistakable tendency of commerce is to employ steam
instead of sails, not only in the transportation of general or mixed freight,
but also for carrying full cargoes of bulky commodities. Moreover, the
canal will so increase the competitive advantages of the steamer as to
render practically certain its general substitution in place of the sailing
vessel for all lines of trade through an isthmian waterway.

As compared with Europe, the United States will derive from the
canal far greater benefits, both commercially and industrially. The
commerce of Europe with the Pacific coast of North, Central, and South
America, under existing conditions, is somewhat larger than the total
volume of the present traffic of the United States that may be considered
tributary to the canal; but this fact does not indicate the relative
advantages which the canal will possess for the trade of Europe and that
of the United States. As soon as it has been opened, our trade with the
west coast of South America will rapidly increase, as will also the volume
of our trade with the Orient. The amount of the American commerce
through the canal will quickly surpass the total amount of Europe's
traffic.

An isthmian canal will strengthen the unity of the national and political interests of the United States, develop its Pacific territory, and
promote the commerce and industries of the entire country. The
benefits which Europe will derive from the canal will be commercial.
In addition to this ours will be political and industrial. By bringing
the eastern and western sections of our country into closer relations, by
reducing the time and cost of transporting our western products to
Europe, and by enabling the Eastern, Southern, and Central States to

reach the raw materials and markets of Pacific countries cheaply and expeditiously, the canal will more fully identify political and social interests and quicken the industrial activity of every section of the United States. The iron and steel, the textiles, and the other manufactures of the Eastern and Southern States, the coal from the mining regions, the cotton from the South, and the grain and forest products from many sections will flow out to foreign countries in an increasing volume, and this larger trade will be shared generally by the ports of all our seaboards — the Atlantic, the Gulf, and the Pacific. The canal will cause the competition of the United States with Europe in the countries of Western South America and the Orient to be much keener, with the result that the trade of our country will increase more rapidly than will that of our rivals. The canal will aid the United States in securing and maintaining a position of primacy in the international trade of the world.

These are the considerations which justify the expenditure by the United States of the sum required to build the canal. They may involve a low tariff of charges and be at variance with the production of a large revenue from the canal. . . .

I. The estimated cost of building the Nicaragua Canal is about $58,000,000 more than that of completing the Panama Canal, leaving out the cost of acquiring the latter property. This measures the difference in the magnitude of the obstacles to be overcome in the actual construction of the two canals, and covers all physical considerations such as the greater or less height of dams, the greater or less depth of cuts, the presence or absence of natural harbors, the presence or absence of a railroad, the exemption from or liability to disease, and the amount of work remaining to be done.

The New Panama Canal Company has shown no disposition to sell its property to the United States. Should that company be able and willing to sell, there is reason to believe that the price would not be such as would make the total cost to the United States less than that of the Nicaragua Canal.

II. The Panama Canal, after completion, would be shorter, have fewer locks and less curvature than the Nicaragua Canal. The measure of these advantages is the time required for a vessel to pass through, which is estimated for an average ship at twelve hours for Panama and thirty-hours for Nicaragua.

On the other hand, the distance from San Francisco to New York is 377 miles, to New Orleans 579 miles, and to Liverpool 386 miles greater via Panama than via Nicaragua. The time required to pass over these distances being greater than the difference in the time of transit through the canals, the Nicaragua line, after completion, would be somewhat the more advantageous of the two to the United States, notwithstanding the greater cost of maintaining the longer canal.

III. The Government of Columbia, in which lies the Panama Canal, has granted an exclusive concession, which still has many years to run. It is not free to grant the necessary rights to the United States, except upon condition that an agreement be reached with the New Panama Canal Company. The Commission believes that such agreement is impracticable. So far as can be ascertained, the company is not willing to sell its franchise, but it will allow the United States to become the owner of part of its stock. The Commission considers such an arrangement inadmissible.

The Governments of Nicaragua and Costa Rica, on the other hand, are untrammeled by concessions and are free to grant to the United States such privileges as may be mutually agreed upon.

In view of all the facts, and particularly in view of all the difficulties of obtaining the necessary rights, privileges, and franchises on the Panama route, and assuming that Nicaragua and Costa Rica recognize the value of the canal to themselves and are prepared to grant concessions on terms which are reasonable and acceptable to the United States, the Commission is of the opinion that " the most practicable and feasible route for " an isthmian canal to be "under the control, management, and ownership of the United States " is that known as the Nicaragua route.

Senate Document, 56 Cong., 2 sess. (Washington, 1900), No. 5, pp. 34-44 *passim*.

------

196. The Future Monroe Doctrine (1901)

BY PROFESSOR ALBERT BUSHNELL HART

This writer, by some occult influence on the editor of the series, has got into the collection among real contributors to a knowledge of our country's history and skilled forecasters of its future.

IS it not possible to rise above temporary and fleeting issues to some understanding as to what the " permanent interest " of the United States demands ? To formulate a state paper expressing such a

2 S

principle is the work of a statesman and not of an essayist; but some clear and definite bases may be laid down for any permanent policy in pan-American affairs.

The first is that the territory of the United States is not to be hemmed in and cut off from its natural outlets : the annexation of Louisiana, of the Floridas, of Oregon, and of California, all resulted from this principle ; at present it is not necessary to appeal to it, because our territory is everywhere accessible. The only exception is the highway of the Great Lakes, which has no natural route to the sea ; but it is easier to make a safe commercial connection through the Mohawk Valley than through the lower St. Lawrence, and we do not need Quebec while we have New York. The only two strategic points which seemed threatening a few years ago have now come into our possession by the control of Cuba and the annexation of Hawaii. We are well protected.

The next principle is that the commerce of the United States with its American neighbors must not be shackled by any restrictions emanating from Europe. We reserve the right to cut off our own trade, and the failure of several successive series of reciprocity treaties in the last twenty-five years seems to show that Congress does not wish to extend our commerce in America at present ; but we do insist that no obstacle shall grow up to at least an equal opportunity in the commerce of the Latin-American states.

In the third place, we must accept the existence of a large territorial part of the British Empire in America, and so far forth must admit that Great Britain is an American power in the same sense that we are an Asiatic power. The annexation of Canada, which has been predicted by many keen-sighted men for a century and a quarter, now seems more distant than ever, because the Canadians are satisfied, and Great Britain desires that they should be satisfied. Next-door intimacy with Canada has always caused, and probably will continue to cause, friction and some heart-burning ; the Oregon question, the San Juan question, the Alaskan boundary question, navigation of the St. Lawrence, the northeastern fisheries, the Maine boundary, transit in bond, rivalries of transcontinental railroads, tariff warfare — all these disagreeable disputes might have been avoided if Montgomery and Arnold had taken Quebec in 1775 ; but they might also have been avoided if Burgoyne had taken Albany three years later. In the balance of national forces it came out that both the United States and Great Britain retained great areas of North American territory. To deny the right of Great Britain to hold Canada and Jamaica is to deny the original Monroe Doctrine, which distinctly disclaims any hostility to those existing colonies.

In the fourth place, we are facing the problem of a canal from ocean to ocean, in which the country most advantaged will be the United States ; whatever the likelihood that the transcontinental railroads would still compete against a water transportation through a locked canal, the necessity of piercing the isthmus is too plain to be disregarded. One cannot quarrel with the people of the United States for the intention of constructing such a canal, although it is a fair question for engineers, statesmen, and financiers whether the cheapest and best route is not the completion of the Panama route. But the canal is not simply a road from the Atlantic coast of the United States to the Pacific ; it is an international benefit which the United States has no right to take upon itself, except as the representative of civilized commerce. The oceans are the property of mankind, and if we try to shut up an artificial strait between them, we may some day find the Bosphorus closed to us.

The next principle must be that in American affairs, as in all affairs, the United States shall stand by its obligations. The Clayton-Bulwer treaty was ratified because it was a fair settlement of a very dangerous question ; and we do not realize how many critical questions have been kept in abeyance by that treaty. The British government unnecessarily aroused the hostility of America by the insistence on territorial right through control of a puppet king of the Mosquito Indians ; but all other interference in the construction of the canal has been warded off ; and now that Great Britain gracefully consents to give up joint guaranty, it leaves a clear field for American ownership.

The next principle is that if the United States is to retain its influence, it must refrain from further annexation of Latin-American territory. The first movement toward the annexation of any part of Nicaragua or of Central America will arouse the hostility of all the other American nations, and undo all the work of commercial conciliation. Neither the Monroe Doctrine nor any other common-sense doctrine delivers our neighbors over to us for spoliation.

These are general principles upon which the " doctrine of permanent interest " must proceed, because they are right, just, and reasonable principles, but also because they lie in the nature of our international conditions. There is no longer the slightest danger of any European intervention in America ; the last suggestion of such a thing was Grant's proposed joint intervention in Cuba in 1875. There is no longer any danger of establishing new European colonies in America ; the Venezuelan incident, with all its unreason, revealed clearly to the rest of the world the temper of the United States on that point. There is no longer any danger of the introduction of European monarchies — and, in fact, no European monarch could teach anything about absolute government to a Latin-American dictator.

Finally, neither the American Doctrine nor any form of American doctrine means that the United States is to do whatever may seem good to it in America, or that its " permanent interest " involves a right to get away from inconvenient restrictions in the law of nations, as established by the practice of civilized peoples. We have too much at stake to raise unnecessary difficulties at home or abroad ; we have to deal with and consider Latin-Americans, British-Americans, and American-Americans ; we have to safeguard our interests in Europe, in the Pacific, and in Asia ; we have to take account of the influence which this nation seems destined to exert on mankind. If there is to be in the coming century a great battle of Armageddon — once more Europe against the Huns — we can no more help taking our part with the hosts of freedom than we can help educating our children, building our churches, or maintaining the rights of the individual. There is no proper and permanent doctrine of foreign policy which does not recognize the United States as the great leader in all American affairs, and one of the great leaders in the affairs of mankind. There is no safe or permanent doctrine which does not recognize our sisterhood with other nations under international law. The " doctrine of permanent interest," therefore, is a doctrine of peace in America, international fellowship in the Eastern Hemisphere, and civilization everywhere.

Albert Bushnell Hart, *Foundations of American Foreign Policy* (New York, 1901).

CHAPTER XXXIII — PROBLEMS OF GOVERNMENT

197. "An Old War Horse" (1880)

BY WILLIAM HENRY McELROY

McElroy, a journalist, has written numerous articles for periodicals under his own name and also under his pseudonym of "Richard Scudder." — Bibliography: Bowker and Iles, *Reader's Guide in Economic, Social, and Political Science*, 115–116.

MY DEAR NEPHEW . . .

WHEN I left you on Commencement Day I urged you to lose no time in getting into politics, promising that I would help you push your fortunes as occasion offered. Since then I have received a letter from you, in which you write that you have read Story on the Constitution, Benton's Thirty Years in the United States Senate, Greeley's American Conflict, two or three works on Political Economy, and De Tocqueville on America. I suppose there can be no objection to such reading. Likely enough it has its value. But what I particularly desire, my dear nephew, is that you should become a practical politician, — a thoroughly practical politician. I never remember reading any of the works you have mentioned, or any like them, unless, indeed, you call Barnum's How to Make Money a treatise on finance. And yet, cast your eyes over the salient points of my career. I have been alderman, supervisor, mayor, state representative, state senator, and congressman. For many years I have been chairman of our state and county committees. I can hardly remember the time when I didn't carry the vote of my own ward in my vest pocket, and of my own city in my trousers pocket, and I've got them there yet. For going on half a century I have had things pretty much my own way in caucuses and primaries, and the like. What has been the secret of my unusual success? I will try — in strict confidence, as you will understand — to give you some plain, blunt, non-partisan hints for your guidance in politics which may serve to answer the question.

I. Never allow yourself to lose sight of the fact that politics, and not poker, is our great American game. If this could be beaten into the heads of some presumably well-meaning but glaringly unpractical people, we should hear less idiotic talk about reform in connection with politics. Nobody ever dreams of organizing a reform movement in poker. . . . And yet political reform clubs, designed to reform politics from the inside or the outside, are springing up on all sides. Of course, it is just as well not to attempt to argue the masses out of their deeply rooted notion that politics is what Noah Webster defines it to be, " that part of *ethics* which has to do with the regulation and government of a nation or state." Ethics is very good in connection with politics. But then Webster, it must be remembered, was simply a learned lexicographer, and not a practical politician. No, no. Don't try to reason with the masses in this matter. The public has no head for such things. It will not understand.

II. Mr. Lincoln, a very estimable and justly popular, but in some respects an impracticable man, formulated another widely diffused error in regard to politics. He held that ours is a government of the people, by the people, for the people. I maintain, on the contrary, that it is a government of politicians, by politicians, for politicians. If your political career is to be a success, you must understand and respect this distinction with a difference.

III. Not a few capable but unpractical people, when they fall to discussing our governmental system, argue that the existence of parties is necessary to the welfare of our country. But long experience has taught me that the more sensible way for a practical politician to look at it is that the existence of the country is necessary to the welfare of parties. Thank Heaven, my dear nephew, that we have a country !

IV. You have received your commission as postmaster of your village. A post-office is a capital political opening for a young man who has sense enough to discover how to make the right use of it. You will of course leave all matters touching the postal service to your deputy. Never forget that your pivotal duty as postmaster will be to nurse the party in your section. As a practical man, you must see, if you reflect a moment, that postmaster and local party-master must be convertible terms with you if you expect to be approved by the great party leaders, and to become a great leader yourself, some day. . . . In your selection of clerks you will be guided primarily by a determination to have only such men around you as will register your will every time at caucuses and conventions. . . .

V. I sincerely hope it is not necessary that I should counsel you always to vote the regular ticket, the whole regular ticket, and nothing but the regular ticket. Hold fast, I beseech of you, to the doctrine of the infallibility of your party in convention assembled. Delegates, like kings, "can do no wrong." The voters who scratch ballots or bolt nominations are to be regarded as the bane of politics, just as certain other reformers have been the bane of religion. They all belong in the same category, and all are equally deserving of the execration of every practical man, as exponents of the pestiferous doctrine of the right of private judgment. And just here a word in reply to the familiar question, Would you vote for the devil if he received the party's regular nomination ? I have no hesitation in affirming that I certainly would. Let's look at it. If the day ever comes when the devil is nominated, the other side will be pretty sure to run Gabriel against him. Of the two, my choice would be the devil. To be sure, it would not be an ideal nomination, — but then, neither is ours an ideal world. I am aware that the devil has split hoofs, pronounced horns, and a bifurcated tail. But do we choose candidates for their good looks ? As to his moral character, I frankly admit it is not all I could desire ; but after criticism has exhausted itself, the fact remains, conceded by both parties, that he is not as black as he is painted. On the other hand, he has many qualities that ought to commend him to practical men. He is self-made, he is thoroughly in earnest in all he undertakes, he is an untiring worker, he is one of the shrewdest of wire-pullers, he possesses vast and versatile accomplishments, he is unsurpassed in ability to find and manipulate the springs that move men, he has a positive genius for making friends. Gifted, popular, magnetic, at home in all circles, from the highest to the lowest, he would be certain to make a splendid run. As for Gabriel, I have only to say that, while his intellectual and moral endowments are undoubtedly of the highest order, there is great reason to fear that he would not succeed in the realm of practical politics. If elected to office, it is more than likely that he would prove more of a botheration than a boon to his party. He would be living up to the promises made during the canvass ; he would resolutely decline to let well enough alone. Let me not be misunderstood. I yield to no one in my regard for Gabriel. But, as a practical man, I would feel called upon to vote against him, and do all I could for his opponent. In my own ward, where my influence is most potent and my political theories most approved of, I feel convinced that the devil would have a very large majority. This hypothetical case is of course an extreme one, and is never likely to occur. I have dealt with it simply for the sake of showing you that the position of those who insist upon the invariable support of regular nominations is sound in the last analysis.

VI. How are scratchers and bolters to be dealt with ? It is an exceedingly difficult question. I myself am at a loss to determine whether it is better to be extremely tender or awfully rough with them. Each policy is good at times, and in making a choice you must be guided by circumstances. In a sterner age than ours, an age that had less stomach for nonsense, gentlemen who were convicted of the crime of private judgment were burned at the stake. It is not permitted us in these latter, laxer days to make it as warm for scratchers and bolters as it was once made for John Huss ; still we can show that we possess the sturdy practical views of those who flung Huss to the fagots, by pelting the scratchers and bolters with jeers, sneers, and innuendoes, by crediting them with the meanest of motives, and insisting that they are either traitorous, inconsequential knaves, or silly, inconsequential fools. As for those upon whom such treatment is lost (and I confess that I suspect it fails with the majority of scratchers and bolters), try what is known to practical politicians as the postponement treatment. . . . Those who employ it with the most gratifying results allow the impression to be produced in the patient's mind at the outset that, although they have never happened to find an election at which scratching or bolting could be indulged in without perfectly harrowing injury to public interests of colossal moment, yet, nevertheless, they heartily and unreservedly approve of scratching and bolting in the abstract. . . .

. . . Be it yours to consult the expedient, leaving it to the purists of the party to consult the highly proper. Beware of those who take sentimental views of unsentimental matters. A man who would "rather be right than be president" by all means ought to decline a presidential nomination, and run for a position in a theological seminary, a Sunday-school, or Vassar College ; while he who holds that "one with God is a majority" antagonizes the system of reckoning which has come down to us from the fathers, and which has the approval of every practical inspector of American elections. Be practical in your politics, be practical, ever more be practical.

[William Henry McElroy] *An Old War Horse to a Young Politician,* in *Atlantic Monthly,* June, 1880 (Boston, etc.), XLV, 761-765 *passim.*

198. Experiences in a State Legislature (1882–1884)

BY THEODORE ROOSEVELT (1888)

Roosevelt began his public career by serving for three terms in the New York legislature. Since then he has been prominent in many phases of public affairs, being noted for his advocacy of practical reforms and, at the same time, for party loyalty. He has been successively national civil-service commissioner, police commissioner of New York City, assistant secretary of the navy, colonel of the "Rough Riders" during the Spanish War, governor of New York, and in 1901 vice-president of the United States. — Bibliography: Bowker and Iles, *Reader's Guide in Economic, Social, and Political Science*, 96–101.

THE representatives from different sections of the State differ widely in character. Those from the country districts are generally very good men. They are usually well-to-do farmers, small lawyers, or prosperous storekeepers, and are shrewd, quiet, and honest. They are often narrow-minded and slow to receive an idea; but, on the other hand, when they get a good one, they cling to it with the utmost tenacity. They form very much the most valuable class of legislators. For the most part they are native Americans, and those who are not are men who have become completely Americanized in all their ways and habits of thought. . . .

It is from . . . great cities that the worst legislators come. It is true that there are always among them a few cultivated and scholarly men who are well educated, and who stand on a higher and broader intellectual and moral plane than the country members, but the bulk are very low indeed. They are usually foreigners, of little or no education, with exceedingly misty ideas as to morality, and possessed of an ignorance so profound that it could only be called comic, were it not for the fact that it has at times such serious effects upon our laws. It is their ignorance, quite as much as actual viciousness, which makes it so difficult to procure the passage of good laws or prevent the passage of bad ones; and it is the most irritating of the many elements with which we have to contend in the fight for good government. . . .

In each of the last three Legislatures there were a number of us who were interested in getting through certain measures which we deemed to be for the public good, but which were certain to be strongly opposed, some for political and some for pecuniary reasons. Now . . . before taking any active steps, we had to "size up" our fellow legislators, to find out their past history and present character and associates, to find

out whether they were their own masters or were acting under the directions of somebody else, whether they were bright or stupid, etc., etc.
As a result, and after very careful study, conducted purely with the object
of learning the truth, so that we might work more effectually, we came
to the conclusion that about a third of the members were open to
corrupt influences in some form or other ; in certain sessions the proportion was greater, and in some less.   Now it would, of course, be
impossible for me or for anyone else to prove in a court of law that
these men were guilty, except perhaps in two or three cases ; yet we
felt absolutely confident that there was hardly a case in which our judgment as to the honesty of any given member was not correct. . . .

. . . it is almost impossible to actually convict a legislator of bribe-
taking ; but at the same time, the character of a legislator, if bad, soon
becomes a matter of common notoriety, and no dishonest legislator can
long keep his reputation good with honest men.   If the constituents
wish to know the character of their member, they can easily find it out,
and no member will be dishonest if he thinks his constituents are looking at him ; he presumes upon their ignorance or indifference.   I do
not see how bribe-taking among legislators can be stopped until the
public conscience, which is, even now, gradually awakening, becomes
fully awake to the matter.   Then it will stop fast enough ; for just as
soon as politicians realize that the people are in earnest in wanting a
thing done, they make haste to do it.   The trouble is always in rousing
the people sufficiently to make them take an *effective* interest, — that is,
in making them sufficiently in earnest to be willing to give a little of
their time to the accomplishment of the object they have in view. . . .

The array of vicious legislators is swelled by a number of men who
really at bottom are not bad.   Foremost among these are those most
hopeless of beings who are handicapped by having some measure which
they consider it absolutely necessary for the sake of their own future to
" get through."   One of these men will have a bill, for instance, appropriating a sum of money from the State Treasury to clear out a river,
dam the outlet of a lake, or drain a marsh ; it may be, although not
usually so, proper enough in itself, but it is drawn up primarily in the
interest of a certain set of his constituents who have given him clearly
to understand that his continuance in their good graces depends upon
his success in passing the bill.   He feels that he must get it through at
all hazards ; the bad men find this out, and tell him he must count on
their opposition unless he consents also to help their measures ; he re-

sists at first, but sooner or later yields ; and from that moment his fate is sealed, — so far as his ability to do any work of general good is con‑ cerned.

A still larger number of men are good enough in themselves, but are "owned" by third parties. Usually the latter are politicians who have absolute control of the district machine, or who are, at least, of very great importance in the political affairs of their district. A curious fact is that they are not invariably, though usually, of the same party as the member ; for in some places, especially in the lower portions of the great cities, politics become purely a business ; and in the squabbles for offices of emolument it becomes important for a local leader to have supporters among all the factions. When one of these supporters is sent to a legislative body, he is allowed to act with the rest of his party on what his chief regards as the unimportant questions of party or public interest, but he has to come in to heel at once when any matter arises touching the said chief's power, pocket, or influence.

Other members will be controlled by some wealthy private citizen who is not in politics, but who has business interests likely to be affected by legislation, and who is therefore, willing to subscribe heavily to the campaign expenses of an individual or of an association so as to insure the presence in Albany of some one who will give him information and assistance. . . .

There are two classes of cases in which corrupt members get money. One is when a wealthy corporation buys through some measure which will be of great benefit to itself, although, perhaps, an injury to the public at large ; the other is when a member introduces a bill hostile to some moneyed interest, with the expectation of being paid to let the matter drop. The latter, technically called a "strike," is much the most common ; for, in spite of the outcry against them in legislative matters, corporations are more often sinned against than sinning. It is difficult . . . in either case to convict the offending member, though we have very good laws against bribery. The reform has got to come from the people at large. It will be hard to make any very great improvement in the character of the legislators until respectable people become more fully awake to their duties, and until the newspapers be‑ come more truthful and less reckless in their statements.

Theodore Roosevelt, *Essays on Practical Politics* (New York, etc., 1888), 10–23 *passim.*

199. Civil Service Reform (1894)

BY CARL SCHURZ

This extract is from an address delivered by Schurz at the annual meeting of the National Civil-Service Reform League. — For Schurz, see No. 143 above. — Bibliography: Bowker and Iles, *Reader's Guide in Economic, Social, and Political Science*, 110-112 ; Brookings and Ringwalt, *Briefs for Debate*, No. xvii.

WHAT Civil Service Reform demands, is simply that the business part of the Government shall be carried on in a sound, businesslike manner. This seems so obviously reasonable that among people of common sense there should be no two opinions about it. And the condition of things to be reformed is so obviously unreasonable, so flagrantly absurd and vicious, that we should not believe it could possibly exist among sensible people, had we not become accustomed to its existence among ourselves. . . .

Looking at the financial side of the matter alone — it is certainly bad enough ; it is indeed almost incomprehensible how the spoils system could be permitted through scores of years to vitiate our business methods in the conduct of the national revenue service, the postal service, the Indian service, the public-land service, involving us in indescribable administrative blunders, bringing about Indian wars, causing immense losses in the revenue, breeding extravagant and plundering practices in all Departments, costing our people in the course of time untold hundreds of millions of money, and making our Government one of the most wasteful in the world. All this, I say, is bad enough. It might be called discreditable enough to move any self-respecting people to shame. But the spoils system has inflicted upon the American people injuries far greater than these.

The spoils system, that practice which turns public offices, high and low, from public trusts into objects of prey and booty for the victorious party, may without extravagance of language be called one of the greatest criminals in our history, if not the greatest. In the whole catalogue of our ills there is none more dangerous to the vitality of our free institutions.

It tends to divert our whole political life from its true aims. It teaches men to seek something else in politics than the public good. It puts mercenary selfishness as the motive power for political action in the place of public spirit, and organizes that selfishness into a dominant political force.

It attracts to active party politics the worst elements of our population, and with them crowds out the best.   It transforms political parties
from associations of patriotic citizens, formed to serve a public cause,
into bands of mercenaries using a cause to serve them.   It perverts
party contests from contentions of opinion into scrambles for plunder.
By stimulating the mercenary spirit it promotes the corrupt use of
money in party contests and in elections.

It takes the leadership of political organizations out of the hands of
men fit to be leaders of opinion and workers for high aims, and turns it
over to the organizers and leaders of bands of political marauders.   It
creates the boss and the machine, putting the boss into the place of the
statesman, and the despotism of the machine in the place of an organized public opinion.

It converts the public officeholder, who should be the servant of the
people, into the servant of a party or of an influential politician, extort-
ing from him time and work which should belong to the public, and
money which he receives from the public for public service.   It cor-
rupts his sense of duty by making him understand that his obligation to
his party or his political patron is equal if not superior to his obligation
to the public interest, and that his continuance in office does not depend
on his fidelity to duty.   It debauches his honesty by seducing him to
use the opportunities of his office to indemnify himself for the burdens
forced upon him as a party slave.   It undermines in all directions the
discipline of the public service.

It falsifies our constitutional system.   It leads to the usurpation, in a
large measure, of the executive power of appointment by members of
the legislative branch, substituting their irresponsible views of personal
or party interest for the judgment as to the public good and the sense
of responsibility of the executive.   It subjects those who exercise the
appointing power, from the President of the United States down, to the
intrusion of hordes of office-hunters and their patrons, who rob them of
the time and strength they should devote to the public interest.   It has
already killed two of our Presidents, one, the first Harrison, by worry,
and the other, Garfield, by murder ; and more recently it has killed a
mayor in Chicago and a judge in Tennessee.

It degrades our Senators and Representatives in Congress to the contemptible position of office-brokers, and even of mere agents of office-
brokers, making the business of dickering about spoils as weighty to
them as their duties as legislators.   It introduces the patronage as an

agency of corrupt influence between the executive and the legislature. It serves to obscure the criminal character of bribery by treating bribery with offices as a legitimate practice. It thus reconciles the popular mind to practices essentially corrupt, and thereby debauches the popular sense of right and wrong in politics.

It keeps in high political places, to the exclusion of better men, persons whose only ability consists in holding a personal following by adroit manipulation of the patronage. It has thus sadly lowered the standard of statesmanship in public position, compared with the high order of ability displayed in all other walks of life.

It does more than anything else to turn our large municipalities into sinks of corruption, to render Tammany Halls possible, and to make of the police force here and there a protector of crime and a terror to those whose safety it is to guard. It exposes us, by the scandalous spectacle of its periodical spoils carnivals, to the ridicule and contempt of civilized mankind, promoting among our own people the growth of serious doubts as to the practicability of democratic institutions on a great scale; and in an endless variety of ways it introduces into our political life more elements of demoralization, debasement and decadence than any other agency of evil I know of, aye, perhaps more than all other agencies of evil combined.

These are some of the injuries the spoils system has been, and still is, inflicting upon this Republic — some, I say; not all. . . .

. . . Every intelligent and unprejudiced citizen, when he candidly inquires into the developments which have brought about the present state of things, will understand that of the evils which have so alarmingly demoralized our political life, and so sadly lowered this Republic in the respect of the world, many, if not most, had their origin, and find their sustenance, in that practice which treats the public offices as the plunder of victorious parties; that as, with the increase of our population, the growth of our wealth, and the multiplication of our public interests, the functions of government expand and become more complicated, those evils will grow and eventually destroy the very vitality of our free institutions, unless their prolific source be stopped; and that this force can be effectually stopped not by mere occasional spasms of indignant virtue, but only by a systematic, thorough and permanent reform. Every patriotic citizen understanding this must be a Civil Service Reformer.

National Civil-Service Reform League, *Proceedings*, 1894 (New York, 1894), 7–37 *passim*.

200. "The President's Message" (1899)

BY FINLEY PETER DUNNE

Dunne is a journalist who by the shrewd political comments of his " Mr. Dooley,"
which made their first appearance in the Chicago *Journal* and *Evening Post,* has
gained a national reputation as a humorist and political critic. — Bibliography as in
No. 198 above.

"DID ye r-read th' prisidint's message?" asked Mr. Dooley.
"I did not," said Mr. Hennessy.
"Well, ye-re r-right," said the philosopher. "I didn't mesilf. 'Tis
manny years since I give up me devotion to that form iv fiction. I don't
think anny wan r-reads a message but th' clerk iv th' house iv riprisinta-
tives, an' he has to to hold his job. But I cud tell ye how 'tis written.
Th' prisidint summons th' cab'net together an' they set ar-round a long
table smokin' seegars excipt th' sicrety iv th' navy, an' he smokes a
cigareet. An' th' prisidint he says ' La-ads,' he says, ' 'tis up to me f'r to
sind a few wurruds,' he says, ' iv good cheer,' he says, ' to thim rilitives iv
th' civil service on th' other side iv town,' he says. ' I'd a great deal rather
set up in th' gall'ry an' hear me frind Grosvenor tell thim,' he says, ' that
I'm no poly-gamist like that there David Harem feller that's thryin' to
break into congress,' he says. ' But ivry other prisidint has done it,' he
says, ' An' I suppose I've got to,' he says. ' What shall I say?' he says,
an' he sets there writin' ' Ye'ers thruly, Willum McKinley,' an' makin'
pitchers iv a house in Canton, Ohio, while th' cab'net thinks.

"Fin'lly th' sicrety iv state, he says, ' Ye might start it off, if ye want
to make it a pop'lar docymint an' wan that 'll be raymimbered,' he says,
' whin ye ar-re forgotten,' he says, ' be mintioning what has been done
be th' state department,' he says. ' They'se a dhray at th' dure with
th' facts,' he says, ' if ye've f'rgotten thim,' he says. ' Thin,' says th'
sicrety iv the threeasury, ' ye might glide aisily into a few remarks about
th' excellent condition iv th' public fi-nances,' he says. ' Something like
this : " Thanks to th' tireless activity iv th' sicrety iv th' threeasury th'
efforts iv those inimies iv pop'lar governmint, th' Wall sthreet bears, has
been onable to mark down quotations an' thus roon th' prosperity iv
th' nation. All his ol' frinds will be glad to know that this pop'lar an'
affable gintleman has his eye on th' ticker again. Lyman is th' boy f'r
th' money," or " I dinnaw what I cud do without Lyman." ' Something
like that 'd hit thim har-rd.' ' In passing,' says th' sicrety iv war, ' ye

might say that ye were late in gettin' hold iv th' right man f'r me place, fr'm th' r-right state, but now ye've got him ye don't know how ye got along without him. Ye may add that I'm th' first sicrety iv war that iver showed that th' constitootion iv th' United States is applicable on'y in such cases as it is applied to on account iv its applicability,' he says. 'F'r further particklars see small bills an' me own report,' he says. 'I don't know,' says th' sicrety iv th' navy, 'whether 'tis gin'rally undherstood, but,' he says, 'ye might point out that th' navy niver was so efficient as at prisint,' he says. 'Th' name iv Jawn D. Long will not soon be f'rgotten be himsilf in common with his fellow-counthrymen,' he says. 'An allusion to th' gradjool extermination iv th' thrusts would be much apprecyated in Noo Jarsey,' says the attorney-gin'ral. 'Those monsthers make their homes there,' he says, 'an',' he says, 'I will say f'r thim, they're good neighbors,' he says.

"'An' while ye're at it,' says a modest voice fr'm th' corner iv th' room, 'don't f'rget to dhrop in a bean f'r th' sicrety iv agriculture — Tama Jim, th' farmers' frind. Gr-reat captains,' he says, 'with their guns an' dhrums,' he says, 'soon pass away, but whin they're gone wan figure will stand out like th' coopoly on a r-red barn,' he says. 'To whom d'ye refer?' angrily demands th' sicrety iv war. 'To mesilf,' says th' sicrety iv agriculture.

"'Gintlemen,' says th' Prisidint, 'ar-re ye all through?' he says. 'We ar-re,' says they. 'An' where do I come in?' he says. 'Why,' says th' sicrety iv state, 'ye sign th' docymint,' says he. 'Well,' says Mack, 'I've heerd ye'er suggistions,' he says, 'an' ye may go back to wurruk,' he says. 'I'll write this message, an' if ye see anny iv ye'er names in it,' he says, 'ye may conclude,' he says, 'that me hand has lost its cunning,' he says. 'I guess,' he says, 'I'm some huckleberries in this governmint mesilf,' he says.

"An' he sets down an' writes: 'Fellow Citizens: I'm glad to see ye here, an hope ye won't stay long. Thanks to ye'er Uncle Bill, times is lookin' up an' will be more so in th' near future. Me foreign relations ar-re iv th' most plisint nature. Ye will be glad to know that th' frindship iv this counthry with Germany planted in Samoa an' nourished at Manila has grown to such a point as to satisfy th' mos' critical German-American. With England we ar-re on such terms as must plaze ivry Canajeen, but not on anny such terms as wud make anny Irishman think we ar-re on such terms as we ought not to be. In other wurruds, we cherish a deep animosity mingled with passionate love, such a feelin' as we must entertain to a nation with common impulses f'r th' same money an' a common language iv abuse.   To'rd our sister raypublic iv France an' our ol' frind an' ally, Rooshia, to sunny Italy an' Austhria an' Boolgahria an' oppressed Poland, to th' Boer, who has manny rilitives here, an' to ivry other nation but Chinnymen an' Indyans not votin', kind regards.   I wud speak to ye on th' subject iv thrusts, but I have nawthin' to say.   If ye want to smash this necess'ry evil, this octopus that with its horrible tentacles is crushin' out an' nourishin' commerce, do it ye'er-silf.   That's what ye'er here f'r.   Something ought to be done f'r th' Nic'ragyooa canal, but what th' divvle it is, I dinnaw.   As f'r our newly acquired possessions, 'tis our intintion to give them a form iv governmint suited to their needs, which is small, an' in short, to do as we blamed please with thim, makin' up our minds as we go along.   So no more fr'm ye'ers thruly, Willum McKinley.'

" An' there's th' message," said Mr. Dooley.

" An' what did congress say? " Mr. Hennessy asked.

" Congress did'nt say annything," said Mr. Dooley.   " Congress yawned. But congress 'll get th' rale message whin it goes over to th' white house wan at a time to see about th' foorth-class postmasthers."

[Finley Peter Dunne], *Mr. Dooley's Philosophy* (New York, Robert Howard Russell, 1900), 103–108.

———◆———

201. How to Regulate Trusts (1900)

BY PROFESSOR JOHN BATES CLARK

Clark is professor of political economy at Columbia University, and was one of the organizers of the American Economic Association.   He has made a specialty of economic theory. — Bibliography : A. P. C. Griffin, *List of Books relating to Trusts.*

THE principle of monopoly itself is not perilous for that investor whose capital is in the monopoly, but it is intolerable for every one else.   It is safe to say that our people will ultimately find or make a way to destroy any genuine monopolistic power that is in private hands ; and it is nearly safe to say that, if we do nothing beyond protecting the investor, the trusts will acquire too much of this power and will become less and less endurable.   The restrictions that now hold them in check are not likely of themselves to grow stronger as time advances, while the trusts are likely to grow much stronger.   Monopoly power that is increasing and restrictions that are diminishing in force point to a time when something positive will certainly have to be done in defense of property rights, if not of personal liberty. The measures that it is possible to take are not many.

First, we may prosecute with more intelligence the effort to break up the trusts into smaller corporations. It has, for example, been suggested that no corporation should be permitted to have more than a certain amount of capital. But if a maximum of capital were fixed for all industries, the difficulty would be that an amount which is too small for prosecuting one type of business would be sufficient to enable a company to monopolize another. A more effective policy would allow capital to vary in different kinds of business, but would so restrict the output of each corporation that no one could produce more than a certain proportion of the whole output of goods of the kind that it makes. If no corporation were allowed to produce more than one-fourth of the goods of a certain kind that were produced in a whole country, we should be sure of having at least four establishments in each department of industry. We should, however, be much less sure that the four competitors might not find a way to act in harmony and to secure the benefit of monopoly under the outward form of competition. Moreover, this forcible regulating of the growth of business establishments is wholly out of harmony with our historical practice and our principles.

Secondly, we might abolish customs duties on all articles manufactured by the trusts. We might in this way appeal to the foreign producer to become the protector of the American consumer. There is no denying the efficacy of such a measure. It is idle to say that, because trusts exist in free-trade countries, our present tariff is not effective in promoting them. Trusts have very little power in free-trade countries. In England there is very little popular objection to them, because in that country they have developed a certain power for good and very little for evil. If interests like those which now resist a very small infringement of our protective system, in spite of the fact that the honor and the welfare of the whole country require it, could be so completely overcome as to allow the sweeping away of a great body of duties, many things would happen : the whole industrial life of the country would be translated to a new plane, and it would be found that the trust problem, for the time being, would be far less troublesome. But the policy of protection will not yield easily ; and, indeed, the system as a whole ought not to be swept away too ruthlessly. Moreover, it may be said that if, in the remote future, trusts should become international in scope, even a free-trade policy would no longer be adequate for the protection of the public.

Thirdly, it is conceivable that we might introduce an elaborate system of price regulation. We might accept monopoly as inevitable, but prescribe, in a minute and detailed way, at what rates goods should be sold. On the supposition that this difficult policy were carried out in a spirit of complete honesty, — on the supposition that the officials of the law remained incorruptible, though placed in positions that offered the maximum inducement for corruption, — there would still remain for determination the question as to what principle they should follow in regulating prices. Customary prices have afforded a standard, where the purpose of the law has been to prevent an individual producer from being extortionate ; and a price may be adjudged reasonable, if it is the one that prevails among competitors ; but such a standard as this is, of course, not available in the case of monopoly. The only available guide for the legal regulation of prices would be the cost of goods ; and it would be incumbent on the officers of the law to ascertain the cost in every instance and to guarantee to the producer a fair profit in addition to it. The first objection to such elaborate price regulation is the obvious technical impossibility of it, but from an economic point of view the fatal objection to it is that it would paralyze improvements. Why should a trust ever discard old machinery and spend its accumulations in getting better appliances, if it would still be allowed to make only the profit it is now making? Arguments on this point are, however, rendered unnecessary, not merely by the impossibility of carrying out such a policy, but by the impossibility of securing from the public any serious consideration of it.

Fourthly, we may put all monopolized industries into the hands of the state and thus, within a very extensive field, carry out the program of the socialists. To a casual observer, this looks easier than the other policy ; and it will certainly find more and more advocates, as the powers of trusts increase. There is, moreover, no doubt that this measure would abolish certain evils that are inherent in private monopoly. Even if it did not succeed in giving the public cheap goods, it might save the people from the necessity of buying goods that were made dear by private producers' grasping policy. But this measure must stand or fall with the general cause of socialism ; and, while so extensive a subject as that is not here to be discussed, it is safe to say that the judgment of the people is against it. It is perhaps safe to add that, if it were once tried, the result that would prevent a repetition of the trial would be the slow but sure reduction of the productive power of the individual worker. With every inclination to make wages rise, the state would be baffled in its efforts by increasing population and by the check on improvements of method and on the accumulation of capital. The sources of gain for labor would dwindle till the "iron law" would begin to assert itself, and a state that would gladly make workers rich would then be unable to keep them out of misery.

Is there no further recourse? There is one; and it has the advantage of being in harmony with the spirit of our people, with the principles of common law and also with the economic tendencies that have made our present state a tolerable one. It is to give to potential competition greater effectiveness — that is, to give a fair field and no favor to the man who is disposed to become an independent producer, leaving him wholly at the mercy of fair competition but shielding him from that which is unfair. Let the trust crush him, if he cannot produce goods as cheaply as it can; but let him bring the trust to terms, if he can produce them more cheaply. This puts the trust in a position where its security will depend, not on its power to destroy competitors, unfairly, but on its power to meet them fairly.

John Bates Clark, *Trusts*, in *Political Science Quarterly*, June, 1900 (Boston, etc.), XV, 187–190.

———◆———

202. The Machine and the Boss (1900)

BY BIRD SIM COLER

Coler was elected comptroller of New York City on the Tammany ticket at the first municipal election under the Greater New York charter. The office is one of great importance and responsibility, and has been administered by Coler wisely and independently of political control. — Bibliography: R. C. Brooks, *Bibliography of Municipal Administration and City Conditions* (*Municipal Affairs*, 1897, I, No. 1); Bowker and Iles, *Reader's Guide in Economic, Social, and Political Science*, 99–101, 115–116.

THE political machine is sometimes made odious to good citizens, but it is never wholly bad in itself. It is a fixture in American politics, and while it may be broken and rebuilt, cleaned and reformed, it can not be eliminated. The men who rail loudest against it, as a rule, are ever ready to use it or its broken parts as stepping-stones to place and power, even to a boss-ship. Its reputation for evil is in every case due to party leaders who have used it for personal purposes and made of it an instrument to defeat the wishes of the people who created it. Contrary to popular belief, a party leader can not make a political machine. The party makes the machine, the machine makes the leader, and then the latter makes himself a boss. A leader of a party is never a boss, because leadership implies followers, and a boss does not lead : he drives, and the machine is his vehicle, the individual members of it his driven cattle.

The corrupt political machine of to-day, controlled by a boss, is contrary to the American system of government, and were it not a terrible reality its creation would be deemed an impossibility. It is, in its present state of perfection, rule of the people by the individual for the boss, his relatives, and friends. It is the most complete political despotism ever known, and yet the political machine on which the boss rises as dictator and despot is based on the fundamental principle of democracy — that system of government wherein all men are supposed to be equal and every voter a sovereign. It is the multiplicity of voting sovereigns that makes the machine a necessity for concerted political action ; and when sovereignty has been centralized by organization, the great majority of our constitutional rulers go about their private affairs, careless of their rights and powers until their personal or property interests are affected by the ukase of a party boss. For a century the division of the voters into political parties has been a part of our system of being governed by the man who runs the machine of the party in office. This division has been carried up or down, according to the point of view, from national politics to the election of township constables. When the sovereigns are divided on party lines the work of partisan organization is made easy, and the majority need not think or act for themselves ; they can leave all such details to the committees. The building of the political machine begins whenever a question of policy seems to demand united party action. The frame is laid in the party caucus or mass meeting, where every voter may be heard. There the necessity for organization is made apparent, and a committee is created. That is the work of the voters of a party in a particular locality, and the first committee is the creation of a majority. So far the plan of procedure is perfect. It is essentially democratic — majority rule. But the committee is too large, and a subcommittee is detailed to carry on the work of the organization. From a subcommittee the task passes to individuals — one, two, or three — and behold, in a day a political machine stands complete, awaiting the guiding hand of a boss !

The committee of the township, county, town, or city mass meetings develops into a small machine, which for a time does its work so well that the people are pleased. When the time comes for holding another mass meeting the voters do not turn out. They are busy with their own affairs, and their confidence in the committee is unshaken. Then the machine grows stronger, and the leader of the first meeting is the boss of the second, dictating nominations and dividing patronage. The smaller committees are represented in the State or city organization, and along the same lines a larger machine is built. It is merely the local and political interests and ambitions merged into one harmonious whole — the machine finished and ready for business.

The party organization created in this way is not wrong in itself, and has no power to move contrary to the wishes of its creators. It is the mechanism of a party ready for work ; but there must be a guiding hand, a directing force provided by the voters as a whole or by a boss. It is only when the rank and file of the party cease to take an active interest in the machine they have created that it ceases to obey their wishes and becomes the tool of the despot. To maintain the organization necessary to keep a political party alive and get out a full vote a large amount of routine work must be done by some one. Men of business have no taste for this labor, and are glad to leave it to those who have no other occupation. When a man takes up politics as a profession usually he expects to make money out of it, and to make money he must get into office himself or put his friends there. It is perfectly natural that the professional politician should become unscrupulous as to means to accomplish his end.

When civic pride and public spirit are withdrawn from the party organization, the modern political machine remains. It stands before the public disguised as a committee ; but every member is there for business, and his first thought is to get all he can out of the party before he is succeeded by some one more unscrupulous. In the scramble for spoils that follows the boss is developed. He is a man with enough force of character to bend the other members of the organization to his will and make the machine a weapon of offense and defense. Once a boss is firmly established in his place his first thought is to take care of the machine, to keep it in good working order, for without it he can not longer retain power.

Bird S. Coler, *Municipal Government* (New York, D. Appleton & Co., 1900), 189-194.

CHAPTER XXXIV — SOCIAL PROBLEMS

203. Political Conditions in the South (1878)

BY SIR GEORGE CAMPBELL, K.C.S.I.

Campbell entered the civil service of India, and rose to be a member of the council of India and later a member of Parliament. He visited the United States in 1878. This extract is from the book in which he recorded his impressions. — Bibliography: Commissioner of Education, *Report for 1893–1894*, I, 1038–1061; Southern Society for the Study of Race Conditions, *Race Problems of the South*, 224–240.

I HAD . . . an opportunity of conversing with a coloured preacher, a clever and influential man. He seems, however, very extreme in his views. He says that during the election there was gross intimidation, and much unfair influence, but in spite of it all the blacks voted Republican as solid as ever. Nevertheless, the boxes were stuffed and the majority stolen. The election commissioners are all on one side, and so are the newspapers, and they openly published violent threats. . . .

I gather that the United States election supervisors were a poor lot — often coloured men ; and they were frequently hustled and insulted. One of them was arrested on some frivolous pretext. According to one Northerner nothing but United States troops at every polling-place will prevent a strong and embittered minority from triumphing over a weak majority. In this part of the country the Republican or Radical party is dead for the present. The victory of the whites is now so complete that there is certainly peace such as there was not before. . . .

I paid a visit to my namesake Mr. C ——, the independent Democrat, who stood for State Senator for this district, but was defeated. He is a lawyer, and all agree that he is a very superior man. I found him very moderate, and not at all inclined to be vituperative, although the election was bitterly contested. He says that he represented the principle of Conciliation against those who would not yield anything. The election was won by simple cheating ; that is, by stuffing the ballot-boxes. At one polling-place not more than a thousand voted, but there were three thousand five hundred papers in the box. There was not much intimidation, but only cheating. . . .

As a general result of all that I have been able to learn about the elections in this part of the country, I may say that there does not seem to be the least doubt that they were won by the most wholesale cheating. That is avowed in the most open way. Most people seem to praise the negroes, and to be on very good terms with them ; but they all admit that, while the blacks will do almost anything else for them, when it comes to voting they cannot be influenced, and insist on voting with their party. At one place that I visited, where a considerable number of Republican votes were recorded, an old Democratic gentleman jocularly remarked that this had been the only honest poll in the whole district. They say the Republicans made the election law to suit their own purpose of cheating, and had arranged the electoral districts so as to swamp the whites with black votes. Now they are hoist with their own petard, and serve them right. The blacks seem to have accepted their defeat as a foregone conclusion, and therefore it is that they are quite good-natured over it. Perhaps, too, they really have to some degree accepted Wade Hampton and his policy, and are not so anxious to fight as they otherwise might be. Both parties seem to assume as a matter of course that whichever controls the machinery of the elections will win the elections. I am told that Wade Hampton generally appointed two Democrats and one Radical as election commissioners ; that the radical was always corrupt and could be bought, and that therefore the Democrats always had it their own way. The Democrats of Charleston have done something to conciliate those blacks who accept the Democratic ticket. In this district seventeen members are sent up to the State Assembly, and of these three are Democratic blacks. The county officers are whites, but there are some blacks in the Charleston municipality. For the State Assembly the Republicans adopted a fusion ticket, including the five best of the Democrats.

Hitherto three Congressional districts in the black part of South Carolina have been represented by black men, and I am told that they were all very fair specimens. The representative of the Charleston district was a well-educated negro, from the North. The Georgetown district was represented by an extremely polished black gentleman, who was formerly a very popular barber in Charleston, and is not at all a bad sort of person. . . .

I observe that in a great number of the elections for county and local offices in these Southern States the opportunity is taken to provide for the veterans of the Confederate army who are not eligible for pensions. I saw several notices of elections of one-legged and one-armed ex-soldiers to county offices. These offices are profitable — if not paid by salaries they have considerable fees.

Looking over the accounts of the elections in other States, of which the papers are full, I observe that Governor Nicholls, of Louisiana, is said to be conciliatory and to have followed the same policy as Wade Hampton; but there the negroes fought more successfully than here; and in some cases the Democrats carried the seats in Congress only by adopting a fusion ticket and giving the blacks a good many county offices. There seems to be more 'bulldozing' in Mississippi than anywhere else. That is called 'the Mississippi plan.' South Carolina seems to be the only State which carried everything solidly Democratic. In all the others there has been more or less success of Republican or independent candidates.

Sir George Campbell, *White and Black: the Outcome of a Visit to the United States* (London, 1879), 321–332 *passim*.

———◆———

204. The Indian Problem (1887)

BY REVEREND JONATHAN BAXTER HARRISON

Harrison is a Unitarian minister who has written several works on economic and social questions connected with the progress of the United States. — Bibliography: Thomas W. Field, *An Essay towards an Indian Bibliography;* Boston Public Library, *Bulletins,* IV, 68–70; Providence Public Library, *Monthly Reference Lists,* III, 5–7. — For other articles on the Indians, see *Contemporaries,* I, Nos. 60, 64, 91, 123, 133, 147; II, ch. xviii; III, No. 139.

EVERY particular reservation and tribe or company of Indians will have to be examined, studied, and dealt with by itself, at least at first. The Indians cannot be understood, nor successfully managed and controlled in detail from a distance. That is the fatal defect of the present system and methods. . . .

Meanwhile . . . the powers of Indian agents should be enlarged, their office made more important, with better pay, so as to make it practicable for men of high character and ability to enter the service on the reservations, and to continue in it while they are successful. I do not think the agency and reservation system should be at once abolished. On the contrary, I think it will be necessary to the very end of our work with the Indians as a separate and special class. The reservation system can be so administered as to prepare the way for its own extinction, by guiding the Indians into conditions in which reservations and agents will no longer be necessary. It *is* so administered, in many cases, at present, as to provide for and require its own permanent perpetuation. The methods of administration maintain and reproduce the conditions and forces which hold the Indians in an undeveloped and parasitic state of life. . . .

What is the Indian problem ? Set forth plainly, without confusing rhetoric or sentimentality, it is the question how the Indians shall be brought to a condition of self-support, and of equal rights before the law, in which they will no longer require the special protection and control of the Government.

The problem has its alternative. If the Indians are not so instructed, educated and guided that they shall become self-sustaining, industrious and law-abiding citizens, they must inevitably sink to a condition of permanent pauperism, and re-enforce, almost in a body, whatever vicious and disintegrating tendencies already exist in our great Western communities. We have more than 250,000 Indians in our country. They are not scattered or distributed in all parts of it. There are enough of them in various restricted regions and districts to become an intolerable curse to the white communities for all time to come, and a burden which will always cripple and depress their vitality. So far as I can now judge, this appears to be the most probable destiny for most of the Indians, unless the people of the country interpose to prevent it.

It will probably be said by and by that nothing better could be done with the Indians or for them. But nobody can know that this is true ; for no reasonable or practical system of management adapted to their guidance through their transition to the conditions of civilized life, has ever been tried. The Indians generally have never had, have not now, and, as I think, are not likely ever to have, what would be half a fair chance or just opportunity for any class of people.

The popular creed on the subject, which clothes itself with the solemn sanctions and imperial authority of science is, that the Indian is doomed and fated to fade away, by reason of his inherent inferiority to the white man. Well, let him fade. Nobody need mourn if any race, justly treated, and with reasonable opportunity for self-perpetuation, comes to an end because its vitality is exhausted and its puny and vanishing representatives no longer reproduce their kind. When a race perishes thus it is time for it to go. But when people numbering hundreds of thousands are destroyed on their own soil by the richest and strongest nation under the sun, crushed and exterminated by means of falsehood and theft, of mountainous fraud and ferocious murder, I do not call that fading out. It is altogether a different matter.

My controversy with a very large proportion of the American people regarding this subject is exactly this : They appear to believe that because we are strong enough to trample upon and destroy the Indians, and there is nobody to call us to account, we may safely do so. I doubt that. I do not believe it. I do not pretend to understand the laws which govern the social world and the course of forces and events in the life of men. But it seems to me that it is by no means plain that we can safely do such deliberate and outrageous wrong. How do people know that it will be safe and profitable, and that there will be no retribution to weary and haunt us by and by ? I do not believe they know at all. They are so greedy for the Indian land, poor as most of it is, that they are willing to leave to their children the added burden of a pauper population of a quarter of a million Indians, idle, vicious and criminal, rather than take the trouble to consider the subject, and to institute a policy which would be best and safest for the white people of the country.

The Indian problem will never be decided rightly until the business men of the country take it up, and apply business principles and methods to its investigation and solution. There is no need of rhetoric or sentimentality in treating the subject sensibly and practically. It would be just as well to vary the terms of the problem so that it would stand thus : What policy, system and methods of management in the conduct of Indian affairs would be best for the white people of the country ? The conclusion would be equally favorable to the Indians, though we should make no distinct claim on their behalf. Of all our people, those of our great and growing Western communities have most at stake in this matter. But we are all one nation, and our business men everywhere should give attention to this pressing and rapidly developing state of things, and should take the matter into their own hands. It will take time and money, but it will save more.

J. B. Harrison, *The Latest Studies on Indian Reservations* (Philadelphia, 1887), 166-173 *passim*.

205. The Negro Question (1888)

BY HENRY WOODFIN GRADY

Grady became one of the most prominent of post-bellum journalists in the South. During his short career he exerted, both through the columns of his newspaper, the Atlanta *Constitution*, and by public addresses, his great ability and oratorical power in promoting reconciliation between the sections of his country. His views on the negro problem, as expressed in his speech at Dallas, Texas, are typical of those of the most enlightened thinkers of the "New South." This extract is from that speech. — For Grady, see J. C. Harris, *Life of Henry W. Grady.* — Bibliography as in No. 203 above.

. . . THE future holds a problem, in solving which the South must stand alone ; in dealing with which, she must come closer together than ambition or despair has driven her, and on the outcome of which her very existence depends. This problem is to carry within her body politic two separate races, equal in civil and political rights, and nearly equal in numbers. She must carry these races in peace ; for discord means ruin. She must carry them separately ; for assimilation means debasement. She must carry them in equal justice ; for to this she is pledged in honor and in gratitude. She must carry them even unto the end ; for in human probability she will never be quit of either. . . .

What of the negro? This of him. . . .

. . . As no race had ever lived in such unresisting bondage, none was ever hurried with such swiftness through freedom into power. Into hands still trembling from the blow that broke the shackles, was thrust the ballot. In less than twelve months from the day he walked down the furrow a slave, the negro dictated in legislative halls, from which Davis and Calhoun had gone forth, the policy of twelve commonwealths. When his late master protested against his misrule, the federal drum beat rolled around his strongholds, and from a hedge of federal bayonets he grinned in good-natured insolence. From the proven incapacity of that day has he far advanced? Simple, credulous, impulsive — easily led, and too often easily bought, is he a safer, more intelligent citizen now than then? Is this mass of votes, loosed from old restraints, inviting alliance or awaiting opportunity, less menacing than when its purpose was plain and its way direct?

My countrymen, right here the South must make a decision on which very much depends. Many wise men hold that the white vote of the

South should divide, the color line be beaten down, and the Southern States ranged on economic or moral questions as interest or belief demands. I am compelled to dissent from this view. The worst thing, in my opinion, that could happen is that the white people of the South should stand in opposing factions, with the vast mass of ignorant or purchasable negro votes between. Consider such a status. If the negroes were skilfully led, and leaders would not be lacking, it would give them the balance of power — a thing not to be considered. If their vote was not compacted, it would invite the debauching bid of factions, and drift surely to that which was the most corrupt and cunning. With the shiftless habit and irresolution of slavery days still possessing him, the negro voter will not in this generation, adrift from war issues, become a steadfast partisan through conscience or conviction. In every community there are colored men who redeem their race from this reproach, and who vote under reason. Perhaps in time the bulk of this race may thus adjust itself. But, through what long and monstrous periods of political debauchery this status would be reached, no tongue can tell.

The clear and unmistakable domination of the white race, dominating not through violence, not through party alliance, but through the integrity of its own vote and the largeness of its sympathy and justice, through which it shall compel the support of the better classes of the colored race, that is the hope and assurance of the South. . . .

One thing further should be said in perfect frankness. Up to this point we have dwelt with ignorance and corruption ; but beyond this point a deeper issue confronts us. Ignorance may struggle to enlightenment ; out of corruption may come the incorruptible. God speed the day when every true man will work and pray for its coming. The negro must be led to know and through sympathy to confess that his interests and the interests of the people of the South are identical. The men who coming from afar off view this subject through the cold eye of speculation or see it distorted through partisan glasses, insist that, directly or indirectly, the negro race shall be in control of the affairs of the South. We have no fears of this ; already we are attaching to us the best elements of that race, and as we proceed our alliance will broaden. External pressure but irritates and impedes those who would put the negro race in supremacy, would work against infallible decree, for the white race can never submit to its domination, because the white race is the superior race. But the supremacy of the white race of the South must be maintained forever, and the domination of the negro race resisted at all points and at all hazards, because the white race is the superior race. This is the declaration of no new truth ; it has abided forever in the marrow of our bones and shall run forever with the blood that feeds Anglo-Saxon hearts. . . .

. . . let us — giving the negro every right, civil and political, measured in that fulness the strong should always accord the weak — holding him in closer friendship and sympathy than he is held by those who would crucify us for his sake — realizing that on his prosperity ours depends — let us resolve that never by external pressure or internal division shall he establish domination, directly or indirectly, over that race that everywhere has maintained its supremacy. Let this resolution be cast on the lines of equity and justice. Let it be the pledge of honest, safe and impartial administration, and we shall command the support of the colored race itself, more dependent than any other on the bounty and protection of government. Let us be wise and patient, and we shall secure through its acquiescence what otherwise we should win through conflict, and hold in insecurity.

All this is no unkindness to the negro — but rather that he may be led in equal rights, and in peace to his uttermost good. . . . Then shall this problem have proved our blessing, and the race that threatened our ruin work our salvation as it fills our fields with the best peasantry the world has ever seen. . . .

Henry W. Grady, *The South and her Problem*, in *Life and Labors of H. W. Grady* (New York, 1890), 179-194 *passim*.

———◆———

206. In the Slums (1890)

BY JACOB AUGUST RIIS

Riis was born in Denmark, and emigrated to America as a young man. He became a police-court reporter, and made a special study of life in the tenements of New York City. Because of the active interest he has taken in alleviating the condition of these congested districts, and of the practical reforms, both public and private, which he has helped to inaugurate, he has been called the " most useful citizen of New York." — Bibliography : R. C. Brooks, *Bibliography of Municipal Administration and City Conditions* (*Municipal Affairs*, 1897, I, No. 1) ; Brookings and Ringwalt, *Briefs for Debate*, No. lxv.

. . . IN the dull content of life bred on the tenement-house dead level there is little to redeem it, or to calm apprehension for a society that has nothing better to offer its toilers; while the patient efforts of the lives finally attuned to it to render the situation tolerable, and the very success of these efforts, serve only to bring out in stronger contrast the general gloom of the picture by showing how much farther they might have gone with half a chance. Go into any of the "respectable" tenement neighborhoods — the fact that there are not more than two saloons on the corner, nor over three or four in the block will serve as a fair guide — where live the great body of hard-working Irish and German immigrants and their descendants, who accept naturally the conditions of tenement life, because for them there is nothing else in New York; be with and among its people until you understand their ways, their aims, and the quality of their ambitions, and unless you can content yourself with the scriptural promise that the poor we shall have always with us, or with the menagerie view that, if fed, they have no cause of complaint, you shall come away agreeing with me that, humanly speaking, life there does not seem worth the living. Take at random one of these uptown tenement blocks, not of the worst nor yet of the most prosperous kind, within hail of what the newspapers would call a "fine residential section." These houses were built since the last cholera scare made people willing to listen to reason. The block is not like the one over on the East Side in which I actually lost my way once. There were thirty or forty rear houses in the heart of it, three or four on every lot, set at all sorts of angles, with odd, winding passages, or no passage at all, only "runways" for the thieves and toughs of the neighborhood. These yards are clear. There is air there, and it is about all there is. The view between brick walls outside is that of a stony street; inside, of rows of unpainted board fences, a bewildering maze of clothes-posts and lines; underfoot, a desert of brown, hard-baked soil from which every blade of grass, every stray weed, every speck of green, has been trodden out, as must inevitably be every gentle thought and aspiration above the mere wants of the body in those whose moral natures such home surroundings are to nourish. In self-defence, you know, all life eventually accommodates itself to its environment, and human life is no exception. Within the house there is nothing to supply the want thus left unsatisfied. Tenement-houses have no æsthetic resources. If any are to be brought to bear on them, they must come from the outside. There is the common hall with doors opening softly on every landing as the strange step is heard on the stairs, the air-shaft that seems always so busy letting out foul stenches from below that it has no time to earn its name by bringing down fresh air, the squeaking pumps that hold no water, and the rent that is never less than one week's wages out of the four, quite as often half of the family earnings.

Why complete the sketch? It is drearily familiar already. Such as it is, it is the frame in which are set days, weeks, months, and years of unceasing toil, just able to fill the mouth and clothe the back. Such as it is, it is the world, and all of it, to which these weary workers return nightly to feed heart and brain after wearing out the body at the bench, or in the shop. To it come the young with their restless yearnings. . . . These in their coarse garments — girls with the love of youth for beautiful things, with this hard life before them — who shall save them from the tempter? Down in the street the saloon, always bright and gay, gathering to itself all the cheer of the block, beckons the boys. In many such blocks the census-taker found two thousand men, women, and children, and over, who called them home. . . .

With the first hot nights in June police despatches, that record the killing of men and women by rolling off roofs and window-sills while asleep, announce that the time of greatest suffering among the poor is at hand. It is in hot weather, when life indoors is well-nigh unbearable with cooking, sleeping, and working, all crowded into the small rooms together, that the tenement expands, reckless of all restraint. Then a strange and picturesque life moves upon the flat roofs. In the day and early evening mothers air their babies there, the boys fly their kites from the house-tops, undismayed by police regulations, and the young men and girls court and pass the growler. In the stifling July nights, when the big barracks are like fiery furnaces, their very walls giving out absorbed heat, men and women lie in restless, sweltering rows, panting for air and sleep. Then every truck in the street, every crowded fire-escape, becomes a bedroom, infinitely preferable to any the house affords. A cooling shower on such a night is hailed as a heaven-sent blessing in a hundred thousand homes.

Life in the tenements in July and August spells death to an army of little ones whom the doctor's skill is powerless to save. When the white badge of mourning flutters from every second door, sleepless mothers walk the streets in the gray of the early dawn, trying to stir a cooling breeze to fan the brow of the sick baby. There is no sadder sight than this patient devotion striving against fearfully hopeless odds. Fifty "summer doctors," especially trained to this work, are then sent into the tenements by the Board of Health, with free advice and medicine for the poor. Devoted women follow in their track with care and nursing for the sick. Fresh-air excursions run daily out of New York on land and water ; but despite all efforts the grave-diggers in Calvary work over-time, and little coffins are stacked mountains high on the deck of the Charity Commissioners' boat when it makes its semi-weekly trips to the city cemetery. . . .

That ignorance plays its part, as well as poverty and bad hygienic surroundings, in the sacrifice of life is of course inevitable. . . .

No doubt intemperance bears a large share of the blame for it ; judging from the stand-point of the policeman perhaps the greater share. . . . Even if it were all true, I should still load over upon the tenement the heaviest responsibility. A single factor, the scandalous scarcity of water in the hot summer when the thirst of the million tenants must be quenched, if not in that in something else, has in the past years more than all other causes encouraged drunkenness among the poor. But to my mind there is a closer connection between the wages of the tenements and the vices and improvidence of those who dwell in them than, with the guilt of the tenement upon our heads, we are willing to admit even to ourselves. Weak tea with a dry crust is not a diet to nurse moral strength. . . .

Perhaps of all the disheartening experiences of those who have devoted lives of unselfish thought and effort, and their number is not so small as often supposed, to the lifting of this great load, the indifference of those they would help is the most puzzling. They will not be helped. Dragged by main force out of their misery, they slip back again on the first opportunity, seemingly content only in the old rut. The explanation was supplied by two women of my acquaintance in an Elizabeth Street tenement, whom the city missionaries had taken from their wretched hovel and provided with work and a decent home somewhere in New Jersey. In three weeks they were back, saying that they preferred their dark rear room to the stumps out in the country. But to me the oldest . . . made the bitter confession : " We do get so kind o' downhearted living this way, that we have to be where something is going on, or we just can't stand it." And there was sadder pathos to me in her words than in the whole long story of their struggle with poverty ; for unconsciously she voiced the sufferings of thousands, misjudged by a happier world, deemed vicious because they are human and unfortunate.

Jacob A. Riis, *How the Other Half Lives* (New York, Charles Scribner's Sons, 1890), 162–175 *passim.*

2 U

207. "Why the Republic may Endure" (1894)

BY PRESIDENT CHARLES WILLIAM ELIOT

As president of Harvard University, Mr. Eliot has introduced extensive reforms in higher education and has also exerted a great influence in improving secondary schools, while in his public addresses and writings he has upheld a high standard of public duty and voiced hopeful opinions of American character and progress.

THE first moral cause of permanence of which the American republic has the advantage is the principle of toleration in religion — a principle which, though not recently enunciated (nobody has ever stated it better than William the Silent), has been very recently put in practice, not, by any means, in all parts of the civilized world, but in a few favored regions, and notably in the United States. On one of the tablets of the Water-gate at Chicago was written this sentence : "Toleration in religion the best fruit of the last four centuries." This statement is no exaggeration but the literal truth. Toleration in religion is absolutely the best fruit of all the struggles, labors, and sorrows of the civilized nations during the last four centuries. . . .

Another mental and moral force which makes for the permanence of our institutions is universal education. This is a new force in the world, not in action in any land before this century. It has not existed more than twenty years in such a civilized country as France ; it dates only from 1870 in England. It is not yet true that education is universal even in our own country ; but the principle of universal education finds general acceptance, and the practical results approximate more and more, as time goes on, to the requirements of the theoretical principle. In all civilized countries continuous effort is made to bring the practice up to the level of the theory. Within three generations immense progress has been made ; and it now seems as if a perfectly feasible development of this principle in practice must work a profound change in human society within a comparatively small number of future generations. . . . It is a commonplace that republican institutions are built on education ; but we hardly realize how new that commonplace is. Plato taught that the industrial and producing classes needed no education whatever. None of the republics which have died had anything more than a small educated class. The masses of their people grew up and lived in crassest ignorance. . . . Universal suffrage prolongs in the United States the effect of universal education ; for it stimulates all citizens throughout their lives to reflect on problems outside the narrow circle of their private interests and occupations, to read about public questions, to discuss public characters, and to hold themselves ready in some degree to give a rational account of their political faith.   The duties of republican citizenship, rightly discharged, constitute in themselves a prolonged education, which effectively supplements the work of schools and colleges.

A third reason for believing that our institutions will endure is to be found in the fact that a better family life prevails among our people than was known to any of the republics which have perished, or, indeed, to any earlier century.   The family, not the individual, is the tap-root of the state, and whatever tends to secure the family tends to secure the state.   Now family life — under which term may properly be included all the complex relations between husband and wife, and parents and children — is gentler in this century, and particularly in the United States, than it has ever been.   Family discipline has become, even within thirty years, much gentler than it ever was before.   The relations of husband and wife have also become juster. . . .

Pursuing the idea that the promotion of diffused happiness promotes governmental stability, we observe next that certain means of public happiness have recently been liberally provided in many American communities, at public expense, with great intelligence and by deliberate design.   During the last twenty-five years, strenuous efforts have been made in many municipalities to promote public happiness by giving opportunities to the multitude for the enjoyment of fresh air and natural beauty.   One of the most striking social phenomena in the United States of recent years has been the sudden creation of public parks and playgrounds, constructed and maintained at public expense.   At bottom, the meaning of this sudden development is that the people seek to procure for themselves, and are procuring, increased means of health and happiness. . . .   The provision of free libraries and museums of natural history and fine arts, at public expense, or by the combination of private endowments with public appropriations, is another evidence of the disposition of the democracy to provide the means of public cultivation and enjoyment. . . .

Another new and effective bulwark of state is to be found in the extreme publicity with which all American activities are carried on. Many people are in the habit of complaining bitterly of the intrusion of the newspaper reporter into every nook and corner of the state, and even into the privacy of home ; but in this extreme publicity is really to be found a new means of social, industrial, and governmental reform and progress. As Emerson said, "Light is the best policeman." There are many exaggerations, perversions, and inaccuracies in this publicity ; but on the whole it is a beneficent and a new agency for the promotion of the public welfare. . . . So new is this force in the world, that many people do not yet trust it, or perceive its immense utility. In cases of real industrial grievances or oppressions, publicity would be by far the quickest and surest means of cure — vastly more effective for all just ends than secret combinations of either capitalists or laborers. The newspapers, which are the ordinary instruments of this publicity, are as yet very imperfect instruments, much of their work being done so hastily and so cheaply as to preclude accuracy ; but as a means of publicity they visibly improve from decade to decade, and, taken together with the magazines and the controversial pamphlet, they shed more light on the social, industrial, and political life of the people of the United States than was ever shed before on the doings and ways of any people. This force is distinctly new within this century, and it affords a new and strong guarantee for the American republic.

Within the past fifty years there has been developed, for the conduct of business, education, and charity, an agency which may fairly be called new — namely, the corporation. . . . In the service of corporations, there is seldom any element of personal devotion, such as existed in other times between subject and sovereign, or between retainer and feudal chief; but there is a large element of fidelity and loyalty, which is becoming of greater and greater importance in the formation of the national character. A considerable portion of all the business, charity, and education carried on in the United States is well conducted by the faithful and loyal servants of corporations, as every one will plainly see so soon as he takes account of his own contacts in daily life with the work of corporations, and compares them with his contacts with the work of individuals or of partnerships. This corporation service affords a new discipline for masses of people ; and it is a discipline of the highest value toward inducing stability and durability in governmental institutions. . . .

. . . The extreme division of labor, which has more and more characterized the normal industrial methods in civilized states since the beginning of the present century, has brought about a mutual dependence of man on man and community on community, which is a strong guarantee of the permanence of free institutions. . . . All civilized

mankind lives under similar conditions of interdependence.   The sense
of dependence is of course mutual, and with it goes some recognition
of common aims and hopes among the different sorts and conditions of
men.   This sense of common interests is something very different from
the sentiment of human equality.   It is a feeling of unity, not of equality.
It has a firm foundation in facts ; whereas the notion that men are
equal is plainly false, unless it be strictly limited to the political significance of equality, namely, to equality before the law and in regard to the
right of suffrage.   It is a feeling which leads naturally to a sense of
human brotherhood. . . .   The doctrine of human brotherhood has
been taught for thousands of years.   It is all contained in two words —
"Our Father " ; but, though accepted by seers and philosophers, it has
been little realized in practice by the multitude.   There are many signs
of the wide and steady spread of the realized acceptance of this doctrine
in practice.   The theory, long current in the world, gets more and more
applied in institutions, in business, and in society.   The fact of intimate
mutual dependence extends to different states and nations.   A federation
of States like the American Union affords a favorable field for the
practical realization by masses of people of the truth of the affirmation
St. Paul frequently repeated, " We are members one of another." . . .
This realization of an ancient truth marks again the progress of society
toward practical acceptance of the conception that there is a genuine
unity of aims and hopes among all men, an acceptance which of itself
will prove a stout bulwark of free institutions.

. . . In recent times, serious changes have taken place in regard to
the highest hopes, aspirations, and ideals of mankind. . . .   The first
change of expectation which claims attention is the changed sentiment
of the people toward what is new, and therefore untried.   The American people, as a rule, approach a new object, a new theory, or a new
practice, with a degree of hope and confidence which no other people
exhibit.   The unknown is to the savage terrible ; the dark has been
dreadful, and evil has always been imagined of it ; many highly civilized
people have an aversion to things novel ; but for us Americans so many
new things have proved to be good things, that we no longer look on
what is novel with suspicion and distrust.   Our continent is new, and
has proved to be rich ; our machinery is new, and has proved to be useful ; our laws are many of them new, but they have proved helpful.
The people have traversed many wilds and wastes, but have passed them
with safety, and found good in the unexplored and unknown.   The untried

is therefore for us no longer terrible, or, at least, to be suspected. Hope
and expectation of good spring in our hearts, as never before in the
hearts of former generations.

Furthermore, the changes which have taken place in the realized
doctrines of Christianity concerning the origin and nature of man are
very reassuring for those who believe in the possibility of developing a
nation of freemen capable of orderly self-government. The old conceptions of the fall of man and of the total depravity of the race were
good foundations for the *régime* of a beneficent despot, but not for the
régime of self-governing freemen. The modern doctrine of the steady
ascent of man through all his history is necessarily welcome to republicans, because it justifies their political beliefs. . . . No cherished ideal
of our race has undergone a more beneficent change during the present
century than the ideal of God ; and this change makes strongly for the
happiness of mankind. The Christian Gospel has just begun to be
realized. We have just begun to understand that God is love. . . .
This ideal promotes happiness and joy. It is not new ; but it is newly
realized by multitudes. Now, these beneficent changes in the spiritual
conceptions of large numbers of men have taken place since our country
took on its present governmental structure ; and they have lent and will
lend to that structure a firm support, because they contribute generously
to the happiness and true spirituality of the people.

Finally, the object of religion and the aim of its ministers have
become wonderfully different, since the American republic was established,
from what they were in ancient or mediæval times, or even down to the
opening of this century. . . . Since the beginning of this century a
revolution has occurred, which has been felt more or less in every branch
of the Christian Church and in almost every Christian nation, but has
had a broad sweep in the United States. The primary objects of religion
and its ministers in our day and country are more and more to soften
and elevate the characters and lives of men in this world, and to amelio-
rate the common lot. . . . Religion, by devoting itself to the elevation
of human character, becomes a prop and stay of free institutions,
because these rest ultimately on the character of the citizen.

These, then, are some of the new principles and forces which make
for the permanence of the republic : toleration in religion ; general
education ; better domestic relations ; attention to the means of public
health and pleasure ; publicity ; corporation service ; increased mutual
dependence of man on man, and therewith a growing sense of brother-

hood and unity ; the greater hopefulness and cheerfulness of men's outlook on man, the earth, the universe, and God ; and finally, the
changing objects and methods of religion and its institutions.   It is
the working of these principles and forces, often unrecognized, which
has carried the republic safely through many moral difficulties and
dangers during the past thirty years.   These things, and not its size and
wealth, make us love our country.   These things, we believe, will give
the American republic long life.   These bulwarks of the commonwealth
will prove all the stronger and more lasting, because women as well as
men can work on them, and help to transmit them, ever broader and
firmer, from generation to generation.

Charles William Eliot, *Some Reasons why the American Republic may Endure*,
   in his *American Contributions to Civilization, and other Essays* (New York,
   1897), 47–67 *passim*.

———◆———

208. The Future of the Negro (1899)

BY BOOKER TALIAFERRO WASHINGTON

Washington was born a slave; but through his indomitable energy and large grasp
of mind in assailing the problems which confront the negro in the South he has
become a leader of his people, a man of international reputation, and a valuable
factor in the future of American progress. — Bibliography as in No. 203 above.

IN the future, more than in the past, we want to impress upon the Negro
   the importance of identifying himself more closely with the interests
of the South, — the importance of making himself part of the South. . . .
In no other way it seems to me, can we get a foundation for peace and
progress.   He who advises against this policy will advise the Negro to
do that which no people in history who have succeeded have done.   The
white man, North or South, who advises the Negro against it advises
him to do that which he himself has not done.   The bed-rock upon
which every individual rests his chances of success in life is securing the
friendship, the confidence, the respect, of his next-door neighbour of
the little community in which he lives.   Almost the whole problem of
the Negro in the South rests itself upon the fact as to whether the Negro
can make himself of such indispensable service to his neighbour and the
community that no one can fill his place better in the body politic.

There is at present no other safe course for the black man to pursue. If the Negro in the South has a friend in his white neighbour and a still larger number of friends in his community, he has a protection and a guarantee of his rights that will be more potent and more lasting than any our Federal Congress or any outside power can confer. . . .

. . . During slavery the Negro was taught every trade, every industry, that constitutes the foundation for making a living. Now, if on this foundation — laid in rather a crude way, it is true, but a foundation, nevertheless — we can gradually build and improve, the future for us is bright. Let me be more specific. Agriculture is, or has been, the basic industry of nearly every race or nation that has succeeded. The Negro got a knowledge of this during slavery. Hence, in a large measure, he is in possession of this industry in the South to-day. The Negro can buy land in the South, as a rule, wherever the white man can buy it, and at very low prices. Now, since the bulk of our people already have a foundation in agriculture, they are at their best when living in the country, engaged in agricultural pursuits. Plainly, then, the best thing, the logical thing, is to turn the larger part of our strength in a direction that will make the Negro among the most skilled agricultural people in the world. The man who has learned to do something better than any one else, has learned to do a common thing in an uncommon manner, is the man who has a power and influence that no adverse circumstances can take from him. The Negro who can make himself so conspicuous as a successful farmer, a large tax-payer, a wise helper of his fellow-men, as to be placed in a position of trust and honour, whether the position be political or otherwise, by natural selection, is a hundred-fold more secure in that position than one placed there by mere outside force or pressure. . . .

. . . What I have said of the opening that awaits the Negro in the direction of agriculture is almost equally true of mechanics, manufacturing, and all the domestic arts. The field is before him and right about him. Will he occupy it? Will he " cast down his bucket where he is "? Will his friends North and South encourage him and prepare him to occupy it? . . . Any individual or race that does not fit himself to occupy in the best manner the field or service that is right about it will sooner or later be asked to move on, and let some one else occupy it.

But it is asked, Would you confine the Negro to agriculture, mechanics, and domestic arts, etc.? Not at all; but along the lines that I have mentioned is where the stress should be laid just now and for many years to come. We will need and must have many teachers and ministers, some doctors and lawyers and statesmen; but these professional men will have a constituency or a foundation from which to draw support just in proportion as the race prospers along the economic lines that I have mentioned. . . .

. . . What bearing will all this have upon the Negro's place in the South as a citizen and in the enjoyment of the privileges which our government confers?

To state in detail just what place the black man will occupy in the South as a citizen, when he has developed in the direction named, is beyond the wisdom of any one. Much will depend upon the sense of justice which can be kept alive in the breast of the American people. Almost as much will depend upon the good sense of the Negro himself. That question, I confess, does not give me the most concern just now. The important and pressing question is, Will the Negro with his own help and that of his friends take advantage of the opportunities that now surround him? When he has done this, I believe that, speaking of his future in general terms, he will be treated with justice, will be given the protection of the law, and will be given the recognition in a large measure which his usefulness and ability warrant. . . . Time, patience, and constant achievement are great factors in the rise of a race.

. . . When a number of Negroes rise to the point where they own and operate the most successful farms, are among the largest tax-payers in their county, are moral and intelligent, I do not believe that in many portions of the South such men need long be denied the right of saying by their votes how they prefer their property to be taxed and in choosing those who are to make and administer the laws.

. . . the Negro must keep a strong and courageous heart. He cannot improve his condition by any short-cut course or by artificial methods. Above all, he must not be deluded into the temptation of believing that his condition can be permanently improved by a mere battledore and shuttlecock of words or by any process of mere mental gymnastics or oratory alone. What is desired, along with a logical defence of his cause, are deeds, results, — multiplied results, — in the direction of building himself up, so as to leave no doubt in the minds of any one of his ability to succeed.

Booker T. Washington, *The Future of the American Negro* (Boston, 1899). 214–235 *passim*.

209. "The Future of the Mississippi Valley" (1900)

BY PROFESSOR ALBERT BUSHNELL HART

. . . WHAT is the likelihood that the population of the Mississippi Valley will continue to increase? Nowhere in the world are the conditions of subsistence more favorable, for the fertility of the soil and the variety of climate make possible an unequalled food-supply, which so far has sufficed not only for the people of the valley, but for their brethren on the sea-coast and for millions of Europeans. For many years to come this food-supply can be steadily increased, both by opening up hitherto untilled lands and by more intensive culture. . . . When . . . we see how easy it is in America to send a surplus from one district to supply a deficiency in another, when we consider the enormous credit facilities which enable the community to endure one or two, or even three, years of bad crops without starvation anywhere, there seems to be no reason why the Mississippi Valley may not some time contain a population of 350,000,000 comfortable people, or ten times its present number. The difficult problem is not to raise sufficient crops, but to keep upon the land a sufficient number of persons to till it; but the Mississippi Valley is the home of a most skilful system of machinery, which amplifies the labor of the farmer twentyfold.

Certainly the West will always be able to clothe itself. Its immense cotton-fields already furnish hundreds of millions of yards of fabrics for men and women; its cattle ranges prepare for everybody a leathern carpet between the foot and the too-adherent soil; and if its sheep still shyly hold back from the encouragement of the wool schedules in the tariff, the West has always a surplus of food products and manufactured goods, with which it may buy its woollen clothing from other lands.

The problem of immigration is different. The free land which drew hundreds of thousands of Scandinavians, Germans, and Europeans to the Western prairies is no longer to be found. Relatively to the total population, the immigrants are already becoming fewer every year; and a generation hence, when the children of the Pole and Hungarian, the Italian, the Dane, the Greek, and the Armenian, have been fused in the crucible of the public schools, and shaped by the mutual hammering of playmates and friends, the population of the valley will be more distinctly American — not the old American descended almost wholly from English ancestors, but a vigorous, active, and probably open-minded composite American.   The negro problem is serious in only half a dozen of the valley States, and does not hem in the future of the Mississippi Basin as it does that of the South Atlantic States.

The greatest checks to the rapid increase of national population in the history of the world have been famine, disease, and war. . . .   Yet, so far as we can look into the future, there will be bread and to spare for the children of this great household. . . .   The advance of medical science makes the Mississippi Valley reasonably safe from devastation by pestilence.   As for war, the Mississippi Valley has now no enemies within the Union, and from invasion St. Louis is as safe as Nijni-Novgorod or Stanley Pool.

Hence the only probable check upon the rapid increase of population is one which has already made itself felt throughout the Union — the increasing difficulty of giving children a good start, and the consequent diminution of the size of families. . . .   This means a slower rate of increase.   The Mississippi Valley has more than doubled its population in every twenty-five years during the last century.   At that rate it would have 560,000,000 in the year 2000, but he would be a bold man who would predict a population of 200,000,000 in that year, for it would be almost as dense as Belgium or Holland.

If the present average scale of living continue, every doubling of the population will mean a doubling of available capital and wealth.   But who can say whether the mechanical discoveries of the next century may not vastly increase the average wealth? and, on the other hand, who can say how far property may be concentrated in a few hands or combined in some kind of national socialism?   The wealth of the Mississippi Valley in arable land already lies beneath the feet of the people, but the upper slopes on the Appalachian rim of the valley are still very little cultivated, though the Tennessee, Kentucky, and Georgia mountains are probably capable of supporting as abundant and as thriving a population as that of the Black Forest or the ranges of the Jura Mountains.   In the lowlands exhausted soils, formerly allowed to go to ruin, are now restored by the wide-spreading use of fertilizers ; and as population grows and land becomes more valuable, a stop will be put to the annihilation of soil through cutting off the timber and the consequent waste of the steep slopes thus exposed to running water.   Everywhere a more intensive cultivation must come in.   The day is past

when twenty-five good crops of wheat can be raised from the same land
except by rotation and skilful husbandry. The amazing heritage of
wealth in the rich soil must be hoarded. . . .

Pork, corn, wheat, cotton, sugar, steel rails, reapers, wagons, shelf
hardware, and shingles will take care of themselves in the West. But
will the Mississippi Valley take its place among the great intellectual
communities of the world? . . .

. . . if popular education, intelligence, and natural keenness make up
civilization, the West is a highly civilized community ; and there are many
reasons for supposing that it has the conditions for a broader intellectual
growth. First of all, it is freer than any other great area of the earth's
surface from the trammels of an official religion ; several of the coast
colonies had established churches, but not one community in the Mississippi Valley except Louisiana. . . .

. . . the district schools in the West are probably as good as those in
the remote parts of New England ; and the great city systems are, upon
the whole, superior to those of the East. . . .

. . . When it comes to universities, the average provision in the West
is excellent, and most of the newer States have a general system of complete government education, for the State universities have direct relations with the public schools, and are superior in equipment and prestige
to the denominational colleges. . . .

The difficulty about intellectual life in the Mississippi Valley is not so
much a lack of interest in the things of the mind as a lack of local traditions. . . . How can there be traditions in a city like Minneapolis,
where not one adult in twenty was born in the place or perhaps in the
State? The North and Northwest are now undergoing a tremendous
social change through the renting of great farms to new-comers, while
the owners live in villages or towns. This means that the children will
not know " the old place," and the grandchildren will have not so much
as a myth of the old oaken bucket. Even in old cities like Albany and
Baltimore it is hard to build up a civic sentiment — a sense of gratitude
to ancestors and responsibility to posterity. Perhaps as population
becomes more stable this feeling will grow up in the West, but it is hard
to realize the effect upon a community of such rapid changes of life that
not one child in twenty will live in the house of his grandfather.

Of the continued material wealth of the Mississippi Valley there is no
reason to doubt, and a political structure designed for small agricultural
communities has somehow proved at least moderately successful for

large States containing great cities. But for ages to come the principal output and wealth of the Mississippi Valley must be agricultural; and the greatest danger is a separation of interest between the tiller of the soil (allied, perhaps, with the workman at the forge) on the one side, and the capitalist and the professional and business man on the other side. At present the social forces are well balanced, and immigration has not brought the great dangers usually ascribed to it; but if the farms are to fall into the hands of a rent-paying peasantry, and the owners are not to live in the midst of that peasantry and to share their interests, as do the land-owners in European countries, then the Mississippi Valley may yet see social contests which will make the French Revolution seem mild. The two bases of the present happiness and prosperity of that great region are — first, the intelligence, honesty, and orderliness of the average man, and secondly, the belief that the farmer and the wage-earner get a fair share of the output.

Albert Bushnell Hart, *The Future of the Mississippi Valley*, in *Harper's New Monthly Magazine*, February, 1900 (New York, etc.), C, 418–424 *passim*.

GENERAL INDEX

TO THE FOUR VOLUMES

[The names of the authors of extracts are in **Boldface**. The titles of the pieces are in SMALL CAPITALS. The titles of books cited are in *Italics*.]

402–403; relations with the Confederate States, iv, 301–303; in Mexico, 301, 571. — See also Canada, Colonies, Indians, Louisiana, Mississippi River, War.

French, Benjamin Franklin, *Historical Collections of Louisiana*, i, 14, 118, 140, 144, ii, 17, 316.

French and Indian War, ii, 352–372.

Freneau, Philip, *Poems*, ii, 19, iii, 119; PEOPLING THE WESTERN COUNTRY, iii, 118–119; *Stanzas on Emigration*, 119.

Friend, The, ii, 293.

Friends. — See Quakers.

Fromentin, Judge E., and Jackson, iii, 487.

Frontier, skirmishes on the, ii, 344–346; settlement of the, 392–393; poverty of people, iii, 97; famine, 98–99; roads, 98; occupation of lands, 100–101; retention of posts, 158–160; Indian hostilities on, 317. — See also Indians, West.

Frothingham, Richard, *Rise of the Republic*, ii, 22.

Fugitive slaves, iii, 630–633, iv, 80–96. — See also Slavery, and next title.

Fugitive-Slave Law, Webster on, iv, 53; Seward on, 57–58; personal-liberty act, 93–96; enforcement of, fosters Republican party, 103; nullification of, a southern grievance, 167; Stephens's remedies, 167–169; changes suggested, 193; Lincoln on, 202–203. — See also Compromise, Slavery.

Fundamental Constitutions, i, 280–282. — See also Carolinas.

Fundamental Orders. — See Connecticut.

Fur trade, in New York, i, 542; Dutch, 584; in Georgia, Carolina, and Virginia, ii, 126; in Canada, 320–324; on Nootka Sound, iii, 56; with Indians, 69. — See also Canada, French, Indians.

GAGE, Lyman Judson, THE GOLD-STANDARD ACT, iv, 539–541; *Gold Standard Law*, 541.

Gaines's Mill, McClellan on battle of, iv, 339–341.

Gallatin, Albert, envoy, iii, 426–429.

Gambier, J., British minister, iii, 426–429.

Gardoqui, Don Diego de, Spanish minister, iii, 170–171.

Garrard, James, speech, iii, 337.

Garrison, William Lloyd, STATEMENT OF

PRINCIPLES, iii, 595–597; THANK GOD FOR WAR, iv, 395–397.

Gates, Horatio, in command of the southern department, ii, 606; recalled, 606; meeting with Greene, 610.

Gates, Sir Thomas, CHARACTER OF THE FIRST COLONISTS, i, 206–208.

General Court. — See Connecticut, Massachusetts, New Haven, Plymouth Colony, Rhode Island.

General histories, lists, i, 26–27, ii, 33–34.

Genet, Edmond Charles, COMPLAINT OF THE FRENCH MINISTER, iii, 307–312.

Geneva (N.Y.), description, iii, 61.

Geneva award, iv, 550–556; rules governing, 551.

Genoa, archives at, i, 8, ii, 10.

Gentleman of the City of New York, LEISLER'S REBELLION, i, 544–547.

George I, poem on his death, ii, 258–260.

George III, value of letters, ii, 2; character as Prince of Wales, 373–374; instances of tyranny, 449–451; AN OBSTINATE GUELPH, 451–453; opinion of Chatham, 452; plans for conduct of the American war, 453; *Correspondence*, 453, 620; THE SUDDEN CHANGE OF SENTIMENTS, 619–620; presentation of John Adams to, iii, 172–176. — See also England, Revolution.

Georgia, reasons for settlement of, ii, 110–113; charter incorporating the trustees for establishing the colony, 111; settlement of, probable aid to England, 112; settlement of, probable aid to conversion of Indians, 113; benefactions solicited for, 114; Salzburg Germans in, 114–116, 283–284; an unfavorable opinion of, 117; **Trustees**, THE QUESTION OF SLAVERY IN GEORGIA, 118–121; Whitefield's orphan-house, 122–124; need of relief in 1749, 124–126; manufactures and trade, 125–126; John Wesley in, 283–287; redemption of, 607; emits bills of credit, iii, 134; Sherman's march through, iv, 428–432; post-bellum condition, 451–452. — See also Slavery, South.

Germanna (Va.), description, ii, 235.

Germans, in Pennsylvania, i, 559; Palatines in New York, ii, 77–79; question of naturalization, 101; the Salzburgers in Georgia, 114–116, 283–284; Washington's de-

During periods of intense activity of external forces, accompanied by increased erosion and leveling of the earth's surface, there took place the opening and the redistribution of the primary ore deposits, and the formation of secondary beds, as well as the creation of new mineral deposits—oil, coal, salts, gypsum, etc.

The overwhelming majority of nonmetallic minerals are associated with sedimentary rocks of marine or continental origin.

The mineral resources most important for the development of the national economy of the USSR are oil, coal, oil shales, peat, iron ore, various ores of nonferrous metals, apatite, phosphorite, potassium salts, sodium chloride, gold, platinum, and ores of other rare metals, as well as various construction materials mined from the earth.

Oil

Oil is associated with rocks of organic origin. But a theory exists that oil was formed inorganically. Nowadays, the majority of scholars adhere to the former theory. The advocates of the organic origin of oil hold that the original materials for its formation were the remains of various animals and plants which were subjected to a process of slow decay with no access to oxygen. Conditions favorable to the accumulation of vast masses of organic matter exist at present in the Black and Caspian seas, whose waters at some depth are contaminated with hydrogen sulphide; organisms which get into those waters provide a source for the accumulation of organic matter.

The eastern and northeastern region of the European part of the USSR, within the East Russian Basin, is very rich in oil. The vast territory of the so-called Volga-Ural oil-bearing area is almost in the center of the USSR, and stretches from the Ural Mountains on the east to the right bank of the Volga on the west. The latest investigations indicate that this extensive oil-bearing area extends to the west of the Volga, the Oka-Tsna divide, and the meridian of Gorky [Fig. 18].

The industrial oil regions in this area extend along the eastern slope of the Timan Ridge, in the region of the Ukhta River and the upper reaches of the Izhma River, near the town of Ukhta (formerly Chibyu), as well as in the Krasnokamsk region, near Perm [Molotov]. Oil deposits here are associated with Upper De-